Social Trends & Indicators USA

Volume 3:
Health & Sickness

Social Trends & Indicators USA

Volume 3: Health & Sickness

Arsen J. Darnay, Managing Editor

Linda Schmittroth, Editor

Helen S. Fisher, Robert Lazich,
Monique D. Magee, and Joyce Piwowarski,
Assistant Editors

GALE®

THOMSON

GALE

Detroit • New York • San Diego • San Francisco • Cleveland • New Haven, Conn. • Waterville, Maine • London • Munich

Social Trends & Indicators USA
Health & Sickness
Linda Schmittroth, Editor

Project Editor
Amanda C. Quick

Editorial
Arsen J. Darnay, Helen S. Fisher, Robert Lazich,
Monique D. Magee, Joyce Piwowarski

Product Design
Pamela A. E. Galbreath

Manufacturing
NeKita McKee

ISBN 0-7876-5906-1 (set)
ISBN 0-7876-5907-X (v.1)
ISBN 0-7876-5908-8 (v.2)
ISBN 0-7876-5909-6 (v.3)
ISBN 0-7876-5910-X (v.4)
Library of Congress Control Number: 2002117074

Printed in the United States of America
10 9 8 7 6 5 4 3 2 1

TABLE OF CONTENTS

Table of Contents v
Introduction vii

PART I 1

CHAPTER 1 - The State of Our Health 1

CHAPTER 2 - Diseases 49

CHAPTER 3 - Prevention 73

CHAPTER 4 - Risky Behavior 107

CHAPTER 5 - Treatments 149

CHAPTER 6 - Drugs 165

CHAPTER 7 - Senior Health 187

CHAPTER 8 - Disability 223

CHAPTER 9 - Our Mental Health 247

CHAPTER 10 - Sexuality 267

CHAPTER 11 - Reproduction 291

CHAPTER 12 - The Environment 315

CHAPTER 13 - Medical Professionals 335

CHAPTER 14 - Medical Infrastructure 363

CHAPTER 15 - Funding 397

PART II 419

Data Presentation 419

Keyword Index 541

Cumulative Keyword Index 561

Introduction

Upon this gifted age, in its dark hour,
Rains from the sky a meteoric shower
Of facts ... they lie unquestioned, uncombined.
Wisdom enough to leech us of our ill
Is daily spun; but there exists no loom
To weave it into fabric.
                                    Edna St. Vincent Millay

Social Trends & Indicators – The Concept

The idea for this series, *Social Trends & Indicators USA*, arose because we are inundated by statistics, but the meaning of the numbers is often elusive. We are getting outrageously obese, for instance, yet we are living longer. Layoffs are devastating sectors, yet the economy seems to be booming. We are the most educated society on earth, yet Johnny can't read. The crime rate is dropping, but we do not feel safe. The workweek is shrinking, yet we never have time.

The Federal Government's many statistical agencies produce a great wealth of superb data. We are undoubtedly the best documented and most measured society that has ever existed. Newspapers attractively box factoids to amaze or to alarm us. Competing interests marshal their data to make their cases, often omitting numbers that do not bolster the argument. Statistics become catch-phrases. The rich fabric of our national experience is thinned by the speed and noise of the mass media attempting to "infotain" us.

But statistics out of context — and without historical background — are often less than informative. They can be confusing and lead to wrong conclusions. Whereas a properly developed presentation on an issue, using what numbers are available, is often very revealing, at times sobering, and frequently reassuring. A balanced presentation of facts within context can serve the public by illuminating hidden facets of an issue and, as often happens, show that beneath the hoopla and the hype is a deeper-lying demographic movement.

This series was born from such considerations, and from our long experience in dealing with, and publishing, statistics. The idea, simply, was to present statistics in context, with as much historical background as possible, in order to answer questions and to pinpoint trends.

Organization of the Series

Work & Leisure deals with the whole economic realm — work, productivity, employment, unemployment, income, and fringe benefits — and with how we organize our leisure time. *Community & Education* covers who we are, where we live, all kinds of family structures, race and ethnicity, politics, religion, and the vast subject of education and the many issues it encompasses. *Crime & Justice* attempts to shine a statistical light into the darker woods of our nature — victimization, crime, law enforcement, the drug war, terrorism, the justice system, and how all these matters affect us. *Health & Sickness*, the current volume in the series, takes on the body and the mind and what can go wrong with us — our state of health and illness, old and emerging diseases, risky behaviors, prevention and treatment, our preoccupation with drugs, disability, sexuality, and the people and institutions that deal with us when we are ailing.

Each volume, of course, is divided into chapters. In their totality, the chapters present a fairly complete picture of the subject in each volume. But the objective is not to create a compendium on health and sickness, for instance, but to deal with issues of current concern. Dealing with the issues of today, of course, often causes us to look backwards — all the way back to the 19th century sometimes. But the focus is on current trends and on indicators of what is likely to happen tomorrow.

Each chapter is divided into several so-called "panels" (see below). Panels tend to come in two flavors: those that provide background information on a subject, including general trends, and those aimed specifically at answering a question: "Is government really growing? Which parts? Why?" "Will future jobs all require an advanced degree? No? Why not?" "Why are today's children suddenly so frequently 'learning disabled'?"

The Mode of Presentation: The Panel and the Tables

Each volume in the series presents statistical information in two forms. In Part I of the book, data are presented in graphic format followed by explanations and commentaries.

The principal unit of presentation in Part I is thus a "panel" — one topic, one main graphic, and a commentary of usually no more than two pages. Panels sometimes also feature additional graphics and statistics laid out in tabular format. The text is a discussion of the topic. It may feature footnotes for additional comment. A source note concludes each panel citing the sources used. In most instances, web addresses are provided pointing to sites where the user can obtain additional information.

Sometimes a single panel is not sufficient to develop a subject. In that case, the discussion continues with another panel, with its own graphic. Groups of panels form chapters, and each chapter has a brief introduction.

Users of such works as *Social Trends & Indicators USA* find graphics a vivid way to show data, but they want to see the actual numbers as well. For this reason, *Health & Sickness* produces all of the data graphed in Part II, the Data Presentation. Here, statistical data are presented in tabular format. Frequently only the data used to create the graphics are shown. Sometimes, however, additional time series are provided as well for a more comprehensive documentation of the subject. Tables in Part II are organized by chapters for rapid access. These chapters are organized to correspond to panels in Part I. The tables are also fully indexed.

Accessing Information

Each volume of *Social Trends & Indicators USA* provides a Table of Contents and an Index. The Table of Contents will guide the user to appropriate chapters. The Index lists important concepts, names, institutions, and issues. Page numbers cited refer to the pages where text or data can be found under the topic listed.

Sources of Information

Data presented in *Health & Sickness*, and in the other volumes, come predominantly, but not exclusively, from Federal or State statistical agencies. Data from not-for-profit organizations and from commercial sources are also sometimes shown. Sources of data are always referenced in footnotes or source notes. Where such data are copyrighted, the copyright notice is provided.

An important feature of this series is that data from different sources are analytically combined and presented together. A typical example might be to show birth data in combination with population data on women of child-bearing age. Another might be to show a flow of expenditures but rendered in constant dollars (for comparability year to year) — for which purpose index data from the Consumer Price Index (or the Gross Domestic Product deflator) may have been used to transform the dollar quantities. Data on alcohol, tobacco, and illegal drug consumption — derived from three sources — might be shown together.

Data were obtained using the Internet or from print sources. Web-based data are "sourced" showing the web site from which they were obtained. The links shown, however, are not guaranteed to be functioning at some later date. Most will be accessible because they are predominantly governmental sites. Historical data were obtained from the *Historical Statistics of the United States, Colonial Times to 1970*, published by the Bureau of the Census.

Authorship and Presentation

Health & Sickness was prepared by five individuals (three women, two men), each responsible for chapter-length segments of the book. The authors are all skilled statistical analysts but none is an expert on the subject presented. All members of the editorial group reviewed and discussed every panel contained in this work. Changes, revisions, and augmentation of the material took place as a consequence of these reviews. Finally, all materials were reviewed and edited by the senior editor in charge. However, no attempts were made — or thought to be desirable — to conform the presentational style of the authors to produce a uniform (and possibly bureaucratic-sounding) voice.

Our aim is to present often complicated and difficult subjects — as these are seen by the educated layperson — the view of the proverbial "man on the street." To the extent that expert opinion was required, it was obtained from the literature and is quoted in the panels. We made a serious effort to present as balanced a view as possible, resisting both the temptation to be politically correct and the temptation to range far off the reservation. No doubt people of all persuasions will find fault with something in these panels, all will find something to applaud.

How to Use this Book

Although *Health & Sickness* is, above all, a reference work, it is best approached by actually *reading* a chapter. Within a chapter, the different panels are closely related to develop the subject. The panels are relatively short. It is not difficult to peruse a chapter from beginning to end.

Use of a panel should begin with a close study of the graphic presented (only very few panels lack a graphic). Each graphic has a title. The meaning of the curves and bars is indicated in legends (or shown in the graph itself). Sometimes both the left and the right scale of the graphic is used to measure data sets that would not otherwise be visible. Please note that some of the graphics are in logarithmic scale. The log scale is used when the lowest value charted would be all but invisible — or in cases where the slope of curves is important to show how one set of data is growing more or less than the other. Some graphics are quite "busy," but a little study will well repay the effort. The general message is usually contained in the chart, although, in a few instances, the graphic is just a way of enticing the user to read the text.

Once the graphic is understood, the text will be more accessible. The objective of the text is to make clear what is depicted and then to add other information to put the subject into perspective. Sometimes parts of the information charted are also shown in tabular form in the text itself. This is done in those cases where the numerical values — not merely the pattern that they form — is of great importance. Sometimes additional, smaller graphics are shown to highlight additional aspects of the data or to present new information.

The user who wishes to look at the numbers charted can immediately refer to Part II, which presents data in tabular format.

The source note at the end of the panel may list one or more web sites for more information. The user might wish to be "distracted" into checking out those web sites — or continue on to the next panel until the entire subject is fully developed.

Introduction to this Volume – *Health & Sickness*

Contemplating the contents of this volume, one is reminded of the opening lines of Charles Dickens' *Tale of Two Cities*: "It was the best of times, it was the worst of times." And one is tempted to quote more: "It was the age of wisdom, it was the age of foolishness."

Our health has never been better. As the 20th century ended and the 21st dawned, we had brought infectious diseases under control and were seeing declines in death rates from the nation's biggest killers, heart disease and stroke. Our programs of immunization were reaching children previously unreachable. Maternal death rates were down. Our babies were healthier. We had made great strides in creating safer places of work. We could expect to live longer than any other population in U.S. history.

Most of the advances we have experienced are due to improvements in sanitation, medical practice, and the public health services provided by our health institutions. If we had to pick one hero for this volume, it would be the Centers for Disease Control and Prevention, one of the stellar performers among the health bureaucracies. But the CDC, in a sense, stands in for a rather extensive array of excellent hospitals, clinics, advocacy groups — and the health professionals who are behind them. Also responsible for the good results that we report in *Health & Sickness* are scientists, researchers, technologists, and pharmacists. In fact, we have done well in all those areas where science, technology, and social organization can effectively reach.

But ours are also, in a sense, the worst of times. We have seen the ravages of new diseases and the reawakening of old ones. Sexually transmitted diseases surged up late in the 20th century. Among them the deadliest is HIV/AIDS, still not under control. In areas where individuals must act, we are not doing quite so well. We are getting more and more overweight and obese. We refuse to exercise and to eat the healthy food we should. Obesity is leading to rising rates of diabetes and related complications. We are still consuming tobacco. Lung cancer rates for women are still climbing. Cancer, in fact, continues to resist. Despite our best efforts, the best we can do is to remove it or try to kill it in place with radiation and chemotherapy. Nature is also fighting back. Tuberculosis, cholera, malaria, and even the bubonic plague have made reappearances, here and there, when our vigilance flagged.

The black community lags some distance behind the majority white community in many important aspects of health — in fact in most, but notably, for instance, in maternal death in childbirth. African Americans are gaining, but the gap is not closing rapidly enough. In some cases it is widening. We explore these issues in various contexts.

We have both surpluses and shortages of doctors ("best of times, worst of times") and, in coming years, a very definite shortage of nurses and other health professionals. Long preparation, stressful environments, overwork, and other factors discourage people from entering and tempt others into leaving these professions. The shortages affect all levels of skill.

The very success of our health regimes is causing problems. Some will intensify as the Baby Boom generation ages. We live longer. We need to be cared for. Alzheimer's disease, one of the dementias of old age, is much more prevalent. The old consume a disproportionately high percentage of total health resource, and the age structure of the population is becoming seriously grey. The aging population is one of the factors putting pressure on our health institutions, which are under economic strain, a subject we also explore, including the subject of malpractice insurance.

While bodily health is improving, our mental health seems to be tanking. Depression among adults and developmental disabilities among the young are one of the subjects we deal with. In these areas there is less light than darkness, but work is underway. Anxieties, eating disorders, learning disabilities, autism, and a number of other ailments point at systemic problems where environment, society, and even the tempo of our lives coincide in what may be imperfect ways.

We cannot provide a final score in *Health & Sickness*. On balance, we are doing well. But much needs to be done. Exactly where the acupuncture needles might be placed is outlined, to the best of our ability, in this book's 15 chapters.

Comments and Suggestions

Those of us who have labored on *Health & Sickness* — and those who have suffered us while we did so — welcome your comments and suggestions. We have made every effort to be accurate, fair, and complete. No doubt we succeeded only in trying. Should errors have occurred, despite best efforts, they will be corrected in future editions. We shall be pleased to incorporate users' suggestions to the extent possible. To reach authors directly, please call Editorial Code and Data, Inc. at (248) 356-6990.

Please address other communications to:

Editor
Social Trends & Indicators USA
Health & Sickness
Gale
27500 Drake Road
Farmington Hills, MI 48331-3535
248-699-GALE
BusinessProducts@gale.com

Chapter 1

The State of Our Health

Somewhat paradoxically, we start to look at the state of our state by looking at the causes of our ultimate demise. The paradox is built into our health statistics. Our best indicators of health are records of mortality. They fix the age at which we die, record that which we die from. Even our life expectancy tables, as we explain in this chapter, are but "inside-out" mortality tables.

The chapter is divided into four broad topics. The first four panels look at causes of death — historically and then in more detail today. We look at differences between men and women, between races and ethnicities, and we examine the special topic of infant mortality. The leading causes of death have changed somewhat — but the heart remains the perennial. When the heart fails, life ceases. The leading causes of death for men and women are the same for the first three causes. After that, *vive la difference.* We explore interesting differences between the races and ethnic groups. The leading cause of infant death is malformations of the body at birth.

We look next more closely at women's health in six panels and zero in on problems that tend to affect women exclusively — including breast cancer and death in childbirth. Along the way we look at problems of obesity. Women tend to be obese, men to be overweight. Men's health is covered next in seven panels. We look at heart disease, lung cancer, cancer of the prostate, and colorectal cancer, and then zero in on deaths by accidents, suicide, and homicide. Many men die of something that science has loosely labeled "testosterone toxicity," meaning a tendency men have to do risky and irrational things. (The women nod.) The last major topic is children's health, covered in four panels. We cover low birth weight, the importance of breast feeding, and crib deaths.

Throughout this chapter — however grim the subject — the news is actually quite good. Our future prospects are excellent. Our state of health is fine and getting better. We don't explore the details — leaving that for chapters that follow — but we sum up the results in the final panel of the chapter which shows show long we are expected to live — and how much longer than our parents, never mind our grandparents.

Causes of Death — Then and Now

Three Top Killers a Century Apart

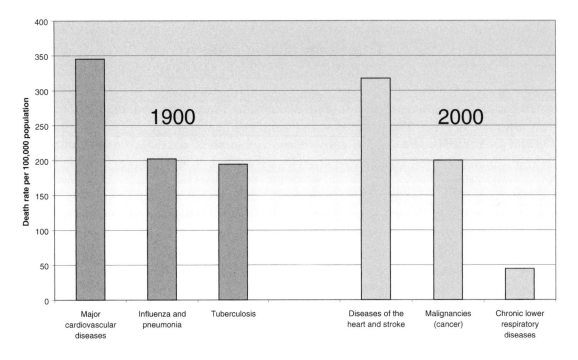

What are we dying of? To begin a look at this topic, let's compare the major causes of death a century apart — in 1900 and in 2000. In a century, methods of classification have changed a little, but the general categories still hold. The leading cause of death, a hundred years ago as now, is the failure of the heart. The heart is a perennial organ — in life as in death. But, thereafter, things are not the same.

Data for the year 1900 combine all of the "major cardiovascular diseases." These include diseases of the heart, stroke (cerebrovascular diseases), hypertension (accompanied or not by renal disease), atherosclerosis, and other forms of heart disease. This combined category also was the leading cause of death in 2000, but data at time of publication were not yet available in full detail to create a matching category. Therefore we show diseases of the heart and stroke in combination. All data are in deaths per 100,000 of population.

In 1900, sulphonamide (sulfa) drugs had not yet been invented and bacterial diseases carried people off in large numbers. Influenza and pneumonia ranked second as a cause of death. The great influenza epidemic of 1918 was still in the future, and pneumonia was known as the "old man's friend" — because the old man (or the old lady) swooned off to death rapidly as the infection, which inflames the pulmonary lining, got into the blood stream and carried people off rapidly and relatively painlessly. It was considered a natural cause of death. Influenza is a severe, contagious, viral respiratory disease that occasionally leads to death, especially for people who already have lung disease or are weak. These diseases were still very much with us in 2000 and still ranked in the top 10 — but in seventh position.

Tuberculosis — once known ominously as consumption, the bloody cough — is an infectious disease that settles in the lungs but can spread from there and attack other organs. According to the National Institutes of Health (NIH), 8 million people are still infected annually around the world, and of these 3 million die. TB, as it is also known, came to be controlled by antibiotics but is now staging a return linked, by NIH, to the HIV/AIDS epidemic (those affected are more vulnerable), crowding (which helps to spread it); poverty (it weakens the constitution); and drug use (which decimates the body). There are also other factors, like immigration. In 2000, TB made news by its reemergence, but it did not rank in the top 10 causes of death.

In 2000, cancer was the second leading cause of death. Among the malignancies, lung cancer is the leading killer. Looking at medical causes only, narrowly construed, heart attack, stroke, and lung cancer take the most lives. It was already present in 1900. In that year, of the top 10 causes of death malignant neoplasms ranked sixth. Lung cancer is associated with smoking. In the 19th century, women largely refrained. The other leading cancers — of digestive organs, genitals, women's breasts, urinary organs, and leukemia — are less clearly linked to behavior.

Chronic lower respiratory diseases include, notably, asthma, bronchitis, and emphysema. Most deaths are associated with a diversity of other lower respiratory ailments, but of those named, emphysema is the leader and is much more likely to have been caused by smoking than by coal dust or other industrial pollution.

Thus in 100 years, we have largely overcome infectious and most viral killers but have replaced them, at least in part, by diseases that may be due to our behavior. The heart's failure, however, then as now, is the leading cause of death.

Source: For 1900 data: U.S. Bureau of the Census. *Historical Statistics of the United States*. Table B149-166, p. 58. For 2000 data: Centers for Disease Control and Prevention. Online. Available: at http://www.cdc.gov/nchs/hphome.htm.

Causes of Death — A Closer Look

10 Leading Causes of Death - 1999

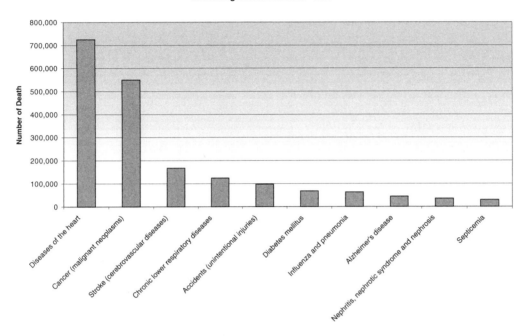

In 1999, nearly 2.4 million people died. Of those, just a shade under 80% (78.8) died of the causes shown in the chart. To get a minimal definition of the disease categories, please consult the table that completes this panel. Note, however, that among the top ten causes of death is a category called "accidents." These are unintentional, fatal injuries caused by motor vehicle crashes, air crashes, falls, drownings, accidental shootings and poisonings, death by fire or smoke inhalation, and other fatal mishaps. Homicides and suicides (*intentional* in nature) are counted among causes of death but don't make the top ten. Nor do military deaths on the battlefield. These data are for 1999, in actual counts. Data for 2000 were only available in very preliminary form at the time of publication.

The list used — as the Department of Health and Human Services points out (see source) — is not perfect but has long been in use. It often hides from view subcategories subsumed under larger headings. Thus it is not obvious, looking at the graphic, that the biggest killer among the cancer categories is lung cancer, associated with smoking, or that motor vehicle accidents lead the "Accidents" categories. Such deaths are, at least in theory, manageable by appropriate behavior.

But much the same may also be said of other things that kill us. Heart disease and stroke can, to some extent, be avoided by proper diet and exercise — and diabetes can be managed in the same way. Among the respiratory diseases, emphysema leads; it is also associated with smoking.

In fact, these leading causes of death are a composite portrait both of our medical/technological achievements and of our habits and follies. In the table that follows, more detail is provided about the categories. In the next panel, we look at interesting differences between men and women.

Diseases of the heart	There are some 23 disease that can affect the function of the heart muscle. The heart supplies oxygen to the cells by pumping the blood through the lungs and maintaining blood pressure. The most common heart disease is ischemic cardiomyopathy, which means that the heart itself is not getting enough blood; myopathy means that the disease affects the heart *muscle*. Lack of blood, in turn, may be caused by coronary artery disease. Ischemic heart disease is the top killer among the cardiac diseases.
Cancer	Also known as carcinoma, malignant tumor, or malignant neoplasm; neoplasm means tumor. This disease is caused by the abnormal multiplication of cells. There are some 200 different cancers, and they may affect most organs of the body. The leading killer is lung cancer.
Stroke	A stroke occurs when the brain fails to get sufficient blood and brain function fails, often with fatal results or permanent disability. Blocked arteries that restrict blood flow or plaques that lead to clot formation are a leading cause, hence stroke is classed as a cardiovascular disease.
Chronic lower respiratory diseases	These include obstructive lung diseases like asthma, bronchitis, and emphysema; restrictive lung diseases (lung elasticity is a problem); and diseases that result in failure properly to oxygenate the blood. There are some 35 diseases in this category, but some, like lung cancer, are classified elsewhere by the Centers of Disease Control and Prevention. The largest killer is emphysema.
Diabetes mellitus	Disease in which the body does not produce enough insulin or resists the action of insulin. High blood sugar results. Excess blood sugar can lead to renal (kidney) disease, blindness, numbness and amputation of feet, and nervous diseases. Type I diabetes is treated by insulin injections, Type II by diet and other forms of medications.
Influenza and pneumonia	Influenza is a viral infection and pneumonia is an infectious disease. See discussion on the previous panel.
Alzheimer's disease	Alzheimer's is an incurable brain disease of unknown cause associated with loss of memory and a progressive, acquired impairment of intellectual functions. The disease causes the destruction of neurons in the brain and inhibits the secretions of chemicals that transmit signals. Parts of the brain no longer communicate. Death eventually results, usually from an infection or the failure of organs.
Nephritis, nephrotic syndrome, nephrosis	Inflammation of the kidneys — diseases of the kidney or diseases that can lead to kidney damage and renal failure. Urinary tract disorders are often associated with these diseases or exhibit symptoms of their presence.
Septicemia	Poisoning of the blood through bacterial toxins caused by severe infections throughout the body, including the lungs, abdomen, and the urinary tract. It can rapidly lead to extremely low blood pressure and death (septic shock).

Source: Anderson, Robert N. "Deaths: Leading Causes for 1999." *National Vital Statistics Reports.* v. 49, No. 11. 12 October 2001. U.S. Department of Health and Human Services.

Causes of Death: Women Compared to Men

10 Leading Causes of Death - Women and Men
(Percent of Deaths and Rank)

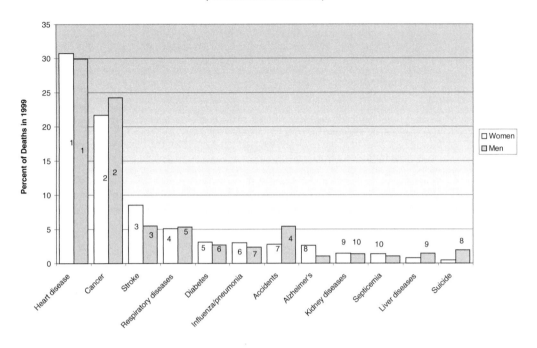

The differences between men and women persist even until death do them part. The similarities do likewise. The graphic shows the ten leading causes of death for women and for men — but since these are not identical, the actual list has expanded by two causes. One of these is "chronic liver disease and cirrhosis"; it is the 9th most common cause of death for males; the other is suicide, the 8th most common cause of male deaths. The list for both genders combined is identical to the list for women — because women outnumber men and more die in any given year. In 1999, 1.175 million men died and 1.216 million women, 103 women for every 100 men.

There are more than 20 liver diseases. Hepatitis A, B, and C, viral diseases, are a common form. Cirrhosis (scarring) of the liver is often associated with the abuse of alcohol. Alcohol use is also associated with hepatitis in some cases.

The differences between men and women are quite interesting and suggest that what some researchers have called "testosterone toxicity" [Perls/Fretts] predisposes males to dangerous and self-destructive activities. The juxtapositions in the graph show, for instance, that, for men, accidents (most of these are vehicular) rank 4th, for women 7th. For males, suicide makes it into the top ten causes of death at the 8th rank. In 1999, 23,458 men committed suicide while only 5,741 women did; suicide, therefore, did not make the top ten causes for women. Males commit suicide proportionally more both in their critical teenage years and in advancing seniority. More males die of cancer than women, a disease category linked to smoking — and of respiratory diseases, in which emphysema is a leading cause. In 1998, 26.4% of men smoked, 21.9% of women.

For men, Alzheimer's disease does not make it into the top ten — a degenerative brain disease of the late years. Women live longer. Septicemia, caused by infections and blood toxicity, is also not one of the top ten killers of the male.

We turn next to the differences between the races.

Source: Anderson, Robert N. "Deaths: Leading Causes for 1999." *National Vital Statistics Reports*. v. 49, no. 11. 12 October 2001. U.S. Department of Health and Human Services. For a discussion of gender differences, see Thomas T. Perls and Ruth C. Fretts, "Why Women Live Longer than Men." *Scientific American*. Online. Available: sciam.com/1998/0698womens/0698perls.htm.

Causes of Death by Race

10 Leading Causes of Death by Races
(Percent of Deaths and Selected Rankings)

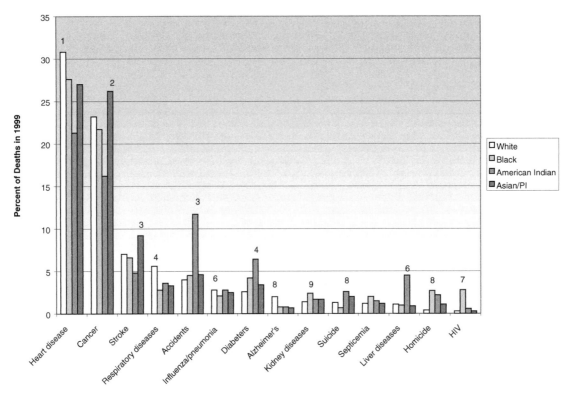

In this panel we continue to look at causes of death in 1999, this time by racial categories. Again, by adding further distinctions, we have to expand the list of causes to a total of 14 to include all the races — this time by adding homicide and HIV (human immunodeficiency virus infection).

Hispanics, who may be of any race, are not broken out as a group in the graphic but are shown in a later table. The races have quite different profiles. Heart disease, cancer, and stroke are the leading causes of death for three of the four groups, in that order. The exception is American Indians. Amazingly, their third-ranking cause of death is accidents.

After the top three, significant differences appear. The graphic shows the rank that the race with the highest percentage of deaths had in the category. To illustrate, American Indians had the highest percentage of deaths from diabetes, and that category was their 4th highest cause of death. One cause is not ranked — septicemia. Blacks had the highest percent of death in the category of the races, but septicemia did not make the top 10 among African Americans.

Sad highlights: Among those who died of heart disease, influenza/pneumonia, and Alzheimer's, whites had the highest percentage. African Americans topped other races in kidney diseases, septicemia, homicide, and HIV. American Indians led in accidents, diabetes, suicide, and liver disease. Asians and Pacific Islanders had the highest rates of deaths from cancer and from stroke.

The overall pattern, of course, is much the same for all the racial groups, but the differences illustrate that there are causes of death that predominate a little more in groups that are poor and — perhaps for that reason — suffer more social dysfunction. High rates of accidental deaths and suicides among American Indians and of homicide and HIV infection among blacks illustrate one end of the spectrum. Leading roles in heart disease, cancer, stroke, and respiratory diseases point more toward causes that accompany wealth and excesses in consumption.

A look at a group that is generally poorer than the national average but may be of any race, the population of Hispanic origin, will further substantiate this observation. The following table shows the leading causes of death for Hispanics, non-Hispanic whites, and non-Hispanic blacks. Data show causes of death in descending rank order for Hispanics and corresponding ranks by the two other groups.

Causes of Death Ranked:

Hispanics and Non-Hispanic Whites and Blacks

Cause of Death	Hispanics	Whites	Blacks
Heart disease	1	1	1
Cancer	2	2	2
Accidents	3	5	4
Stroke	4	3	3
Diabetes	5	7	5
Liver disease	6	...	...
Homicide	7	...	8
Respiratory ailments	8	4	6
Influenza/pneumonia	9	6	10
Adverse perinatal conditions	10	...	...

... indicates that cause did not reach top 10.

Adverse conditions originating in the perinatal period (near time of birth) affect the newborn, either because of maternal conditions or developmental or other causes. The fact that this cause makes it to the top ten among Hispanics indicates a high incidence of neonatal deaths. Among Hispanics, this cause accounted for 2.1% of all deaths — among African Americans for 1.8%, among whites for 0.3%.

Note that among Hispanics accidents are the third highest cause of death and homicide is ranked 7th, higher than among African Americans. But among this grouping of the population, as among all, the top four are still heart disease, cancer, and stroke. Only among American Indians is stroke ranked in 5th place.

We look, finally, more closely at infant deaths. Infant deaths are included in the statistics shown to this point, but to look at causes, we must separate the category from the much more numerous adults who pass on.

Source: Anderson, Robert N. "Deaths: Leading Causes for 1999." *National Vital Statistics Reports*. v. 49, no. 11. 12 October 2001. U.S. Department of Health and Human Services.

Causes of Death: Infants

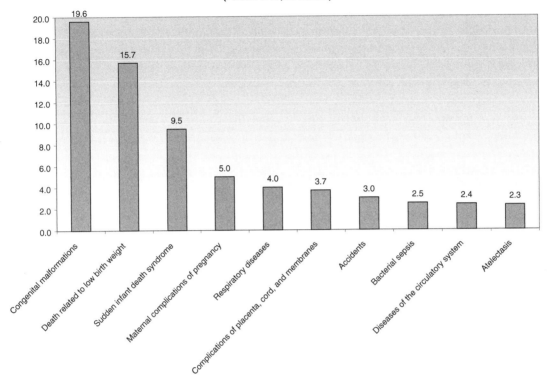

Leading Causes of Infant Deaths - 1999
(Percent of 27,937 Deaths)

In 1999, 3.959 million babies were born — and 27,937 infants died. Of these, 67% (18,728) died before they had reached 28 days of age. Neonatal deaths thus dominate infant deaths. The most common causes of death of all infants, defined as children less than 11 months of age, are congenital malformations, deformations, and chromosomal abnormalities. These categories comprise an umbrella term for several hundred malformations of body systems (nervous, respiratory, circulatory, digestive) as well as disturbances in the chromosomes that produce, for instance, Down's Syndrome, which shortens life, retards development, and is associated with congenital heart problems.

Among neonatals (less than 28 days of age) disorders due to low birth weight — not specifically pinpointed — is the leading cause. Among infants (28 days to 11 months old), the leading cause is Sudden Infant Death Syndrome (SIDS). Congenital malformations are the second cause of death of both groups and thus the leading cause for all infants.

Low weight at birth is one of the factors tracked by the U.S. Department of Health and Human Services as part of its "Healthy People 2000" (more recently "Healthy People 2010") program. Improvements in neonatal care — from technology — are keeping more and more of such babies alive. Babies may simply be small or may have low blood sugar, low body temperature, and polycythemia (increased level of red blood cells), all contributing to low birth weight. High blood pressure in the mother, heart disease, malnutrition, and drug addiction are thought to contribute to low birth weight.

The cause of SIDS is unknown. Deaths occur when infants are thought to be asleep. There is speculation that the babies may have problems with sleep arousal and that their bodies cannot detect the build-up of carbon dioxide in the blood. The incidence of SIDS has dropped since 1992 when parents were told to put their babies to sleep on their sides — because, as MEDLINEplus puts it, "risk factors include babies who sleep on their stomachs (up to 4 months. of age)." MEDLINEplus continues, citing other risk factors as including "soft bedding in the crib (up to 1 yr. of age), multiple births, prematurity, a history of a sibling who had SIDS, maternal smoking, maternal substance abuse, young maternal age, short intervals between pregnancies, late prenatal care and low socioeconomic status."

Among the leading causes are two not heretofore defined. Bacterial sepsis is an infection of the blood stream caused by bacteria. Atelectasis is a partial collapse of the lungs sometimes caused by shallow breathing.

The number of neonatal deaths (less than one half of one percent of total births – 0.47%) is thankfully small; nature is imperfect. It is much more disturbing to note that humans are too: among infants who survived the first 28 days of life in 1999 but died before age one, the seventh most common cause of death was homicide. In 1999, 272 of 9,209 infants in this age group were killed.

Death is a painful subject. We continue, now, on a more hopeful note, by examining progress in the health status of the nation overall as measured by various indicators, for women, men, and children — and what progress has meant for us in extended life expectancy. We begin with a look at women's health issues.

Source: Anderson, Robert N. "Deaths: Leading Causes for 1999." *National Vital Statistics Reports*. v. 49, no. 11. 12 October 2001. U.S. Department of Health and Human Services. Quotations from MEDLINEplus. Online. Available: http://www.nlm.nih.gov/med lineplus/ency/article/001566.htm.

Women's Health: Tracking Causes of Death

Female Death Rates from Heart Disease, Stroke, Breast Cancer, and Diabetes

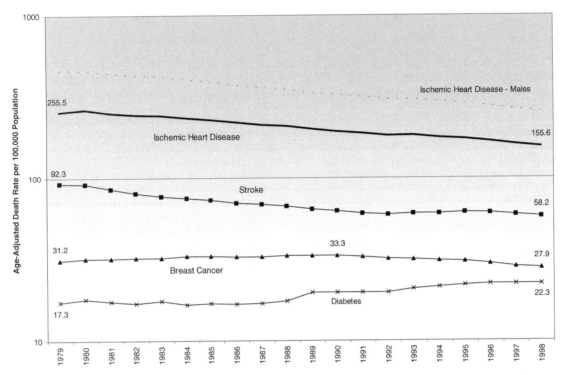

We begin our look at women's health by examining trends in death rates for heart failure (ischemic heart disease) — the leading cause of death among women — stroke, breast cancer, and diabetes. For comparison only, the death rates of males from heart disease are also shown in a dotted line at the top (more men die of heart disease than women).

Age-adjusted death rates enable comparison of deaths from a cause over multiple years. These rates are indexes which adjust actual death rates (the "crude death rate") to a "standard population." Thus fluctuations in the age groups, one year to the next, do not produce unusual results. Data are shown on a logarithmic scale so that slopes are comparable and data are more easily seen.

A 20-year period is provided. In the field of health statistics, data that are four years old, at this level of detail, are considered to be "current." Data for 2002 will come along, slowly, around about 2006.

These indicators paint a hopeful picture. Of the four causes of death shown in this graphic, all display a declining tendency except diabetes.

Those suffering from ischemic heart disease die because their hearts do not receive sufficient oxygen. This condition is the largest killer among those who die of cardiac diseases. New pharmaceuticals that control the undesirable type of cholesterol, early detection of the condition through diagnostic means, and technological interventions (more and more non-invasive), are bringing this condition under control. But heart failure continues to be the leading killer. We shall look at it more closely in the next panel and show differences between the races.

Stroke ("cerebrovascular disease") is another of the cardiovascular diseases and is controlled by much the same treatment as heart disease generally. Stroke comes about because the brain is denied oxygen by a blockage in the arteries or because blood clots are formed in the brain. Death rate due to stroke has declined at a slightly lower rate than ischemic heart disease. Among adults, it has decreased most in the age groups between 65 and 84. It has also declined among those 85 and older, the largest group that dies of stroke.

Breast cancer is the second most common cancer among women (next to lung cancer). With the exception of skin cancer, survival rates of those who have this condition are the highest. Breast cancer is related to hormonal influences. Women 50 years and older have 77% of new cases; 84% of those who die of breast cancer are 50 or over. The slow decline in death rates is in part due to failure of early detection and an increase in the population of those most subject to this condition.

Adult-onset diabetes (Type II) accounts for 90% of cases. Type I appears in childhood and is treated by insulin injections. Type II diabetes appears most commonly with advancing age; obesity and lack of exercise are factors. As the population is aging — and with obesity dramatically on the rise (a subject we cover elsewhere) — diabetes is a disease on the march. It has an increasing death rate. Its incidence — as a cause of death — has increased most in the 55 to 64 age group. A troubling aspect of the rise in this disease is that it is closely associated as a contributor to heart disease, stroke, blindness, and kidney failure.

Females, over all, have a lower death rate from diabetes than males because white females have a lower death rate than males and whites dominate the statistics. Among minority populations, but most notably among African Americans, females have a higher diabetes death rate than do males.

We turn next to a closer look at heart disease among women, looking at racial differences.

Source: Centers for Disease Control and Prevention. National Center for Health Statistics. National Vital Statistics System. Online. Available: http://www.cdc.gov/nchs/default.htm. May 29, 2002.

Women's Health: Heart Disease

Age-Adjusted Death Rates of Females from Ischemic Heart Disease

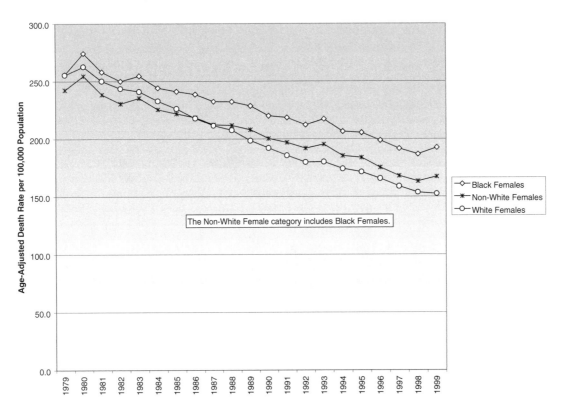

The death rate from ischemic heart disease (IHD is the cause of most coronary deaths) is down among women of all races in the 1979 to 1999 period, as shown in the graphic above.

In 1999, the age-adjusted[1] death rate of African-American females was 192.5 per 100,000 population, 26% higher than the death rate for white females, 152.5. But at the beginning of the period shown, in 1979, the black and white death rates were nearly identical, 255.8 for blacks, 255.4 for whites. As shown, the rates began to diverge after that year. The death rate dropped for both populations, but at a much more rapid rate for whites.

Several factors are associated with the prevention of early death from IHD. These include appropriate nutrition ("heart-healthy foods" low in cholesterol), adequate exercise, controlled body weight, abstinence from tobacco, and control of hypertension and diabetes. Blacks have a higher incidence of high blood pressure and diabetes. They are less likely to be diagnosed early with the disease or to receive proactive therapeutic treatment. They

---

[1] Age-adjusted death rates are indexes so that the rates can be compared from one year to the next. The so-called "crude" death rate is influenced by changes in the age structure and does not lend itself well to comparison of data over longer periods.

---

are also more likely to die suddenly and outside of hospitals from coronary heart disease.[2] Socioeconomic factors, including poverty, thus play a role in the difference between the death rates of white and black females from heart disease.

The series shown in the graphic does not break out death rates for Asians and Pacific Islanders, American Indians, or people of Hispanic origin. The curve showing Non-White Females includes the black population, which is its largest component. This shows that the Asians and Pacific Islanders and American Indian groups have lower death rates than blacks. Their inclusion brings the death rate down. Hispanic women had the lowest death rate due to IHD in 1999 as shown in the table:

1999 Age-Adjusted Death Rates of Females from IHD

Population Group	Death Rate in 1999 per 100,000 population
White Females	152.5
Non-Hispanic	153.7
Black Females	192.5
Non-Hispanic	196.6
Hispanic Females	112.8

The median Hispanic household income in 1999 was only slightly higher than that of blacks ($30,735 versus $27,910) and 72% of whites ($42,504). It is evident, therefore, that life-style or genetic endowment are more important in avoiding death by coronary heart disease than other factors. Note, in the table above, that Hispanic females in the white and black populations caused overall death rates for white and black females to be lower than for the non-Hispanic portions of those populations.

Source: Centers for Disease Control and Prevention. National Center for Health Statistics. National Vital Statistics System. Online. Available: http://www.cdc.gov/nchs/default.htm. May 29, 2002.

---

[2] Reported in Centers for Disease Control's *Morbidity and Mortality Weekly Report, 1998; 47:945-949.*

Women's Health: Weighty Trends

Obesity - 1960 to 1999
(Persons 20-74 years, age adjusted to 2000 population)

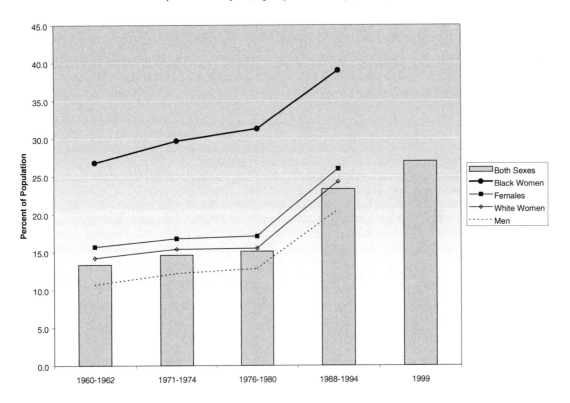

The graphic shows the stately march of obesity over the past 30 years or so. Data for 1999, from the National Health and Nutrition Examination Survey (NHANES) conducted by the Centers for Disease Control (CDC), is still preliminary, and details by sex and race are not yet available. (Obesity trends for men as a group are shown here for illustrative purposes only. More specific information on men is provided in other panels.)

How is obesity measured? Divide your weight by your height in inches; divide the result by your height in inches again; multiply the result by 703. A person 5 feet and 7 inches tall, weighing 134 pounds will have the following calculation:

$$134 \div 67 \div 67 \times 703 = 21.$$

In this calculation, 5 feet and 7 inches have been converted to 67 inches. The resulting value, 20.985, rounded to 21, is the so-called Body Mass Index or BMI. A BMI of less than 25 is considered to be healthy weight. A BMI of 25 to 29.9 is considered to be overweight. A BMI of 30 or above indicates obesity.

The metric calculation is to divide the body weight, in kilograms, by metric height squared. The same person, above, weighs 60.8 kg and has a height of 1.7 meters. The formula is therefore $60.8 \div 1.7^2 = 21$.

A higher percentage of men are *overweight* than women (39.9% men, 25.7% women in the 1988-1994 period), but, as the graphic shows, a higher percentage of women are *obese*. The percentage of African-American women who are obese is much higher than the percentage of white women (39.1% and 24.3%). Obese black and white men represent almost the same percentage of the male population (21.1% and 21.0%)[3].

We're eating the wrong kinds of food and we're not moving around enough. First the automobile, then the TV, finally the Internet. Obesity was trending up, but at a slow rate, in the 1960 to 1980 period. Then it started heading up steeply, growing 54% in about a decade and another 16% in the next five years or so. Not surprisingly, the CDC labels this phenomenon a public health epidemic.

Obesity is a woman's health issue because more women are obese and hence at risk. The relative risk of diabetes increases by about 25% for each BMI index point above 22. Sixty-seven percent of people with Type II diabetes (the most common form) have a BMI of 27 or higher; 46% of these women are obese. Among obese women, 32.2% have high blood pressure, 24.7% have high blood cholesterol.

More information on weight problems and obesity is presented elsewhere in this book. We note here the troubling trend toward more body weight, with its adverse consequences and relationship to heart disease, the leading killer of women (and men). Once the 1999 survey data are available, it is almost certain that women, as before, will be leading the parade, achieving (if that's the right word) very high obesity scores.

[1]*Sources*: Centers for Disease Control and Prevention. National Center for Health Statistics. Division of Health Examination Statistics. Unpublished data. Online. Available: http://www.cdc.gov/ June 1, 2002. Obesity and disease correlations from "Statistics Related to Overweight and Obesity." National Institute of Diabetes and Digestive and Kidney Diseases (NIDDK). Online. Available: http://www.niddk.nih.gov/health/ nutrit/pubs/statobes.htm.

---

[3] These data are taken from actual measurements. When asked to judge themselves, more men report that they are obese than women, as shown by the CDC's Behavioral Risk Factor Surveillance System (BRFSS). Men are too honest, women too modest. For details, see http://www.cdc.gov/nccdphp/dnpa/obesity/trend/ prev_char.htm.

.

Women's Health: Cancer Trends

Mammograms and Breast Cancer Death Rate

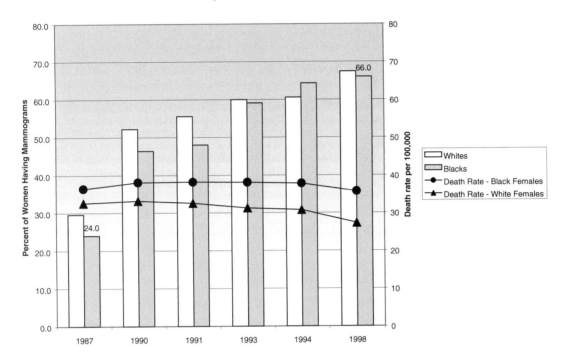

The cancer that takes most women's lives (not counting lung cancer, the top category for both sexes) is cancer of the breast. Some types of cancer are difficult to detect and, consequently, survival rates after detection are quite low. Breast cancer can be detected early by mammograms. It has one of the highest survival rates. In the 1987-1994 period (most recent available data), if the survival rate of the population as a whole is taken as 100, those with breast cancer have an 84.6 survival rate. The rate for those with cancer of the pancreas is 4.2.

The chart shows the percentage of women aged 40 years or older who reported having a mammogram within the past two years. In the 12-year period shown (1987 to 1998), the number of women having this test has increased dramatically. Among white women, 29.6% reported undergoing a mammogram in 1987, 67.4% in 1998, a 128% increase. Blacks have done even better, going from 24% of women aged 40 or older to 66%, a 175% increase.

Deaths attributable to breast cancer have also declined in both groups. Among African American women of all ages, the death rate has dropped from 36.4 per 100,000 population (albeit after first rising to a 38.2 rate first) to 35.7%, a 2% decline. Among white women the rate has gone from 32.6 to 27.6, a 15.3% improvement. All death rates are age-adjusted, therefore comparable between the periods.

Declines in death rates clearly do not correlate strongly with the frequency of undergoing the mammography procedure. Other factors than detection are involved, clearly. As discussed earlier, socioeconomic factors play an important role in the higher incidence of death for black females.

Breast Cancer Survival Rates

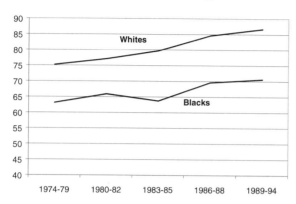

We can trace this further by looking at cancer survival rates in the 1974 to 1994 period in five time periods. Whites have a significantly higher survival rate than blacks for the same condition — and the white survival rate has a more even progression, implying a more consistent application of diagnostic measures and therapeutic interventions.

The table below provides a numerical view of the chart, with survival rates added for four other cancers that take women's lives — lung cancer, cervical cancer, cancer of the uterus, and ovarian cancer. In all cases, black women have a lower survival rate than whites.

Survival Rates for Selected Cancer Sites, 1974-79 and 1989-94

Type of Cancer	Whites		Blacks	
Period	1974-79	1989-94	1974-79	1989-94
Lung	16.7	*16.5*	15.4	*13.9*
Breast	75.2	86.7	63.1	70.6
Cervix uteri	69.4	71.5	63.0	*59.0*
Corpus uteri	87.5	*86.5*	59.2	*54.4*
Ovary	37.1	50.1	**40.4**	46.3

Bold indicates Blacks higher than Whites. *Italics* indicate a declining rate of survival.

Note here that lung cancer and ovarian cancer are difficult to detect. The symptoms of ovarian cancer are "vague and non-specific" according to MEDLINEplus. Pap smears can detect precancerous conditions in the cervix and in the uterus (in combination with pelvic exams). Among both groups, survival from lung cancer has declined. Among African Americans survival rates have declined in cervical and uterine cancer. Uterine cancer survival rates among whites have also dropped.

Detection is obviously only the first step — however, vital — to survival from cancers that take women's lives.

Source: U.S. Department of Health and Human Services. *Health United States, 2001*, p. 279. Online. Available: http://www.cdc.gov/nchs/products/pubs/pubd/hus/tables/2001/01hus082.pdf. Survival rates, same publication, are from National Institutes of Health, National Cancer Institute, Cancer Statistics Branch, Bethesda, Maryland 20892. Quotations from MEDLINEplus: Online. Available: http:// www.nlm.nih.gov/med lineplus/ency/article/001566.htm.

Women's Health: Fat, Sugar, and Salt

High Cholesterol Levels - Women, by Race

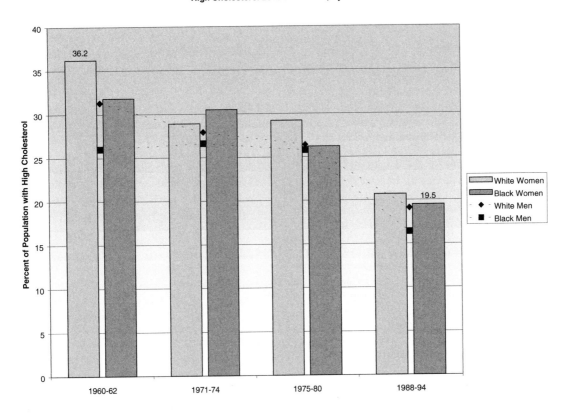

Cholesterol is good. Our body makes it in our liver from meat and animal products that we eat. The body then sends the cholesterol to other regions in the blood. The body turns cholesterol into hormones, bile acid, and Vitamin D. So what's all the controversy about? Too much of a good thing.

Excess cholesterol deposits in our arteries lead to atherosclerosis, the deposit of fatty substance that interferes with and that also can block blood-flow; this leads to heart disease. Cholesterol comes in two forms. High Density Lipoprotein (HDL) is known as "good cholesterol," low density (LDL) as "bad." HDL is good because it is the body's way of "packaging" excess cholesterol for return to the liver for recycling. LDL is not such a package, and high levels of it in the blood ("serum cholesterol") correlate with heart disease.

As shown on the graphic, serum cholesterol has been dropping both for white and black women in the period shown. This is the biomedical counterpart of the "fat free" promotions launched by every purveyor of food. Since only animal products end up as cholesterol in blood, by way of the liver, reducing our intake of animal fats (and organ meats, like liver, which contain high amounts) also reduces the level in us. Fats and oils from plants do not contain cholesterol.

Of course, it is precisely animal fats that give food taste. If the producer removes the fat, he or she also removes some of the pleasure. All three substances that improve "eatability," to borrow a phrase from advertising — fat, sugar, and salt — are on the healthy eater's list of "no-nos." In practice, when fats are removed, sugar or salt (or both) are added in compensation. If sugar is removed, fat can lift the taste. This has turned diet-conscious Americans into avid and sometimes frustrated readers of labels on cans and on jars.

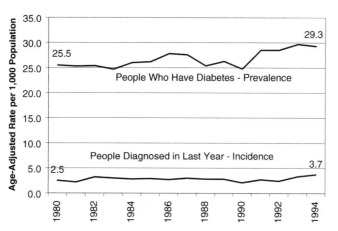

Prevalence and Incidence of Diabetes

Increased levels of sugar in the blood (blood glucose) worsen the condition of those with diabetes (people whose pancreas does not produce enough insulin to handle the "overdose" or whose body does not respond effectively to insulin). Those without insulin problems get fat. Both diabetes and obesity are up sharply. The chart on the left shows the prevalence and incidence of diabetes for the years 1980 to 1994. It is worth noting that age-adjusted rates of prevalence are up 14.9%, of incidence (new diagnoses) up 48%. Actual people with diabetes increased 40.1%. Obesity expanded 54% between the periods 1976-1980 and 1988-1994. Meanwhile, cholesterol levels for all women are down, from 1975-80 to 1988-1994 by 28.8%.

The correlation between diet, weight, and exercise is well established. The growing prevalence of diabetes cannot be directly blamed on people eating more sugar, but controlling sugar-intake mitigates the damages of diabetes. Diabetes is more common now because the population is aging, does not exercise, and is getting obese. Some of that may be related, indirectly, to other dietary stratagems that bring down cholesterol.

Salt, which is very high in fast foods and abounds in many prepared foods and sauces, contributes to high blood pressure in some. The recommended daily intake (National Academy of Sciences) is 1,100 to 3,300 milligrams for adults. Not surprisingly, the average intake of American adults is 4,000 to 5,000 milligrams a day. Pass the salt.

Balance, obviously, is everything. The choice for those among us who love fat, sugar, and salt may be to live long but dreary lives — or grossing out and dying young but happy.

Source: Centers for Disease Control and Prevention. *Morbidity and Mortality Weekly Report.* October 31, 1997. Online. Available: http://www.cdc.gov/mmwr/preview/mmwrhtml/00049741.htm.

Women's Health: Death in Childbirth

Maternal Mortality

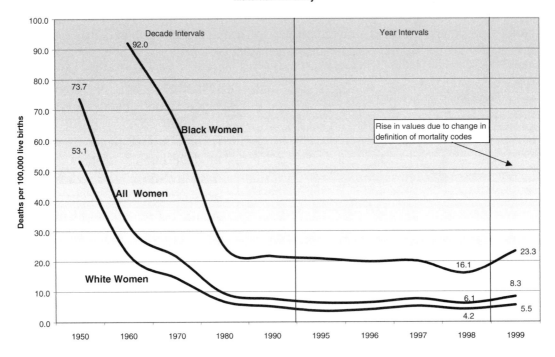

The spectacular drop in maternal deaths since the 1930s to the 1980s, of which the portion from 1950 onward is shown in the graphic, is one of the more laudable achievements of 20th-century medical practice. The persistently higher maternal death rate of African American women is a continuing source of concern. The graphic shows deaths per 100,000 live births in an age-adjusted fashion, meaning that data from year to year are comparable despite changes in the age composition of the population. Age-adjustment is important to see the age stratification of women dying of this condition. Typically, women 35 years old and older have the highest maternal mortality rate.

In 1950, 2,960 women died in childbirth. In 1998, 281. In 1999, maternal deaths began to be classified under the International Classification of Diseases 10 (ICD-10) which caused more women to be classified as having died because of "complications of pregnancy, childbirth, and the puerperium [the period during and just after labor]" in 1999. Under the previous ICD classification, the number would have been lower than in 1998.

First, why has maternal mortality dropped so dramatically? The process began in 1933 when a report, issued by a White House conference, stimulated changes. Cited as causes for high mortality rates were poorly trained medical practitioners, unsanitary deliveries at home, excessive surgical and obstetric interventions (induced labor, use of forceps, episiotomy [incision to enlarge the vagina during delivery], and cesarean deliveries). Forty percent of deaths were due to infections of the bloodstream caused by unsanitary interventions (sepsis); of these, half occurred after illegal abortions. The rest of the deaths were caused by hemorrhage and pregnancy-related hypertension (toxemia), which occurs in about 8% of all pregnancies.

Dramatic results were achieved as hospital-delivery of babies became more and more prevalent, as certification procedures for practitioners improved, as antibiotics came into use, better drugs were found to induce labor (oxytocin, a contraction-inducing hormone), better methods to provide blood transfusion became established, and improved techniques for managing pregnancy-induced high blood pressure took hold. Septic death from illegal abortions dropped dramatically when induced abortions were legalized in the 1960s.

Rates of maternal mortality have been more or less level since the 1980s. There are still too many. The Centers for Disease Control estimates that more than half could be prevented using accepted interventions. Twenty countries have lower maternal mortality rates than the United States. Leading causes are hemorrhage caused by ectopic pregnancy (the egg is implanted outside the uterus, usually in the Fallopian tubes), other severe bleeding, high blood pressure (toxemia), and pulmonary embolism (clotting — blood fails to reach the lungs).

The other question that needs to be addressed is the persistently higher maternal mortality rate of black women. Black women begin with a disadvantage. Nonwhite women have a 1.6 times higher risk of maternal complication than white women. Risks are associated with physical condition that may, in turn, be linked to socioeconomic factors — nutrition, the prevalence of diabetes, bacterial vaginosis (an infection of the vagina in nubile women – 23% of pregnant blacks suffer from it, 9% of whites), high blood pressure, and other factors. Blacks have a higher risk factor *before* childbirth (almost twice the risk of whites). But they are *four times* as likely to die in childbirth as whites. The Centers for Disease Control concludes: "This suggests that access to and use of health-care services for early diagnosis and effective treatment, if complications develop, may be a factor." Indeed, it might. One is tempted to put it more bluntly: Black women are just are not getting the proper care, for whatever reason. It may be economic, cultural, or societal in nature. The gap between whites and blacks is narrowing, but it is happening very slowly.

Source: U.S. Department of Health and Human Services. *Health, United States, 2001*. Online. Available: http://www.cdc.gov/nchs/products/pubs/pubd/hus/tables/2001/01hus044.pdf. History: "Achievements in Public Health, 1900-1999: Healthier Mothers and Babies." *MMWR Weekly*. Centers for Disease Control. 1 October 1999.

Men's Health: Hearty Progress

Ischemic Heart Disease Death Rate for Men

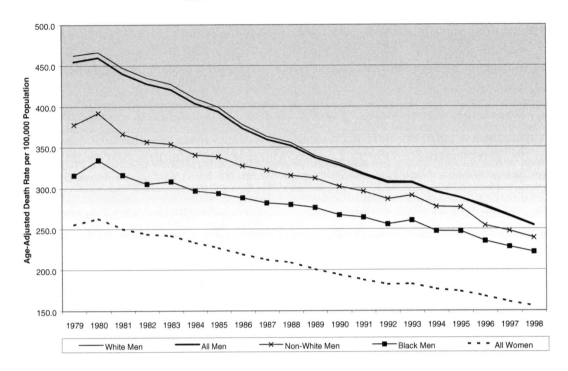

The top killer of men, as of women, is heart disease, of which ischemic heart disease (the heart muscle is starved of oxygen) is the leader. The graphic shows overall progress in reducing the death rate for this disease by a variety of interventions — new technology and surgical techniques, better management of the condition through pharmaceuticals, and postponement of death by regimens of diet and exercise.

In this as in the other panels that follow, data are shown for "all men" — men of all races — for whites, blacks, and "non-white men." The comprehensive data set used for these assessments does not break data down by Asians, Pacific Islanders, and Native Americans. Typically the values for "all men" will be close to those for whites because whites, by sheer numbers, dominate the statistics. Similarly, the non-white category, which includes African Americans, is dominated by blacks, who are the majority. It is the difference between values for blacks and total non-whites that is, by inference, the Asian/American Indian category in combination. Data for women are included, where appropriate, as a dotted line as are data for women of all races.

This chart shows that the prevalence of heart disease is greatest among whites. Asian and American Indian men have a higher death rate from coronary heart disease than black males. Black males are, on the whole, the most physically active and least over-weight group in the U.S. population. This shows up rather vividly in this graphic. Exercise pays dividends. But black males still have a higher death rate from heart disease than black females; in 1998, the difference was 35 deaths per 100,000 population.

Between 1979 and 1998, the death rate has declined nearly 45% for white males, 37% for non-white males as a group, and 30% for black males. Black men are less likely to be diagnosed early or to be treated as intensively as other racial groups — a phenomenon we have remarked on before. The death rate for women of all races dropped 39% in this same period (40% among white women, 32% among non-whites, which includes blacks, and 27% among blacks viewed as a separate grouping).

More men than women are at risk for heart disease. Past age 40, 49% of men and 32% of women are likely to have heart disease. Heart disease can run in families. Vigorous exercise, a healthy, low-fat diet, abstention from tobacco, and stress-control are actions individuals can adopt for keeping coronary heart disease at bay and controlling its ravages after it appears.

Surgical/technological interventions for controlling heart disease are making great strides and are no doubt reflected in the results on the chart.[4] These methods are becoming less and less invasive and produce longer-lasting results, beginning with balloon angioplasty, a procedure that opens clogged arteries by the expansion of a tiny balloon, the insertion of tiny tubes that hold the artery open (stents), and most recently stents coated so that they inhibit the re-clogging of the opening after some period of time (not yet available in the U.S.). These interventions do not involve major surgery.

Surgical interventions now include minimally invasive direct coronary artery bypass surgery (MIDCAB): the heart continues to beat while surgery is performed. Conventional coronary bypass surgery "bypasses" clogged arteries in the heart; during the procedure, blood is circulated by a pump. Eventually, no doubt, minute little robots will be launched into the arteries that chew away or dissolve the build-up of plaque. But in the meantime, a word to the wise: Eat sensibly and exercise, exercise, exercise...

Source: Centers for Disease Control and Prevention. National Center for Health Statistics. National Vital Statistics System. Online. Available: http://www.cdc.gov/nchs/default.htm. May 29, 2002. Background information obtained from MEDLINEplus. Online. Available: http:// www.nlm.nih.gov/med lineplus/ency/article/001566.htm.

---

[4] The author of these lines was able to write them because of an intervention not yet attempted when he gave away his first daughter in marriage.

Men's Health: Lung Cancer

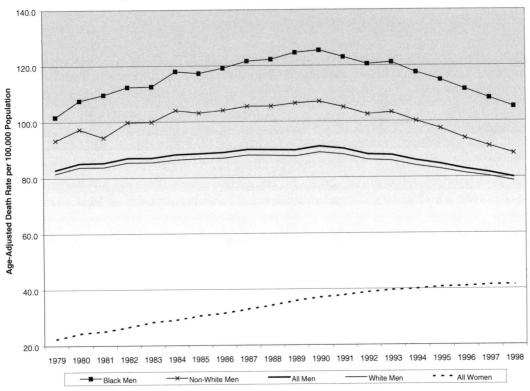

Lung Cancer Death Rates of Men
(Death due to malignant neoplasms of trachea, bronchus, and lung)

Y-axis: Age-Adjusted Death Rate per 100,000 Population

Legend: Black Men · Non-White Men · All Men · White Men · All Women

Cancer is the second leading cause of death, and lung cancer the leading cause of death from cancer among both men and women. In 1999, 171,600 cases of lung cancer were reported, and 152,480 people died of the disease, 59% males, 41% females.

Death rates for men have been dropping since about 1990. There are causes other than cigarette-smoking for lung cancer, but cigarette smoking is by far *the* cause of the disease. A thorough look at smoking is presented in Chapter 4 of this volume. Here we would note the disturbing pattern shown in the graphic for the 1979 to 1998 period. Death rates for males are down but climbing for women. Women have a significantly lower death rate for lung cancer than men — because fewer women smoked. But the use of cigarettes is climbing among women, as we shall show elsewhere.

Detection of lung cancer is difficult, hence survival rates after the onset of the disease are very low. Survival rates are measured by comparing the survival rate of the total population to that of the affected group in increments of five years. Among whites, survival rate was 11.6% of patients in the 1974-1979 period (88.4% died); survival had improved by the 1989-1994 period to 13%. Among blacks, the rate was 9.9% in 1974-1979 and had worsened to 9.7% by 1989-1994, having improved in the intervening period.

Black males have the highest death rate from lung cancer followed by Asians/American Indians, then whites. There is a correlation between the decline in lung cancer death rates and incidence (new cases) of lung cancer, as shown in the inset graphic on the next page. New cases are dropping for each of the major population groups: whites, blacks, and Asians/Pacific Islanders. Decreases in new incidents are greatest for whites, least for Asians as is evident from the graphic.

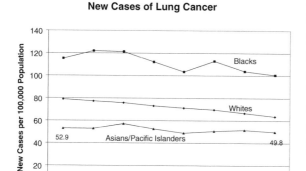

New Cases of Lung Cancer

Lung cancer death rates are highest for those in advanced years. Highest rates are associated with the 75 to 84 age group, next with those aged 85 years and older, and third with those between 65 and 74. This pattern holds for whites and non-whites. Among black males, the 65 to 74 age group has a higher death rate than the 85 and older group.

Lung cancer comes in many forms and survival rates depend on the type of cancer and the stage at which it has been detected. Chemotherapy, radiation therapy, and surgical interventions are used to control the disease. In the elderly, the interventions can lead to debilitating complications as well.

Source: Centers for Disease Control and Prevention, National Center for Health Statistics, National Vital Statistics System, accessed at http://www.cdc.gov/nchs/default.htm, May 29, 2002. Background information obtained from MEDLINEplus at http://www.nlm.nih.gov/med lineplus/ency/article/001566.htm.

Men's Health: Prostate Cancer

Prostate Cancer Death Rates

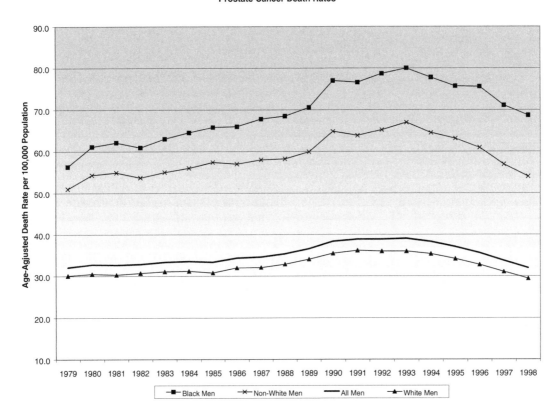

Prostate cancer is the second leading cause of deaths of men by cancer (after lung cancer). It is the leading cause of cancer death among men 75 years or older. The graphic shows age-adjusted death rates per 100,000 population. In 1999, one year beyond the time frame of the graphic, there were 179,300 cases of prostate cancer and 31,728 men died of the disease.

Roughly midway through the period shown, a new prostate cancer screening method was approved by the FDA. This method, commonly known as the PSA blood test ("prostate specific antigen"), may in part explain both the spike in the death rate and its decline. The logic is laid out by the National Institutes of Health in a News Advisory (see source note). The essence, in summary, is as follows:

Prostate cancer mortality rates have been increasing gradually since 1977, sped up in the mid-1980s, and began to drop slightly in 1992 for white males, in 1994 for black males. The PSA test was approved in 1986, but did not come into wide use until after 1989, when new diagnoses of preclinical prostate cancer shot up. (Clinical diagnoses actually detect the formation of a tumor.) The test added a five-year lead-time to the detection of prostate cancer and may be producing a decline in mortality rates late in this period. However, the blood test may also have produced the spurt in mortality due to what the NIH labels "attribution bias." To quote:

Attribution bias is "a distortion of true mortality rates that occurs when the stated cause of the death is incorrect. A recently diagnosed cancer may be recorded as cause of death, even if, as in the case of preclinical prostate cancers, it is almost certainly not the true cause of death. The death of an elderly man might thus be wrongly attributed to prostate cancer simply because a recent diagnosis is in his files and no other underlying cause could be identified."

The cause of the cancer is not known, although an interesting correlation has been observed. Testosterone levels increase with the intake of dietary fat. At the same time, lowering testosterone levels — by surgical removal of testicles or medication — can cause prostate cancer to regress. At this time the medical community is not willing to go further than simply stating these relationships. A lay person might observe, however, that we are becoming more obese — and that prostate cancer is encountered least among fish-eating Japanese men and vegetarians.

The higher mortality rate of black men, and the lag-time in the down-turn of the mortality rate of blacks, again shows that the African American community is not receiving the same health care — for whatever reasons — than the wider community.

Death rates from prostate cancer increase with age and are highest among those 85 years old and older. Longevity may have its downside.

Source: Centers for Disease Control and Prevention. National Center for Health Statistics. National Vital Statistics System. Online. Available: http://www.cdc.gov/nchs/default.htm. May 29, 2002. Background information: MEDLINEplus. Online. Available: http://www.nlm.nih.gov/med lineplus/ency/article/001566.htm. Information from the NIH is taken from: "Recent Trends in Prostate Cancer Incidence and Mortality." Press Release. 21 November 1997. National Institutes of Health. National Cancer Institute.

Men's Health: Colorectal Cancer

Colorectal Cancer Death Rates - Men

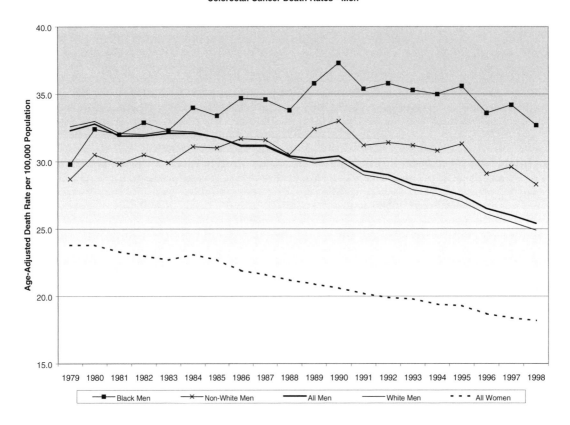

Cancer of the colon or the rectum, combined into the "colorectal" category, is the second leading cause of death from cancer for the population as a whole and the third most common cancer death for men (coming after lung and prostate cancer respectively). It also ranks third among women (coming after breast cancer and lung cancer).

The graphic shows death rates per 100,000 population for different categories of men and for all women (dotted line). For all men, the death rate has declined 21.4% from 1979 to 1998, but results for racial groups are mixed: for white males, the rate is down 23.6%, for black males it is up 9.7%. For females as a whole, it has declined 23.5%.

Colorectal cancer is a disease strongly correlated with animal fat consumption. Less pronounced is the correlation with the consumption of red meat and meats prepared at high temperature (broiling and frying). Colorectal cancer rates are significantly lower in underdeveloped countries — but high among their upper socioeconomic strata.

In the United States, at the beginning of the period shown, blacks, whose median income is lower than that of whites, had a lower colorectal death rate. By 1982, the situation was reversed. Active promotion of colorectal screening, changes in diet, the push to eat more "high-fiber" foods and less fat, had begun to bring down the death rate of white males. The improved earnings of blacks caused a movement in the other direction for African

Americans. Declines in the death rate, from a peak in 1990, did not begin until much later. The non-white group, which includes blacks, had a similar pattern but at a delay in time; that group also includes Asian Americans and American Indians, populations that have a lower colorectal death rate than whites.

Here, again, we observe different health outcomes for the races. Again, we see that women's death rate is lower, perhaps due to a generally healthier style of life or a greater willingness to undergo medical procedures.

As is the case in most cancers, survival depends on early detection. Colorectal cancer screening can be done by the individual by collecting a fecal sample (as instructed) and submitting it for a fecal occult blood test (FOBT). The doctor can examine the rectum and the lower colon with a lighted instrument in a sigmoidoscopy. A colonoscopy is similar in nature but enables the doctor to examine the entire colon. X-ray examination of the colon and rectum, after a barium enema, provides a picture of these organs (DCBE or, Double-Contrast Barium Enema). A digital rectal exam (DRE) is used to detect abnormal areas in the rectum. Energetic efforts are made by the government (CDC, National Cancer Institute) to persuade people over 50 to undergo screening at least once a year.

Colorectal death rates are heading down because significant numbers of people are willing to change their diets and to undergo tests the names of which are acronyms or run on for five Greek syllables. Better that than the alternative...

Source: Centers for Disease Control and Prevention. National Center for Health Statistics. National Vital Statistics System. Online. Available: http://www.cdc.gov/nchs/default.htm. May 29, 2002. Background information: MEDLINEplus. Online. Available: http://www.nlm.nih.gov/med lineplus/ency/article/001566.htm and National Cancer Institute, Schatzkin, MD, Arthur G., "Risk Factors: Colon and Rectum." Online. Available: http://rex.nci.nih.gov/NCI_Pub_Interface/ratrisk/risks129. html.

Men's Health: Accidents

Male Death Rate from Accidents

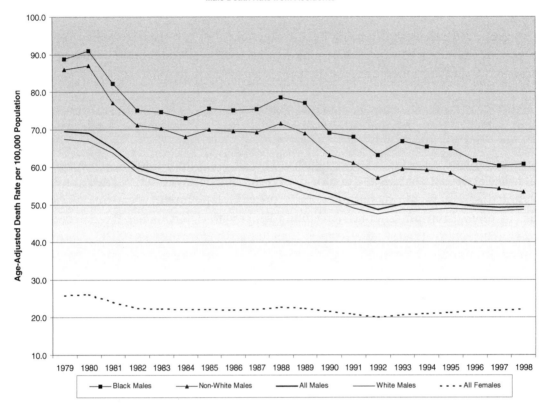

In 2000, 93,592 people died of unintentional injuries suffered in accidents of all kinds. Of these, just shy of 45% were motor vehicle fatalities — 41,804 deaths. The rest were due to other events. Accidents are most common from falls (17%), accidental poisoning from drugs or medicines (10%), drownings (4.2%), inhalation or ingestion of objects (3.7%), and fires (3.5%).

Those aged 75 to 84 have a 2.8 times higher accidental death rate than all ages combined. Those aged 85 or older have a 7.6 times higher death rate. Men's death rates in 1998 were 46.5 deaths per 100,000 population, women's 23.8, so men are nearly twice as likely to die of accidents than women — hence accidents are highlighted here as a men's health issue.

The graphic shows the general pattern for groupings of men from 1979 to 1998 and for women of all races (dotted line). Accidental death rates are down for all groups, most noticeably for women: fewer women die in automobile accidents. And auto accidents are down significantly, probably because males aged 15 to 24 have become a lower percentage of the total population. This group of males has a higher death rate from motor vehicle accidents than any age group except those 85 years old or older. The graphic on the following page shows accidental death rate trends and the percentage of this age group of the population.

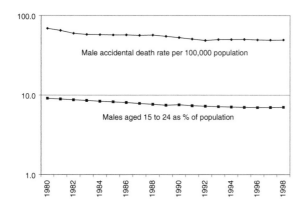

Note the similarity of the curves on this logarithmic chart — which preserves the change between the two sets of data despite difference in scale.

The decline in accidental death rates, however, is not explained simply by a decrease in an especially "accident-prone" age cohort as a percentage of the population. While males aged 15 to 24 declined in the 1980 to 1998 period by 8% overall, males aged 75 and older increased by nearly 65%. Death rates in both groups dropped. Improvements appear to be due to many factors working together. As shown elsewhere in this series, occupational fatalities are down in part as a consequence of vigorously enforced safety programs — which were, in part, instituted to avoid expensive litigation. Accidental fatalities are down for motor vehicles, railroads, airlines (except for a sharp uptick in 1995), recreational boating, and water-borne transportation. In general, accidents and accidental fatalities have diminished during the past two decades.

In this series, as in others, we note that the experience of African Americans is worse than that of whites. In 1998, blacks had a 12.5% higher accidental death rate than whites, a slight spreading in the gap between the groups: in 1979, blacks had an 11.5% higher death rate in this category. Both races, however, have seen an overall decline in the death rate.

Source: Centers for Disease Control and Prevention. National Center for Health Statistics. National Vital Statistics System. Online. Available: http://www.cdc.gov/nchs/default.htm. May 29, 2002.

Men's Health: Suicide

Suicide Death Rates of Men

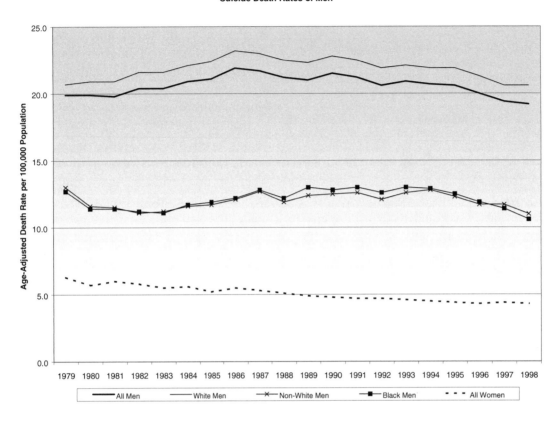

Around 30,000 people commit suicide every year. To give this number some dimension, consider that around 42,000 people die each year in motor vehicle accidents. There is a "National Strategy for Suicide Prevention." It was published in 2001. But the initiative bridges the last two administrations under the leadership of the Surgeon General.

Nonetheless, in a book on social trends, one is impelled, first of all, to emphasize that the incidence of suicide is very much a wave-like phenomenon statistically. The death rate (expressed as deaths per 100,000 population) goes up and down over time. In 2000 the rate was 10 deaths per 100,000. In 1900, it was 10.2. It rose to a peak of 17.4 in the Depression year of 1932. It was 10 in 1944, during World War II and under 11 in 21 years of the 20th century. Suicide appears to be a perennial phenomenon. Having said that, some observations.

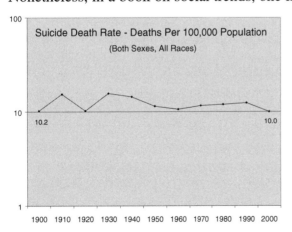

In 1999, when the death rate was 10.7, 29,199 people committed suicide. Of these 80% were males. Most suicides now — and as far back as measurements extend — are males. Suicides also take younger lives. This is illustrated in the graphic on this page. The two ten-year age groups that have the most suicides are those aged 25 to 34 and 35 to 44. Data graphed are for males in 1999.

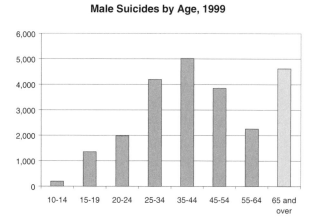

Male Suicides by Age, 1999

Suicide has long fascinated students of human nature and behavior. Perhaps the most comprehensive treatment of the subject — one of the founding acts of the science of sociology — came from the pen of the Frenchman, Émile Durkheim. His 1897 work, *Suicide*, made a strong case for the interaction of social forms — not least social integration — and individual behavior. Durkheim's observations should be pursued in their detail, but here a very rough summary must suffice.

Studying data from a number of nations, Durkheim observed that the individual is protected from suicide when his or her integration within the social community is well in balance with the moral regulation provided by that community. He noted that high suicide rates are associated with men more than women, professionals more than laborers, unmarried status more than married status, Protestant faith more than Catholic or Jewish. His theories, interestingly enough, are still modern enough to explain suicide bombers, for instance.

Durkheim identified four types of suicide. *Altruistic* suicides are those who have lost their identity to the group and can be persuaded to give their lives for a group's goals — suicide bombers, religious cult suicides. In these cases, integration is high and social regulation very dominant. *Fatalistic* suicides are people who are very strictly regulated but do not share the views of those who dominate them: prisoners, inmates of concentration camps, and also, by extension, those subject to an incurable disease. *Egoistic* suicides are people who have lost the meaning of life but lack support mechanisms — religion, marriage, children, the security of a stable family, economic means. Many suicides during the Depression appear to have been caused by sudden loss of wealth. Finally, *Anomic* suicides are people who have ample means, much talent, and great freedom — yet lack sufficient moral regulation to channel wealth or talent.

Thus far with Durkheim. No one, needless to say, has the last word on the mysteries of life and death, but some of these concepts are useful in explaining the patterns shown by the statistics. One of these is the low suicide rate of women, whether married or single. Women, based on Durkheim's theory, would appear to be more socially integrated, males more aberrantly individualistic.

The experience of the African American community also appears to support Durkheim's general thesis. The black suicide death rate has been consistently lower than that of the white population as a whole. This is shown for males in the main graphic of this presentation and for both sexes below. The black experience is usually worse than the white. Here is the reverse of that.

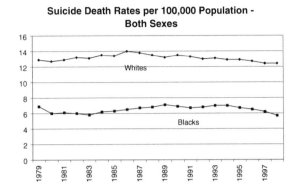

Suicide Death Rates per 100,000 Population - Both Sexes

The black population, large portions of which are concentrated in densely settled urban enclaves, appears to provide more cohesion and support to its members in a number of different ways: extended family groups living together, a greater struggle for economic survival which limits anomie, the important role that churches play in the acculturation of black youths, probably even the "life of the street" which causes more social contact and sense of community.

Interestingly, one study published by the Centers for Disease Control (see source note), observes that in the 1980 to 1995 period, the suicide rate among black youths aged 10 to 19 years of age increased from 2.1 to 4.5 per 100,000 population. In 1980, white youths in the same age bracket had a 157% higher rate than blacks; by 1995, the difference was only 42% higher. The CDC's comment is telling.

In explaining the closing of the gap, the agency says:

> One possible factor may be the growth of the black middle class. Black youths in upwardly mobile families may experience stress associated with their new social environments. Alternatively, these youths may adopt the coping behaviors of the larger society in which suicide is more commonly used in response to depression and hopelessness.

This is not a cheerful note. As the life of the African American community comes more and more to resemble that of the white community, the suicide rate may become more and more the same.

Source: Centers for Disease Control and Prevention. National Center for Health Statistics. National Vital Statistics System. Online. Available: http://www.cdc.gov/nchs/default.htm, May 29, 2002. U.S. Bureau of the Census. *Historical Statistics of the United States.* 1975. Centers for Disease Control and Prevention. "Suicide Among Black Youths — United States, 1980-1995." *Morbidity and Mortality Weekly Report.* 20 March 1998.

Men's Health: Death by Murder

Death Rate by Homicide for Men

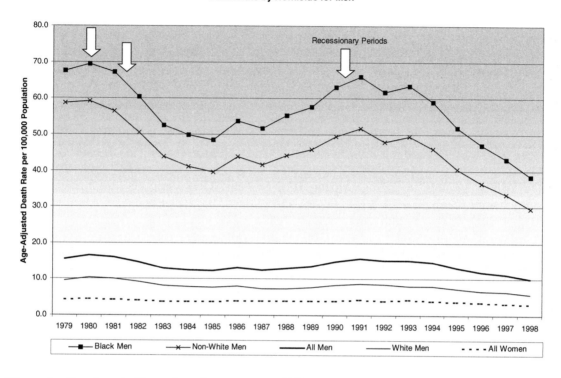

Those inclined to believe that there are no differences between the sexes need only consult homicide statistics for a corrective. In the period shown in the graphic, men were 3.5 times more likely to die by homicide than women were. The ratio fluctuates. In times of economic stress, men are nearly 4 times as likely to meet such an end than women.

As we have had occasion to note before in this series, men's generally shorter lifespans, greater tendency to die in accidents, to commit suicide, to be killed by others (and to kill others) is viewed by medical experts as at least partially due to the male hormone, testosterone. This hormone has been linked to aggressive and competitive behavior, not just strong libido, and has led some to use the phrase "testosterone toxicity."[5] Needless to say, we transcend our chemical nature — but it produces tendencies society strives to channel.

Ours is a high-tech society much given to pharmaceutical interventions (Ritalin, Prozac) and to nurturing types of coping mechanisms (counseling, therapy, support groups). But Mother Nature may have her reasons for unevenly distributing traits between the sexes — even if behavior, beneficial for survival over millennia — produces awkward results in our times.

---

[5] Perls, Thomas T. and Ruth C. Fretts, "Why Women Live Longer than Men," *Scientific American*, June 1998, accessible at http://www/sciam.com/1998/0698womens/0698persl.html.

Some quick facts about homicide. More is provided in *Crime and Justice*, another volume in this series. Males are the victims of 75.2% of all homicides, around 11,553 males in 2000[6]. Of these 87% were killed by men, 13% by women. When a woman kills, she is four times more likely to kill a man than to kill another woman. Estimated data for 2000 are shown in the table below:

Offender/Victim	Homicides in 2000	% of all homicides
Male/male	10,001	65.1
Female/male	1,552	10.1
Male/female	3441	22.4
Female/female	369	2.4

Men invariably kill more people than women, but rankings are interesting. The highest ratio "favoring" men is in the killing of an elder; women rank highest in killing a child. When circumstances are considered, men have the highest ratio as offenders in a gang-related killing, women in killings during an argument. Men use guns, arson, and poison — in that order. Women use poison, arson, and guns — in that order.

Unlike the suicide death rate, the homicide death rate is much more variable. It appears to respond to social disturbances, rising in "exciting" times, becoming less visible in quiet periods. It may also have intensified with urbanization. Measured in deaths per 100,000 population, it was 1.2 in 1900, rising to 4.6 by 1910, to 6.8 by 1920. It rose to 9.2 by 1931, continued high during the Depression, dropped to 5.0 as World War II ended, reached a low of 4.7 in 1960, and began to rise again. The highest rate in the 20th century was in 1980 (10.6). Most recently it has been dropping again during the Internet boom.

Black males have a very low suicide rate but a high death rate from homicide. In 1998, the black male death rate was 38.4 per 100,000 people, the white male rate was 5.8. A black male was nearly 7 times more likely to die a violent death by homicide than a white. The same cultural and economic conditions that hold down suicide may produce a higher homicide rate in the African American community. Economic stresses may translate into higher rates of social disorder and personal stress for some. Periods of economic recession, therefore, are indicated on the graphic.

Source: Centers for Disease Control and Prevention. National Center for Health Statistics. National Vital Statistics System. Online. Available: http://www.cdc.gov/nchs/default.htm, May 29, 2002. U.S. Bureau of the Census. *Historical Statistics of the United States*, 1975. "Homicide trends in the U.S.: Gender." Bureau of Justice Statistics, for 1976-1999: Online. Available: http://www.ojp.usdoj.gov/bjs/homicide/gender.htm.

---

[6] Please use with caution. Preliminary 2000 totals are used, distributed using 1976-1999 averages for occurrence. Data are intended to be illustrative only.

Children's Health: Low-Birthweight

Low-Birthweight Live Births
(Less than 2,500 grams by races, less than 1,500 grams for all races)

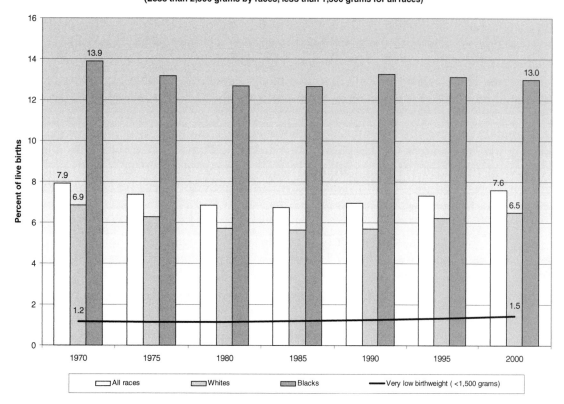

Children's health begins before birth. Low weight at birth (less than 2,500 grams, 5 lbs. 8 oz.) is not only the cause of 70% of infant deaths and a third of all handicapped conditions, it also affects the life of the child as an adult — for the worse. Low-birthweight is usually abbreviated as LBW.

Trends in low-weight births have not changed much in the last 30 years despite dramatic increases in multiple births (one cause of LBW). Among whites, 6.5% of all live births are low-weight. Among blacks this figure is 13.0%. The rate is very high — it is higher than the low-birthweight ratio in Rwanda in 1992 (11.7%) — and is another indicator showing the generally poor state of health of black Americans.

Causes. In 2000, 44% of LBW births were premature — the baby born before the 37th week of gestation. LBW is also associated with multiple births — which have been increasing rather dramatically — 26% for twins, 138% for triplets, 174% for quadruplets, and 492% for higher-order multiples in the 1990-2000 period. Many such births are due to new medical interventions ("assisted reproductive techniques," ART).

Low-birthweight singletons, when born at normal term, suffer from intrauterine growth retardation — which is due to many factors, including maternal malnutrition, anemia, infectious disease (not least those sexually transmitted and those of the urinary tract), kidney disease, high blood pressure, and other ailments of the mother. The mother is often underweight at conception and does not gain sufficient weight as pregnancy progresses. The fetus also may have genetic/chromosomal defects.

Very young mothers (under 15) and those at the end of their reproductive cycle (45+) have the highest percentage of LBW babies. Women who smoke, drink alcohol, and take drugs put their babies at risk. Low-birthweight girls survive to give birth to LBW babies themselves. There is a definite cycle to this phenomenon, observable especially in underdeveloped regions of the world or in communities in the U.S. that resemble them.

Consequences. Low-birthweight has been found to impair the immune system. LBW children may experience poor cognitive development. Those who survive into adulthood are more at risk for developing chronic diseases. Dr. David J.P. Barker, a British physician, first proposed the "fetal origins of disease hypothesis," also known as the Barker hypothesis. The hypothesis states that:

> "... fetal undernutrition at critical periods of development in the intrauterine environment and during infancy leads to permanent changes in body structure and metabolism. These changes result in increased adult susceptibility to coronary heart disease and non-insulin dependent diabetes mellitus. There is also growing evidence that those adults born with low birthweight suffer an increased risk of low blood pressure, obstructive lung disease, high cholesterol and renal damage."[7]

Thus childhood — indeed prenatal — problems cast their shadow over later life.

American Indians and Alaskan Natives have a slightly higher rate of LBW births than whites. In 1999, their rate was 7.15% of live births versus a white rate of 6.57%. Asians and Pacific Islanders have a rate slightly higher than American Indians, 7.45% in 1999. Within this group, those of Chinese extraction had the lowest rate of any racial group, 5.19%; Filipinos had the highest rate--second only to blacks--of 8.3%.

In 1999, cigarette smokers as a group had a 12.1% rate, nonsmokers 7.2%.

Sources: Centers for Disease Control and Prevention. *Health, United States, 2001*. For 2000 data: *National Vital Statistics Report*. v. 50, no. 5. 12 February 2002.

---

[7] United Nations, ACC/SCN (2000) Low Birthweight: Report of a Meeting in Dhaka, Bangladesh, 14-17 June 1999. Eds. Pojda J and Kelley L.

Children's Health: Mother's Milk

Breastfeeding by Mothers Aged 15 to 44

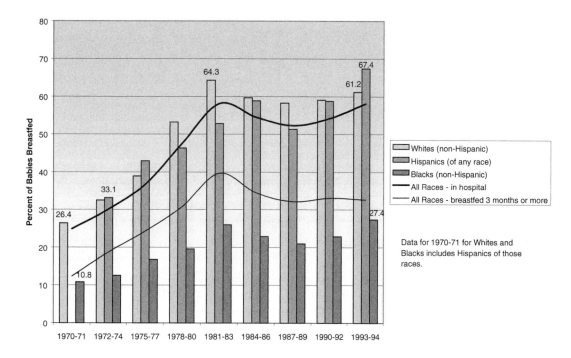

The graphic shows just a quarter century of breastfeeding statistics for non-Hispanic whites and blacks and for Hispanics of any race. The bars and the top curve show initial feeding of the babies following birth. The lower curve shows babies who were still being breastfed three months after birth and beyond.

This period is one of resurgence. In the 1955 to 1971 period, breastfeeding of infants declined. At the beginning of this period less than 25% of babies were fed mother's milk at birth and only 12% were breastfed three months after birth or later.

This resurgence coincides with the Baby Boom's entering its reproductive years. One is inclined to see it as a cultural response — which no doubt it was — the children doing what their parents had avoided doing. In 1971, La Leche League (which started in 1956) hosted Princess Grace of Monaco at its 4th International Conference in Chicago. Her speech seems to have been the spark that set off a fire, albeit with the fuel abundantly available for a conflagration — because breastfeeding began to surge and appears still to be blazing. This phenomenon is the more remarkable since in the 1970 to 1994 period, female participation in the labor force went up from 43.4% to 59.2%.

The surge faltered in the 1983 to 1989 period — no one seems to have an explanation. But the climb in breastfeeding resumed thereafter. To bring the data as close to up-to-date as possible, the results for 1994 through 1998 are presented on the next page.

Percent of Babies Breastfed

Year	In Hospital	At home, 6 months	At home, 12 months
1994	57.4	19.7	-
1995	59.7	21.6	-
1996	59.2	21.7	-
1997	62.4	26.0	14.5
1998	64.3	29.0	16.0

The benefits of breastfeeding are enormous and — in a way — obvious: millions of years of evolution have developed mother's milk for the baby — and the cow's milk for the baby — and the cow's milk for her calves. It is the natural and best possible food for a child. The La Leche League enumerates specific benefits thus:

> Breastfeeding has been shown to be protective against many illnesses, including painful ear infections, upper and lower respiratory ailments, allergies, intestinal disorders, colds, viruses, staph, strep and e coli infections, diabetes, juvenile rheumatoid arthritis, many childhood cancers, meningitis, pneumonia, urinary tract infections, salmonella, Sudden Infant Death Syndrome (SIDS) as well as lifetime protection from Crohn's Disease, ulcerative colitis, some lymphomas, insulin dependent diabetes, and, for girls, breast and ovarian cancer.

One key benefit of breastfeeding is that antibodies made by the mother's mature immune system reach the baby through mother's milk while the baby's immune system is still developing. The mother's body responds to germs from the baby by synthesizing antibodies and passing them through the milk.

The breastfeeding experiences of whites and Hispanics (who may be of any race) are very similar. Black mothers breastfeed at lower rates than white and Hispanic mothers — which, in turn, translates into lower overall health status in the African American community.

Data collected by the government indicate that mothers with the highest education breastfeed most (Bachelor's degree or higher – 80.6%, no High School — 43%). Those oldest breastfeed most (30-44 — 71.1%, under 20 — 45.3%). This suggests, indirectly, that breastfeeding is highest at the highest economic strata of the society and lowest at the lowest levels of income and education.

Breastfeeding around the world shows no particular pattern. Rates in the U.S. are better than in India (51%), are about the same as in China (64%), are better than in France (50%), and much worse than in Sweden (98%). The rate in Great Britain is 63%, in Ireland 31%, in Nigeria a surprisingly low 2% — as in Thailand (4%), Paraguay (7%), and the Dominican Republic (10%). Concerning the children who fall into these percentages, we can only agree with Coleridge, that they "on honeydew have fed and drunk the milk of Paradise."

Source: Centers for Disease Control and Prevention. Data from National Survey of Family Growth, published in *Health, United States, 1994* and *2001*. Data in table from Ross Laboratories Mothers Surveys, by Ross Products, an element of Abbot Laboratories. Benefits quoted from La Leche League International. Online. Available: http://www. lalecheleague.org.

Children's Health: Infant Mortality

Infant Mortality - Children Under 1 Year of Age

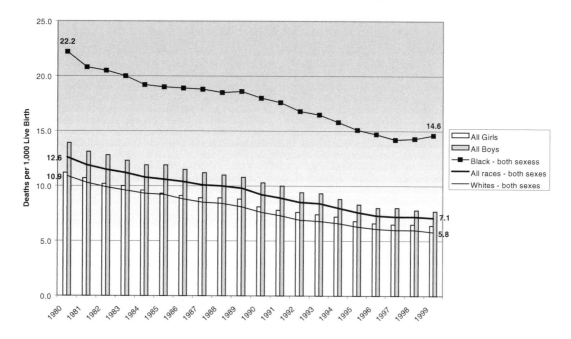

With the near-conquest of infectious diseases, most childhood deaths take place early in life. In 1999 (the year of the most recent complete statistics) 27,937 children died before reaching their first year, the definition of "infant mortality."

Infant mortality is divided into neonatal deaths, those occurring less than 28 days after birth, and postneonatal, infants who survive the first 28 days but die before they reach their first year. More than two-thirds of infant deaths (18,728 in 1999) are neonatal. Most neonatal deaths are associated with (1) low birth weight, (2) congenital malformation, deformations, and chromosomal abnormalities, (3) conditions caused by complications in the mother's pregnancy, (4) respiratory distress, and (5) by complications of placenta, cord, and membranes. Such causes account for more than 62% of all neonatal deaths.

One third of infant deaths (9,209 in 1999) were postneonatal. The leading cause of death was sudden infant death syndrome (SIDS) followed by congenital malformations, deformations, and chromosomal abnormalities. The third cause was accidents.

Male infants have a higher death rate than female — as men have a lower life expectancy, generally, than women.

Data by race for all races and groups were not available in detail for 1999 as of this writing. Data that follow are for 1998, except as indicated. The highest rates experienced are by African Americans (13.9 per 1,000 live births, 14.6 in 1999), the lowest by Asians and Pacific Islanders (5.5); the lowest rates in 1999 mentioned by the Centers for Disease Control were for Chinese infants (2.9) and for Japanese infants (3.4). White non-

---

Hispanics had a rate of 6.0 (5.8% in 1999). People of Hispanic origin were slightly lower than whites (5.8 vs. 6%). American Indians and Alaskan Natives had a 9.3% infant mortality rate in 1998.

While the subject here is mortality, the good news is that the trend in infant deaths is down — from 12.6 per 1,000 live births in 1980 to 7.1 twenty years later. This is a good sign. As a CDC article states, "infant mortality is one of the most widely used general indices of health in the United States and other countries."[8] A low infant mortality rate indicates that healthy, well-fed mothers brought more children to full term, that the children had a normal weight at birth, that the mother received prenatal care and education, that she did not smoke or indulge in alcohol and drugs, that the infant was breastfed after birth and received appropriate medical care, that complications, if present, were detected early and treated with modern interventions — because the mother had access to proper medical care. The CDC is certainly very active in its efforts to bring about this happy state. At the time when the article cited was written (1991), the infant mortality rate was 8.9 and the goal was to achieve a rate of no more than 7 per 1,000 live births. In 1999, that goal had been almost achieved.

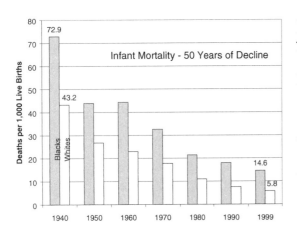

A look further back, to 1940, illustrates just how far we have come. In that year, the white infant mortality rate was 43.2 and the black rate 72.9. Whatever else may be said about the U.S. healthcare system, it seems to work.

The differences between blacks and whites, however, continue to be great. The black rate in 1999 was more than twice that of the overall rate and 2.5 times the white rate — despite a downward trend overall. The gap, observed before in these pages, is not fully explained by the lower average household income of blacks but points as well to other factors. In 1999, black median household income was $27,910, that of Hispanics $30,735. Yet the Hispanic rate was just slightly lower than the white infant mortality rate as already mentioned above. White income was $42,504.

We conclude this series by a closer look at SIDS — crib deaths — which illustrate the CDC's — and state health departments' — efforts to lower infant mortality — even in an absence of clear knowledge.

Sources: Centers for Disease Control and Prevention. *National Vital Statistics Report*. v. 49, nos. 8 and 11. 21 September 2001 and 12 October 2001.

---

[8] "Current Tends in Infant Mortality – United States, 1988," *Morbidity and Mortality Weekly Report,* September 21, 1991, Centers for Disease Control and Prevention.

Crib Deaths: A Closer Look

SIDS Death Rates

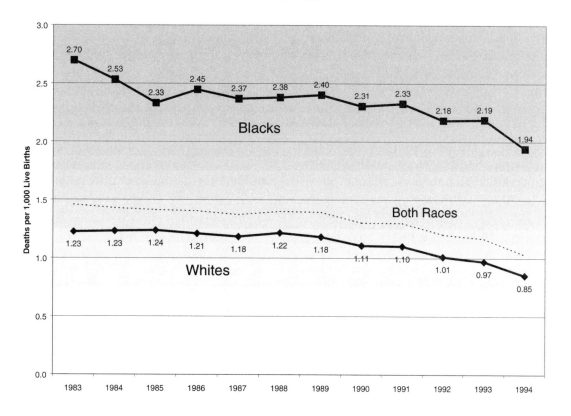

Among infant deaths — death before the first year — crib death, formally known as Sudden Infant Death Syndrome (SIDS), is the third leading cause of death. The two leading causes are congenital malformations, deformations, and chromosomal abnormalities (a single category) and disorders due to short gestation and low birth weight, not elsewhere classified (another single category).

Until 1992, SIDS was the second leading cause of infant mortality. In the 1980s, more than 5,300 babies died of SIDS every year. In the first half of the 1990s, this average had dropped to 4,880. Death rates are shown for the 1983 to 1994 period from a special study conducted by the Centers for Disease Control (see source).

According to an expert panel convened by the National Institute of Child Health and Human Development, SIDS is defined as "the sudden death of an infant under 1 year of age which remains unexplained after a thorough case investigation, including performance of a complete autopsy, examination of the death scene, and review of the clinical history." In other words, SIDS is not understood. SIDS is described as "a diagnosis of exclusion and of unknown etiology." Etiology is the science of demonstrating causes. Risk factors are known. The following is the wording used by MEDLINEplus:

Risk factors include babies who sleep on their stomachs (up to 4 months. of age), soft bedding in the crib (up to 1 yr. of age), multiple births, pre-maturity, a history of a sibling who had SIDS, maternal smoking, maternal substance abuse, young maternal age, short intervals between pregnancies, late prenatal care and low socioeconomic status. Male infants are affected more than females. While studies show an increase in these factors, the impact or importance of each factor is not well defined or understood in sudden infant death syndrome.[9]

A strong association between SIDS and babies sleeping on their stomachs had been ob-served by 1990. This led to a national campaign, initially spear-headed by the American Academy of Pediatrics. Mothers were advised to put their children to sleep on their backs or sides (the "Back to Sleep" campaign). Declines in the SIDS death rate began to reflect this education/campaign — which was widely backed by the federal government and state health departments throughout the nation in hard-hitting campaigns, some tailor made for racial groups. Similar declines in crib deaths were also observed in other coun-tries where similar efforts were launched.

The campaign to bring SIDS under control is an excellent example of the manner in which the health authorities, governmental and private, cooperate, first, in sifting through data and observations to understand intractable and difficult to understand health prob-lems — and then launching effective programs that save lives by outreach and education alone. Other risk factors — like low birth weight and socioeconomic and cultural factors (poverty, youth pregnancy) — are more difficult to manage. It is also clear that the mes-sage is not reaching as many mothers in the black community as in the white.

Source: Centers for Disease Control and Prevention. National Center for Chronic Disease Prevention and Health Promotion. "Sudden Infant Death Syndrome, United States, 1983-1994." Published in *Morbidity and Mortality Weekly Report,* v. 45, no. 40, 11 October 1996.

---

[9] "Sudden infant death syndrome," MEDLINEplus, accessible at http://www.nlm.nih.gov/medlineplus/ency/article/001566.htm

The Payoff: Life Expectancy Trends

Life Expectancy

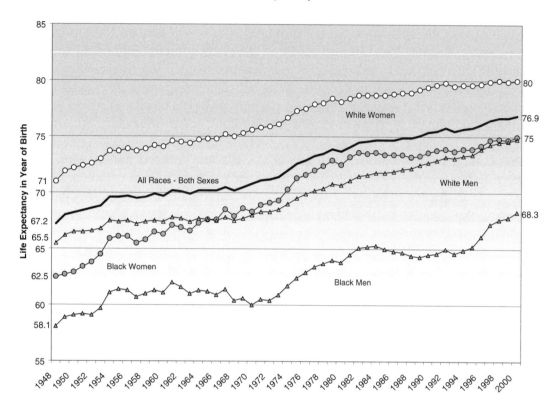

The immediate reward of good health is quality of life — a concept difficult to define, but, where health is concerned, we all know it when we have it. Good health usually manifests when we don't notice it at all.

These days the long-term measure of good health is life expectancy. Data on the life expectancy of men and women, white and black, are shown in the graphic for a 50-year period. For the nation as a whole, life expectancy has increased from just over 67 years at birth to nearly 77 years between 1948 and 2000. In a word, the combination of our regimens of nutrition, exercise, and health care have added ten years to our life span on average.

Black women have made the greatest gains. Their life expectancy has increased 20% in this period, from 62.5 years in 1948 to 75 in 2000. White women (from 71 to 80) show the smallest gains, but white women have the highest longevity rates of any of the subgroups shown. (Notice, incidentally, that in 1948 the Social Security System was doing just fine. Men retired at 65 and then obligingly died six months later.)

Black men had the second best improvement in life expectancy, up 17.6% in this period, from a low 58.1 years in 1948 to 68.3 in 2000. Indeed, the gap between whites and blacks has narrowed in this period. At the beginning, all whites could expect to live 8 years longer than blacks. By the end of the period, the difference had narrowed to 5.6 years.

If "current trends continue," as they say, can we expect to live forever? Don't bet on it. As space travel seems to be limited by the speed of light, so human cellular reproduction seems bounded by the Hayflick Limit. Exceeding the first may be as difficult as breaking through the other. In 1961, Dr. Leonard Hayflick at Stanford found that human cells have a limited life. Different kinds of cells have a different lifespan, but the number of divisions is around 60. We die, ultimately, because, in old age, dying cells far outnumber newly formed cells, and our organs lose functionality. Many theories exist on why and how this happens. Immortalists are hard at work, but don't hold your breath.

More specifically, we're creatures built of cells. Cells are grouped into tissues, tissues into organs. Other tissues connect organs and provide structure to our bodies. Cells divide. Cells age with each division. Over time, cells accumulate pigments and fatty substances inside their walls. They deform — growing larger. Or they deform — growing smaller. They take on abnormal shapes and sizes, called dysplasia. When cells atrophy other cells enlarge or multiply in compensation. Over time, disorder increases in the tissues and in the organs of which the tissues are the components. Organs gradually lose first their "reserve" capacity — their ability to function at high rates in emergencies — and then some of their basic functionality. Connective tissues grow stiff. All this appears to be the consequence of normal cell reproduction and the stresses and strains our cells suffer living in the "big city," our bodies.

There are early indications, particularly in the life expectancy data for white women, that growth in life expectancy may be slowing, flattening out. This may be a temporary phenomenon or may mean that we are nudging up against the Hayflick Limit. Once we reach it, progress is bound to be slow. At present there isn't even a consensus on the number of cells we have in our bodies. Estimates range from 7.5 trillion on up to 100 trillion, although the lower number appears to be closer to the truth and is the result young people get when doing estimates in Biology Class, using body mass and cell volume. In any case, there are many, many cells we must fix, train, or reinvent before we routinely dress for our morning jog at age 155.

Source: National Center for Health Statistics. National Vital Statistics Report, v. 47, no. 28. 13 December 13 1999. Population data from the U.S. Bureau of the Census.

Chapter 2

Diseases

This chapter attempts to discover trends in the diseases that afflict us — and what they may signify — not by following some kind of classification of diseases but by looking at diseases — or groupings of diseases — that have caused concern in recent years.

We begin with a look at sexually transmitted diseases (STDs). These affect by far the largest numbers of people and have been most persistent and *resistant* to control. The most recently emerging STD is HIV/AIDS — which is also one of the most deadly modern diseases not counting the Ebola virus which, thank heaven, has not touched our shores. The first panel is a broad look at STDs. The second focuses on AIDS. AIDS receives further coverage in Chapter 10, where we look more closely at sexuality.

The Centers for Disease Control and Prevention (CDC) maintains a register of so-called "notifiable" diseases. These are the infectious diseases that can be passed from person to person and are therefore of great interest in preventing epidemics. STDs belong in this group. In the next three panels, we take a look at trends in these diseases under three headings: Diseases of Childhood, Old Diseases, and Emerging Diseases.

We are living in an era of transition. Many serious diseases have been brought under control by modern antibiotics and by vaccination and immunization. The panel on childhood diseases displays curves all headed downward. At the same time, the microbial world is also adapting to our medications. Our standard drugs are wearing out. And our methods of sanitation and control have, here and there, shown signs of neglect or breakdown. Surprisingly, as shown in the panel on old diseases, ancient diseases like the bubonic plague and cholera have made their reappearance in the United States. Leprosy is with us and malaria has been rising in recent years. We attempt to explain what is going on.

Nature produces new diseases to challenge our medical arts. The fifth panel in this chapter takes a look at the subject. We make a stab at explaining how new diseases are discovered and what gives them rise. Not surprisingly, in this area, curves are rising: it takes time to discover ways to handle new diseases.

Ours is also an age of mental distress. In the sixth panel we look at depression, in the seventh at attention deficit disorder and learning disability. We have means of dealing with these ailments (mitigating their effects, treating their symptoms), but we do not genuinely understand them yet.

Very much the same thing can be said of one of the more deadly diseases afflicting us — cancer. Our methods of approach to cancer resemble those we use against terrorism. We try to kill the cancer wherever we encounter it. A look at diseases that afflict the elderly — and will probably face the Baby Boom — completes our look at diseases. Last we look at Alzheimer's, one of the newer diseases of old age, although long recognized, simply, as dementia.

In trying to sum up this chapter, one thinks of "on the one hand, on the other." We see the consequences of past medical breakthroughs and the virtual disappearance of diseases. We see the emergence of new diseases from various causes, including our own technologies. We see bacteria and viruses fighting back and the plague reappearing — and diseases that have become prominent because, alas, we live so much longer than once we used to.

Sexually Transmitted Diseases

Sexually Transmitted Diseases

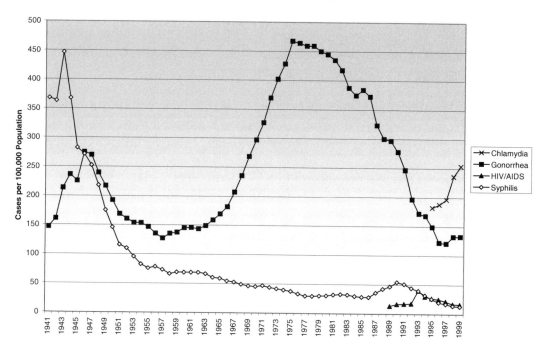

The nearly 60-year history of four major sexually-transmitted diseases shows that STDs have a cyclical pattern — produced by a complex interaction between bacterial/viral adaptations, medication, cultural patterns, economics, and demography.

Chlamydia, a bacterial infection of the genitals, is a disease of long standing but was not one of the "notifiable" diseases until 1985 — hence historical data on chlamydia are not available for earlier years. HIV/AIDS, which appears on the graphic for the first time in 1989, was first diagnosed in the United States in 1981. The name dates to 1982. Like Legionnaire's disease, which appeared in 1976, it is a newcomer. Epidemics are required to draw attention to the causative agents before diseases became classified.

First, some perspectives. HIV/AIDS has the fewest cases per 100,000 population among the STDs, but it is causing a large number of deaths. In 1999, AIDS resulted in 14,802 deaths, up from 13,426 in 1998. By contrast, syphilis, with about the same number of cases in 1998, produced 45 deaths. Gonorrhea, with a much larger number of cases, only produced 4 deaths in 1998, chlamydia none. AIDS has no cure. The other STDs are curable — although the future is less certain, as we shall see.

In the context of a presentation on social trends and indicators, three issues are worth noting about STDs: (1) anti-bacterial/viral medications appear to have a wear-out factor (bacteria and viruses develop new, resistant strains); (2) sexual behavior patterns have a major influence on who falls prey to a sexually transmitted disease; (3) populations that do not actively seek medical help — for cultural or economic reasons — experience a higher incidence of STDs because they pass on the diseases to more people.

The pattern of cases of gonorrhea is an illustration of the first two issues. In the 1970s, varieties of the disease-causing bacterium, *Neisseria gonorrhea*, began to occur. Incidence then began to grow. The downturn in cases did not take place until the use of variant treatments came to be introduced. The period of case-expansion also coincided with changes in sexual behavior, especially in the black population. Blacks became sexually active at increasingly younger ages. Gonorrhea is associated with young people who have multiple partners, do not use condoms, and are slow to seek medical help. Two trends, one bacteriological, one social/demographic, caused a rise in cases.

There are indications that this pattern may repeat. We may be entering a period when more and more strains of bacteria develop resistance to the tried-and-true antibiotic of the 20th century, penicillin. Periods of sexual freedom/license cause peaks in STD cases.

The black population is much more subject to STDs than other racial groups as shown by the following table. This result is traceable to different behavioral patterns — sexual and health-care seeking.

Percent of Cases by Race, 1999

	Indian	Asian	Black	White	Unknown
AIDS	0.4	0.8	48.5	32.8	17.5
Chlamydia	1.3	1.4	34.8	20.9	41.6
Gonorrhea	0.5	0.5	61.4	11.4	26.3
Syphilis	0.8	0.6	73.0	15.2	10.4

Considering the relatively small size of the black population, these data show very high STD rates in the black community — 12% of the population, 61% of gonorrhea cases, for instance.

Even the STDs that do not kill have significant negative consequences for the affected person. Third, final-stage **syphilis** can cause coronary heart disease. **Gonorrhea** is a common cause of pelvic inflammatory disease (PID) in women. PID can cause infertility, damage to the Fallopian tubes, and increases the risk of pregnancies outside the womb (ectopic pregnancies). Babies born to women with gonorrhea may catch the disease during delivery, may die of blood infections, and may go blind. In men, untreated gonorrhea can lead to infertility and urinary difficulties. The disease can affect the blood and the joints and is then life threatening. Among the diseases that must be reported to the government, **chlamydia** produces the most cases of *any* disease, the vast majority of those affected being women. It produces the same problems as gonorrhea and often appears in the same person. The disease can cause pneumonia and lead to blindness. Approximately 30% of women do not have symptoms, which endangers their babies. Chlamydia can cause premature labor and delivery, hence low birth weight, hence infant mortality.

Source: Centers for Disease Control and Prevention. Data for 1999 and HIV/AIDS data from *Summary of notifiable diseases*, United States, 1999. MMWR 1999; 48 (No. 53). Data from 1941 through 1993: Online. Available: http://wonder.cdc.gov/wonder/ STD/OSTD3202/ Table_1.html.

HIV/AIDS Close-up

AIDS Deaths by Sex and Exposure Category

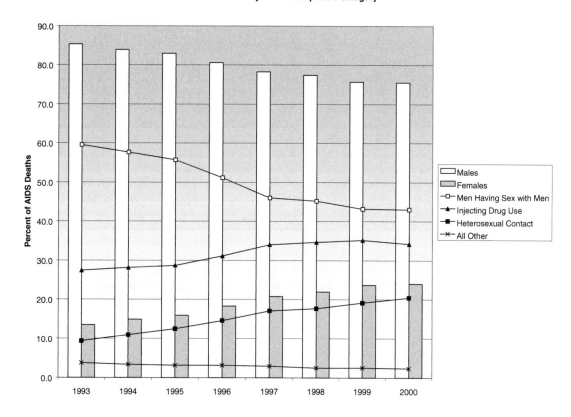

The Human Immunodeficiency Virus (HIV) causes Acquired Immune Deficiency Syndrome (AIDS). HIV infection occurs first. If left untreated, it rapidly develops into AIDS. A very small percentage of people with the infection ("non-progressors") remain unaffected. AIDS is the last and most serious stage of HIV. People often use the abbreviations HIV and AIDS interchangeably and sometimes combine them as HIV/AIDS. AIDS is the most deadly of the sexually transmitted diseases. Blood, semen, vaginal secretions, and breast milk transmit it. It also can be transmitted when infected blood is passed to drug users via unclean needles.

AIDS is incurable and invariably fatal. HIV infection, which occurs first, can be treated but not cured. It is not proved — but generally held — that HIV infection will progress to AIDS except in a small minority of cases. Progression can be delayed. The onset of AIDS may take up to 10 years.

HIV destroys the body's immune system. This manifests itself in the reduced presence of a cell in the bloodstream called CD4 lymphocyte. Its presence prevents many deadly infections and cancers. Its absence leads to death from any number of infections, cancer of the lymph glands, tuberculosis, pneumonia, brain infections, and the wasting of the body through weight loss and anorexia.

The main tool in fighting HIV/AIDS today is Highly Active Anti-Retroviral Therapy (HAART). It reduces HIV in the blood and thus preserves high CD4 counts. HAART prolongs life but is a regimen of multiple medications with disagreeable side effects. Strict adherence to the regimen is required to avoid HIV resistance to the treatment. Some strains of HIV easily mutate. We're not there yet, in other words. But life is being extended by the therapy.

Some general indicators. New HIV infections in 2000 were 70% men, 30% women. Men who have sex with men (MSM, as the CDC abbreviates this) had 42% of new infections; 33% were traced to heterosexual contacts, 25% to needle use in drug injections. Lesbian sexual acts do not seem implicated — although they are theoretically possible means of transmission. Seventy-five percent of females infected are infected in heterosexual acts; 25% by needle use. Of women, 64% are black. Among men, 60% are infected in homosexual contacts, 15% by needles, 15% in heterosexual acts. Of men, 50% are black.

Looking at both sexes, African Americans had 12% of the U.S. population in 2000 but had 54% of all new HIV infections, whites 26%, all other races 1%. HIV is thus becoming a major health problem in the black community.

As shown in the main graphic, deaths associated with gay male activity have been dropping as a percentage of total deaths, those associated with needle use and heterosexual contact have been rising in percentage. Women are infected because they are drug users or because they have sex with those infected by needles or by bisexual individuals who also have sex with men. The women pass the disease on to yet others.

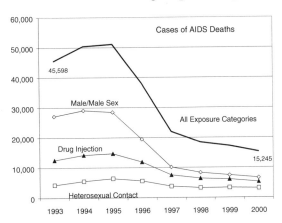

Total deaths, fortunately, are down significantly, as shown in the inset. In 1993, 45,598 people died of AIDS. In 2000 the number was down to 15,245, a 66% decrease. New infections in 2000, however, were around 40,000 — we are delaying but not preventing deaths.

To some extent, these numbers hide the total impact of HIV/AIDS. If we look back over the entire history of the disease — which first surfaced in 1981 — we note that 774,467 cases of AIDS have been reported — 82.6% men, 17.4% women, 42.6% white, 37.8% black, and 18.3% Hispanic. We're adding to this total at the rate of 40,000 a year.

A total of 448,060 deaths have been reported as of the end of 2000: 85.2% men, 14.8% women, 46.2% white, 35.5% black, and 17.3% Hispanic. In other words, nearly 58% of those with AIDS have died.

Source: Centers for Disease Control and Prevention. National Center for HIV, STD and TB Prevention. Online. Available: www.cdc.gov/hiv/stats/hasr 1301/table30.htm.

Childhood Diseases: No Permanent Victories

Selected Childhood Diseases

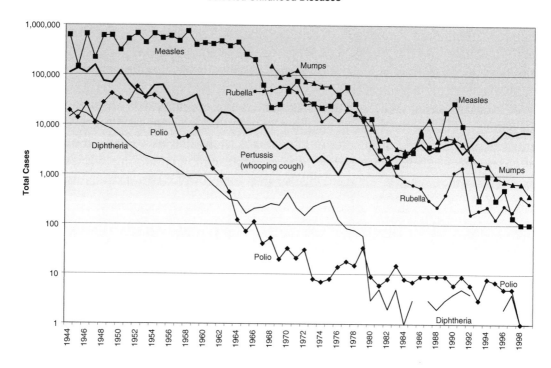

Over the last 60 years or so, we have seen science and communal effort lower the incidence of childhood diseases in a dramatic, reassuring fashion. In 1944, we had 630,291 cases of measles — in 1999 100! In 1944 we had 19,029 cases of crippling polio — in 1999 not a single one! Not one.

Scientific creativeness, discovery, and hard work produce the vaccines. The health community provides leadership in disseminating the news. Responsible parents assume the job of having their children vaccinated. And the cases tumble.

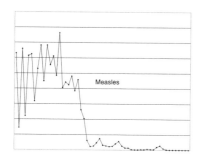

The data above are graphed on a logarithmic scale so that details at low incidence rates are still visible too. This form of presentation understates the great change that has taken place — shown in the small chart to the left (for measles) using ordinary scale. These diseases — affecting hundreds or tens of thousands of children, now affect two or three hundred — or none. Smallpox is not shown at all. It virtually disappeared before 1950. But in the area of health, it appears that victory should not be declared too soon or too confidently. Bacteria are resilient, and people sloppy.

As we point out in Chapter 3, Prevention, as of 1999, 4% of children were not immunized against diphtheria, 8% were not vaccinated against measles, and 10% were not protected from polio. But the interesting trend and indicator, shown in the graphic, is the "contrar-

---

ian" movement of pertussis, whooping cough. After a period of long decline, cases of pertussis began to climb again after 1981 in a pattern that professionals refer to as the "reemergence" of the disease.

One of the important actors in the control of diseases is the virus or the bacterium that causes it. In Australia, Canada, and in The Netherlands — all countries with highly vaccinated populations — the disease has reemerged. A comprehensive study in The Netherlands (see Mooi in source), has shown that adaptations of the bacterium, *Bordetella pertussis,* have permitted it to increase its circulation in the population. Pertussis is an endemic disease, meaning that it is always present in the population. Vaccination had evidently reduced its prevalence but adaptation has allowed it to "expand" again and to infect more people. In the U.S. the growing incidence of the disease may have other causes — possibly other adaptations. It has increased substantially among adolescents and adults. No vaccines specific for these age groups have been developed. Thus the battle continues (see Todar in source).

A brief note about the diseases shown in the graphic. **Diphtheria** is an infection that attacks the respiratory tract. The bacterium, *Corynebacterium diphtheriae*, produces a toxin that can damage the nerves and the heart. Recovery is slow. Diphtheria is a serious disease —it has a 10% death rate.

A virus causes measles, also known as rubeola. After a person is vaccinated or has the disease, he or she becomes immune. People are feverish, cough, and have inflamed eyelids. Measles produces a rash. A serious complication of the disease — which happens in about 1 case out of 3000 — is encephalitis, an inflammation of the brain.

Mumps is another viral disease. It causes painful swelling of the salivary or parotid glands. Parotid glands are those located between the ear and the jaw and also produce saliva. This is a childhood disease (children 2 to 12) but can also affect adults. Those affected gain lifetime immunity.

Pertussis, whooping cough. The disease gets its common name because, during convulsive coughing, one of the symptoms of the disease, children make a sound as they breathe in. Severe cases of the disease, when left untreated, can have a poor outcome. About 1 to 2% of children die of the disease.

Polio, formally poliomyelitis, infantile paralysis, is a viral infection with variable outcomes depending on the form of the disease. Polio is classified into subclinical, nonparalytic, and paralytic types. Subclinical polio may produce no symptoms or relatively mild symptoms of discomfort, fever, headache, and sore throat for about three days. Nonparalytic polio lasts from one to two weeks, has symptoms similar to but more intense than the subclinical variety, and causes considerable muscular pain, stiffness, and rashes. Of greatest concern is paralytic polio. It can lead to death, usually because the patient cannot breathe. More usually, a permanent disability is more likely than death.

Rubella, also known as German measles, is another viral disease. It has relatively mild symptoms but, in some special cases, can lead to serious results. Rubella produces a rash.

It is less contagious than measles. The same vaccine, MMR, is used to immunize children against measles, mumps and rubella — hence its name. Children have few symptoms. The most dangerous outcome is for babies born to unvaccinated mothers who have rubella during early pregnancy. About a quarter of such babies develop congenital rubella. The disease damages the embryo and can result in heart defects, which may be repairable later, and in nervous system problems which are not reversible.

Source: Centers for Disease Control and Prevention. *Summary of notifiable diseases*, United States, 1999. MMWR 1999 and earlier years. Kenneth Todar, "Bordetella pertussis and Whooping Cough." University of Wisconsin-Madison. Online. Available: http://www.bact.wise.educ /Bact330/lecturebpertussis. Frits R. Mooi, Inge H.M. van Loo, and Audre King, "Adaptation of Bordetella pertussis to Vaccination: A Cause for its Reemergence?" National Institute for Public Health and the Environment (RIVM) Bilthoven, The Netherlands, http:// www.cdc.gov/ncidod/eid/vol7no3_supp/mooi.htm.

Old Diseases: Still Going

Diseases of History

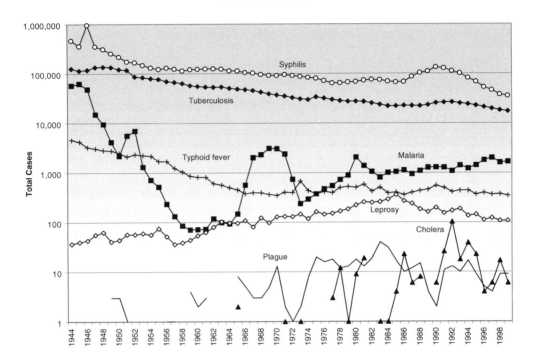

At a time when news periodically reaches us that now this bacterium and now that virus have become resistant to our antibiotics or antivirals, it may be useful to look at some diseases that the 19th century would have immediately recognized — and some that stem from Biblical times. The graphic charts actual cases of seven such diseases from 1944 to 1999. They are still with us. We are still getting cholera and the bubonic or pneumonic plague. In 1999, for instance, there were 35,600 new cases of syphilis and 17,500 people were diagnosed with tuberculosis; more than 1,600 cases of malaria were documented, up from the year before; 350 new cases of typhoid fever were reported, and more than 100 people came down with leprosy. That year, doctors notified the Centers for Disease Control of fewer than 10 cases each of plague and cholera — but these diseases were beginning to show up in some numbers toward the latter part of this 56-year period — having been virtually absent in the 1940s, 50s, and 60s.

The battle against disease is still going on. The climbing rates of some diseases, the persistence of others, and the reemergence of lethal ailments all illustrate that modern medicine has its limits. We also are aware that if we relax our vigilance — or if the social arrangements that keep disease at bay loosen — the plague can come back and consumption can once more waste us.

No exhaustive treatment of these diseases is possible in a single panel. We show these data to hint at possibly adverse social trends. We have touched briefly on sexually transmitted diseases. The presence of **syphilis** in the population, and its occasional flare-ups, illustrates the tenacity of the syphilis spirochete — a tubular bacterium that bores into broken skin or mucous membranes and causes havoc — the unruly form of our passions, and the limits of the antibiotics with which we combat this disease.

Tuberculosis — the ravages of which were mourned by Verdi in *La Traviata*, and by Puccini in *La Bohème* — has been showing a resurgence (not well seen in this graphic). There are several likely causes for this resurgence, including increased HIV infection (which reduces immunity), homelessness, other forms of extreme poverty, poor nutrition, and the appearance of drug-resistant strains of the disease. Crowding and unsanitary habits and conditions contribute to TB's spread: coughing or sneezing spreads infected droplets. Most people recover — but some few still succumb to the disease. As strains of the tuberculosis bacterium become resistant, major efforts must be made to find new, still effective antibiotics. One hopes that an industry busy inventing new drugs — that reduce our obesity or prop up our potency — will keep up with the demand for drugs that are used predominantly by the lower socioeconomic classes.

The incidence of **typhoid fever** is still very high for a country with modern water treatment facilities and high levels of sanitation. The Salmonella typhi bacterium found in poorly treated water and spread from water to food and drink causes this disease. Typhoid is also exhibiting drug resistance. Complications of the disease (intestinal hemorrhage, intestinal perforation, kidney failure, and peritonitis, inflammation of the abdominal lining) can be fatal. A few people can carry the bacteria without being affected. The bacteria appear in their feces. The most famous of these unfortunates was Mary Mallon, a cook who worked in New York in the early part of the 20th century. Wherever she went, people came down with typhoid. Many died. This was Typhoid Mary. She spent many years of her life in quarantine. The continued presence of the disease is blamed on foreign travel.

Malaria also is a communicable disease associated with travel to the tropics. Malaria is a parasitic disease. Mosquitoes spread it. Mosquitoes pass the parasites (sporozoites) to people. The parasites, after many travels in the human body and long colonization of the liver, eventually return to the mosquitoes by way of human blood and have another career in the mosquitoes' stomachs and salivary glands — then it's time to immigrate again. It is interesting to see that peaks in the incidence of the disease appear at the time of World War II, the Korean War, and the Vietnam conflict. Increased travel to tropical regions causes the disease to claim more and more victims of late. Travelers can prevent the disease with certain drugs. Mefloquine, specific for the most dangerous type of malaria, falciparum, can cause confusion and other mental side effects — just the sort of things you need to experience as you take boat into Joseph Conrad's *Heart of Darkness*. Indeed, studying malaria — or the spirochetes of syphilis — one gets the idea that humankind's conquest of the earth has a ways to go yet.

Like typhoid fever, **cholera** reaches people by way of contaminated water. It causes diarrhea and kills by dehydration, which can occur very rapidly, unless counter-measures — rehydration, antibiotics — are taken. One type of cholera bacterium, *Vibrio*, is associated with shellfish, especially raw oysters. Of special note, in our graph, is the reappearance of cholera in 1991. Until then it was fairly sporadic — and in the period 1944-1964 no cases were reported at all. Suddenly, in 1992, we had more than a hundred cases. The cholera epidemic broke out in South America and spread to the United States. One cannot help but wonder if some kind of control is breaking down. In our eagerness to detect terrorists, inspections of contaminated seafood may be lapsing even more radically in the future. As it says in the musical, *Hair,* "Don't drink the water and don't breathe the air."

The **plague**, which some of us have thought was "history," is still going too. The word is not a generic for any or all kings of serious disease epidemics. There is a real plague. It comes in a bubonic and pneumonic variety. Bubonic plague gets its name from swollen lymph glands (buboes); pneumonic plague causes pneumonia. Half of all cases of bubonic and all cases of pneumonic plague lead to death if no treatment is provided. Antibiotics are used to treat these types of plague. Fluids are provided intravenously, oxygen and other forms of respiratory support are used. With treatment, 5% of all cases die — but during the outbreak in the 1980s, according to the Centers for Disease Control, one person in 7 died, which is 14%. This death rate suggests problems of detection and failure to report for treatment.

Lice living on rats pass the plague. The agent is the bacterium *Yersinia pestis.* Rat infestations suggest inadequate housing and pest control — children and adults living close enough to rats so that the lice can make the leap to humans and bite them. Thus the much higher prevalence of the plague in the latter part of the 56-year period shown in the graphic should give us pause. The incidence is still low, hovering around 10 cases a year.

Finally, we come to **leprosy**. The incidence of the disease peaked in 1985 with 361 new cases, corresponding to an influx of Indo-Chinese refugees reaching the U.S. in the 1978-88 period. Worldwide there were 640,000 new cases in 1999, 738,284 cases in 2000. The disease is growing worldwide possibly because the cause, *Mycobacterium leprae,* has been showing up in drug-resistant varieties. The disease damages nerves in the extremities. People lose sensation in their hands and feet and often, for that reason, injure themselves. Their muscles weaken. The mechanism of transmission is still not known with certainty but is thought to be through respiratory droplets. Thus close contact with those who have the disease is a risk factor.

In the next panel, we look at new diseases.

Source: Centers for Disease Control and Prevention. *Summary of notifiable diseases*, United States, 1999. MMWR 1999 and earlier years.

Emerging Diseases: Many Pathways

Recently Emerging Diseases

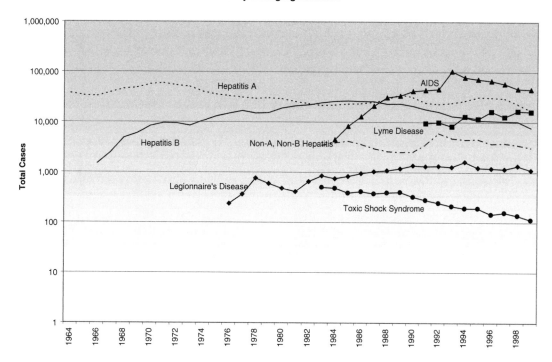

Historic diseases continue on — and new diseases emerge seemingly out of nowhere — from other diseases, from animals, from air-conditioning systems, and from our latest sanitary devices. New cases for seven such new diseases are shown in the graphic. Their histories illustrate the many ways in which new diseases are "born."

Several new varieties of **viral hepatitis** emerged in the 1960s, then in the 1980s. Hepatitis A, B, and C are now well identified. Hepatitis D is a defective virus (it cannot reproduce unless B is present). Hepatitis E is not very common in the United States. These diseases illustrate how, through scientific inquiry, a generic ailment, "viral hepatitis," came to be known first as having an "infectious" and then a "serum" variety (passed by blood transfusion). These two varieties came to be associated with viral forms A and B. Other cases that remained, the so-called Non-A, Non-B instances, were eventually examined closely enough to isolate Hepatitis C as the principal agent of disease.

Hepatitis is a disease of the liver. The liver controls sugar, produces bile and coagulating agents, makes certain hormones, filters, detoxifies blood, makes vitamins, etc. Diseases of the liver have wide ramifications. Hepatitis A is the least dangerous; B and C can be transmitted through blood — as well as sexual contact, and needle sharing. The diseases often occur in conjunction with AIDS. Both are dangerous and can be lethal. Hepatitis C is the most serious of the three and is associated with the majority of liver transplants.

Legionnaire's disease came to be recognized when, in 1976, a deadly outbreak of pneumonia occurred at a convention of the American Legion in Philadelphia. The disease may equally well have become known as the "air-conditioning" disease. The bacterium, *Legionella pneumophila*, lives in water systems but reaches high numbers in the stagnant, warm waters found in plumbing systems, hot water tanks, and cooling towers of large buildings. The disease illustrates how changes in the physical structures of our lives can cause the concentrations of bacteria that have been around for a very long time. Those who smoke and have other underlying diseases (kidney, cancer, diabetes, or respiratory diseases) are most at risk. About 15% of those who contract pneumonia die. The disease has not been associated with home or auto air-conditioning systems.

Toxic shock syndrome appeared in the early 1980s in association with a kind of "super-absorbent" tampon no longer on the market. The agent is the bacterium called *Staphylococcus aureus*. The disease is abbreviated as TSS. The bacteria produce a toxin that results in shock and multiple organ dysfunction or failure (kidney, liver). Low blood pressure, confusion, seizures, nausea, vomiting, and diarrhea are associated with TSS. Treatment is by intravenous fluids, blood pressure support, and dialysis (if kidney dysfunction is present). To prevent the disease, women are advised to use tampons only intermittently in the menstrual cycle and to avoid highly absorbent tampons. The actual cause for the concentration of the bacterium is still being debated. Tampons are said to cause small ulcerations that aid the entry of the bacterium into the body. Other theories hold that stagnating blood in or behind the tampon facilitates bacterial growth. A few men and children have also shown up with the disease. *Staphylococcus aureus* — like *Legionella pneumophila* — are making use of human inventions in order to proliferate.

AIDS may have reached us by way of the monkeys. Simian immunodeficiency virus (SIV) *may* have migrated, adapted itself to humans in Africa where contact with monkeys, including consumption of monkey meats, sometimes happens. The Chimpanzee variety of SIV is very similar in structure to AIDS, but the origin is not well established. **Ebola virus** also was also to have come from monkeys — but the disease, absent in the United States, fortunately, is now being traced to lower forms of life, possibly bats. Our fervent hope is that this disease will never make it into the U.S. statistics on notifiable diseases. Ebola made its appearance in 1972. Two serious outbreaks have occurred (1976, 1995) in Africa, with hundreds dead. Lesser outbreaks occurred as recently as 2001. Death rates are in the 70-80% range.

Lyme disease was first discovered in Old Lyme, Connecticut, in 1975. This is another disease that reaches humans through an animal linkage — this time the deer tick. The disease has flu-like symptoms and is treated with antibiotics. Secondary and tertiary stages appear if the disease is left untreated and causes arthritis-like symptoms in the joints and nervous symptoms like speech impairment, hallucinations, decreased consciousness, and confusion. Another animal-based disease, **Hanta** virus, appeared in 1993, spread by mice. No data are shown for the disease because it is not contagious and is, therefore, not routinely reported on by the Centers for Disease Control.

Source: Centers for Disease Control and Prevention. *Summary of notifiable diseases*, United States, 1999. MMWR 1999 and earlier years.

Depressing Statistics

Physician Visits for Depression

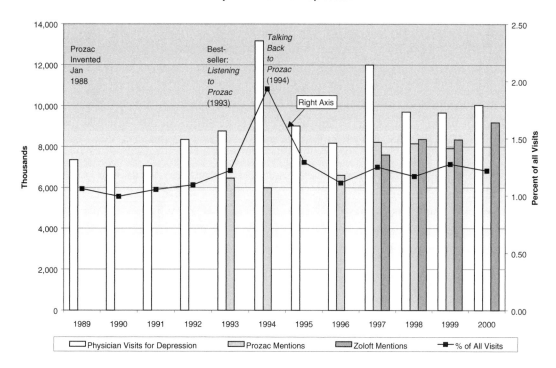

How real is depression? A few people genuinely suffer from a mental condition known as major or clinical depression. They are passive, withdrawn, and cannot work. They sleep poorly and have suicidal impulses. They lose interest in pleasure, including sex. They lose or gain weight. The condition lasts for several weeks at a time and is recurrent or chronic. Such people cannot function normally. Major depression may eventuate in suicide. In reading what follows, it is well to keep in mind that there are real cases of depression that require medical attention. People with the symptoms just described may be a small or a large proportion of those who have depression.

It is difficult to find believable statistics about this condition. Numbers are thrown about without much evidence: 15 or 19 million people suffer from depression; 800,000 children have clinical depression. So it goes. The closest thing to a statistical tracking comes from the National Ambulatory Medical Care Survey (NAMCS) conducted by the Department of Health and Human Services. Trained interviewers talk to physicians engaged in private patient care. The survey reports, among many other things, the reason why patients visit doctors and what drugs the physician mentions on the patient's record.

The graphic shows the number of patients who went to doctors because they felt depressed. In 1989, for instance, 7.4 million visits to doctors were motivated by depression — of a total of 693 million visits, or 1.06%. In 2000, 10 million visits out of 824 million (1.22%) were occasioned by depression. This is a 37% increase in depression-driven visits. Population has only creased 12% in this period. How real is depression?

In the period 1989 to 1992, antidepressants did not make it into the top 20 drugs mentioned by doctors on their patient records in any single year. In 1999, two antidepressants made the top 20: Zoloft was 14th, Prozac 16th.

Prozac was introduced in January 1988 — a year before the data shown here. Before that time — and still continuing — serious depression was/is treated using tricyclic antidepressants (TCAs), monoamine oxidase inhibitors, and selective serotonin re-uptake inhibitors. These medications all affect brain chemistry and are used to treat a variety of mental problems. Older versions have more undesirable side effects than the newer medications; some require special dietary cautions. For these reasons, the medical community has closely monitored their use. Lithium and thyroid supplements must sometimes be used in conjunction with the older antidepressants.

Prozac became a popular drug for the treatment of depression. It caught some kind of public mood or wave. A best-selling book, *Listening to Prozac*, was published in 1993. Sales of Prozac — and possibly patient visits to doctors — may have shot up in response. The next year a book with a more negative message — *Talking Back to Prozac* — had the opposite effect, suggesting that, above a certain clinical level, where real suffering is going on, depression, and its medication *du jour*, may be a social response to the stresses and strains of ordinary life.

This impression is backed by the demographic profile of those who make appointments with their doctors to have depression treated. The largest group (41% to 44% of visits, depending on year) is aged 25 to 44. These are people in the prime of life — and the women are in the childbearing range. They are overwhelmingly white (92%) and two-thirds are women. One imagines millions of mothers raising children while working in high-stress jobs, more and more of them single mothers... As discussed elsewhere in this book, a version of Prozac, with another name, has been introduced specifically to treat premenstrual syndrome.

The rising incidence of depression — and the methods and hype associated with its treatment — appear to be a social trend: to convert life's ordinary and extraordinary stresses into medical conditions that create lucrative markets. A minority have a clinical condition — a majority may be seeking relief from stress. Many seem to welcome this approach, others find it depressing, but we may just be undergoing a change in our drugs of choice. In 1990, North American alcohol consumption was twice the world average. In 1999, U.S. alcohol consumption was the same as the world average. And cigarette consumption per capita in the U.S. fell nearly 28% between 1989 and 2000.

Source: U.S. Department of Health and Human Services. *National Ambulatory Medical Care Survey*, 1989 through 2000. Online. Available: http://www.cdc.gov/nchs/about/major/ahcd/adata.htm.

Attention Deficit and Learning Disability

ADD and Learning Disability

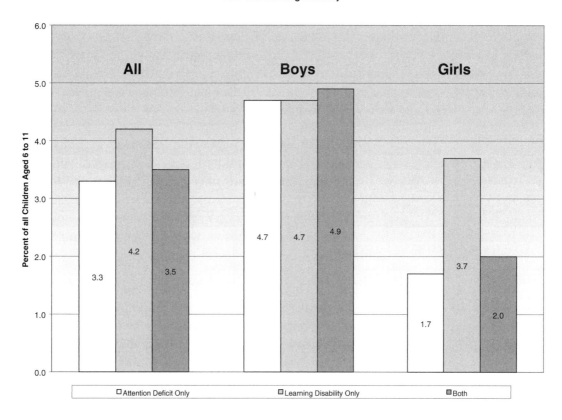

Attention Deficit Disorder, more recently re-Christened Attention Deficit/Hyperactivity Disorder, is another medical or quasi-medical phenomenon of recent decades. Coupled with Learning Disability, it is said by the U.S. Department of Health and Human Services to affect 2.6 million children. Data distilled from the 1997 and 1998 National Health Interview Survey are presented in the graphic showing the prevalence of this disorder for all children, boys, and girls.

Children with ADD cannot concentrate, listen, pay attention, follow instructions, organize activity, or remember things from one minute to the next. They shy from tasks that require mental effort. This syndrome occurs with hyperactivity — constant fidgeting and squirming, inability to stay seated, to have a "quiet time." Hyperactive children are "driven," in motion, and talk excessively; they can't wait their turn, blurt out answers, and butt into others' games or activities. The learning disabled suffer from psychological disorders that make it difficult or impossible for them to process language and mathematical concepts; the term specifically excludes those who have difficulties because of physical or brain dysfunctions — hearing problems, visual impairment, brain damage, etc. The learning disabled often cannot listen, think, write, read, or spell effectively. Their traits merge, at the edges with ADD.

The disorder seems to have emerged about 30 years ago. The Centers for Disease Control (see source), cites numerous academic and other sources that, taken together, appear to assign the cause to transformations in families, marital instability, inadequate day care (day care itself necessitated by changes in the economy), and poverty. Schools and the medical profession are credited, by the CDC's authors, for recognizing and diagnosing the problem. In another volume in this series (*Community and Education*), we take a close look at changes in our family structure. Elsewhere in this volume (see Chapter 6, Drugs), we deal with our methods of sedating children who are afflicted with ADHD — and also those who do not have the symptoms. The object in this panel is to trace the characteristics of this socio-behavioral disorder.

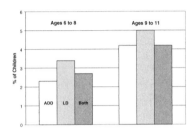

Notice, for instance, that the disorder is much more prevalent in older children than in younger, suggesting that more parental care may be available to children earlier in age than as they grow and become more independent. Their exposure to TV, possibly inadequate nutrition, and family stresses grows with time, manifesting in dysfunctions.

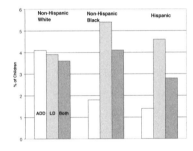

Attention Deficit Disorder is highest among non-Hispanic whites, least among Hispanics. Learning disabilities are most pronounced among non-Hispanic blacks. One can only speculate about causes for these differences. The disorders have been under study for some time, but considerably more work, with larger populations, will be required to understand differences between racial/ethnic groups.

Finally, family structure also plays a role. Children with ADD are 3.8% of total where the family is headed by the mother alone, 3% in families with mother and father both present. Learning disability is 6.1% in mother-only families, 3.5% in father-mother families. And where both ADD and LD are present, the one-parent home has a 4.6% rate versus a two-parent family with a 2.9% rate. ADD is higher among the better off ($20,000 or more family income) and lower among the poor (less than $20,000). Learning disability shows the reverse pattern.

Source: Pastor, P.N. and C.A. Reuben. Attention deficit disorder and learning disability: United States, 1997-98. National Center for Health Statistics. Vital Health Statistics 10(206). 2002.

Cancer Trends

Selected Cancer Death Rates

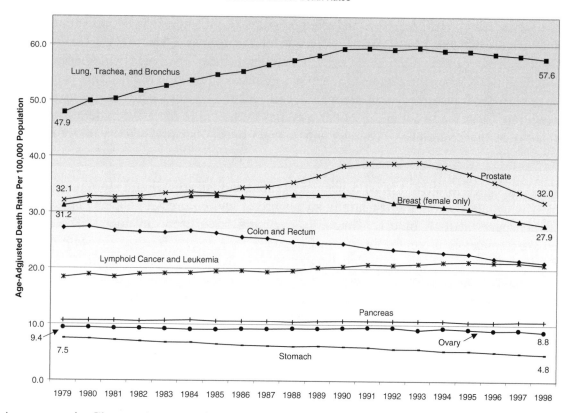

As we saw in Chapter 1, cancer is the second most common cause of death in the United States. The graphic shows a 20-year history of the eight most common cancers. Trends are expressed as death rates per 100,000 population. Death rates are age-adjusted so that results from one year to the next are comparable despite changes in the population's age structure. A value of 57.6 for lung cancer means that of a population of 100,000, 57.6 people die of lung cancer. If only females are reported (breast cancer), only the female population is used.

What trends do we see? In cases in which new diagnostic methods are available and used, cancers are being detected earlier, survival rates are improving, and the death rate is trending down. Cancers that arise from — or are in some way linked with — human pleasures have been gaining ground. Difficult-to-detect cancers continue to have roughly the same death rate at the end as they had at the beginning of the 20-year period shown.

Death rates from **lung cancer** and **lymphoid cancer** and **leukemia** (the last two shown in combination) have been increasing. Lung cancer survival rates ("still alive 5 years after diagnosis") have improved slightly for whites, from 13.1 to 14.5% of patients from 1974-1979 to 1989-1996. For blacks the rate in these two periods has been the same, 11.3% of patients. Primary lung cancer — cancer that has not spread to the lungs from other organs

— is principally caused by cigarette smoking. Note that since 1990 the death rate has flattened and now seems to be declining — as smokers quit.

Lymphoid cancer, or, Non-Hodgkin's lymphoma, has shown increased survival rates, from 48.2% to 52.6% of whites — but a decline from 50.5% to 41.9% for blacks. The disease is treated with radiation and chemotherapy. Leukemia survival has improved for both whites and blacks — 36.7% to 45.4% for the former, 31% to 34% for the latter. Leukemia is a cancer of the blood cells. Treatment usually involves chemotherapy. Lymphoma appears when the immune system is suppressed; one kind of leukemia is produced by a sexually transmitted virus (human T-cell leukemia virus). Thus the uptrend in the death rate for these two families of cancers may be linked to the HIV epidemic and loosening of sexual restraints — younger and younger onset of sexual activity, more partners, etc.

Prostate cancer in men, **breast** cancer in women, and **colorectal** and **stomach** cancer in both sexes are down — substantially so for breast and colorectal cancers. These are all cases where methods of early diagnosis/screening have been developed. The story of prostate cancer is presented in full in Chapter 1 (see *Men's Health: Prostate Cancer*). Breast cancer has been declining because mammography works. Excellent screening tools have been developed for colorectal cancer. Stomach cancer requires an upper-GI examination; barium is swallowed, X-rays are taken. The highest survival rates are seen (1989-1996) by white men for prostate cancer (94.1%); breast cancer survival is high as well (86.3% for whites and 71.4% for blacks). Stomach cancer survival is lowest for whites (15.9%) and only somewhat better for blacks (21.6%). (All survival rates are shown in Part II in tabular format.)

Pancreatic cancer causes loss of appetite, weight loss, abdominal discomfort, and nausea. Diagnosis may require a biopsy, and may be delayed because the initial symptoms are not very specific. Only about 20% of cases can be treated surgically. Survival rate is quite low. In the 1989-1996 time frame, it was 4.2% of patients. The disease is thought to be linked to smoking in some way. The death rate has been virtually unchanged in the last 20 years. It was 10.7 in 1979 and 10.6 in 1998.

Ovarian cancer is rare. Its symptoms are vague. It often has spread by the time of diagnosis. Outcomes are often poor although slight decreases in the death rate have been seen. Rates for **cervical** cancer and **uterine** cancer (not shown on the graphic) have both improved. Deaths from cervical cancer have dropped from 4.6 to 3.0 between 1978 to 1998; those from uterine cancer from 5.0 to 4.1. Pap smears are used to screen for cervical cancer. Uterine cancer usually requires dilation and curettage (D&C). Survival rates are high.

Source: Centers for Disease Control and Prevention. National Center for Health Statistics. National Vital Statistics System. Online. Available: http://www.cdc.gov/nchs/default.htm. May 29, 2002; and MEDLINEplus. Online. Available: http:// www.nlm.nih.gov/medlineplus/ency/article/001566.htm. Survival rates are from the National Institutes of Health, National Cancer Institute, from *Health, United States,* 2002, Table 57.

Diseases of an Aging Baby Boom?

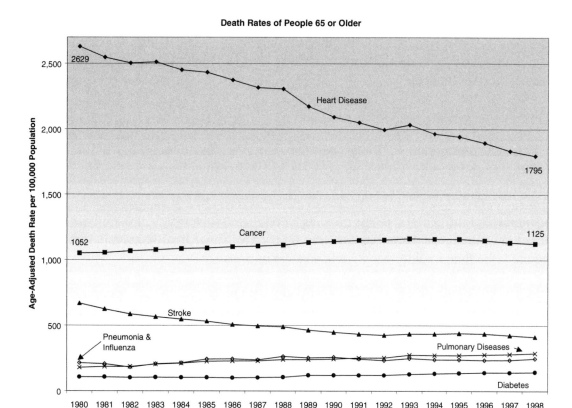

Death Rates of People 65 or Older

Diseases are not all created equal — and they do not affect all age groups in the same way. With the exception of childhood diseases, sexually transmitted diseases (which affect, initially, the sexually active), and maternal mortality, most chronic ailments fall on the aging with special force. Some, like Alzheimer's disease, carry off the oldest age group by preference, those aged 85 and older.

We are entering a period when the post-war Baby Boom is approaching its seniority. In our times, the Baby Boom has been, directly or indirectly, *the* social indicator *par excellance*. Therefore we present trends in major disease groupings in this panel for those aged 65 and older. Data are for nearly two decades and show age-adjusted death rates (comparable one year to the next) per 100,000 population.

Two trends come to the fore immediately. The first is presented by the significant decline in the death rate for **heart disease** and for the closely related killer, **stroke**. Heart disease, the nation's foremost killer, in a sense paces the death rate. As heart disease and stroke decrease, so life expectancy goes up. Heart disease is under attack from all kinds of directions — medical interventions and techniques are preventing its onset and mitigating its consequences; we know more about the links between nutrition and heart disease/stroke; and we know that exercise is an important element in postponing heart conditions. This trend suggests that the Baby Boom will also affect the "senior scene" for a longer time and in a deeper way than other, earlier cohorts. Its members will live longer, will have the votes, and will almost certainly transform health care yet again.

The second important trend is that the death rate from **cancer** continues to grow — suggesting that more members of the Baby Boom will die from it than previous age cohorts. Cancer is a complex disease and is proving toughly resistant to the kinds of medical strategies that have brought infectious diseases to heel (at least until bacterial and viral strains develop resistance).

Chronic, obstructive pulmonary diseases are trending up. The term covers primarily emphysema and chronic bronchitis, both associated with smoking — also, to a lesser extent, with industrial pollution. The growth rate, however, is declining. In the 1980 to 1984 period, the death rate rose 17.9%, in the 1994 to 1998 period, it rose 5.5%. The effects of the programs against smoking are showing up in disease statistics.

Pneumonia and influenza also are growing, albeit at a slower pace. Pneumonia is an inflammation of the lungs caused by bacteria, viruses, or fungi. **Influenza** is a viral disease Both tend to be fatal in older people whose constitutions are weakened.

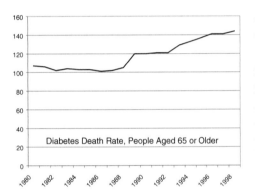

Diabetes Death Rate, People Aged 65 or Older

Although the main graphic does not show it, the death rate for **diabetes**, in this age group, has shown rather dramatic growth, as shown in the insert to the left. The rate remained roughly flat from 1980 to 1988. Then it shot up. So did our collective weight. Americans are more obese now than ever before in history — and there is a clear link between our weight, our lack of movement, and the onset of Type II (non-insulin-dependent) diabetes.

Obesity, at present, is getting close national scrutiny — as is the increase in the incidence of diabetes. The disease is much easier to bring under control using known techniques and pharmaceutical regimens than is cancer. No doubt, therefore, the focus of the next two decades will be on bringing cancer under control. The Baby Boom will see to it. We hope.

Source: National Institute on Aging, drawing data from the National Vital Statistics System. National Center for Health Statistics. U.S. Department of Health and Human Services. Online. Available://www.nia.nih.gov/.

Alzheimer's Disease: Curious Patterns

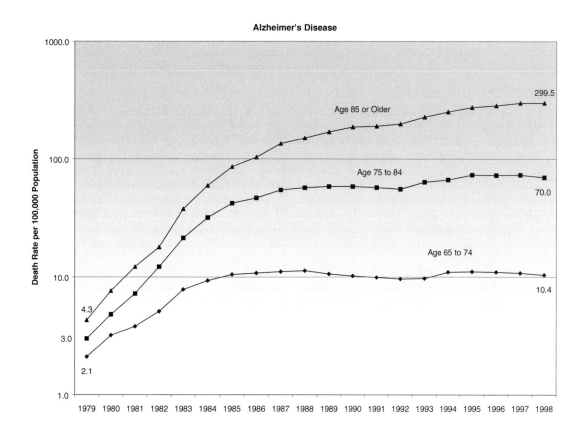

Alzheimer's Disease

Alzheimer's Disease was the 8th leading cause of death in 1999. More than 44,500 people died of AD that year. The disease properly belongs on the graphic of the previous panel, but this disease has a curious pattern and history and is thus best treated as a separate topic.

In a sense Alzheimer's also belongs among the "new" diseases (see *Emerging Diseases: Many Pathways* in this chapter). Dr. Alois Alzheimer, a German physician, initially described it in 1906. It has come to be known as the leading cause of dementia — a term that generally describes symptoms of a decline in a person's ability to think, remember, make judgments, produce speech, and generally to function normally. Although the graphic shows a steep rise in the AD death rate for the most affected age groups (somewhat understated by the use of a logarithmic scale here — to show the data clearly), the disease has not grown quite as dramatically as might appear — except in recognition.

AD cannot be confirmed with certainty except by autopsy. Dementia, generally, means that brain function is impaired — which causes death by other means. The underlying cause, which may be Alzheimer's, has not made it on the death certificates as often in the past as it does today — now that the disease has become well known by the medical community.

The incidence of the disease, however, is also growing in absolute terms, not simply because it is better recognized and reported. It is a disease of advanced old age, as the graphic shows: those 85 and older are much more likely to die of the disease. People are living longer — women longer than men. The disease is more prevalent among women. We are seeing here one of the curious by-products of an extended life expectancy. As people survive to higher and higher ages, they are more likely to die of Alzheimer's disease than of disease now being brought under better and better control — like heart disease and stroke.

AD comes in an "early onset" and a "late onset" variety. Early-onset AD is traceable to inherited genetic traits. Symptoms begin to manifest before age 60. Late onset AD is more common; the genetic transmission is less clear. At present the disease is not preventable and has no cure.

The disease may last from three to 20 years. If it is of long duration, it imposes heavy costs — economic and emotional — on the families in which the sufferer lives. The rising incidence of this disease in the future is a certainty — unless breakthroughs produce a cure or, possibly, a vaccine (one is under test). A future social trend may well be an increase of those who experience the disease at second hand — watching the slow deterioration of a once vital and vibrant human being.

Source: Centers for Disease Control and Prevention. National Center for Health Statistics. National Vital Statistics System. Online. Available: http://www.cdc.gov/nchs/default.htm, May 29, 2002. For background and support, contact Alzheimer's Association. Online. Available: http://www.alz.org.

Chapter 3

Prevention

In 1900, at the dawn of the era of scientific medicine, our life expectancy at birth was just a shade over 47 years. We turned away from folkways and came to rely on science and reason in the treatment of disease and illness. The discoveries that allowed medical science to extend our lives occurred at a dizzying pace. By 1998, our life expectancy at birth had risen to nearly 77 years.

Medical treatment used to respond to illness or to injury. Today, it helps us prevent the things that made us ill or killed us. Mothers rarely perish while giving birth; the infant mortality rate is down. Immunizations and antibiotics protect us from deadly diseases so efficiently that we forget they ever threatened us. Some aspects of the aging process are now treatable. Pharmaceuticals extend life and enhance its quality. How much further can science take us?

Government plays an active role in urging us to protect our own health. The government's 700-page report called *Healthy People 2000* (1990) explains that "the health of a people is measured by more than death rates. Good health comes from reducing unnecessary suffering, illness, and disability. It comes from an improved quality of life. Health is thus measured by citizens' sense of well being. The health of a Nation is measured by the extent to which the gains are accomplished for all the people." The report calls for "mobilizing the considerable energies and creativity of the Nation in the interest of disease prevention and health promotion."

The government cajoles us: Make sure you're fully immunized; exercise regularly, eat fruit, vegetables, and fiber. Know what the leading causes of death are in order to plan for a healthy life. Health and Human Services Secretary Tommy Thompson tells us that "good health is literally a walk away." Are we paying attention?

We know that food nourishes us and new evidence shows it can help prevent disease, even the scourge of cancer. But regular food may not be enough. We're told: Take vitamins and supplements, eat superfoods, buy organic. Dr. Thomas Perls, director of the New England Centenarian Study and co-author of *Living to 100*, tells us the real key to longevity: "Good genes."

We know that it is far more economical to practice prevention — to pay now rather than pay later. Then again, perhaps genetic engineering will eventually do away with all of our health concerns. Or will it be the stuff of horror movies?

Despite what science has done for us, a growing number of people do not believe that science has all the answers when it comes to preventing illnesses, curing diseases, or even just making life more pleasant. They complain that doctors no longer make house calls, and patients are handed from specialist to specialist as though they were diseases, not whole persons. Modern managed medical care is cold and distant, but alternative practitioners listen, care, and get results. Believers have spearheaded one of the most significant public health developments of the end of the 20th century — the boom in complementary and alternative medicine (CAM), coupled with the move to integrate popular alternative healing methods into standard Western medical practice.[1] Alternative therapies are currently sought out by individuals who have AIDS, arthritis, back pain, cancer, and other medical conditions conventional medicine cannot cure.

The age of the miracle cure is upon us. Entrepreneurs, drug companies, and hucksters have been quick to exploit the unwillingness of an aging population to succumb gracefully to the pain, discomfort, distress, and inconvenience of illness and old age.

We open our chapter with a discussion of the alternative medicine phenomenon ("Validated by science, tested by the American people," claims the cover of the alternative health magazine *The People's Pharmacy*). We then look at trends in the American diet and exercise. We will see how new vaccines make for increasingly complex immunization schedules, and how federally funded community health centers are proliferating to meet the health care needs of underserved Americans.

We conclude our prevention chapter with a discussion of the Human Genome Project. We will see how the events of September 11th made bioterrorism the latest prevention watchword.

---

[1] The act of defining alternative medicine and CAM is politically charged. The scientific medical establishment contends that there cannot be two kinds of medicine — there is only medicine that has been adequately tested and that works. The Alternative Medicine Home Page informs us that "In 2002, the Medical Subject Headings (MeSH) Section staff of the National Library of Medicine classifies alternative medicine under the term complementary therapies. This is defined as therapeutic practices which are not currently considered an integral part of conventional allopathic medical practice. They may lack biomedical explanations but as they become better researched some, such as physical therapy, diet, and acupuncture, become widely accepted whereas others, such as humors or radium therapy, quietly fade away, yet are important historical footnotes. Therapies are termed as Complementary when used in addition to conventional treatments and as Alternative when used instead of conventional treatment" (definition retrieved May 31, 2002, from http://www.pitt.edu/~cbw/altm.html.

If It's "Natural," It Must Be Better, Or
Every Man His Own Doctor

Top-Selling Medicinal Herbs (in millions of dollars): 1995-1999

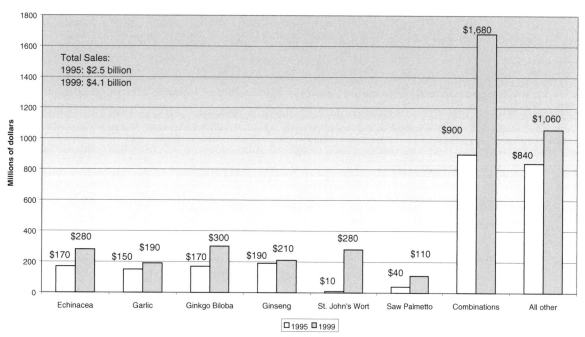

Probably the most common form of alternative medicine is the ingestion of dietary supplements. A dietary supplement, as defined by the U.S. Office of Dietary Supplements, "contains one or more of the following dietary ingredients: a vitamin, mineral, amino acid, herb or other botanical." Dietary supplements have been around for a long time. The trends in the way of self-medicating are megadoses (remember Dr. Linus Pauling and Vitamin C?) and the growing use of medicinal herbs.

The American Medical Association reported that the market for herbal remedies was $1.13 billion in 1993. The chart shows growth in sales of herbal remedies between 1995 and 1999. Sales rose 121% between 1993 and 1995 (to $2.5 billion), then rose another 64% between 1995 and 1999 (to $4.5 billion).

Dietary supplements are big business ($15 billion a year, says the U.S. Health and Human Services Department), and herbal remedies are a rapidly growing component of it. A joint survey by Harvard's Kennedy School and National Public Radio estimated that in 1999, more than 50% of adult Americans looked favorably upon supplements and would continue to take them even if their doctor recommended otherwise.[2]

We see from the chart that the most explosive growth in herbal remedies was in the use of St. John's Wort, touted as a treatment for depression. When the media point out that

---

[2] Supplementquality.com. See Source notes.

prescription drug prices have skyrocketed and suggest that cynical drug manufacturers are passing off modified versions of existing drugs as new to protect patents and profits, is it any wonder people turn to herbal remedies? The treatment of clinical depression is a $44 billion a year business. A dose of St. John's Wort is far less expensive than a prescription pharmaceutical like Prozac (on which Americans spend over $1 billion a year.)[3]

This brings to mind the placebo effect. The Skeptic's Dictionary (http://skepdic.com/placebo.html) tells us:

> The placebo effect is the measurable, observable, or felt improvement in health not attributable to treatment. This effect is believed by many people to be due to the placebo itself in some mysterious way. A placebo (Latin for "I shall please") is a medication or treatment believed by the administrator of the treatment to be inert or innocuous. Placebos may be sugar pills or starch pills.

The Skeptic's page then refers us to an article from the *Washington Post* reporting that "After thousands of studies, hundreds of millions of prescriptions and tens of billions of dollars in sales, two things are certain about pills that treat depression: Antidepressants like Prozac, Paxil and Zoloft work. And so do sugar pills…. The new research may shed light on findings such as those from a trial last month that compared the herbal remedy St. John's wort against Zoloft. St. John's wort fully cured 24 percent of the depressed people who received it, and Zoloft cured 25 percent — but the placebo fully cured 32 percent."

An area of concern for health care practitioners is the potentially harmful side effects and interactions of herbal home remedies. The Dietary Supplement Health and Education Act of 1994 allows manufacturers of herbal products to make general claims about well-being and the effects of substances on bodily function without evaluation or approval by the FDA. The act made manufacturers responsible for ensuring that a dietary supplement is safe before it is marketed. Is this confidence-inspiring?

A little later, Congress also has put the Federal Government into the business by establishing the National Center for Complementary and Alternative Medicine (NCCAM) as one of the National Institutes of Health (October 1998). Among other things, NCCAM is conducting tests on — yes — St. John's Wort. More on this later in this chapter and in Chapter 5.

The General Accounting Office credits soaring sales of dietary supplements to the passage of the Dietary Supplement Health and Education Act but warns that "Some companies promote their products to senior citizens by using 'antiaging' or 'cure-all' claims for which there is little or no supporting scientific evidence of either safety or efficacy." But there may be no stopping an aging population from self-medicating. *Health Care Man-*

---

[3] Caution: St. John's Wort may interact with other drugs and render them ineffective.

ager reports a 130% increase in the use of herbal remedies between 1990 and 1997. Let us look next at growth in the number of practitioners of alternative medicine

Sources: "Alternative Medicine." *World Almanac and Book of Facts*. Annual 2001. p. 508; National Center for Complementary and Alternative Medicine. National Institutes of Health. *Nutrition Business Journal*. Peter Golden, "St. John's Wort Versus Prozac — All A Matter Of Perspective."(February2000). Online. Available: http://www.supplementquality.com/editorials/stjohns_vs_prozac.html. May 24, 2002. NIH Office of Dietary Supplements. "What Are Dietary Supplements?" Online. Available: http://ods.od.nih.gov. May 23, 2002. Jennifer Ouellette, "The Scrooge of Science."Online. Availble: http://www.salon.com/books. May 27, 2002. Shankar Vedantam, "Against Depression, a Sugar Pill Is Hard to Beat." Online. Available: http://www.washingtonpost.com. May 27, 2002. Donald J. Sutherland, "The Continuing Rise in Prescription Drug Expenditures." Online. Available: http://www.socioeconomic. org/Publi cations/ Perspectives/drug price.pdf. May 30, 2002.

Alternative Medicine Practitioners

Licensed Alternative Health Care Practitioners: 1999

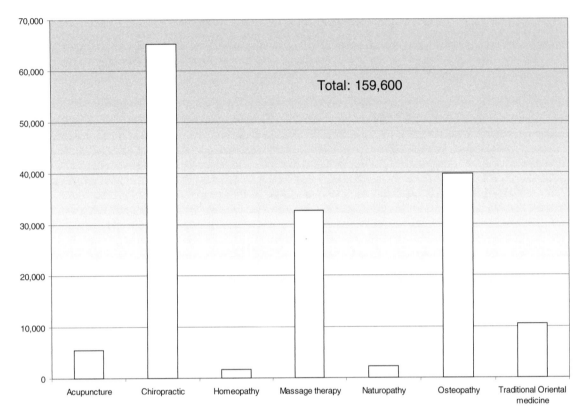

Total: 159,600

Health Care Manager tells us that people visited primary care physicians 386 million times in 1997. Alternative care practitioners received 629 million visits.[4] The chart shows whom we visit when we seek alternative medical care. Of a total of 159,600 alternative care practitioners at work in 1999, most were osteopaths, chiropractors, and massage therapists.

Comparing the chart to data from the U.S. Bureau of Health Professions, we learn that there has been growth in the number of osteopaths[5] and chiropractors.[6] The Bureau does not keep statistics on the other alternative medical practitioners shown on the chart.

---

[4] A Centers for Disease Control report issued in June 2002 found that Americans visited doctors 823 million times in 2000 and those doctors ordered or provided alternative medical care in 31 million visits.

[5] *Merriam-Webster* defines osteopathy as "a system of medical practice based on a theory that diseases are due chiefly to loss of structural integrity which can be restored by manipulation of the parts supplemented by therapeutic measures (as use of medicine or surgery)."

[6] *Merriam-Webster* defines chiropraxis as "a system of therapy which holds that disease results from a lack of normal nerve function and which employs manipulation and specific adjustment of body structures (as the spinal column)."

Government data show 12,600 osteopaths in 1980 and 37,300 in 1996. The chart shows 39,800 osteopaths in 1999, an increase over 1980 of 216%. By way of comparison, there were 701,200 MDs and 154,900 dentists in 1996.

Government data show 25,600 active chiropractors in 1980 and 47,200 active chiropractors in 1996, an increase of 84%. The chart shows 65,300 chiropractors in 1999, only three years later. This figure, from *World Almanac and Book of Facts*, seems high.

Practitioners of alternative therapies have long been at loggerheads with the scientific medical community. The latter is represented by the 300,000-member American Medical Association (AMA). AMA takes credit for the 20th-century movement that "led to the acceptance of the biological, disease-oriented models that dominate medicine" and "limited the practice of medicine to graduates of accredited institutions." That acceptance caused alternative medical practices to fall out of favor. Although they are enjoying renewed interest, critics complain that practitioners fall under too little state and federal regulation. The exception is osteopaths.

Osteopathy: Osteopathic training is similar to that for an M.D., and the AMA counts osteopaths among its members. Many would argue that osteopaths do not belong in the category of "alternative" medical practitioners. The Osteopathic Association's web page[7] tells us: "D.O.s practice a "whole person" approach to medicine. Instead of just treating specific symptoms or illnesses, they assess the overall health of their patients including home and work environments. Osteopathic physicians focus on preventive health care." When your primary care physician tells you to lose weight, stop smoking, and eat better, (s)he is using osteopathic philosophy.

Chiropraxis: According to *CQ Researcher*, "one in 20 Americans now uses the spinal manipulations [performed by chiropractors] to remedy supposed misalignments of vertebrae.... Recent studies by the RAND Corp... and others have found that chiropractors can do more for back pain than traditional medical treatment." This alternative group has the largest number of practitioners. In 1992 the AMA reversed its longstanding opposition to chiropraxis and declared that it was ethical for doctors to refer patients to chiropractors who have "denounced unscientific methods used by many of their colleagues" (for example, promoting manipulation as a cure for disease). The AMA concedes that "manipulation has been shown to have a reasonably good degree of efficacy in ameliorating back pain, headache, and similar musculoskeletal complaints."

Massage therapy: Who doesn't enjoy a relaxing massage? *Health Care Manager* tells us that in 1997, somewhere between $4 and $6 billion was spent on massage therapy. The chart shows that massage therapists are the third largest group of alternative practitioners. The AMA approves of massage therapy when performed by a licensed practitioner.[8]

---

[7] See (http://www.aoa-net.org).

[8] See http://massage_cpt.com.

Traditional Chinese medicine and acupuncture[9]**:** These specialists are fourth and fifth on the chart, with 10,500 and 5,500 practitioners respectively. The AMA says "practitioners of traditional Chinese medicine use acupuncture, a host of herbal remedies, and sometimes include substances derived from sources such as the gallbladder of bears, tiger teeth and bones, and rhinoceros horn, increasing the hazards facing these endangered species."

Regarding acupuncture, *U.S. News & World Report* tells us: "American doctors have tolerated acupuncture practitioners in their midst since the 1930s, mostly with suspicion. According to The Academy of Chinese Culture and Health Sciences, in 1998 there were 50 schools of acupuncture in the United States, 7,000 licensed acupuncturists, hundreds of acupuncturists had been approved by HMOs and PPOs, and after 20 years of debate, the AMA has finally changed its position and accepted acupuncture as an effective medical treatment." Laws governing the administration of acupuncture vary from state to state.[10] Americans made more than 5 million visits to acupuncturists in 1998.

Naturopathy: Number six on the chart with an estimated 2,200 practitioners in 1999 is naturopathy. According to the AMA: "Naturopaths practice various treatments such as manipulation and massage, and use herbs, acupuncture, and traditional Oriental medicine. Its practitioners treat underlying causes of illness by facilitating the body's response to disease through its 'life force' … Naturopaths are licensed in 11 states, but most third-party payors, including Medicare, do not cover their services." In the early 20th century there were about 20 schools of naturopathy. Today there are five North American schools of naturopathy.

Homeopathy: Last on our chart, with 1,700 practitioners, is homeopathy. Based on the theory that "like cures like," homeopathy treats patients with an extremely diluted version of what ails them. During the anthrax scare of 2001, hundreds of web sites offered homeopathic cures for anthrax. The National Center for Complementary and Alternative Medicine (see next panel) warned that it was "unaware of any scientific basis that these or other CAM therapies would be effective in protecting the public from biological or chemical weapons." According to the AMA, in order to "ferret out fraud," a few states have validated certain CAM therapies, including homeopathy.

Sources: "Alternative Medicine." *World Almanac and Book of Facts*, Annual 2001, p.508; National Center for Complementary and Alternative Medicine. National Institutes of Health, *Nutrition Business Journal.* Bureau of Health Professions, National Center for Health Workforce Information and Analysis, *United States Health Workforce Personnel Factbook.* Online. Available: http://bhpr.hrsa.gov/healthworkforce/. May 22, 2002. American Medical Association. "CSA Reports: Report 12 of the Council on Scientific Affairs (A-97) Full Text: Alternative Medicine." Online. Available: http://www.ama-assn.org. June 3, 2002. Jay Greene, "FSMB developing guidelines for complementary care." amednews.com, May 8, 2000. Online. Available: http://www. ama-assn.org/sci-pubs/amnews/. June 10, 2002.

---

[9] Acupuncture is defined by *Merriam-Webster* as the "Chinese practice of puncturing the body (as with needles) at specific points to cure disease or relieve pain (as in surgery).

[10] For more information, go to http://acupuncture.com/StateLaws/StateLaws.htm

---

Alternative Medicine in the Mainstream

Budget Appropriations, National Center for Complementary and Alternative Medicine, 1992-2002

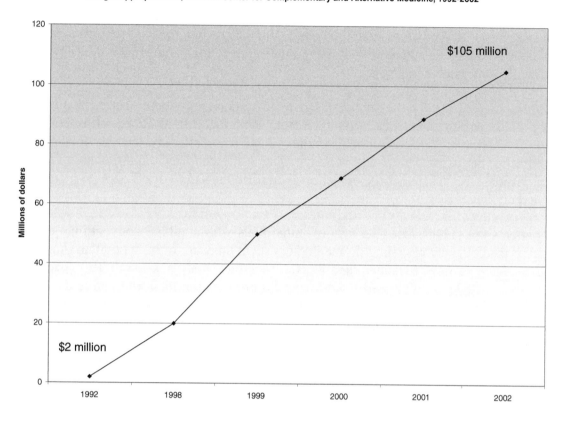

With so many people apparently using alternative medicine, something jogged the political system into action. In 1998, Congress voted to expand the already existing Office of Alternative Medicine, a part of the National Institutes of Health (NIH), into a National Center for Complementary and Alternative Medicine (NCCAM). According to the NCCAM, this marked "a watershed in medical history in America. Not only was the founding of the Center an acknowledgment that Americans are increasingly receptive to forms of healthcare outside Western medicine, it was an acknowledgment that rigorous research on these forms could enrich Western medicine."

The chart shows budget appropriations for alternative medicine research grants. Funding rose from $2 million in 1992 to $105 million in 2002. This is small potatoes compared to the total NIH budget of $23 billion — but enough to generate grumbling by some about this use of finite research funds. One particularly controversial award in FY 2000 went for research into "Distant Healing Efforts for AIDS by Nurses and 'Healers'." In 1997 Duke got $4.3 million to study St. John's Wort in the treatment of depression.

In 1998, the *Journal of the American Medical Association* published the results of a survey about American medical schools' alternative medicine offerings. Sixty-four percent of 117 medical schools responding offered elective courses in complementary therapies. Close to one-third of the classes were part of required courses; 68% were stand-alone electives. The most common topics were acupuncture, chiropractic care, herbal therapies, homeopathy, and mind-body techniques.

Like it or not, the medical establishment understands that it must learn alternative medicine — if only to be aware of what its patients are up to. Therapeutic touch is now taught in nursing schools. And more than 75 American and Canadian medical schools now teach students how to blend alternative therapies and conventional medicine — a new technique called integrative medicine.

According to a survey by the American Hospital Association, the number of hospitals offering alternative therapies nearly doubled from 1998 to 2000, to 15.5% of all hospitals. They offer therapies that some doctors believe have some efficacy, such as acupuncture, chiropractic, herbal medicine, and massage. The American Medical Association's lukewarm response is: "There is little evidence to confirm the safety or efficacy of most alternative therapies."[11]

But patients are enthusiastic. Surveys of individuals who combine conventional and alternative medicine are revealing. Some doctors seem unaware of how popular alternative remedies have become. Eisenberg and Kessler found a "Don't Ask-Don't Tell" pattern in their survey of 831 people; nearly two-thirds did not mention their alternative therapy to their doctor, because "It wasn't important for the doctor to know," "The doctor never asked," and "It was none of the doctor's business." A survey of cancer outpatients in New Zealand showed that 46% were using alternative therapies. More than half of that 46% didn't tell their doctor about the therapies. They used four or more alternatives, unaware that some therapies could have side effects or could interact adversely with chemotherapy or radiotherapy treatments.

CAM proponents claim that America can cut out-of-control heath care costs by focusing on alternative medical care. Maybe so, maybe not. Both CAM and the scientific medical community agree on at least one issue: Diet and exercise play an important role in an individual's wellbeing. We will look next at trends in diet and exercise.

Sources: Budget of the United States Government. Online. Available: http://www.whitehouse.gov/omb/budget/fy 2003/pdf/hist.pdf. July 2, 2002. Villarosa, Linda. "Verdict Is Still Out on Some Alternative Therapies." *New York Times*, 13 April 2002 p.C3. Clark, Charles S. "Alternative Medicine." *CQ Researcher* 31 January 1992. Eisenberg, D.M., R.C. Kessler, et al., "Perceptions About Complementary Therapies Relative to Conventional Therapies Among Adults Who Use Both: Results of A National Survey. *Ann Intern Med*, p. 135, 344. "Cancer Patients Using Alternative Therapies." *Natural Life Magazine*. Online. Available: www.life.ca. May 23, 2002. National Center for Complementary and Alternative Medicine. Online. Available: http://nccam.nih.gov. May 24, 2002. Abelson, Reed. "Alternative Medicine Is Finding Its Niche in Nation's Hospitals." *New York Times*, 13 April 2002, p.C1.

---

[11] Quoted in Villarosa, *New York Times*; see Source notes.

The American Diet: How Has It Changed?

Percent Change in Per Capita Consumption of Various Foods: 1970-1997

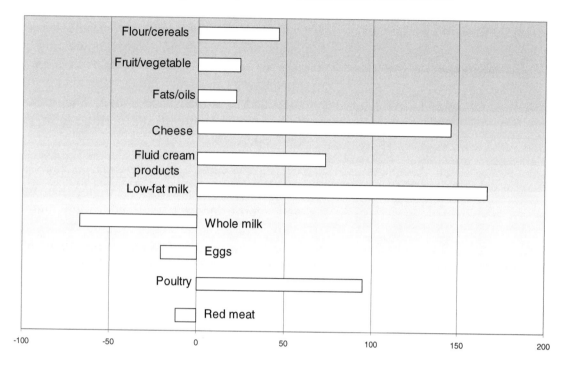

The U.S. government is watching what we eat and thinks we can do better. Thanks to a media blitz from the office of the U.S. Surgeon General,[12] most people are aware of the advice regarding the importance of diet and exercise for health and disease prevention. Many can picture in their heads the government's "Food Guide Pyramid"[13] outlining what we are supposed to be eating each day for optimal health. Who doesn't know that public health officials thinks we should eat more fruits and vegetables than red meat and less fats, oils, and sweets?

Have we changed our diets to reflect the latest dietary wisdom? The chart shows changes in the consumption of various food commodities between 1970 and 1997. Consumption of red meat, eggs, and whole milk is down, a response to warnings about dangerous cholesterol. We're eating more of everything else, though. Is our diet healthy enough?

---

[12]Health information is available at http://www.surgeongeneral.gov/sgoffice.htm.

[13] The USDA releases Dietary Guidelines every five years. The 2000 version is available at http://www.nal. usda.gov/fnic/dga/. Go to http://www.nal.usda.gov:8001/py/pmap.htm for a look at the Pyramid. A non-governmental group has put forth its own "food pyramid," based on the traditional Mediterranean diet. Absent from this pyramid is milk, and red meat appears in the tiny point at the top, to be eaten in very small amounts only a few times a month.

Apparently not. The USDA reports that "contrary to recommendations, Americans are consuming record-high amounts of caloric sweeteners and some high-fat dairy products, and near record amounts of added fats…. a hefty increase in grain consumption reflects higher consumption of mostly refined, rather than high-fiber, whole-grain products."

The USDA summarizes data about Americans' overall diet quality in a Healthy Eating Index (HEI). The pie chart shows how we scored in 1996: 71% of people were in the "needs improvement" range, 12% had a good diet, and 17% had a poor diet. Our greatest failings? Not enough fruit, too little milk, says the USDA.

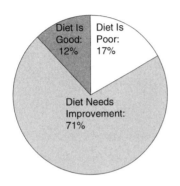

Healthy Eating Index Rating: 1996

Diet Is Good: 12%
Diet Is Poor: 17%
Diet Needs Improvement: 71%

Who has the best scores? Children aged 2 to 3 score highest, women score higher than men, and scores increase with education and income. Do we have a bad attitude? When surveyed between 1991-94 about their diets, 62% of men and 38% of women indicated they had no interest in improving their diets. Sixty-nine percent of respondents said "too much emphasis is placed on nutrition" and "eating healthfully is too complicated."

At the other end of the dietary spectrum are the "worried well," the segment of the population that may be overly preoccupied with health and nutrition. They are the ones who snap up the latest dietary trends — the antioxidant vitamins and fortified foods, for example. Sometimes these food additives are a response to a real public health issue — calcium-fortified orange juice, for example, is a response to an observed inadequate intake of calcium among certain groups of people. Other food additives have dietary experts scratching their heads — ginkgo biloba- or ginseng-fortified beverages, for example.

Whereas a century ago, our nutritional problems were due to inadequate intakes of certain vitamins and minerals, we may now be in danger of nutrient overload. The American Dietetic Association cautions that people should monitor what they consume; they may be getting the same nutrients in their fortified foods as they get out of their vitamin bottle.

Whatever the level of our knowledge of nutrition, there are many factors that contribute to our food consumption patterns. We have far more choices available to us now than the traditional meat-and-potatoes fare of the early 20th century. We eat for pleasure as well as from biological need. And the poor spend their grocery dollars differently, as we shall see next.

Sources: Center for Nutrition Policy and Promotion. Online. Available: http://www.ers.usda.gov/ Lino, Mark, P. Peter Basiotis, et al. "The Diet Quality of Americans: Strong Link With Nutrition Knowledge." *Family Economics and Nutrition Review (1999)*. v. 12, no. 1, p. 49. Dinkins, PhD, Julia M. "Beliefs and Attitudes of Americans Toward Their Diet." *Family Economics and Nutrition Review* (June 2000), p. 98. (survey conducted by Market Research Corporation of America; sample size, 1,851 adults 18 years old and over). "Functional foods — Position of ADA." *J Am Diet Association* 1999. Online. Available: http://www.eatright.com/adap1099.html. June 4, 2002. Spake, Amanda. "Natural Hazards." *U.S. News & World Report*. 12 February 2001.

Income and Grocery Purchases

Percentage Variance From the National Average for Grocery Expenditures in Low-Income Cities

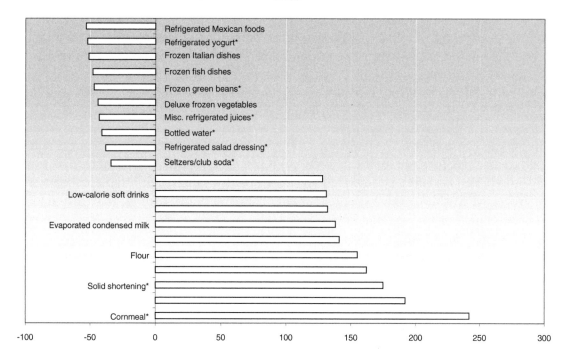

The type of groceries we buy is influenced by our income, among other things. The graphic shows items that get above- and below-average spending in low-income cities compared to the national average.[14] Asterisks indicate items that show up as high priorities here but show up as low priorities for high-income cities (see table) — and vice versa.

Percent Variance from the National Average for Expenditures on Grocery Products in High-Income Cities

Above-average expenditures		Below-average expenditures	
Seltzers/club soda*	197	Solid shortening*	48
Misc. refrig. juices*	171	Canned meat stew	56
Bottled water	171	Canned pie filling*	56
Refrig. orange juice	160	Refrig. biscuits*	57
Refrig. drinks	155	Spoonable salad dressing	60
Frozen green beans*	154	Cornmeal*	61
Dried rice	152	Canned green beans	68
Refrig. yogurt*	147	Dry toaster items	68
Butter	147	Refrig. pastries	69
Refrig. salad dressing*	142	Canned poultry	69

For example, the table shows that in high-income cities[15] like New York, the average household spent 48% below the national average on solid shortening, while we see from the graphic that low-income cities spent 192% above

[14] Representative low-income cities were Scranton, PA; Charleston, WV; Shreveport, LA; and El Paso, TX.

[15] Representative high-income cities were New York, NY; Chicago, IL; Miami, FL; and San Francisco, CA.

the national average. On the other hand, low-income cities spent 52% below the national average on yogurt, while high-income cities spent 147% above the national average. What can we infer from this chart and table?

Jekanowski and Binkley found "that grocery categories that are relatively important in high-income areas tend to be relatively unimportant in low-income markets, and vice-versa." They concluded that in high-income areas, more money is spent on high-value, discretionary items like seltzers, juices, and bottled water, while people in low-income areas spent more money on staples that require further preparation at home. They also concluded that higher expenditures on flour, cornmeal, shortening, and condensed milk suggested more cooking and baking "from scratch."

High-income consumers favor items associated with current thinking on what constitutes a health-conscious lifestyle: bottled water and juices and yogurt, for example. The refrigerated salad dressing must be intended for their healthy salads. High-income consumers favor frozen vegetables, which are generally considered better-tasting, but canned vegetables, the choice of low-income consumers, tended to be less expensive. Will that calorie-laden butter on the high-income list flavor those frozen green beans? If so, it is the rare fatty indulgence of the high-income consumer, from whose kitchen it appears the art of baking has disappeared.

Purchases in low-income cities tend to be higher in calories (canned sausage and lunchmeat). The charted data were collected in 1990. Given a few more years of media bombardment about good nutrition, would spending habits change?

The USDA collected data on average annual per-person expenditures on various food items by income quintile. In 1997-98, dissimilarities are still seen between the lowest and highest income groups. The lowest group was less favorably disposed to cereal and bakery products, except for flour ($3.27 versus $3.16). Not surprisingly, the highest-income group spent more on meats, poultry, fish, and eggs, with the highest dollars going to red meat ($177.85 versus $193.73). Pork was second ($60.15 versus $61.57), followed by the healthier poultry ($56.56 versus $64.80) and fish ($33.78 versus $46.40).

The lowest-income people spent less on dairy products ($112.07 versus $149.15) and fruits and vegetables ($180.15 versus $223.15). Recall that the USDA has identified too little milk and fruit as our greatest nutritional failings. (See Chapter 1 in this volume for a further discussion of how our diet affects our health.)

Good nutrition may be hampered by income, but other factors are involved. Lack of knowledge is a problem. Studies suggest that low-income people are less likely to read nutrition labels. Many of us dine out more (and less nutritiously; see Chapter 4 for more on this). Next we will look at the growing interest in organic foods.

Sources: Jekanowski, Mark D. and James K. Binkley. "Food Spending Varies Across the United States." *Food Review* (January-April 2000), p. 38; Selling Area Marketing Incorporated (SAMI), 1990. "Food Resource Management Practices and Needs of Low-Income Households: A Summary of Research." (April 2002). Online. Available: http://www.uwex.edu/ces/wnep/p4/pdfs/03rsmgmt.pdf. June 7, 2002. Noel Blisard. *Food Spending in American Households, 1997-98 / SB-972*. Economic Research Service/USDA. Online. Available: http://www.ers.usda.gov/publications/sb972/sb972a.pdf. June 7, 2002.

Growing Interest in Organic Foods and Farmers' Markets

Certified Organic Farmland Acreage (1,000) and Certified Growers: 1992 to 1997

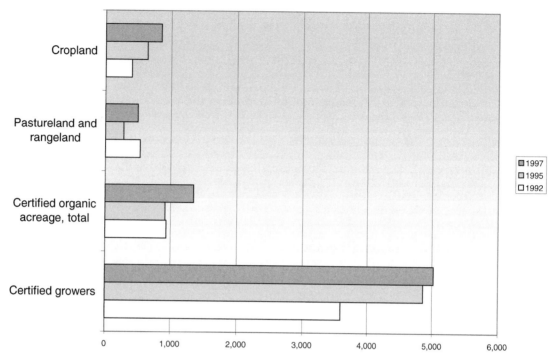

Concern with healthier eating and nutrition can be credited for increased interest in organic foods and farmers' markets. The number of farmers' markets more than doubled between 1994-2002 according to the USDA. In an age when the produce sections of our supermarkets are bursting with tasteless goods from around the globe, produce from farmers' markets is perceived as fresher and healthier. Since the government wants to see everyone better nourished, the 2002 Farm Bill appropriated $40 million (double the 2001 amount) for Farmers Market Nutrition Programs to help low-income mothers and seniors.

The chart shows the increase between 1992 and 1997 in the number of certified growers of organic foods and the rise in the number of acres certified organic. Farmers in 49 states dedicated 1.3 million acres of farmland (about 0.2% of all U.S. cropland) to organic production in 1997, an increase of 39% over 1992. Farmers used two-thirds of such land for crops, the rest for raising certified organic livestock.

Why buy organic? People have been concerned about pesticides in food since Rachel Carson's *Silent Spring* (1962) sounded an early alert about the unknown effects of widespread pesticide use. Today, organic agriculture is one of the fastest-growing segments of the food sector. With consumer demand rising at the annual rate of 20% since the 1980s, by 2000 organic farming accounted for $7.7 billion of Americans' annual $400 billion+ food expenditures. Sales were expected to top $9 billion in 2002. Among the favorite organic crops are lettuce, tomatoes, carrots, grapes, apples, and St. John's Wort.

The USDA defines certified organic crops as those that "have been grown and processed according to the specific standards of various State and private certification organizations." The 1990s saw considerable legislative and regulatory activity because of the lack of consistent national standards for pesticide regulation and organic production.

Joel Bourne tells us in *Audubon*: "The USDA created a firestorm within the organic community in December 1997 with its first draft proposal [of national standards for organic labeling], which left open the possibility of using irradiation, sewage sludge, and genetic engineering to produce 'organic' foods. These processes and materials, rarely if ever used by organic growers, have strong supporters in the food industry. Irradiation involves bombarding food with gamma rays, which kills most bacteria, but because of public concerns over safety and radioactive waste, it hasn't become widespread."

Studies show that while organic produce is more attractive than it used to be and contains less pesticide residue, there is little evidence that it is more nutritious than conventionally grown produce, and there is no discernable taste difference. Proponents contend that buying organic produce supports farming practices that are better for the environment. A large-scale conversion to organic farming is not foreseen.

Michael Pollan contends that "the rapid growth of organic closely tracks consumers' rising worries about the conventional food supply — about chemicals, about additives and, most recently, about genetically modified ingredients and mad cow disease; every food scare is followed by a spike in organic sales."[16] Pollan confesses: "I like buying organic, for the usual salad of rational and sentimental reasons."

Organic products tend to be more expensive. Are we paying more for an inferior product? *U.S. News & World Report* suggests the higher price may buy peace of mind and recommends targeting organic spending on fruits and vegetables that harbor the most chemicals. Check out watchdog lists like those published by Consumers Union (www. consumersunion.org/food/food.htm) and the Environmental Working Group (www.foodnews. org). The American Council on Science and Health says the health benefits of fruits and vegetables "dramatically overwhelm the theoretical risks of tiny amounts of pesticides in food." That advice and your taste buds might be the best guides.

Sources: U.S. Bureau of the Census. *Statistical Abstract of the United States 2001*. 121ˢᵗ ed. "Greener Greens? The Truth About Organic Foods." *Consumer Reports* (January 1998). "Organic Farming and Marketing: Questions and Answers." Online. Available: http://www.ers.usda.gov/briefing/Organic/Questions/orgqa1.htm. June 10, 2002. Bourne, Joel. "The Organic Revolution." *Audubon* (March/April 1999). Pollan, Michael. "Naturally: How Organic Became a Marketing Niche and a Multibillion ..." *New York Times Magazine*. 13 May 2001. Marcus, Mary Brophy. "Organic Foods Offer Peace of Mind — At a Price." *U.S. News & World Report*. 15 January 2001. Winter, Ph.D., Carl K. "Eat Apples—Give Up Junk Food and Junk Science." American Council on Science and Health. Online. Available: http://www.acsh.org/press/editorials/eatapples030399.html. July 10, 2002.

---

[16]Bioterrorism is the most recent food scare; go to http://www.usda.gov/homelandsecurity/response.html for the government's response.

Diet and Weight

Percent of Individuals 2 Years and Over Consuming More than the Recommended Energy Allowance (REA; Calories), Average Fat Intake (% of Calories), Average Saturated Fat Intake (% of Calories), and Average Calorie Intake: 1987-1995

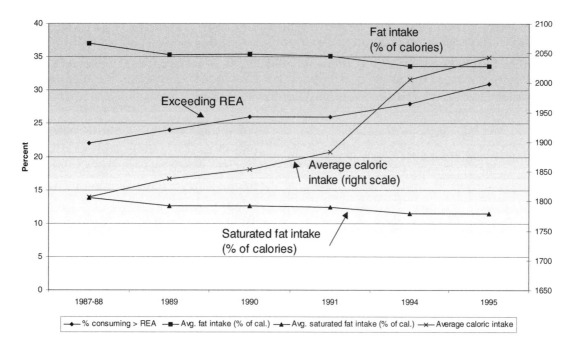

Americans are blessed with the world's most abundant food supply. And how we take advantage of it! The graphic shows the percentage of those aged two and older who consumed more than their daily recommended energy allowance — their REA. This new acronym just means the number of calories that we need in order to live. We also exceed what we should consume in the way of ordinary and saturated fat. Data are from 1987 to 1985 and are based on USDA surveys. In these surveys, people report on their household food consumption. People tend to be a little shy. Caloric intake is thus subject to underreporting, and actual caloric intake is actually higher.

The USDA's recommended caloric intake varies by age, sex, and activity level. The chart shows that average per-person caloric intake rose steadily from 1,807 calories per day in 1987-88 to 2,043 in 1995. The percentage of the population that consumed more than the recommended number of calories rose from 22% to 31%, a 41% increase.

We are told that fat intake should not exceed 30% and saturated fat should account for fewer than 10% of total calories. Indeed, we have reduced the fat in our diets. Average per-person fat intake dropped from 37% to 33.6% and average saturated fat intake dropped from 13.8% to 11.5% of total calories. This is still over the recommended intake. The USDA attributes the increase in caloric and fat intake to away-from-home eating.

There is, however, some contrarian opinion as well. A cover story in the July 7, 2002, *New York Times Magazine* examines the question "What If It's All Been a Big Fat Lie?"

Author Gary Taubes reports on how researchers are beginning to suggest that maybe Dr. Atkins (proponent of a controversial, high-fat, low carbohydrate diet) was right after all. The same story refers to an alternative Food Pyramid proposed by Dr. Walter C. Willett, chairman of the department of nutrition at the Harvard School of Public Health. For more on this view, see www.hsph.harvard.edu/now/aug24/.

Nearly one-third of us take in more than our recommended daily dose of calories. At the same time, we expend fewer calories than our parents did. The inevitable result? More of us are overweight or obese — and the lower our income, the more likely this is to be so. Excess weight may be the prelude to Type II diabetes and heart disease. For a discussion, see Chapter 1, *Women's Health: Weighty Matters.*

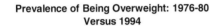

Prevalence of Being Overweight: 1976-80 Versus 1994

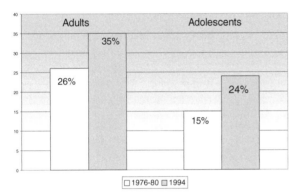

According to the USDA, more than one-third of adults and nearly one-quarter of adolescents were overweight in the early 1990s, compared to one-quarter and one-seventh in the late 1970s (see left). The National Center for Chronic Disease Prevention & Health Promotion reports that by 2000, the prevalence of obesity among adults was 19.8%, reflecting a 61% increase since 1991. The culprits? We're told: too much fat, too much sweetener, refined flour, not enough exercise.

Eating for Disease Prevention Versus What We Really Eat

Time's Top 10 "Foods That Pack a Wallop"	What We're Eating
Tomatoes	Oranges, apples, bananas
Spinach	Iceberg lettuce
Red wine	Cola drinks
Nuts	Potato chips
Broccoli	Fresh and frozen potatoes
Oats	Cookies
Salmon	Beef
Garlic	Salt
Green tea	Carbonated drinks
Blueberries	Melons

So what are we supposed to be eating? Fruits and vegetables are repeatedly mentioned by experts. And if we want to get really serious about our diet and maximize its disease-prevention capabilities, *Time* magazine showed how in a January 2002 report on foods that contain phytochemicals; they may help prevent serious diseases. Phytochemicals are found in abundance in certain foods, foods that *Time* labeled the top 10 "Foods That Pack a Wallop." They are shown on the table next to USDA data showing what we actually spend our food dollars on.

Thanks to the media, we have a pretty good idea of what we should be eating. We've also heard we should be exercising. We will look next at Americans' exercise habits.

Sources: Lin, Biing-Hwan, Joanne Guthrie, and Elizabeth Frazão, "Nutrient Contribution of Food Away From Home." ERS. NFCS 1977-78, NFCS 1987-88, CSFII 1989-91, and CSFII 1994-95; 1-day intake data; Online. Available: www.ers.usda.gov/publications. July 3, 2002; Lino, Mark et al.," The Diet Quality of Americans: Strong Link With Nutrition Knowledge." *Family Economics and Nutrition Review (1999),* p. 49; Horowitz, Janice M. "10 Foods That Pack a Wallop." *Time*, 21 January 2002. USDA. "Food expenditures by selected demographics, 1997-98: Average annual per person expenditures of urban households." Online. Available: www.ers.usda.gov/. June 10, 2002.

Exercise Trends

Percentage of Adults Who Meet Recommended Activity Level, By Gender, Race/Ethnicity, Education Level, and Income: 1998

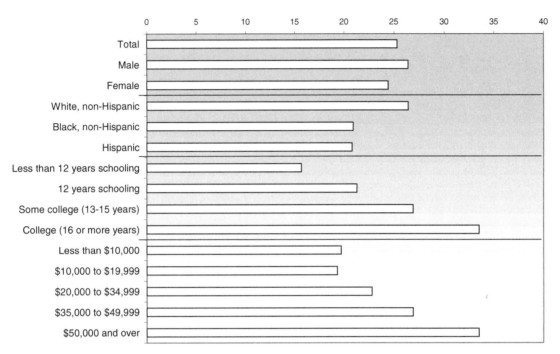

The U.S. government has been promoting the benefits of physical activity since the 1950s, when it emphasized team sports. Cardiovascular fitness was the emphasis in the 1970s: We took up jogging. In the 1980s, new studies showed the health benefits of moderate-intensity activities: We took up aerobic dancing. Exercise machines took off in the 1990s: We joined health clubs. Well, some of us did.

The graphic shows the percentage of people who met a specified activity level in the prior month, by various characteristics.[17] Only 25.3% of respondents met the recommended activity level. The CDC currently recommends at least 30 minutes of moderate activity on most days of the week. The graphic also shows that those most likely to meet the recommendations are white, college-educated, high-income males.

The table on the next page shows the activity breakdown by gender and age. Male senior citizens were more likely to meet recommended levels than men in the other age groups, while about one-quarter of women in every age group were active. Large percentages of all people did not meet the recommended activity level or reported no physical activity whatsoever.

---

[17] Survey size was about 147,000 people aged 18 and over. Recommended activity level for purposes of the survey was physical activity at least five times a week for 30 minutes, or vigorous physical activity for 20 minutes at a time at least three times per week.

Percentage of Men and Women Engaging in Leisure-Time Physical Activity, by Age: 1998

	Met activity level	Insufficient activity	Physically inactive
Males:			
18 to 29 years old	27.7	54.2	18.1
30 to 44 years old	22.8	52.7	24.5
45 to 64 years old	25.4	44.1	30.5
65 to 74 years old	32.1	36.8	31.1
75 years old and over	32.1	26.9	41.0
Females:			
18 to 29 years old	24.5	50.0	25.5
30 to 44 years old	24.7	47.4	27.9
45 to 64 years old	23.9	44.7	31.4
65 to 74 years old	23.6	0.5	35.9
75 years old and over	25.3	26.8	47.9

The CDC findings are summarized in a 300-page tome, *Physical Activity and Health*. Its main point: "People of all ages can improve the quality of their lives through a life-long practice of moderate physical activity."

Why aren't we exercising? Researchers reported in *American Attitudes Toward Physical Activity & Fitness* that our number-one excuse is lack of time. This was mentioned far more often than any other factor.

How do we reconcile this inactivity and the obesity figures from the previous panel with the growth in health clubs?[18] In *Bowling Alone*, Robert D. Putnam tells us that the rise in the number of health clubs has been offset by a decline in jogging and exercise classes. Walking more than a mile is more popular than all other forms of exercise combined, he notes, but golf ranks highly, too, due to the fitness boom among older Americans.

The CDC says that lack of activity contributes to an estimated 300,000 preventable deaths each year. But Americans are an optimistic people. An MSNBC poll shows that 13% of respondents think exercise is "just a passing fad." Fourteen percent are waiting for "a magic pill" that brings weight loss without the sweat.[19] Education is key, concluded researchers; without it, many people do not make the connection between exercise and good health.

We move now to another vital preventive — immunizations.

Source: *Statistical Abstract of the United States: 2001*, Table 198. *Physical Activity and Health*: http://www.cdc.gov/nccdphp/ *American Attitudes Toward Physical Activity & Fitness.* Council on Physical Fitness & Sports and Sporting Goods Manufacturers Association: http://www.fit ness.gov/american. Robert D Putnam, *Bowling Alone,* Simon & Schuster, 2000. MSNBC survey of 1,200 adult Americans: http://www.msnbc.com/news/569883.asp

[18] The International Health, Racquet & Sportsclub Association reported that the number of health clubs reached a record 17,807 facilities as of January 2002. There was a 41% increase in the number of clubs from 1992-2002: http://www.ihrsa.org/.

[19] Obesity and exercise may "have little in common" suggests Gary Taubes *in The New York Times Magazine,* July 7, 2002: "What If It's All Been a Big Fat Lie?" He notes that obesity rates climbed in the 1990's but exercise activity remained unchanged from the 1980s.

Childhood Immunizations Save Lives

Number of Cases ofSelected Vaccine-Preventable Diseases (Estimated) in the United States, Various Years Before Vaccines Were Widely Used

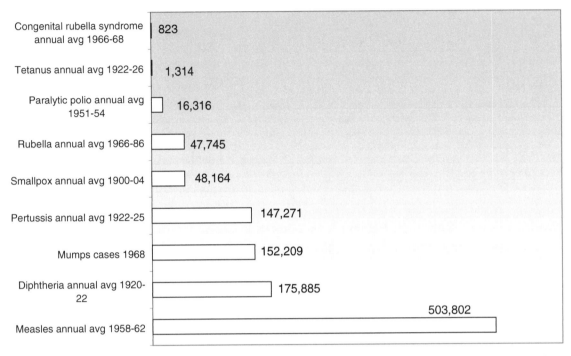

Congenital rubella syndrome annual avg 1966-68	823
Tetanus annual avg 1922-26	1,314
Paralytic polio annual avg 1951-54	16,316
Rubella annual avg 1966-86	47,745
Smallpox annual avg 1900-04	48,164
Pertussis annual avg 1922-25	147,271
Mumps cases 1968	152,209
Diphtheria annual avg 1920-22	175,885
Measles annual avg 1958-62	503,802

As once widely dispersed people began living close together, infectious diseases (like those shown on the chart) proliferated. Improvements in sanitation and quarantine were early methods of controlling the spread of disease. In 1796 Edward Jenner developed a vaccine against smallpox. Millions around the world were then dying of the disease each year, most of them children. By the early 20th century, five vaccines existed (against smallpox, rabies, diphtheria, typhoid fever, and plague), but they were not widely accepted or used. The chart shows the annual number of cases of various infectious diseases in various years before vaccines were widely used.

Disease epidemics cause great suffering. The 1918 influenza outbreak, first observed in a U.S. Army barracks, led to 675,000 American deaths and at least 20 million worldwide. A popular theory of the time held that enemy German agents had unleashed this affliction on us. There was no treatment; the disease disappeared as mysteriously as it appeared.[20]

The graphic shows that between 1951 and 1954, cases of paralytic polio averaged more than 16,000 annually. Polio, also called infantile paralysis, is a dreadful disease that sen-

---

[20]Dr. Jeffrey Taubenberger, chief of molecular pathology at the Armed Forces Institute of Pathology, reported in 1997 that the 1918 flu virus "does not match any strain of influenza virus isolated since, but it is most related to the kind of influenzas that infect swine, suggesting that this influenza entered the human population after being passaged through pigs." He said: "this kind of thing could certainly happen again" (http://www.pbs.org/newshour/bb/health/march97/1918_3-24.html).

---

tenced some of its young victims to a lifetime inside an "iron lung." No one knew where it came from, and parents lived in fear of its appearance. Ironically, the more highly developed a country's system of sanitation, the more vulnerable it was to the disease. In 1954 Dr. Jonas Salk presided over history's largest-ever field trial of a vaccine when 1.8 million American schoolchildren voluntarily received his remedy against polio.

Since 1946, the Centers for Disease Control has been orchestrating large-scale public health efforts to reduce the number of cases of infectious diseases around the world. The small graphic shows the results of these efforts in the United States — a dramatic decline in just 10 years (1990-99) in the number of cases of all vaccine-preventable diseases except pertussis (whooping cough).

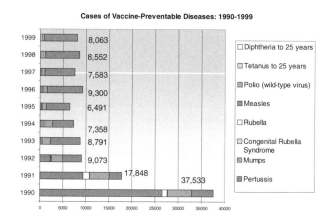

Cases of Vaccine-Preventable Diseases: 1990-1999

Smallpox and polio are absent from this chart but are shown on the large graphic. The last case of smallpox in this country was reported in 1949. There has not been a single reported case of polio caused by the wild virus in this country since 1979. Cases of diseases that were once seen as a normal and unavoidable part of growing up fell 365% in a decade. Immunizations are called one of the greatest public health achievements of the 20th century.

Today vaccines against more than 20 diseases have been developed or licensed. Most are administered to children (adults are discussed later in this chapter). The success of vaccination programs inspired a new way of thinking about disease —"disease eradication," which holds that selected diseases can be eradicated from all human populations through worldwide cooperation. Smallpox was the first disease proclaimed eradicated by the World Health Organization. The debate now is whether the smallpox virus should be destroyed. Worldwide polio eradication is the new goal.

As infectious diseases seemed to disappear, we grew complacent. The past few decades have brought us Lyme disease, Rocky Mountain spotted fever, AIDS, genital herpes, chlamydia, Ebola, Hantavirus, and Legionnaire's disease. Current causes of concern are the growing problem of bacterial resistance and its effects on the treatment of infectious disease, and the possibility of bioterrorism. Next we look at immunization prevalence.

Sources: Chart 1: "Impact of Vaccines Universally Recommended for Children." CDC Fact Sheets. April 2, 1999: www.cdc.gov/od/oc/media/fact/impvacc.htm. Chart 2: National Center for Health Statistics. *Healthy People 2000 Final Review*. Table 20.: http://www.cdc.gov/nchs/. "A Brief History of Infectious Diseases.": http://www.bayerpharma-na.com/healthcare/. National Institute of Allergy and Infectious Diseases: http://www.nih.gov/niaid.

Childhood Immunizations: How Are We Doing?

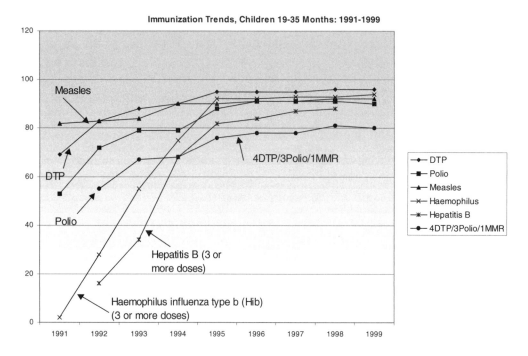

Immunization Trends, Children 19-35 Months: 1991-1999

This chart shows childhood vaccination trends in the 1990s for five of the childhood immunizations now recommended by the American Academy of Pediatrics. (Also recommended are varicella (chicken pox) after 12 months for susceptible children, hepatitis A in certain regions and for certain high-risk groups, and pneumococcal and influenza vaccines.) This graphic demonstrates that (1) as medicine advances, more childhood vaccinations are recommended (the latest, Hepatitis B and *Haemophilus*, are discussed below), and (2) a campaign to increase vaccination rates, like the one that began in 1993, leads to higher rates.

The graph shows that at the beginning of the decade, immunization rates for polio, DTP and measles ranged from 53% to 82%. DTP combines agents against diphtheria, tetanus toxoids, and acellular pertussis; MMR stands for "measles, mumps, and rubella." By the end of the decade, more than 90% of infants had received their recommended series of polio, DTP, and measles shots. "4DTP/3Polio/1MMR" constitutes the entire series of DTP, polio, and MMR vaccinations, which are administered at intervals from infancy to 35 months of age. The rate for this vaccination series went from 55% in 1992 to 80% in 1999.

The chart shows Hib immunizations at zero in 1991, just before the Hib vaccine was approved for young children. At the time, *Haemophilus influenzae* type b was the leading cause of bacterial meningitis (infection/inflammation of the membranes and fluid surrounding the brain and spinal cord). About 15,000 children under five got meningitis from Hib each year; about 500 died. By 1999 more than 90% of infants had gotten Hib shots. The incidence of Hib infection declined to an estimated 54 cases in 1998.

The chart shows childhood hepatitis B doses rising from 16% in 1992 to 82% in 1999. Hepatitis B virus (HBV) is a liver infection transmitted by sexual contact with an infected person or through the use of infected needles during injection drug use. About one third of chronic HBV infections are acquired around the time of birth or during early childhood and can result in chronic liver disease or liver cancer during adulthood. A vaccine developed in 1982 was recommended only for persons at high risk, including infants born to infected mothers. Unfortunately, infected individuals seldom seek medical attention, and it became apparent that prevention could not be achieved by immunizing only those at risk. A new, long-term strategy to prevent HBV is now aimed at all infants.

In 1993 universal childhood immunization became a legislative priority and the passage of the Childhood Immunization Act brought about the highest vaccination rates in history. The result was a decline in the incidence of all vaccine-preventable diseases except whooping cough (pertussis).

What led to the campaign to get more infants and children immunized? The measles epidemic of 1989-1991 may have had something to do with it. During this two-year period, more than 55,000 children succumbed to measles and more than 150 children died. A CDC investigation found that the epidemic started among pre-school-age children. Fewer than two thirds of them were fully vaccinated, while most older children were protected because state laws required vaccination for school entry. The CDC also found that immunization rates for low-income, minority children were lower than the national average, with the result that the number of epidemic measles cases among Hispanic and African-American populations was four to seven times higher than among non-Hispanic whites.

One might ask: If a way is known to prevent a disease, what stands in the way of implementing it? Politics is blamed. For example, it was alleged that Reagan administration cost-cutters saw rates of preventable diseases declining and cut funding for immunizations. Parents are blamed. Medical advances lead to increasingly complex vaccination schedules; many parents fail to get their children immunized until forced to do so by schools. Vaccine manufacturers are blamed. Fear of lawsuits drove some manufacturers out of the vaccine business; prices went up and shortages occurred.

Adverse reactions to vaccines happen — for example, between eight and 10 cases of vaccine-related paralytic polio are still reported in the United States each year. The National Vaccine Injury Compensation Program (1988), which assists the families of victims, is a no-fault alternative for resolving claims. Adverse reactions, although rare, have sparked a small but vocal anti-immunization movement. Joining this movement are those who oppose immunization for religious, philosophical, or other reasons.

Source: Chart: National Center for Health Statistics, *Healthy People 2000 Final Review*, Table 20, retrieved June 13, 2002, from http://www.cdc.gov/nchs/. Mary Graham, "Public Health: Unprotected Children," *Atlantic Monthly*, March 1993. Linda A. Moyer and Eric E. Mast, "Hepatitis B: Virology, Epidemiology, Disease, and Prevention," *American Journal of Preventive Medicine,* Oct. 1994, p45-55. Gretchen Flanders, "Vaccinations: Public Health's 'Miracle' Under Scrutiny," *State Legislatures*, March 2000, p20+.

Immunization Trends: Adults

Epidemic-Related Pneumonia and Influenza Deaths (per 100,000 aged 65+), and Pneumococcal and Influenza Immunizations (Last 12 Months) of Non-Institutionalized People 65 Years and Over in the 1990s

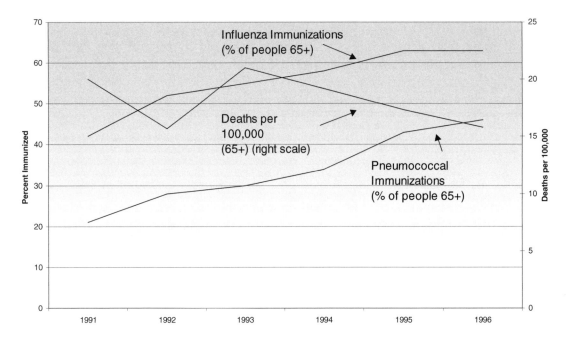

Immunizations are not just for kids. According to the Centers for Disease Control (CDC), they can save adult lives. This graphic shows trends relative to two of the most common vaccine-preventable diseases afflicting adults: influenza (flu) and pneumonia. Flu shots are also recommended for all adults 50 and up and pneumococcal polysaccharide vaccine (PPV) shots are recommended to protect against pneumonia for all adults 65 and up. The CDC also recommends that all adults receive the Tetanus-diphtheria toxoid immunization every 10 years. The CDC publishes a list of recommended immunizations for adolescents and adults, including those who have not been immunized against childhood diseases, travelers, homosexuals, and illegal drug users. For more information, please see http://www.cdc.gov/nip/recs/adult-schedule.pdf.

The graphic shows epidemic-related pneumonia and influenza deaths among people 65 years and over (per 100,000) and percentages of that population who were immunized in the 1990s. The years are not precisely comparable, but the trend is clear: epidemic-related pneumonia and influenza deaths went down while the percentage of older adults who were immunized went up. Is this just a coincidence?

Kristine Severyn has this to say: "Considering that more than 90 percent of pneumonia and influenza deaths occur in persons 65 years of age or older, but that about 65 percent of all deaths (from any cause) occur in this age group anyway, it is nearly impossible to prove if flu shots significantly increase life expectancy in the elderly.... Congress and the American taxpayer have been defrauded about the alleged advantages of flu shots."

The CDC Web site tells us that flu and pneumonia are the fifth leading cause of death among the elderly. The CDC has been strongly urging immunizations for senior citizens since the early 1990s. Medicare has paid for pneumonia vaccinations since 1981 and flu vaccinations since 1993. By 1998, only 63% of the population over age 65 received the flu vaccine and only 46% received the pneumococcal vaccine. Even fewer African-Americans and Hispanics were immunized, as the table below shows.

Pneumococcal and Influenza Immunizations: 1991-1998

	1991	1993	1994	1995	1997	1998
Pneumococcal immunizations						
Noninstitutionalized people 65 years+	21%	28%	30%	34%	43%	46%
a. Black 65 years+	14%	14%	15%	23%	22%	26%
b. Hispanic 65 years+	12%	12%	14%	23%	23%	23%
Influenza immunizations (in last 12 months)						
Noninstitutionalized people 65 years+	42%	52%	55%	58%	63%	63%
a. Black 65 years+	27%	33%	39%	40%	45%	46%
b. Hispanic 65 years+	NA	47%	38%	50%	53%	50%

According to CDC data published in *JAMA*, flu vaccination levels are higher among people with more than a high school education.

Some immunizations are now available at the corner pharmacy for a nominal fee. Why, then, are immunization rates so low? *NursingWorld* offers these explanations: "Misconceptions about vaccine safety, efficacy and inadequate knowledge of indications"; "'Well adults' often lack awareness of the need for immunization"; "Financial barriers"; "Current low mortality rates of tetanus and diphtheria as compared with other vaccine-preventable diseases may not appear to justify cost and practice of periodic TD [tetanus-diphtheria] vaccination"; "High costs of hepatitis B vaccine and the failure of most insurance companies to pay for its use… populations at greatest risk for hepatitis B are often hard-to-reach populations who lack regular health care"; and "Access to health care."

The great weight of expert opinion is on the side of immunizations as recommended by the CDC. We live in a world where, contrary to what many of us may believe, infectious diseases have not been eradicated and are easily spread through global travel. Advances in modern medicine are keeping us alive longer but leaving us vulnerable to infection. Chemotherapy, for example, or drugs taken after organ transplants, can weaken the immune system and leave a patient unprepared to fight a powerful virus.

Next we look at community health programs. They are the major sources for knowledge about disease prevention for much of the population.

Sources: National Center for Health Statistics, *Healthy People 2000 Final Review*, Table 20: http://www.cdc.gov/nchs/. Severyn, R.Ph.,Ph.D.,Kristine."AreFluVaccinesBeneficial?" *Spotlight*:http://www.spotlight.org/01_07_00/Vacc/vacc.html. "Position Statements: Adult Immunization.": http://www.nursingworld.org/readroom/position/social/scaltimm.htm. "Influenza and Pneumococcal Vaccination Levels Among Persons [greater than or equal to] Aged 65 Years — United States, 1999." *JAMA, the Journal of the American Medical Association*, 25 July 2001. p.413.

Prevention Through Community Health Centers

Estimated Growth in the Number of Federally-Funded
Community Health Centers: 2001-2006
(Figures in parentheses are projected total new health care delivery sites since 2001)

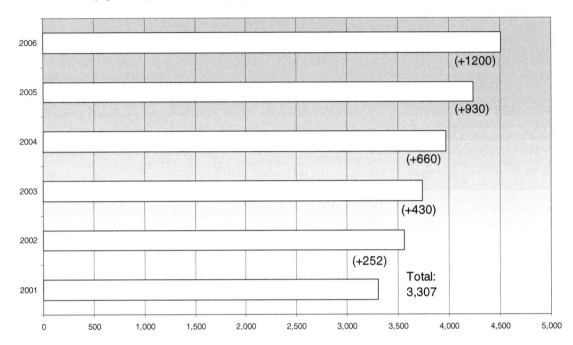

President Johnson's War on Poverty was the inspiration for the first federally funded community health centers (CHCs). Their aim, according to Johnson's 1965 State of the Union Address, was "to help the mentally ill and improve health care for school-age children from poor families, including services for the mentally retarded." Today CHCs aim to improve the health status of all underserved populations and provide access to health care services for the uninsured. Uninsured people numbered 38.9 million in 2001; 8.5 million of them were children (about 11.2% of children under age 18).

The CHCs are supported by Federal grants. The FY 2002 appropriation was $1.3 billion. The program coordinates cooperative agreements and grants with national, state, and regional health and primary care organizations. Those wishing to find such a center can begin by looking at http://www.bphc.hrsa.gov/databases/fqhc/default.htm.

In 2001, there were more than 1,000 CHCs in operation. The chart shows that they offered care at 3,307 delivery sites. The Department of Health and Human Services projects growth to 4,507 sites by 2006, an increase of 37%. There are CHCs in all 50 states, the District of Columbia, Puerto Rico, Guam, and the U.S. Virgin Islands.

CHCs served some 11 million patients in 2001. It is estimated that an additional 6.1 million will be served by 2006, for a total of 17 million served. Well-known sites include St. Vincent's Hospital in New York, Cook County Hospital in Chicago, and COTS in Detroit. Because services are tailored to community needs, delivery sites have been established specifically for the homeless, for women, for migrants, for subsets of the population (Native Americans, for example), and others.

Why do we have CHCs? The Centers for Disease Control tells us: because society has an "interest in assuring conditions in which persons can be healthy." This falls under the heading of public health. According to CDC: "Public health engages both private and public organizations and individuals in accomplishing this mission. Responsibilities encompass preventing epidemics and the spread of disease, protecting against environmental hazards, preventing injuries, encouraging healthy behavior, helping communities to recover from disasters, and ensuring the quality and accessibility of health services."

A hundred years ago, major public health threats were infectious diseases associated with poor hygiene, sanitation, and nutrition; high infant and maternal death rates; and diseases or injuries associated with unsafe workplaces. Today, major threats to health are chronic diseases and risky behavior; these can be prevented. Because the health problems of untreated individuals can have far-reaching consequences, everyone must be cared for. And when preventive care is made available, Medicaid disbursements are lowered.

President George W. Bush's 2003 budget cites this evidence of the benefit of CHCs: "While health center patients typically have high blood pressure rates far exceeding that of comparable racial, ethnic and socioeconomic groups, they are more than three times as likely to report that their blood pressure is under control compared to non-health center patients." Untreated, high blood pressure can cause stroke, heart attack, kidney or eye problems, or death.

Not everyone agrees with the practices of community health centers. For example, some centers offer needle exchanges to prevent HIV, a practice that is supported by the CDC, the American Medical Association, and the National Institutes of Health. Critics contend that needle exchanges encourage drug use. There are those who argue that the confidentiality guaranteed to a child in a health center suspends parental rights and that the parent should be the only health educator.

What are emerging threats to public health? According to the Public Health Threats and Emergencies Act of 2000, they "may include new or resurgent infectious diseases, dangerous microbes resistant to antibiotics, or deliberate terrorist attacks using biological weapons." Vast numbers of uninsured people without access to health care would be a threat to public health in any of these dire events. Hence the need for more CHCs.

We will now take a look at the rising number of health care programs offered in schools.

Sources: Chart: The White House Office of Management and Budget, retrieved June 26, 2002, from http://www.whitehouse.gov/omb/budget/fy2003/bud15.html. CDC, "Achievements in Public Health, 1900-1999: Changes in the Public Health System," retrieved June 26, 2002, from http://www.cdc.gov/mmwr/preview/mmwrhtml/mm4850a1.htm. Lyndon Johnson's 1965 State of the Union Address, retrieved July 2, 2002, from http://lone-star.net/mall/jcitychamber/union65.htm.

School-Based Health Care

Selected Services and Policies of School-Based Health Centers: 1998-99

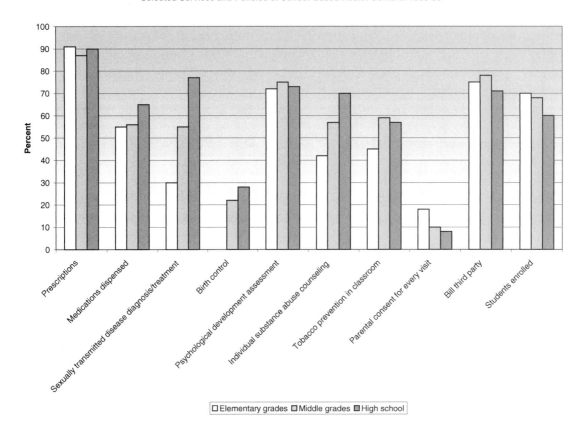

Should schools engage in health care? Or health care education? Here are two justifications: The General Accounting Office reports that Medicaid pays for the health care of 21 million children, more than one in four. Medicaid screens children for various conditions — to detect and treat conditions early. But many children are not getting these services. They lack service providers. More teens are indulging in risky behavior. Easy availability of health care services might help alleviate both of these problems.

School-based health centers (SBHCs) are on the increase. They provide medical care and education for the approximately 1 million enrolled students, particularly low-income students.

The graphic shows data from the National Assembly on School-Based Health Care (NASBHC); 806 school-based health centers completed questionnaires. The average center was located in a school with 1,004 students, with 64% of students enrolled in the center; 537 students used their center at least once. The median age of the centers was four years; the average six. SBHCs served 1.1 million students (2% of the total school enrollment), nearly two-thirds of them minorities.

SBHCs began in the 1970s as a response to poor access to health care and alarming statistics about risky behaviors and teen pregnancy. SBHCs are sponsored by health departments, community health centers, hospitals, university medical centers, and nonprofit health care agencies.

The graphic shows some of the services provided by SBHCs in the elementary, middle, and high school grades. Specifically, the centers provide basic preventive services, including vision, hearing, and dental screenings, immunizations, and so on. The centers also do mental health screening (suicide is a leading cause of death among high school students).

The chart shows that birth control information is provided by a small percentage of schools (22% of middle and 28% of high schools). Why so few? SBHCs are constrained by citizen complaints that the centers are a front for family planning activities and that the sex education offered encourages teenage pregnancy and promiscuity. President Bush's solution to the problem of unintended pregnancies and sexually transmitted diseases: "A substantial investment in abstinence education," included in his 2003 budget.

We know that teen sex is problematic; we cannot agree on what ought to be done about it. The NASBHC reports that once an SBHC has established itself and earned community trust, it is more likely to offer family planning services. Not shown on this chart is their finding that 41% of SBHCs more than 10 years old (20% of centers) offer such services.

A survey conducted by Making the Grade[21] found that in school year 1999-2000, the number of SBHCs had grown to 1,380, operating in 45 states and the District of Columbia, up from only 120 centers in 1988. The majority (58%) are located in urban school districts; 24% are in rural districts, and 18% are in suburban districts.

SBHCs traditionally relied on private funding and grants from local, state, and federal governments. Recently, third-party payers like Medicaid have become an important source of support. The chart shows that more than 70% of SBHCs sought third party reimbursement for services in 1998-99. Medicaid contributed $9 million in 1997-98.

Where SBHCs are in place, they are accepted by the majority of students — 70% of students in elementary grades, 68% in middle grades, and 60% in high school were enrolled in the centers, and 83% of enrolled students actually used the centers.

Are kids getting the prevention message? The table below shows that greater percentages of students reported engaging in risky behaviors in 1999 than in 1991.[22] These students are at risk for major killers like cardiovascular disease, cancer, and diabetes, as well as unwanted pregnancy, HIV, and sexually transmitted diseases. This is a strain on the health care system and a threat to the public health.

---

[21] Now The Center for Health and Health Care in Schools at George Washington University.

[22] Data from CDC, Youth Risk Behavior Survey, 1999. Included were students in grades 9-12 in 42 states, 16 large cities, and 4 territories. The average sample size was 2,200.

Do SBHCs help reduce risky behaviors? Study results reported in *Journal of School Health* indicate that "SBHCs have been effective in addressing health care needs but less effective in reducing risky behaviors. Focusing interventions on selected, individual high-risk behaviors such as substance use and pregnancy prevention without giving consideration to the student's social, environmental, and cultural situations resulted in minimal positive behavior change." Sounds like a tall order.

Youth Risk Behaviors That Worsened Between 1991-1999					
	1991	1993	1995	1997	1999
Frequent cigarette use	12.7	13.8	16.1	16.7	16.8
Episodic heavy drinking	31.3	30.0	32.6	33.4	31.5
Lifetime marijuana use	31.3	32.8	42.4	47.1	47.2
Current cocaine use	1.7	1.9	3.1	3.3	4.0
Lifetime illegal steroid use	2.7	2.2	3.7		3.7
Used birth control pills at last intercourse	20.8	18.4	17.4	16.6	16.2
Attended physical education class daily	41.6	34.3	25.4	27.4	29.1

What about parental consent? In surveys, teens repeatedly mention the need for a place they can go for health information when they cannot go to their parents. The chart at the beginning of this discussion shows that 18% of young children, 10% of middle schoolers, and 8% of high school students needed parental consent to visit their SBHC. Parental consent to enroll was required in 94% of responding centers. The survey asked health centers to identify services a student could receive without parental consent. Those most frequently mentioned were emergency care, sexually transmitted disease treatment, drug and alcohol counseling, family planning, mental health counseling, and prenatal care.

Public schools must be concerned about their vulnerability to costly legal challenges when dispensing health care services. It is well known that condoms can prevent HIV/AIDS, the eighth leading cause of death for 15-24-year-olds. Yet condom availability in schools remains a controversial issue. In a recent national survey of school superintendents, 64% said they would seek legal counsel before developing condom availability programs.

Next we will look at what genetic engineering might hold in store for us relative to disease prevention.

Source: Chart: National Assembly on School-Based Health Care, "Creating Access to Care for Children and Youth: School-Based Health Center Census 1998-1999," June 2000, retrieved June 25, 2002, from http://www.nasbhc.org/. Table: National Youth Risk Behavior Surveys, 1991–1999, in "Reducing the Burden of Chronic Disease: Promoting Healthy Behaviors Among Youth," *Diseases Notes and Reports*, National Center for Chronic Disease Prevention and Health Promotion, Volume 14, Number 1, Winter 2001, retrieved May 31, 2002, from http://www.cdc.gov/nccdphp/cdwin2001. General Accounting Office, "Medicaid: Stronger Efforts Needed to Ensure Children's Access to Health Screening Services," GAO-01-749, July 2001; retrieved June 26, 2002, from www.gao.gov/. M.J. Friedrich, "25 Years of School-Based Health Centers," *JAMA, The Journal of the American Medical Association*, March 3, 1999, v281 i9 p781(1). Pamela A. Shuler, "Evaluating Student Services Provided by School-Based Health Centers: Applying the Shuler Nurse Practitioner Practice Model," *Journal of School Health*, October 2000, v70 i8 p348. The Alan Guttmacher Institute, "School-Based Health Centers And the Birth Control Debate," *Issues in Brief*, 2000 Series, No. 3, , retrieved June 25, 2002, from http://www.agi-usa.org/pubs/ib_1200.pdf. "The Untapped Power of Schools to Improve the Health of Teens," retrieved June 26, 2002, from http://www.healthinschools.org/ejournal/2002/may02_1.htm.

Genetic Engineering: The Future of Preventive Medicine?

U.S. Human Genome Project Funding: Total and Contributions of Department of Energy (DOE) and National Institutes of Health (NIH): 1988-2002

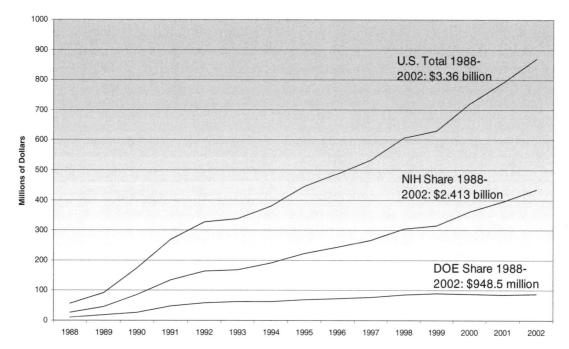

On June 26, 2000, *The New York Times* reported thus: "In an achievement that represents a pinnacle of human self-knowledge, two rival groups of scientists said in a joint announcement today that they had effectively deciphered the genome, the set of genetic instructions that defines the human organism."

This remarkable achievement resulted from ongoing work by researchers on the federally funded Human Genome Project (HGP) and the private company Celera Genomics. There are genome research centers all over the world, financed by governments, pharmaceutical and other industries, and private investors. They espouse goals both lofty and practical. The HGP Web site states: "Treating gene-related diseases and conditions is a major hope of the Human Genome Project." Somewhat less altruistically, a Clinton-Gore Web site predicted that resulting "sales of DNA-based products and technologies ... are projected to exceed $45 billion by 2009."

The graphic shows the U.S. budget for the HGP from 1988 to 2002. The original estimate was $3 billion, with the ultimate goal "to discover all the more than 30,000 human genes and render them accessible for further biological study." The project started with an appropriation of $27.9 million in 1988 and grew to $434.3 million for the year 2002, bringing total spending to more than $3.3 billion. The lion's share goes to the NIH and a smaller amount is allotted to DOE. Why is DOE involved? Ever since the Manhattan Project, which produced the first atomic bombs, the DOE has been interested in learning how radiation affects genes.

The implications of HGP research are profound and far reaching. Philosopher Georges B. Kutukdjian says the project "is giving rise to anxieties that may in some cases be justified but are more often irrational." How to make proper use of the discoveries has been a concern from the very beginning. The DOE and NIH devote 3% to 5% of their genome project budgets to ethical, legal, and social issues.[23]

As was true of big projects like the superconducting supercollider, a major criticism of the HGP is that the high cost is not justified where research dollars are finite. Nevertheless, the Clinton and Bush administrations have been supportive of the HGP. Since 9/11, the funding of certain research projects over others has assumed a new urgency. In a government memorandum dated May 30, 2002,[24] it was noted that genome research is a priority because: "This basic research is leading to new applications in health care, agriculture, energy, and environmental management. [Genome] sequence data are also critical for homeland security forensic purposes."

The HGP has brought both cooperation and conflict between nations.[25] Cooperation is evidenced by the international sharing of data from genome labs around the world.[26] Conflict is evidenced by the uproar that arose when NIH applied for a gene patent in 1991. Cook-Deegan wrote of the furor: "Sanctimonious claims were made about direct links between human genes and human dignity." A patent gold rush ensued. John J. Doll, director of biotechnology for the U.S. Patent and Trademark Office, told *Scientific American* that more than 20,000 patents on genes or other gene-related molecules have been granted and 25,000 applications were pending.

What does the HGP mean to preventive medicine? Gene therapy might be used for diseases ranging from cancer to AIDS and even for aging. Stem cells (generic cells that develop into all parts of the body) might be the answer to previously untreatable ailments.

Sources: Human Genome Project Budget, retrieved June 26, 2002, from http://www.ornl.gov/hgmis/project/budget.html. Nicholas Wade, "Scientists Complete Rough Draft of Human Genome," NYT Update, June 26, 2000, retrieved June 27, 2002, from www.nytimes.com/library/national/science/062600sci-human-genome.html. Georges B. Kutukdjian, "UNESCO and Bioethics," *UNESCO Courier*, September 1994. Robert Mullan Cook-Deegan, "Origins of the Human Genome Project," retrieved June 27, 2002, from www.fplc.edu/risk/vol5/spring/cookdeeg.htm. "Human Genome Research," retrieved June 27, 2002, from http://www.er.doe.gov/production/ober/hug_top.html. Office of Science and Technology Policy Memorandum, May 30, 2002, retrieved June 27, 2002, from http://www.ostp.gov/html/. Mae-Wan Ho, "The Human Genome Sellout, *Third World Resurgence* Nov./Dec. 2000. "Talking Gene Patents," retrieved June 28, 2002, from http://www.sciam.com/techbiz/0801patents.html.

---

[23] See ELSI (Ethical, Legal, and Social Issues) Web page: http://www.ornl.gov/hgmis/elsi/elsi.html.

[24] From the Office of Scientific Policy; see Source notes.

[25] Some companies are accused of keeping their own human genome data secret while benefiting from free access to the public database; Mae-Wan Ho, see Source notes.

[26] Access the data at http://www.ncbi.nlm.nih.gov/.

Chapter 4

Risky Behavior

In the following pages, we look at risky behaviors that can carry us to early graves. We know these behaviors are risky because the public health establishment tells us so — and often. Public health efforts shifted in the 20th century from sanitation and preventing communicable diseases to advising us how to extend our lives by correcting our behavior. The government's redefined role crystallized with the 1964 U.S. Surgeon General's *Report on Smoking and Health*, the first widely publicized official recognition that cigarette smoking is a cause of cancer and other serious diseases. The report stated: "Cigarette smoking is a health hazard of sufficient importance in the United States to warrant appropriate remedial action."

Since then, the government has insinuated itself into other behavioral arenas, launching a war on drugs in 1971 and declaring "a smoke-free society" an achievable goal in the 1980s. Our sex lives are not immune to governmental scrutiny: In 1995 Surgeon General Joycelyn Elders caused an uproar when she said: "I think that [masturbation] is something that is a part of human sexuality and it's a part of something that perhaps should be taught." In 2001 Surgeon General David Satcher told us: "Overweight and obesity may soon cause as much preventable disease and death as cigarette smoking."

Our mental health is now also the government's concern. In her introduction to the 1999 Surgeon General's report on mental health (marking the end of the Congressionally mandated Decade of the Brain), Health and Human Services Director Donna Shalala declared: "We are poised to take what we know and to advance the state of mental health in the Nation." The report went on to assure us that the government "will continue to attend to needs that occur across the lifespan, from the youngest child to the oldest among us."

In this chapter we look at some of the "new epidemics": trends in diet and obesity, and smoking, drug, and alcohol abuse. The government collects statistics on all of them.[1]

---

[1] A caveat about drug use data: Different methods of calculating the number of drug users can produce widely different estimates. The *Washington Post* reports that "Measuring the drug war with any precision is a daunting task. Hard-core drug users are hard to find, much less question." In the same article is a quote from David Musto, Yale University medical historian and an expert on drug trends: "You really can't tell from the big debate that goes on in public what the big picture is ... When I tell people about it, they're completely surprised by the fact there has been a decline [in drug use] since 1980." Jeff Leen, "Number Jumble Clouds Judgment of Drug War," *Washington Post*, January 2, 1998, pA01.

Diet: Our first panels explore the risky way we eat. We have so many obligations and so little time. We must eat, so we eat out. But that is not a healthy way to eat and is blamed for current rates of obesity.

Drug and alcohol abuse: We continue with a look at drug and alcohol abuse. One theory has it that we are all looking for nirvana; some approach it through exercise, others through alcohol or drugs. Attempts to regulate drinking and drugs are not new and such attempts have always met with resistance. Our latest "war on drugs" is criticized as endless, excessive, costly, and ineffectual. In the following panels, we will see why the war on drugs has been called a war on African Americans and a war on children.

We cannot agree on whether risky behaviors are diseases to be treated, character flaws to be condemned, or criminal problems worthy of the harshest punishment. Attitudes change with accumulated knowledge. Yesterday's vilified drug becomes today's socially accepted drug, with the result, for example, that in 2001 the American Medical Association called for more studies of the benefits and risks of using marijuana as a medicine. Several states now allow marijuana to be used for medical purposes, and polls show strong support for this initiative.

Times and attitudes change. Before 9/11, there was talk of alternative approaches to the war on drugs. In 2002 terrorism replaced drug enforcement as the FBI's top priority and President George W. Bush linked drugs to patriotism, announcing that "if you're buying illegal drugs in America, it is likely that money is going to end up in the hands of terrorist organizations."

Smoking: We've known for a long time that smoking is bad for us. Commenting on an 1893 court decision, *The New York Times* opined: "The smoking of cigarettes may be objectionable, as are many other foolish practices, and it may be more injurious than other modes of smoking tobacco, but it is an evil which cannot be remedied by law… cigarettes are not a legitimate subject for legislative action."[2] That is no longer true. By 1992, the 50 state and DC had laws governing tobacco sales and distribution to youths. On June 6, 1996, prevalence of cigarette smoking was added to the list of conditions designated as reportable by states to the CDC, marking the first time a behavior, rather than a disease or illness, was considered nationally reportable. In this chapter, we will examine smoking trends.

Stress: Our chapter continues with a look at stress. Hans Seyle, Viennese physician and pioneer in the study of stress, wrote that "without stress, there would be no life." We will chart a course through a typical working-person's day and enumerate some of the events that can cause stress. We conclude the chapter by looking at two more risky behaviors that have experienced a surge in popularity lately: tanning and tattooing.

---

[2] "Cigarette Prohibition in Washington, 1893-1911," retrieved July 22, 2002, from http://www.history link.org/output.

Dining Out May Be Hazardous To Your Health...

Percentage of Americans Aged 2 and Over Who Ate Meals Away From Home, and Percent Contribution of Away-From-Home Foods to Daily Calorie, Fat, and Saturated Fat Intake: 1977-1995

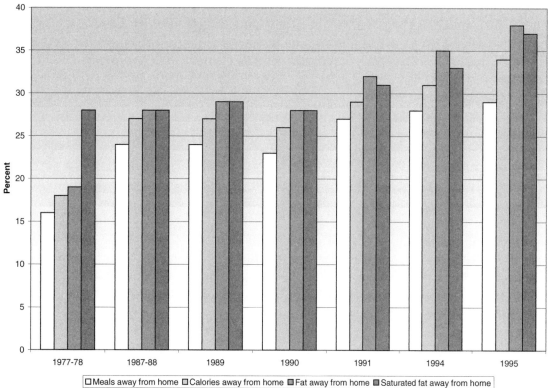

☐ Meals away from home ☐ Calories away from home ■ Fat away from home ■ Saturated fat away from home

Are Americans the fattest people on earth? Some Europeans think so. Michael Fumento, author of *The Fat of the Land*, writes: "Any European who has recently arrived here will gladly regale you with stories about how stunningly fat he thinks we are. No European country even comes close to us in terms of obesity." Obesity, says the CDC, is "the most urgent challenge to nutritional health during the 21st century."

How did we get this way? According to the U.S. Department of Agriculture (USDA), a major culprit in our bulging is foods prepared outside the home. About 57% of us eat away from home on any given day.

The graphic shows that the proportion of our meals consumed away from home rose from 16% in 1977-78 to 29% in 1995. This accounted for 34% of daily calorie intake and 38% of total fat consumption in 1995, up from 18% and 19% in 1977-78 respectively.

One of the biggest problems in the American diet today is trans fat, the kind found in fast foods — says Walter Willet of the Harvard School of Public Health Department of Nutrition. Trans fat is the artery-clogging variety. The USDA reports that between 1982 and 1997, the amount of money we spent on fast food grew at an annual rate of 6.8%, compared to 4.7% growth in table service restaurant expenditures. The proportion of expenditures on fast food increased from 29.3 to 34.2%, while the restaurant proportion decreased from 41 to 35.7%. At about $109.5 billion in 1997, fast food sales approached the amount spent at table service restaurants ($114.3 billion in 1997, including tips).

Kids love fast food. Right now, millions of children around the world are eating Happy Meals at one of 29,000 McDonald's restaurants.[3] In terms of health, according to Robert A. Vogel, M.D., "A Happy Meal … is roughly the equivalent of smoking two cigarettes."[4] By advertising to children while they are watching television and not exercising, the fast-food industry skillfully manipulates new generations of consumers. Some say that this is particularly egregious because companies advertise to low-income children.

Fumento's theory as to why we are so fat? "Our food portions look like something out of Jurassic Park." Geocities.com says two frequently expressed fast-food customer complaints are: "They don't give you enough meat," and "The hamburgers are too thin."

On the other hand comes this advice from Walter Willett: Eliminating all fat from our diets "can be really dangerous. Not all fats are bad." Another popular alternative — replacing fats with sugar or refined carbohydrates — is not a good solution either.

Must we stop dining out? Not necessarily. One can find something resembling healthy food in most restaurants. Eric Schlosser (*Fast Food Nation*) suggests we make our preferences known: "The executives who run the fast food industry are not bad men. They are businessmen. They will sell free-range, organic, grass-fed hamburgers if you demand it. They will sell whatever sells at a profit."

Sources: Biing-Hwan Lin, Joanne Guthrie, Elizabeth Frazão, "Nutrient Contribution of Food Away From Home." ERS. NFCS 1977-78, 1987-88, CSFII 1989-91, 1994-95; www.ers.usda.gov/. "Unhappy Meals." *Atlantic Monthly*. December 14, 2000: http://www.theatlantic.com/. Eric Schlosser, "Fast-Food Nation: Meat and Potatoes." *Rolling Stone*, 3 September 2001: http://www.ericsecho.org. "Fast Food Facts."http://www.geocities.com/mcdonaldization/facts.html. "Nutrition Book Author Willett Rebuilds USDA Food Pyramid." *Harvard Public Health Now*: http://www.hsph.harvard.edu/. Michael Fumento, "On the Thin Side of the World: Europeans Eat Less Than We Do, Exercise Informally.": http://www.fumento.com/plainfat.html. Mark D. Jekanowski, "Causes and Consequences of Fast Food Sales Growth.." www.ers.usda.gov/publications/.

---

[3] McDonald's is not the only purveyor of fast-food meals. It recently introduced "What's On Your Plate," a series of twelve different public service announcements on "eating right," produced in partnership with the U.S. Society for Nutrition Education; see http://www.mcdonalds.com/countries/usa/food/eating_right

[4] Vogel was commenting for WebMD on an Australian study reported in the June 2001 *Journal of the American College of Cardiology*. The study of 32 "healthy volunteers" showed that "After eating a simple meal of a ham and cheese sandwich with butter, and a serving of whole milk and some ice cream, the ability of the body's arteries to expand and accommodate the blood and fat traveling through them is reduced by about 25%. See http://content.health.msn.com/content/article/1728.80751.

... But Dining In May Sicken You

Cases of the Four Major Bacterial Food-Borne Illnesses (per 100,000 population) in Five States: 1996-2000

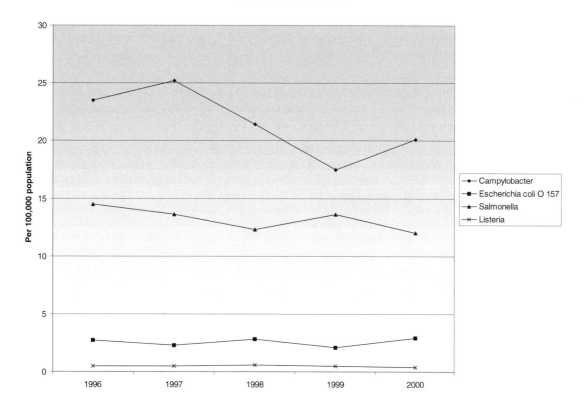

The graphic shows incidences of the four major bacterial food-borne illnesses from 1996 through 2000 (see Chapter 2 for definitions). FoodNet first began collecting this data in 1996.[5] It is plain to see that we are living in a microbial world. Estimates vary, but the CDC reports that every year there are 76 million cases of food poisoning in the United States and about 30,000 Americans are hospitalized each year for *Salmonella* and *Campylobacter* infections (they are the two major villains) they got from tainted food. An estimated 5,000 people die. Most at risk are infants and young children. All this despite the fact that Americans are said to have the world's safest food supply.

---

[5] Defined at http://www.cdc.gov/foodnet/: "The Foodborne Diseases Active Surveillance Network (Food-Net) is the principal foodborne disease component of CDC's Emerging Infections Program (EIP). FoodNet is a collaborative project of the CDC, nine EIP sites (California, Colorado, Connecticut, Georgia, New York, Maryland, Minnesota, Oregon and Tennessee), the U.S. Department of Agriculture (USDA), and the Food and Drug Administration (FDA). The project consists of active surveillance for foodborne diseases and related epidemiologic studies designed to help public health officials better understand the epidemiology of foodborne diseases in the United States." The project began in five states and surveilled laboratory-confirmed cases. Each year the surveillance area, referred to as the "catchment," expands. By 2002 it covered 38 million persons in nine states. Incidence rates for all food-borne pathogens can be found in table form at the back of this book.

The fact is, like fast food, home cooking can be hazardous to your health. In reviewing Eric Schlosser's book *Fast Food Nation*, Nicols Fox wrote: "Given the dangers of cross-contamination and under-cooking, it seems to me very likely safer, from a microbial perspective, to eat the fast-food version of a hamburger than one prepared at home."

Many food-borne illnesses are the result of poor hygiene and bad decisions on the part of the cook. Poorly canned foods, undercooked meat and eggs, groceries past their sell-by date, unpasteurized dairy products — all are breeding places for sickening pathogens.

It is likely that millions of cases of food poisoning go unreported each year. Remember that little stomach upset you experienced after you ate Aunt M—a's (underdone) fried chicken at the Fourth of July picnic? You recovered without official notice being taken. But the CDC wants precise numbers so it can track outbreaks and protect consumers. Therein lies another problem — too many government cooks, too little communication. FoodNet and HACCP[6] are just two recent government measures intended to address concerns about the nation's food supply.

Irradiation as a way to prevent food contamination is one controversial solution. The FDA is for it: "The process has been shown to be safe and to significantly reduce bacterial contamination." The Organic Consumers Association is against it: "Science has not proved that a long-term diet of irradiated foods is safe for human health."

The good news? A year after releasing the data that appear on the graph, Health and Human Services Secretary Tommy Thompson released new data showing a 23% drop in incidences of the four major food-borne illnesses between 1996-2000. In the wake of 9/11, however, and the threat of food-borne terrorism, Thompson told *U.S. News & World Report*: "I am more fearful about this than anything else."[7]

Sources: "Preliminary FoodNet Data on the Incidence of Foodborne Illnesses—Selected Sites, United States, 2000," MMWR Morbidity and Natality Weekly Report, April 6, 2001:http://www.cdc.gov/mmwr/. Nicols Fox, "Feeding Frenzy," January 28, 2001; p. T03: http://www.washingtonpost.com. "Foodborne Illnesses Post Dramatic Six-Year Decline." *HHS News*. April 18, 2002: http://www.hhs.gov/news/ "What's Wrong With Food Irradiation." Organic Consumers Association. February 2001: http://www.purefood.org/irrad/irradfact. "FDA Approves Irradiation of Meat for Pathogen Control, *HHS News*: http://www.cfsan.fda.gov/~lrd/hhsirrad.html. Foodborne Illness Education Information Center:http://www.nal.usda.gov/foodborne/index.html.

---

[6] Hazard Analysis and Critical Control Points, the U.S. Department of Agriculture's system for ensuring that meat and poultry plants meet food safety standards.

[7] There actually was a terrorist attack on the food supply in the 1980s. An Oregon cult (followers of the Indian guru Bhagwan Shree Rajneesh) contaminated salad bars with salmonella bacteria. Cult members hoped that by incapacitating enough voters (750 people fell ill), they would see their candidates win in county elections.

School Lunch: Maybe Kids Were Right All Along

K-12 Enrollment and Participation in the National School Lunch Program: 1970-2001

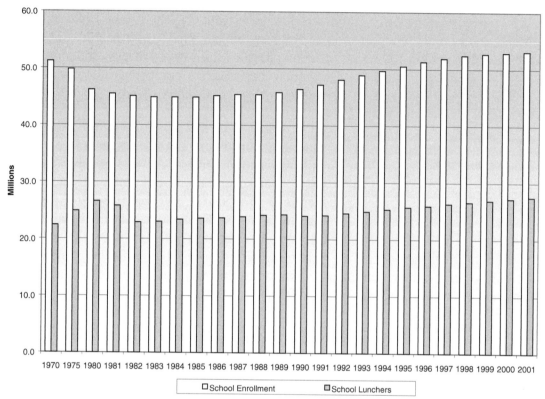

The chart shows total enrollment in grades K-12 and average participation in the National School Lunch Program (NSLP) for the years 1970-2001. The NSLP is a federally assisted meal program operating in public and nonprofit private schools and residential child care institutions. NSLP, established by President Truman in 1946, cost taxpayers $5.56 billion in FY 2000, "less than the price of three stealth bombers," according to Kelly Patricia O'Meara, who investigated the program for *Insight on the News*, a conservative current events magazine. The chart shows that in 2000, more than half of all schoolchildren dined on lunches provided through this program (27.2 million of 52.9 million students). In the charted period, participation in the program rose from a low of 20.7% of all students (1970) to a high of 57.8% (1998).

The NSLP's avowed purpose is to provide "nutritionally balanced, low-cost or free lunches." What could be risky about a school lunch? A number of things. Schools have been plagued by outbreaks of food poisoning and questions about the nutritional value of the food they serve. The emerging trend is for schools to earn extra dollars by offering soft drinks, snacks, and fast food — in other words, unregulated junk food that provides little or no nutritional value, competes with more nutritious offerings, and contributes to unhealthy weight gain. The USDA registered turf alarm over this trend in a report to Congress entitled "Foods Sold in Competition With USDA School Meal Programs."

The NSLP uses donated commodities. *Insight on the News* reports that in 1999 nearly 1 billion pounds of food were donated to NSLP schools. The magazine quotes Nancy Donley:[8] "Recent data show that 40 percent of the samples [of meat supplied for NSLP] being taken by the USDA's Food Safety and Inspection Service are turning up positive for E. coli 0157:h7, an often deadly bacterium." The magazine charged that USDA policies for inspecting donated commodities were inefficient. In school year 1997-98, 17 outbreaks of food-borne contamination in the program affected 1,600 people.[9] The Sierra Club charged in a June 2001 report that hundreds of millions of federal dollars had been awarded for NSLP to companies that had been involved in large food safety recalls.

Most Likely to Become "Plate Waste"	
Cooked vegetables	42%
Salads, raw vegetables	30%
Fresh fruit	22%
Canned/processed fruits	21%
Meat alternatives	21%
Meats	14%
Breads/grains	13%

Food donated for the NSLP is surplus — not purchased by consumers and not necessarily based on a child's nutritional needs. A 1993 government report found that school foods did not meet the government's *Dietary Guidelines for Americans*, being too high in fat and sodium and low in fiber and calcium. Legislation went into effect in the 1996-97 school year to modify school foods to fit the guidelines. By 2001, 82% of elementary schools participating in the NSLP offered meals that met dietary guidelines for fat, up from 34% in 1993.

Studies show that children who eat school meals are getting a more nutritious lunch than those who bring a sack from home, but it's still not nutritious enough. Some students don't eat their lunches, as we see in the table. It shows the discard rate for foods served through the NSLP.[10] The most popular school lunch item was pizza — in goes the fat, out go the fruits and vegetables. A report from the Physicians Committee for Responsible Medicine stated that public school lunches remain "a major risk to our children's health."

Sources: "National School Lunch Program: Participation and Lunches Served." National School Lunch Annual Summary: http://www.fns.usda.gov. *Statistical Abstract of the United States 2001*, Table 205. Kelly Patricia O'Meara. "What Is Being Fed to Schoolchildren?" *Insight on the News*, April 3, 2000. "Compared to Home-Brought Meals." *Food Service Director*, August 15, 2000. Biing-Hwan Lin et al., "Quality of children's diets at home and away from home: 1994-96," *Food Review*. (January-April 1999). Jean C. Buzby and Joanne F. Guthrie, "Plate Waste in School Nutrition Programs: Final Report to Congress.": http://www.ers.usda.gov. "School Lunch Program Fails to Make the Grade." Physicians Committee for Responsible Medicine (Fall 2001), based on a survey of 12 school districts: http://www.pcrm.org/news/health010. Russell Mokhiber. "Spoiled Lunch." *Multinational Monitor*. (July 2001). Online data retrieved July-August 2002.

---

[8] A member of the National Advisory Committee for Meat and Poultry Inspection. Donley's six-year-old son Alex died in 1993 after eating a hamburger contaminated with E. coli 0157-H7.

[9] For example, a 1997 outbreak of hepatitis in Michigan schoolchildren was traced to frozen strawberries from Mexico. The USDA vowed a crackdown on suppliers. NSLP products must be U.S.-grown.

[10] Data are based on a 1996 Government Accounting Office report described in *The Food Institute Report*; see Source notes.

Weighty Obsessions

Percentage of Adult Americans Who Were on a Diet: 1986-2000

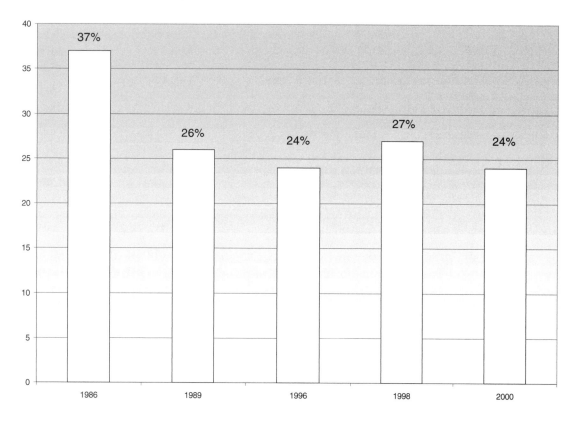

We know we're overweight (61% of adults in 1999) and some of us try — and keep on trying — to do something about it. The chart presents data from the Calorie Control Council's biannual survey of American eating and weight control habits.[11] It shows that 24% of adults (51 million people) were dieting in 2000. This figure includes people on any of the ubiquitous "lose weight fast — without trying — while sleeping" types of fad diets. The Calorie Control Council interprets the decline from 37% in 1987 as a positive sign, indicating that people "understand that traditional dieting (deprivation, short-term solutions) spell failure." Calorie Control Council's survey showed that women are more likely to blame themselves when they are unable to lose weight (41% cite "lack of self-discipline" versus 30% of men), while men are more likely to blame external sources such as their inability to find a proper meal at a restaurant.

Preoccupation with weight can be harmful to one's health and can lead to eating disorders like anorexia nervosa, bulimia nervosa, and obesity. According to the *Diagnostic and Statistical Manual of Mental Disorders*[12]:"Individuals with [anorexia nervosa] keep their

---

[11] Based on "a nationally projectable sample of 1,200 people aged 18 and older."

[12] American Psychiatric Association; Fourth Edition.

body weight below a minimal normal level by exercise, control of food intake, and other means.... Individuals with [bulimia nervosa] control their body weight in spite of binge overeating by purging (self-induced vomiting) or use of laxatives, diet pills or other means."

The table shows eating disorder statistics amassed by the National Institute of Mental Health (NIMH) and ANRED.[13] NIMH concludes that females are more likely than males to develop an eating disorder. The statistics are necessarily estimates;

Statistics About Eating Disorders from NIMH and ANRED	
% of females who suffer from anorexia nervosa in their lifetime	0.5 to 3.7
% of female adolescents who have anorexia	1
% of college-aged women who have bulimia	4
% of people with anorexia and bulimia who are male	10
% of females who suffer from bulimia nervosa in their lifetime	1.1 to 4.2
% of Americans who experience binge-eating disorder in a 6-month period	2 to 5
% of women who seek treatment to lose weight who have binge eating disorder	30
% of alcoholic women under 30 who also have eating disorders	72
% of people with serious untreated eating disorders who die	up to 20
% of people with serious treated eating disorders who die	2-3
% of people with treated eating disorders who recover	60
% of people with serious treated eating disorders who make only partial recov-	20

many of those affected will not admit they have a problem and do not seek treatment. Eating disorders often go hand in hand with other risky behaviors such as smoking, cutting (injuring oneself regularly and deeply enough to draw blood) and psychiatric problems such as clinical depression, anxiety, personality or substance abuse disorders, or obsessive-compulsive disorder (OCD); many sufferers are at risk for suicide.

Public awareness of eating disorders rose over the last few decades, apparently as a result of the women's movement. "Eating disorders" appears on college syllabuses as a feminist issue, but Arnold Andersen, M.D., co-author of *Making Weight,* asserts that it is a men's issue as well. His book examines eating disorders and compulsive exercise and claims that as many as 25% of people with eating disorders are men.

Eating disorders are called a modern disease, a product of our society's over-emphasis on thinness, but Rudolph Bell's book *Holy Anorexia* points out that people of medieval times were elevated to sainthood after starving themselves, sometimes to death.[14]

Another area of concern for health experts is the current movement in some circles to make women in particular feel comfortable in their (fat) skin. When all is said and done, there seems to be one best way to take off excess pounds: You have to expend more calories than you take in. And it doesn't hurt to get moving.

Sources: Chart: Calorie Control Council, retrieved July 11, 2002, from http://www.caloriecontrol.org/dietfigs.html. National Institute of Mental Health, *Eating Disorders: Facts About Eating Disorders and the Search for Solutions,* retrieved July 12, 2002, from http://www.nimh.nih.gov/publicat/eatingdisorder.cfm. University of Iowa Health Care, "Book co-written by UI physician can help men with conflicts about weight, appearance, food," retrieved July 12, 2002, from http://www.uihealthcare.com/.

---

[13] Anorexia Nervosa and Related Eating Disorders, Inc (http://www.anred.com/stats.html).

[14] Bell is a history professor at Rutgers, The State University of New Jersey.

Popular Illicit Substance Use Trends: Young People

Percentage of 12-17-Year-Olds Who Reported Being a Current User of Alcohol, Cigarettes, and/or Marijuana/Hashish: 1985-1999

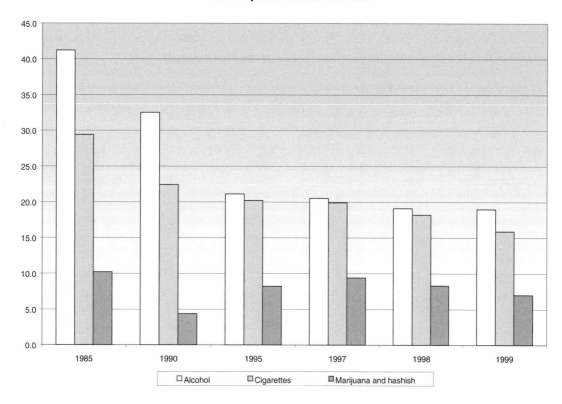

The war on drugs notwithstanding, young people like to experiment with illicit drugs, and some young people like drugs so much that they become regular users.[15] Certain drugs may wax and wane in popularity ("crack" cocaine, for example), but the three that never go out of style are alcohol, tobacco, and marijuana. The public health community and parents are concerned because unhealthy habits like these are difficult to change once acquired. There may be cause for celebration, though, because the data shown on the chart indicates that the number of 12- to-17-year-old current users[16] of alcohol and cigarettes has steadily declined since 1985. Decline in drug use among young people suggests future declines in all age groups.

The data are shown in tabular form below. Note the upsurge in marijuana use in the mid-1990s. The U.S. government attempts to explain it[17]: "the coming of age of a new gen-

---

[15] We use the definition of drug from *Merriam-Webster* online: "something and often an illegal substance that causes addiction, habituation, or a marked change in consciousness." Use of any of these substances is illegal for this age group.

[16] Current users are those who used a drug at least once within the month prior to the study.

[17] "Parental Influences…"; see Source notes.

---

eration of youths who have had little direct exposure to the negative consequences of drug use in an era of declining drug use ... a decrease in drug prevention efforts; and reduced governmental and media attention to the drug problem. Another relevant factor might be the influence of parents who, as members of the Baby Boom generation, belonged to cohorts heavily involved in marijuana use in their own youth." The same report refers to studies showing similar patterns of behavior between parents and children in regard to alcohol and cigarettes. Our society has an ambivalent attitude toward drugs, an attitude that has led lately to increased calls for decriminalization.

Percentage of 12-17-Year-Olds Who Ever Used and Currently Use the Three Most Popular Drugs

Drug	Ever used			Current user					
	1985	1990	1998	1985	1990	1995	1997	1998	1999
Marijuana/hashish	20.1	12.7	17.0	10.2	4.4	8.2	9.4	8.3	7.0
Alcohol	56.1	48.8	37.3	41.2	32.5	21.1	20.5	19.1	19.0
Cigarettes	50.7	45.1	35.8	29.4	22.4	20.2	19.9	18.2	15.9

A note about drug use data: The data shown above were collected in classrooms by researchers for the Monitoring the Future Survey (they have been collecting such data since 1975). Among the best known other organizations collecting substance use data are the National Household Survey on Drug Abuse (NHS), which has collected data in homes since 1971, and the Pride Survey,[18] which collects data in classrooms. Such data are often contradictory and are subject to underreporting for many reasons, including the likelihood of drug users being truant, homeless, or unwilling to be candid with interviewers.

In *Monitoring the Future*, the authors state: "In the last third of the twentieth century we saw an epidemic of illicit drug use among American young people that is unparalleled in this country's history." The "epidemic" was noticed in the late 1960s, when recreational drug use became popular among young, white, middle-class youths. President Nixon declared drug abuse "public enemy number one" in 1971. The war on drugs began with a government campaign to educate people about the dangers of drug use. At the time, heroin was a scourge in urban, black communities. We look at discrimination based on choice of drugs later in this chapter, but first we will look at trends in youth experimentation with the less common illegal substances.

Sources: NCES. *The Condition of Education 1999;* U-M. Survey Research Center. Institute of Social Research. Monitoring the Future Study: http://nces.ed.gov/; Bureau of Justice Statistics. "Drug and Crime Facts." Monitoring the Future National Results on Adolescent Drug Use: Overview of Key Findings 2001, 2002: http://www.ojp.usdoj.gov/ "Parental Influences on Adolescent Marijuana Use and the Baby Boom Generation: Findings from the 1979-1996 National Household Surveys on Drug Abuse.": http://www.samhsa.gov.

---

[18] Pride is designated by Federal law "as an official measure of the effectiveness of the White House drug policy." Their 2001-2002 survey of 101,882 students in grades 6-12 showed a significant decline over the previous year in alcohol, tobacco, and other drug use, a phenomenon attributed to family togetherness since September 11. Pride researchers claim that while their data tend to agree with the Monitoring the Future Survey, the NHS tends to show significantly lower drug use in the 12-to-17-year-old age group.

Uncommon Substance Use Trends: Young People

Percentage of High School Students Using Illicit Substances in the Last Year: 1976-1998

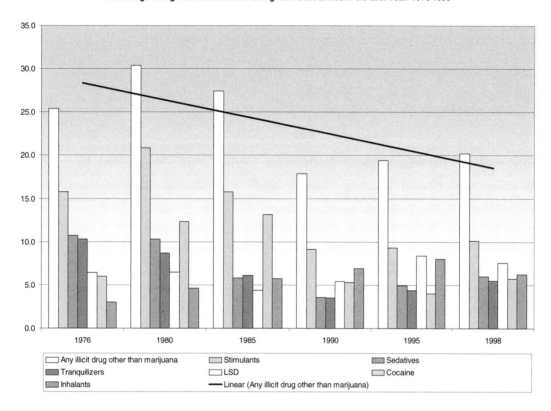

The chart uses data from the Monitoring the Future Study (see previous discussion). It shows trends in drug use among high school seniors (percentage using the named drugs at any time during the previous year). The data are shown in tabular form below. Notice that drug use was up slightly in 1998 over 1995. Recent studies show that all drug use among students declined in the aftermath of September 11.

Percentage of High School Seniors Who Used Drugs in the Last Year

Type of drug	1976	1980	1985	1990	1995	1998
Any illicit drug other than marijuana	25.4	30.4	27.4	17.9	19.4	20.2
Stimulants	15.8	20.8	15.8	9.1	9.3	10.1
LSD	6.4	6.5	4.4	5.4	8.4	7.6
Cocaine	6.0	12.3	13.1	5.3	4.0	5.7
Sedatives	10.7	10.3	5.8	3.6	4.9	6.0
Tranquilizers	10.3	8.7	6.1	3.5	4.4	5.5

Use of LSD and inhalants was up in the 1990s. The rise and fall of a drug's popularity often follows this course: A new drug comes on the scene (for example, LSD in the 1970s, "crack" cocaine in the 1980s, Ecstasy in the 1990s). News of the drug's "benefits" is disseminated by word of mouth and now by way of the Internet. More young people begin using the drug. Evidence accumulates about the risks and is broadcast. Researchers begin collecting statistics. Use of the drug declines. Sometimes a drug is revived, as happened with LSD in the 1990s. Researchers for Monitoring the Future call this type of revival "generational forgetting."

Use of inhalants ("sniffing" or "huffing") has been around for a long time (nitrous oxide, ether, chloroform, amyl nitrite, and gasoline have all had their day as popular inhalants). The intoxicating possibilities of common household products became widely recognized in the 1960s. Huffing is especially popular today among the very young (as early as 7 according to studies).[19] This disturbing behavior has introduced a new medical diagnosis: Sudden Sniffing Death Syndrome, more common in boys than girls.

Also making headlines in the 1990s were MDMA (Ecstasy) and Rohypnol (the "date rape" drug), called "club drugs" because they are popular at all-night parties called "raves." Monitoring the Future researchers report that in 2000, 8.2% of 12th graders and 9.1% of college students surveyed confessed to using Ecstasy in the last year.

It is unlikely that drug experimentation by young people will ever disappear completely, despite widespread anti-drug advertising. Meanwhile, teens who are tired of hearing the constant refrain: "Don't do this, don't do that," were dealt a blow in June 2002 when the U.S. Supreme Court ruled to allow random drug testing of public high school students who take part in any extracurricular activities. Critics questioned the benefits of such an invasion of the privacy of this particular group of students. Supporters point to polls showing that Americans consider drugs to be one of the greatest problems facing America's children today.

Next we will look at drug and alcohol use trends among adults.

Sources: Chart: National Center for Education Statistics, *The Condition of Education 1999* (Primary source: University of Michigan, Survey Research Center, Institute for Social Research, Monitoring the Future Study), retrieved July 19, 2002, from http://nces.ed.gov/pubs99/condition99/SupTables/supp-table-27-1.html. Siri Carpenter, "Teens' risky behavior is about more than race and family resources," *Monitor on Psychology*, retrieved July 17, 2002, from http://www.apa.org/monitor/jan01/teenbehavior.html. National Institute on Drug Abuse, *Monitoring the Future National Results on Adolescent Drug Use, Overview of Key Findings*, retrieved July 19, 2002, from http://monitoringthefuture.org/pubs/monographs/overview2001.pdf.

---

[19] A *Newsweek* interview with soldiers stationed in Afghanistan elicited the information that some have resorted to huffing air freshener because alcohol is forbidden. In a somewhat similar vein, a 1971 report on a heroin "epidemic" among soldiers in Vietnam made headlines.

Substance Use Trends: Adults

Percentage of Adults in Three Age Groups Who Are Current Users of Marijuana/Hashish and Cocaine: 1985-1999

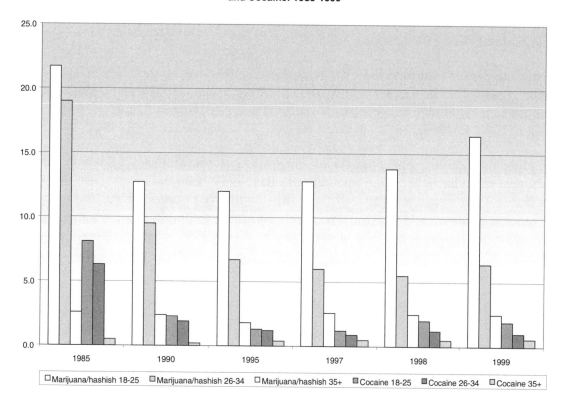

☐ Marijuana/hashish 18-25 ☐ Marijuana/hashish 26-34 ☐ Marijuana/hashish 35+ ■ Cocaine 18-25 ■ Cocaine 26-34 ☐ Cocaine 35+

This chart shows trends in the use of marijuana/hashish and cocaine — the most commonly used illicit drugs — among three adult age groups from 1985-1999, according to the National Household Survey on Drug Abuse (NHSDA).[20] The data are shown in tabular form below (the table below also shows alcohol and tobacco trends by age group).[21] Rates of use of all forms of drugs — legal and illicit — tended to be lower at the end of the time period among all age groups. Despite the overall decline, we observe a seesaw pattern. For example, marijuana use was on the rise in the late 1990s among the older children of the Baby Boom, who were perhaps enjoying those prosperous times. The tabular data show that as with teens, alcohol and cigarettes (legal for most adults) and marijuana are the most popular drugs, and the young use more drugs than do the old.

Alcohol use trend 1985-1999 (table): The youngest adult age group showed the greatest decline in alcohol use (a 14% decline compared to 12% and 7%).

---

[20] Survey of those who confessed to being current users, defined as those who used drugs at least once within the month prior to the survey. Based on a representative sample of the U.S. population aged 12 and over, including persons living in households and in some group quarters.

[21] Current users are those who used a drug at least once within the month prior to the study.

Cigarette and marijuana/hashish trends 1985-1999: The 26-34 age group showed the greatest decline in both cigarette smoking (25% compared to 13% and 20%) and use of marijuana and hashish (registering an impressive 122% drop compared to 24% for the youngest group and 4% for the oldest group). As was true with 12-17-year-olds, marijuana use rates rose in the 1990s among the 18-25 group. While the teens then showed a decline, this is not so for the 18-25 group. Marijuana has a reputation for being a relatively harmless illicit substance.

Cocaine use trend: Cocaine use by the youngest adult age group fell 76% and use by the middle group fell 84%. Cocaine use by the oldest age group actually rose 20%, but only a small percentage of that age group ever reported using cocaine (a low of 0.2% in 1990 to a high of 0.6% in 1999).[22]

The table includes the phenomenon of binge alcohol use among 18-25-year-olds. No doubt this behavior is ages-old, but statistics have only been collected since the 1980s. Media headlines would lead us to believe that binging is rampant on college campuses, and indeed, a rate of 31% of 18-25-year-olds admitting to binging in 1999 might justify alarm. Not shown here is NHSDA data indicating that in 1999, 15% of all people aged 12 and over admitted to being bingers (some 32 million people). Secondhand effects of binging include noise, vandalism, and public disturbances.

Percentage of Persons 18-25, 26-34, and 35+ Who Are Current Users

Age/Drug	1985	1990	1995	1997	1998	1999
18 to 25 Years Old						
Marijuana/ hashish	21.7	12.7	12.0	12.8	13.8	16.4
Cocaine	8.1	2.3	1.3	1.2	2.0	1.9
Alcohol	70.1	62.8	61.3	58.4	60.0	60.2
Binge alcohol use	34.4	(NA)	29.9	28.0	31.7	31.1
Cigarettes	47.4	40.9	35.3	40.6	41.6	41.0
26 to 34 Years Old						
Marijuana/ hashish	19.0	9.5	6.7	6.0	5.5	6.4
Cocaine	6.3	1.9	1.2	0.9	1.2	1.0
Alcohol	70.6	64.4	63.0	60.2	60.9	61.9
Cigarettes	45.7	42.4	34.7	33.7	32.5	34.4
35 Years and Over						
Marijuana/ hashish	2.6	2.4	1.8	2.6	2.5	2.5
Cocaine	0.5	0.2	0.4	0.5	0.5	0.6
Alcohol	57.5	49.5	52.6	52.8	51.7	53.4
Cigarettes	35.5	28.9	27.2	27.9	25.1	28.5

According to *BoozeNews*: "For current alcohol use, binge drinking [5 or more drinks] and heavy alcohol use, 21 [the legal drinking age in every state] is the age of peak prevalence" before these behaviors decline. The prevalence of cigarette and marijuana smoking and use of cocaine also tends to decline with age.

---

[22] A *Washington Post* story cited in the introduction to this chapter alleges "discrepancies in the habitual cocaine-use figures ... but the discordant numbers keep appearing."

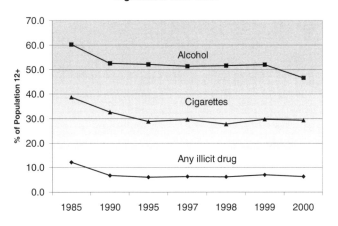

Current Users Aged 12+, Illicit Drugs, Alcohol, and Cigarettes: 1985-2000

This graphic shows the downward trend in the rates of use of all illicit drugs[23] and alcohol and cigarettes among people 12 years old and over between 1985 and 1990. Rates of use of these substances held fairly steady through the 1990s.

Earlier panels showed substance use trends in younger age groups and this panel covers adults. What about older adults? A government report on substance use among older adults showed that in 2000, some 568,000 people aged 55+ (1%) had used illicit drugs in the month before the survey, and more than 5 million (9%) were "binge" alcohol users, including more than 1 million (<2%) who were heavy users of alcohol. It is predicted that the aging of the baby boom generation will increase the number of older users of illicit drugs.

Interesting survey results about illicit drug use on the job are worth noting. Drug Strategies, a private research group that promotes "more effective approaches to the nation's drug problems," reports that 75% of U.S. drug users are white and working. (Since 80% of the population is white, whites represent less than their share of drug users.) The Substance Abuse and Mental Health Services Administration (SAMHSA) states that the highest rates of illicit drug use on the job are reported by construction and food service workers (17.3% and 16.3%, respectively), the lowest rates by police officers, teachers, and child care workers (1%, 2.3%, and 2.6% respectively). In a poll taken by Minnesota-based Hazelden Foundation, 60% of respondents reported knowing someone who had gone to work under the influence of alcohol or drugs.

Is there a drug crisis? When the media talk about one, they are usually referring to increases in emergency room visits for drug-related problems. We look at those next.

Sources: Chart and Table: *Statistical Abstract of the United States: 2001*, Table 189; primary sources, U.S. Substance Abuse and Mental Health Services Administration, National Household Survey on Drug Abuse. Harvard School of Public Health, "Secondhand Effects of Student Alcohol Use Reported by Neighbors of Colleges: The Role of Alcohol Outlets," retrieved July 23, 2002, from http://www.hsph.harvard.edu/cas/Documents/secondhand/. "Key Findings on Adolescent Alcohol Use From the National Household Survey on Drug Abuse and the Parents' Resource Institute for Drug Education Survey," *BoozeNews,* retrieved July 23, 2002, from http://www.cspinet.org/booze/adolescent_statistics2.htm. "Illicit drug use down; varies by job," *Public Health Reports,* V111 (Sept/Oct 1996), pp. 385-6. "Substance Use Among Older Adults," The NHSDA Report, November 23, 2001, retrieved July 24, 2002, from http://www.samhsa.gov/oas/facts/olderadults.htm.

---

[23] Any illicit drug includes the following: Marijuana/hashish, cocaine and crack cocaine, inhalants, hallucinogens including PCP and LSD, heroin, stimulants, sedatives, tranquilizers, and analgesics.

Illicit Drugs Can Land You in the Hospital

Emergency Room Drug Episodes, 12-17-Year Olds and Ages 18+: 1994-2000

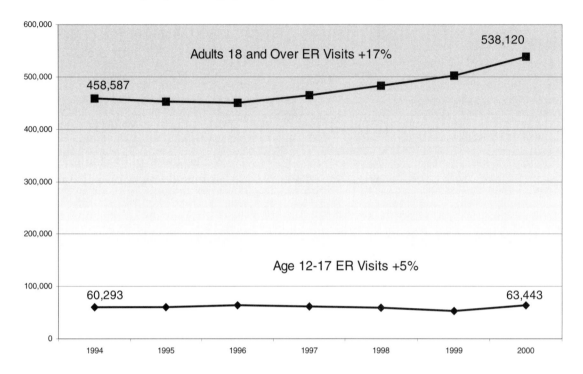

DAWN is the benign acronym for the government's Drug Abuse Warning Network. It has been collecting data on drug abuse-related visits to emergency rooms since 1972. The graphic shows that between 1994 and 2000, emergency room visits related to drugs increased 5% for teens (their total population rose 13%). Emergency room visits by adults increased 17% (their population increased 39%). The trend in drug use may be down overall, but drugs still send people to the emergency room. The 1990s were boom times. Research suggests that when there is disposable income, drugs will be readily available.

The DAWN report summarizes the 1999-early 2001 period, noting that in 2000, the four illicit drugs of abuse that most often took users to the emergency room were cocaine, heroin/morphine, marijuana/hashish, and methamphetamine/speed. Alcohol in combination with illicit drugs is frequently mentioned as a contributing factor to the visit. Not surprisingly, the illicit drug most often mentioned by teens in connection with their emergency room visits is marijuana. When asked why they took the substance, the majority of patients answered either "dependence" or "suicide." When it came to marijuana-related visits, however, "psychic effects" was the most common motive for taking the drug.

DAWN reports that in just the one-year period from 1999 to 2000, drug-related emergency room visits for 12-17-year-olds increased 20% to 272 per 100,000 population, lagging behind the 18-25 age group (426 episodes per 100,000) and the 26-34 age group (411 episodes per 100,000). Substances of abuse that had substantial increases in that time period were MDMA (Ecstasy, up 58%) and PCP (up 48%). Drugs like Ecstasy have an undeserved reputation among young people for being safe and non-addictive, and they are relatively affordable. An estimated 12% of 12-18-year-olds have experimented with Ecstasy.

Overall, in the 1999-2000 period, there were significant increases in mentions of heroin (15%), amphetamines (37%), and methamphetamine (29%) in connection with the visits.

Alcohol and cigarettes lead to undramatic deaths after prolonged use — but annual deaths are in the hundreds of thousands. A rash of emergency room visits for drug overdoses will bring headlines about a "drug crisis," even though the actual number of cases might not be very high. For example, the 58% rise in Ecstasy-related visits mentioned above refers to a rise from 2,850 visits in 1999 to 4,511 visits in 2000 (out of the total of 554,767 and 601,563 visits in those years, respectively). If we look back to 1994, we find that Ecstasy, the "club drug" of the 90s, was mentioned in only 253 visits (an increase in visits of 1683% by 2000).

Some of the risk involved with drugs lies in the possibility of ingesting more than one bargained for and ending up in the hospital or dead. It also lies in the possibility of being arrested, as we see next when we look at misconceptions about drug use among African Americans.

Sources: Graphic: Emergency Department Trends from the Drug Abuse Warning Network, Preliminary Estimates January-June 2001 with Revised Estimates 1994-2000; Primary source: Office of Applied Studies, SAMHSA, Drug Abuse Warning Network, 2001 update; retrieved July 24, 2002, from http://www.samhsa.gov/oas/dawn/TrndED/2001/Text/TrndEDtxt.PDF. Mortality Data from DAWN, retrieved July 24, 2002, from http://www.samhsa.gov/oas/DAWN/mortality2k.pdf.

Illicit Substance Use Trends and Misconceptions: Race

Percentage of Black and White Persons Aged 12-17 Years Who Used Marijuana and Cocaine in the Past Month: 1985-1996

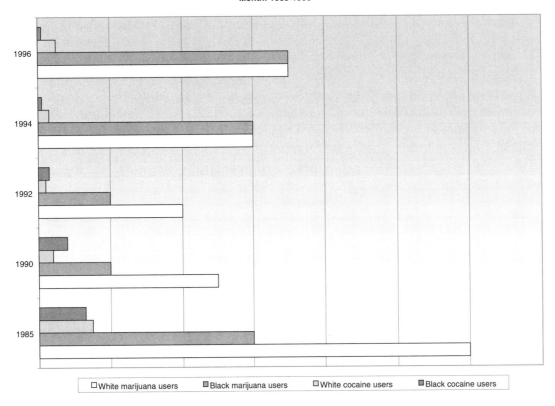

☐ White marijuana users   ◪ Black marijuana users   ☐ White cocaine users   ◪ Black cocaine users

The chart shows prevalence rates for recent use of cocaine and marijuana by whites and blacks aged 12-17 (1985-1998). The table shows data for the same age group and for adults aged 18-25. Since 1985, blacks in both age groups have reported equal or lower rates of marijuana use than whites. Except among black teens in the early 1990s, cocaine prevalence has also been lower among blacks.

Researchers for Monitoring the Future (discussed earlier) point out: "Contrary to popular assumption ... African American youngsters have substantially lower rates of use of most licit and illicit drugs than do whites. These include any illicit drug use, most of the specific illicit drugs, alcohol, and cigarettes." However, in 1998, recent illicit drug use was more common among black adults (8%)

Percentage of Persons Reporting Use of Marijuana or Cocaine in the Last Month

	1985	1990	1992	1994	1996	1998
Marijuana						
Age 12-17						
White	12	5.0	4.0	6.0	7.0	10.0
Black	6	2.0	2.0	6.0	7.0	9.0
Age 18-25						
White	NA	NA	NA	13.0	14.0	15.0
Black	NA	NA	NA	12.0	14.0	15.0
Cocaine						
Age 12-17						
White	1.5	0.4	0.2	0.3	0.5	0.9
Black	1.3	0.8	0.3	0.1	0.1	NA
Age 18-25						
White	NA	NA	NA	1.2	2.3	2.2
Black	NA	NA	NA	0.7	1.1	0.6

than among white adults (5.7%).

The perception of heavy drug use by blacks comes from the reality of higher arrest rates in inner cities for using and selling drugs. Selling drugs tends to be an inner-city business, although customers are more often white. The sale and use of crack cocaine, the cheap, smokable form of powder cocaine, exploded in inner cities in the 1980s before declining in the mid-1990s. Crack is highly addictive and often leads to violent behavior. Selling and/or using such a drug is the type of behavior that tends to attract the attention of police. According to federal law, it takes 100 times more powder cocaine than crack to trigger the same mandatory minimum prison sentences.[24]

According to Orange County Superior Court Judge James P. Gray[25]: "The typical drug case is a small amount of drugs that is being sold by somebody to support his or her habit … mostly it's just the low-level users and the low-level drug sellers. And we fill our prisons with them."

The Justice Policy Institute (JPI; a research/public policy organization) notes that at the end of the 1990s America had more people behind bars than ever before in its history, though the economy was good and crime rates were down. The black community is disproportionately affected. "In 1997, even though African Americans made up only 13% of the population, half of the 1.2 million state and federal prisoners were African American (548,900).… Even though surveys continue to show similar drug usage rates for young blacks and whites, drug commitment rates for black males ages 15-29 increased six-fold [from 1980 to 1997] while the comparable rates for young whites doubled" (JPI). Racism? The problem, says JPI's Vincent Schiraldi, is "that we've focused on imprisonment as the near-exclusive solution to substance abuse, while giving short shrift to treatment and prevention."

Commenting on a similar 1996 report, conservative author Michael Fumento stated: "There's no doubt there's something pathologically wrong in a society in which a third of the members of the second-largest race are involved in the criminal justice system. Throwing young men in prison or putting them on probation or parole doesn't solve this problem."

Sources: *Health, United States 2001*, Table 63; SAMHSA, NHS: http://www.cdc.gov/. Justice Policy Institute, "The Punishing Decade: Prison and Jail Estimates at the Millennium," and "Poor Prescription: The Costs of Imprisoning Drug Offenders in the United States." http://www.cjcj.org. "Closing the Health Gap." HHS Fact Sheet. http://www.healthgap.omhrc.gov. "New report blasts media coverage of Contra-crack story." FAIR (Fairness & Accuracy In Reporting) news release, 18 December 1996: http://www.hartford-hwp.com. Michael W. Lynch. "Battlefield Conversions." *Reason*. (January 2002). Michael Fumento, "Crime Study Doesn't Show Racism." http://www.fumento.com/.

---

24 Legislation mandating this punishment was passed after the 1986 cocaine (mistakenly believed to be crack) overdose death of University of Maryland basketball star Len Bias, which allegedly gave ammunition to congressional drug warriors. Legislation introduced in December 2001 (the Drug Sentencing Reform Act) seeks to reduce the penalties for both powder cocaine and crack cocaine offenses.

25 Quoted in *Reason*; see Source notes.

Abuse of Over-the-Counter and Prescription Medications

Percent of Population Aged 12 and Over Who Are Current Nonmedical Users of Prescription Drugs: 1985-1999

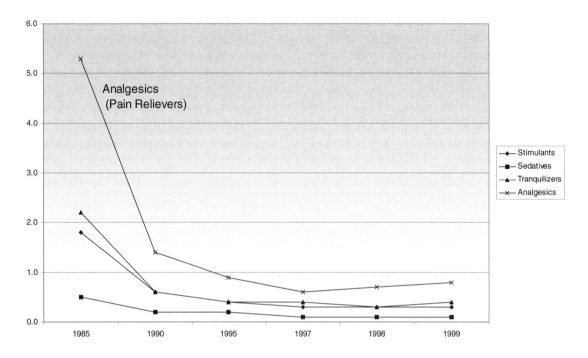

The National Institute on Drug Abuse (NIDA) reports that the number of people who abuse prescription drugs far surpasses the 2.1 million people who use heroin, cocaine, and/or crack cocaine. NIDA says an estimated 9 million people aged 12 and older used prescription drugs for nonmedical reasons in 1999, which constitutes abuse and signals a public health crisis in the making. NIDA bases its conclusions on recent data from the National Household Survey on Drug Abuse (NHSDA). The survey was completely re-designed in 1999, so comparisons to earlier data (like that on the chart above and the table below) cannot be made.

Percent of Population Aged 12 and Over Who Are Current Users: 1985-1999

Drug	Ever Used				Current User					
	1985	1990	1995	1998[26]	1985	1990	1995	1997	1998	1999
Stimulants	7.3	5.5	4.9	4.4	1.8	0.6	0.4	0.3	0.3	0.3
Sedatives	4.8	2.8	2.7	2.1	0.5	0.2	0.2	0.1	0.1	0.1
Tranquilizers	7.6	4.0	3.9	3.5	2.2	0.6	0.4	0.4	0.3	0.4
Analgesics	7.6	6.3	6.1	5.3	5.3	1.4	0.9	0.6	0.7	0.8

The chart shows the percentage of the population aged 12 and over who reported being current nonmedical users of prescription drugs in the period 1985-1999 (earlier data are

---

[26] Comparable data for 1999 are not available.

not available).[27] The table adds data on persons who ever used the named substance. Data are for stimulants (e.g., Ritalin; Adderall), sedatives (e.g., Seconal), tranquilizers (e.g., Valium), and analgesics (e.g., Oxycontin, Percodan). It appears from the chart and the table that nonmedical current use and lifetime use of all the named types of substances declined between 1985 and 1999. The high percentages of users in 1985 and the abrupt drop between then and 1990 simply may be due to what the *Washington Post* described in 1998 as "different methods of calculating the number of drug users [which] continue to produce widely gyrating estimates."

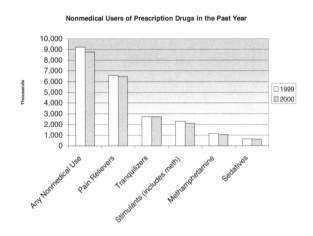

The small chart shows data for 1999-2000 obtained using the new NHSDA survey methods. Media Awareness Project has this to say about the new method: "Teasing out precise trends is difficult." The chart shows 9.2 million past-year users in 1999, falling to 8.7 million in 2000. In 2000, an estimated 3.8 million people — almost 2 percent of the population aged 12 and older — were currently (use in past month) using certain prescription drugs nonmedically: pain relievers (2.8 million users), sedatives and tranquilizers (1.1 million users), and stimulants (0.8 million users).

The three most commonly abused prescription drugs are pain relievers (6.6 million past-year users in 1999, 6.5 million in 2000), tranquilizers (2.7 million past-year users in 1999 and 2000), and stimulants (including methamphetamine). The three groups most at risk for prescription drug abuse are older adults, adolescents, and women. Older adults are most likely to abuse tranquilizers and sleeping pills; usually the drug has been prescribed but in a too-high dosage, and frequently it is abused accidentally because the patient does not follow instructions. Adolescents favor painkillers like Oxycontin7 and stimulants like methamphetamine (see below). Studies suggest that women are more likely than men to be prescribed easily abused prescription drugs such as narcotics and anti-anxiety drugs.

Of the approximately 2 million past-year users of stimulants in 1999 and 2000, half used methamphetamine, commonly known as speed, meth, or chalk. In its smoked form, it is often referred to as ice, crystal, crank, or glass. The substance is easily and illegally manufactured using inexpensive, over-the-counter ingredients found in nasal decongestants and bronchial inhalers. The government reports that methamphetamine abuse reached alarming proportions in the 1990s based on deaths and emergency-room episodes related to its abuse. Also of concern is a recent trend among adolescents to illegally purchase the stimulant Ritalin from individuals who have been prescribed the medication.

---

[27] Total population aged 12 and over in 1990 was 199,956,202.

Of particular concern to the Drug Enforcement Agency (DEA) is abuse of Oxycontin7, a sustained-release formulation of oxycodone, an opium-based drug of abuse since the early 1960s. According to DEA, the number of emergency room visits involving oxycodone was stable from 1990-1996 but more than tripled from 1996-2000 (from 3,190 visits to 10,825). When drug enforcement authorities and the media get hold of evidence showing that a legitimate and effective legal prescription drug like Oxycontin7 is being widely abused, doctors grow leery about prescribing it, even for people who have a compelling need for it. Carolyn Kleiner[28] summarizes the medical establishment's dilemma this way: "Pain care in this country is already characterized by widespread undertreatment and stigma, and the worry is that doctors, pharmacies, and insurance companies will overreact — to avoid addicting patients or to avoid prosecution, or both."

Reinforcing its fears that prescription drug abuse is on the rise is this NIDA conclusion: "In 1998, an estimated 1.6 million Americans used prescription pain relievers nonmedically for the first time. This represents a significant increase since the 1980s, when there were generally fewer than 500,000 first-time users per year. From 1990 to 1998, the number of new users of pain relievers increased by 181 percent; the number of individuals who initiated tranquilizer use increased by 132 percent; the number of new sedative users increased by 90 percent; and the number of people initiating stimulant use increased by 165 percent."

Over-the-counter drugs of abuse include aspirin, cough syrup (may contain alcohol and dextromethorphan, an opium-like agent used as a cough suppressant), diet pills, athletic performance-enhancing substances like creatine and androstenedione, and any other legally-obtained nonprescription medication. The University of Michigan Institute for Social Research estimates that up to 4% of boys and 2% of girls use performance-enhancing legal and illegal drugs.

Sources: Graphic/table: *Statistical Abstract of the United States: 2001*, Table 189. Primary source: U.S. Substance Abuse and Mental Health Services Administration, National Household Survey on Drug Abuse, annual. "Drugs and Chemicals of Concern," http://www.deadiversion.usdoj.gov/. Small chart: SAMHSA, Office of Applied Studies, National Household Survey on Drug Abuse, 1999 and 2000, http://www.samhsa.gov/oas/NHSDA/2kNHSDA/appendixf1.htm. NIDA Research Report, "Prescription Drugs: Abuse and Addiction, http://www.nida.nih.gov/ResearchReports/Prescription/Prescription.html. Analyses of Substance Abuse and Treatment Issues, http://www.samhsa.gov/oas/NHSDA/Treatan/httoc.htm. "Muscles now, problems later: Performance-enhancing drugs may put teens at future health risk," http://www.med.umich.edu/opm/newspage/1999/perfen.htm. Carolyn Kleiner, "A Curse and a Cure," *U.S. News & World Report*, July 27, 2001. Media Awareness Project, "US: Mixed Message On Prescription Drug Abuse," http://www.mapinc.org/drugnews/v01/n776/a06.html. Jeff Leen, "Number Jumble Clouds Judgment of Drug War," *Washington Post*, January 2, 1998, http://washingtonpost.com. All information retrieved August 14, 2002.

---

[28] In *U.S. News & World Report*; see Source notes.

Drinking, Smoking, Driving: Riskier Than Drugs

Comparative Causes of Annual Deaths in the United States

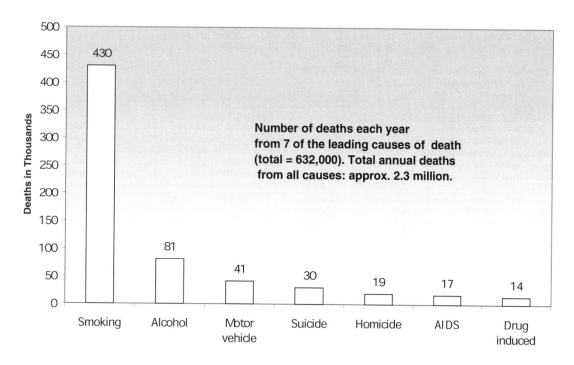

If death is the ultimate measure of the riskiness of a behavior, then smoking,[29] drinking, and operating a motor vehicle — legal activities all — have taken a far deadlier toll than drugs. (This is not to say, as some do, that drug/substance abuse is just another lifestyle choice; abusers are a risk to others as well as self.) The chart shows that the first three activities account for 87% of deaths from seven leading causes of death, while drug-induced deaths rank seventh.[30] For young people, the risk behaviors most likely to result in death are related to driving behavior (with/without alcohol involved): failure to fasten seatbelts, riding with a person who has been drinking, and the like). The Centers for Disease Control (CDC) points out that about three-quarters of all deaths among persons aged 10-24 years result from four causes: motor-vehicle accidents, "other unintentional injuries" (e.g., falls, drowning, fires), homicide, and suicide.

Source: "Comparative Causes of Annual Deaths in the United States," retrieved July 26, 2002, from http://www.cdc.gov/tobacco/research_data/health_consequences/andths.htm.

---

[29] Smoking deaths from lung cancer, cardiovascular and respiratory diseases, and burns.

[30] The category "drug-induced deaths" includes deaths from legal and illegal use of drugs and also poisoning from medically prescribed and other drugs. Drug-induced deaths excludes accidents, homicides, and other causes indirectly related to drug use. Also excluded are newborn deaths due to mother's drug use.

Teens' Experience of Marijuana

Percentage of Teens Who Reported These Drug Opinions

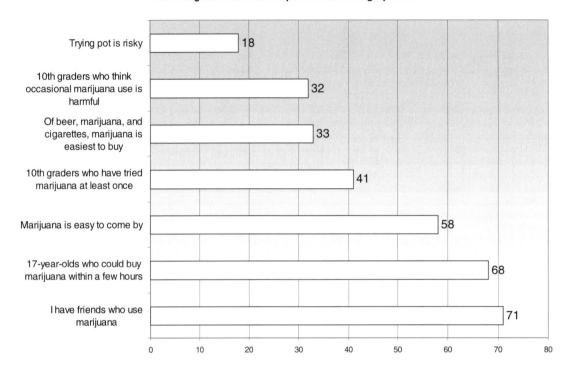

At the beginning of this discussion of drug use, we saw data from the Monitoring the Future Survey (MTF) indicating that the use of marijuana by 12-17-year-olds was up in the 1990s after declining between 1985 and 1990. MTF tells us that by the time they graduate from high school, more than half of the young people in America have tried an illicit drug, usually marijuana. This is about the same percentage as in 1975, when the "drug crisis" was in its infancy.

The graphic above presents statistics (1) from a Partnership for A Drug-Free America[31] survey of 10,000 parents and children and (2) from MTF (2000). If they are right, 41% of 10th graders have tried marijuana at least once, and 58% of teenagers find it easy to procure marijuana (easier to get than beer and equally as easy to come by as cigarettes, kids say, despite a trend toward adoption of punitive measures for the sale of tobacco to minors). In fact, MTF reports: "Every year from 1975 to 1999, at least 82% of high school seniors surveyed have said they find marijuana 'fairly easy' or 'very easy' to obtain... marijuana has been almost universally available to American high school seniors (from 83% to 90%) over at least the past 25 years."

---

[31] A nonprofit coalition of media professionals that produces most of the White House's anti-drug ads.

We've passed the 30-year mark in the multibillion-dollar war on drugs. Marijuana remains a Schedule I controlled substance.[32] The Supreme Court recently approved random, suspicionless drug testing of students wishing to participate in extracurricular activities. We send drug-sniffing dogs into schools. Minor marijuana offenses can mean time spent in prison.[33] The government has spent nearly $2 billion on anti-drug advertising, warning that today's marijuana is more potent (thus dangerous) than it was when boomers were using it. Boomer parents order hair and urine drug test kits to surprise their kids, because, as DrugFreeTeenagers.com assures them, "FACT: Drug Users Lie!" But kids still don't get it? In fact, in a display of post-modern irony, teens have turned the 1936 propaganda film "Reefer Madness" into a cult favorite. What's going on here?

Today's pot experimenters are yesterday's D.A.R.E. graduates. D.A.R.E. (Drug Abuse Resistance Education) reaches an estimated 60-75% of elementary school children in the United States and is employed in more than 50 other countries. Hundreds of millions of dollars are spent each year on D.A.R.E. But is it effective? As far back as 1993 the General Accounting Office found that there was little evidence that "resistance training" programs like D.A.R.E. have reduced the use of drugs by adolescents, and studies still question its effectiveness. What does D.A.R.E. do? "A Different Look at D.A.R.E." quotes a Portland, Maine, D.A.R.E. police officer: "I tell kids they can smoke dope if they want to, as long as they consider the consequences." Conservative Phyllis Schlafly complains that D.A.R.E. does not tell children that drug use is morally wrong. "Their bottom line is, 'Kids, make up your own mind.'" Critics say D.A.R.E. employs lurid scare tactics, demonizing all substance users rather than encouraging moderation and responsibility, and sometimes stimulates the very behavior it seeks to discourage. Some say D.A.R.E. owes its continued existence to politicians' unwillingness to appear "soft on drugs."

What do kids hear about the consequences of early marijuana use? Voluminous literature and pervasive advertising warn that marijuana is addictive, harmful, risky, is a "gateway" to the use of other illegal drugs, and impedes one's ability to develop into a well-adjusted adult. Less voluminous and disseminated is the literature downplaying the risks.[34] At

---

[32] Schedule I is the most restrictive schedule under the Controlled Substances Act. According to the U.S. Drug Enforcement Agency (DEA), such a substance has a high potential for abuse, no officially accepted medicinal uses, and no safe level of use under medical supervision. On May 24, 2002, the U.S. Court of Appeals for the District of Columbia Circuit issued a ruling upholding DEA's determination that marijuana must remain a Schedule I controlled substance. DEA also seeks to declare hemp, an ingredient used in certain brands of pretzels, beer, bread and granola, a controlled substance.

[33] Thomas (see Source notes) presents an estimate of the number of "marijuana only" (no other drug involved) prisoners in state and federal prisons in 1998: 27,600.

[34] A 1997 report by researchers at Demos, a British public policy think tank, used data from a survey of more than 850 young people to compare the attitudes of 16- to 24-year-olds who consume drugs with the attitudes of young people in general. The surveys found that users "trusted and respected their families in much the same way as other teenagers; tended to be more independent and less introverted than those who did not use drugs; made their own decisions about drug use and disapproved of 'out of control' behaviour by problem users; led active lives, viewing drug-taking as an integrated part of certain social events; were no more fatalistic than other young people or lacking in self-esteem." (Source: "'Czar' warned to beware of

some point between D.A.R.E. and high school, though, large numbers of young people experiment with drugs (or observe the behavior by others) and find that the dire warnings they have heard were blown out of proportion. There comes the realization "that smoking one joint will not ruin their lives, so telling them that it will can only make them more cynical than they already are" (Sager).

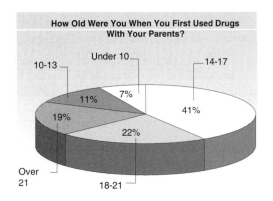

How Old Were You When You First Used Drugs With Your Parents?

Under 10 — 7%
14-17 — 41%
18-21 — 22%
Over 21 — 19%
10-13 — 11%

The Baby Boomer parental dilemma: As charter members of the drug generation, how to talk to their children about drugs? The chart demonstrates what the parents of 20% of 582 young drug rehabilitation clients in four states did — they bonded with their kids through drugs. Other surveys show that as many as half of high school students have not discussed drugs with their parents.

Cannabis sativa (marijuana), says The Honest Cannabis Information Foundation, "is one of the most widely used substances around the world." A 1995 report from the World Health Organization (WHO) tells us: "The US has higher rates of illicit drug use by young people than European nations, as noted by the Monitoring The Future survey... All the participating European countries had a considerably lower rate of lifetime use, averaging 17% [compared to 41% of U.S. tenth graders].... The US also had one of the lowest proportions of students seeing marijuana use as carrying a risk of harm to the user, and one of the lowest proportions saying that they personally disapprove of marijuana use." If they try it, are they hooked? WHO says the risks of cannabis use "are unlikely to produce public health problems comparable in scale to those currently produced by alcohol and tobacco," and "it is unlikely that the proportion of cannabis users who become very heavy users would ever be as high in industrial societies as it often [is] for stimulants such as tobacco or cocaine, since heavy use of a stimulant fits more easily into the rhythms of daily life in such societies." Is there a teen drug crisis? In opting for incarceration over treatment, do we have our priorities straight?

Sources: Chart: Partnership for A Drug-Free America , "The Boomer-Rang: Baby Boomers Seriously Underestimating Presence of Drugs in Their Children's Lives ; retrieved August 1, 2002, from http://www.mediacampaign.org/newsletter/fall98/update13.html; and Johnston, Lloyd D. Johnston., PhD, et al., *Monitoring The Future: National Survey Results on Drug Use, 1975-2000, Volume 1: Secondary School Students* (Bethesda, MD: National Institute on Drug Abuse, August 2001). QEV Analytics, *National Survey of American Attitudes on Substance Abuse VI: Teens* (New York, NY: National Center on Addiction and Substance Abuse at Columbia University, February 2001). Chuck Thomas, "Marijuana Arrests and Incarceration in the United States," retrieved August 1, 2002, from http://www.mpp.org/arrests/fas61699.html. U.S. GAO, *Confronting the Drug Problem*, retrieved August 1, 2002, from http://www.gao.gov/. "A Different Look at D.A.R.E.," retrieved August 1, 2002, from http://www.drcnet.org/DARE/index.html. Ryan H. Sager, "The Drug War: Teach Them Well," *National Review*, May 1, 2000, p30+. Terry O'Neill, "Redesigning DARE," *Report Newsmagazine* (Edmonton, Canada), March 19, 2001. Wayne Hall et al., "WHO Project on Health Implications of Cannabis Use: A Comparative Appraisal of the Health and Psychological Consequences of Alcohol, Cannabis, Nicotine and Opiate Use," August 28, 1995, retrieved July 31, 2002, from http://www.druglibrary.org/schaffer/hemp/general/who-index.htm. The Honest Cannabis Information Foundation, retrieved July 31, 2002, from http://www.thc.nl. Donna Leinwand, "Teen Addicts Point to Parents," *USA Today*, August 24, 2000, p. 1 (primary source: Penn, Schoen & Berland Associates' survey in April 2000 of 582 drug rehabilitation clients.

myths about young people who use drugs, Joseph Rountree Foundation, retrieved August 2, 2002, from http://www.jrf.org.uk/pressroom/releases/051197.asp).

Smoking Trends: Adults

Percentage of the Population Who Smoked

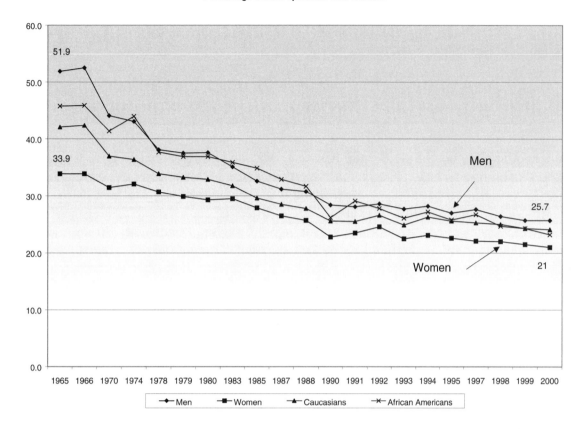

Of all the risky behaviors one can indulge in, smoking must be the riskiest. It is the source of more disease and death than any other cause. One out of five deaths each year is linked to smoking — 442,000 deaths a year (264,000 men, 178,000 women). The average male smoker sacrifices more than 13 years of life; the average female smoker gives up 14.5 years. According to the Centers for Disease Control (CDC): "If current smoking patterns continue, an estimated 25 million persons in the United States who are alive today will die prematurely from smoking-related illnesses, including an estimated 5 million persons now under age 18 years."

In light of this ominous information, a hint of which must have permeated the consciousness of every American, who among us cannot summon the grit to quit? The chart shows that in 2000, 25.7% of men, 21% of women, 24.1% of the white population, and 23.2% of the black population were smokers. That's about 46.5 million adult Americans who may be addicted to tobacco. Half of them will die of it if they continue.

Concerning addiction, back in 1997, *Harvard Mental Health Letter* bluntly stated: "By now everyone knows that nicotine is addictive, and only tobacco salesmen deny it.... Spokesmen for the tobacco industry, using their own special definitions, prefer to say that their product is merely 'habituating.' If they are correct, and nicotine is not addictive, then nothing is."

Before research in the 1950s showed that cigarette smoking caused heart disease and lung cancer, it was seen as glamorous, though not without risk. Surgeon General Luther Terry's 1964 *Report on Smoking and Health* "hit the country like a bombshell," Terry stated. "It was front page news and the lead story on every radio and television station in the United States." The report seems to have sparked a brief rise in smoking behavior (see graphic), followed by a decline among all groups by 2000 (50% for men, 38% for women, 43% for whites, 49% for blacks).

Not shown on the graphic are 1955-1965 statistics (available for men/women only). In 1955, 56.9% of men and 28.4% of women smoked. By 1965 more men had given up smoking (men down 9%), but more women took it up (women up 19%).

Did something happen in the decade between 1955 and 1965 to cause more women to take up smoking? Actually, the increase in women smokers had already started. In the early 20th century, tobacco companies began a successful campaign to hook women on smoking; later women started working in smoke-filled offices. The 1920s slogan "Reach for a Lucky instead of a sweet" linked smoking with staying thin. Lucky Strike sales allegedly went up 300% in the first year of the campaign. "The number of women aged 18-21 years who smoked tripled between 1911 and 1925 and more than tripled again by 1939" (Powers). In 1968 Philip Morris got on the women's movement bandwagon when it introduced Virginia Slims cigarettes with the slogan: "You've Come a Long Way" ("Baby" was added later). Indeed, we had come a long way since a Civil War-era etiquette book admonished: "Ladies should NEVER smoke in public; it is shocking and unheard of!" Congress banned TV and radio ads for cigarettes in 1971. In 1982 Surgeon General C. Everett Koop announced that smoking was the major cause of cancer death.

Here's the good news and the bad news about smoking from *Harvard Health Letter*: "The good news is that heart disease risk is cut in half within a year of quitting and lung cancer risk is halved within 10 years. The not-so-good news is that former smokers are still much more likely than nonsmokers to develop these diseases for at least 15 years after they've stopped smoking."

The CDC breaks down smoker demographics in many ways. This is what the agency tells us about the groups who have a "disproportionately high" smoking prevalence: "In 1998, more than one of three American Indians/Alaska Natives, people with low income, and people with less than a high school education smoked cigarettes." CDC reports that 7 in 10 smokers want to quit; the higher one's education level, the more likely one is to succeed. The CDC also knows a great deal about teen smokers. We look at that issue next.

Sources: Chart: "Smoking Prevalence Among U.S. Adults," CDC, retrieved August 6, 2002, from http://www.cdc.gov/tobac co/research_data adults_prev/prevali.htm. Pamela Powers, MPH, *Women & Smoking: Historical & National Trends & Issues*, retrieved August 6, 2002, from http://128.196.174.132/bigfiles/maternalhealth.pdf. Howard Bell, "Surgeons General: Defenders of Public Health," *New Physician*, Jan./Feb. 2002, p10+. CDC, *Healthy People 2000 Final Review*, retrieved August 6, 2002, from http://www.cdc.gov/nchs/. "Will You Pay for Your Past As a Smoker?," *Harvard Health Letter*, June 1998, p1-3.

Smoking Trends: Teens

Percentage of High School Seniors Who Smoked in the Last 30 Days

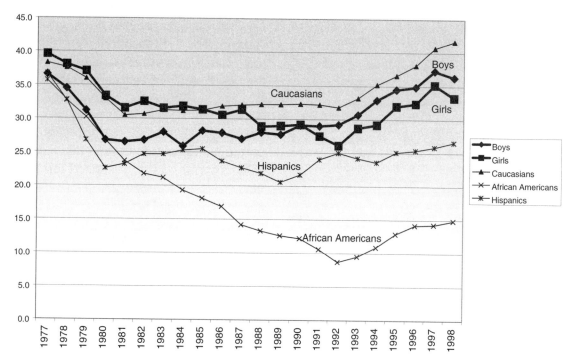

This chart shows smoking trends among high school seniors between 1977 and 1998. The data come from Monitoring the Future Project, which first began collecting data in high schools in 1975. Youth is a time for experimenting. This was true for smoking, especially for girls. The graphic shows that in 1977, 37.1% of girls had smoked in the last 30 days, compared to 31.2% of boys. Overall prevalence declined among both boys and girls until the early 1990s, but girls continued smoking at higher rates than boys until 1990.

Smoking prevalence has been consistently lower among blacks and Hispanics. Smoking by blacks declined precipitously from 37% to 9% between 1977-1993 before it began to rise again, reaching 15% in 1998. Hispanic rates fell from 36% in 1977 to a low of 21% in 1988 before starting a rise to 27% in 1998. Smoking among white teens also rose in the 1990s. A booming economy may account for this.

The table on the next page compares smoking prevalence among students and adults. The data are not precisely comparable because high school students reported smoking in the last 30 days; adults reported being current smokers. From 1979-1988, a smaller percentage of boys than men smoked and a higher percentage of girls than boys smoked. From 1979-1998, more girls than women smoked.

Are Joe Camel and his ilk responsible for hooking the young? *Multinational Monitor* tells us: "R.J. Reynolds' enormously successful Camel cartoon advertising campaign [is] one of the most blatant efforts by tobacco companies to market cigarettes to teens and children. Launched … in 1988, the Camel ads feature a cartoon camel character called Joe

High School Seniors and Adults Who Smoked (%)

	Students		Adults	
Year	Boys	Girls	Men	Women
1979	31.2	37.1	37.5	29.9
1980	26.8	33.4	37.6	29.3
1983	28.0	31.6	35.1	29.5
1985	28.2	31.4	32.6	27.9
1987	27.0	31.4	31.2	26.5
1988	28.0	28.9	30.8	25.7
1990	29.1	29.2	28.4	22.8
1991	29.0	27.5	28.1	23.5
1992	29.2	26.1	28.6	24.6
1993	30.7	28.7	27.7	22.5
1994	32.9	29.2	28.2	23.1
1995	34.5	32.0	27.0	22.6
1997	37.3	35.2	27.6	22.1
1998	36.3	33.3	26.4	22.0

Camel, who appears in hot tub and as a player in a band, often with women nearby. Many of the ads feature the Hard Pack, a blues band consisting of Joe and four other cartoon characters. The Joe Camel character is based on a Camel cartoon used in France in the early 1970s to circumvent a prohibition on the use of human models in tobacco advertising."[35][36]

Centers for Disease Control recently reported that the number of high school students who said they smoked fell more than 20% between 1997-2001, from about 36% of all students to 28%. The decline is attributed to higher cigarette taxes, anti-smoking campaigns aimed at teens, and state efforts to reduce rates of tobacco use. The government hopes to see high school smoking prevalence fall to 16% or lower by 2010 and believes a $2-a-pack excise tax on cigarettes by that year will help in the achievement of that goal.

Pierce and Gilpin studied national survey data to determine how long adolescent smokers can expect their addiction to last. They concluded that adolescents "may not fully understand that quitting this addiction is very difficult.... smoking will be a long-term addiction for many adolescents who start now."

Sources: Chart: "Smoking status of high school seniors — United States, Monitoring the Future Projects, 1976-1998," retrieved August 6, 2002, from http://www.cdc.gov/tobacco/research_data/youth/. Adam Marcus, "Teen Smoking Rates Drop Sharply: Higher cigarette taxes a big contributor to the trend," *HealthScoutNews*, May 16, 2002, retrieved August 6, 2002, from http://www.drkoop.com/. John P. Pierce and Elizabeth Gilpin, "How Long Will Today's New Adolescent Smoker Be Addicted to Cigarettes," *American Journal of Public Health*, Feb. 1996, p. 253-256. Karen Lewis, "Addicting the Young: Tobacco Pushers and Kids, *Multinational Monitor*, Jan./Feb. 1992, p. 13-17.

---

[35] In 1991, the *Journal of the American Medical Association* charged R. J. Reynolds Tobacco Company with targeting children through the Joe Camel campaign. That year Attorney Janet C. Mangini became the first person to challenge the tobacco industry for targeting minors through advertising.

[36] How successful is this kind of advertising? Before Joe Camel (1988), Marlboro targeted kids and Camel sales trailed Marlboro. By 1993 the three most heavily advertised brands were Marlboro, Camel, and Newport (CDC). While those brands accounted for 35% of overall cigarette sales, 86% of adolescent smokers bought one of the three brands. Between 1989-1993, Camel sales to adolescents were up 64%, Newport sales were up 55%, but Marlboro sales declined 13%.

Stress in the Morning

Morning Habits That Can Cause Stress

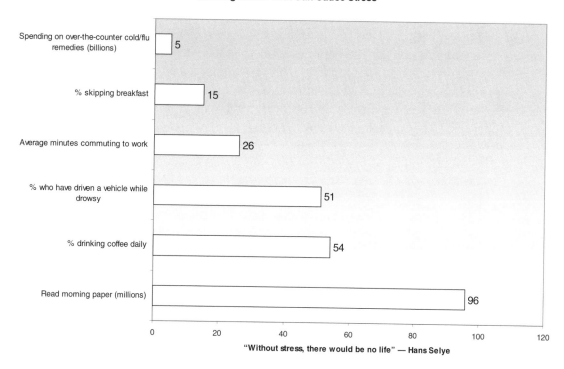

"Without stress, there would be no life" — Hans Selye

Stress is subjective, with little hard data available. It can be defined as "a state of tension that is created when a person responds to the demands and pressures that come from work, family and other external sources, as well as those that are internally generated from self-imposed demands, obligations and self-criticism."[37] There are so many stress-inducers. We will consider some that might confront a working person on a typical day.

The graphic presents some typical morning stress-inducers. We start with breakfast. The U.S. Department of Agriculture (USDA) reports that 85% of Americans eat breakfast. But what kind of breakfast, exactly? The USDA does not specify. Oats, the perfect food? Or bacon, eggs, toast? But the agency does go on to say: "Coffee and fluid milk are still the most popular foods consumed at breakfast." The National Coffee Association reports that 54% of American adults drink coffee every day, while 79% (161 million people) drink coffee at least occasionally. Reuters Health Information reports on a finding that "people who consume caffeine may experience an increase in blood pressure, feel more stressed and produce more stress hormones than on days when they opt for decaf." An estimated 85% of American adults consume caffeine every day in their coffee, soft drinks, and tea.

---

[37] Definition retrieved July 23, 2002, from http://www.stressfree.com/stress.html.

The 15% of Americans who skip breakfast have their own set of problems, including the tendency to eat more later to make up; being less productive and less efficient than those who eat breakfast; suffering impaired memory, mental performance strength, and endurance in the late morning; and exhibiting a negative attitude toward school or work.

Pharmacy Today reports on a New Zealand study showing that people who skip breakfast are more likely to get a cold or flu.[38] In the United States, $5 billion will be spent each year (see graphic) on cold and flu remedies with drowsiness as a typical side effect. Fifty-one percent of adults surveyed by the National Sleep Foundation reported "driving a car or other vehicle while feeling drowsy in the prior year while 17% report actually falling asleep at the wheel." There's a stress-inducing concept!

Fifty-six million households subscribe to a daily newspaper (down from 62.1 million in 1970), and more than half of American adults (96 million) read the newspaper on a typical weekday. Reading the daily paper can be a stress-inducer. For example, if you are one of more than 1.1 million people who subscribe to *The New York Times*, you might feel your stress level rising at headlines like these: "Retirement Money: Irate at Scandals and Big Losses, Pension Funds Are Going to Court" or "U.S. Attacked: Hijacked Jets Destroy Twin Towers and Hit Pentagon in Day of Terror."

Having digested the news (if nothing else), get ready for your commute to work. The 2000 census showed that Americans spent nearly 26 minutes on average commuting to their job, up from 22 minutes in 1990. If you live in Elliott County, Kentucky, plan on spending an average of 48.7 minutes traveling, the longest travel time in the country. Are you watching out for the driver with "road rage?" It may not even exist, according to Michael Fumento, who pours water on an AAA Foundation for Traffic Safety study showing a 60% increase in "aggressive driving" between 1990 and 1996. Still, the idea of ubiquitous outraged drivers has caught on with the public — definitely a stress-inducer.

If you're flying somewhere, be prepared for flight delays and "air rage." The Bureau of Transportation reported that 73.4% of flights arrived on time in 2001. Research by Andrew Thomas for his book, *Air Rage: Crisis in the Skies*, suggests that the FAA might have handled as many as 9,431 "probable instances of 'interference with a flight crew' in 2000. That number might include cases of disruptions at the gate as well as on planes."

Sources: Chart: USDA, Results from the 1994-96 Continuing Survey of Food Intakes by Individuals, http://www.barc.usda.gov/bhnrc/foodsurvey/96result.html; Kelvin Pollard, "Going to Work: Americans' Commuting Patterns in 2000," Population Reference Bureau, http://www.ameristat.org/; "Coffee drinking in U.S. hits all-time high of 79% of all adults — study," http://starchefs.com/news /press_releases/html/a_14.shtml Blake Morrison, "Reporting of violence lacks standards," *USA Today*, December 5, 2001, http://www.usatoday.com/news/attack/2001/12/05/air-side.htm. All online articles retrieved August 7, 2002. Michael Fumento, "'Road Rage' Versus Reality," *The Atlantic* online, August 1998, http://www.theatlantic.com/issues/98aug/road rage.htm. "Skip Breakfast — Get More Flu," Pharmacy Today, March 8, 2002, http://www.pharmacy-today.co.nz/news. Alison McCook, "Caffeine Boosts Stress Level All Day Long: Study," Reuters Health Information, http://www.nlm.nih.gov/medline plus/news/.

---

[38] Based on a study of 500 healthy volunteers at Cardiff University. The 188 participants in the study who developed colds were also more likely to drink alcohol and smoke than were those who stayed healthy.

Totally Stressed by Noon

Indicators of Stress at Work (in % except for number)

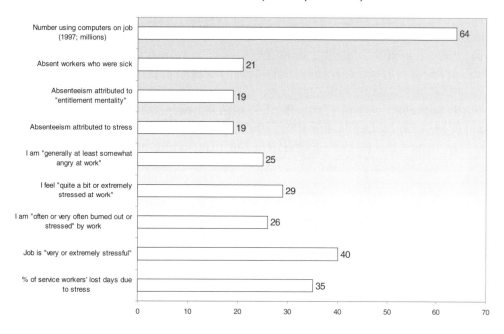

Number using computers on job (1997; millions)	64
Absent workers who were sick	21
Absenteeism attributed to "entitlement mentality"	19
Absenteeism attributed to stress	19
I am "generally at least somewhat angry at work"	25
I feel "quite a bit or extremely stressed at work"	29
I am "often or very often burned out or stressed" by work	26
Job is "very or extremely stressful"	40
% of service workers' lost days due to stress	35

Your job can cause stress (and so can being unemployed). The National Institute for Occupational Safety and Health (NIOSH) defines job stress as "the harmful physical and emotional responses that occur when the requirements of the job do not match the capabilities, resources, or needs of the worker." Job stress, says NIOSH, is not the same as challenge, which can be invigorating. The early warning signs of job stress are headache, sleep disturbances, difficulty in concentrating, short temper, upset stomach, job dissatisfaction, and low morale.

The chart shows survey statistics reflecting stress on the job. Two-thirds of workers reported stress in degrees ranging from "quite a bit" to "extremely."[39] Nearly 25% of workers polled (Gallup poll of 1,000 adults employed full- or part time) were "generally at least somewhat angry at work." Reasons why workers were off the job on short notice: 21% were actually sick, 19% felt stressed, and 19% felt they deserved a day off ("entitlement mentality").[40]

The Bureau of Labor Statistics offers data indicating that service is the most stressful type of work, with 35% of service workers' lost days due to stress. If left untreated, workplace

---

[39] Surveys conducted by Northwestern National Life, Families and Work Institute, and Yale University; reported by NIOSH (see Source notes).

[40] CCH Inc., a Chicago research firm, survey of human resources managers at 305 firms representing 800,000 employees. Other issues were family or personal needs. CCH reports that worker stress more than tripled between 1995-1999 (from 6% to 19%).

stress can lead to workplace rage or violence. According to the Bureau of Justice Statistics, Americans suffered an annual average of 1.7 million violent workplace victimizations between 1993-1999, including about 900 on-the-job homicides.

What brings this on? NIOSH finds that "job stress results from the interaction of the worker and the conditions of work." The relative importance of the two is debatable; "NIOSH favors the view that working conditions play a primary role in causing job stress." NIOSH delineates possible causes: (1) Heavy workload, long work hours/shift work; hectic/routine tasks with little inherent meaning that do not utilize workers' skills/provide little sense of control. (2) Lack of worker participation in decision making, poor communication, lack of family-friendly policies. (3) Poor social environment, lack of support or help from coworkers/ supervisors. (4) Conflicting/uncertain job expectations, too much responsibility.(5) Job insecurity, lack of opportunity for growth/advancement/promotion; rapid changes for which workers are unprepared.

Juliet Schor (*The Overworked American*, 1992) concluded that in 1990 Americans worked nearly a month longer per year than in 1970. Less than ten years later, "Workers in the United States [were] putting in more hours than anyone else in the industrialized world" (International Labor Organization). In 2000, the average American worked 1,978 hours, up from 1,942 in 1990 (nearly a week longer).[41] At least 64 million Americans use computers on the job. A survey of 501 workers[42] found that nearly half believe technology increases stress and 51% report that "the possibility of losing documents due to computer crashes causes them 'a lot' or 'some' stress." This can lead to "IT (information technology) rage"; 83% of IT managers surveyed reported that they had seen outraged workers attack their computer equipment — the most common targets were keyboards, followed by mouses, then monitors. The knowledge that one's every keystroke is being monitored can cause stress, as can the fear of being replaced by a computer. Computers also cause repetitive stress injury.

Having come to the end of our overlong and stressful day on the job (unless we work the night shift), some 115 million of us head for home. Is there more stress to come?

Sources: NIOSH, *Stress at Work*, www.cdc.gov/niosh/stresswk.html. Nancy Rivera Brooks, "Most Workers Who Call in 'Sick' Aren't, Study Finds," *Los Angeles Times*, Sept. 23, 1999, pC1+. Bureau of Justice Statistics, http://www.ojp.usdoj.gov/bjs/pub/press/vw99pr.htm. "Technology Increases Workplace Stress," Kensington Product News Releases, http://www.kensington.com. Porter Anderson, "Study: U.S. employees put in most hours," August 31, 2001, http://www.cnn.com/. All sources retrieved August 13, 2002. Chris Wood, "Dealing with Tech Rage: Ever Feel Like Hurling Your Computer Out the Window," *Maclean's*, March 19, 2001, p40.

[41] The trend in other industrialized nations is downward. In Australia, Canada, Japan, and Mexico, the average worker puts in about 100 hours per year less than we do. In Brazil and Britain, it's 250 hours less; in Germany, 500 hours less.

[42] Kensington Technology Group, designers/manufacturers of computer accessories.

Stress at Night

Indicators of Nighttime Stress

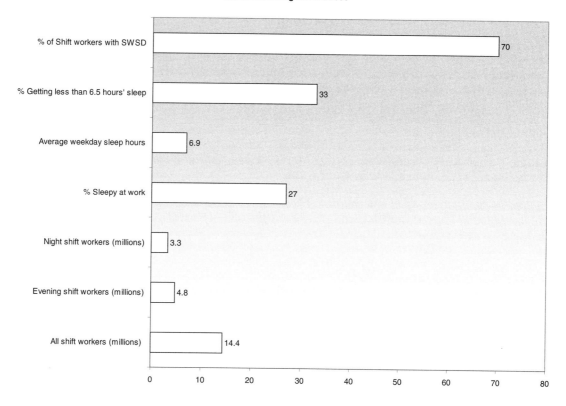

"O Sleep, rest of all things, mildest of the gods, balm of the soul..."

Iris to Hypnos. Ovid, Metamorphoses 1.623

Suppose you have survived your average 26-minute commute home, have listened calmly to the evening news (was it bad?), and have enjoyed a delicious, nutritious, stress-free family dinner. What other nighttime stresses might lie in wait for you? You might be one of "many millions" with insomnia, or one of 10 to 15 million more with sleep apnea, according to the National Institutes of Health (NIH).[43] You can expect to get insufficient sleep, if the National Sleep Foundation is to be believed. Their exhaustive 2002 "Sleep in America" poll provides some of the data on the graphic above. Poll respondents slept an average of 6.9 hours on weekdays, although 33% reported less than 6.5 hours, and 27% felt sleepy at work. NIH sleep experts believe you should be getting somewhere in the range of 7 to 8 hours of sleep a night.

---

[43] James P. Kiley, Ph.D., Director of the National Center on Sleep Disorders Research, says there could be as many as 1,500 fatalities and 100,000 sleep-related automobile accidents annually in the United States.

If you are one of 14.4 million people classified by the Bureau of Labor Statistics as a shift worker, you are likely to suffer from a different kind of sleep problem: Shift Work Sleep Disorder (SWSD), caused by fighting the internal clock that signals you to sleep at night. Jed Black of the Stanford Sleep Disorders Clinic estimates that 70% of shift workers suffer from SWSD. Many of them are working multiple jobs.

Australian/New Zealand researchers report that insufficient sleep can have some of the same effects as being drunk (it affects coordination, reaction time, and judgment). Consider this in light of the fact that shift workers include police officers and firefighters, doctors and nurses, and transportation and public utility workers. There's a stress-inducing concept!

Another reason for shift workers to feel stress: Researchers at the Fred Hutchinson Cancer Research Center report that women who work the "graveyard shift" (beginning at 11:00 p.m. or thereabouts) may have an increased risk of breast cancer ranging from 60% to 130%. A study in Antarctica suggests that night shift workers are at increased risk of developing heart disease.

Worker fatigue is blamed for an estimated $18 billion each year in lost productivity. The destruction of the space shuttle Challenger, the Chernobyl radiation disaster, the nuclear reactor accident at Three Mile Island, and the *Exxon Valdez* oil spill have all been linked to worker fatigue. But rest easy. Researchers are studying whether a drug called modafinil might benefit shift workers by allowing them to go 40 hours without sleep.[44]

We have seen that there are plenty of exposures to potential stressors in a 24-hour-day. Ready for a vacation?

Sources: Graphic: National Sleep Foundation, 2002 "Sleep in America" Poll, nationally representative telephone survey of 1,010 adults living in households in the continental United States, http://www.sleepfoundation.org/; and U.S. Department of Labor, "Full-time wage and salary shift workers by reason for working a non-daytime schedule, May 2001," http://www.bls.gov/news.release/. "Stanford researchers study drug to help shift workers stay focused and rest easy," Stanford Hospital & Clinics news release, November 26, 2001, http://www.stanfordhospital.com/. "Sleep deprivation as bad as alcohol impairment," CNN.com health, September 20, 2000, http://www.cnn.com/2000. Warren King, "Graveyard shifts may raise risk of breast cancer, October 17, 2001, http://seattle times.nwsour. "Shift work link to heart disease," BBC News, December 27, 2001, http://news.bbc.co.uk. Jan Ehrman, "A Good Night's Sleep? Merely a Dream for Millions," http://www.nih.gov/news/WordonHealth/jun98/story02.htm. All data retrieved August 13, 2002.

---

[44] Modafinil is approved by the Food and Drug Administration as a treatment for narcolepsy (brief attacks of deep sleep). According to *washingtonpost*.com: "In trials on healthy people like Army helicopter pilots, modafinil has allowed humans to stay up safely for almost two days while remaining practically as focused, alert, and capable of dealing with complex problems as the well-rested. Then, after a good eight hours' sleep, they can get up and do it again — for another 40 hours, before finally catching up on their sleep." A possible application? "The Defense Advanced Research Projects Agency is searching for ways to create the 'metabolically dominant soldier.' Among the projects it is pursuing is the creation of a warrior who can fight 24 hours a day, seven days straight." (Source: http://www.washingtonpost.com/wp-dyn/articles/A612 82-2002Jun16.html)

Stress All Year 'Round

Why Vacations Are Stressful

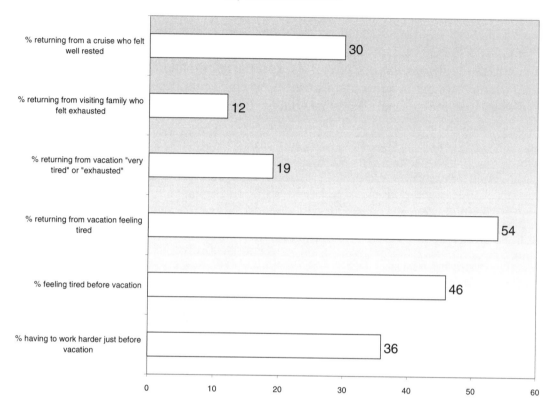

% returning from a cruise who felt well rested	30
% returning from visiting family who felt exhausted	12
% returning from vacation "very tired" or "exhausted"	19
% returning from vacation feeling tired	54
% feeling tired before vacation	46
% having to work harder just before vacation	36

Every man who possibly can should force himself to a holiday of a full month in a year, whether he feels like taking it or not. ~ William James

The chart shows results of a Gallup poll asking about Americans' vacation experiences. Do we return from vacation refreshed? No. Americans are more tired after their vacations than before they left. A little over a third of working adults said they had to put in more hours in the office the week before their vacation, contributing to the finding that 46% of those surveyed felt tired before the vacation began; and 54% of those polled described themselves as tired on returning home. Happily, 30% of those who went on a cruise felt well rested on their return. Of those visiting family, 12% were exhausted on return.

A 1995 survey of Americans elicited this information: 23% worked while on vacation, 40% caught up on work-related reading, 35% called in to check with the boss, 29% caught up on paperwork, 18% learned a new work skill. The survey did not report how many took their laptops on vacation, but we know from a 2001 survey conducted by travel planners VacationCoach, that 33% of 400 adults polled online felt they had too much work to go on vacation, 11% were concerned that their job wouldn't be there when they got back, and 20% said they never take vacations.

Vacations are supposed to be good for us. Do these findings mean that we should cross them off our agenda? Perhaps our vacations are too short to do us good. According to the

Bureau of Labor Statistics, full-time employees in medium and large private establishments averaged 9.6 days of paid vacation per year after one year on the job (1997). At 10 years, vacation days rose to 16.9. Compare this to the 4 to 6 weeks of paid vacation enjoyed by Europeans and Australians each year.

The consequences of overwork and no vacation? Arthur Waskow, caretaker of the Free Our Time Web site (www.freeourtime.org), notes that "the workings of American society work increasingly to squeeze dry the time for spirit, family and community. Without [a] sense of dignity, rooted in economic as well as spiritual realities, work becomes ill-paid, ill-respected, dishonored, and degrading, rather than dependable, financially sustaining, meaningful, honorable." No wonder we are stressed!

Top Ten Stress-Inducting Events

Life Event	Value
1. Death of spouse	100
2. Divorce	73
3. Marital separation	65
4. Jail term	63
5. Death of close family member	63
6. Personal injury or illness	53
7. Marriage	50
8. Being fired from work	47
9. Reconciliation with spouse	45
10. Retirement	45

In these four panels, we have looked at some of the events in a typical working person's life that might cause stress. What about major life stresses? In 1967, Holmes and Rahe introduced a scale that ranks life events according to how stressful they are. The table shows the top 10 (of more than 40) with their point value. It was discovered that in 79% of the persons studied, when more than 300 stress points accumulated in one year, major illness followed.

Are there ways to mitigate stress? Exercise is an oft-mentioned remedy. And if you're a woman, you're ahead of the game — German researchers think that female sex hormones may blunt the impact of stress. Or try cooperation. *The New York Times* notes: "Scientists have discovered that the small, brave act of cooperating with another person, of choosing trust over cynicism, generosity over selfishness, makes the brain light up with quiet joy."

Before concluding this chapter on risky behavior, we will take a look at two risk behaviors that have gained popularity despite warnings against them: tanning and tattooing.

Sources: Chart: John O'Neill, "Vital Signs: Reactions: Needing Vacation After a Vacation," *The New York Times*, July 23, 2002, (describes a survey of 1,000 Americans who had taken a vacation in the last year, sponsored by Sanofi-Synthelabo Inc., manufacturers of a sleep medication and other pharmaceuticals). Natalie Angier, "Why We're So Nice: We're Wired to Cooperate," *The New York Times*, July 23, 2002. Holmes, T.H. and Rahe, R.H. The social readjustment rating scale. *Journal of Psychomatic Research* 1967; 11: 213-17. Table: "Divorce Recovery," http://www.divorcerecovery.net/resources/change/Soc.readj.scale.PDF. Joe Robinson, "4 Weeks Vacation for Everyone!" *Utne Reader*, Sept/Oct 2000. BLS, "Paid vacation and length of service," http://www.bls.gov/. "Females handle stress better than males," *UPI*, November 13, 2001. Steelcase/Bruskin Goldring Research 1995 survey (http://www.isdesig net.com). For VacationCoach survey results, see (http://www.vacationcoach.com/aboutvaco/ewsroom/pressrel_hr survey.html).

Tall and Tan, Young, Lovely, and Tattooed

Incidence of Invasive Melanomas of the Skin (Per 100,000 Population) By Year of Diagnosis: 1975-1999

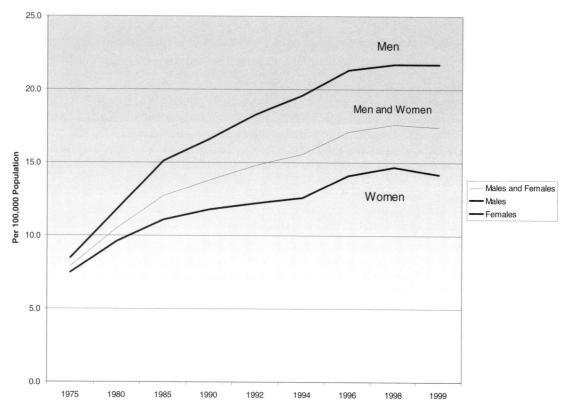

A tan is a sign of damage to the skin. Yet every day millions of Americans deliberately put themselves at risk for skin cancer, the most common type of cancer in the United States. Particularly alarming is that fact that while incidence and mortality rates for most other types of cancer are declining, skin cancer is on the rise. The Centers for Disease Control predicts that in 2002, 53,600 persons will be diagnosed with malignant melanoma, the most serious form of skin cancer. The chart shows that between 1981 and 1999, the incidence of melanoma increased from a rate of 11.1 per 100,000 to 17.4, an average of 7% per year. Melanoma is the most common cancer among people 25 to 29 years old, and it affects 40 to 50% of Americans who live to age 65 at least once.

Tanning salons are blamed for some of the increase. The American Academy of Dermatology estimates that every year, 30 million Americans visit the nation's more than 49,000 tanning parlors. About 7 out of 10 patrons are women between 16 and 60. A 15-to-30-minute session under the sunlamp, experts say, is the equivalent of a full day at the beach. Marie-France Demierre, M.D., director of the skin oncology program at Boston University Medical School, calls the trend "tanning bed addiction and sun worship."

According to the *Looking Fit Tanning Fact Book 2002-2003,* indoor tanning made its way to this country from Germany in 1979. By 1985, "The industry was very cosmopolitan and many people were making money." Tanning parlor patrons believe a tan makes them look fit and healthy. Says the National Institute on Aging: "The simplest and cheapest way to keep your skin healthy and young looking is to stay out of the sun....UV radiation from the sun is the main cause of skin cancer [and] artificial sources of UV radiation — such as sunlamps and tanning booths — can cause skin cancer."

Dermatologist Mark Naylor says: "Right now people think it's not a problem. [They think:] If I get a skin cancer, I can just go to my dermatologist and he can just take it off." Acknowledging that melanoma can be treated if it's caught early and hasn't spread, Naylor says to those whose melanoma is advanced: "Good luck." Donald L. Smith (North American Alliance of Tanning Salon Owners) responds to "the dermatology community": "...over 100 people die prematurely each year because of the adverse consequences associated with underexposure to ultraviolet radiation (UVR) for every one person who dies prematurely each year because of overexposure to UVR... [and] there is not one scintilla of evidence to show that sensible, moderate and responsible exposure to UVR is anything other than beneficial to human beings."

Like tanning, tattooing has entered the mainstream. According to Hoag Levins ("The Changing Cultural Status of Tattoo Art"): "The cultural status of tattooing has steadily evolved from that of an anti-social activity in the 1960s to that of a trendy fashion statement in the 1990s." He cites a Canadian study of the clientele at a popular Toronto tattoo art studio where "80% of the customers were 'upper middle-class white suburban females.'" He quotes *U.S. News & World Report*: "...tattooing was the sixth-fastest-growing retail business in 1996, after Internet, paging services, bagels, computer, and cellular phone stores. Since then, the industry has been expanding by more than one studio a day, a 13.9 percent increase in nine months."

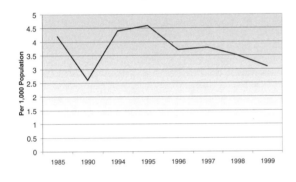

Incidence of Hepatitis C: 1985-1999

The inset graph shows reported cases of hepatitis C. What does hepatitis have to do with tattooing? *Hepatitis Weekly* reports on a study showing that "getting a tattoo could be a key infection route for hepatitis C, the most common viral infection affecting almost 2% of the United States population." The newsletter points out that hepatitis C attacks the liver and is potentially fatal. Be trendy at your own risk.

Sources: Charts: Centers for Disease Control, National Cancer Data, Table XVI, "Melanomas of Skin (Invasive), http://seer.cancer. gov/csr/1973_1999/melama, and *Statistical Abstract of the United States: 2001*, Table 181. National Institute on Aging AgePage, http://www.nia.nih.gov/health/agepages/skin.htm. Lisette Hilton, "Get the Word Out to Patients About Melanoma," http://www. healthcarehub.com/. "Indoor Tanning Casts a Year-Round Shadow," American Academy of Dermatology, http://www.aad.org/erm nsights/. Centers for Disease Control, Facts and Statistics About Skin Cancer, http://www.cdc.gov/ChooseYourCover/skin.htm. John Jesitus, "Melanoma rates are on the rise : Other forms of cancer, meanwhile, take downward trend," *Dermatology Times*, September 2000, p. 23. Hoag Levins, "The Changing Cultural Status of Tattoo Art," http://www.tattooartist.com/history.html. "Study Finds Tattooing a Major Route of Hepatitis C Infection," *Hepatitis Weekly*, April 16, 2001. All Internet information retrieved July 12, 2002. *Looking Fit Tanning Handbook*, http://www.lookingfit.com/factbook/.

Chapter 5

Treatments

One can say — guardedly — that the health status of Americans is generally very good indeed. The caution comes because it is never safe to crow when it comes to matters of health. But a look at our methods of treating diseases certainly bears out the general judgement. We begin this chapter by looking at operations and medical procedures in hospitals — and looking at data a distance of ten years apart — in 1990 and in 2000. During this time the population grew substantially. We added more people than Canada has population. Yet in 2000 we had fewer operations than in 1990.

In one sense this happy outcome is due to our better health status in general, in part due to better diagnostic tools (we detect diseases earlier), in part we cure diseases by pharmaceutical and therapeutic interventions that do not require hospital stays. Thus, for instance, although cardiac procedures have increased sharply, they were less invasive in 2000 than they had been in 1990.

The largest numbers of procedures have to do with childbirth — one of nature's most demanding performances. Giving birth — and its complications — are likely to hold a commanding lead over other procedures in the years to come as well — but here, too, there has been a drop in overall numbers.

We take three panels to examine treatment methods — and outcomes — for cancer. Cancer remains a tough opponent of medical intervention. We look at progress through the lens of so-called survival rates. The government keep track of people diagnosed with cancer, and checks on them to see how they are doing at five-year intervals. From these data we learn that we are doing a better job keeping people alive despite the absence of any breakthroughs. But our "weapons" for killing cancer cells are getting better — and our "intelligence" in detecting their presence has also improved. We are getting the best results with the white population — but improvements are present for both whites and blacks. We are also making much better progress with cancers we can more easily detect.

The chapter concludes with a brief look at alternative medical treatments. There, too, progress is being made.

My Operation? Let Me Tell You...

Operations in 1990 and 2000

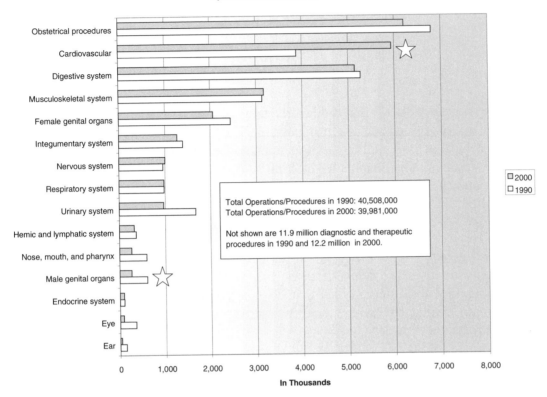

What are the most common operations — and what has changed over the last ten years? The graphic attempts to answer this question. In 2000 we underwent nearly 40 million operations. Ten years earlier, the number was just over 40 million. During that period, our population grew by 32.7 million people. We are having fewer operations — and we are possibly suffering less. Some trends are discernible, but let's first take a closer look at these data.

The largest number of operations in 1990 and again in 2000 took place in connection with childbirth — possibly the most complex and miraculous event in human biological experience. Rankings for other categories are somewhat different between 1990 and 2000, however. Operations on the musculoskeletal system, female genital organs, and the respiratory system, have retained their ranks — 4th, 5th, and 8th respectively. Others have shifted in rank.

Most notably, perhaps, two changes should be noted — and are marked with stars in the graphic. **Cardiovascular** operations are second in rank in 2000, displacing operations on the digestive system. Much of this change is due to an increase in catheterization — used for diagnosis — and procedures for removing obstructions (similar to catheterization) including use of the newly invented stents. Stents are tiny metallic inserts that keep arteries open in the heart. Catheterization is a process whereby the doctor can enter a beating heart using a wire (inserted in the thigh region) and examine the "environment."

Operations on the **male genital organs** have dropped in rank from 10th to 12th place — largely because of a drop in prostatectomy (prostate removal). This may be due to improvements in the detection of prostate cancer and experience gained in how to manage the disease, which has a very slow progression.

When we look at operations in detail — rather than by major groupings — we note that the single most common operation is a **catheterization**, mentioned earlier. This is a straw in the wind, as it were, because it signals the rise of procedures that will be less and less invasive (no large incisions, no bones sawed). As our ability to look inside the body with lasers and to manipulate miniaturized instruments by tiny motors increases, operations will change in character.

The third rank in specific procedures also goes to the cardiac category — **angioplasty** and stent insertion — also non-invasive procedures. The second most common operation is the mending of tissues cut during childbirth — **repair of obstetric lacerations**. The fourth-ranked procedure belongs to obstetrics as well. This is **episiotomy**. In some cases of difficult birth (944,000 such difficult cases took place in 2000), the vagina must be cut so that the baby will not tear the tissue as it comes out or is extracted. The cut is sewed up after the baby is delivered. To round out this ranking, the fifth most common operation is **endoscopy** of the small intestine. And endoscope is a device inserted through the anus to look at the small intestine from inside the body. A biopsy may be performed as part of an endoscopy. The 6th ranking procedure is the famous **Cesarean** section. The 7th is also obstetrical — the **artificial rupture of membranes** to aid the birthing process. It looks as if the delivery room and the heart have it.

Trends in operations reflect changes in society. A down-turn in deaths from heart disease appears to have its reflection in more — but less invasive — cardiac operations. Better methods of disease detection or screening have their echoes in the operating room.

Let us end with some glossary notes. "Hemic and lymphatic system" refers to the blood circulating system and the lymph nodes. Lymph nodes return water and protein from tissues back to the blood stream. The "pharynx" is the throat. The "endocrine" system, as MEDLINEplus defines it, consists of "glands that produce and secrete hormones into the blood or lymph systems. These glands include the thyroid, parathyroid, hypothalamus, pineal, pituitary, adrenal, islands of Langerhans in the pancreas, and the gonads (testes and ovaries). The effects of these hormones may affect one organ or tissue, or the entire body." The "integumentary system" includes the skin, hair, nails, and the sweat and oil glands.

Source: *2000 National Hospital Discharge Survey*, Advanced Data from Vital and Health Statistics, Number 329, June 19, 2002. 1990 data from *National Hospital Discharge Survey: Annual Summary, 1990*, Series 13, Number 113. Vital and Health Statistics, U.S. Department of Health and Human Services. MEDLINEplus quote taken from http://www.nlm.nih.gov/medlineplus/ency/article/002351. htm.

Diagnostic and Therapeutic Procedures

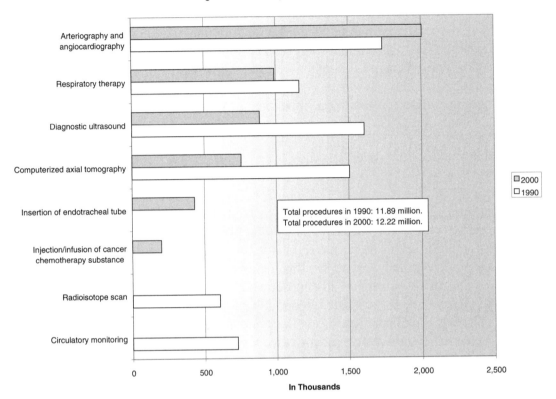

Diagnostic and Therapeutic Procedures

Arteriography and angiocardiography

Respiratory therapy

Diagnostic ultrasound

Computerized axial tomography

Insertion of endotracheal tube

Injection/infusion of cancer chemotherapy substance

Radioisotope scan

Circulatory monitoring

□ 2000
□ 1990

Total procedures in 1990: 11.89 million.
Total procedures in 2000: 12.22 million.

0   500   1,000   1,500   2,000   2,500

In Thousands

The database that provides an insight into operations also lets us see a little into the details behind some 12 million diagnostic and therapeutic procedures carried out in 2000. Roughly the same number were performed ten years earlier in 1990.

In a sense we see here the rather dynamic transformations that have taken place in the treatment of diseases in just a ten year period. Looking into the arteries and into the inner workings of the heart, using contrast materials — **angiography and angiocardiography** — are the top ranking diagnostic procedures in both benchmark years. We saw in the previous panel that heart-related operations have increased. Here we see a reflection of that in diagnostic procedures — which are more numerous in 2000 than ten years before.

Total procedure are up slightly, but the leading procedures — heart-related procedures alone excepted — are down. Fewer respiratory therapy procedures were performed. Ultrasound seems to have lost ground. CAT scans seem to have lost their popularity. The administration of chemotherapy substances has come to the fore — a therapeutic procedure.

To be sure, the procedure shown — and selected by the compilers of the *National Hospital Discharge Survey* — are a limited part of all procedures counted. In 1990, the NHDS showed 64% of such procedures in detail, in 2000 only 43%. One inference of that (no explanations are offered in the source) is that in 2000 many more procedures were in use, suggesting that both diagnostic and therapeutic methods have proliferated, have become more specific, and are applied with more discrimination these days. Tools are being refined.

This, in fact, appears to be a trend in medicine these days — and may well continue in the future. It is reflected in better understanding of diseases (see the panel entitled *Emerging Diseases: Many Pathways* in Chapter 2) and the corresponding fine-tuning of pharmaceutical treatments and medical interventions. Thus well-known tools are applied more sparingly and others are, one imagines, too numerous to mention.

A brief note about procedures that may not be familiar. Endotracheal intubation is a procedure whereby a tube is inserted through the nose into the throat to help a patient breathe. Radioisotope scans require the introduction of radioactive materials into the body — say by injection, by a drip. Cameras placed close to the organ being studied can obtain images. Diagnostic ultrasound makes use of high-frequency sound waves, beyond human hearing, to create images of organs and bones. Several different imaging systems may be used in conjunction.

We turn next to take a look at the age-distribution of those who undergo operations now — and then.

Source: *2000 National Hospital Discharge Survey*, Advanced Data from Vital and Health Statistics, Number 329, June 19, 2002. 1990 data from *National Hospital Discharge Survey: Annual Summary, 1990*, Series 13, Number 113. Vital and Health Statistics, U.S. Department of Health and Human Services. MEDLINEplus quote taken from http://www.nlm.nih.gov/medlineplus/ency/article/002351.htm.

Operations/Procedures: By Age

Age Distribution of Operations and Procedurers

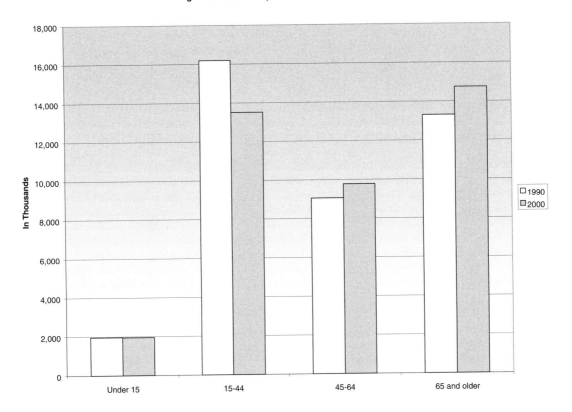

Children, thank heaven, have the fewest operations and the oldest age group, those 65 years old and older, had the highest number in 2000. In 1990, the 15 to 44 age group ranked highest, but there is an explanation for that.

Fifteen to 44 is the childbearing period of women. In 2000, nearly 55% of all operations in the 15-44 age group were related to obstetrics and operations on the female genital organs. These two areas accounted for less than 21% for all ages. In 1990, women in this age group were 23.5% of the population, in 2000 21.8% — which goes far in explaining why this age group had more operations in 1990 than ten years later.

What is surprising is that, in this period, population increased by 10.7% but total operations recorded in the National Hospital Discharge Survey actually *decreased* 1.3%. We must note here, again, that we are having fewer operations — which must be good news. Had the ratio for 1990 still held in 2000, we would have had nearly 5 million more operations than we actually had. As the ads constantly besiege us, these days, "See your doctor." — And tell your doctor what a good job he or she is doing!

While women in the nubile period of their lives have decreased as a percent of total — and this group has also aged within the group (more women aged 35-44, for instance) — those aged 65 and over have increased by 11.8% in this ten-year period. The population as a whole is aging — and we are seeing the results in the graphic. Both those in the 45-64 and especially those in the 65-plus age groups, are having most of the operations in 2000.

Among the oldest, the three categories that represent the most operation are operations of the cardiovascular system (heart disease is still the leading killer), operations on the digestive system, and operations on the musculoskeletal system. The older people have bypass operations, catheterizations, and angioplasty procedures. They have most problems with the small intestine and suffer fractures. It is a little sad to realize that when you're finally ready to be put out to pasture, you will most likely find it crowded with operating theaters and CAT scan machines.

The people in the middle, those aged 45 to 64, exhibit a pattern very much like that of their seniors. The people in this age group have the same operations, in the same proportions, as the growing 65-plus crowd. They are simply early in the process. Those more hardy have their operation a little later.

Source: *2000 National Hospital Discharge Survey*, Advanced Data from Vital and Health Statistics, Number 329, June 19, 2002. 1990 data from *National Hospital Discharge Survey: Annual Summary, 1990*, Series 13, Number 113. Vital and Health Statistics, U.S. Department of Health and Human Services.

Cancer Treatment: Prolonged Life

Cancer Survival

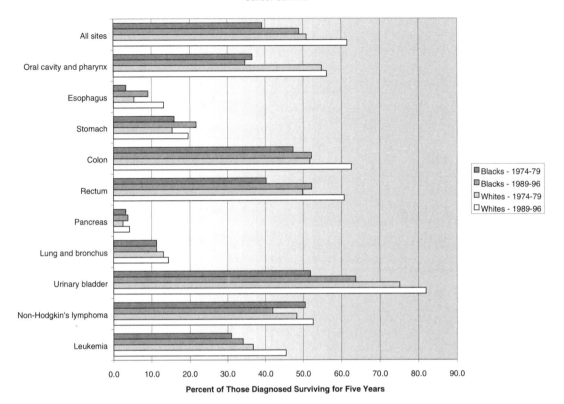

Percent of Those Diagnosed Surviving for Five Years

Cancer has no cure, but cancer can be treated. Cancer is the uncontrolled multiplication of cells, beginning in one of the body's organs ("the site"). Multiplying cells produce a tumor ("malignancy"). Cancer can spread from one site to other parts of the body. When that happens, the cancer is said to "metastasize" (Greek for moving from one place to another).

Modern medicine fights the destructive character of a cancer — by cutting it out in surgical procedures or trying to kill it with radiation directed at the site or by trying to destroy the cells with chemicals. Chemotherapy works on a wider front than radiation and can thus also destroy metastasizing cancers.

Cancer in the body is in a way analogous to a fire in a building. The sooner it is noticed, the easier it is to put out. Early detection through screening or inspection — mammography, pap smears, lung X-rays, PSA blood tests (for prostate cancer), a fecal occult blood and colonoscopy (for colon cancer), etc. — are really part of the treatment. As in buildings unsafe practices invite fire, so also in the body smoking and obesity, to name two risk conditions, can be controlled and thus prevent cancer.

How goes our fight against cancerous cells? One general view of outcomes is to look at cancer survival rates. The graphic shows five-year survival rates for whites and blacks during two periods 15 years apart: for the 1974 to 1979 period and the 1989 to 1996 period. This measure, in percent, shows what percentage of individuals diagnosed with a cancer were still alive five years later. The worst results shown here were for whites with pancreatic cancer in the 74-79 period (2.5% — 97.5% died). The best results shown are for whites with urinary bladder cancer in the 89-96 period: 81.9% survived for five years.

Survival rates for whites improved across the board. Survival rates for blacks are lower than for whites in all but one instance — stomach cancers in the 89-96 period. In the case of mouth and throat cancer, the black survival rate has worsened between the two periods.

In the next panel, where we shall look at female-male differences (and cancers specific to each sex), we shall discuss specific treatments in some moderate detail. In what follows, please note some of the following points:

- The easier it is to detect a cancer early, the higher, generally, will be the survival rate. Early detection requires (a) strong, early symptoms, (b) screening tests that catch the disease before its onset or just at onset, and/or (c) a combination of the two. Pancreatic cancer produces symptoms like stomach ache, fatigue, loss of appetite, and back pain.

- Where surgery is easiest to perform, survival rates will be highest. In the case of pancreatic cancer, for instance, only 20% of cases are operable. Colorectal cancer is relatively easy to detect — and screening methods are available. Early detection means that surgical intervention is possible — hence a high survival rate. Lung cancer manifests as a cough, a shortness of breath, breast pain, blood in the sputum. Here, again, surgical intervention is possible if the disease is detected early. Once the cancer has spread, only chemotherapy and radiation therapy remain.

- Where the treatment is primarily by chemical or radiological means, survival rates are lower.

Black survival rates are probably lower than white because detection of the disease happens at a later point. This may be due to less access to health care which, in turn, may have economic and social causes for at least a portion of the black population.

We continue exploration of this subject in the next panel.

Source: National Institutes of Health, National Cancer Institute, from *Health, United States*, 2001, Table 56.

Cancer Treatment: Women Do Better

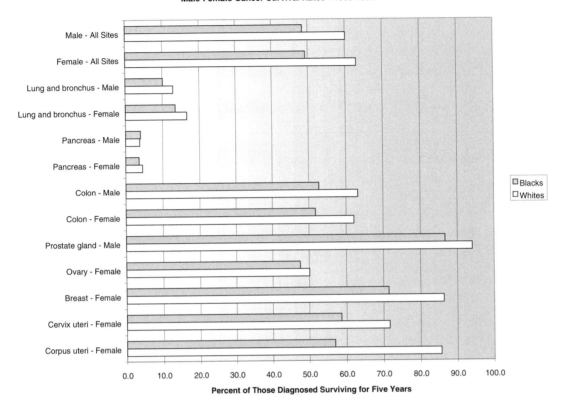

Male-Female Cancer Survival Rates - 1989-1996

Percent of Those Diagnosed Surviving for Five Years

Legend: Blacks / Whites

Categories (top to bottom): Male - All Sites, Female - All Sites, Lung and bronchus - Male, Lung and bronchus - Female, Pancreas - Male, Pancreas - Female, Colon - Male, Colon - Female, Prostate gland - Male, Ovary - Female, Breast - Female, Cervix uteri - Female, Corpus uteri - Female

In the previous panel, we saw progress made over a 15-year period in treating cancers. In this graphic, we show survival rates for a single period, 1989 to 1996, comparing men and women, white and black. Cancers specific to sexes are shown — prostate cancer for men, ovarian, breast, cervical, and uterine cancers for women.

The two clear messages of the graphic are that women, black and white, have a higher survival rate than men and that blacks, of both sexes, have a lower survival rate than whites. This graphic shows only selected cancer sites. All data are presented in Part II in tabular format.

The highest survival rates are shown for prostate cancer. The malignancy now has a new early-warning screen, the PSA blood test. The disease spreads slowly. Surgery can be used to remove the malignancy in most cases — i.e., when the cancer has not metastasized. Ovarian cancer is difficult to detect early, has often spread by the time it is discovered. Symptoms are vague. Symptoms of cervical and uterine cancer speak louder, as it were. And breast cancer detection has been greatly aided by mammography, which is strongly promoted by the health authorities. The only cancer where males survive fractionally longer than females is with cancer of the colon: men lead by 1.1% survival.

It is noteworthy, in contemplating this graphic, that in *no* case does the survival rate reach 100%. This means that our methods of prevention, surveillance, and treatment are not working very well. Cancer is a killer. A brief look at the important methods of treatment show us why.

Once cancer has begun, it is analogous to our current war on terrorists. We claim we don't know why terrorists hate us. Similarly, we don't understand why cancer cells multiply. We are left with the task of destruction. Our ability to see is limited. Areas we have pacified can revive. In the process of destroying the enemy, we harm the innocent. Thus radiation therapy damages healthy cells — and can sometimes, after years of delay, cause leukemia. Chemotherapy designed to attack and to destroy rapidly growing cells also destroys healthy cells, damages tissue. Both treatments have severe side-effects and weaken the body.

The treatment of cancer is, in this preferred order: surgery, radiation, and chemotherapy. Each technique is less specific, going from left to right, and has greater side effects. Sometimes the last two are used in preparation for or during surgery as well.

Surgery is indicated when the disease is localized and hasn't spread. Radiation therapy, similarly, is applied to the cancer site itself. Chemical agents are useful when the disease has spread — because the chemicals can reach cells beyond localized points.

Leukemia and lymphatic cancers are treated by radiation therapy and chemotherapy exclusively. Only about of fifth of pancreatic cancers can be treated surgically. In lymphoma, bone marrow transfers are a treatment, in leukemia blood transfusions. Hormone therapy is associated with uterine and breast cancer. In cervical cancer, cryotherapy (freezing cancer cells), electrocoagulation (burning the cells), and laser ablation (cutting them with concentrated light) are also used. New radiological techniques are in testing now. These techniques are designed to be more accurate in reaching the target, make use of sophisticated computer targeting of tumors, and operate so that surrounding tissues do not suffer "collateral damage."

The object in all of these cases — except the replacement strategies of bone marrow transfer and blood transfusions — is destruction. Even very sophisticated new techniques like antiangiogenesis therapy — which starves cancer cells of blood — are meant to destroy. A cure for cancer would be to prevent the defective cells from forming in the first place.

Not surprisingly — in the absence of a cure — much emphasis is on managing risk factors — especially for those major cancers known to be caused by or are linked to behaviors like smoking and obesity. We conclude our look at cancer treatments by looking at prevention in the next panel. Much more information on prevention is presented in Chapter 3.

Source: National Institutes of Health, National Cancer Institute, from *Health, United States,* 2001, Table 56. Background data from American Cancer Society, accessible at http://www.cancer.org.

Cancer Treatment: The Case for Prevention

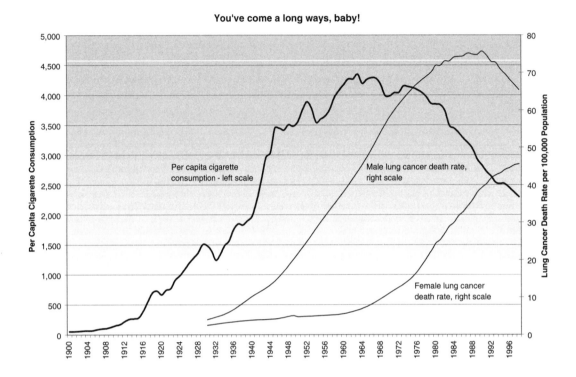

You've come a long ways, baby!

Treatment helps people survive cancer longer. Our methods of destroying cancers are becoming sophisticated. But cancer survival rates are still not at 100%. Not surprisingly, the health authorities are laboring to *prevent* the disease — by trying to change our behavior.

The graphic illustrates the correlation between cigarette smoking and lung cancer. Tobacco became the drug of choice the world over when Columbus set foot in the New World and the natives offered large, brown leaves as welcoming gifts. The leaves had a pleasant odor, but the discoverers didn't know what to do with them. They did by the time they were returning home again. Tobacco has been an integral part of the American experience from the start — but it was cigarette smoking that has had the most massively lethal impact on the U.S. population. Women at first modestly refrained — except the most daring — so much so that in the sixties a cigarette advertising slogan was, "You've come a long ways, baby!"

We deal with this subject in more detail elsewhere in this volume (see Chapter 4, *Risky Behavior*). In the case of cigarette smoking — and other forms of tobacco consumption — we're making a certain amount of progress. Other areas are not quite so clear. Let's look at some of the risk factors over which people have some degree of control..

Obesity. According to the American Cancer Society (ACS), "in 1981, approximately 2% of all cancer deaths ... were attributed to overweight, and more than one-third of all cancer deaths to dietary factors in adulthood." Obesity increases cancer risks for post-menopausal breast cancer (50% higher risk for obese women), colon cancer for men

(40% increase in risk), cancer of the gallbladder and endometrium (uterine cancer), and there may also be positive association between obesity and cancer of the kidneys, pancreas, rectum, esophagus, and liver. The ACS puts it like this: "Obesity alters complex interactions among diet, metabolism, physical activity, hormones, and growth factors."[1]

The Centers for Disease Control has labeled obesity "an epidemic." We deal with the subject elsewhere; see for instance *Women's Health: Weighty Trends* in Chapter 1. When it comes to obesity, we are *losing* the battle against one of the cancer risk factors.

Alcohol. Consumption of alcohol — especially in combination with smoking, use of snuff, and chewing tobacco — increase the risks of mouth and throat cancer. Alcohol consumption also appears to increase the risk of breast cancer. The mechanism is not understood, but alcohol may influence the estrogen level in a woman's body.

Diet and Exercise. The right kind of food and vigorous exercise keep off the pounds — hence the obesity-related risks are lower. People who like diets high in fat put themselves at greater risk for colorectal cancers, cancer of the prostate, and uterine cancer. It is not yet clear which kind of fat is the culprit. The risks of colon and prostate cancer are higher for people who eat red meat. Prostate cancers are associated with high levels of testosterone — which seem to be more prevalent in men who eat large amounts of fat. Prostate cancer rates are lowest in Japanese men. They eat a lot of fish.

Modern Drugs, Treatments, Pastimes. Relatively low risks are associated with hormone replacement therapies and oral contraceptives for women. More risk is associated with having been exposed to high-dose ionizing radiation to the chest (breast cancer). Tanning, whether in salons or on the beach, increases the risk of skin cancer.

Staying trim, avoiding fat, tobacco, alcohol, and some drugs doesn't guarantee a cancer-free life. Cancer can appear anywhere in the body — even in the heart and in the bones. In the digestive system alone, in 2002, estimated new cases of cancer were as follows: in the esophagus (gullet) – 13,100; stomach – 21,600; small intestine – 5,300; colon – 107,300; rectum – 41,000; anus, anal canal, and anorectum – 3,900; liver and bile duct – 16,600; gallbladder – 7,100; pancreas – 30,300; and other digestive organs – 4,400.

Many stresses to the body may trigger the onset of cancer — one of these may be the cumulated stresses of aging. Cancer kills those in advancing years. One strategy of prevention may be to stay forever young — but that may be more difficult than finding a cure for cancer.

Source: U.S. Department of Agriculture (cigarette consumption). CDC Wonder data base for cancer mortality rates. Background data from American Cancer Society publications available at http://www.cancer.org, especial *Cancer Facts* or *Cancer Facts & Figures* for various years.

---

[1] Both quotes and information in this paragraph from *Cancer Facts and Figures 2001*, American Cancer Society, Inc., Atlanta, GA, p. 20.

Alternative Treatments

NCCAM Clinical Trial Leaders

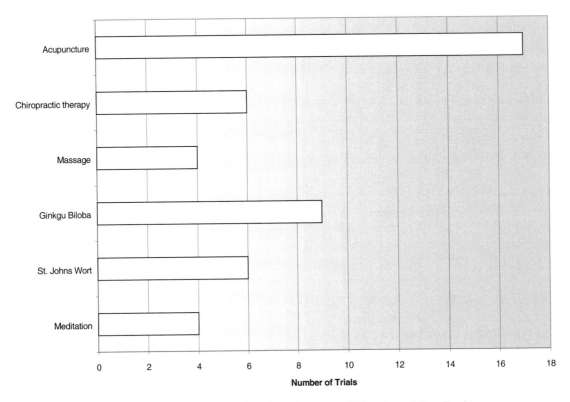

Number of Trials

An' the dawn comes up like thunder outer China 'crost the Bay!
Rudyard Kipling, *Mandalay*

By October 1998, alternative and complementary treatments of things that ail us had reached a certain maturity. At that time Congress established the National Center for Complementary and Alternative Medicine (NCCAM) as one of the National Institutes of Health (see also Chapter 3, *Alternative Medicine in the Mainstream*). Since then such things as art therapy, ginseng, and laying on of hands have taken on a certain respectability and are being studied in double-blind, randomized, highly rigorous clinical tests. No doubt NCCAM is the consequence of popular disaffection with conventional, western, "allophatic" medicine — the popularity of herbal remedies — and the Baby Boom's always dominant biases. But NCCAM is also, perhaps, a belated response to objective experience. Namely that many of the treatments and the natural medicines that have reached us from the Orient may actually work — and while we're at it, we might as well examine such home-grown (meaning Western) practices as chiropraxis and homeopathic medicines.

Since the National Center for Health Statistics does not (as yet) track such matters as acupuncture and our consumption of chamomile tea — and the benefits we gain from such treatments — one way of gauging the interest in alternative and complementary medicines might be to look at the clinical trials that NCCAM funds.

NCCAM's budged in Fiscal Year 2003 was $113.2 million. We note that here because clinical trials are *not* cheap. The average cost in 1996 for all National Institutes of Health was $605,088. One should keep that number in mind in reading what follows — while remembering that costs of individual trials vary all over the lot.

NCCAM lists some 65 different categories of clinical tests conducted under its auspices or with other agencies — from acupressure to Yoga. Six of these categories have four or more clinical trials going on at present. They are shown in the graphic above. By far the most trials are clustered around acupuncture (17), the Chinese method of curing the body and of relieving pain by inserting needles at points in the body that correspond to a theoretical river-system of energies believed to circulate through the body.

In addition to the management of pain at various sites, acupuncture is being tested to control arthritis, cancer, cerebral palsy, depression, diarrhea in HIV patients, heart disease, and high blood pressure.

The leading categories also include such western practices as chiropractic manipulation and massage, the effects of the herb (leaf) ginkgu biloba on a variety of diseases, St. John's Wort as an antidepressant, and meditation techniques (which derive from Indian, Japanese, and western traditions) on mental and physical health.

All told, 22 categories (of the 65) have two or more trials under way. These include a variety of herbs (e.g., ginseng, echinacea), substances like shark cartilage, healing techniques like the Japanese "body energy" balancing, Reiki, the Chinese Tai-Chi, the Hindu Yoga. They include the western hypnosis as well as mind-body techniques blended from various cultural roots, minerals like selenium, and practices of naturopathic medicine. The remaining 43 categories have one trial running each. That list includes, to pick at random, garlic, distance healing, guided imagery, borage oil, and music therapy.

Do these alternative methods work? The answer must be a very qualified yes. Certainly the NCCAM is putting its money where its needles go — as regards acupuncture. Clinical trials have shown that St. John's Work works as well as patent medicines and sometimes much better than placebos. We can all attest to the benefits of a good massage — and chiropractic medicine is very much a going concern. Are there data to show the effectiveness of all of these techniques? The answer is an unqualified No. But someday large parts of alternative and complementary medicines will be just as much a part of normal medicine as are aspirin and radiation therapy.

Source: National Center for Complementary and Alternative Medicine, accessible at http://www.nccam.nih.gov/.

Chapter 6

Drugs

"Pill-Popping Nation." This was the title of an October 2000 article in the magazine *Forecast*.[1] Is it a true description of the United States? In 2001, 3.1 billion prescriptions were dispensed in the United States, a 1.2 billion increase since 1991. By 2004, the number of prescriptions dispensed is expected to reach 4 billion. In the first panel we look at the most dispensed prescriptions in 1995 and 2000. Were we being treated for the same conditions? Are the most dispensed drugs used for the most prevalent conditions?

Antidepressants made the top 10 of dispensed drugs — for in 1995 and 2000. The number of people diagnosed with depressive disorders rose by 3.7% from 2000-2001, but the number of prescriptions dispensed rose by 13.2% Why this discrepancy? The next panel examines the antidepressant market (and possible over-marketing of the drug).

Ritalin is a drug to treat attention deficit hyperactivity disorder (ADHD). It was/is a controversial drug for a controversial diagnosis. Between 1975 and 2000 there was a 3,900% increase in children taking this drug. The next panel examines the reasons behind this astronomic rise.

Another controversial issue we examine from various angles is the price of prescription drugs. We start by presenting the pharmaceutical industry's argument: research and development costs drive up the cost of prescription drug prices. Then, we look at the public's claim: drug advertising is causing the skyrocketing prescription drug prices. Next, we examine other angles of the issue to discover just where our prescription drug dollar is going. Is the pharmaceutical industry's argument correct, is the public's, or is there another reason for the rise in prescription drug prices?

And finally, with all the talk of overuse, misuse, and over-charging of prescription drugs, are they worth the price we pay for them? Do they drive down the costs of health care as the pharmaceutical industry claims? We attempt to shed some light on these issues in the last panel.

---

[1] Stein Wellner, Alison. "Pill-Popping Nation." *Forecast*, October 2000.

Most Dispensed Prescription Drugs

Number of Top 10 Prescriptions Dispensed, 1995-2001

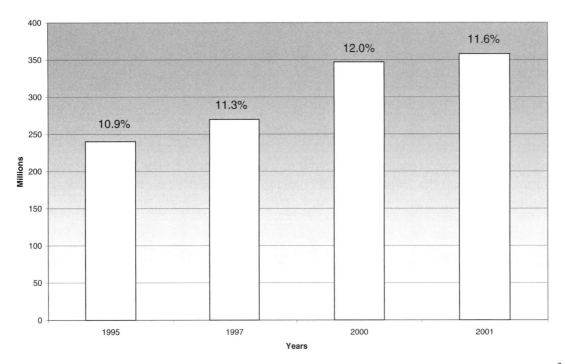

In 2001, 3.1 billion prescriptions were dispensed, up from 1.9 billion a decade earlier.[2] The graphic shows the number of prescriptions dispensed for the top 10 drugs and the percentage that that number represents in terms of all prescriptions dispensed in that year. In 2001, 11.6% of all the prescriptions dispensed were for the top 10 most dispensed drugs. What drugs were dispensed the most? The table beginning on the next page shows the top 10 prescriptions for the years 1995 and 2000. Following the table is a discussion about some of the more noteworthy (and in some cases newsworthy) drugs on the list.

In 1995, Trimox and Amoxil represented 12-14% of all prescribed drugs despite objections to their widespread use, "well demonstrated" lack of effectiveness, and concerns about antibiotic resistance.[3] In 2000, not one drug in the top 10 was an antibiotic, suggesting that antibiotic use (or overuse) was down considerably.

---

[2] Some estimate that the number of prescriptions written will increase to 4 billion by 2004. Source: *Psychiatric Times*. Full citation in source note.

[3] Source: "The Top 10." Retrieved July 16, 2002 from http://www.chiroweb.com/archives/15/04/24.html. For more information about antibiotic drug resistance see the chapter entitled "The Environment" in the current volume.

Top 10 Prescription Drugs, 1995 and 2000

Rank	1995		2000	
	Drug name	Use	Drug name	Use
1	Premarin	Estrogen replacement	Lipitor	Lowers cholesterol
2	Trimox	Antibiotic	Premarin	Estrogen replacement
3	Synthroid	Thyroid hormone replacement	Synthroid	Thyroid hormone replacement
4	Amoxil	Antibiotic	Hydrocodone/APAP	Analgesic
5	Zantac	Acid reflux, ulcers	Prilosec	Acid reflux, ulcers
6	Lanoxin	Digitalis preparation	Norvasc	Antihyperintensive
7	Procardia XL	Antihypertensive	Albuterol	Bronchodilator[4]
8	Vasotec	Antihypertensive	Glucophage	Diabetes medication
9	Prozac	Antidepressant	Claritin	Antihistimine
10	Proventil-Aerosol[5]	Bronchodilator	Zoloft	Antidepressant

Lipitor blocks an enzyme in the liver that the body uses to make cholesterol. As a result, the medication begins to work almost immediately. Doctors feel that this immediate positive feedback leads more people to continue taking the medication. The reason for Lipitor's popularity may have as much to do with advertising and increasing consumer awareness of the health benefits of lowered cholesterol as with the drug's effectiveness. In May 2001, the National Cholesterol Education Program (a division of the National Institutes of Health) lowered the total cholesterol level at which drug therapy is recommended. Because of this, Pfizer, the maker of the drug, estimates that the number of patients eligible to take their drug more than tripled. And Pfizer is capitalizing on this. Pfizer has 5,000 sales representatives who promote this drug to doctors. From 1999 to October 2001, Pfizer spent close to $150 million to market this drug to consumers, not only by promoting Lipitor outright but also by educating the consumer about the importance of early diagnosis and treatment for high cholesterol. According to Pfizer's estimates, less than one-third of those who could benefit from cholesterol-lowering drug therapy are actually being treated.[6]

Prilosec replaced Zantac as the medication of choice to treat Gastroesophageal Reflux Disease (GERD) and peptic ulcer disease. Prilosec, according to doctors at Robert Wood Johnson Medical School (RWJMS) in New Jersey, represented a considerable improvement in the treatment of these diseases. It's also considered the most effective drug in its class. But marketing must have played a role in its success as well. Spending on direct-to-consumer marketing more than doubled from 1997 to 2000 ($41.9 million to $107.9 million).

Premarin and Synthroid maintained their status as two of the top 3 prescription drugs. Premarin has been around since 1942. Doctors tend to feel comfortable with its effectiveness. It gained popularity among women in the 1960s who no longer wanted to endure menopausal symptoms. In the 1970s-90s, research showed that hormone replacement

[4] Rescue inhaler for asthmatics.

[5] The active ingredient is Albuterol.

[6] According to Pfizer, 52 million Americans are in need of cholesterol-lowering drug therapy. More information about drug advertising will appear in later panels.

therapy (HRT) prevents osteoporosis, cardiovascular disease, and Alzheimer's disease, and lowers the risk of uterine and cervical cancers. Other positive effects were also observed. As a result, the popularity of the drug continued to rise, coinciding with the aging of the Baby-Boomers (5.1 million women become eligible for HRT each year). However, on July 17, 2002, results of long term studies of women on HRT were published in the *Journal of the American Medical Association*. Researchers found that women on HRT showed increases in breast cancer, heart disease, stroke, blood clots, and ovarian cancer. How this will impact on the drug's prescriptions is yet to be seen. Will more women shun prescription therapies in favor of lifestyle changes and alternative medications? Or will women feel that the benefits of HRT outweigh the risks?

Synthroid's appearance as number three on the list may be surprising, since hyperthyroidism is not very common. This disease is characterized by fatigue, weight gain, hair loss, and sensitivity to cold. Without the proper amount of thyroid hormones, the heart, liver, and kidneys don't work properly. Synthroid is also used in the management of some types of thyroid cancer. According to Marvin Kirschner, chief of endocrinology at the University of Medicine and Dentistry of New Jersey, the reasons for Synthroid's popularity are (1) brand recognition by physicians and (2) the overprescribing of this drug as an obesity treatment. Dr. Kirschner states that Synthroid has been proven as an ineffective treatment for weight loss, but millions of Americans still use that drug for that purpose. Initially, there is a temporary weight loss, but instead of getting rid of extra fat tissue, muscle and bone tissue and lean body mass break down. According to Dr. Kirshner, "overweight patients tell their physicians, 'I don't know why I'm so heavy, I must have a glandular problem.' In response to these pleas, the physician prescribes Synthroid." (Iozzia).

In 2001, the total number of prescriptions dispensed per capita in the United States equaled 10.9 (28 states exceeded this rate). This was up from 9.9 prescriptions per head a year earlier. What is behind the rise in the number of prescriptions dispensed? Part of the rise may be due to the aging of the population. But how much of the rise in prescriptions dispensed is needed and how much is not? Next, we will look at the issue of the overuse of medications in our society.

Sources: IMS Health. "US Top 10 Products by Prescriptions" and "Leading 10 Products by Total U.S. Dispensed Prescriptions, 2001." Retrieved July 16, 2002 from http://www.imshealth.com. Alan Cook, DC. "The Top 10" and "The Top 10 Drugs -- 1997." Retrieved July 16, 2002 from http://www.chiroweb.com/archives. Barbara Iozzia. "Top 10 Prescription Drugs in the U.S." *HealthState*, Winter/Spring 2001. Retrieved July 17, 2002 from http://www.undnj.edu/umcweb/hstate/winter_spring01/features/feature01_drugs.htm. National Institute for Health Care Management. *Prescription Drug Expenditures in 2001: Another Year of Escalating Costs*, May 6, 2002. Retrieved July 17, 2002 from http://www.nihcm.org. Frank Scussa. "On its way to $10 billion: LIPITOR." Retrieved July 17, 2002 from http://www.medadnews.com/pharma_month/flash/ 3011.asp. "Increased Risk of Ovarian Cancer Is Linked to Estrogen Replacement Therapy." *ScienceDaily Magazine*, July 17, 2002. Retrieved July 17, 2002 from http://www.sciencedaily.com. Richard Frank, et. al. The Henry J. Kaiser Family Foundation. *Trends in Direct-to-Consumer Advertising of Prescription Drugs*, February 2002. The Henry J. Kaiser Family Foundation. *State Health Facts Online*. Retrieved July 17, 2002 from http://www.state health-facts.kff.org/. Per capita data for 2000 extrapolated using population data from the U.S. Census Bureau. Retrieved July 17, 2002 from http://www.census.gov. Michael Montagne. "Patient Drug Information from Mass Media Sources." *Psychiatric Times*, May 2002. Retrieved July 18, 2002 from http://www.psychiatrictimes.com/massme-dia.html

Treatments for Depressive (and Other?) Disorders

Depressive Disorders and Their Treatment, 2000-2001

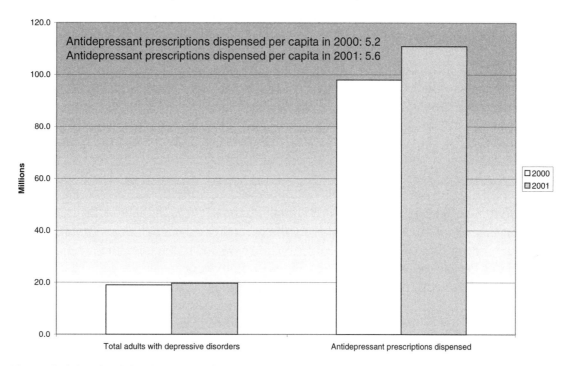

About 9.5% of adults in the United States suffer from depressive disorders in a given year. In 2001, this equaled 19.7 million people.[7] The graphic shows the estimated number of adults who suffer from depressive disorders and the number of prescriptions dispensed to treat their condition. The per capita numbers at the top of the table are based on the total number of people who have these disorders. In 2001, an average of 5.6 prescriptions (Prozac, Zoloft, etc.) were dispensed for each person who suffers from these disorders, up from the year before.

An increase in the number of people taking antidepressants continued a trend seen since the late 1980's. In 1987, Prozac was approved for the treatment of depression. The medication was found to be more effective than previously prescribed medications. It also had fewer side effects. "Patients reported feeling 'better than well.' It not only eased their depression, but seemed to give them a new look at themselves."[8] Within two years, 65,000 Prozac prescriptions a month were being filled. In 1987, 37% of depressive disorder patients were treated with antidepressants. By 1997, 75% of patients were taking antidepressants. During this time period, the percentage of patients receiving psychotherapy, however, went down (from 71% in 1987 to 60% in 1997). Are more doctors looking for the "quick fix" when it comes to depressive disorders? Are more patients?

---

[7] Based on a July 2001 U.S. Census Bureau population estimate of 207,197,000 for those 18 and over.

[8] Source: "Antidepressant Prozac introduced 1987." Retrieved July 18, 2002 from http://www.pbs.org.

"The imagery and symbolism in advertising and mass media sometimes suggest to patients that a specific medication promises to solve health and life problems in magical ways" (Montagne). From 1997 to 1998, Eli Lilly and Co., makers of Prozac, the most prescribed antidepressant, spent over $60 million in direct-to-consumer advertising for the drug. In 2000, the makers of Paxil, another antidepressant, spent over $92 million dollars to tout its benefits.

One antidepressive medication is also being marketed to those who do not have depressive disorders. In a controversial move, Eli Lilly started advertising a "new" medication for premenstrual dysphoric disorder (PMDD) in 2000. The ad campaign for Sarafem ("the first and only prescription medication for PMDD", according to the ads) claimed that the medication helps women who suffer from severe discomfort, mood swings, and tension every month.

Sales of the drug soared as 202,000 prescriptions were written from July 2000 to January 2001. Sarafem, however, was not new. It contained the same ingredient as Prozac. Critics claim that this was just a marketing ploy by the company to extend the profitability of its most popular drug[9]. Laura Miller, an Eli Lilly spokeswoman, defended the creation of the new brand of Prozac saying: "We asked women and physicians, and they told us that they wanted a treatment with its own identity. Women do not look at their symptoms as a depression, and PMDD is not depression but a separate clinical identity. Prozac is one of the more famous pharmaceutical trademarks and is closely associated with depression" (Vedantam). But, in 2002, second quarter sales for all brands of fluoxetine hydrochloride (two of which are Sarafem and Prozac) were down 72% from the second quarter of 2001. Eli Lilly blames the drop in sales on competition from generic forms of the drug. The importance of a "treatment with its own identity" may have been overstated.

And PMDD: Is it a real disorder? In the 1980s, the American Psychiatric Association (APA) considered listing PMDD as an official condition in its *Diagnostic and Statistical Manual of Mental Disorders*. Backlash from women's groups (fearing women's competence may be questioned in the workplace and in court rulings) led the APA to leave PMDD out of the *Manual*. "When men get mood shifts, no one says let's call it mental illness," said Paula Caplan, a PMDD critic who wrote the book *They Say You're Crazy*. But, many doctors argued that PMDD is a serious problem that interferes with women's lives. The disorder was put in the appendix of the APA *Manual* when the FDA approved Prozac to treat the condition. However, the debate still goes on. Speaking about the difficulty of distinguishing between PMDD and PMS[10], Nada Stotland, a psychiatrist at Rush Medical College in Chicago said: "Unlike any other kind of psychiatric condition, most women believe they have PMS, and most people believe women have PMS. We now

---

[9] In 2000, sales of Prozac grossed $2.6 billion.

[10] PMS: premenstrual syndrome, a milder form of PMDD. An interesting note: Eli Lilly's fact sheet for Sarafem states that it's "to treat the symptoms of premenstrual dysphoric disorder (PMDD)." However, some pharmacy web sites state that this drug may be used "to treat PMS."

have a psychiatric disorder with [symptoms] that people believe all women have" (Vedantam).

Does this mean that more people will be taking this mood-altering drug?[11] What about side effects? Besides the usual headache, drowsiness, and fatigue that almost any medication has a possibility of causing, more than 200 lawsuits have been filed against Eli Lilly claiming that Prozac (or Sarafem, or fluoxetine hydrochloride) causes suicide and violence. Most cases have been settled out of court, but in one case that went to court in 2000, the president of Eli Lilly's neuroscience product group testified under oath that there was no correlation between Prozac and suicidal thoughts and violence. The jury ruled in Eli Lilly's favor. Later that year, Eli Lilly decided to stop development of a new, improved version of Prozac. The patent for this new, improved version claimed that "it would reduce the 'usual adverse effects' of the original Prozac, including 'suicidal thoughts, self mutilation, [and] manic behavior'" (Huffington). When this was made public, a lawsuit was filed against the company charging fraud in the court case mentioned above.

All this did not slow sales for antidepressant drugs overall. The number of antidepressant prescriptions dispensed increased by 13.2% from 2000-2001, while the number of people diagnosed with depressive disorders increased by only 3.7%, suggesting that more people were being treated for other disorders with these drugs.

Ritalin has been controversial in recent years. It's used for the treatment of Attention Deficit Hyperactivity Disorder (ADHD). However, some have claimed that doctors are prescribing this drug to children who do not have ADHD. The next panel will discuss this issue in more depth.

Sources: Chart data: IMS Health. *National Disease and Theraputic Index, 2002* and *National Prescription Audit Plus,* 2002. Retrieved July 18, 2002 from http://www.imshealth.org. Number of adults with depressive disorders extrapolated based on a figure of 9.5% of the population suffers from depressive disorders. Population data: "Projections of the Total Resident Population by 5-Year Age Groups, and Sex with Special Age Categories: Middle Series, 1999 to 2000." and "Projections of the Total Resident Population by 5-Year Age Groups, and Sex with Special Age Categories: Middle Series, 2001 to 2005. Retrieved from U.S. Census Bureau website at http://www.census.gov. Panel data: Richard Frank, et. al. The Henry J. Kaiser Family Foundataion. *Trends in Direct-to-Consumer Advertising of Prescription Drugs,* February 2002. Michael Montagne. "Patient Drug Information From Mass Media Sources." *Psychiatric Times,* May 2002. Retrieved July 18, 2002 from http://www.psychiatrictimes.com/massmedia.html. National Institute of Mental Health. "The Numbers Count: Mental Disorders in America." NIMH Publication No. 01-4584, January 2001. Retrieved July 18, 2002 from http://www.nimh.nih.gov/publicat/numbers.cfm. Nancy Schute. "Tripling Treatment." *U.S. News & World Report,* January 21, 2002. Retrieved July 18, 2002 from http://www.usnews.com/. Shankar Vedantam. "Renamed Prozac Fuels Women's Health Debate." *Washington Post,* April 29, 2001. Retrieved July 18, 2002 from http://www.washingtonpost.com. "FDA Panel Recommends Fluoxetine for PMDD." *Psychiatric News,* December 3, 1999. Retrieved July 19, 2002 from http://www.psych.org/pnews/99-12-03/pmdd.htm. Arianna Huffington. "Prozac: Unsafe At Any Price." *Arianna Online,* October 23, 2000. Retrieved July 19, 2002 from http://www.ariannaonline.com/columns/files/102300.html. Eli Lilly & Co. "Information for the Patient: Sarafem™." Retrieved July 18. 2002 from http://pi.lilly.com/us/sarafem.ppi.pdf. Pharmacy information retrieved from http://www.walgreens.com and http://www.drugstore.com. "Lilly Announces Second-Quarter Earnings Per Share of $.61." *Lilly Newsroom,* July 18, 2002. Retrieved July 19, 2002 from http://newsroom.lilly.com/news/.

---

[11] In June 1995 the *New England Journal of Medicine* estimated that PMDD affects 3-8% of women of childbearing age. In 2000, this equaled 1.8-4.8 million women. Prozac is in a class of medications called SSRIs. This stands for selective serotonin reuptake inhibitors. These medications alter the serotonin levels in the brain. This brain chemical affects a person's mood and emotions.

Sedating Our Children

Children with ADHD and Children Taking Ritalin, 1975-2000

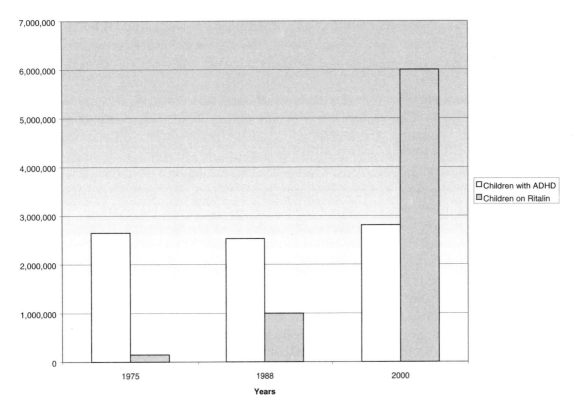

The National Institute of Mental Health (NIMH) estimates that attention deficit hyperactivity disorder (ADHD)[12] affects 3-5% of children under 18 years of age.[13] In 2000, this was between 2.1 and 3.5 million children. The chart shows the estimated number of children who have ADHD and the number of children presumed to be taking Ritalin, the most popular medication prescribed for this disorder. Why were there nearly three times as many children taking this drug in 2000 as the estimated cases of ADHD?

A 1998 study by researchers Adrian Angold and E. Jane Costello found that the majority of children and adolescents who take Ritalin (and other stimulants) for ADHD do not fully meet the criteria for ADHD. The increases in the use of these medications coincided with a three-fold increase in the number of children 4-15 years old diagnosed with emotional or behavioral problems: from 6.8% in 1979 to 18.7% in 1996. Diagnoses for attention problems increased from 32% of all children diagnosed with emotional or behavioral

---

[12] For more information on ADHD and Ritalin use see the chapters entitled "Diseases" in this volume and "Special Needs and Issues" in the *Community and Education* volume.

[13] Different sources cite different numbers. Unfortunately, no one knows the exact number of children taking Ritalin. The chart estimates for the number of children with ADHD are based on 4% of the population 0-17 years old.

problems to 78% in this same time period. Daniel Safer, adjunct associate professor of pediatrics and psychiatry at Johns Hopkins Medical Institutions stated in a Maryland Department of Education report on ADHD: "You don't have to be ADHD to be on stimulants. Other kids may benefit from stimulants, which are quite safe." (Dunne). An interesting comment considering methylphenidate, the stimulant in Ritalin, is classified as a Schedule II[14] drug by the U.S. Drug Enforcement Agency (the same classification as amphetamines). Safer goes on to explain that the increase in children taking Ritalin is due to the expanded criteria of symptoms for ADHD and better awareness of those symptoms by doctors. And by schools. The American Psychiatric Association published a checklist of symptoms characteristic of those with ADHD. The problem: the symptoms are vague and are common in normal children also. Yet many schools rely on this checklist to identify children with ADHD.

Critics claim that schools avoid providing special services to students who may need them by insisting that the children be placed on Ritalin. Studies show that regardless of their intelligence, 12-60% of children with ADHD also have a learning disorder. David Gaffney, a social worker who specializes in ADHD treatment in Saginaw, Michigan, states: "Treating the child's ADHD with medication often does not change the underlying learning disabilities. It just makes the child less likely to be a behavior problem while he fails to learn." In 2000, a parent of a 5-year old Michigan kindergartner was encouraged by the school to place her child on Ritalin. Her doctor, however, determined that the child did not have ADHD and did not need medication. The parent was then fearful that her child would not be passed on to the next grade unless her son was put on the medication. A Federal subcommittee heard many parents of 5-7 year olds testify to similar stories in a congressional hearing on Ritalin in 2000. Some school districts warned parents that their children would be expelled if they were not put on the drug.

This case also points to another problem: the overmedication of children under 6 years old. Ritalin is not approved for children under 6 years old and yet a study published in the *Journal of the American Medical Association* found that the use of Ritalin with 2 to 4-year olds increased 150% from 1991 to 1995.[15] Are we now able to "cure" the "terrible twos"? Do we really want to?

Some have linked the rise in the number of diagnosed ADHD cases to children's sedentary lifestyles and the modern classroom environment. Perhaps, many of these children just need to get outside and play to expend some of their natural energy? This was the

---

[14] A drug is classified as Schedule II by the DEA when it has the potential for abuse. In recent years, there have been reports of methylphenidate abuse, mostly among middle and high school students in many large cities. Those with ADHD, however, do not become addicted to the drug if it is taken properly.

[15] Ritalin isn't the only mood-altering drug physicians are prescribing to preschoolers. In 1997, 40,000 children below the age of 6 were taking the antidepressants Prozac, Zoloft, and Paxil. This is a 400% increase from the year before. Source: IMS Health. None of these drugs have FDA approval for use with children and only 8% of physicians reported that they had adequate training in treating children with depression. 57% said that they prescribed an antidepressant for a diagnosis other than depression in patients younger than 18. Source: "SSRI Use Common in Children." *JAMA,* May 16, 1999.

theory in the 1950s, according to Patti Johnson, a Colorado State Board of Education member in 1999. Elementary school students had a short morning recess, a recess after lunch, and an afternoon recess. The theory was that children naturally have short attention spans and lots of energy. Children needed a break from time to time in order to concentrate better on academics. (How many adults can sit through a grueling 8-hour workday without so much as a 15-minute break to chat with a co-worker? Should we expect our children to do the equivalent?) In the wake of the report *A Nation At Risk*[16], high-stakes standardized testing became the norm. Reading, writing, and math were emphasized and music, art, gym, and recess were gradually being cut back or eliminated. Kindergartners were expected to learn to read.

Is Ritalin a useful drug? Yes. Despite being a stimulant, this drug has the opposite effect on those with ADHD. A child's hyperactivity is calmed and his ability to concentrate is increased. A study published in *Experimental and Clinical Psychopharmacology* in 2001, found that adolescents with ADHD who took Ritalin improved their test scores by an average of 17%, which is equal to two or three letter grades. However, researchers cautioned that Ritalin wasn't the only factor in the jump in test scores. William E. Pelham, Jr., a psychology professor at the State University of New York, stated that students in the study were placed in "a highly structured, well-run classroom, and they had been taught how to take notes and become better organized. The message is that schools need to do both" (Viadero). A study published in the December 1999 issue of *Archives of General Psychology* found that academic and social skills only improved in ADHD patients when combined with behavioral treatment in the home and school. Unfortunately, in 2000, one national HMO no longer approved psychotherapy for ADHD. Medication was declared the "treatment of choice."[17] Are schools, doctors, and insurance companies really doing what is in the best interest of our children?

Sources: National Council for Community Behavioral Healthcare. National Mental Health Association. "Key Facts and Statistics." Retrieved July 18, 2002 from http://www.nmha.org/children/green/facts.cfm; Leonard Sax. "Ritalin: Better Living Through Chemistry?" *The World and I Online,* November 2000. Retrieved July 22, 2002 from http://www.worldandi.com/public/2000/November/sax.html. "Michigan ranks third in U.S. Ritalin use." *Michigan Education Report,* Winter 2001. Retrieved July 22, 2002 from http://www.educationreport.org. "Preschoolers in the Prozac Nursery." Retrieved July 22, 2002 from http://www.healthatoz.com/atoz/healthupdate/alert03252000.html. Chiropractic Wellness Center of Macomb. "Treatment of U.S. Children With Antidepressants Becoming More Common." Retrieved July 22, 2002 from http://www.wellnesschiro.com/children_and_antidepressants.htm. "SSRI Use Common in Children." *JAMA,* May 26, 1999. Debra Viadero. "Study Points to Academic Benefits For Adolescents Taking Ritalin." *Education Week,* June 6, 2001. Retrieved July 22, 2002 from http://www.edweek.org. Diane Weaver Dunne. "Statistics Confirm Rise in Childhood ADHD and Medication Use." *Education World,* December 12, 2000. Retrieved July 19, 2002 from http://www.education-world.com/a_issues/issues148a.shtml. National Institute on Drug Abuse. National Institutes of Health. U.S. Department of Health and Human Services. "Methylphenidate (Ritalin)." *NIDA InfoFacts.* Retrieved July 22, 2002 from http://www.nida.nih.gov/Infofax/ritalin.html. Patti Johnson. Independence Institute. "Too Much Ritalin," October 20, 1999. Retrieved July 18, 2002 from http://i2i.org/Publications/Op-Eds/HealthCare/ritalin.htm.

---

[16] A report published in 1983 that outlined the problems with the United States educational system and proposed solutions to these problems.

[17] The HMO was unnamed in the source: "a major national HMO operating in Michigan." Source: "Michigan ranks third in U.S. Ritalin Use." *Michigan Education Report,* Winter 2001.

Researching the Rise in Prescription Drug Prices

Average Retail Prescription Prices in Constant 2001 Dollars, 1990-2001

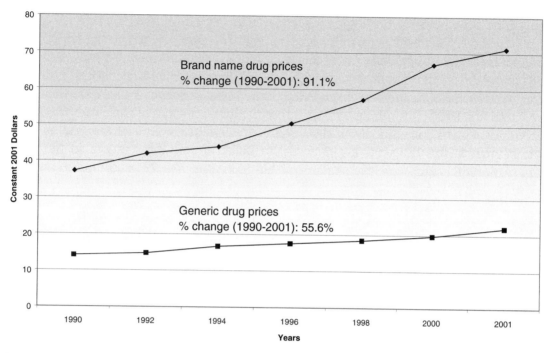

The graph charts the rise in prescription prices from 1990 to 2001. The prices of both generic and brand name drugs went up, but brand name prices rose at nearly twice the rate of generics. According to the Pharmaceutical Research and Manufacturers of America (PhRMA), the cost of research and development (R&D) is one cause for the increase in brand name drug prices. Researchers at Tufts University Center for the Study of Drug Development found the average cost of bringing a new drug to market in 2001 was $802 million. Adjusting for inflation, that's a 166% increase from 1991, and a 469% increase from 1979. (A Public Citizen study, however, found that the average cost in 2001 was only $240 million.)

Why did R&D costs rise so much? The average number of clinical trials more than doubled from 1977-1994 (from 30 to 68) and the average number of patients per clinical trial nearly tripled (from 1,576 in 1977 to 4,237 in 1994). Every new drug goes through 7 stages of development. Discovery of substances that may be effective in treating illnesses usually takes about 2-10 years. Typically 5,000-10,000 drugs then go through laboratory and animal testing. About 250 of these drugs reach the Phase I clinical trial stage. Phase I testing involves about 20-80 healthy volunteers. At this stage safety and dosage is determined. Only about 5 drugs reach Phase II trials. These involve 100-300 volunteers for about 2 years. At this stage researchers determine efficacy and side-effects. Phase III trials usually last about 4-5 years. Adverse reactions and long-term side-effects are studied in about 1,000-5,000 patients. If a drug passes Phase III it goes through U.S. Food and Drug Administration (FDA) review for about 2 years and, if found safe and effective, the drug is approved for sale. The process doesn't stop when the drug is distributed to consumers. Post-consumer testing is a part of drug development also. That usually lasts about 2 years. Each of these stages incurs expenses that are then passed along to the consumer.

The passage of the Drug Price Competition and Patent Term Restoration Act of 1984 increased the time between FDA approval and patent expiration. But, significantly, it also decreased the time between patent expiration and the approval of generic copies of the branded drugs. Drug companies now had less than 12 years to recoup their R&D and to build reserves for future drug development.[18] And drug companies are doing just that, in some cases. Lipitor, a cholesterol-reducing drug, was introduced in 1997. Sales from 2000-2001 totaled $11.5 billion, over 14 times the amount spent on R&D for a new drug in 2001 (or 48 times the amount, if the Public Citizen study was accurate). According to some estimates, this drug has the potential to make double that amount in the next 3 years. A month's supply of Lipitor ranges from $59.86 to $93.92 according to dosage.[19] This leads one to wonder about the continued need for such high prices on this drug.

Admittedly, not all drugs sales are as successful as Lipitor. A 1994 study by economists at Duke University revealed that only 3 out of 10 drugs introduced from 1980 to 1984 had returns higher than their average after-tax R&D costs. But, the study was done before 1997 when the regulations dealing with drug advertisement were relaxed. Since then, prescription drug sales have nearly doubled in the United States, from $78.9 billion in 1997 to $154.5 billion in 2001. The number of prescriptions filled, however, rose only 29.2%. Are drug companies pushing more people towards the newer, more expensive drugs? We'll look at the issue of drug advertising in the next panel.

Sources: Levitt, Larry. The Henry J. Kaiser Family Foundation. *Prescription Drug Trends,* February 2001. Retrieved July 24, 2002 from http://www.kff.org. "The Inflation Calculator." Retrieved July 24, 2002 from http://www.westegg.com/inflation. National Association of Chain Drug Stores. "Industry Statistics." Retrieved August 1, 2002 from http://www.nacds.org. Pharmaceutical Research and Manufacturers of America. *Pharmaceutical Industry Profile 2000.* Retrieved July 24, 2002 from http://www.pharma.org. "On its way to $10 billion: LIPITOR." *PharmaBusiness.com.* Retrieved July 17, 2002 from http://www.medadnews.com/pharma_month/flash/3011.asp. "Global Pharmaceutical Sales by Region, 2001." Retrieved July 18, 2002 from http://www.imshealth.org. Tufts Center for the Study of Drug Development. *Outlook 2002.* Retrieved July 25, 2002 from http://csdd.tufts.edu/InfoServices/OutlookPDFs/Outlook2002.pdf. National Institute for Health Care Management. *Prescription Drug Expenditures in 2001: Another Year of Escalating Costs,* May 6, 2002. Retrieved July 17, 2002 from http://www.nihcm.org. Department of Health and Human Services. *Report to the President: Prescription Drug Coverage, Spending, Utilization, and Prices,* April 2000. Retrieved July 25, 2002 from http://www.aspe.os.dhhs.gov/health/reports/drugstudy. National Center for Policy Analysis. "Costs to Develop New Drugs Soar." *Daily Policy Digest,* December 3, 2001. Retrieved July 24, 2002 from http://www.ncpa.org/iss/hea/pd120301b.html. Kris Hundley. "Trials and transformation." *The St. Petersburg Times,* April 8, 2002. Center for Drug Evaluation and Research. U.S. Food and Drug Administration. "Generic Drugs: Questions and Answers." Retrieved July 26, 2002 from http://www.fda.gov.

---

[18] Competition from generics may only hurt 50% of the brand name comparable sales. According to the FDA, 50% of the generic drugs are manufactured by brand-name firms. "They frequently make copies of their own or other brand-name drugs but sell them without the brand name." Source: Center for Drug Evaluation and Research.

[19] Data retrieved July 25, 2002 from http://www.drugstore.com.

Prescription Drug Advertising

Prescription Drug Advertising Expenditures, 1996-2000

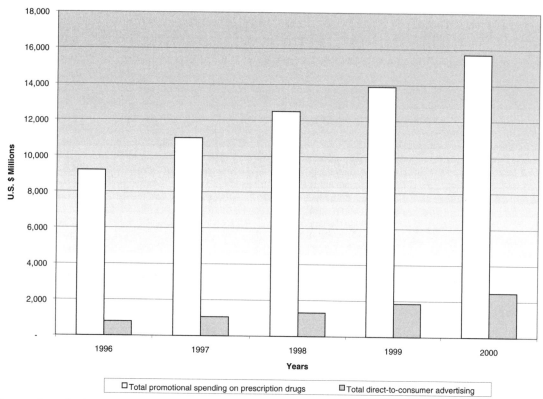

☐ Total promotional spending on prescription drugs ☐ Total direct-to-consumer advertising

If you thumb through nearly any magazine, browse the daily newspaper, or relax in front of the TV you are bound to run across an ad for the latest prescription drug to battle everything from allergies to high cholesterol to depression. As the graphic shows, both overall prescription drug promotion and direct-to-consumer advertising[20] expenditures increased during this time period: 70.7% and 211.9%, respectively. The drug industry's marketing staff increased just as dramatically. In 1996, there were a total of 60,539 marketing professionals working in the drug industry. By 2000, this number rose to 87,810.

In 1993, 39% of us said that we had seen at least one prescription drug ad. By 2000, 91% of us said this. This may have something to do with the newly found popularity of television advertising. In 1994, a mere $36 million (13.5% of all direct-to-consumer advertising) was spent on TV ads. By 2000, spending for this type of advertising reached nearly $1.6 billion, or 63.6% of all direct-to-consumer advertising.

---

[20] Overall promotion includes free samples and other promotional efforts aimed at medical professionals and direct-to-consumer advertising. Direct-to-consumer advertising involves newspaper, magazine, radio and television advertising.

But, is this an outrageous amount? Some critics of the drug industry point to the 4,258% increase in overall advertising expenditures from 1994 to 2000 as one of the reasons for rising prescription drug prices. But, is the amount spent on prescription drug advertising outrageous? The next table compares the amount spent on advertising for some prescription drugs with the amount spent on advertising other products. The number in parentheses represents the ranking of the drug in terms of direct-to-consumer advertising expenditures. The advertising budget allocated to promote a single drug in many cases exceeds the total ad budget for an entire large company.

Amount of Advertising Expenditures on Prescription Drugs vs.

The Advertising Budgets of Companies in Other Industries, 2000

Product	$ million
Vioxx (1) ad budget	**160**
Dell Computer's ad budget for its top brands	160
Budweiser's total ad budget	146
PepsiCo's ad budget for Pepsi	125
Zocor (5) ad budget	**91**
Nike's total ad budget	78
Meridia (10) ad budget	**65**
Campbell's total ad budget	58

But, does a high advertising budget translate into higher prices for the drug? If we look at two anti-inflammatory drugs, Vioxx and Celebrex, there does seem to be a connection. A month's supply of Vioxx at its lowest dosage ranges from $73.29 to $80.99. Celebrex ranges from $42.48 to $47.79 for a month's supply of its lowest dosage tablets.[21] The amount spent on direct-to-consumer advertising in 2000 for Celebrex was $78.8 million, $82 million less than Vioxx. A comparison of prices and advertising budgets of the leading prescription antihistamines, Claritin and Allegra, yields the same results. Whether this is true for all advertised prescription drugs and their counterparts requires further study, however — there are nearly 9,600 prescription drugs on the market.

But, does most of the money spent on prescription drugs go towards advertising? Or does more of it go for research and development? The next panel will examine just where our money goes when we buy a prescription drug.

Sources: National Institute for Health Care Management. *Prescription Drug Expenditures in 2001: Another Year of Escalating Costs*, May 6, 2002. Retrieved July 17, 2002 from http://www.nihcm.org. National Institute For Health Care Management. *Prescription Drugs and Mass Media Advertising, 2000*, November 2001. Retrieved July 26, 2002 from http://www.nihcm.org. Larry Levitt. The Henry J. Kaiser Family Foundation. *Prescription Drug Trends*, November 2001. Alan Sager and Deborah Socolar. Boston University School of Public Health. "Drug Industry Marketing Staff Soars While Research Staff Stagnates." *Drug Data Brief*, December 6, 2001. Retrieved July 29, 2002 from http://rxpolicy.com/studies/bu-rypromotion-v-randd.pdf. Prescription prices retrieved July 29, 2002 from http://www.drugstore.com, http://www.cvs.com, and http://www.eckerd.com.

---

[21] All prescription prices obtained July 29, 2002 from http://www.cvs.com, http://www.eckerd.com, and http:://www.drugstore.com.

Where is Our $71.18 Going?

U.S. Retail Prescription Drug Sales and Monies Allocated by Percentage of Retail Sales, 1996-2001

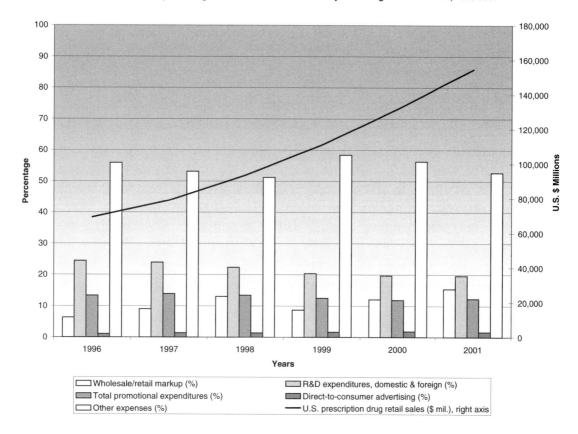

Legend:
- Wholesale/retail markup (%)
- Total promotional expenditures (%)
- Other expenses (%)
- R&D expenditures, domestic & foreign (%)
- Direct-to-consumer advertising (%)
- U.S. prescription drug retail sales ($ mil.), right axis

In 2001, the average brand name prescription drug price was $71.18.[22] In that same year U.S. consumers spent $154.5 billion on prescription drugs, up from $69.1 billion in 1996.[23] Where is our money going? The chart above tracks the percentage of money drug companies spent on research & development (R&D), promotional efforts, and other expenses. It also tracks the percentage of money that went into wholesale and retail markup.[24] The table on the next page shows the dollar amount allocated in each category. Total pharmaceutical company expenditures include all monies allocated for R&D, total promotional expenses, and other expenses. This is equal to PhRMA's figures for domes-

---

[22] The average generic prescription drug price in 2001 was $21.96.

[23] Not all of this increase can be attributed to higher prescription prices. According to the Barents Group analysis of Scott-Levin Source Prescription Audit Data for 1993-1998, 64% of the increase in prescription drug spending is due to increase in prices and 36% is due to increased utilization of prescription drugs. The Barents Group, a part of KPMG Consulting, provides financial and economic advisory services. Scott-Levin, Inc. is a research firm specializing in pharmaceutical marketplace data.

[24] Wholesale and retail markup was extrapolated from domestic sales figures, reported by the Pharmaceutical Research and Manufacturers of America, and U.S. retail spending figures, reported by the National Institute for Health Care Management. See source notes for complete citations.

tic sales reported in their *Industry Profile 2002*. Total promotional spending includes direct-to-consumer advertising and professional promotion (free samples to doctors, for example). Data are in millions of U.S. dollars.

Prescription Drug Monies Allocated by Category, 1996-2000

	1996	1997	1998	1999	2000	2001
U.S. retail sales	$69,100	$78,900	$93,400	$111,100	$131,900	$154,500
Wholesale/retail markup	4,359	7,138	12,111	9,638	16,018	23,826
Total pharmaceutical company expenditures	64,741	71,762	81,289	101,462	115,882	130,674
Total R&D expenditures	16,906	18,958	20,967	22,691	26,031	30,343
Total promotional expenditures	9,200	11,000	12,500	13,900	15,700	19,059
Direct-to-consumer advertising	791	1,069	1,317	1,848	2,467	2,679
Other expenditures	48,044	53,886	59,838	73,168	89,753	102,262

Only about 20% of total prescription drug revenues went toward expenditures for R&D over this time period. And, the percentage allocated for R&D has been decreasing: from 24.5% in 1996 to 19.6% in 2001. Total promotional expenses accounted for about 12-13% of drug revenues during this time period, and this share dropped from 1997 to 2000. In 2001, the percentage went up slightly. Direct-to-consumer advertising, a part of the total promotional package, rose from 1996 to 2000 (from 1.1% to 1.9% of retail sales), but then declined by 0.2% in 2001. The percentage of revenues allocated for wholesale and retail markup fluctuated: rising from 1996 to 1998, then dropping in 1999, and again rising from 1999 to 2001.

By far, the biggest share of the prescription drug cost goes into the "other" category. Presented here are a few of the expenses in this category.

Cost of operation. According to the Internal Revenue Service (IRS), in 1998 (the latest year for which tax information was available), pharmaceutical (and medical) manufacturing companies claimed that the *cost of goods sold* equaled $87.2 billion. This was 46% of their total business receipts.

Another cost of operation is *employee (and employer) salaries*. In 2000, 315,000 people were employed in the pharmaceutical industry. The total number of employees is expected to increase by 23.8% from 2000 to 2010. The average weekly salary in 2000 for workers in the pharmaceutical industry was $766 compared to $597 for employees in other manufacturing industries. What about executives? In 2001, the average salary including bonuses was $631,000. But that doesn't mean that some CEOs aren't making more. The top paid executives in nine pharmaceutical companies[25] averaged $20.9 million in compensation and $47.9 million in unexercised stock options.

Taxes. We all have to pay them. But are we all paying our fair share? The Congressional Research Service report *Federal Taxation of the Drug Industry from 1990 to 1996* stated that the average tax rate for the drug industry from 1993 to 1996 was 16.2%, compared to an average 22.6% for all manufacturing industries, and 27.3%

---

[25] Merck & Co., Inc., Pfizer, Inc., Bristol-Myers Squibb Company, Abbott Laboratories, Wyeth, Pharmacia Corporation, Eli Lilly & Co., Schering-Plough Corporation, and Allergan, Inc.

for all industries. In 1998, this still held true: the pharmaceutical (and medical) manufacturing industry had an average tax rate of 19%, compared to 21.4% and 27.4% respectively. Why? Before deducting tax credits, all three averaged a tax rate of around 35%, but pharmaceutical companies tend to benefit more from deductions for research, experimentation, and development. After all taxes were paid, the pharmaceutical industry had the highest profit margin[26] of all industries in 2000: 18.9%. The average profit margin of the Fortune 500 companies in that year was a mere 4.9%.

(Tax-deductible) Philanthropy. According to the Conference Board, a New York-based corporate research organization, pharmaceutical companies contributed 2.2%[27] of their pre-tax income to charities since 1991. This is 1.4% more than corporations in general.

Pharmaceutical companies routinely provide goods and services to disaster areas. The tragedy of September 11, 2001 was no exception. Pharmaceutical companies donated $85 million in cash plus medicines, medical supplies, and other goods and services to help in the relief and recovery efforts. From 1998 to 2001, the pharmaceutical industry donated nearly $2 billion in financial assistance and medical products to developing countries to fight the spread of AIDS, tuberculosis, and other diseases. More than one billion people in 80 countries are at risk of contracting elephantiasis (a disease of the lymph system spread by mosquitoes), according to the World Health Organization. Drug companies have already donated 4-5 billion doses of medicine in an attempt to eliminate the disease in the next 20 years.

Pharmaceutical companies also contributed $1.5 billion worth of prescription medications to patient-assistance programs in the United States in 2001, up from $374 million in 1997. 3.5 million patients were served in 2001, up from 1.1 million in 1997. These programs (through hospitals, clinics, and community pharmacies) provide prescription medications to indigent patients. Admirable, but is it enough? In *PhRMA Industry Profile 2002,* the Pharmaceutical Research and Manufacturers of America (PhRMA) stated: "A number of companies have pledged that no patient in need of their medicines will do without them." One wonders, then, why thousands of senior citizens must decide every month between filling their prescriptions and putting food on the table. But, are pharmaceutical companies the only ones to blame for high prescription drug prices?

The table on the next page shows the growth rates in each of the categories shown in the previous graph. Wholesale and retail markup fluctuated yearly throughout this time period. However, from 1996 to 2001, the total growth rate was greater than four times the growth rate of pharmaceutical company expenditures. From 1998 to 1999, wholesale and retail markup fell more than 20%. But, from 1999 to 2001, wholesale and retail markup

---

[26] Profits as a percentage of revenue.

[27] The six drug companies that answered the survey contributed an average of $426 million a year to charity.

again grew at a faster rate than any other category. Except for 1999, growth rates for wholesale and retail markup averaged 4-6 times that of total pharmaceutical company expenditures.

But does this higher growth rate translate into a greater share of the total markup? No. If both wholesale/retail and pharmaceutical growth rates would stay the same for 2001 to 2002, the wholesale/retail markup on a prescription costing $71.18 would be $4.19 and the pharmaceutical company markup would be $8.01. This is nearly twice that of the wholesaler and retailer, and in this case, contributes 66% to the total markup.

Growth Rates (%), 1996-2001

	1996-1997	1997-1998	1998-1999	1999-2000	2000-2001	1996-2001
Number of prescriptions dispensed	4.3	8.3	3.8	7.4	6.9	34.8
U.S. retail sales	14.2	18.4	19.1	18.7	17.1	123.6
Wholesale/retail markup	63.8	69.7	-20.4	66.2	48.7	446.6
Total pharmaceutical company expenditures	10.8	13.3	24.8	14.2	12.8	101.8
Total R&D expenditures	12.1	10.6	8.2	14.7	16.6	79.5
Total promotional expenditures	19.6	13.6	11.2	12.9	21.4	107.2
Direct-to-consumer advertising	35.1	23.2	40.3	33.5	8.6	238.7
Other expenditures	12.2	11.0	22.3	22.7	13.9	112.9
Average inflation rate[28]:	2.7	1.9	1.9	2.8	3.0	15.4

In the next panel we will discuss some of the benefits of new medications.

Sources: Levitt, Larry. The Henry J. Kaiser Family Foundation. *Prescription Drug Trends*, November 2001. Retrieved July 24, 2002 from http://www.kff.org. National Institute for Health Care Management. "Factors Affecting the Growth of Prescription Drugs Expenditures," July 1999. Retrieved July 26, 2002 from http://www.nihcm.org. National Institute for Health Care Management. *Prescription Drug Expenditures in 2001: Another Year of Escalating Costs*, May 6, 2002. Retrieved July 17, 2002 from http://www.nihcm.org. Pharmaceutical Research and Manufacturers of America. *Pharmaceutical Industry Profile 2000, 2001,* and *2002.* Retrieved July 24-August 2, 2002 from http://www.phrma.org/. National Science Board. National Science Foundation. Science and Engineering Indicators -- 2000, 2000. Retrieved July 26, 2002 from http://www.nsf.gov/. National Association of Chain Drug Stores. "Industry Statistics." Retrieved August 1, 2002 from http://www.nacds.org. IMS Health. "Total U.S. Promotional Spending by Type, 2001." Retrieved July 16, 2002 from http://www.imshealth.org. National Institute for Health Care Management. *Prescription Drugs and Mass Media Advertising, 2000.* Retrieved July 26, 2002 from http://www.nihcm.org. Alliance for Retired Americans. *The Profit in Pills: A Primer on Prescription Drug Prices,* June 2002. Gary Guenther. Congressional Research Service. "Memorandum: Federal Taxation of the Drug Industry from 1990 to 1996," December 13, 1999. Retrieved August 2, 2002 from http://rxpolicy.com/studies/crs_pharm_tax_memo.pdf. Bureau of Labor Statistics. U.S. Department of Labor. *Career Guide to Industries.* Retrieved August 1, 2002 from http://www.bls.gov/oco/cg/cgs009.pdf. Internal Revenue Service. U.S. Department of the Treasury. "1998, Returns of Active Corporations." Retrieved August 2, 2002 from http://www.irs.gov. Families USA. *Profiting from Pain: Where Prescription Drug Dollars Go,* July 2002. Retrieved August 1, 2002 from http://www.familiesUSA.org/PPreport.pdf. "Revenues, Schmevenues. Why Biotech's CEOs Lead the Salary Race," April 2, 2002. Retrieved July 26, 2002 from http://www.genomeweb.com/articles/. National Institute of Allergy and Infectious Diseases. National Institutes of Health. "Lymphatic Filariasis (Elephantiasis)" Retrieved August 2, 2002 from http://www.niaid.nih.gov/newsroom/focuson/bugborn01/filar.htm. Economic History Services. "What Was The Inflation Rate Then?" Retrieved August 7, 2002 from http://www.eh.net/ehresources/howmuch/inflationq.php.

---

[28] Inflation rate for first five columns calculated by averaging the inflation rates of the two years. Last column is the cumulative inflation rate from 1996-2001.

Are Prescription Drugs Worth The Expense?

U.S. Per Capita Expenditures on Health Care in Constant 2000 Dollars, 1993-2000

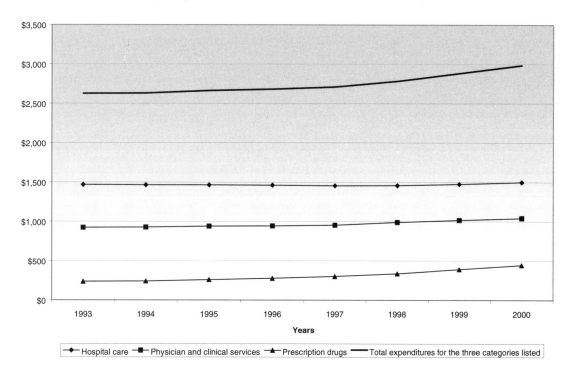

The graphic shows the per capita expenditures on various health-related services in the United States. Numbers are in 2000 constant dollars. "High-price new drugs may be the cheapest weapon we have in our struggle against rising overall medical expenses" according to J.D. Kleinke, a health care analyst.[29] The graph doesn't seem to confirm this, however. From 1993 to 2000, the amount spent on prescription drugs rose, but so did total health care expenditures. From 1993 to 1997, the amount spent on hospital care did decrease as preventative care (prescription drug and physician and clinical service) expenditures increased. But the decrease was miniscule compared to the increase in preventative care expenditures: -0.8% for hospital care, 3.4% for physician and clinical services, and 27.7% for prescription drugs. After 1997, expenditures in all three categories rose.

Contrary to popular thinking, new medical advances may not necessarily be contributing to the rising cost of health care. Although some new medical procedures and diagnostic procedures may be costly, the alternatives would be much costlier. Electron beam tomography (EBT), a new diagnostic procedure to predict heart attacks and other potential health problems costs from $500 for a heart scan to $1,200 for a scan of the whole body. If the heart scan is performed and plaque formation is discovered, the condition can be

---

[29] Source: Kleinke, J.D. "The Price of Progress: Prescription Drugs in the Health Care Market." *Health Affairs,* September/October 2001.

reversed by medications such as aspirin, certain vitamins, or in more advanced cases prescription cholesterol-lowering drugs. Coronary stenting and open bypass surgery, procedures a patient may need if the problem wasn't diagnosed early, cost around $15,000 and $27,000, respectively. Although many patients who undergo EBT may not need prescription medications, those who do can expect to pay $18,000 or more over their lifetime for cholesterol-lowering drugs.[30]

Prescription drug therapy for AIDS patients may reduce health care costs by a third. Protease "cocktail" therapies cost about $16,000 a year. In contrast, before the availability of drug therapy, an AIDS patient averaged $24,000 a year in hospital costs. The average hospital stay for an AIDS patient in New York state dropped from 23.4 days in 1983 to 9.6 days in 1999. $16,000 a year for drug therapy? How can we (patients, insurance companies, federal health programs) pay for it? According to Samuel A. Bozette, M.D., who headed a study of antiretroviral therapy for AIDS patients that was published in *The New England Journal of Medicine*: "'The drugs are almost a perfect substitute for hospital care. We can afford them because, in fact, we are already spending the money on HIV care' in the form of hospitalization."

Can this be said about other prescription drug treatments? If there were a direct link between prescription drug treatment and hospitalization costs, perhaps. Money spent on one treatment could be funneled into another, less costly treatment. But, looking at the previous graph, our health care system seems much more complicated.

The lack of a steeper downturn in hospital care expenses, despite cost saving diagnostic and pharmaceutical treatments, may partly be attributed to the aging of the population. In 1999, the hospitalization rate for those 65 years old and over was greater than three times that of the general population: 370 vs. 116 per 1,000. The number of hospital discharges for the elderly increased 11% from 1990 to 1999. And, the baby-boomers haven't yet reached age 65. As that generation ages and more and more will need hospital care, per capita hospitalization costs (and as a consequence, total health care expenses) will continue to rise.

Are we better off with new drug therapies? Yes. Overall life expectancy is trending upward. In many cases chronic conditions are now manageable with drug therapy, allowing patients to live longer, more active lives. But, not all diseases and conditions can be managed (or cured) simply by having new diagnostic procedures and pharmaceutical treatments available. Despite the availability of cholesterol-lowering drugs, people still have heart attacks. Despite medical innovations and drug therapies to diagnose and treat cancer, people are still hospitalized for and dying of the disease. The same can be said for many other health conditions and diseases.

---

[30] If a person was diagnosed at age 45, put on Lipitor or Zocor (two of the most advertised drugs in this class) daily for the rest of his life, and lived until 75 years old: Zocor 5mg (the smallest dosage) would cost him $17,982; Lipitor 10mg (the smallest dosage) would cost him $21,550. This assumes that prices stay constant over this 30-year period. Prices obtained August 7, 2002 from http://www.drugstore.com.

Why? In some cases, it's a patient's lack of access to proper health care. In other cases, it's people's attitudes about their own health (and consequent behaviors). But, in many cases, this may simply be nature winning over our attempts to control it.

Sources: Centers for Medicare & Medicaid Services. U.S. Health and Human Services. "Table 9: Personal Health Care Expenditures, by Type of Expenditure and Source of Funds: Calendar Years 1993-2000." Retrieved August 5, 2002 from http://www.cms.hhs.gov/statistics/nhe/historical/t9.asp. "The Inflation Calculator." Retrieved August 5, 2002 from http://www.westegg.com/inflation/. U.S. Census Bureau. *Statistical Abstract of the United States: 2001*. Pharmaceutical Research and Manufacturers of America. *The Value of Medicines*, 2001 and *PhRMA Industry Profile 2002*. Retrieved July 16, 2002 and August 2, 2002 from http://www.phrma.org. National Center for Health Statistics. Centers for Disease Control. "Hospital Stays Grow Shorter Heart Disease Leading Cause of Hospitalization," April 24, 2001 and *1999 National Hospital Discharge Survey*. Advance Data Number 319, 2001. Retrieved August 7, 2002 from http://www.cdc.gov/nchs/. Advanced Medical Technology Association. "The Promise of Medical Technology" Retrieved August 7, 2002 from http://www.himanet.com/aboutourindustry.shtml. R.J. King. "'Visual Tour' can predict heart attack." *The Detroit News*, June 23, 2002. Retrieved August 7, 2002 from http://detnews.com/2002/health/. Johnson & Johnson. "Putting a Price on Health Care Progress." *Health Care Issues*, May 16, 2002. Retrieved August 6, 2002 from http://www.jnj.com/issues/putting_price.html.

Chapter 7

Senior Health

Until the middle of the 20th century, men worked until they died or fell terminally ill (after which they soon died). The women left behind managed as best they could with the help of family. Life expectancy crept up. In 1960, America counted its first 1 million citizens over the age of 85. In 2050, there will be 1 million Americans over the age of 100. As the huge Baby Boom generation struggles to care for its aging, long-lived parents and confronts its own prospects for old age, senior health and care at the end of life have become big issues.

In an extensive 2001 report entitled *An Aging World*, researchers for the U.S. Department of Health and Human Services reported: "Population aging represents, in one sense, a human success story; societies now have the luxury of aging. However, the steady, sustained growth of elderly populations also poses myriad challenges to policymakers in many societies."[1] How are our policymakers doing at addressing those challenges?

This chapter opens by looking at where we live in the longer and longer twilights of our years. We shall see that the most fortunate among us will remain in our own homes, and especially if we are men, we will do so with our loving spouses at our sides. Others — most often women — will end up in the nursing homes that since World War II have replaced a family setting as the last residence of those of us who linger on into great old age. Like many aspects of elder care in our society, nursing homes have been insufficiently regulated. In 1980, Bruce C. Vladeck's *Unloving Care: The Nursing Home Tragedy* chronicled 50 years of government mismanagement of nursing homes. Vladeck called for a restructuring of the nursing home system and increased emphasis on home-based services for the independent elderly. We will explore the question: Are nursing homes really as bad as we've heard they are? And what are the alternatives? We also explore the painful topic of elder abuse.

For our third topic, cost of healthcare versus quality of life in the end, we will look at indicators of quality of life, what government has done to improve life for the elderly, and what seniors can do to help themselves. We then explore trends in end-of-life care — the hospice movement, pain control, and the growth of the patients' rights movement.

---

[1] U.S. Department of Health and Human Services, "An Aging World," November 2001, www.census.gov/prod/2001pubs/p95-01-1.pdf.

Throughout history, doctors have striven to prolong life. We look at the question: Has technology brought us to the point where the medical establishment is prolonging life to no good purpose? According to the National Institutes of Health: "Defining when these technologies and treatments shift from life saving interventions to burdensome and futile procedures that negatively impact quality of life has proved elusive."[2]

The case of Karen Ann Quinlan illustrates the type of ethical dilemma that has emerged in our era of modern medicine. Decisions about ending the lives of individuals for whom quality of life has ceased to be an issue used to be made quietly, privately. In Quinlan's case, in our new age of dying in institutions, a court of law got involved when permission to remove her from a respirator was sought and granted. So began an era of social, ethical, and legal controversy, and the phrases "the right to die" and "death with dignity" became part of the national vocabulary. Such phrases are used to describe a variety of end-of-life decision-making issues. This chapter will look at two places that are on the vanguard of the physician-assisted suicide movement: Oregon and Holland.

Government and the medical establishment have been slow to respond to the issue of quality of care at the end of life. Medical schools are not graduating geriatricians and the National Institutes of Health (NIH) reports: "Results of two separate surveys found on average only 2% of the content of nursing … and medical … text books was relevant to end-of-life care."[3] And what about cost of care at the end of life? In 2002 George P. Smith, II, B.S., J.D., wrote: "The government does arguably have a duty, based on a collective social obligation, to help people live out a natural life span. Yet, without a limit on investments into health care for the elderly, younger generations will suffer based on an inadequacy of available health care resources."[4] Conservative John Hood grumps: "Statistical fact: America spends more on its old than on its children."[5] Michael Fossel asks in *Futurist*: "What will happen when people can live on and on for centuries?"[6] Who pays for care at the end of life? Who should pay for it?

We end the chapter on a lighter note with a look at how media images of senior citizens have evolved from "Help, I've fallen and I can't get up" to something more positive. Aging Baby Boomers will say that old age begins at 79 and would no doubt agree with the view expressed by the International Longevity Center: "It is not enough for people to live long. They should also live well."

---

[2] National Institutes of Health, "Quality of Life for Individuals at the End-of-Life," August 2000, http://grants1.nih.gov/grants/guide/pa-files/PA-00-127.html.

[3] National Institutes of Health, ibid.

[4] George P. Smith, II, "Allocating Health Care Resources to the Elderly," *Elder Law Review*, Vol 1 (2002).

[5] John Hood, "Senior Slump," *National Review*, October 23, 2000, p56+.

[6] Michael Fossel, "Reversing Human Aging: It's Time to Consider the Consequences," *Futurist*, July/Aug 1997.

Geographic Distribution of the Population in Their Golden Years

Geographic Distribution of the Population Aged 65+: 1980, 1990, 2000

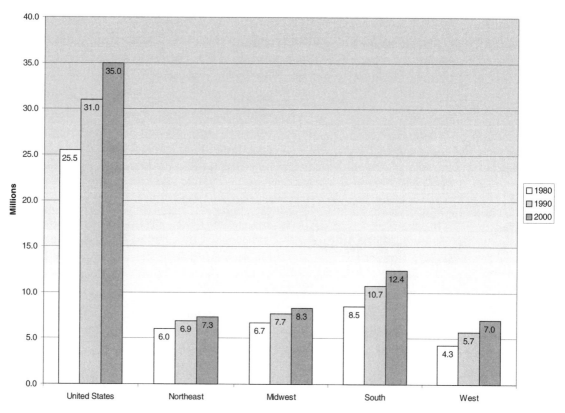

In the year 2000, there were 35 million Americans aged 65 and over. This age group comprised about 1 of every 8 Americans, about the same proportion as in 1990 and a substantial increase over 1900, when the 65+ group comprised 1 in 25 Americans (3.1 million).

The graph above and the table below show the geographic regions where the older population chose to live in 1980, 1990, and 2000. The warmer climate of the South is a big draw, with 35% of the total older population choosing to live there in 2000 (up from 33% in 1980). Between 1980 and 2000, the West saw the biggest gain in the percentage of the total older population living there (up 3%, from 17 to 20%). The biggest losers were the Midwest (down from 26 to 24%) and the Northeast (down from 23 to 21%).

Population 65 Years and Over and Percent Change, by Region: 1980-1990 and 1990-2000

Region	1980	1990	2000	Percent Change 1980-90	Percent Change 1990-00
U.S.	25,549,544	31,078,895	34,991,753	21.6	12.0
Northeast	6,071,865	6,948,232	7,372,282	14.4	5.4
Midwest	6,692,026	7,725,193	8,259,075	15.4	6.6
South	8,487,699	10,668,679	12,438,267	25.7	16.0
West	4,297,954	5,736,791	6,922,129	33.5	19.9

The number of older people increased in every state from 1980 to 1990 and again from 1990 to 2000. This is a pattern that will continue as 75 million Baby Boomers start turning 65 in 2010. It is projected that by 2030, 1 in 5 Americans will be age 65 or older.

What states do we retire to, if we decide to move? Between 1980 and 1990, the greatest percentage increases in the older population were in Western states (Nevada, Alaska, Hawaii, Arizona, and New Mexico, in descending order) and Southern states (Florida, South Carolina, Delaware, North Carolina, Virginia). The pattern repeated between 1990 and 2000 but with some different states showing greater gains. The greatest Western percentage increases between 1990 and 2000 were in Nevada, Alaska, Arizona, New Mexico, and Hawaii. In the South, South Carolina, Texas, Georgia, North Carolina, and Virginia saw the greatest percentage increases between 1990 and 2000.

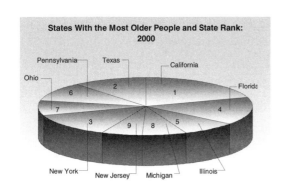

The small chart shows the nine states with the greatest number of older people in 2000. Of a total 34.9 million people aged 65 and older , more than half (18.1 million) lived in the nine states shown. These are the same 9 states that had the largest number of older people in 1990. Not surprisingly, these are the 9 most populous states. Their 2000 ranking is shown on the chart.

According to the Census Bureau, in 1999, about 50% of older persons lived in the suburbs, 27% lived in central cities, and 23% lived in nonmetropolitan areas.

It appears that most older people prefer to remain in the place where they have ties rather than move to a more hospitable climate. This phenomenon is called "aging in place." The Census Bureau reports that only about 5% percent of older Americans move in any year, and older people comprised less than 4% of all movers in the United States in 2000. A large majority of those elderly who moved (78%) had moved to another home in the same state.

Next we look at the places older people call "home."

Sources: Graphic: U.S. Census Bureau, http://www.census.gov/population/www/socdemo/age.html; Primary sources: U.S. Bureau of the Census, unpublished data consistent with *U.S. Population Estimates, by Age, Sex, Race, and Hispanic Origin: 1980 to 1991*, Current Population Reports, P25-1095, U.S. Government Printing Office, Washington, DC, 1993, and Census 2000 Summary File 1; 1990 Census of Population, *General Population Characteristics* (1990 CP-1). Small chart: U.S. Census Bureau, Census 2000 Summary File 1.

Where and With Whom We Live in Our Golden Years

Homeownership Rates, All Households and Householders Aged 65 and Over: 1950-2000

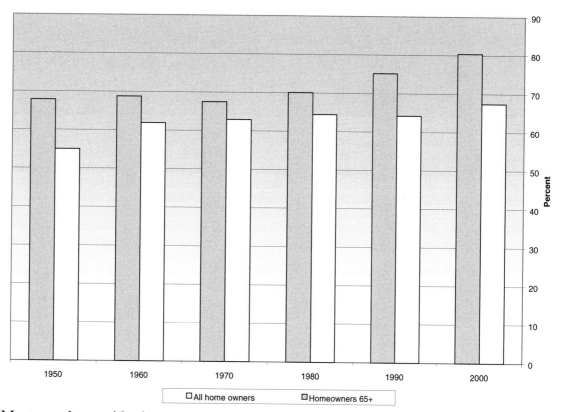

All home owners   Homeowners 65+

Most people consider home ownership to be the most desirable residential option. Older people are no exception. Men who were 65 in the year 2000 could expect to live another 16.3 years, and women could look forward to 19.2 more years (up from 11.5 and 12.2 years, respectively, in 1900). A majority of older Americans report that their health is good if not excellent and 84% of older householders plan to remain in their own homes as long as they can, according to AARP.[7][8]

The information on the chart comes from the American Housing Survey, which dates back to 1940. Data regarding home ownership rates are shown for each decade from 1950

---

[7] Older African Americans and older Hispanics are less likely to rate their health as good to excellent. In 1999, 26% of older whites said their health was fair or poor; the figures were 41.6% for blacks and 35.1% for Hispanics.

[8] The Older Americans Act, first passed in 1965 and reauthorized from time to time afterwards, is designed to help seniors stay in their homes as long as possible by providing such services as home-delivered meals, home health care, and so on. According to AARP: "In fiscal year 2001, the total federal appropriation for the OAA is $1.1 billion, up from $830,000 in 1997. Funding has generally increased slightly each year, but has not kept pace with inflation and the growth of the older population." For more information, go to http://www.aoa.gov/aoa/pages/aoafact.html.

Living Arrangements of Men 65+

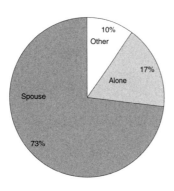

Living Arrangements of Women 65+

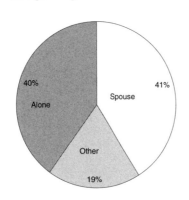

to 2000. We see that people aged 65+ have always had higher rates of home ownership than the population as a whole, and home ownership rates rose for everyone, from 55% in 1950 to 67.4% in 2000. The rise for older householders has been more rapid, from 68% in 1950 to 80% in 2000.[9]

The Census Bureau tells us that older minority Americans are less likely to be homeowners than older white Americans. In 2000, about 66% of older black and 59% of older Hispanic households were homeowner-households.

The AARP (formerly American Association of Retired Persons) analyzes housing censuses to find out whether older Americans are adequately housed, an important consideration in allowing them to maintain their independence. AARP reports that in 1997, about 77% of older owners owned their homes outright and lived in single-family homes with a median value of about $89,294. More than one-fifth of older households are rented. Regardless whether they were renters or owners, most older householders said they had few problems with the quality of their residences. Only 6% of older households reported "moderate or severe physical problems" with their housing.

The pie charts show the living arrangements of noninstitutionalized older Americans in 2000. Nearly three-quarters of elderly men live with their spouse, but fewer than half of elderly women have a spouse to look out for them. Older women often live and die alone.

Next we will look at living arrangements of the frailest older Americans.

Sources: Charts: U.S. Census Bureau, "Historical Census of Housing Tables, Ownership Rates, Ownership Rates by Household and Structure Type, http://www.census.gov/hhes/www/housing/census/historic/ownrate.html., and Administration on Aging, U.S. Department of Health and Human Services, "A Profile of Older Americans 2001: Living Arrangements," http://www.aoa.dhhs.gov/aoa/stats/profile/2001/4.html. AARP, "A Profile of Older Americans 2000," http://research.aarp.org/general/profile_2001.html. Data retrieved August 21, 2002.

---

[9] An emerging trend among seniors and others is home sharing. The National Shared Housing Resource Center, a network of more than 300 programs under the auspices of nonprofit agencies across the United States, matches home providers and seekers; see http://www.nationalsharedhousing.org/.

Where Do the Frailest of the Old Live?

Nursing Home Residents 65 Years of Age and Over: 1973-74-1999

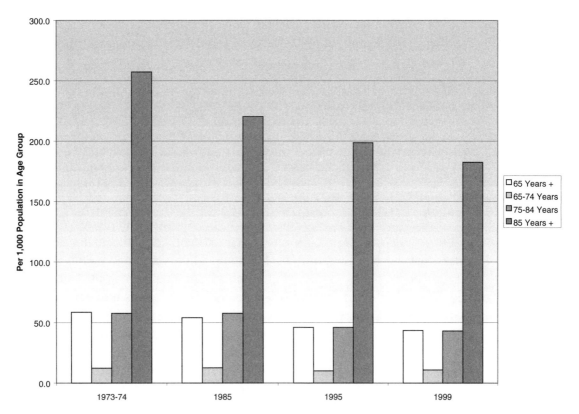

We have seen that the majority of people aged 65+ live in homes they own. Poor health increases with age, and there comes a time when some older people may no longer be able to care for themselves. The chart shows data on the population aged 65+ who were in nursing homes from the period 1973-74 to 1999. The data are presented in tabular form below. According to the source, in crude numbers, there were 961,500 residents of nursing homes at the time of the survey in 1973-74 and 1,469,500 in 1999.[10] In 1999 there were an estimated 18,000 licensed nursing homes. Their population is disproportionately female.

One trend is immediately obvious: If you are 85 years or older, you have a far greater chance of finding yourself in a nursing home. However, the data show that there was a decline among all age groups in the ratio of people confined to nursing homes.

---

[10] According to a 2002 General Accounting Office report: "Nursing homes in the United States play an essential role in our health care system, caring for 1.6 million elderly and disabled persons who are temporarily or permanently unable to care for themselves but who do not require the level of care furnished in an acute care hospital."

The *Nursing Facility Sourcebook 2001* summarizes results from a 1997 study showing: "[M]ore than a quarter of our nation's population currently over the age of 25 can anticipate at least one stay in a nursing facility in their lifetime.... The typical nursing facility patient is a white female Medicaid beneficiary aged 75 years or older.... Forty-two percent of nursing facility patients suffer from some level of dementia and 33% have documented symptoms of depression." The National Council on the Aging says: "A person turning 65 in the year 1990 had about a 40 percent lifetime chance of living in a nursing home."

Nursing Home Residents Aged 65+

Age	Residents per 1,000 population			
	1973-74	1985	1995	1999
65 years+[1]	58.5	54.0	45.9	43.3
65-74 years	12.3	12.5	10.1	10.8
75-84 years	57.7	57.7	45.9	43.0
85 years +	257.3	220.3	198.6	182.5

The modern nursing home dates back to the 1940s; they expanded in the 1950s thanks to federal subsidies. Why the decline in nursing home residence? More people are taking advantage of home health care, and more people are taking advantage of the rising number of alternative facilities that are considered more desirable. This is a phenomenon that dates back to the 1980s and corresponds to the rising numbers, income, and clout of senior citizens. Where once older people had few options when health problems made running their household too hard to handle, today there is a variety of retirement communities that provide health-related services. They go by various names, the most common being continuing care retirement communities (CCRCs) or assisted living facilities (ALFs). CCRCs are the most expensive option and tend not to accept individuals with serious disabilities. According to AARP, most CCRCs require an entrance fee and monthly payments. The fees can range from $20,000 to $400,000; monthly payments range from $200 to $2,500.

The Assisted Living Federation of America (ALFA) says there are about 1 million older adults and individuals with disabilities residing in about 20,000 ALFs nationwide.[11] The average resident is age 83 and in need of assistance with at least one activity of daily living. An estimated 50% of residents have some form of cognitive impairment. It is usually a health care crisis or death of a spouse that prompts the move to assisted living.

Sources: Chart: *Health, United States, 2001*, Table 97, http://www.cdc.gov/nchs/hus.htm. *The Nursing Facility Sourcebook 2001*, http://www.ahca.org/research/nfbook.htm. National Council on the Aging, "Facts About Older Americans," http://www.ncoa.org/press/facts.html. ALFA, http://www.alfa.org/. U.S. Department of Health and Human Services, "Continuing Care Retirement Communities: A Background and Summary of Current Issues," http://aspe.os.dhhs.gov/daltcp/Reports/ccrcrpt.htm#admissions. "Continuing Care Retirement Communities, AARP, http://www.aarp.org/confacts/housing/ccrc.html.

---

[11] Assisted living facilities (ALF) are defined by ALFA "as a special combination of housing, personalized supportive services and health care designed to meet the needs ... of those who need help with activities of daily living." Daily fees range from $15 to $200, paid by residents/families. Costs may be reimbursed by health insurance or other policies; some residences have financial assistance programs. Government payments for ALFs have been limited, but some state/local governments offer subsidies for rent or services and/or use Medicaid waiver programs to help pay for such services.

Where Do the Poorest of the Old Live?

Distribution of Older Renter Households: 1980-1995

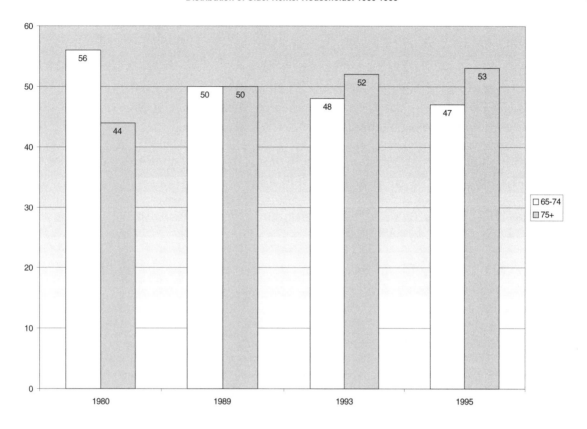

"Poverty — the most deadly and prevalent of all diseases." — Eugene O'Neill

More than 5 million elderly households are rented. As the chart shows, older renter households are increasingly headed by those aged 75+. In 1980, that age group comprised 44% of older renters. The percentage grew steadily, and by 1995, the over-75 segment comprised 53% of renters. As we live longer, the percentage of over-75 renters will grow.

Elderly rental households tend to be poor and headed by women/minorities. Renters have higher housing costs and lower (usually fixed) incomes than homeowners.[12] They have reached old age with few assets and little chance now of acquiring any. Where once they might have moved in with relatives, they now must rent. A Cornell University study found that the percentage of elderly women who moved in with family declined from

---

[12] Of the 21.4 million households headed by older persons in 1999, 20% were renters. In 1999, about 1.7 million households headed by a person age 62 or older benefited from some kind of federal rental housing program, according to AARP. Data from the 1999 American Housing Survey (AHS) show that 55% of older renter households incurred "excessive expenditures" for housing, defined as housing costs in excess of 30% of income. In 1999 the median family income of older renters was $12,566. To be eligible for federally subsidized housing, the household income must be less than $18,375.

46% of women over 75 in 1960 to 19% in 1990. For more, see http://www.news.cor nell.edu/science/Sept95/st.poorseniors.html.

Women, minorities, and the oldest old (age 85+) are the largest and fastest growing segments of the older population.[13] There will be an increasing demand by the most economically vulnerable people for decent, affordable rental housing with features adapted to meet the needs of the old. Can the market meet those demands?

By most accounts no, not if present trends continue. The biggest problem is that housing costs are simply too high. The U.S. Conference of Mayors (who should know as well as anyone) summarizes the problem this way:

• "1.4 million elderly and 2 million people with disabilities pay more than 50% of their incomes for housing or live in substandard housing.

• Section 202[14] elderly funding has been flat at $679 million for several years, despite rapid growth in the elderly population.

• Section 811[15] funding for the disabled has declined by nearly $100 million in the past decade, from $387 million to $271 million.

• In the past five years, about 100,000 units of Section 8 housing for the elderly have been converted to more expensive market rate housing."

AARP Board Member Keith Campbell notes: "If we fail to meet these challenges, the likely result will be a crisis in both affordability and availability in housing, creating the possibility that we will see an America with a significant increase in underhoused, underserved older citizens. And a result of this could be a substantial increase in costly and premature institutionalization of older people."

Sources: Chart: "Housing Characteristics of Older Households," AARP calculations from American Housing Surveys, AARP. "Section 202 Supportive Housing for the Elderly," AARP. AARP data retrieved August 23, 2002, from http://research.aarp.org. U.S. Conference of Mayors, Mayors National Housing Forum Fact Sheet, Frank B. Hobbs, "The Elderly Population," U.S. Census Bureau, http://www.census-gov/population/www/pop-profile/elderpop.html.

---

[13] Between 1980 and 1997, the elderly population grew 33%, but the number of persons age 85+ grew 73%, and the total U.S. population grew by 18%. The oldest Americans made up less than 9% of the elderly population in 1980; they comprised more than 11% of the elderly in 1997 and may make up 23% by 2050. In 1997, 15% of the U.S. elderly population were minorities — 8% were African American. By 2025, 24% will be minorities.

[14] A U.S. Department of Housing and Urban Development (HUD) program of federally subsidized apartment units for senior citizens. It is the only federally funded program designed specifically for the elderly.

[15] A HUD program for the disabled.

Reporting Domestic Elder Abuse

Reported Cases of Domestic Elder Abuse: 1986-1996

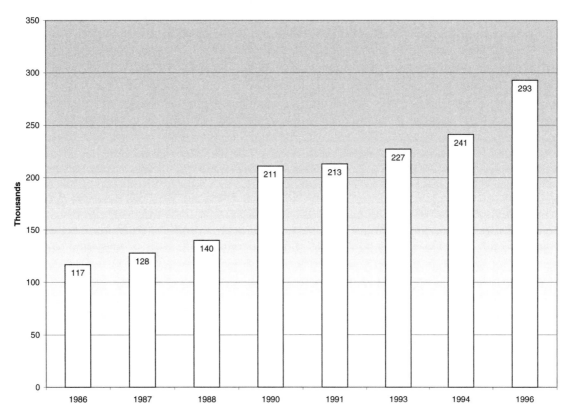

The figures on the graphic were collected by the National Center on Elder Abuse (NCEA) from state adult protective service agencies and state units on aging.[16] From 1986-1996, there was a steady rise in the number of reported cases of domestic elder abuse, from 117,000 to 293,000, an increase of 150%.

In 1987 the American Medical Association defined elder abuse as "an act or omission that results in harm or threatened harm to the health or welfare of an elderly person."[17] No doubt elder abuse has been with us as long as we have had an elderly population. Domestic elder abuse can happen when an elderly, once independent family member suc-

---

[16] NCEA is funded by a grant from the U.S. Administration on Aging, and consists of a consortium of six partners: National Association of State Units on Aging (NASUA), the lead agency; Commission on Legal Problems of the Elderly of the American Bar Association (ABA); the Clearinghouse on Abuse and Neglect of the Elderly of the University of Delaware (CANE); the San Francisco Consortium for Elder Abuse Prevention of the Institute on Aging (IOA); the National Association of Adult Protective Services Administrators (NAAPSA); and the National Committee to Prevent Elder Abuse (NCPEA).

[17] "Elder abuse can be classified into 6 categories: (1) physical abuse, (2) sexual abuse, (3) neglect, (4) psychological abuse, (5) financial and material exploitation, and (6) violation of rights" (Collins et al.; see Source notes).

cumbs to injury, illness, or dementia; when a man feels emasculated by retirement and takes it out on his wife; when an elderly person lives with dysfunctional family members. Since the 1980s elder abuse has gotten more attention, but it is impossible to know the true extent of the problem. Elder abuse may be aggravated by a poor economy, cutbacks in social services, and drug abuse. Because we expect old people to decline, mistreatment that results in impairment or disability is often not recognized by medical personnel.

Efforts by law enforcement personnel to deal with the issue of elder abuse are complicated by the fact that victims are poor witnesses on their own behalf. We can expect the problem of elder abuse to get worse as the number of older Americans increases to 70 million by 2030, more than double the number in 1990, with fewer young people proportionately to take care of them.

In the 1970s the British press brought "granny bashing" out of the closet. States began compiling estimates on cases of suspected elder abuse in the early 1980s after Rep. Claude Pepper's House Select Committee on Aging held hearings and coined the term "elder abuse." Efforts to come up with national data are complicated by the fact that each state has its own laws regarding elder abuse, its own policies for reporting suspected cases (sometimes mandatory, sometimes not), and its own definitions of what constitutes elder abuse. Our next panel shows some results from the first national study.

Sources: National Center on Elder Abuse, *Elder Abuse Information Series*, www.elderabusecenter.org/. Kim A. Collins, MD; Allan T. Bennett, MD; Randy Hanzlick, MD; and the Autopsy Committee of the College of American Pathologists, "Elder Abuse and Neglect," *Archives of Internal Medicine*, Vol. 160 No. 11, June 12, 2000 http://archinte.ama-assn.org/issues/v160n11/ffull/iam90005.html. Data retrieved August 22, 2002.

How Are the Elderly Abused?

Types of Elder Maltreatment Substantiated by Adult Protective Services (Percent): 1996

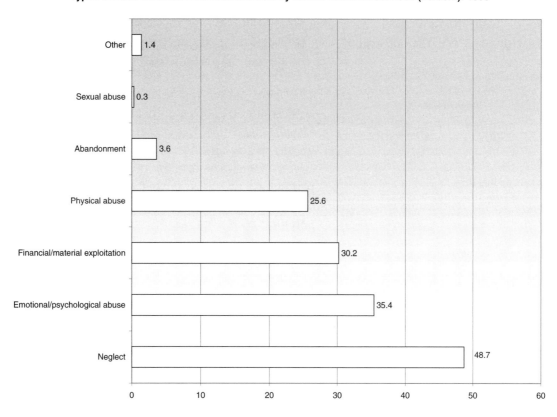

"How sharper than a serpent's tooth it is to have a thankless child."— W. Shakespeare

The Family Violence Prevention and Services Act of 1992 required that the U.S. Administration on Aging (AoA) conduct a study of the national incidence of abuse, neglect, and exploitation of elderly persons. AoA issued its first-ever National Elder Abuse Incidence Study (NEAIS) in 1998, which stated: "This study estimates that at least one-half million older persons in domestic settings were abused and/or neglected, or experienced self neglect during 1996, and that for every reported incident of elder abuse, neglect or self neglect, approximately five go unreported."

NEAIS collected data from two different sources in a nationally representative probability sample of 20 counties: (1) local Adult Protective Services (APS) agencies or the Area Agencies on Aging (AAA); and (2) approximately 1,100 trained "sentinels" from public and private agencies that had frequent contact with elderly community residents.

The NEAIS examined the incidence of newly filed reports of abuse and neglect during calendar year 1996. The graphic shows the types of elder maltreatment involved in the total of 70,942 reported incidents substantiated by Adult Protective Service agencies. Nearly a half of the incidents involved neglect, a little over one-third involved emotional/psychological abuse, and nearly a third involved financial/material exploitation.

NEAIS also reported the ages of elder abuse victims for selected types of maltreatment. The oldest of the old — those aged 80 and over — were the most likely to be neglected (51.8% of cases) or to experience emotional, physical, or financial exploitation (41.3%, 43.7%, and 48% of cases, respectively). However, a slightly younger group, those aged 75 to 79, were the most likely to be abandoned (58.8%). NEAIS cannot explain why this is so. However, NEAIS does report that in 96.1% of cases of abandonment, the victim's income was less than $10,000.

Relationship of Alleged Perpetrators

of Elder Abuse

Relationship	Percentage
Child	30.8
Spouse	30.3
Parent	24.0
Friend/Neighbor	5.7
Service Provider	4.2
Sibling	0.3
Not Determined	0.6

The table shows the relationship of the alleged perpetrators of abuse. In nearly equal proportions (30.8% and 30.3%), it is the child or spouse of the victim who committed the abuse. In 24% of cases, it was a parent involved. In a far smaller percentage of cases, it was either a friend/neighbor, grandchild, or service provider who was the perpetrator.

Sources: The National Elder Abuse Incidence Study; Final Report, http://www.aoa.gov/abuse/report/GFindings-01.htm#P131_7832. Administration on Aging, http://www.aoa.gov/aoa/PAGES/aoa.html.

Elder Abuse in Nursing Homes

Statistics About Nursing Homes, Their Residents, and Their Staffs (in percent, except dollars and ranking)

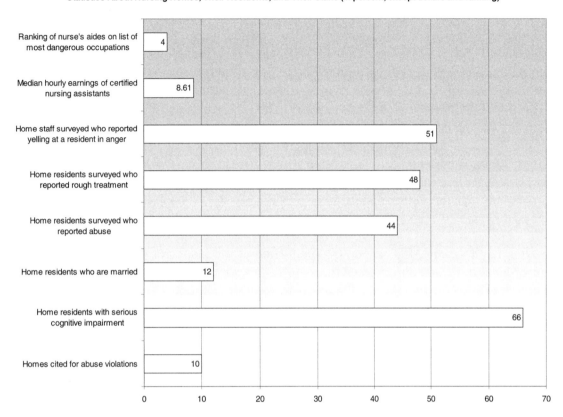

We've seen the headlines: "Nursing Home to Pay After Death." "Relatives of Victims of Nursing Home Neglect Say $2-Million Penalty Against Chain's Owner Isn't Enough to Force Industry Reforms." Perhaps we've heard a relative say: "I'd rather be dead than in a nursing home." Are they really as bad as all that?

The graphic shows some statistics about nursing homes, their staffs, and their residents. The data were reported by Catherine Hawes, PhD, in testimony before the U.S. Senate Committee on Finance in June 2002. Hawes told the committee: "There are no reliable data on the prevalence of abuse or neglect in nursing homes or residential long-term care facilities. However, the piecemeal evidence we do have suggests the problem is serious and widespread." Later, Hawes stated: "The daily misery, indignity, preventable decline, and premature death caused by neglect in nursing homes is truly a national tragedy. Moreover, it is probably more widespread than abuse."

Nursing Homes: A government report asserted that abuse of residents is a major problem in nursing homes. The report analyzed data for a two-year period (1999-2000) showing that 10% of nursing homes "were cited for abuse violations that caused actual harm to residents or placed them in immediate jeopardy of death or serious injury." The percentage is increasing.

Reports From Residents: An Atlanta Long Term Care ombudsman interviewed 80 residents in 23 Georgia nursing homes and elicited the information that 48% had experienced rough treatment and 44% experienced abuse.

Reports From Staff: Nurse's aides make up about 85% of the staff in a nursing home. A 1993 survey of certified nursing attendants found that more than half (58%) had seen a staff member yell at a resident in anger. What little information is available on the causes of abuse and neglect in nursing homes suggests that the foremost reasons are staff shortages, staff burnout, and poor staff training. The chart shows that the median hourly earnings of Certified Nursing Assistants is $8.61. The title is usually applied to caregivers in a nursing home or hospital setting. This rather low wage may go some way toward explaining the staff contribution to the problem. The fact that two-thirds of nursing home residents have some cognitive impairment from diseases like Alzheimer's and other dementias may help explain their contribution to the problem. Only 12% of nursing home residents are married with a spouse who presumably would be concerned about the resident's care.

Christine L. McDaniel, J.D., reports: "The Office of the Inspector General of the Department of Health & Human Services has identified seven different types of elder abuse of nursing home residents: physical abuse, misuse of restraints, verbal/emotional abuse, physical neglect, medical neglect, verbal/emotional neglect, and personal property abuse (material goods)." Something to look forward to in our old age?

Expect to see lawsuits against nursing homes explode, and cost of liability insurance policies for nursing homes skyrocket. Will this help? What will surely help is the increasing political clout wielded by older Americans. The issue of nursing home quality is now on the front burner. Thanks to public demand, the government recently initiated a six-state pilot project as part of the Health and Human Services' Nursing Home Quality Initiative. Quality data on nursing homes will be collected and published.

Sources: "Abuse In Residential Long-Term Care Facilities: What Is Known About Prevalence, Causes, And Prevention," Testimony Before the U.S. Senate Committee on Finance," Catherine Hawes, Ph.D., http://finance.senate.gov/hearings/testimony/061802chtest. pdf. Christine L. McDaniel J.D., *Elder Abuse In The Institutional Setting,* May 1997 http://www.keln.org/bibs/mcdaniel2.html. "HHS Releases Quality Data About Individual Nursing Homes: Pilot Project in Six States to Help Consumers Make Informed Health Decisions," HHS News, April 24, 2002, http://www.hhs.gov/news/press/2002pres/20020424.html. All data retrieved August 2002.

Health-Related Quality of Life As Life Winds Down

Percentage of Adults Aged 70+ With Hearing and Vision Limitations: 1994

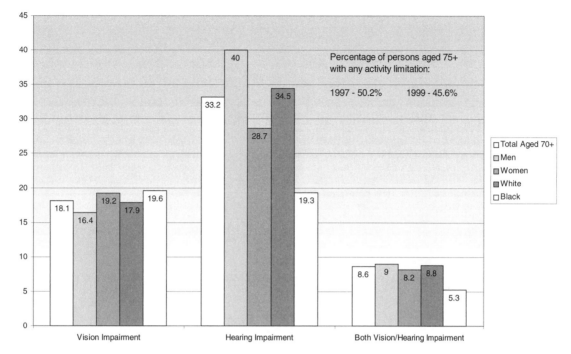

Advancing age is accompanied by periods of diminished health and functioning. Quality of life consequently suffers. How many elderly are affected? The chart shows the results of Centers for Disease Control (CDC) researchers' examination of data collected in 1994 (CDC has been asking quality-of-life questions only since 1993). Sensory impairment is common among the elderly — 18.1% of those aged 70+ had impaired vision, 33.2% had impaired hearing (more men are affected than women and only 11.6% of adults used a hearing aid), and 8.6% reported both hearing and vision impairments. African Americans had a slightly higher rate of vision impairment but a lower rate of hearing impairment.

Vision and hearing impairments are just the tip of the iceberg. With these and other common chronic conditions of old age (e.g., arthritis, hypertension, heart disease, diabetes) comes difficulty in performing the normal activities of daily life.

Percentage of Older Adults With Activity Limitations: 1994

Sex/Race	75-84	>=85	75-84	>=85	75-84	>=85
	Functional Activities		ADL		IADL	
Male	37.0	50.0	10.6	21.0	21.9	42.1
Female	46.2	65.6	13.5	29.2	32.3	57.9
Black	42.1	59.5	11.9	25.8	27.8	52.1
White	52.5	76.3	19.0	35.0	24.3	67.4

The table shows data on older adults who reported limitations in basic functional activities, activities of daily living (ADL), and instrumental activities of daily living (IADL). Functional activities include lifting, climbing stairs, walking, sustained standing, bending, reaching, and grasping. Activities of daily living (ADL) include bathing, dressing, getting around inside the home, toileting, eating, and getting in and out of beds and chairs. Instrumental activities of daily living (IADL) include shopping, managing money, using the telephone, performing household chores, and preparing meals. Whites and women are affected more than blacks and men — three quarters of Caucasians and two-thirds of women aged 85+ reported difficulty getting around (total population 85+ is about 3 million; two-thirds are women).

Coping with chronic illness on top of activity limitations and life events like loss of teeth,[18] financial problems, or the death of a spouse can lead to dementia, depression, and suicide. Between 25-50% of persons aged 85+ are affected by dementia, most commonly Alzheimer's disease. Depression, which is treatable, is often not recognized in the elderly (in 2000, 19% of persons aged 85+ had depressive symptoms, according to the Health and Retirement Study). Research has shown that over a period of four years, depressive symptoms in persons aged 70+ resulted in a 55% greater decline in physical abilities than might otherwise be expected. Elderly suicides (aged 65+) account for 20% of the total, though the elderly make up only 12% of the population. Men aged 85+ are particularly vulnerable.

The Administration on Aging reports that while the picture presented above may be "disheartening," the future promises something better: "Future cohorts of older Americans are expected to have fewer disabilities than past generations. Findings from the National Long-Term Care Surveys regarding the health and disability status of Americans, conducted by Duke University under the auspices of the National Institute on Aging, show that disability rates among older persons are falling, and this trend is expected to continue." This finding is bolstered by CDC: In 1997, half of all persons aged 75+ reported some kind of activity limitation, a figure that had fallen to 45.6% in 1999.[19]

Sources: Chart/Table: Vincent A. Campbell, Ph.D., et al., "Surveillance for Sensory Impairment, Activity Limitation, and Health-Related Quality of Life Among Older Adults — United States, 1993-1997," Tables 3 and 4 CDC, http://www.cdc.gov/mmwr/preview/mmwrhtml/ss4808a6.htm#top, and Health, United States, 2001, table 57, updated, http://www.cdc.gov/nchs/products/pubs/pubd/hus/tables/2001/01hus057.pdf. Marjorie Valbrun, "As America Ages, Abuse Grows Old," Philadelphia Inquirer, Feb. 6, 1994. CDC, "New Findings on Health, Quality of Life of U.S. Seniors Released," December 17, 1999, http://www.cdc.gov/od/oc/media/pressrel/r991217a.htm. JAMA Patient Page, "Depression — Symptoms of Depression in the Elderly Contribute to Physical Decline," http://www.medem.com. Online data retrieved September 2002.

---

[18] In 1997–98, 34% of low-income seniors in central counties of large metro areas had lost all their teeth, compared with 47% in the most rural counties. The prevalence of tooth loss is declining; persons aged 45-64 in 2000 can expect a better dental outcome than this as they age.

[19] According to CDC: "Limitation of activity is assessed by asking respondents a series of questions about limitations in their ability to perform activities usual for their age group because of a physical, mental, or emotional problem. Respondents are asked about limitations in activities of daily living, or instrumental activities of daily living, play, school, work, difficulty walking or remembering, and any other activity limitations. For reported limitations the causal health conditions are determined and respondents are considered limited if one or more of these conditions is chronic."

Perceptions of Health-Related Quality of Life Among the Elderly

Percentage of People Aged 75+ Who Reported Their Health Was Only Fair or Poor: 1993-97

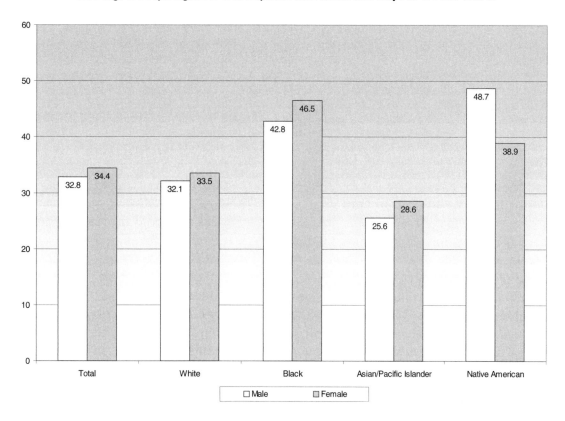

"Health is a state of complete physical, mental, and social well-being—not merely the absence of disease, or infirmity." — World Health Organization, 1948

The human spirit is remarkably resilient and power comes from positive thinking. The elderly may be debilitated in one way or another, but it may not matter much as long as they feel good. How do they feel?

The chart shows data from the Behavioral Risk Factor Surveillance System for the years 1993-1997. The BRFSS people describe this activity as "an ongoing, state-based, random-digit-dialed, telephone survey of U.S. civilian, noninstitutionalized persons aged greater than or equal to 18 years, which tracks health- and safety-related characteristics." The self-reports of health discussed here were obtained from 46,458 men and women aged 75+.

Each respondent was asked: "Now, thinking about your physical health, which includes physical illness and injury, for how many days during the past 30 days was your physical health not good?" and "Now, thinking about your mental health, which includes stress, depression, and problems with emotions, for how many days during the past 30 days was your mental health not good?"

Percentage of People 75+ Who Felt Only Fair or Poor

Item	Male	Female
Educational Level		
Less than h.s. grad	43.3	44.8
H.S. grad	30.7	32.7
Some college	29.0	27.2
College graduate	23.1	22.3
Annual Household Income		
<$15,000	42.9	41.6
$15,000-$24,999	34.2	31.7
$25,000-$34,999	25.3	25.5
$35,000-$49,999	24.6	22.5
>=$50,000	27.3	32.2
Marital Status		
Married	32.0	32.8
Divorced	37.7	35.6
Widowed	34.3	35.3
Separated	37.5	35.1

Sadly, about a third of men and women aged 75+ reported that their health was only fair or poor. For African Americans and Native Americans, the percentages were much higher. Nearly half of older black women and Native American men did not feel well, nor did somewhat smaller percentages of black men and Native American women.

The table shows self-reported health status data by gender according to educational level, annual household income, and marital status. It would appear that the best indicator for feeling better than fair is to be a married college graduate with a household income of at least $25,000. Using complete survey data of all adults aged 55+, the researchers summarized: "Older black or Hispanic adults and adults who had less than a high school education, earned less than $15,000 annual household income, were unable to work, were without health-care coverage, lived in the south, reported diabetes mellitus or consistently high blood pressure, were underweight or overweight, were current smokers, or did not participate in leisure-time activities were consistently more likely than the overall group to report fair or poor health status."

The Administration on Aging has data showing that, in 1999, 26.1% of all older persons (65+) surveyed reported only fair or poor health, a decline since the 1993-97 surveys. The sexes were pretty much equal, but older African-Americans (41.6%) and older Hispanics (35.1%) were still far more likely to report only fair or poor health. Black and Hispanic elderly persons are more likely to be poor, to have higher rates of smoking, poor nutrition, inadequate housing, and reduced access to/use of preventive health care services. Fortunately, blacks and Hispanics have stronger social support networks and are more likely than whites to receive care from family members when their health declines. We look next at trends in the way society has viewed its responsibilities toward improving the quality of life of the elderly.

Sources: Chart: Chart/Table: Vincent A. Campbell, Ph.D, et al., "Surveillance for Sensory Impairment, Activity Limitation, and Health-Related Quality of Life Among Older Adults — United States, 1993-1997," Tables 3 and 4 CDC, http://www.cdc.gov/mmwr/preview/mmwrhtml/ss4808a6.htm#top. Administration on Aging, "A Profile of Older Americans: 2001," http://www.aoa.gov/aoa/stats/profile/2001/12.html. Brenda F. McGadney, "Family and Church Support Among African American Family Caregivers of Frail Elders," http://www.rcgd.isr.umich.edu/prba/perspectives/spring1995/bmcgadney.pdf. "Family Structure Key to Care," http://www.asaging.org/at/at-232/RT_Family_Structure.html. Online data retrieved September 2002.

What Can Be Done to Improve the Quality of Life of the Elderly?

Medicare Benefits by Type of Provider: 1980-2000

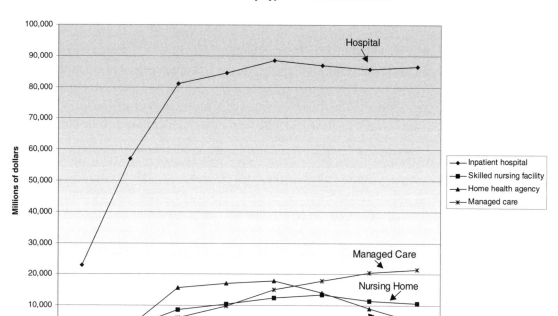

"Through this new law, every citizen will be able, in his productive years when he is earning, to insure himself against the ravages of illness in his old age. This insurance will help pay for care in hospitals, in skilled nursing homes, or in the home." Lyndon Johnson

When it comes to improving life's quality in the golden years, both society and the elderly have responsibilities. Elders' responsibilities are discussed in the next panel. Society's role is spelled out in programs like Social Security (1935), Medicare (1965), and the Older Americans Act (1965). This panel looks at Medicare.

The access to medical care that Medicare guarantees to the elderly, especially low-income beneficiaries, has improved their quality of life immeasurably. Medicare is one of our most popular and expensive entitlement programs, and it becomes more popular and more expensive as the elderly population grows. Today, Medicare serves about 39 million people (34 million seniors and 5 million others), about 14% of the total population.[20]

---

[20] The poorest Medicare recipients ("dual eligibles") have their medical costs partly paid through the Medicaid program. Unlike Medicare, this coverage includes benefits like prescription drugs, hearing aids, and payment for nursing home services. Medicaid coverage must be applied for; many eligible but unaware individuals do not receive it.

The chart shows major services that Medicare covered from 1980-2000.[21] About 12% of the elderly are hospitalized each year, so it is not surprising that hospitals received the lion's share of Medicare benefits —$22.8 billion in 1980, rising to $86.5 billion in 2000.

Services covered by Medicare may change depending on how the political winds blow or how the budget balances. When the public outcry for government action is loud, or when special interest groups prevail, Medicare is amended or reformed.[22] This is evident in the ebb and flow of payments to nursing homes, home health agencies, and Health Maintenance Organizations (HMOs, a k a managed care). The chart shows that managed care was not even an option before 1980 but by 2000 was number two in line for Medicare payments. Payments to HMOs rose from $2.3 billion in 1990 to 21 billion in 2000.

The chart shows that from 1980 to 1990 skilled nursing facilities (nursing homes) were third in line for Medicare payments but were overtaken by managed care and home health care (then home health care declined in the 1990s). Nursing homes are a phenomenon of the second half of the twentieth century. Most elderly people used to live either with their families or in boarding houses, where landlords might provide rudimentary assistance. Legislation passed in 1950 forbade Social Security payments to residents of institutions (including boarding houses) if the institutions did not provide health care. Encouraged by this and by Medicare/Medicaid, nursing homes gradually became the primary institutional setting for the care of the elderly.

Medicare Benefits: 2000

When prescribed by a physician, Medicare will pay for a short stay in a nursing home after a hospital stay. Medicare payments to nursing homes rose from $392 million in 1980 to $13.8 billion in 1998, then fell to $10.6 billion in 2000. Why the decline? The 1997 Balanced Budget Act (BBA) reduced the Medicare budget by $115 billion over five years. Payments to all health care providers were reduced.

Elderly people would rather be cared for at home by family, friends, or volunteers than be confined in institutions. In the last few decades, in the face of hugely rising Medicare

---

[21] Services under Medicare Part A only, which include inpatient hospital services, nursing facility care following a hospital stay, certain home health services, and hospice care (hospice care for the terminally ill is not included on the chart). A yearly deductible of $792 on hospital stays must be paid, and beneficiaries also pay a substantial portion of the cost for long hospital and nursing home stays. All those eligible for Part A may choose Part B coverage (most do). Part B, Supplementary Medical Insurance, is financed through general tax revenues and through monthly premiums paid by beneficiaries.

[22] A major issue in the 2000 presidential campaign was prescription drug coverage under Medicare.

costs and horror stories about the dehumanizing care in nursing homes, there was a shift in thinking about how elder care should be delivered. It is now generally accepted that public monies ought to be concentrated on home- and community-based services (e.g., adult day care, respite care, transportation services, and meals-on-wheels), rather than on institutional care. This shift in thinking is reflected in the chart data showing a rise in Medicare payments to home health agencies,[23] from $524 million in 1980 to $8.9 billion in 2000. Peter Uhlenberg wrote: "The rapid expansion of home-care services reflects demographic change (increasing number of disabled persons), technological change (increasing feasibility of delivering services within the home), and public-policy changes (increasing willingness of Medicare and Medicaid to pay for home health care."

The chart shows that between 1990-1997, there was a huge rise in payments to home health agencies, from $3.2 billion to $17.9 billion. In 1998 payments fell to $14.1 billion, because the BBA required beneficiaries to assume part of the cost of some home health care services. The George Washington University Medical Center reports: "Medicare home care beneficiaries generally are sicker, older, and poorer than Medicare beneficiaries in general.... The reductions in care ... [under the BBA] potentially could affect their health status."

Other ways to approach the delivery of elder care are suggested by Uhlenberg, who contends that alternatives such as assisted living, group homes, and rehabilitation are not as plentiful as they should be "due to misguided public policy"; namely, too much government support of nursing homes (a multibillion-dollar industry with a powerful lobby).

Doctors are seeing more and more elderly patients and geriatricians are in short supply. With the focus now on the elderly, some hospitals and clinics are working to enhance quality of care. For example, some offer geriatric evaluation and management units (GEMU) and clinics (GEMC), where teams of medical professionals address the particular physical and emotional needs of the 20% of the elderly who are frail. Drug companies are doing their part too, seeing a profit to be made on treatments for urinary incontinence (it has been associated with depression) and other conditions of the elderly.

Sources: Chart: *Statistical Abstract of the United States, 2001*, Table 135. Administration on Aging, "Older and Younger People With Disabilities," http://www.aoa.dhhs.gov/factsheets/disabilities.html. Peter A. Corning, *The History of Medicare*, http://www.ssa.gov/history/corning.html. *Medicare Basics*, The Century Foundation, http://www.medicarewatch.org/Basics/MedicareBasic.pdf. Joseph V. Agostini, M.D., et al., "Geriatric Evaluation and Management Units for Hospitalized Patients" http://www.ahcpr.gov/clinic/ptsafety/chap30.htm. Peter Uhlenberg, "Replacing the Nursing Home," *Public Interest*, No. 128, Summer 1997. George Washington University Study's Executive Summary, http://www.nahc.org/NAHC/NewsInfo/ 99nr/gwexecsum.html.

---

[23] Home health agencies provide skilled nursing care and other services in the home for the treatment of an illness or injury.

What Can the Elderly Do to Improve Their Quality of Life?

Risk Behaviors, Elderly Population: Latest Year

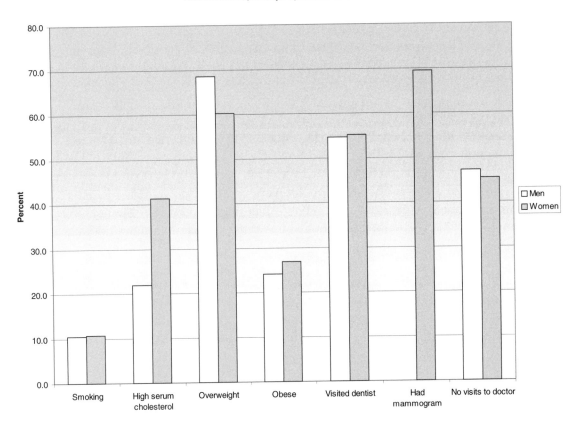

"God helps them who help themselves." — Benjamin Franklin

Average life expectancy may soon reach 85 years or more, but will the additional years be satisfying, or will old age be a degraded time of life?. In some ways, that is up to the individual.

Just like everyone else, older Americans could do more to optimize their own health and quality of life. As shown on the chart, about 10% of Americans aged 65+ are still smoking (1999). More than one-fifth of men and 41.3% of women aged 65-74 had high serum cholesterol (1988-94). In that same age group, 68.5% of men and 60.3% of women were overweight, while 24.1% of men and 26.9% of women were obese (1988-94). Among all people aged 65+, only a little over half had seen a dentist in the last year (1999). Among women 65-74 years old, 69.4% had a mammogram within the past 2 years, and only 57.2% of women aged 75+ had their mammogram (not shown) (1998). Women's risk of breast cancer increases as they age.

More than a third of people aged 65+ had not seen a doctor within the last year (1997). Screening older adults for the treatable chronic conditions that are the major causes of death for this population (e.g., cardiovascular disease and cancer) might help prolong life and improve its quality.[24] In addition to vaccinations and breast cancer screening, the Centers for Disease Control (CDC) recommends screening for colorectal cancer. In 1999, fewer than a third of people aged 55+ had received a simple screening test for colorectal cancer — their lives may be shortened or they may be living their last years with poor quality of life.

In 1999 CDC identified three specific areas in which older Americans are falling down, prevention-wise. They don't eat enough fruits and vegetables, they smoke too much, and they don't get enough exercise. More than 30% of people aged 65+ are not eating five or more servings of fruits and vegetables a day — easier said than done, since the elderly are often housebound, lack access to transportation, reside in a long-term care facility, or are unwilling/unable to attempt excursions to the market. About a third of 55- 74-year-olds are physically inactive, and 46.% of those aged 74+ report no physical activity what-soever. Exercise might help prevent falls, the most common cause of injuries and injury deaths among older Americans(nearly 10,000 seniors die each year because of fall inju-ries). Special exercise programs have been developed for the frail elderly. The Administration on Aging suggests that people think ahead about their probable future need for the modifications that make a home safer. AoA recommends that the frail elderly use as role models younger people with disabilities who refuse to be relegated to the sidelines.

CDC reports that too little is known about quality of life issues of the elderly. The government funds Prevention Research Centers and has established partnerships with states to move research findings into communities. An example of this initiative is the North-west Prevention Effectiveness Center at the University of Washington, which works with senior centers to help older adults exercise, eat well, and preserve their independence.

The elderly can improve the quality of their dying by executing living wills (a.k.a. advance directives), documents that state what limits a person wishes to place on the treatment (s)he would receive at the end of life. We have looked at quality of life; next we will look at the quality of dying in America.

Sources: Chart: *Healthy People 2000, Final Review*, Table 20; *Health, United States, 2001*, Tables 60, 68, 69, 80, 82; Primary sources: (Smoking data) CDC, National Center for Health Statistics (NCHS), National Health Interview Survey; (Cholesterol, smok-ing, obesity data) CDC, NCHS, Division of Health Examination Statistics. Unpublished data. (Dental and mammogram data) CDC, NCHS, National Health Interview Survey.

---

[24] Medicare coverage for most preventive services was increased or initiated on January 1, 1998. Medicare has reimbursed one lifetime pneumococcal vaccination, including the cost of the vaccine since 1981 and the cost of administration since 1992. Since May 1, 1993, Medicare has reimbursed health-care providers for the cost of influenza vaccine and its administration. Having teeth that are well cared for is important to quality of life, but retired persons are less likely to have dental insurance. With few exceptions, Medicare does not cover dental care services, and few states provide adult dental coverage under their Medicaid pro-grams.

What Can Be Done to Improve the Quality of Dying?: Hospice Care and Pain Control

**Medicare Benefits for Hospice Care:
1990-2000**

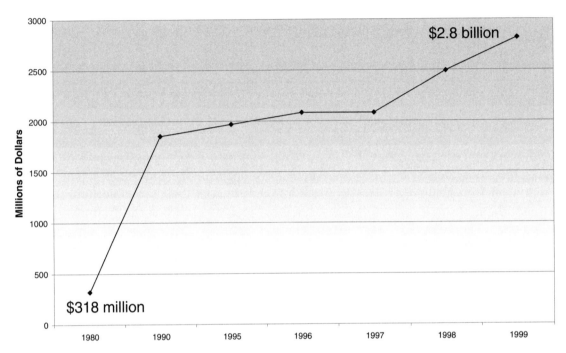

"We know with near certainty that the majority of patients who die in this country die with pain that they do not need to have, with dyspnea [difficulty breathing] that could be relieved, in isolation rather than in the comforting presence of loved ones, with desperate meaningless, last-ditch therapies they do not want and that cannot help them." — Donald M. Berwick, MD

Almost 2.5 million Americans die each year. Most of them are over the age of 65. Eighty percent die in hospitals. In "the place of solitary death,"[25] we succumb to acute illnesses that often involve interventions like intensive care, mechanical ventilation, or major surgical procedures — whether we want them or not. Hospice care is an alternative to this kind of death. The chart shows Medicare payments for hospice care from 1980-1999. Payments rose 786%, from $318 million to $2.8 billion.

Hospice care has grown rapidly since the nation's first hospice opened in 1974. Five years earlier, Elisabeth Kübler-Ross argued in her book *On Death and Dying* that for most people at the end of life, hospice care is a better alternative to dying in an institu-

---

[25] So called by French social historian Philippe Ariès, according to Nuland; see Source notes. Furthermore, Ariès wrote: "The hidden death in the hospital began very discreetly in the 1930's and 1940's and became widespread after 1950.... Although it is not always admitted, the hospital has offered families a place where they can hide the unseemly invalid whom neither the world nor they can endure...."

---

tion. Most people, when questioned about dying, will cite dying alone and in prolonged pain as their greatest fears. Hospice care addresses both of these issues. Hospice care is intended exclusively for the terminally ill and their families and takes place primarily in the patient's home. A team of doctors, nurses, home health aides, social workers, counselors, and trained volunteers provides pain treatment and palliative care (care that reduces the violence of a disease) with the aim of easing dying. Although it sounds like a good (and less expensive) alternative to an institutional death, hospice care accounts for only about 1% of total Medicare outlays. The reason has to do with longstanding attitudes toward death on the part of the medical establishment.

Today, the American medical community stands accused of prolonging life past all hope through technology (thereby extending the process of dying), of failing to respect dying patients' wishes for their own care, of making decisions based on financial considerations rather than compassion for the dying, and of failing to make full use of hospice care.

A CDC survey showed 52,100 patients receiving hospice care in 1992. By 1998, there were 79,837 patients being served by about 3,000 hospice organizations, a 53% increase. The small chart shows the primary admission diagnosis of hospice patients in 1998. According to Dr. Jill A. Rhymes: "Only approximately one third of cancer patients receive formal hospice care, often in the last few weeks of their illnesses. Patients with other terminal illnesses (eg, progressive neurological illnesses, end-stage cardiac or pulmonary disease, and acquired immunodeficiency syndrome [AIDS]) are even less likely to be admitted into hospices, and palliative care may be unavailable or inadequate for those outside of hospices."

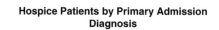

Hospice Patients by Primary Admission Diagnosis

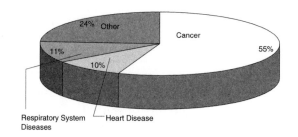

How many dying people actually experience unbearable pain? Dr. Timothy Quill, a spokesman for the assisted-suicide movement, estimates that only 2-5% of terminally ill patients find themselves in intractable pain (and that doctors have a moral duty to help them). A 1997 study called SUPPORT[26] e. Nine thousand patients were studied; 46% died during the study. Of that 46%, about 40% "were in either severe or moderate pain for most or all of the last three days of life — pain … that could have been alleviated through medication." Nearly half of the 4,100+ patients who died were subjected to aggressive measures to keep them alive (tube feeding, mechanical ventilation, attempted resuscitation). Dr. Albert W. Wu, who collaborated on the study, said: "We talk about he-

[26] Study to Understand Prognoses and Preferences for Outcomes and Risks of Treatment. Researchers from Johns Hopkins School of Public Health, George Washington University, and Beth Israel Hospital in Boston studied 9,000 individuals; their findings were published in the January 1997 *Annals of Internal Medicine* and are described by Marcus; see Source notes..

roic measures, extraordinary measures, but most of those words don't have negative connotations. We don't say that people were tormented until they died, but if we're to believe the results of this study, people were in pain until the end."

The attitude of the medical establishment towards hospice care and pain control is problematical. Why are medical practitioners so willing to prolong life in a hospital and so loathe to prescribe pain medication? Nuland writes of doctors' fear of failure, their "need to control [the dying process] that exceeds in magnitude what most people would find reasonable," their view of themselves as warriors and death as "an implacable enemy" that must be vanquished. Often cited is doctors' very real fear of losing their license,[27] or fear of patient addiction or the sedative or respiratory depression side effects of narcotics.

Why have doctors been slow to refer patients to hospice care? One reason is a Medicare requirement that doctors say with certainty that a hospice candidate has six months or less to live. Evidence that hospices are underused may be found in statistics like these from Michigan: The average length of hospice care in 1997 was 20 days and 30-40% of patients died within 7 days of initiating hospice treatment, although Medicare provides for a six-month stay. This means patients were nearly dead when they came to hospice care, when they might have benefited from the comfort to be found in such a program.

There has been criticism of current hospice care. Dr. Rhymes complains that hospice care is not well integrated into the established health care system and is underrepresented in inner cities and rural areas. She contends that "formal palliative care is available only in a package that many patients and families may be unable or unwilling to accept." She says hospice care teams may consist of completely different people from those who had cared for a patient previously, causing a separation trauma when patient and family are already traumatized. Furthermore: "To enter a hospice, patients and families must forfeit other forms of or access to health care, accept only palliative care, and make no attempt to prolong life."

This is the modern way of dying. Next we look at the movement to put some decisions about dying in the hands of those most intimately affected.

Sources: *Statistical Abstract of the United States 2001*. Nuland. *How We Die*. New York: Vintage Books, 1995. Adam Marcus, "Death Be Not Painful." *Johns Hopkins Magazine* (September 1997). Jill A. Rhymes, M.D., "Barriers to Palliative Care," http://www.moffitt.usf.edu Gregory Brusstar, "Michigan: Toward Physician-Assisted Living — Improving End of Life Care," http://www.medem.com. JAMA Patient Page: Decisions About End-of-Life Care, http://www.medem.com.

---

[27] Doctors have lost their licenses for what drug regulators call over-prescribing of narcotics. After California voters approved the Medical Marijuana Initiative in 1996 (which holds that the state's criminal laws against marijuana do not apply when a seriously ill patient uses marijuana on the advice of a physician), the federal government announced that as part of the war on drugs, it would use its authority under the Controlled Substances Act to revoke a doctor's right to prescribe *any* drugs if the doctor recommended marijuana to a patient. A group of doctors and patients sued. In 2002 the case awaited a decision by the U.S. Supreme Court. See http://www.conantfoundation.org/commentary.html for more information.

Improving the Quality of Dying: The Patients' Rights Movement

Patients' Rights Timeline

1906	First euthanasia bill is drafted in Ohio.
1968	First living will bill is introduced in Florida.
1973	American Hospital Association creates Patient Bill of Rights, which includes informed consent and right to refuse treatment.
1976	11 states pass "natural death" laws giving legal standing to living wills and protecting doctors from being sued for failure to treat incurable illnesses.
1980	"Dear Abby" publishes letter from anguished relative of dying loved one. Society for the Right to Die receives 30,000 requests for advance directives.
1984	Advance care directives have been recognized in 22 states and District of Columbia.
1987	California State Bar Conference is the first public body to approve of physician aid-in-dying.
1988	Unitarian Universalist Association of Congregations is the first religious body to affirm a right to die.
1990	American Medical Association adopts the position that with informed consent, a physician can withhold/withdraw treatment from a patient who is close to death, and may discontinue life.
1990	U.S. Supreme Court decision recognizes the constitutional right of a competent patient to refuse medical treatment (including artificial nutrition and hydration).
1990	Patient Self-Determination Act is passed, requiring hospitals that receive federal funds to tell patients that they have a right to demand or refuse treatment.
1991	Gallup poll finds that 75% of Americans approve of living wills.
1994	Oregon voters approve the first Death With Dignity Act. All states + District of Columbia have recognized some type of advance directive.
1997	Voting unanimously, the U.S. Supreme Court rules that states may outlaw doctor-assisted suicide - that Americans do not have a "constitutional right to die" with the aid of a physician. It is now widely recognized that better care for the dying is crucially needed.

"Death belongs to the dying and to those who love them.... within the limits of my ability to control, I will not die later than I should simply for the senseless reason that a highly skilled technological physician does not understand who I am." — Sherwin B. Nuland, *How We Die*

A living will (a.k.a. advance directive) spells out a person's wishes for terminal care and takes effect when the person is no longer able to communicate those wishes.[28] Living wills are a product of the patients' rights movement of the twentieth century, some highlights of which are charted above. Patients' rights include the right to demand or refuse medical treatment when one is faced with inevitable death and the right to secure a doctor's help in ending suffering (sometimes called euthanasia or doctor-assisted suicide). These rights have legal, moral, medical, and ethical components, as reflected in the timeline above. Since the early twentieth century, courts of law, religious bodies, the medical establishment, voters, and newly-formed societies have weighed in on the emotional issue of appropriate end-of-life care and the patient's role in it.

The timeline shows that the right of the terminally ill to refuse treatment is now established — by 1994 all states had recognized some type of advance directive. Physician-

---

[28] Other names for living will include special medical power of attorney; power of attorney; verbal directions for future care; durable medical power of attorney; DNR — do not resuscitate; and organ donation.

Oregonians Choosing Death With Dignity: 1998-2001

Item	Number (%)
Age — Median, years (range)	69 (25-94)
Race	
White, non-Hispanic (%)	88 (97)
Asian (%)	3 (3)
Sex	
Male (%)	44 (48)
Marital status	
Married (%)	40 (44)
Widowed (%)	22 (24)
Divorced (%)	23 (25)
Never married (%)	6 (7)
Education	
Less than high school grad (%)	10 (11)
High school grad/some college (%)	42 (46)
College graduate (%)	27 (30)
Post-baccalaureate education (%)	12 (13)

assisted suicide is another matter entirely. Except in Oregon, it is illegal to choose a physician-assisted, peaceful death over a life of unbearable pain and suffering.

Oregon became the first state to legalize physician-assisted suicide in 1994. The Death With Dignity Law[29] requires an annual report on the year's experience with the law. The first report stated that 23 people received legal prescriptions for lethal medications; 15 of them used the medication.[30] Six people died before using the drug and two others were still alive at the time the report was filed. Non-use of the drug has been interpreted to mean that people want a choice, whether or not they take advantage of it.

By 2001 a total of 91 Oregonians were reported to have availed themselves of a physician's assistance in dying. The table shows some demographics of that population of 91. Median age was 69, the majority were white, female, married, and had attended college. Seventy percent of those who died had cancer.

The American Medical Association holds that physician-assisted suicide is "fundamentally incompatible with the physician's role as a healer." Anonymously, many doctors will concede that there have been times when they assisted someone to die. Sometimes the assisted death has been notorious rather than anonymous, as in the deaths presided over by Jack Kevorkian (Michigan's Dr. Death). A 2002 ABC News poll found 48% of Americans opposed and 40% in favor of physician-assisted suicide. However the patient's rights movement plays out, appropriate end-of-life care is an issue that will no longer be ignored. Next we look at how patients' rights are handled in Holland.

Sources: Chart: Doctor-Assisted Suicide: A Chronology," Longwood University, http://www.lwc.edu/administrative/library/death.htm. Small chart: "Oregon's Death with Dignity Act — Annual Report 2001," http://www.ohd.hr.state.or.us/chs/pas/ar-tbl-1.htm. National Center for Health Statistics, *Health, United States, 1998*, www.cdc.gov/nchswww/products/pubs/pubd/hus/hus.htm. National Institutes of Health, "Quality of Life for Individuals at the End of Life, August 2, 2000, http://grants1.nih.gov/grants/guide/pa-files/PA-00-127.html. Faye Girsh, "Death With Dignity: Choices and Challenges," *USA Today*, March 2000/. Data retrieved September 13, 2002.

---

[29] After passage of Oregon's law, U.S. Attorney General John Ashcroft declared that writing lethal-dose prescriptions was not "legitimate medical practice." In May 2002 a federal judge ruled that Ashcroft had overstepped his authority in making that declaration.

[30] It has been alleged that the Oregon data are sketchy and incomplete because of physician non-reporting and privacy concerns. By way of comparison, in 2000, 493 total suicides were reported in Oregon (http://www.ohd.hr.state.or.us/chs/finalabd/00/deathman.htm). The 2001 report and earlier data can be found at http://www.ohd.hr.state.or.us/chs/pas/ar-index.htm.

The Dutch Way of Death

Statistics About Death in Holland: 1991

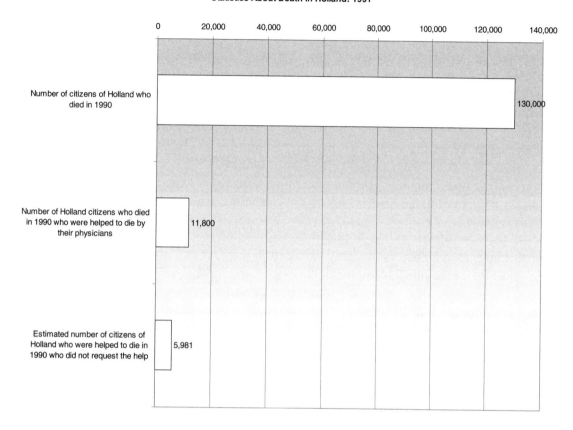

Number of citizens of Holland who died in 1990 — 130,000

Number of Holland citizens who died in 1990 who were helped to die by their physicians — 11,800

Estimated number of citizens of Holland who were helped to die in 1990 who did not request the help — 5,981

"We Beatrix, by the grace of God, Queen of the Netherlands, Princess of Orange-Nassau, etc., etc. etc. Greetings to all who shall see or hear these presents! Be it known: ... We have considered that it is desired to include a ground for exemption from criminal liability for the physician who with due observance of the requirements of due care to be laid down by law terminates a life on request or assists in a suicide of another person..." — from Holland's euthanasia law, which went into effect on April 1, 2002

We have looked at the American way of death. Is there a better way? The chart shows death statistics collected in Holland in 1991. When Holland passed the world's first euthanasia law in 2002, the practice of physician-assisted death in that country was longstanding. Although a criminal act, it had been openly tolerated since 1973 according to the International Task Force on Euthanasia and Assisted Suicide.

In Holland, physician-assisted death legally requires the consent of the patient, but according to the task force, a Dutch study found that "55% of the Dutch doctors interviewed in 1995 indicated that 'they had ended a patient's life without his or her explicit request' or 'they had never done so but that they could conceive of a situation in which they would.'"

On the day the Dutch senate approved the law, Dutch health minister Els Borst said in a newspaper interview that she is in favor of "Drion's pill" "if it can be carefully regulated so that it only concerns those people of advanced age who are done with life." Drion's pill is named after Hulb Drion, the former vice-president of the Dutch High Court, who in 1991 proposed that a suicide pill be made available to elderly people upon request.

The United Nations Human Rights Committee is "concerned that, with the passage of time, [Holland's] practice may lead to routinization and insensitivity to the strict application of the requirements in a way not anticipated." The London *Daily Telegraph* opined: "It is no mercy to get rid of the patient instead of the disease." The German newspaper *Frankfurter Allgemeine* warned: "When a sick person sighs: 'I wish I were dead,' it will no longer elicit sympathy and nursing care, but provide the opportunity to bind the patient to these words and begin legal proceedings, with the full approval of the state." The London *Times* predicted the growth of a new industry — death tourism — one-way euthanasia trips to Holland (the law does not prohibit doctors from administering euthanasia to non-residents).

Under the law, Dutch doctors are not permitted to suggest euthanasia as an option and a patient must be aware of all other medical options and have sought a second professional opinion. The request must be made voluntarily, persistently and independently while the patient is of sound mind. Patients may also execute a written request (advance directive) for a doctor to use discretion regarding euthanasia in the event the patient becomes too physically or mentally ill to make the decision. Children aged 12 through 15 can be euthanized or assisted in suicide with the consent of at least one parent or guardian. No parental consent is required for minors 16 or 17 years old.

Is this sound, humane policy to end unnecessary suffering? Does it constitute freedom to die, or freedom to be killed? Is this slippery slope legislation, from which a sequence of increasingly unacceptable events will follow?

Before leaving the topic of health care at the end of our days, we will look at the cost of health care for seniors.

Sources: Chart: Statistics from "a 1991 report by the attorney general of the High Council of the Netherlands," cited in "The Dutch Way of Death," by Richard Miniter, The Wall Street Journal, April 28, 2001, retrieved September 11, 2001, from http://opinionjour nal.com/editorial/feature.html?id=95000390. International Task Force on Euthanasia and Assisted Suicide, http://www.international taskforce.org/holland.htm. United Nations Human Rights Committee, http://www.unhchr.ch/.

The Price We Pay for Health Care for Senior Citizens

Net Medicare Outlays 1967-1996 in 1995 Constant Dollars

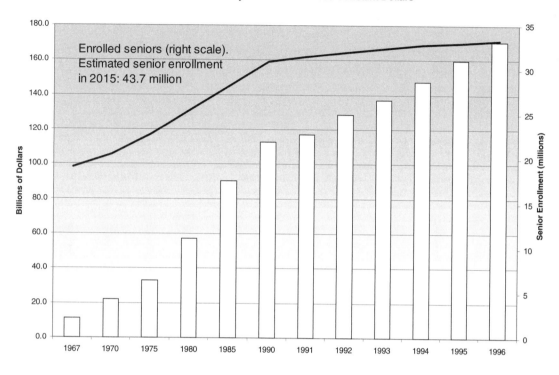

"Free medicine is medicine paid for by somebody else." — William F. Buckley Jr.

In 1964, the Johnson administration projected that Medicare would cost $12 billion by 1990. The chart shows that the actual figure was close to $113 billion, and it keeps on growing. "More ominously," grouses conservative John Hood, "Medicare conditioned an ever growing legion of elderly recipients to think that health care could and should be obtained at virtually no apparent cost. Because of this development, 20 percent of the voters in our elections — the retirees — now believe that they paid for their benefits throughout their working lives and deserve them, or even enhanced versions of them." And this is despite the fact, says Hood, that the elderly are better off financially than any other segment of the population.

Perhaps you have heard some of the grumbling or seen the headlines, like this one: "The Coming War Between the Old and the Young": 'The elderly ...12 percent of the population ... consume 60 percent of federal social spending.'" And there's nowhere to go but up. The first of 76 million Baby Boomers will retire in 2011, will start to collect Social Security, will become eligible for Medicare. They will live longer than earlier generations, and they will have access to medical innovations that may keep them alive well past what has long been thought of as the proper time to go. (In 1975 the average age of death among Medicare beneficiaries aged 65+ was 78.8; in 1997 it was 81.2). The number of Medicare beneficiaries is projected to nearly double to 72 million by 2030.

The chart above does not include substantial Medicaid expenditures on the elderly. Medicaid is the government health care safety net program for lower-income people or those impoverished by high medical expenses. Medicaid payments for the elderly came to $142 billion in 1998, up from $65 billion in 1990, a 118% jump in just 8 years.

Rettenmaier and Wang analyzed Medicare expenditures between 1965 and 1997 to determine (among other things) whether the rapid growth could be blamed on "the extraordinary sums spent on patients nearing the end of life." They found that Medicare spending in the last two years of life among those who died in 1997 averaged $28,616.[31] This does not include substantial out-of-pocket expenditures by the patient and his/her family.[32] While the cost of dying is high, it "does not appear to be growing any faster than the rest of Medicare spending," despite expensive technological innovations.

The Congressional Budget Office (CBO) estimates that net mandatory spending for Medicare will total $223 billion in 2002 and $3.2 trillion from 2003 through 2012, if the law governing Medicare spending in 2002 remains unchanged. In testimony before the U.S. Senate Committee on the Budget in February 2002, David M. Walker, Comptroller General of the United States, stated: "Absent structural changes in entitlement programs for the elderly, in the long term persistent deficits and escalating debt will overwhelm the budget." Can anyone summon the political will to effect these changes? AARP, the nation's most powerful seniors organization with 30 million+ members, favors adding a prescription drug benefit to Medicare. CBO estimates that a basic Medicare drug benefit for low-income beneficiaries[33] would increase Medicare spending by a total of $57 billion over the 2003-2012 period (on top of the $3.2 trillion already projected for Medicare). As Senator Everett Dirksen is alleged to have said: "A billion here, a billion there, and pretty soon you're talking real money."

An increasing number of Americans are elderly and frail. Who should pay for long-term care services for them? It might be prudent to start saving money for a long retirement.

Sources: Chart: *Medicare and Health Care Chartbook*, U.S. House of Representatives, Committee on Ways and Means, February 27, 1997, http://www.access.gpo.gov/congress/house/ways-and-means/. John Hood, "Senior Slump," *National Review*, October 23, 2000, p56+. "Entitlement Programs Will Overwhelm the Budget, Cato Daily Comment, March 14, 2002, http://www.socialsecurity.org/dailys/03-14-02.html. Andrew J. Rettenmaier and Zijun Wang, "Explaining the Growth of Medicare: Part II," National Center for Policy Analysis, Brief Analysis No. 408, August 6, 2002, http://www.ncpa.org. Robert Wood Johnson Foundation, Grant Results Report, Monograph on High-Cost Illness at the End of Life. Summary, http://www.rwjf.org/reports/grr/021577s.htm.

---

[31] The average amount spent on Medicare enrollees who did not die was $3,663.

[32] "On average, it costs Americans more than $30,000 above any insurance coverage to pay for the care required in their last year of life." *Annals of Internal Medicine*, March 2000: 132:451-459.

[33] A prescription drug benefit like the one proposed in President George W. Bush's 2003 budget. See http://www.cbo.gov/showdoc.cfm?index=3304&sequence=0. In 1996 the lowest fifth, income-wise, of Medicare beneficiaries spent an average $12,602 on health care, compared to $6,371 for the highest fifth.

Trends in Media Images of Senior Citizens

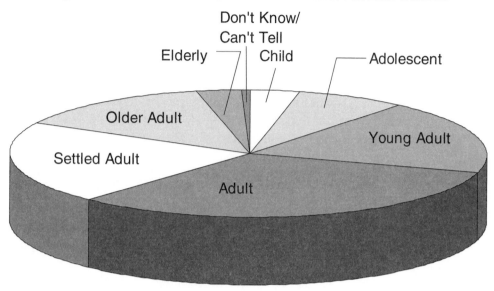

Age Distribution of Prime-Time TV Characters: Fall 2000 Season

Television is America's most popular medium — we spent 3,491 hours per person watching television in 2000.[34] How many senior citizens did we see? The chart presents data from a survey of prime-time television shows during the fall 2000 season. Children Now, the child advocacy group that carried out the survey, observed that a television viewer would see "A world overwhelmingly populated by able-bodied, single, heterosexual, white, male adults under 40." (Perhaps the people who create these television shows are offering us the characters they know best — themselves.)

The television survey found that among the total prime-time population of 2,251 characters, only 67, or fewer than 3%, were aged 70 or older, and 13% were "older adults" roughly between the ages of 50 and 69. An earlier survey of prime-time characters on view during the decade 1982-1992 did not even make a distinction between "older adult" and "elderly" but simply reported that over that period, 1.9% of prime-time casts were "old males" and 2.5% were "old females." Semantically and numerically, seniors are making a little progress.

In 2000, 20.4% of Americans were age 55 or older. On prime-time television that fall, one-third of male characters were older than 40, while only 19% of the women were that age or older — even though in real life, older women outnumber older men.

---

[34] Veronis, Suhler & Associates; see Source notes.

There is more to the media than television, of course. Are we seeing plenty of positive images of older adults elsewhere? In the movies, perhaps? Maria D. Vesperi points out in *Generations* (Journal of the American Society on Aging) that the current image of older Americans has been honed for retirement community advertising. Those ads show older adults as "slender, healthy, financially secure, at leisure, casually but conservatively dressed, and heterosexual — usually depicted as couples or in leisure-time association with children and grandchildren." Similar images of senior citizens appear in ads for potency drugs (minus the children) or in ads for a nutritional supplement featuring senior citizen couples playing sports and frolicking on the beach. These advertisers may have heeded the advice of Paul Kleyman of the American Society on Aging to "Wake up and smell the demographics," but does anyone other than seniors see the ads? The ads were most likely placed in newspapers and magazines. We spent 152 hours per person reading newspapers and 80 hours per person reading magazines in 2000.[35] Isn't it likely that the ads depicting senior citizens in a positive way were overlooked by everyone but seniors?

If it is true that the media can influence the way we feel about ourselves, do the images they see make the majority of senior citizens feel inadequate? Vesperi dates the current, more positive depiction of seniors to the late 1980s, when "the public dialogue shifted from discussion of the fragile, dependent aged to a focus on healthy older people with self-serving 'lifestyles.'" Vesperi calls this group "woofies" — well-off older folks. How many senior citizens fit the bill? Is there really a huge population of well-off, "active elders" out there, ready to strap on their backpacks and explore the backcountry? The median older householder income in 2000 was $23,048, not exactly in the jet-setting realm. And according to the Centers for Disease Control, the vast majority of senior citizens have chronic health conditions that do not permit strenuous physical activity, although they may enjoy a reasonably good quality of life.[36]

Whether positive media depictions of senior citizens are accurate or even absorbed by a wide audience, the huge Baby Boom generation is about to join the rank of senior citizens. For them, we end on this positive note from Elizabeth Benedict: "Old age seems poised to become a period associated with liberation, innovation, the next cool thing: a sort of Woodstock Nation redux. Except, of course, we won't want to thrash around half-naked in the mud anymore."

Sources: Maria D. Vesperi, "Media, Marketing, and Images of the Older Person in the Information Age," http://www.generationsjournal.org/gen25-3/intro.html. Small chart: "Fall Colors: 2000-01 Prime Time Diversity Report," http://www.childrennow.org/media/fc2001/fc-2001-report.pdf. "Comparison of prime time casts of 1982-92 and 1994-1997, by age group and gender," Screen Actors Guild, http://www.sag.org/diversity/Table3.html. Elizabeth Benedict, "When Baby Boomers Grow Old," *The American Prospect*, vol. 12 no. 9, May 21, 2001, http://www.elizabethbenedict.com/boomers.html. *Statistical Abstract of the United States: 2001*, Table 1125, "Media Usage and Consumer Spending: 1995 to 2004," primary source: Veronis, Suhler & Associates Inc., New York, NY, *Communications Industry Forecast* annual.

---

[35] *Ibid.*

[36] For example, more than 65% of Americans aged 65 years or older have some form of cardiovascular disease; half of all men and two-thirds of all women older than 70 have arthritis.

Chapter 8

Disability

The history of how human societies have treated their handicapped and disabled members is not a pretty tale. The disabled have often been misunderstood, shunned, locked away, feared, and kept on the margins of society.

With medical advances made during the 20th century, many more people with severe disabilities were saved from an early death, particularly those disabled through injury. For example, of soldiers suffering spinal cord injuries in World War I only 2% survived. By World War II that figure had risen to 85%. The United States was faced with a growing number of disabled people. With the rise of the civil rights movement in the 1960s, a movement for the rights of the disabled began to grow. The movement culminated in the passage of the Americans with Disabilities Act (ADA) in 1990.

The ADA is intended to provide all disabled people with protection against discrimination and to help them achieve full integration in mainstream society. One important outcome of the legislation was the recognition that more needed to be known about our disabled population. In the early 1990s, new data collection systems were put in place. As more data become available, we will be able to track the progress of the ADA.

The first panels in this chapter measure the disabled population and list the causes of disability both for adult-onset disability and childhood disability. Schools are categorizing an ever-growing number of children as disabled. The fifth panel poses the question: Are more of our children disabled or have definitions of disability changed?

Disabled workers grew 253% between 1970 and 2001. We explore the reasons why in two panels. The next three panels cover the differences in educational attainment and earnings that exist between the disabled and general populations.

We're making progress towards the integration of disabled people into all aspects of society. At the same time, we're labeling more people as disabled, be that for mental disorders, weight problems, or drug addiction. While severely disabled people are finding employment in greater numbers, the number of people on disability is rising. These seeming contradictions are difficult to reconcile. In this chapter we simply present the situation as it is today and try, where possible, to explain how we got here.

The Number of Us with Disabilities

Disabled Americans as a Percentage of the Population, 1997

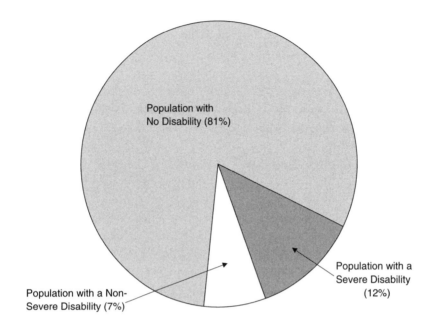

Population with
No Disability (81%)

Population with a Non-
Severe Disability (7%)

Population with a
Severe Disability
(12%)

How many of us live with an impairment serious enough to be considered a disability? The Americans with Disabilities Act of 1990 defines disability as a substantial limitation in a major life activity. More specifically, and according to the U.S. Bureau of the Census, a person is considered disabled if he or she has one or more of the following:

> Difficulty performing certain basic functions (for example: seeing, hearing, talking, walking, climbing stairs and lifting and carrying).

> Difficulty performing activities of daily living (for example: eating, bathing, dressing, and handling toiletry needs).

> Difficulties with certain social roles (for example: doing school work for children, working at a job and around the house for adults).

The designation of *disabled* is one that covers a large range of impairments. In 1997, 52.6 million people had some level of disability. This figure is 19% of the population or close to one in every five Americans. Of this total, almost two thirds (32.9 million) had what are categorized as severe disabilities[1] and the rest (19.6 million) had non-severe disabilities.

---

[1] A person with a severe disability is one who is unable to perform one or more activities of daily life, or who uses an assistive device to get around, or who needs assistance from another person to perform basic activities.

The distinction between severe and non-severe disability is somewhat fluid. It depends to a large degree on how people self-identify themselves in census counts and surveys. For example, an older woman who has difficulty walking due to leg pain from arthritis may or may not be counted as disabled. But if she uses a cane or wheelchair, she will be categorized as having a severe disability.

Persons with the *most* severe disabilities usually need another person's assistance with one or more activities of daily living, often referred to as ADLs. In this group are those paralyzed by accident or disease, those born with a crippling disorder (cystic fibrosis, metal retardation, and cerebral palsy to name but three), and those suffering from advanced cases of such degenerative diseases as Alzheimer's, Parkinson's, and multiple sclerosis. These are the people whose impairments so dramatically impact their lives as to make independence impossible. In 1997, 10.1 million people lived with this level of disability, 3.8% of the U.S. population.

Among the young, men have a higher rate of disability than do women. In the age group 15 to 24 years, the prevalence of disability among women in 1997 was 9.8% and among men 11.6%. Young men, as we saw in Chapter 1, tend to engage in dangerous activities at higher rates than young women do. This may explain why they suffer more disabling accidents.

The situation changes as we age. Among those aged 55 to 64 in 1997, women had a rate of disability of 37.2% and men of 34.0%. Overall more women than men of all ages are disabled, 28.3 million women to 24.3 million men.

The fact that women live on average longer than men may have a lot to do with their higher rates of disability. As we age we experience more disabling diseases and accidents, both as a result of more life experience and because with age comes deterioration. Next we will look at the rate of increased disability with age.

Source: U.S. Bureau of the Census, *Americans with Disabilities, 1997,* Table 1, "Prevalence of Disability by Age, Sex, Race, and Hispanic Origin: 1997," February 2001, p. 10. Much of the data in this report originated in another Bureau of the Census report, the *Survey of Income and Program Participation* (SIPP).

Aging and Disability

Percent of Population That is Disabled by Age Group, 1997

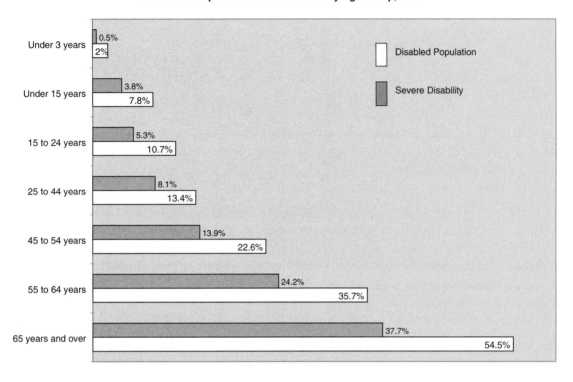

As we age our chances of being disabled increase. For those under 15 years of age in 1997, 7.8% were disabled while more than half (54.4%) of those 65 or older were disabled. The severity of the disability also rises with age. Of the youngest group charted, 0.5% has a severe disability, a quarter of all disabled children under 3 years of age. For the 65 and over crowd, more than half of those with some kind of disability had a severe kind of limitation.

What are the leading causes of disability among adults? We look at that subject next. Children's disabilities will have their own distinct panel.

Source: U.S. Bureau of the Census, *Americans with Disabilities, 1997,* Table 1, "Prevalence of Disability by Age, Sex, Race, and Hispanic Origin: 1997," February 2001, p. 10.

What Disables Us?

Top 15 Causes of Disability in Those 15 or Older

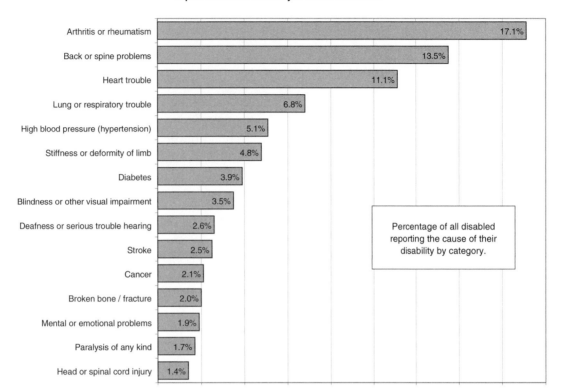

Arthritis or rheumatism	17.1%
Back or spine problems	13.5%
Heart trouble	11.1%
Lung or respiratory trouble	6.8%
High blood pressure (hypertension)	5.1%
Stiffness or deformity of limb	4.8%
Diabetes	3.9%
Blindness or other visual impairment	3.5%
Deafness or serious trouble hearing	2.6%
Stroke	2.5%
Cancer	2.1%
Broken bone / fracture	2.0%
Mental or emotional problems	1.9%
Paralysis of any kind	1.7%
Head or spinal cord injury	1.4%

Percentage of all disabled reporting the cause of their disability by category.

As we saw in the last panel, our likelihood of being disabled increases as we age. It is, therefore, not surprising that the leading cause of disability in adults is arthritis and rheumatism[2]. There were 7.2 million people disabled by arthritis and rheumatism in late 1991 and early 1992.

Spine problems come next. Back and spine problems caused disability in 5.7 million adults. Such problems should not be confused with paralysis; paralysis affects many fewer people. Back and spine problems include serious chronic stiffness or deformity of the back or spine. Paralysis of any kind represents the 14th leading cause of disability in adults. There were 716,000 people with some form of paralysis in 1991 and 1992.

---

[2] The terms arthritis and rheumatism are often used interchangeably to describe conditions involving stiff, swollen, and inflamed joints. In actuality, each of these is a form of disease that falls into the larger category called rheumatic diseases. These diseases share similar symptoms and can leave their sufferers crippled. The causes of rheumatic diseases are not known but treatments to ease the pain they cause and reduce their crippling effects are available.

Once we have dealt with arthritis, rheumatism, back, and spinal problems, we enter a group of disabilities that have a good deal to do with behavior — although unlucky genes cannot be discounted either. The heart exceeds the lungs in causing disability. High blood pressure disables more people than does diabetes. But all four of these conditions are high on the list of causes that disable us.

The adult causes of disability are most often related to aging, accidents or injury. Lung and respiratory problems are very often linked to smoking. Heart disease can also be traced back to smoking, lack of exercise, and poor diet. Some people, of course, have genetic heart conditions. High blood pressure is a potentially disabling condition is frequently made worse — if not brought on — by bad diet, smoking, and lack of exercise. Unwise behavior builds up as we age. Eventually it presents some of us with a bill as we reach a certain age.

For children the situation is different. In the next panel we'll look at childhood disabilities.

Source: U.S. Department of Health, Centers for Disease Control, "Prevalence of Disability and Associated Health Conditions, United States, 1991-1992," *Mortality and Morbidity Weekly Report*, 1994, Volume 43, Number 40, available online at http//www.cdc.gov/mmwr/preview/mmwrhtml/00033002.htm.

What Disables Our Children?

Top 15 Causes of Disability in Those 17 or Younger

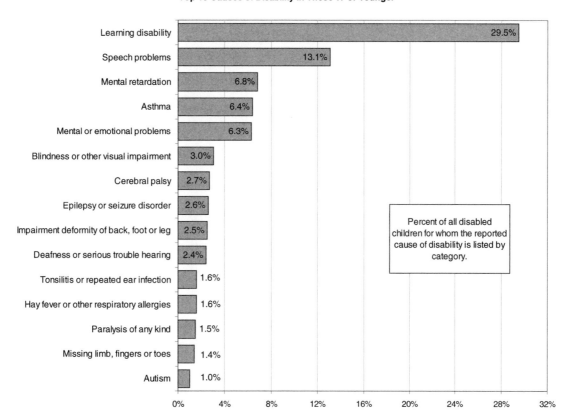

The leading type of disability among the young, those 17 years old or younger, is learning disability. This one category — it covers a range of cognitive disabilities — accounts for almost one third of all child disabilities. The data in this graph are from the same 1991-92 report from which we took disability causes for adults in the last panel. In 1991 and 1992 a total of 3.8 million children had some disability. Of these, 1,435,000 were afflicted with a learning disability, not including mental retardation or autism.

Other leading causes include (1) speech problems (634,000 children in 1991-92; (2) mental retardation (331,000); (3) asthma (311,000); and (4) mental and emotional problems (305,000 children). Of the top five causes of childhood disability, all but one originate with a malfunction in the brain.

The subject of childhood disability is one that merits a much closer look. The dramatic increase in the number of children being served in programs designed for the disabled is alarming. Is the increase due to growing incidence of disability? Or are we just serving the disabled more effectively?

Source: U.S. Department of Health, Centers for Disease Control, "Disability Among Children Aged Less than or Equal to 17 Years, United States, 1991-1992," *Mortality and Morbidity Weekly Report*, 1995, Volume 44, Number 33, available online at http//www.cdc.gov/ mmwr/preview/mmwrhtml/00038522.htm.

Growing Numbers of Disabled Children?

Number of Disabled Children by Category of Disability, 1977-2000

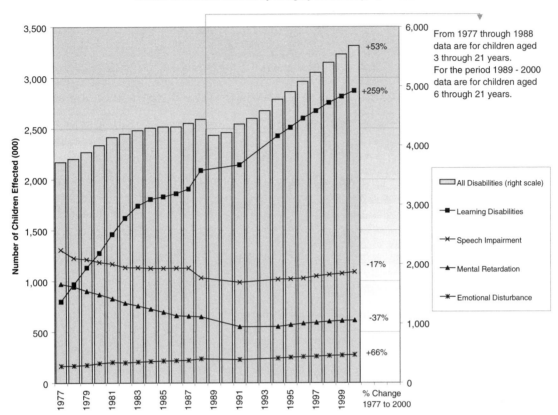

The number of children being served by educational programs for the disabled rose sharply between 1977 and 2000. The graph presents, as bars and against the right scale, the total number of children enrolled in some program for the disabled. The curves are measured on the left scale and show the number of children by the type of disability being addressed in the program the children attend. On the right side of the graph we are showing the 1977 to 2000 percentage change for each of the items charted.

The overall number of children served by such programs grew from 3.72 million in 1977 to 5.68 million in 2000, an increase of 53%. During this same period, the total number of children in the age ranges covered[3] grew by only 8% in the population. In terms of number of children served per 100,000 children, the increase between 1980 and 2000[4] was 57%, rising from 6.1 in 1980 to 9.5 children per 100,000 in 2000.

---

[3] For the period 1977 through 1988 the range covered is 3 years to 21 years of age. From 1989 through 2000 that range changed to all children 6 to 21 years of age.

[4] Detailed population figures for the period 1977-2000 are not available so data for the period 1980-2000 were used for this measure.

If we looks at specific disabilities separately, a variable pattern emerges. The curves in the graph present data on the number of children participating in the four largest program areas — those serving the greatest number of children. There are eleven program areas for which data are collected and reported by the U.S. Department of Education. For the 6 areas not charted ,the number of cases in each were too small to be usefully included in the graph. All 11 areas are presented in the table below.

In most areas the number of disabled children being served is up, in some dramatically. In two areas, numbers are down. The table provides percentage change figures for each category. The change measured is the change in number of children served per 100,000 children — the data are thus normalized for shifts in population.

Percentage Change in Participation Rate per
100,000 Children by Type, 1980-2000

Program Type	% Change	Period if other than specified
Other Health Impairment	169	
Learning Disability	148	
Multi-handicapped	108	
Emotionally Disturbed	58	
Orthopedic Impairment	23	
Speech Impairment	1	
Deaf and Hearing Impaired	-1	
Mentally Retarded	-8	
Developmental Delay	398	1998-2000
Autism	215	1994-2000
Traumatic Brain Injury	137	1994-2000

All but three areas have seen a marked increase. Are we experiencing an epidemic level increase in number of children with disabilities? If so, where is the outcry? Or, are we instead properly diagnosing more children and enrolling them in special programs at a higher rate? If so, this could be a good thing.

The questions posed are difficult to answer. It has only been since the mid-1990s that data collection systems have been designed to gather information systematically about the disabled population. Passage of the Americans with Disabilities Act in 1990 made these new systems necessary. "We have never had a national population-based survey that focused on all ages or on all causes of disability. As a result, we know almost nothing about some very important policy-relevant groups, such as children with disabilities and people with developmental disabilities.[5]"

This will change as we gather the appropriate data through new surveys and census forms. In the meantime, one way to try and make sense of the ever-growing numbers of children participating in programs for the disabled is to look at the legislation behind these programs.

---

[5] This quote is from a paper published in late 1992 by the Office of Disability, Aging and Long-Term Care Policy, part of the U.S. Department of Health and Human Services. See source notes for a full citation.

Some of the key legislation governing special education is listed here.

1966   Congress established the first Federal grant program specifically for children with disabilities. It also established the **Bureau of Education of the Handicapped**.

1970   The **Education of the Handicapped Act** was passed. This act recognized under a single law programs that had been established by the new Bureau of Education of the Handicapped in the intervening years.

1973   The **Rehabilitation Act** was passed, a civil rights statute for persons with disabilities.

1975   The **Education for All Handicapped Children Act** was passed. This law mandates specific provisions for all handicapped children. These include access to a free appropriate public education in the least restrictive environment possible and an individualized education program for each child, the design of which is to involve parents or guardians.

1990   The **Individuals with Disabilities Education Act** (IDEA) was passed. This law is an extension (and renaming) of the Education for All Handicapped Children Act. It reauthorizes and expands the discretionary programs and mandated services covered in the original law. It also adds *autism* and *traumatic brain injury* to the list of disabilities covered. Amendments were added in 1992 to increase coverage so that infants and toddlers with disabilities are included.

1997   The **Individuals with Disabilities Education Act** was amended. Changes were made to increase the parental role, assist education agencies with funding, guard against mislabeling of children due to racial, ethnic, and linguistic differences, and encourage non-adversarial means of dispute resolution between parents and educators.

It is absolutely no surprise — given this level of effort, attention, and funding — that the number of disabled children participating in special programs has risen sharply.

Once data become available from the new surveys and census forms put into place in the mid-1990s, we will begin to count all disabled children. And that is when we will be able to determine whether or not a growing number of our children are disabled.

For more about disabled children see a panel in Chapter 2 on "Attention Deficit Disorder and Learning Disability," as well as several panels on "Special Education" in Chapter 13 of the companion volume *Community and Education*.

Source: Data for the graph were taken from four different editions of the U.S. Bureau of the Census, *Statistical Abstract of the United States*, editions 1980, p. 363, 1990, p. 146, 1995, p. 171, 1999, p. 186, and 2000, p. 175. The Quote is from U.S. Department of Health and Human Services, Office of Disability, Aging and Long-Term Care Policy, Federal Disability Data: Creating a Structure in the 1990s to Further the Goals of the ADA, December 1992, available online at http://aspe.hhs.gov/daltcp/report/feddd.htm.

Disabled Workers on the Rise

Disabled Workers Receiving Disability Benefits, 1970-2001

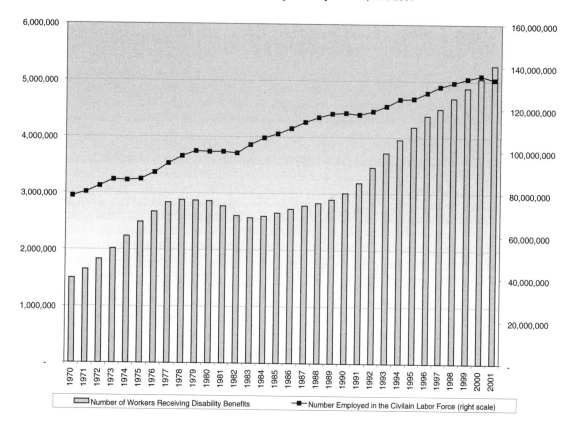

Tracking the number of disabled workers receiving Social Security disability benefits is one way to gauge the disability status of adults in the U.S. It should be noted, however, that not all disabled adults have work experience, a requirement for disability benefits through the Social Security Administration. Nor do all disabled workers received disability benefits[6]. Figures on the number of Social Security Disability Beneficiaries are used to assess a trend, not by way of counting *all* disabled workers or *all* disabled adults. The subject of employment among the disabled will be covered in another panel.

The graph presents the number of workers on disability benefits (bars) and the total employment in the non-farm sector (curve). The patterns produced by these two series are very similar. Both rise dramatically over the period 1970 through 2001. Civilian Employment rose by 71%. The number of workers receiving disability benefits rose by 253%. If we express disability as disabled workers per 1,000 workers, the increase was

---

[6] The Social Security Administration regularly denies disability claims. In 2001, 691,300 new claims were awards. This was 46.1% of all claims received. Between 1970 and 2001 the average annual percent of claims awarded was 42.2%.

107%. In 1970 there were 19 disability beneficiaries for every 1,000 workers in the civilian labor force. In 2001 there were 39.

It might be assumed that the aging of the workforce may be a factor in the increasing numbers of disabled workers. Disability, after all, rises with increased age. But the average age of disabled workers actually fell during this period. In 1970 the average age of a disabled worker was 52 years. In 2000 it had fallen to 49 years.

The number of disabled workers per 1,000 receiving benefits has risen most sharply during the 1990s. It rose 54% over the 11-year period 1990 through 2001, from 26 per 1,000 to 39. Why this increase? More specifically, why this increase following legislation[7] designed to assist disabled people to participate fully in society and more specifically for disabled workers to stay on the job or attain work suitable to their disabilities?

A look at the sorts of disabling conditions that lead a worker to apply for disability benefits may be helpful in understanding the sharply rising numbers of disabled workers.

A look at the educational level of disabled workers may be useful as well. According to some analysts, Social Security disability insurance is becoming an alternative to unemployment for the less educated in the labor force. According to Morley White, an administrative judge who rules on disability claims, when you've lost your low skill job, can't find another and are sitting around on the sofa, you might easily become preoccupied with ailments. The ailments "do qualify in many cases as legal disability but while you were working did not come into your mind."[8] This situation is probably exacerbated by the fact that as you sit on your sofa and watch TV, you are bombarded by pharmaceutical industry advertisements reminding you of the many possible ailments for which they can provide a cure. In the past, many less educated employees[9] would have worked through injuries or chronic pain. Now, they often choose to apply for disability benefits instead.

The next panels will address these matters further by looking at (1) disabling conditions for which workers are being awarded benefits and, (2) the level of education of beneficiaries.

Source: U.S. Social Security Administration, *Social Security Beneficiary Statistics*, "Number of beneficiaries receiving benefits on December 31, 1970-2001, available online at http://www.ssa.gov/OACT/STATS/OASDIbenies.html. Uchitelle, Louis. "Laid-off Workers Swelling the Cost of Disability Pay" *The New York Times*, September 2, 2002, p. 1.

---

[7] In 1990 the American with Disabilities Act was passed.

[8] This statement by Judge Morley White appeared in an article by Louis Uchitelle on the swelling roles of disability beneficiaries. See the source note for a full citation.

[9] Of all workers on disability benefits in 2000, 75% had a high school degree or *less* education.

What Keeps Us from Working

New Disability Beneficiaries Annually as a Percentage of All New Benefit Awards by Diagnostic Group, 1960-2000 by Decade

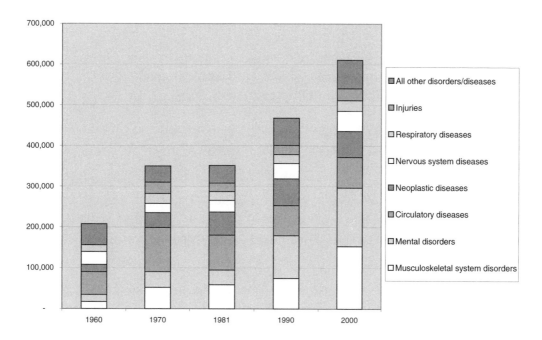

The number of newly awarded disability benefits varies from year to year. The number in 1960 was 207,805. By 2000 it reached 610,700. The conditions suffered by the new beneficiaries are categorized by the Social Security Administration into 15 diagnostic groups. The 7 most common for the period 1960 through 2000 are presented in the graph, along with an 8th category covering all other conditions.

The distribution of work disabilities by the conditions causing the disability has changed greatly over the last decades. The leading causes in 1960, circulatory diseases and nervous system disorders, have given way to two new sets of disabling disorders, musculoskeletal and mental. To better understand this trend it may be helpful to look briefly at the ailments associated with each of the diagnostic groups listed.

Musculoskeletal system disorders are all those related to the muscles and bones as well as the ligaments and tendons which link these structures together within the human body. The most common forms of disorders in this category are joint problems often related to arthritis, soft tissue ailments, fractures, disorders of the spine, and repetitive strain injuries like carpal tunnel syndrome. Ailments in this category are the leading cause of work disabilities.

Mental disorders are the second leading cause of work disabilities and include a full range of impairments from severe retardation and autism to personality or anxiety-related disorders and substance addiction disorders.

Circulatory diseases are all those related to the heart and vascular system — the movement of blood through the body. Examples of such conditions include heart disease, diabetes, peripheral vascular disease, hemophilia, and thrombosis.

Neoplastic diseases are all those resulting from malignant tumors. These are, in short, cases of cancer.

Nervous system disorders are all those involving the nervous system. Disorders in this category include such things as epilepsy, spinal cord lesions, cerebral palsy, muscular dystrophy, peripheral neuropathies, and multiple sclerosis.

Respiratory diseases include asthma, bronchiectasis, lung infections, chronic pulmonary insufficiency, as well as all other serious breathing impairments.

The final category, **All other disorders and diseases,** includes digestive system diseases; infectious diseases; endocrine diseases (ailments resulting from over or underproduction of hormones); genitourinary system diseases (disorders of the genital or urinary organs); skin diseases and congenital anomalies which together accounted for 11.26% of all new disability awards in 2000.

If one looks at the bottom two segments of each of the columns in the graph it is easy to see how the rising numbers of musculoskeletal disorders and mental disorders account for much of the annual increase in number of new beneficiaries. Between 1990 and 2000 alone, the number of disability beneficiaries resulting from musculoskeletal disorders more than doubled, from 74,500 to 153,600 cases. Much of this rise is attributable to arthritic conditions and to the rising numbers of repetitive strain injuries; many of these are the result of working with keyboards.

Personal computers and computers terminals have become ubiquitous in the workplace. Programmers and others who key for long stretches of time are particularly susceptible to carpal tunnel syndrome. It is a treatable condition but can disable a person for long periods of time if not treated early. And carpal tunnel syndrome is only one of a growing number of repetitive strain injuries.

In the case of mental disorders, the largest rise occurred between 1981 (36,318 new cases) and 1990 (105,173 new cases), an almost three fold increase. The number of cases in this category continued to rise during the 1990 but at a somewhat slower pace, reaching 143,200 cases in 2000. Why exactly is difficult to say.

One reason for this dramatic rise may have to do with changes made to the medical manual published by the American Psychiatric Association called the *Diagnostic and Statistical Manual of Mental Disorders*. This book is the main reference used by mental health professionals in the United States. In 1980 it was updated to include many mood disorders which had not previously been listed as clinical disorders.

In 2000, more men than women receive disability benefits based on mental disorders, but 34% of female beneficiaries have clinically diagnosed mental disorders compared to 33% of males.

The diagnostic category that led all others in 1960 was circulatory system diseases with 31.1% of all cases. This category saw a 60% decline in its representation as a category, accounting in 2000 for only 10.44% of new cases. The likely reason for this decline is increasingly successful medical treatments for circulatory system ailments. These treatments include cardiac catheterization and other similar procedures that clean out obstructed arteries and blood vessels.

These procedures, apart from saving many lives, make many circulatory conditions suffered less likely to disable a person for a long period of time. According to a paper published by Duke University Medical Center in early 2000, an estimated 600,000 angioplasty procedures (one form of cardiac catheterization) are performed in the United States annually. Our circulatory health, if not improving, is being managed more successfully and thus fewer people are being kept from gainful employ due to poor circulatory health.

The data in this panel show trends in new disability beneficiaries. The next panel will look at all beneficiaries as of the year 2000.

Source: U. S. Social Security Administration, *Annual Statistical Report on the Social Security Disability Insurance Program, 2000*, Table 18, "Awards to Disabled Workers by Diagnostic Group, 1960-2000," September 2001, p. 56. Twombly, Renee. *Inside Duke University Medical Center 2000*, "Duke's Other ACC — Also a Winner," April 2000, Vol. 9, Number 7, available online at http://www.inside.mc.duke.edu/archives/2000/ 20000403/5.html.

Mental Illness and Rising Disability in the Workforce

All Disability Beneficiaries by Disagnostic Group, 2000

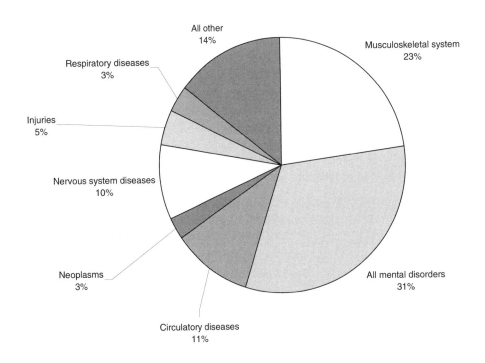

In December 2000, a total of 5,042,333 people received disability benefits through the Social Security Administration's Disability Insurance program. The graph presents a breakdown by percentage of beneficiaries by the diagnostic group under which they were found to have a covered disability. The largest single category, by far, is the one covering mental disorders. Almost one third of beneficiaries (1,618,758) are disabled by mental illness.

In the previous panel we saw that trends in new beneficiaries over the past 40 years. Here we are looking at all beneficiaries receiving benefits at the end of 2000.

A person on disability benefits may remain on the disability rolls for a short period of time or may stay on disability benefits until retirement age. For some diagnostic groups the longevity of the disabling condition is greater than for others. This appears to be the case for those with mental disorders. Therefore, over time these beneficiaries grow as a percentage of all beneficiaries. Those, for example, receiving benefits because of a neoplasm, have a greater chance of dropping off the beneficiary rolls because they are cured or, quite the opposite, because they succumb to their ailments and die. In the case of musculoskeletal disorders, again, the rate of successful treatment and return to work is higher than for mental disorders.

Our mental health appears to be causing us a great deal of trouble. It is difficult to say exactly why so many people are unable to work due to mental disorders. Is it the nature of the modern workplace? Or are our mental health problems originating from some other area of our lives? What is clear is that the workplace is losing workers as a result of deteriorating mental health in the workforce. Mental disorders are difficult to diagnose. A skeptic might conclude that the rise in mental disorder related disability is the result of fraudulent claims. But the claims process is arduous and fewer than half of those claiming benefits are ever awarded disability benefits.

All we can say with certainly is that, based on these data, the state of our mental health is keeping far more people from earning a living than was the case in the past.

Source: U. S. Social Security Administration, *Annual Statistical Report on the Social Security Disability Insurance Program, 2000*, Table 4, "All Disabled Beneficiaries by Diagnostic Group and Sex, December 2000," September 2001, pp. 32 and 33.

Education Level and Disability Status

Disability Beneficiaries by Highest Level of Education Attained, 1998

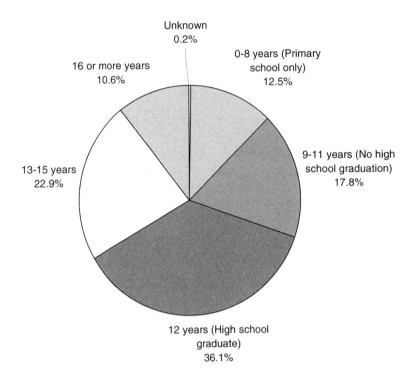

The pie graph presents the breakdown of all disabled workers receiving Social Security disability benefits in 1998 by highest level of education attained. A total of 5,158,545 adults were receiving disability benefits in 1998. The education level breakdown falls pretty close to a one-third, one-third, one-third split.

Nearly one third (30.4%) of beneficiaries had never completed high school. Those who had completed high school represent roughly another third, 36.1%. Finally, beneficiaries who had attained at least some schooling after high school made up the final third, 33.5%.

This breakdown does not follow the pattern present in the adult population generally. Those with no high school diploma represent 30.4% of workers on disability and only 19.6% of the general adult population[10]. At the other end of the spectrum, those with more than a high school degree, we see the opposite situation. Of disability beneficiaries, only 33.5% have done any study beyond the high school level whereas in the adult population generally more than half (51.8%) of adults have done some study beyond high school.

---

[10] General population figures are for the year 2000 and include all persons 25 years old or older.

Many of those with limited education hold down manual jobs. Not surprisingly, their bodies pay a price. When an accountant gets arthritic pain and stiffness in her knees, she can keep on trucking, but the ready-mix concrete truck driver can not. Thus it's not surprising that the majority of those who have disabilities also have a lower educational attainment.

The rise in mental disorders as a cause of work disability may begin to change this educational attainment differential. But, that is yet to be seen. Depression often follows a serious illness. If the patient is a middle aged man or woman, recently laid-off of a well paid job at which he or she worked for many years, and finds that he or she is ill prepared for any other job, the depression may well be even more severe.

In this panel we focused on disabled workers receiving disability benefits. What about the overall disabled population? Do they have the same educational opportunities as the population at large? That is what we will address in the next panel.

Source: U.S. Social Security Administration, "Annual Statistical Report on the Social Security Disability Insurance Program, 2000," September 2001, Table 45, available online at http://www.ssa.gov/statistics/di_asr/2000/sect6.html.

Disability and Educational Attainment

Educational Attainment by Highest Level Reached Among the Severely Disabled Population, 1995 and 2001

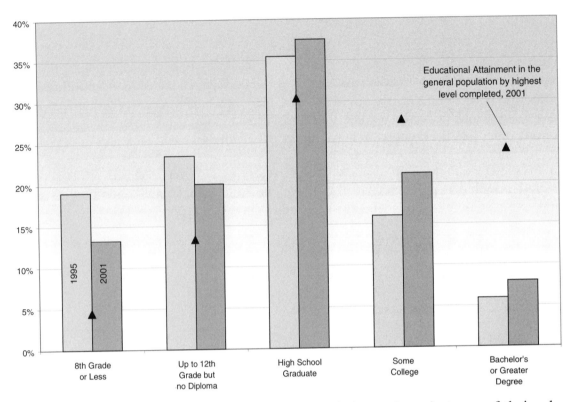

Disabled American adults lag behind the adult population at large in terms of their educational attainment. The graph presents two year's worth of data on educational attainment of the severely disabled by highest level of education completed. Triangle markers have been charted for the educational attainment of the general population in 2001 for comparison.

Some progress has been made in reducing the gap during the period shown, 1995 and 2001. The lighter bars are for the year 1995. The darker bars are for the year 2000; they show that a growing percentage of severely disabled people are taking college courses and earning degrees. Nonetheless, in 2001 among severely disabled adults aged 16 through 64 years one third had never finished high school (33%) and more than two thirds had *at best* a high school degree (71%). For the general adult population these figures were 18% and 48% respectively.

As one moves up the educational ladder this difference increases. In 2001, within the general population, 52% of adults aged 16 through 64 years had taken some college courses after graduating from high school, and 24% of them had earned a bachelor's or higher degree. Of the severely disabled population, fewer than one third of adults (29%) had studied at the college level and only 8% had a bachelor's or higher degree.

Although these differences are large, it's worth noting that parity in educational attainment for the general population and the severely disabled population is not a realistic goal. The category "all severely disabled persons" includes many people with serious cognitive impairments. By their very nature many of these impairments make scholastic achievements impossible. Cognitive impairments cover a range of diseases and disorders such as dyslexia, Alzheimer's disease, mental retardation, Parkinson's disease, stroke, autism, head injury, and/or AIDS dementia.

What might be far more instructive is to compare educational attainment in the general population with attainment by those with a physical disability, precluding all those with a cognitive impairment. This, however, is not possible with the data now available.

A person's educational attainment has direct bearing on his/her employment opportunities. The next panel will look at employment rates in the disabled community.

Source: U.S. Bureau of the Census, *Disability: Selected Characteristics of Persons 16 to 74: 2001*, Table 1.,"Selected Characteristics of Civilians 16 to 74 Years Old with a Work Disability, by Educational Attainment and Sex: 2001," October 2000, available online at http://www.census.gov/hhes/www/disable/cps/cps101.html.

Disability and Employment

Employment and Earnings by Disability Status, 1997

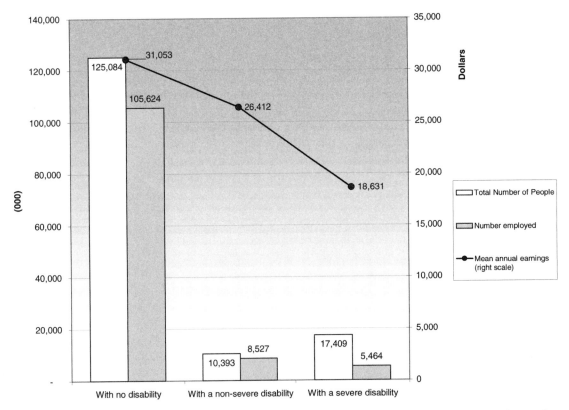

The graph presents data on the number of people 21 to 64 years of age, the number who are employed, and their average annual earnings in 1997. Data are shown for all adults, those with non-severe disability, and for those with a severe disability.

Although these percentages are not shown in the graphic, those without any disability and those only somewhat disabled have similar rates of employment: 88% of the first group and 82% of the second have jobs. But only 31% of those with severe disability are employed. These data go far in explaining why the nearly a third of the severely disabled (aged 25 to 64) live in poverty.

Average earnings of these groups follow the pattern. The more disabled, the lower the income.

"Severe disability" stands for a range of limitations on the ability of the individual to function in society. The type of disability from which an individual suffers affects employment potential and earnings. Those who have speech impairments, for instances, are less employable than those with sight impairments. The table on the following page provides a closer look at the conditions that impact on the severely disabled.

Disability Status, Employment, and Annual Earnings

of Individuals 21 to 64 Years of Age, 1997

Severe Disability Status	% Employed	Mean Annual Earnings
Needed assistance to move around inside	9.3	8,122
Impaired by mental retardation	31.5	8,191
Speech impaired	24.1	10,712
Severe difficulty walking	22.5	18,222
Sight impaired	29.9	19,714
Used a wheelchair	22.2	28,307
Hearing impaired	46.5	31,889

Someone who cannot hear well but is aided by a hearing aid (or is able to read lips) is less likely to encounter barriers to employment than someone who has difficulty communicating verbally. The table shows the supreme importance of mental and communications skills and the ability of the person to move on his or her own without assistance. Someone able to move about in a wheelchair is much, much better off than someone who needs another person to move around indoors — at least as measured in employment and earnings.

Since the passage in 1990 of the American's with Disabilities Act, more has been done to facilitate the integration of disabled persons into the workplace. And these efforts are having an impact. The rates of employment among the disabled, shown in the graph and table, are still relatively low, but they are higher than they were just 4 years earlier. In 1994, 26% of severely disabled people were employed compared with 31% in 1997.

Progress is being made. Some worry that the economic vigor of the late 1990s was the motor behind increasing employment rates among disabled persons. The fear is that as the economy cools the recently hired disabled person will be the first to be laid off. However, with the aid of new high tech tools and equipment and changing attitudes about what disabled people are capable of doing the prospects for better integration of those with disabilities is at least fair.

Source: U.S. Bureau of the Census, *Americans with Disabilities: 1997*, Table 4, Disability Status, Employment, and Annual Rate of Earnings: Individuals 21 to 64 Years Old: 1997," February 2001, available online at http://www.census.gov/hhes/www/disable/sipp /disab97/ds97t4.html.

Chapter 9

Our Mental Health

Four of the top ten disabilities in the United States are mental health issues: major depression, bipolar disorder, schizophrenia, and obsessive-compulsive disorder. Many people suffer from more than one mental disorder a time — depression, for example, tends to accompany any illness that diminishes one's quality of life. More than 44 million men and women (1 in 5 adults) are thought to have a diagnosable mental disorder.

Some readers may raise their eyebrows at such statistics.(*Is* everyone crazy, after all? — It certainly confirms a long-standing suspicion!) The first panels in this chapter will discuss some of the leading mental disorders: depression, social phobias, post-traumatic stress disorder, obsessive compulsive disorder and eating disorders. Many of these disorders have been discussed in the media. But how many people really have them? Such numbers are difficult to pin down precisely. Those who suffer from disorders may not always seek treatment. How are they diagnosed? Another question to ask: Are we too quick to label some behavior a disorder? When is a diet an eating disorder? Is shyness a social phobia?

The themes of stress, depression, and social isolation are present in this chapter as they are in others in this book. What roles do they play in our mental health? This chapter also contains panels on psychotherapy and mental health hospitals.

The chapter includes a look at bipolar disorder — which has begun to surface in our children and young people as well. Autism appears to be on the rise. Some may argue that we are simply just more aware of the disorder. The chapter also examines suicide. Rates are down, but some groups still are at high risk.

Our Mental Health

The State of Our Mental State: Estimates of Cases in a Given Year

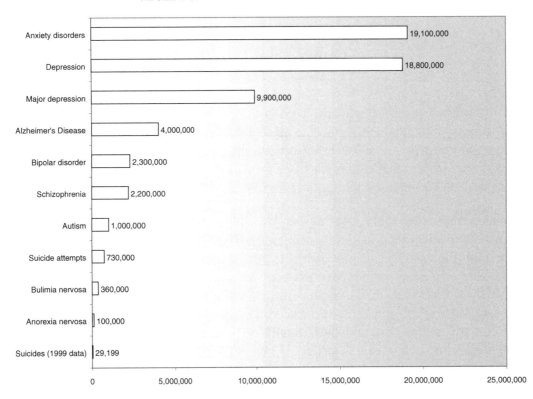

According to the National Institute of Mental Health (NIMH), 4 out of the top 10 leading causes of disability in the United States and developing countries are mental disorders such as those seen in the graphic — major depression, bipolar disorder, schizophrenia, and obsessive compulsive disorder. Some of these illnesses are well understood, some less so. In many cases we don't even have good estimates of the number afflicted. This panel serves as an introduction to the whole area of our mental health. Some of these disorders/illnesses will be examined more closely in panels to come.

Depression and anxiety disorders top the list. They also cast wide nets. According to the NIMH, nearly 19 million adults suffer from some kind of depressive disorder. These can include major depressive disorders, dysthymic disorders (chronic, mild depression), and bipolar disorder. (The topic of depression is introduced in Chapter 2, *Depressing Statistics*.) **Bipolar disorder** affects roughly 2.3 million Americans, or slightly more than 1% of the population. Unlike depression, men and women are equally likely to develop bipolar disorder. The first manic episode usually occurs in the early 20s.

Anxiety disorders includes panic disorders, obsessive-compulsive behavior, post-traumatic stress disorder and specific phobias. Again, about 19 million Americans between 18 and 54, or 13% of the age group, have some affliction in this category. Anxiety disorders, according to NIMH, frequently appear coupled with depression — which tends to accompany any physical/mental issue that diminishes the quality of one's life in some way. Women again lead in this category. Females being twice as likely as males to suffer from a panic disorder, phobia, and post-traumatic stress.

An estimated 4 million seniors are affected by **Alzheimer's Disease**. The disease destroys portions of the brain that control thought, memory, and language. The cause of the disease is unknown. As we continue to live longer, and the number of seniors grow, many in the health industry expect to see an increase in the incidence of Alzheimer's disease, largely a disease of old age. The disease has become so talked about — with many of us caring for our aging parents, etc. — that its early symptoms are well known: confusion with names, forgetting how to do simple everyday tasks, and problems in speaking and reading.

Roughly 1% of the population, or 2.2 million adults are afflicted by **schizophrenia**. The causes of schizophrenia are not known, although some combination of genetic predisposition and profound disturbance to the brain during development appear to be implicated. Drug use may set off schizophrenia in those predisposed to it. The disease affects the sexes equally, although it tends to manifest in males in their late teens or early 20s; women come down with schizophrenia in their 20s and early 30s.

Autism is a developmental disability that usually appears in the first three years of life. The disability affects the development of the brain responsible for social interaction and communication skills. Children and adults typically have difficulties communicating at all levels (verbal, non-verbal). This manifests in play and social interactions. Those with autism may display repeated body movements (their hands flap, they rock), display unusual reactions to people, become highly attached to objects, and they exhibit unusual sensitivities in vision, hearing, touch, smell, and taste. The Autism Society of America estimates that 500,000 to 1,500,000 individuals may be affected.

There are three main types of eating disorders: **binge eating, anorexia nervosa,** and **bulimia**. These disorders are tough to track. The behavior takes place behind closed doors. Initial symptoms are so subtle, they can be missed easily. Between 1 and 2% of women are thought to develop anorexia nervosa. The figure for bulimia ranges from 1.1%-4.2%. One source claims that 4% of college age women suffer from the disease. Roughly 9 million women fall into this age range, meaning that 360,000 women may be abusing their bodies in this manner. Is this to be believed?

Suicide, of course, is what may happen when we can no longer cope with the world around us. It was the 11th leading cause of death in 1999, beating chronic liver disease and even homicide. We kill *ourselves* more than each other. Men are four times more likely to take their own life than women. There are thought to be 730,000 attempts annually — nearly three quarters of a million — but this is an estimate, again, because so much of this takes place behind closed doors and goes unreported. How many make an attempt and then seek help? How many make multiple attempts? Also, the 730,000 figure is an estimate. No one tracks attempted suicide.

Some of these numbers may quite rightly prompt the reader to raise a skeptical eyebrow. More than 19 million Americans suffer from some sort of anxiety disorder. Really? We seem to have a disorder for everyone: panic disorder, obsessive compulsive, and generalized anxiety disorder. One could argue most of this nation's population could fall into one of these important but vague sounding categories. Women in particular seem to carry a difficult burden in balancing personal and professional lives. We all lead lives with stress and worries. But where does the line get drawn between a difficult life and a disordered one?

We'll now take a closer look at some of the mental states shown in this panel.

Source: Chart data are estimates. Data for bulimia refers to college age women. "The Numbers Count: Mental Disorders in America." Retrieved May 2, 2002 from http://www.nimh.gov.

Mood Disorders: Life Out of Control

Some important dates the treatment of depression and mood/anxiety disorders:

Mid 19th to the early 20th century: reports of childhood-onset "circular insanity" or "mania and melancholia" are common in European psychiatric literature.

1930s. Freud dominates psychiatric thought. The standard psychoanalytic theory dictates that classical depressive syndrome could not occur in children before puberty.

1942: Carl Rogers publishes *Counseling and Psychotherapy*, suggesting respect and non-judgmental approach to therapy is the foundation for effective treatment of mental health issues.

1952: The *Diagnostic and Statistical Manual of Mental Disorders* (DSM) is first published.

1960s: Articles begin to appear in medical literature to suggest that adult manic-depressive adults have been ill since adolescence.

1968: The second edition of the DSM is published.

1970: Lithium is approved by the FDA to treat mania.

1970: The mass deinstitutionalization of mental hospitals begins ("mainstreaming").

1979: National Alliance for the Mentally Ill is founded.

1980: The Mental Health Systems Act is passed, dramatically increasing federal funding for mental health programs.

1980: Bipolar disorder replaces manic-depressive disorder as a diagnostic term. Other mental disorders that are included in the third edition of the DSM: bulimia, post-traumatic stress disorder, panic disorder, and anxiety disorder.

1988: Prozac is invented.

1992: The term binge-eating disorder is officially introduced.

1994: Childhood mood disorders are included in the DSM IV.

1997: Researchers identify genetic links to bipolar disorder, suggesting that the disorder is inherited.

The standard manual used for diagnosis of mental disorders in the United States is the *Diagnostic and Statistical Manual of Mental Disorders (DSM)*. The first edition was published in 1952 by the American Psychiatric Association. It was published as a way to encourage physicians to use the same standards to diagnose mental illness. It was not until the third edition in 1980, however, that the *DSM* actually published clear criteria for diagnosing mental disorders (the first two editions had been heavy on Freudian theory). Criteria used to define mental disorders are based on the majority view of psychiatrists and other mental health professionals.

The *DSM* features descriptions of more than 300 mental disorders. Every edition includes new disorders, or refined definitions of those included earlier. It was in 1980 that a number of new mood and anxiety disorders received official classification: bulimia, post traumatic stress disorder, anxiety disorder, panic disorder, and bipolar disorder. With these disorders given official classification, the National Institute of Mental Health

(NIMH) now estimates that more than 19 million adults between 18 and 54 suffer from some sort of diagnosable disorder:

What are these new mood and anxiety disorders? The estimated annual numbers are

Estimated Number of 18-54 Year Olds With Disorder Annually

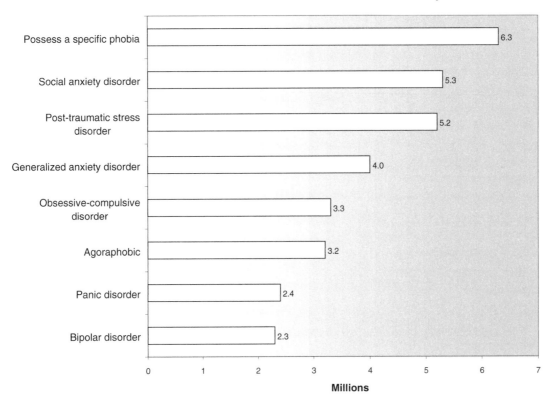

shown above. **Social anxiety disorder** — often referred to with its telling acronym, SAD, is the third largest mental health care problem in the world. Social anxiety, according to the Social Anxiety Association, is the "fear and anxiety of being judged and evaluated by other people." People with SAD are often perceived as "shy, quiet, backward, withdrawn, inhibited, unfriendly, nervous, aloof or disinterested." Those with the disorder experience constant, intense anxiety in the face of public speaking, meeting people in authority or potential criticism. Their hearts beat faster, they can't breathe, or their bodies ache in these situations. SmithKline Beecham marketed Paxil, the first drug ever approved for social phobia, with the slogan "Imagine being allergic to people."

More than 5 million Americans allergic to people? Another 4 million people have something called **Generalized Anxiety Disorder** (called GAD for short). The possibility of experiencing deep anxiety can happen across the life cycle, according to government statistics, but the highest risk occurs between childhood and middle age. There are, of course, numerous gradations of shyness; many people get nervous at job interviews or while making a speech. The qualifier here seems to be the intensity of the anxiety. But the line between anxiety and dysfunctional thinking is certainly a thin one — and open to interpretation.

Doctors had begun to make distinctions between patients with unexpected anxiety attacks and patients with other anxiety disorders as early as the 1960s. **Panic disorder** received official recognition by the mental health community when included in the *DSM* in 1980. Panic disorder typically develops in late adolescence or early adulthood. Roughly 1 in 3 people with panic disorder develop agoraphobia. **Agoraphobia** is often defined as a fear of public places. It turns out that there's more to it. Those with the condition become afraid of being in any place or situation from which it might be difficult to escape — or where they might not be able to get help in the event of a panic attack. It is the fear of having fear, in a sense — and being unable to find help.

The first symptoms of **obsessive-compulsive disorder** generally appear in childhood or adolescence. Worries and doubts so overwhelm sufferers that their regular lives are impaired. Some people with OCD have described it as having "mental hiccups." Common obsessions include fear of germs, imagining having harmed oneself or others, excessive or intrusive thoughts (usually about sex or religion), and a need to have things "just so." Those with OCD are then compelled to perform some act in order to relieve the anxiety. They wash hands repeatedly, for instance, to get rid of germs.

As already stated, the mental health community continually renames conditions as it comes to understand them better. **Post traumatic stress disorder** (PTSD) is often seen as an attempt at describing the plight of some Vietnam veterans. PTSD is, at least in some circles, a more precise explanation of the difficulties of shell-shocked soldiers in World War I or those with combat stress or battle fatigue in subsequent wars. Those with PTSD experience sleep deprivation, depression, guilt at having survived battles, and a number of related issues (alcohol abuse, for example). But has the disorder taken on a life of its own? The ailment can be assigned to anyone who has difficulty coping with life after some traumatic event: violent assault, rape, robbery, terrorism, natural or human-made disasters. Eric Dean points out in his book *Shook Over Hell: Post-Traumatic Stress, Vietnam and the Civil War*, how far off some of the comparisons are. He quotes sources that suggest some professional football players who find their careers suddenly ended as having "developed post-traumatic stress disorders comparable to those experienced by Vietnam veterans." According to one study, 60% of men and 50% of women will experience a traumatic event in their lifetime. Some wont be able to cope with trauma or with loss. Do they have post-traumatic stress?

What about **phobias**? Over 6 million people between 18 and 54 — more than 4% of the age group — have a specific phobia regarding an object or situation. We all have such fears — we avoid freeways where we've had an accident. But the key, of course, is that some fears take on an irrational intensity. The fear is exaggerated in relation to the actual threat. Fear then comes to disrupts the sufferer's life.

Research (Ost & Hugdahl) suggests that half of all people with phobias have never had a painful experience with the object that they fear. Martin Seligman (1971) argues that we may be "prepared" to learn certain phobias. People learned to avoid snakes, rats, and heights to evade the potential dangers that they pose. Man survived as a species, and the fear has been passed on in our genes. Specific phobias are generally treated with behavioral therapy. The patient is exposed to the object of his fear in safe surroundings. In "flooding," a patient is exposed to the trigger until the fear goes away. The patient may be trained to substitute a feeling of calm and relaxation for the fear and panic. This is called "counter conditioning." A patient may be gradually introduced to the object of his fear. This is called "systematic desensitization."

More than 2 million Americans suffer from **bipolar disorder** — the old manic-depression. Those with the disorder experience sudden and sharp mood swings, from abysmal "lows" to exuberant "highs." These phases can last for months. The shifts often become more dramatic with time (roughly 8 to 10 years are thought to elapse from onset of the disorder to diagnosis). People may be deeply depressed, or have grandiose thoughts, pick fights, drive indiscriminately or be hypersexual.

The illness was thought to affect only adults, but there has been a disturbing rise in the number of children and adolescents diagnosed as bipolar. Indeed, in a generation, *Time* reports, the average age of onset has fallen from early 30s to the late teens. Children diagnosed with the illness exhibit a variety of symptoms: hyperactivity, a fascination with blood and gore. Giddy mood states, complaints of boredom, and poor handwriting are all included on *The Bipolar Child*'s checklist of possible behavior for bipolar children. Some of these symptoms, of course, are exhibited by every child at some point. But where's the line between normal development and a child potentially at risk? As well, some symptoms are so generic that that the child can be misdiagnosed. Is a hyperactive child bipolar or is he suffering from attention deficit hyperactivity syndrome? Or is he just an energetic child? One study suggests that 15% of those with ADHD actually are bipolar. The distinction is important; Ritalin is a useful treatment for attention deficit syndrome but has sent some bipolar children into emotional tailspins.

What causes bipolar disorder? As with many of these illnesses, researchers simply don't know. There is certainly evidence of genetic predisposition to the illness. Researchers have just begun to solve some of the riddles of how the brain functions. Some scientists point to something in "modern lifestyles": a child overcome by a stressful home, difficulties in school, etc. Any recreational drug that disrupts body chemistry may trigger those with a genetic predisposition. How is the illness usually treated? Anticonvulsants and antipsychotics are very useful. Lithium is still an effective tool. Those who are bipolar also receive intensive therapy.

Why were these disorders included in the updated version of the DSM in 1980? The manual is used as a tool to diagnose mental disorders. The inclusion of all these new ailments speaks to something that may have happened in society in the preceding years. Were counselors and clinicians suddenly besieged by a sudden number of deeply anxious people? It's tempting to point to a bad economy, a high suicide rate, or the rise of "dysfunctional" families as a potentially easy answer to this question. Were they visited by the millions of mentally ill who were being moved out of institutions? Did mental health officials start seeing a dramatic rise in depressed teenagers, or young women who had stopped eating? Considering the violent crime rate in the 1970s, were doctors seeing patients who were stressed over being victimized?

The issue of cost is an additional consideration. If these conditions were legitimized, would it be easier for mental health organizations to obtain vital dollars to treat them? In the coming years, managed care would further complicate the issue of the mentally ill being able to afford to get treatment.

Are we just giving new names to old problems? In some cases, No. Scientists are making significant discoveries that warrant tailoring standard definitions. For example, another term included in the *1980 DSM* was Pervasive Developmental Disorder, which is used to suggest the multi-faceted issues around autism and its related disorders (a topic addressed later in this chapter).

But one might argue that the labels are getting out of control. Is social anxiety just a fancy term for shyness? What one calls a bipolar of bipolar child, another calls a classic case of "the terrible twos." Is a victim of a traumatic incident suffering from post-traumatic stress disorder or is he just traumatized? Are doctors — with the best of intentions — misdiagnosing marginal patients? Some disorders have such generic symptoms, one might fear this is the case. Why do we have so many organizations to address the needs of sufferers? The Social Anxiety Institute, the Social Anxiety Network, Social Phobia/Social Anxiety Association, the Child and Adolescent Bipolar Foundation, and the Depressive and Manic Depressive Association are but a few. Does an official organization make us feel better about our dysfunction? Does having "a name for it" perhaps absolve us of being responsible for our behavior — or our pain?

Data from the National Institute of Mental Health show that more than 19 million Americans between 18 and 54 have some *diagnosable* (there's that word again) disorder. But what of the younger and older age groups? Are we even more troubled than we realize?

Sources: Chart figures come from the National Institute of Mental Health located at http://www.nimh.nih.gov; Ost Hugdahl & Martin Seligman theories on phobias taken from http://www.phobialist.com; "What is OCD?" at http://www.ocfoundation.org. "Social Phobia Fact Sheet." Retrieved from http://www.socialphobia.org; Kluger, Jeffrey and Sora Song. "Young and Bipolar." Time, August 19, 2002, p. 38. Fay Flam. "Gene Plays Role in Anxiety, Scientists Discover." *Knight-Ridder/Tribune News Service*, July 18, 2002.

Eating Disorders: Healthy Body, Healthy Mind

Number of women over the age of 15 in 1999: 111 million

Percent of females who suffer from anorexia in lifetime: 0.5 to 3.7%

Percent of females who suffer from bulimia in lifetime: 1.1 to 4.2%

Percent of men with eating disorder: 5.0 to 15.0%

Spending on weight loss products in 1999: $32 billion

Estimated number of dieters in 1999: 51 million

Percent of 10-12 year old girls who say they are slightly or very overweight: 34%

Percent of 22-24 year old women who say they are slightly or very overweight: 51%

There are three main types of eating disorders: anorexia nervosa, bulimia nervosa and binge-eating disorders.

Hard numbers on those afflicted are hard to find. Sufferers are secretive, early-stage symptoms difficult to detect. Those with **anorexia nervosa** will starve their bodies of food. Those with **bulimia** will eat a large quantity of food and then take laxatives or induce vomiting. As the names suggests, those with **binge-eating disorders** will eat large quantities of food in a short period of time. But they don't purge as bulimics do. All of these disorders are characterized by low self-esteem. Food is used to fill some psychological void in the person; they literally "hunger" for love and acceptance. By embracing the old myth that "I'm fat and no one will ever love me" these overeaters are keeping people and potential relationships at bay — stresses that they simply cannot handle.

According to the National Institute of Mental Health, 0.5 to 3.7% of women will develop anorexia in their lifetime. An estimated 1.1 to 4.2% of women will develop bulimia at some point. Somewhere between 2 to 5% of Americans will experience a binge-eating disorder in a 6 month period.

How does one develop an eating disorder? It appears to be a complex process, of course, and researchers are unable to point to a single trigger. In various studies, a significant number of women talk of getting messages about food (and their bodies) from their mothers. Some mothers may be openly critical of their daughter's weight. Other messages involve family meals. No one leaves the table until everyone's plate is cleared. No snacks. Dessert with every dinner. Family functions always involve food. Or worse, mother herself is anorexic or bulimic, and the daughters continue the cycle.

But it isn't just Mom's fault. For some, it is a critical husband or boyfriend. For others, a psychological response to their changing adolescent body. Recent research does suggest that genetics and brain chemistry may trigger certain segments of women to starve themselves.

Society is a factor as well. To be thin is to be attractive. We spent in excess of $34 billion on weight loss products and services in 1999, a figure that grows every year. Spending on diet pills and meal replacements have increased 160% since 1996. The number of dieters has grown in recent years as well. When women were asked "Why do you diet?" in a recent University of Michigan survey, 43% said they diet for themselves, 16% out of exposure to media images. When asked what they thought caused eating disorders, 30% said family or peer pressure, 30% said pressure from media images, and 23% named poor self image. It's easy to see how a woman may feel overweight compared to the models in fashion magazines. The average American woman is 5'4" tall and weighs 140 pounds. The average model is 5'11" and carries a scant 117 lbs. Most fashion models are thinner than 98% of American women!

Eating disorders are killers. An estimated 50,000 people currently suffering from such disorders will die from them. Anorexics can suffer heart attacks, arthritis, and osteoporosis. Bulimics can destroy the linings of their stomachs and esophagus through the use of laxatives and vomiting. It is possible for a woman to destroy her body chemistry to the point where it ceases to work.

There has been a disturbing response to the issue of eating disorders. A small segment of young women have embraced anorexia as a lifestyle. Some web sites feature photos of emaciated young women with protruding ribs and backbones to chart the progress of their weight loss. In 2001, the National Association of Anorexia Nervosa and Associated Disorders contacted web hosts at Yahoo! to ask them to remove pro-anorexia web groups with names like skin n'bones and anorexiarocks from their site. In these groups, women traded starvation tips, advice on how to fool parents into thinking they are eating, and extolled the virtues of anorexia: "Being thin is more important than being healthy," "Being thin and not eating are signs of true willpower and success."

Source: Chart data from the National Eating Disorders Association, located at http://www.nationaleatingdisorders.org; statistics from the National Institute of Mental Health located at http://www.nimh.nih.gov. "Weight Loss Industry Enjoys Its Best Gains In A decade." *Research Alert*, March 2, 2000; "Girls More Likely to Feel Overweight, Less Likely to Exercise Than Boys." located at http://www.harrisinteractive.com; Text from "Survey of Teen Girls Shows Disturbing Trends." Retrieved from http://www.umich.edu. Lubrano, Alfredo. "Pro-anorexia Forums Popping Up on the Web." *Knight-Ridder/Tribune News Service*, August 26, 2001. Emily Sohn. "The Hunger Artists." *U.S. News & World Report*, p. 45. Erica Goode, "Anorexia Strategy: Family as Doctor." *New York Times*, June 11, 2001, P. D7.

The Rise of Autism

Number of Children with Autism Logged by California Department of Developmental Services

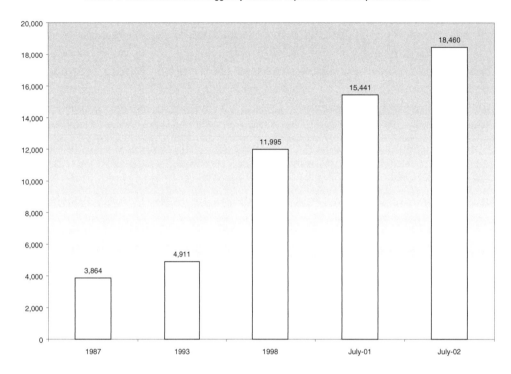

The number of children entering California's developmental services system has been steadily increasing. Do the increases suggest autism is on the rise in this country?

The organization provides a number of services to the handicapped in the state. It took 25 years (1970-1995) for them to add 6,527 cases of people with autism into their system. It took only 3 years to add virtually the same number of cases — 6,596 new cases were added from 1999 to 2001. From 1987-1998, cases grew over 200%. Such figures do not include related autism-like disorders, such as Asperger's Disorder and Rett's Syndrome. Autism is now the top disability entering California's developmental system, surpassing mental retardation, cerebral palsy, and epilepsy.

The increase in autism is not just limited to California. States such as Illinois, Pennsylvania, and Missouri have seen striking increases in autistic students. Indeed, the number of autistic students served under the Individuals with Disabilities Education Act (IDEA) increased 320% nationwide from the 1992-1993 fiscal year to 1999-2000. The growth in the under 18 population in the United States, meanwhile, increased about 10% over the same period.

The obvious question here: is autism on the rise, or are we just more aware of the disorder? Researchers seem to think both factors play a part. "We're in the middle of an autism epidemic," said Dr. Bernard Rimland of the Autism Research Institute in 1999 to the *Los Angeles Times*. But a doctor at UC Irvine made this remark the same year: "I heard the 'A word" twice in seven years of postgraduate education, and never in medical school."

Autism is a disorder that typically appears in the first three years of life. The disease was first described by child psychologist Leo Kanner in 1943 at Johns Hopkins University. He who used the word autism — from the Greek word self, *autos* — to describe a group of his patients who were deeply withdrawn and exhibited some highly idiosyncratic behavior. Children with autism exhibit difficulty with verbal and non-verbal communication. Other symptoms include repeated body movements (hand flapping, rocking), short attention spans, being preoccupied with routines, no spontaneous playing, no eye contact, and social isolation. Boys are four times as affected as girls. The exact cause is not known, although mercury poisoning, pollution, and vaccinations have all been blamed. The latest research links it to biological and neurological disturbances in the brain. The most recent clinical study's outcome (October 2002) might be characterized as a wringing of hands and a shake of heads. Experts have no clue.

Autism has traditionally been thought to appear in every 4 to 5 out of 10,000 births, but recent studies suggest that as many as 1 in 150 kids age 10 and younger may suffer from autism or related disorders — a total of about 300,000. If these new numbers are accurate, the disorder is five times as common as Down's Syndrome and juvenile diabetes.

Wired magazine offered up an intriguing analysis of the rise in autism and related disorders in California, particularly in the Silicon Valley area. They theorized that those with autism and Asperger's Disorder are well suited to the rigid life of a computer programmer (those with Asperger's Disorder are as withdrawn as autistic people, but they also tend to be obsessed with literal thinking about complex subjects such as weather, music, astronomy, history, etc.). They are adept at working with the logical commands of computer codes. They work in walled-off cubicles, limiting their contact with people. E-mail replaces the potentially tricky process of face to face communication. Then, some researchers suspect, something known as assortive mating takes place. Basically, smart men tend to meet and marry smart women; or, more crudely stated, "geeks of a feather flock together." This mating then leads to an overload of genes that predispose their children to autism and related disorders (and potentially unrelated ones, such as dyslexia).

Researchers continue to try to unravel they mystery of autism. One question scientists have yet to solve: why do roughly 25% of autistic children respond strongly to intensive speech and social communication therapy, when the rest do not?

Source: California Health and Human Services Agency, Department of Developmental Services: Changes in the Population of Persons with Autism and Pervasive Developmental Disorders in California's Developmental Services System, March 1, 1999; Nash, J. Madeleine. "The Secrets of Autism." *Time*, May 6, 2002, p. 46; Steve Silberman. "The Geek Syndrome. " *Wired*, December 2001, p. 1; "What is Autism?" Retrieved July 31, 2002 from http://www.autism-society.org; "Schools Contend with Increase of Autistic Children." Retrieved August 13, 2002 from http://www.nsba.org; Thomas H. Maugh II, "State Study Finds Sharp Rise in Autism Rate." *Los Angeles Times*, April 16, 1999, p. 1; "Autism Epidemic Continues to Expand in California." Retrieved from http://www.mer cola.com.

Suicide: Men and Seniors at Risk

Suicide Rates for Selected Groups

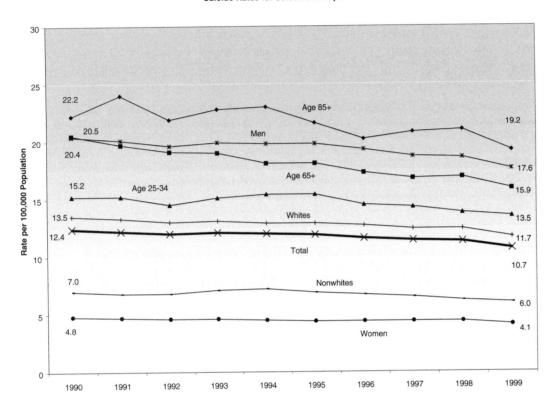

A total of 29,199 Americans killed themselves in 1999, making suicide the 11th leading cause of death. Men and seniors seem particularly vulnerable.

The suicide rate fell in the 1990s, from 12.4 to 10.7 people per 100,000. It is the lowest rate since 1968. One factor thought to affect suicide rates is the health of the country. In short, good times equal low rates, bad times high rates. The highest suicide rate occurred in 1932, when the Depression helped push the rate to 17.4 per 100,000. Just after World War II, with the war over and the economy growing, the rate lingered at about 10.0. In the following decades, the rate did increase, fluctuating between 11.1 and 13.3. Population increased during this time, of course. But with changing work and social structures — divorces, job demands and losses, spread out families, the rise of the suburbs — so did the possibility of feeling completely overwhelmed, depressed and socially isolated.

Men are four times more likely than women to take their own life. White males have the highest rate of any group, 19.1 per 100,000, a rate far above black males (10.0), Native Americans (12.1) or any segment of females (white females 4.5, black females 1.6). Of the 29,199 suicides in 1999, about 72% (21,107) were committed by white men.

Seniors also have high suicide rates. There were more than 35 million Americans over the age of 65 in 1999, and their suicide rates are roughly double the national rate. While seniors represent 13% of the population, they represented 18.8% of all suicides. Seniors are perhaps particularly vulnerable to the sense of despair that can lead to suicide. Many older persons suffer from some illness that has diminished their quality of life. Most are no longer working, and not enjoying the sense of purpose that a job provides. Many are suffering from loneliness and depression. Many have lost a spouse. Government statistics offer some correlation between marital status and suicide rates. During the period 1980 to 1992, the suicide rate for married persons increased 4%, increased 3% for never married persons and 9% for widowed or divorced persons. Again, men seem particularly prone to suicide. In 1992, the rate for divorced/widowed men age 65 and higher was 2.7 times that for married men, 4 times the rate of never married men and 17 times the rate for married women.

There has been significant increase in the rates among young people. For 15-19 year olds, the rate grew nearly 120% from 1950 to 1970, from 2.7 deaths per 100,000 in 1950 to 5.9 in 1970. The rate hit its high point in 1991 with a rate of 11.1 per 100,000, an increase of over 300% from 1950. Again, it is men who overwhelmingly turn to suicide. Disturbingly, men in their early 20s kill themselves at rates higher than all men and seniors.

Suicide Rates: Young Men in Crisis (Rate per 100,000)

	1990	1991	1992	1993	1994	1995	1996	1997	1998	1999
Men 15-19	18.1	18.0	17.8	17.5	18.1	17.3	15.6	15.2	14.6	13.3
Men 20-24	25.7	25.5	25.6	26.6	28.5	27.7	24.8	23.0	23.0	21.6
All men	20.4	20.1	19.6	19.9	19.8	19.8	19.3	18.7	18.6	17.6
All 65+	20.5	19.7	19.1	19.0	18.1	18.1	17.3	16.8	16.9	15.9

Suicide is the third leading cause of death for the 19.1 million men between 20-24 years of age. For 20-24 year old white males, it is the second leading cause. Why? Are some men overcome by the stress of starting their adult lives? Quite possibly these young men have been troubled since their adolescence. A recent National Institute of Mental Health survey found that among adolescents who suffer from depression, potentially as many as 7% will commit suicide in their adult years.

Women have far lower suicide rates than men. Are we, as a society, more accepting of women discussing their feelings? For all the talk of men getting in touch with "their feminine side" do we still expect boys and young men to be the "strong, silent type"?

Source: "USA Suicide Official Final Data" Retrieved August 22, 2002 from http://www.suicidology.org; Table 3 "Suicide Rate (per 100,000 persons in each age group." From http://www.albany.edu/sourcebook/1995/pdf/t1315.pdf; causes of death from *National Vital Statistics Report 1999*, table 1, 7. "Suicide and Homicide Rates in the U.S. 1900-1994." Retrieved August 22, 2002 from http://www.suicidemethods.net. "Suicide Among Older Persons." *MMWR*, January 12, 1996.

Buddy, I Think You Need Professional Help

Visits to Psychiatrists by Age Group, 1989-90

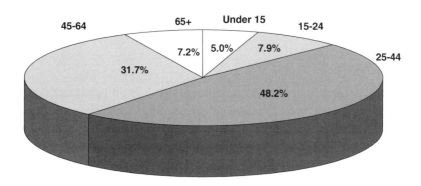

Psychiatrists had an estimated 37.6 million office visits in 1989-1990. Who goes to therapy? Why?

Those between the ages of 25-64 made up over three quarters of the visitors to psychiatrist offices for the period shown. In short, many people who seek counseling tend to be of the Baby Boom generation — sometimes unkindly labeled the "me" generation. Their rates for 25-44 year olds and 45-64 year olds were fairly comparable, with the older segment seeing a slightly higher rate: 11.4 visits per 100 people for those aged 25-44 and 12.8 visits per 100 people for those aged 45-64.

59.1% of the visits were made by women and 40.9% by men. The willingness of women to talk about their feelings seems to be a rather clear distinction between the sexes. This gender gap has changed little over the decades; in 1975-76, the split was 60.1 and 39.9%. Patients are also overwhelmingly white. Whites make up more than 95% of visitors.

What was the top reason cited for seeking professional help? Depression topped the list; 36.8% of men and women cited depression as their motivation. Anxiety or nervousness was the second most popular reason (13.4% of cases); more than 8 million visits were made to psychiatrists for these reasons. In looking at the age groups, it's easy to guess potential reasons for the visits: those 25-44 years old are starting their adult lives, getting married, having children, climbing the corporate ladder. Those 45-64 may be coping with the flip side: a divorce, a job loss, the death of a loved one, or handling a seriously ill parent.

One curious statistic: an additional 4 million visits were made to physicians other than psychiatrists for the treatment of depression and anxiety. Indeed, in the panel called *De-*

pressing Statistics (Chapter 2), we saw the rise in doctor visits for the treatment of depression. These visits coincide with the rise of Prozac and other mood altering medications. Were these patients prescribed medication when they should have really received counseling? The mental health industry has argued that antidepressants and similar drugs — now a billion dollar industry — merely change a patient's symptoms, not the reason for them.

How do we feel about therapy? Some of its stigma is gone, certainly. A generation of us have come of age listening to psychologists and self-help gurus like Dr. Joyce Brothers, Oprah Winfrey, Phil Donahue, and Dr. Sonya Peterson (Dr. Phil from the Oprah show, is the current rage). But for every nurturer of his or her dysfunctional inner child, there are those who shake their head at the psychobabble. In an *American Demographics* survey of 1,000 adults, 19% said psychotherapy was for people with serious psychological disorders, 13% claimed it was a waste of time, and 3% said it was for "the rich and famous."

Money, of course, is a significant issue surrounding therapy: 32% in the poll claimed they had avoided treatment because of the cost. Ivan Miller points out that A National Medical Expenditure Survey found that 45-48% of the money spent on psychotherapy was out of the patient's pocket. The study was done before managed care. However, most insurance companies have some sort of cap on payments for mental health services. A 1997 survey in *Psychotherapy Finances* found that 44% of therapists' income comes from direct payments from their patients. Is seeking treatment from a counselor just too expensive? The average length of treatment for therapists is about 8 to 11 sessions. But what of those people in need of long-term treatment? Eventually, insurance companies stop paying and the patient must go it alone. Or worse, some insurance companies have tried to dictate treatment for a patient, by urging therapists to move patients to less costly group therapy or to simply prescribe medication for a patient.

Source: Schappert, Susan M. "Office Visits to Psychiatrists: United States, 1989-90." U.S. Department of Health and Human Services, *National Ambulatory Medical Survey*. Ivan J. Miller, Ph.D. "The Death of Independent Practice Has Been Greatly Exaggerated." Retrieved August 27, 2002 from http://www.nomanagedcare.org; John Fetto. "What Seems to be the Problem?" *American Demographics*, April 2002, p. 8.

Mental Health Facilities

Mental Health Organizations: The Move to Outpatient Care

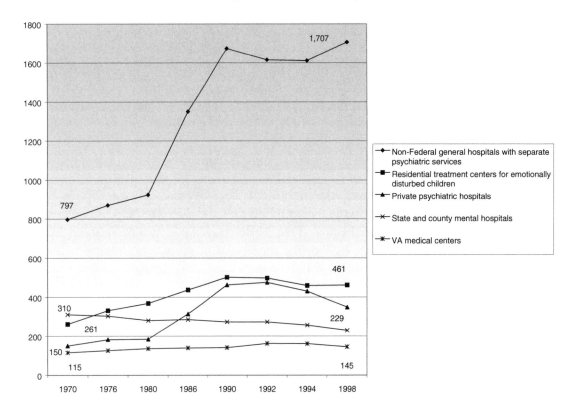

From 1970 to 1998, we moved from residential to outpatient treatment of our mental health needs.

Nearly all types of mental health establishments grew during this nearly 30 year period. The number of private psychiatric hospitals rose 132%, the number of non-federal hospitals with separate psychiatric services rose 114%. Residential centers for emotionally disturbed children rose 77%. The number of other types of organizations — psychiatric outpatient clinics, partial care organizations and multiservice mental health organizations — (data not shown in the panel) grew 141%. Only the number of state hospitals saw a decline, helped along by mergers, consolidations, and closings. The growth rates far exceed the growth rate in the general population, which was about 33%.

This growth took place as the number of beds in all hospitals and treatment centers were on the decline. Beds for residents fell 50% overall, from 524,878 to 261,903. But there were also fewer patients in them; the number of resident patients also fell during this period, from 471,451 to 215,798 (down 54%).

The move from state facilities to community care began much earlier. Mental hospitals had been the cornerstone of mental health policy in the years before World War II. There were significant changes taking place within the population of state mental hospitals just before 1950. Previously, they were home to schizophrenics who required life long care and seniors with dementia. (The aged sometimes had other afflictions that were not necessarily related to mental health. In the 19th century, senility was redefined as a mental illness, allowing local communities to ship the aged off to state facilities.) Post World War II, state hospitals were now seeing more patients with short and intermediate term care needs.

Shortly after the war, a push came to strengthen outpatient and community clinics, led by shifts in funding and psychiatric thinking (and, no doubt, the needs of returning servicemen). The effect of this thinking on these clinics — which pre-1940 had dealt primarily with children, not adults — was dramatic. Before 1948, more than half of all states had no clinics; a year later, all but five had one or more. By 1959, there were more than 1,400 clinics serving more than 500,000 people. Certainly, the clinics had value, but how adept was staff at spotting mental illness in the people it treated?

In 1948 came the film, *The Snake Pit*. In the midst of all these changes in the mental health field, it was one of the first films to treat mental illness and hospitalization in insightful, compassionate terms. But by the 1960s, some were openly challenging the entire concept of mental illness. In 1961, psychiatrist Thomas Szasz and sociologist Erving Goffman each argued that there is no such thing as mental illness. Goffman felt that people in mental hospitals exhibit psychotic behavior as a result of the hospitalization. In 1962, Ken Kesey wrote *One Flew Over the Cuckoo's Nest*, based on his experiences working in a psychiatric ward in a Veteran's Administration hospital. He makes the same arguments as Szasz and Goffman: the patients aren't mentally ill, they just behave in ways that aren't socially acceptable.

In the mid-1960s, many of the seriously mentally ill began to be removed from institutions to local mental health facilities. Antipsychotics such as Thorazine aided in this transition. Antipsychotics were first developed in the 1950s, and while they did not cure the mentally ill, they proved to be highly effective in reducing symptoms of psychosis in many patients. The Mental Retardation Facilities and Community Mental Health Centers Construction Act was passed in 1963. It provided federal funds to establish a network of mental health centers so the recently deinstitutionalized could seek out treatment. But many released patients did not do so. Without proper care, some mentally ill people end up homeless. Two decades later, roughly one-third of those living on the streets are thought to be mentally ill, with the vast majority of them suffering from schizophrenia.

There is perhaps a reason for the growth in hospitals with separate psychiatric wards — as shown in the panel. Some mentally ill people show up in general hospitals looking for help. They put such institutions under stress. Detroit Receiving Hospital in Michigan is one of the busiest in the nation, serving up to 12,000 psychiatric patients annually. "For people who have lost it all, this is their house," stated Dr. Alireza Amirsadri, the medical director of high intervention programs. Of the 1,000 patients evaluated monthly in the psychiatric ward, 250 are repeat patients.

Some mentally ill also end up somewhere else: in jail. A 1992 survey found that 7.2% of inmates (about 100,000 people) suffer from serious mental illness. Cook County Jail and

Riker's Island, located in Illinois and New York respectively, have been described as the largest psychiatric facilities in their states.

Where do things now stand? The growth of local mental health facilities surely must speak to the need for such places. But state and county mental hospitals still remain the largest provider of psychiatric treatment in this country. Numbers have fallen, to be sure: in 1970, they treated 185.8 people per 100,000 and now treat about 21.2. Roughly half of the residents, argue some experts, would be better off somewhere else. A recent Supreme Court decision, *Olmstead v. L.C.,* has opened the door for this. It was successfully argued before the Supreme Court that the mentally ill need better access to homes and small community centers.

What are likely to be future trends? In the West we appear to cycle between "holding" the mentally ill in institutions that are little better than prisons — and simply letting them roam free. "Mainstreaming," was a phrase used during deinstitutionalization. Money is an issue, always. For the foreseeable future, a combination of "mainstreaming" and use of drugs seems to be the precarious balance we have settled on. The mentally ill march on — these days the armies of the "homeless."

Sources: Chart statistics come from Chapter 14 of *Mental Health in the United States, 2000* by the U.S. Department of Health and Human Services located at http://www.mentalhealth.org. Chamberlain, Claudine. "Out of the Cuckoos Nest." Retrieved August 7, 2002 from http://www.abcnews.go.com; Sarah Webster. "Mentally Ill Pouring into City Streets." *Detroit News*, August 29, 1999, P.1.Fred Kaplan. "For Mentally Ill, Jail Means Care." *Boston Globe*, July 26, 2000. "The Cost of Madness on the Streets, *Chicago Tribune*, June 7, 1999.

Chapter 10

Sexuality

The subject of sexuality would probably merit a book on its own, but in the panels that follow, we shall only be able to peek at a few issues — our attitudes and some of behavior. Are our views changing? For all the talk of sex in the media, how sexually active are we?

The first panel will explore our attitudes to premarital sex, and how they have changed over recent years. The next panel looks at sexual activity among adults. There are plenty of myths out there on this subject: men don't think they get enough (to put it delicately), women think they get too much, married people don't have sex, all young people are very sexually active. How true are all these common beliefs?

The chapter will then shift slightly from behavior to attitudes. We'll examine surveys on sexual fantasies and performance. Are we good lovers? Are we comfortable with sex? Recent data show a significant segment of the population experience some level of dysfunction with their sex lives. We'll deal with the issue of dysfunction in other ways. We'll study Viagra's effect on the drug industry and on the sex lives of millions of men. We'll also examine plastic surgery. Looking for the perfect body? Trying to get rid of wrinkles and stay young? You'll see that you are not alone.

We'll examine teenagers' lack of knowledge about sexual health and reproduction. We'll also look at AIDS. The disease was covered in an earlier chapter (along with sexually transmitted diseases). This chapter will look at the disease through a different lens. AIDS has been with us for (at least) two decades and has had a dramatic impact on the gay community and our sexual behavior.

The reader will, we hope, start to see patterns convergent patterns. There is a substantial number of depressed people in the nation. Is it possible that they're not interested in sex? How will this affect our primary relationships? If we feel that premarital sex is acceptable, do we then encourage births out of wedlock? Is a teenager who doesn't know the facts about sex at a higher risk of becoming pregnant or becoming infected with a sexually transmitted disease?

Our Changing Attitudes

How Do We Feel About Premarital Sex?

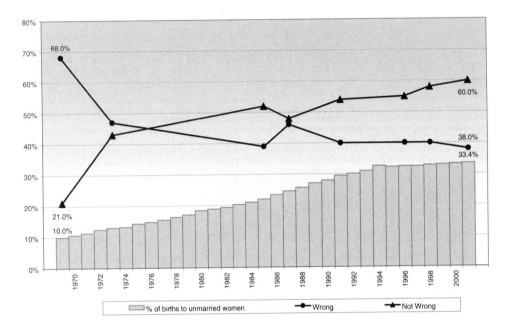

If polls reflect reality, the American public has changed its mind about premarital sex. The data chart opinion between 1969 and 2001. In 1969, according to Gallup polling, 68% of us saw sex outside of marriage as unacceptable behavior. Thirty-two years later, 60% felt that premarital sex was not wrong at all. It took a while for this reversal in public attitudes. In 1987, it was still a toss-up, half leaning in one direction, half in the other. During the 1969-1987 period, the Baby Boom was coming into its own: it was in its teens and early 20's. The sexual revolution was in full swing. After 1987, Baby Boom attitudes probably dominated adult opinion, and we have a drift toward permissiveness.

Are polls on target? They appear to be. Charted as bars on the graphic above are the percent of all births to unmarried women. In 1969 one baby in 10 came to an unmarried woman. In 1987, a quarter of all babies were born out of wedlock; in 2001, fully a third. Single-mother homes have been on the increase — as have cohabiting but unmarried couples — one consequence of the new sexual freedom. Other consequences have been charted in the rising incidence of sexually transmitted diseases. Sexual attitudes have also had a significant impact on the nature of families, as we shall see in the next chapter, Reproduction.

Source: "Majority Considers Sex Before Marriage Morally Okay." Retrieved August 23, 2001 from http://www.gallup.com. "Nonmarital Childbearing in the United States 1940-99, *National Vital Statistics Report*, October 18, 2000, p. 28.

Loving The One You're With

Sexual Activity for Men and Women in 1994

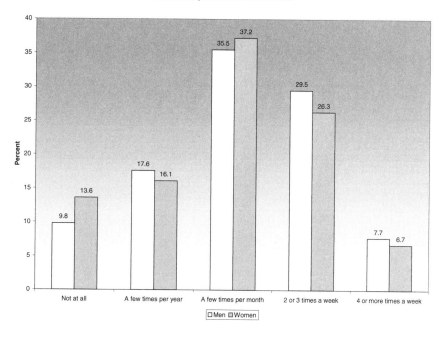

How often are we having sex?

A survey in 1994 was conducted as a part of a study called *The Social Organization of Sexuality* and was also included in a later report to the Centers for Disease Control. A total of 1,330 men and 1,664 women were asked about their sex lives over the previous year. About half were married, about a quarter had never married, and the rest either were divorced, separated, or widowed. Nationally, according to the Census Bureau, 59% of men and 56% of women were married in 1994.

Perhaps the most interesting point is that a significant percentage of respondents were not very sexually active. 9.8% of men and 13.6% of women reported having no sex in the previous year. 17.6% of men and 16.1% of women said they had sex only a few times during the year. More men than women reported being sexually

Sexual Activity of Women, 1994

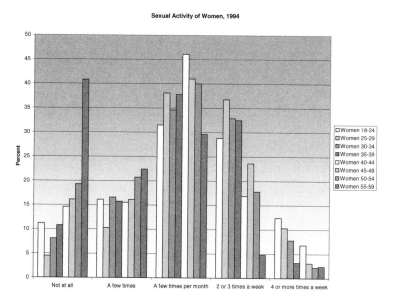

active 2 or more times a week. More women than men reported having sex just a few times a month. They were usually married, although a significant portion was single.

The panels below compare sexual activity by age. Men who were not active sexually fell into the 18-24 or 55-59 groups. This makes sense. Young men probably are not married or may not have a partner. Older men may be without a partner because of divorce or a deceased wife. They also may not be interested. The levels of men who had not had intercourse were roughly comparable over the age groups. This is more striking when compared to the levels of women who have not had sex. The share of women who had been celibate over the year increased steadily by age group. The jump between women from 50-54 and 55-59 is particularly striking.

The most sexually active seem to be between 18-24 years of age. They were more likely to be having sex four times a week or more (they also have the most sexually transmitted diseases). Activity for both decreased with age. More men than women had sex four times a week. Women 40-44 years of age were the exception for their sex. The share of women reporting this level of sexual activity increased noticeably for women in their thirties and fifties.

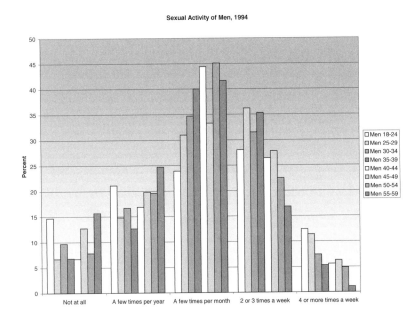

Sexual Activity of Men, 1994

Common responses were "a few times a month" or "two or three times a week" The highest levels were reported for men and women between 40-44 years of age. Those in their forties and fifties saw the highest levels in general — in short, people most likely to be married. Most couples, on average, probably have intercourse once a week.

Sexual activity is influenced by a number of issues. People are getting married later in life; this (potentially) delays the start of their sex lives. A second marriage may trigger a jump in sexual activity later in life. A woman trying to get pregnant will also probably be more sexually active in an effort to conceive.

Source: U.S. Department of Health and Human Services. *Report to Congress on Out-of-Wedlock Childbearing.* (September 1995), Table IV; Laumann, E.O., et. al. 1994. *The Social Organization of Sexuality.*

Americans and Their Sexual Behavior

I Have This Fantasy....

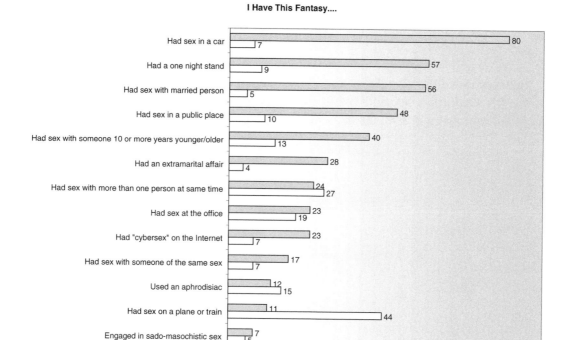

Had sex in a car — 7 / 80
Had a one night stand — 9 / 57
Had sex with married person — 5 / 56
Had sex in a public place — 10 / 48
Had sex with someone 10 or more years younger/older — 13 / 40
Had an extramarital affair — 4 / 28
Had sex with more than one person at same time — 24 / 27
Had sex at the office — 19 / 23
Had "cybersex" on the Internet — 7 / 23
Had sex with someone of the same sex — 7 / 17
Used an aphrodisiac — 12 / 15
Had sex on a plane or train — 11 / 44
Engaged in sado-masochistic sex — 7 / 5

Percent of Survey Respondents

☐ Would like to   ☐ Have done

We've seen some statistics on sexual activity of Americans. But what are they really doing behind closed doors? What would they *like* to do?

Tracking such behavior, of course, is quite difficult. People may not always admit their sexual behavior and interests out of fear of being labeled too far out of the ever-shifting norm. One recent survey, conducted by Durex (the condom maker) and Euro RSCG Worldwide, potentially sheds some light on what has been happening in the dark.

Some of the data is not too surprising: 80% of the respondents confessed to having had sex in a car. As quickly as cars appeared in our nation's garages in the 1950s, America's teenage males were borrowing the keys from Dad and driving their girlfriends out to "Lookout Point" (or some other spot to park). Fifty-seven percent claimed to have had a one night stand; again, hardly surprising information in light of the rise of casual sex and easier access to contraception.

Other data will trouble some a little more. More than half have had sex with a married person (5% would like to!); 28% have had an extramarital affair (4% would like to!). With computers finding their way into more homes, 23% confess to having "cybersex" on the Internet. For all the pleasures of this new technology, it's putting Americans on a slippery moral slope. Is cybersex cheating?

What interests Americans sexually? Americans would like to try sex on a plane or a train (having already done so in a car, of course). They would also like to try sex with multiple partners. The third most popular activity was to have sex at the office. Amazingly, 23% of the respondents actually have done so (for, um, information on America's productivity standards, see this series companion volume *Work & Leisure* — actually, productivity is *way* up!).

Now, for some questions: People want to have sex on train or a plane. Why are boats not on the list? If a pilot has sex on a plane, is he also having sex at the office? If I have cybersex at an Internet café, am I also having sex in a public place?

Source: "Love and Lust: A Euro RSCG Global Study." Retrieved March 18, 2002 from http://www.eurorscg.com.

How Do We See Ourselves?

How Americans Describe Themselves Sexually

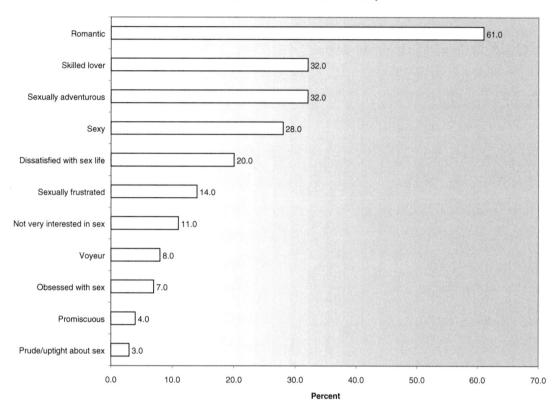

The Durex and Euro RSCG Worldwide asked Americans to describe themselves sexually. What do the results say about Americans sexual activity?

A majority of respondents regard themselves as romantics. They're all for holding hands, candle light dinners, love letters, and sending flowers to their sweetheart. Thirty-two percent of those surveyed think they are skilled lovers, 32% said they were sexually adventurous, and 28% said they were sexy.

But wait. These are actually rather low numbers, one could argue. The rest of the survey indicates that there is potentially a sizeable portion of the public that is having trouble with its sex lives. Twenty percent reported being dissatisfied with their sex life, 14% reported feeling sexually frustrated, and 11% reported being not very interested in sex. In this book and its companion volumes, the issues of depression, stress, and social isolation have been aspects of many topics in a number of issues. How common are such conditions? Does a significant segment of the population have problems with sex?

A recent study in the *Journal of the American Medical Association* seems to suggest that many people do. Sociologist Edward Laumann analyzed data from the *1992 National Health and Social Life Survey.* In interviews with 1,749 women and 1,410 men ages 18-59, 43% of women and 31% of men reported some degree of sexual dysfunction. Problems cited included pain during intercourse, difficulties with erections, inability to achieve orgasm and — perhaps most significantly — lack of interest in sex.

There were about 100 million men and 108 million women over the age of 18 in the United States. How does this figure apply to them? Laumann has already raised an obvious question: because of people's unwillingness to seek out help for their sexual problems, could the figures actually be higher?

Sources: "Love and Lust: A Euro RSCG Global Study." Retrieved July 22, 2002 from http://www.eurorscg.com; Laumann, Edward O.; Anthony Paik; Raymond C. Rosen. "Sexual Dysfunction in the United States: Prevalence and Predictors." *Journal of the American Medical Association*, February 10, 1999, p. 537.

Viagra Offers Men Some Help

New Prescriptions of Viagra Written for Selected Months

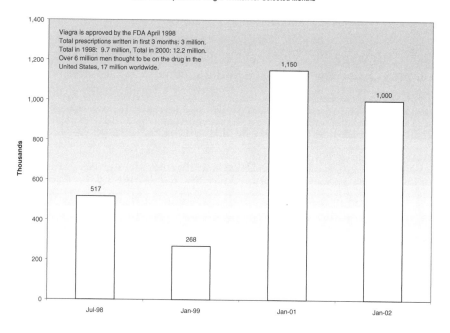

Viagra is approved by the FDA April 1998
Total prescriptions written in first 3 months: 3 million.
Total in 1998: 9.7 million, Total in 2000: 12.2 million.
Over 6 million men thought to be on the drug in the
United States, 17 million worldwide.

An estimated 10 to 20 million men are thought to have an inability to achieve and/or sustain satisfactory erections in the United States. Some sources have placed this figure even higher. One in 10 men are thought to have erectile dysfunction worldwide (what was once called impotence).

Viagra was seen as a wonder drug when it first became available in April 1998. Until that time, men often had to use pumps or injection therapies for sexual intercourse. In its first three months on the market, Viagra sales hit $411 million and 3 million prescriptions were written. It is the second highest prescription drug launch in health care history (Celebrex beat it roughly a year alter).

A great deal of snickering was done in the media in their coverage. Women were now going to have to "fight off" their suddenly randy husbands, we were told. Senator Bob Dole's admission that he was using the drug offered even more opportunity for jokes. One article opened in this way: "Former Senator Bob Dole thinks Viagra is the greatest thing since the invention of the wheel. And he ought to know…he's lived to see both in a single lifetime."

After the initial rush of men to their urologists, the number of prescriptions did fall. In July 1998, a total of 891,000 prescriptions were filled, with 517,000 being new and 374,000 refills. By January 1999, the numbers had fallen, with a total of 676,000 pre-scriptions written, only 268,000 being new and 408,000 refills.

There are several reasons this. The drug probably did not prove effective for some men. Some men might have been alarmed by the 242 reports of fatal heart attacks suffered by

Viagra users, although the drug was never proven to have any link to the deaths. Others might have been turned off by the expense. The pills cost about $10 each, and some insurance carriers do not provide coverage. But men were clearly using the drug. By the end of 1999, a reported one out of three doctors had written a prescription for Viagra.

The number of prescriptions has increased recently. Pfizer, the maker of the drug, has recently boosted ad spending for Viagra, helping it achieve the household name status that other branded drugs enjoy (just to provide a little context, 44 million prescriptions were written for Lipitor in 2000, 25 million for Claritin, 23.4 million for Zoloft and 12.2 million for Viagra). Advertising may help explain the increase in new prescriptions in recent years. It could also be that more men are simply finally coming forward.

The erectile dysfunction market will become all the more important with our aging male population. The average age of a Viagra user is 55. According to the Census, there is expected to be 29.5 million in this age group in 2005 and 34 million in 2010. Such numbers don't even include the number of younger men who need the drug.

Viagra also raises another interesting point. What about sexual dysfunction in women? (Viagra has not been shown to aid women's sexual performance). According to a recent *Journal of the American Medical Association* article, 43% of women experienced dysfunction in their sex lives. According to many in the health care field, research is already under way on medication to benefit them.

Sources: Chamberlain, Claudine. "Happy Birthday, Viagra." Rose Pike. "Better than Cigars" both Retrieved August 6, 2002 from http://www.abcnews.go.com; "All Signs are Good for OTC Sales in Wake of Huge Viagra Success." *Drug Store News*, June 22, 1998, p. 53. Andrew Humphreys. "Marketer of the Year." *Med Ad News*, March 2002, p. 6; Frank Scussa "Making History." *Med Ad News*, March 2000, p. 3. "Facts About Erectile Dysfunction." Retrieved August 6, 2002 from http://www.mmhc-online.com. "Heavy Hitters of 2000." *Drug Topics*, April 16, 2001, p. 30.

Plastic Surgery: Are Men Becoming the New Women?

Percent Increase in Cosmetic Procedures for Men, 1998-2001

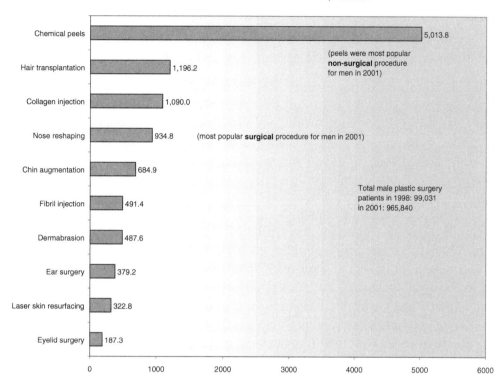

Chemical peels — 5,013.8

(peels were most popular **non-surgical** procedure for men in 2001)

Hair transplantation — 1,196.2

Collagen injection — 1,090.0

Nose reshaping — 934.8 (most popular **surgical** procedure for men in 2001)

Chin augmentation — 684.9

Fibril injection — 491.4

Total male plastic surgery patients in 1998: 99,031 in 2001: 965,840

Dermabrasion — 487.6

Ear surgery — 379.2

Laser skin resurfacing — 322.8

Eyelid surgery — 187.3

Once upon a time it was snickered about: *oh, she's had work done* someone might whisper about a woman's facelift. *Look at that bad wig*, we might whisper about the man with a toupee. But as we live longer, and lead increasingly more active lives, we don't want to just feel young. We want to look young as well. Plastic surgery has become a viable way to turn back the clock on aging — and more men are seeking surgical and non-surgical treatments.

The American Society of Plastic Surgeons began tracking trends in the field in 1992, when 412,901 men and women sought some sort of enhancement surgery. In 2001, a little more than 7.4 million had some sort of surgical or non-surgical work done, an increase of 1,692%. (Plastic surgery is different from reconstructive surgery. Reconstructive surgery deals with such things as tumor removal, hand surgeries and laceration repair. 1.4 million such operation were performed in 2001).

Roughly 99,000 men had plastic surgery in 1998, representing 9% of patients. In 2001, more than 965,000 went for some nips and tucks, an increase of 875%. Their share of total cases more than doubled to 20%. Admittedly, we are talking about a small subset of men — there are about 50 million men between the ages of 20 to 49. But a growing number of men have become concerned about their looks. Men are being held to standards of physical beauty the way women have been: men need flat stomachs and have suddenly started to count calories. For some older men, a red sports car when they hit 40 or 50 simply won't do any more.

What kind of work are men getting done? Mostly procedures to smooth out wrinkles in the face and make them appear younger. **Chemical peels**, the most popular non-surgical procedure, improve skin texture by removing damaged layers of skin. It is most helpful for those with wrinkles, blemishes, or uneven skin pigmentation.

Hair transplantation was the second fastest growing procedure. It was the fourth most popular surgical procedure for men. The hair transplant industry has been conservatively estimated at $1 billion. Men want a full head of hair because our culture sees baldness in negative terms: a man without hair is boring and unsexy. The number of transplants does not even address the chemical treatments, such as Rogaine.

Dermabrasion is a process of surgical scraping to "refinish" the top layers of skin. Treatments can soften scars or lines in the face, particularly around the mouth. Collagen and fibril injections are rather similar. Collagen, which gives skin its elasticity, diminishes naturally as the body ages. In **collagen injections**, the substance is injected under the skin to smooth out lines and wrinkles. **Fibril** is used to fill in facial lines and creases and restore the skin's natural healthy look. Fibril is a gelatin powder compound that is mixed with the patient's own blood then injected to plump up skin. **Chin augmentation** involves adding synthetics or biologicals to the area below the lower lip to make the face more prominent or to perhaps give it greater symmetry.

Women aren't letting their numbers um…sag, however. The panel on the next page shows the fastest growing plastic surgeries for women. Females clearly still fuss over their features, with the number undergoing procedures increasing 587% from 1998 to 2001, from 946,784 to 6.5 million. Chemical peels were the most performed non-surgical procedure for women in 2001, with the numbers increasing from nearly 65,000 to 1.1 million in this four-year period. Other procedures remain popular: facelifts, liposuction, and eyelid surgery. Breast augmentation remains so popular — it was the top surgical procedure in both 1998 and 2001 — that its growth was minimal during this period.

Who goes for these procedures? In 2001, the largest category was for those between 35 and 50, with slightly more than 600,000 patients falling into this segment (37% of total patients). This really isn't surprising, as this is when the aging process first begins to show on the body. This was the top age bracket in 1998 as well. Most patients underwent procedures to slow/erase the aging process — to "grow old gracefully" as the saying goes. This age group got excess fat removed, lines smoothed from around their eyes, new breasts, and their tummies tucked. The next age group with the most patients was 19 to 34. They seemed slightly more interested in improving their looks. This age group got the most nose reshapings (151,092) and breast enlargements (122,045).

In looking at the youngest age group (18 or less) one can't help but wonder how many of these teenagers, still growing into both their bodies and their sexuality, are influenced by fashion and fitness magazines. There were nearly 24,000 ear surgeries, nearly 2,600 breast augmentations, over 1,000 chin augmentations, and over 43,000 nose reshapings performed on these young men and women in 2001. Many of these could be legitimate, certainly, but how many of these surgeries were borne out of teenage insecurities?

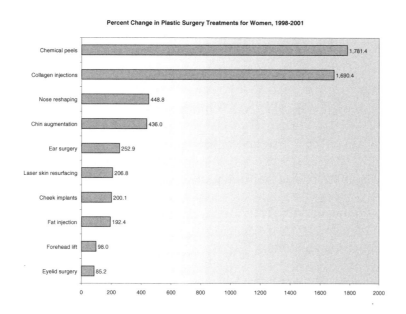

Percent Change in Plastic Surgery Treatments for Women, 1998-2001

These procedures — which are usually out of pocket costs for the patient — are not cheap either. A facelift is the most expensive of the common procedures, with the national average physician fee running roughly $5,000. Breast augmentation averages $3,043. Nose reshaping is $2,947. The prices remained fairly constant over the period, with some procedures becoming less expensive as the treatment is perfected. A chemical peel suddenly starts to sound like a bargain at $516, about half of what it cost in 1998.

New treatments are being discovered all the time. Botox became the most popular procedure in 2001, after the FDA approved the drug for cosmetic use. Botox is short for botulism toxin, the substance that causes botulism, a potentially fatal form of food poisoning. (It is administered in small enough doses so that it is fairly harmless). This "facelift in a syringe" has given birth to Botox parties, where a group of women (and sometimes men) get together, witness a demonstration, and then have the procedure performed on each of them. Botox does reduce wrinkles, true, but it only lasts a few months, and the $300 to 1,000 treatments can add up. Also, the drug can paralyze the nerves in the forehead, potentially diminishing the user's range of facial expressions. You can't frown, look surprised or squint, but, hey …. you look ten years younger.

In any discussion of who is a suitable plastic surgery candidate, some version of this line invariably appears: patient must be in good physical *and* emotional health. That last point is a good qualifier. Why do we get our tummies tucked, and our love handles zapped and a new jaw? Just to be beautiful and young? To help in the competition for mates? Many patients profess to being pleased with their new and improved physical selves. Great. But how many expect their new face to grant them a new life?

Source: Data come from the American Society of Plastic Surgeons, located at http://www.plasticsurgery.org.

Does Sex Really Sell?

Estimated size of pornography market in 1970: $5-10 million

Estimated size of pornography market in 2000: $10 billion

Estimated size of the legal global sex industry: $56 billion

Number of adult movie rentals in 1975: 75 million units

Number of adult movie rentals in 1996: 665 million units

Percent of adult films rented by men alone: 71%

Percent of adult films rented by women alone: 2%

Number of adult films produced in 1990: 1,275

Number of adult films produced in 1998: 8,948

Under President Reagan, Attorney General Edwin Meese III's Commission on Pornography released a report stating that sexually explicit materials are harmful and calling for the strict enforcement of obscenity laws. The hard-core pornography market was estimated at between $5-10 million in a federal study. In 1998, total spending on adult entertainment was placed at $10 billion, a figure that has been cited in a variety of sources such as *Time* and *The New York Times*.

Technology played an important role in the growth of the pornography industry. Previously, if one wanted to see an X-rated film, one had to visit a theater in the bad part of town (and purchase a raincoat and hat, too, presumably). But then Sony released the video cassette recorder in 1975, and a decade later roughly 75% of homes in America had one. The home video market came into existence — and with it the market for blue movies. A person could now watch adult films in the privacy of his own home.

There is still the potentially embarrassing moment of having to go and rent a pornographic film at the local video store. Technology has come to the rescue again. Cable and satellite programmers feature a number of sexually oriented cable stations, including The Playboy Channel, The Spice Channel, and the Hot Network. The financial incentives are just too enticing for companies. It isn't just back alley companies enjoying these revenues either. General Motors owns DirecTV, a satellite broadcaster, that sells $200 million annually in pay-per-view sex films to its customers. AT&T owns a company that sells sex films to nearly a million hotel rooms, according to the *New York Times*. Several conservative groups have launched campaigns against upscale prominent hotel chains to rid themselves of the adult pay-per-view services (which are in 60% of mid and upper level hotel chains).

But we do we really spend $10 billion a year on hard-core videos, peep shows, sexual devices, magazines and Internet porn? We spent slightly over $4 billion on diapers and $10 billion on heroin in 1999. The motion picture industry had revenues of $8 billion. If the $10 billion figure is accurate, has pornography really become mainstream? Could Nadine Strossen of the ACLU be correct when she said of the $10 billion figure: "It's not 10 perverts spending $1 billion a year."

More than a few people have questioned this figure. Dan Ackman in *Forbes* cites a variety of industry data to peg the industry at about $4 billion. Is this still too high? Perhaps too low?

Another staggering figure is a study published in *Forbes* that attempted to measure the value of the legal sex industry: $56 billion spent on videos, magazines, adult clubs, escort services, phone lines, sexual devices and the Internet. Is this to be believed?

Source: Egan, Timothy. "Technology Sent Wall Street Into Market for Pornography." *New York Times*, October 23, 2000; Dan Ackman. "How Big is Porn?" *Forbes*, May 25, 2001, Richard C. Morais. "Porn Goes Public." *Forbes*, June 14, 1999.

What Do Teens Know About Sex?

What They Don't Know CAN Hurt Them: Percent of Teens Answering Correctly

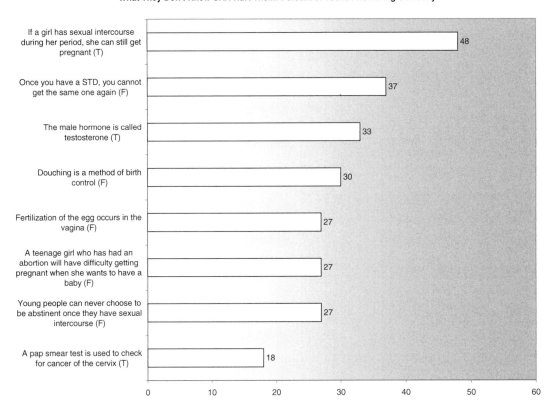

A recent study was conducted of 661 teenagers aged 13 to 15 in seven major communities[1]. The group was administered 75 true or false questions on reproduction and sexual health (respondents were instructed not to guess at answers they did not know). Overall, the young people averaged a score of 40% correct. Some of the questions in which less than half the adolescents answered correctly are shown above (T or F indicates a true or false statement).

The test revealed a lack of knowledge about basic human sexuality. More than half did not know a women can still get pregnant during her period (it's a very small chance, but possible). Only 33% of the teens were able to identify testosterone as a male hormone. Only 27% understood that the egg is not fertilized in a woman's vagina. Only 27% of the teens understood that one can still choose abstinence after sexual activity. This final revelation is rather surprising, considering the public debate about sex education and ab-

---

[1] The communities were Hollywood, FL; Bronx, NY, Portland, OR; Rochester, NY; Seattle, WA, Baltimore MD and Houston, TX. Many came from high risk or disadvantaged areas. Over 40% were African American or Caribbean Black and another 29% were Latino or Hispanic. Almost half lived with two parents. Almost a third had had sexual intercourse at least once.

stinence in our nation's schools. The adults may be talking, (or shouting), but are their sons and daughters listening?

The responses around sexually transmitted diseases and pregnancy are more troubling. There is still misinformation about how and when a woman can get pregnant. More than half did not know a woman can get pregnant during her period. More than half did not know an abortion generally plays no role in woman's ability to conceive in the future.

The teens did show some knowledge of sexual issues. However, even these answers could give one pause. What of those who did not know the answers or responded incorrectly?

Question	Percent Answering Correctly
Pregnancy happens when a sperm fertilizes an egg. (T)	79
Girls cannot get pregnant the first time they have sex (F)	73
If a girl only has sex once in a while, she really doesn't need birth control (F)	73
You cannot get HIV from someone you know really well (F)	70
Sexually transmitted diseases usually go away on their own (F)	49

According to the results, over 20% did not understand how a pregnancy occurs, nearly 30% don't use birth control when necessary, 30% don't understand how HIV is transmitted and over 50% don't understand how to treat a sexually transmitted disease.

What does this survey potentially say about adolescents in general? Do the old myths about pregnancy and STDs persist? Not knowing the facts about sex can be a costly — even deadly — mistake. 27% of the teens in the survey thought a girl doesn't need contraception if she is occasionally sexually active. Let's ask the girl if she needed it in nine months when the baby is born. 30% of the teens thought you can't get HIV from someone you know well? Half of new HIV infections occur among the young, no doubt from people they thought they knew well too. A sexually transmitted disease goes away on its own? You may not know you even have one until after you've passed it on to someone else!

Source: "Knowledge about Reproduction, Contraception, and Sexually Transmitted Infections among Young Adolescents in American Cities." *Social Policy*, Spring 2000, p. 41.

Teens and Sex: What's Really Going On

Sexual Activity Among Teenagers, 1993-2001

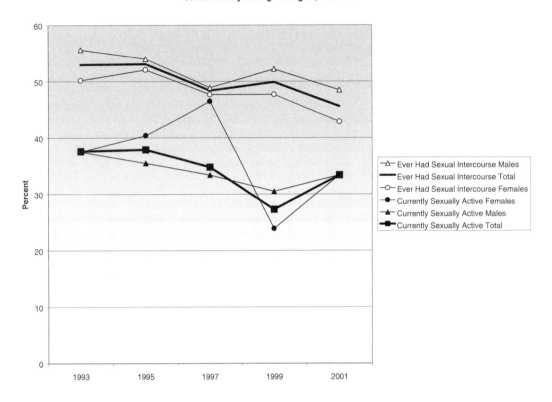

Sexual activity was generally on the decline among high school students in the 1990s, according to data from the Center for Disease Control.

The percentage of high school students who have ever had sex has been declining since 1993. In that year, 50% of females had had intercourse, while slightly more than 42% had done so by 2001. More young men were delaying the start of their sexual lives as well. 55.6% of males had had sex, while 48% of them had had sex in 2001.

The percent of young men and women who remain sexually active peaked in the middle of the 1990s for both sexes and then began to decline.[2] Figures fell steadily across this period for all races, according to the CDC, although in the case of blacks it was quite dramatic. According to the study, 89% of females and 80% of males reported having had sex in 1993, although just 69% and 60% of males reported having had sex in 2001. So, what is going on here?

Explaining sexual behavior is a complex issue, of course. Young people get their messages about morality and sex from a variety of sources: parents, friends, the church, and the media. Fear of pregnancy or a sexually transmitted disease still are powerful motiva-

---

[2] Sexually active is defined as having had intercourse in the three months preceding the survey.

---

tors to refrain from intercourse. Some young people have intercourse and realize they have "gotten in over their heads" so to speak. A survey in *Psychology Today* found that of those high school boys and girls who have had sex, 55% of boys and 72% of girls regretted the decision. There has also been dialogue in recent years about remaining a virgin. Some young people have decided that sexual activity is something they will only share with their husband or wife. The "virgin message" also appears in popular entertainment. Pop music stars such as Brittany Spears and Jessica Simpson have been open about their decision to remain virgins until marriage.

Why has there been a sudden jump between 1999 and 2001 in sexually active teenagers? Why the dramatic rise in sexually active girls in the first years of the survey? Some studies have pointed out that sexual maturation has been happening at startlingly early rates for some pre-teen girls. Once a young girl hits puberty, the door opens to potential sexual experimentation much earlier.

Some have theorized that we are just more accepting of female sexuality, at least in the context of a relationship. The numbers do suggest that teenagers are more interested in relationships; the percent of teenagers with a history of four or more sexual partners fell from 18.8% in 1993 to 14.2% in 2001. A boy is now potentially more likely to have his first sexual experiences with a girlfriend as opposed to a "girl of ill repute" as he might have had before the sexual revolution. That's potentially good news for young people learning that sex is just one part of an intimate relationship. More alarming is anecdotal evidence of boys and girls engaging in other forms of sex — oral, for example — because this is seen as safe behavior and relatively harmless.

It's important to remember we are looking a fraction of our 15 to 17 year olds. Less than half have had sex. About a third remain sexually active. Most teenagers are waiting to have sex — whether they like it or not.

Source: "Youth Risk Behavior Surveillance." Centers for Disease Control and Prevention, Surveillance Summaries, June 28, 2002.MMWR 2002: 51 (No. ss-4); "Behind Closed Doors." *Psychology Today*, November 2000, p. 10; "Number of Teens, Primarily Boys, Having Sex in 90s as Adolescent Girls Lead Way in Redefining Relationships." Retrieved August 8, 2002 from http://www.washington.edu.

Two Decades of AIDS

Reported Cases and Deaths in the United States

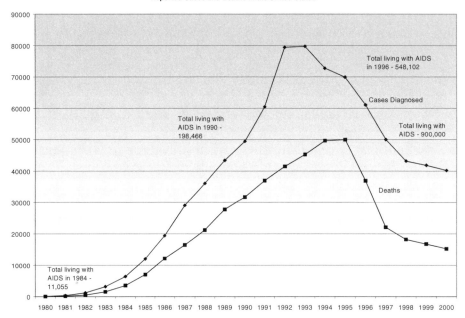

On June 5, 1981, doctors reported a strange and deadly disease that had begun to show up in gay men in Los Angeles. A peculiar aspect of the cases was that the men were the victims of the types of infections traditionally found in cancer patients, transplant patients, and those with severely compromised immune systems. It would not be until 1984 that doctors and researchers would be able to link AIDS to the human immunodeficiency virus (HIV). Over the 20 year period, we have lost 457,667 men and women to AIDS, and 900,000 are thought to be living with the AIDS/HIV at the end of 2001 (a fraction of the 40 million worldwide). Where have we been? Where are we headed?

Some scientists believe HIV made the jump from monkeys to humans somewhere between 1926 and 1946. The earliest case appears to have been in 1959. Scientists recently discovered a blood sample from an adult Bantu male from what is now the Democratic Republic of Congo that tested positive for HIV-1.[3] The graphic shows how quickly the disease spread: a year after the first 335 cases were diagnosed in 1981, cases rose 841% to 3,153 in 1983, and then 281.4% to 12,026 in 1985. That same year, the blood supply was screened for the virus for the first time (284 people were exposed to HIV through transfusions in 2000, down from a peak of 1,098 in 1993). Also in 1985, Rock Hudson announced he had the disease. In 1987, the FDA approved AZT, the first drug to treat

---

[3] Nature reports that "the sample taken from the Bantu man has a viral sequence that lies near the ancestral node of subtypes B and D in the major group, suggesting that these HIV-1 subtypes may stem from a single introduction into Africa soon after 1959. The team notes that given the large genetic differences between HIV-1 and HIV-2, the divergence of these viruses could not have occurred in the late 1940s; that branching point must have come considerably earlier."

AIDS. In 1988, the National Institute of Health established the first Office of AIDS Research. There were other attacks on the spread of the disease, some more controversial: the first comprehensive needle exchange program for IV drug users began that year as well.

How did the homosexual community respond to the crisis? There was grieving to be done, to be sure. In 1986, the first panel of the AIDS Memorial quilt was created. This quilt features panels sewn by family members and friends to commemorate the deceased. It currently has more than 44,000 panels and is the length of 16 football fields. Some gay men did not just grieve, however; they got angry. In 1987, the Aids Coalition to Unleash Power (ACT UP) was formed, a group of activists who called attention to the disease in dramatic (and, some may argue, counter-productive) protests. The phrase Silence = Death is associated with this organization.

Other public figures brought visibility to the disease. After being criticized for his silence on the issue, President Reagan spoke of AIDS for the first time in 1990. In 1991, Magic Johnson announced he was HIV positive. A year later Arthur Ashe announced he had AIDS. Also in 1992, Mary Fisher, who is HIV positive, addressed the Republican National Committee. The year 1993 saw the highest reported number of cases: 79,752. AIDS was killing 14.5 per 100,000 people, a rate higher than suicide (12.1), homicides (10.1), and nearly as many as motor vehicle accidents (16.3). By 1994, AIDS was the leading cause of death for all Americans 25 to 44. More than 335,000 Americans were living with the disease.

Prevention strategies and drug therapies have helped to reduce the spread of HIV and to extend the life of those with AIDS. Deaths fell dramatically in the middle 1990s. Indeed, the drug cocktails were so effective that those with AIDS had to start worrying "not about dying but about living" to quote one source — paying rent, finding a job, getting insurance policies. People were starting to ask: is AIDS finally over? Journalist Andrew Sullivan wrote a 1996 piece in the *New York Times Magazine* called "When Plagues End — Notes on the Twilight of an Epidemic." *Newsweek*'s cover asked: "The End of AIDS?"

AIDS may no longer be a plague as long we keep it (and ourselves) under control. The number of new infections in the United States has leveled off at roughly 40,000 annually — still an enormous number. Mortality is dropping as well, from 22,067 cases in 1997 to 15,300 in 2000. But the disease is far from over. The number of Americans living with the disease increases by about 25,000 a year. The CDC is in the process of launching programs to halve the rate by 2005. Plans include education about high risk behaviors and on-the-spot testing. But will we listen?

Sources: Chart data from *United States of America Epidemiological Fact Sheets on HIV/AIDS and Sexually Transmitted Infections, 2002 Update, HIV/AIDS Surveillance Report*, Vol. 11 no. 2, table 22. 1980 figure is actually for total cases pre-1980. Zhu, Tuofo; Korber, Bette T.; Nahinias, Andre J.; et al. "An African HIV-1 Sequence from 1959 and Implications for the Origin of the Epidemic." Nature, February 5, 1998, p. 594. Sternberg, Steve. "AIDS Approaches Grim Anniversary." May 29, 2001, p. 8D. Charlene Laino. "1 in 4 Infected with HIV don't know." Retrieved July 24, 2002 from http://www.msnbc.com/news/715645.asp.

HIV: The New Cases

Estimated New Annual Infections

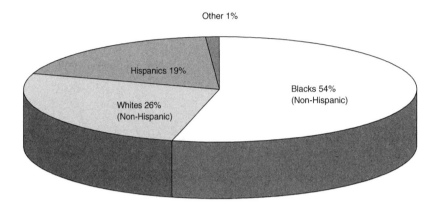

Other 1%

Hispanics 19%

Whites 26%
(Non-Hispanic)

Blacks 54%
(Non-Hispanic)

Roughly 40,000 new HIV cases are diagnosed each year, according to the Center for Disease Control and Prevention. Who are the new cases? Why are they happening?

Men make up 70% of new HIV infections. Male-to-male sex remains the primary method on transmission, with 42% of annual cases believed to fall into this category. AIDS has found a disturbing home in minority communities: over half of new cases involve blacks and nearly 20% are Hispanics. The percentage of blacks with AIDS surpassed the percentage of whites for the first time in 1996.

Minorities are disproportionately affected by HIV. In 2000, blacks accounted for 43% of AIDS cases, although they make up 12% of the population. Hispanics accounted for nearly 20% of the cases, while they make up only 13% of the population. American Indians and Alaska natives make up less than 1% of the total population. After several years of decline, the number of adult cases have been increasing steadily since 1998 (150 in 1998 to 184 in 2000), while the other ethnic groups have been on the decline. These groups have traditionally had low access to health care and information. How does one tailor health information to a group of people that cover many tribes, each with its own language and culture?

Rate of AIDS Cases Per 100,000 Population		
	1994	2000
Blacks	101.0	74.2
Hispanics	51.0	30.4
American Indian/Alaska Natives	12.0	12.7
Whites	17.0	7.9
Asians/Pacific Islanders	6.0	4.3

The spread of AIDS was controlled in part through prevention efforts: learn how to use condoms, get tested, know your partners. But a generation of young gay men have come of age who were babies during the epidemic. They didn't see stories on HIV ever day in the newspapers, did not attend funerals of friends, or saw sex as a potentially lethal activity. This lack of vigilance comes at a price: Half of the new cases occur among people 25 years old and younger. Reaching young black and Latino men may be particularly difficult, although it is vital that the health industry (and community leaders) do so. Among gays and bisexuals, men of color make up a growing share of the new cases: they made up 52% of cases, up from 31% in 1989, while whites represented 48% of cases, down from 70% in 1989.

There are several issues that complicate prevention strategies. Minorities may not have access to quality and consistent health care. Also, homosexuality is such a stigma that men of color may be unwilling to identify themselves as gay. Some don't, either: according to a CDC study, 24% of blacks and 15% of Latinos who have sex with other men identity themselves as heterosexual (indeed, this is why the health industry uses the men who have sex with other men category in the first place — terms like gay or homosexual contact just don't fit the context).

Another factor is testing. According to the CDC, one in four do not know they are infected with the virus. Again, there are striking racial differences: One recent study of over 5,700 gay men in selected large cities found that of those that tested positive, 91% of black men 16-29 were unaware of their status, compared to 77% for Hispanics and 60% for whites. Look at the potentially deadly combination here: a man does not believe AIDS will "happen to me"; he does not know his HIV+ status because he is never tested, and spreads the virus to partners of both sexes.

It isn't just tailoring the AIDS message to a new generation. Any prevention strategy faces political, financial, and social challenges, of course. The dollars for minority community initatives were fairly small until 1998, when the Congressional Black Caucus urged President Clinton to declare AIDS a "state of emergency" in 1998 for their community. Some have criticized the black community for mobilizing so late in the crisis, arguing that they looked the other way when the primary sufferers were intravenous drug users and gay/bisexual men. Action came only when the disease then began to affect straight women and more middle/upper class blacks. Congress now spends $245 million to target minority communities. Some argue this still is not enough.

This leads to another point: women. The men who have sex with men also have sex with women — who make up the remaining 30% of the 40,000 annual cases. Three quarters of women receive the virus through heterosexual contact. About 65% of the women are black, while 18% are Hispanic. The number of cases for women overall grew 159% from 1993 to 2000, nearly double the rate for men.

In 1999, for men 35 to 44, HIV was the leading cause of death for black men, the third for Hispanic men, and the fifth for white men. It routinely ranks in the top 6 causes of death for various age brackets of both sexes.

Are we ready to have some frank discussions about our lives and behavior, as we did a decade ago?

Sources: Schreiber, Chris. "Demographic Shift." Nurse Week, March 2000. Kai Wright. "AIDS and Black New Yorkers." Village Voice, June 14, 2000, "First 500,000 Cases." MMWR, November 24, 1995. "A Glance at the New Epidemic." "New CDC Studies Shed Light on Factors Underlying High HIV Infection Rates Among Gay and Bisexual Men." Retrieved July 19, 2002 from http://www.cdc.gov.

Chapter 11

Reproduction

Many factors influence the decision to have children. The very fact that we now *decide* whether or not to have a child is, in itself, a sign of the change in attitude about reproduction that have taken place over the 20th century.

The century saw two Baby Booms, one after each World War, the second being of epic proportions. The first two panels provide an overview of these two patterns. In the 1960s, reliable contraceptives became readily available and a sexual revolution followed. The fertility rate dropped sharply. The other panels in the chapter focus on the period since 1960 — as the Baby Boom generation comes of age.

The correlation between fertility rates (number of children born to 1,000 women of child-bearing age) and female participation in the workforce is analyzed in the third panel. At the end of the century, most women's magazines offered regular columns of advise on balancing work and family while Martha Stewart provided an ideal of domesticity that most women only dream about.

As the women of the Baby Boom reached childbearing age they decided to put off motherhood. Two panels look at the rising age of mothers and some side effects thereof; assisted reproductive technology (ART) and the rise of twins and higher order multiples.

Although the use of ART is on the rise, more women are trying to prevent pregnancy than to conceive. Always ready to oblige, we look at the most popular contraceptives. The next panel then reviews figures on abortion and its rise and fall since becoming legal nationwide in 1973.

Sharply rising rates of cesarean births are covered in the next panel. The explanation of this increase reminds us that having babies is still one of life's more physically challenging endeavors. Happily, both infant and maternal mortality rates are down.

Low birth weight babies are, however, on the rise. This is explained in another panel that also discusses the fact that low birth weight is one of the leading causes of infant mortality and disability. Other birth defects are covered in a separate panel.

The chapter ends on an upbeat note. We look at the dramatic decline in infant mortality over the last 50 years. As one of the most widely used indicators of a society's general health, it is reassuring to see that the infant mortality rate has fallen more than 400% from 1950 to 2000 — a trend that is going in the right direction.

Our Reproductive Patterns

Live Births, Fertility Rate, and Birth Rate
1909 to 2000

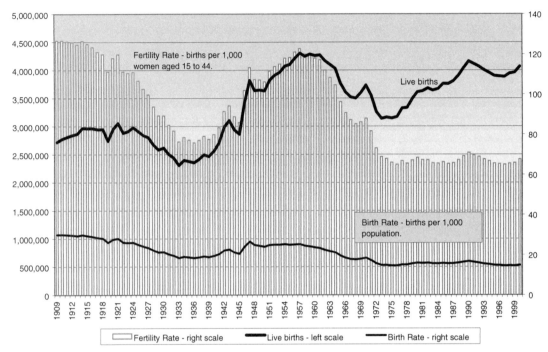

A look at the history of births — and birth rates — may be a suitable way to introduce a chapter titled Reproduction. Most of the panels in this chapter will focus on the later part of the 20th century. By taking a look at a longer sweep of time, we can see the fluctuating nature of our reproductive patterns.

The fertility rate was high during and after World War I. The Roaring 20s produced a slide in fertility and births. Both measures began to climb during the dark days of the Depression as people drew back to basic values. This flattened briefly as Johnny marched off to another war and Rosie the Riveter went to the factory. When the boys came back from war we had a Baby Boom of historic size, defining the demographic landscape of a century. It stands like a mountain in the center of this century of births.

As the 1960s began, fertility began to drop reaching record lows by the mid-1970s. This was an era of change as reliable contraceptives made control over pregnancy possible. Norms regulating sexual activity were questioned by many. The issue of the Baby Boom was coming to its own age of reproduction and decided to consider other options.

The falling fertility rate leveled out in the last 15 years of the century. The constant ebb and flow of generations continues. But, are we producing enough babies to replenish our numbers? That is what we will look at next.

Source: "Vital Statistics of the United States, 1998," Volume I, Natality, National Center for Health Statistics (NCHS), U.S. Department of Health and Human Services, updated from later issues of National Vital Statistics Reports and Monthly Vital Statistics Reports also published by the NCHS.

Are We Breeding Enough to Sustain Our Numbers?

**Total Fertility Rate in the United States
1940 to 2000**

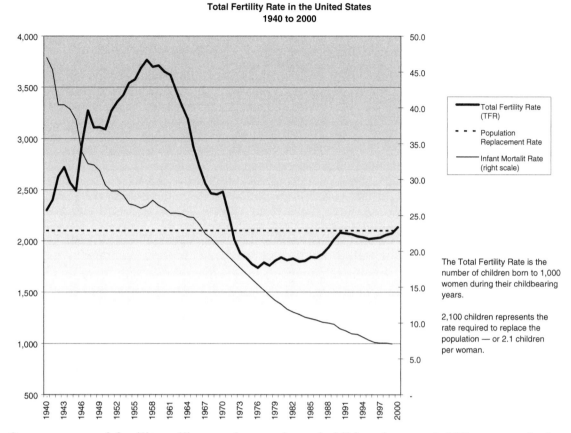

The Total Fertility Rate is the number of children born to 1,000 women during their childbearing years.

2,100 children represents the rate required to replace the population — or 2.1 children per woman.

One measure of fertility tallies up the number of children born to 1,000 women during their childbearing years, 15 to 44. This is called the Total Fertility Rate (TFR). In order for a population simply to replace itself (neither to grow nor to shrink) it needs to maintain a TFR of 2,100, or 2.1 children per woman.

During the last 60 years of the 20th century the United States' TFR averaged 2,560, well over the level required to replenish our numbers. The answer to the question posed in the title of this panel is, yes. The chart shows the Total Fertility Rate each year from 1940 through 2000. The replacement level of 2,100 is highlighted with a dotted line towards the center of the graph. Wherever the TFR is above the replacement level, the society is breeding enough to at least replace its numbers. Where the TFR drops below the 2,100 line, the population is shrinking (before counting immigration and emigration). As an interesting point of reference, the infant mortality rate is also provided in the graph. This rate is the number of infants who die per 1,000 live births.

What is clear is that the TFR during the post World War II period far-exceeded population replacement levels. This was the generation that produced the Baby Boom.

On the right side of the graph, for the years 1970 through 2000, the TFR dips below replacement level for many years, slowly creeping back towards the 2,100 line and crossing it again in 2000 for the first time since 1971. This later period is the time during which the Baby Boom was reproducing. This generation was clearly less willing to raise large families than was its parents' generation.

Many factors influence the fertility rate. Industrialized countries have all seen sharp declines in their total fertility rates. Declines in fertility are understood to result from "broadening horizons for girls and women, who respond by delaying childbearing; health care advances that keep babies alive, reducing the need for more; broad availability of reliable and inexpensive family planning services; and urbanization."[1] All of these have been experienced in the United States in the 20th century.

One of the most important of these factors is our ability to control procreation. Throughout human history many methods have been used to try and prevent pregnancy. They were somewhat effective but abstinence was the only truly reliable means of preventing pregnancy... until the 1960s.

Birth control became reliable in the 1960s. Although not 100% reliable — abstinence still being the only 100% certain way to avoid pregnancy — the oral contraceptives introduced in the 1960s made it possible to engage in sexual intercourse with more than a 97% certainty that pregnancy would not occur. This marked a watershed in family planning and the beginning of sharp declines in fertility rates.

What is clear from this panel is that the TFR in the United States, after falling below the replacement level, has again reached that level in 2000. Even without the inflow of new people through immigration to the U.S., we are breeding at levels that will sustain us.

The next panel will look at another of the factors influencing fertility rates; women's growing participation in the paid workforce.

Source: U.S. Department of Health and Human Services, National Center for Health Statistics (NCHS), "Vital Statistics of the United States, 1998," Volume I, *Natality*, updated from later issues of *National Vital Statistics Reports* and *Monthly Vital Statistics Reports* also published by NCHS. International Planned Parenthood Federation, *The Myth of Shrinking Population*, September 1999, available online at http://www.ippf.org/resources/6billion/myth.htm.

---

[1] This statement is from a report entitled *The Myth of Shrinking Population* published by the International Planned Parenthood Foundation. The report does not show an author. See source note for a full citation.

Women: Working 9 to 5 and Having Fewer Babies

Total Fertility and Women in the Workforce, 1940 -- 2000

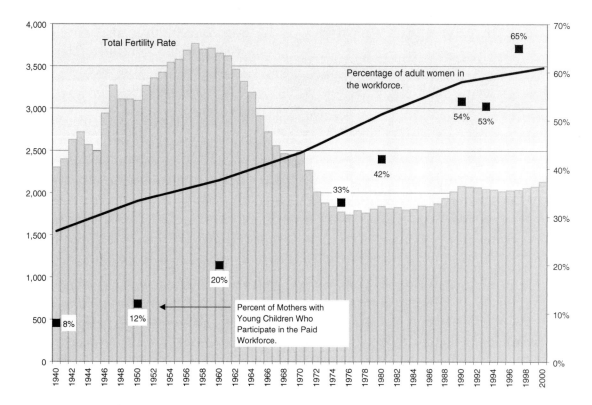

This graph again presents the Total Fertility Rate (TFR)[2] annually from 1940 to 2000. We have added to this background a curve showing the percentage of women that participate in the workforce. Finally, we placed square markers in the few years for which data are available on the percentage of mothers with young children who participate in the workforce, part- or full-time[3].

In the last panel we focused on trends in the TFR. Here the focus is on the relationship between fertility rates and women's participation in the workforce. The extent to which female participation in the workforce impacts the fertility rate is not clear. The likelihood that increasing female participation in the workforce *does have* an impact on fertility is not disputed. The undulating pattern of the TFR is not directly mirrored by the rate of female participation in the workforce. Women have been entering the workforce in steadily greater numbers throughout the 20th century while the TFR has varied greatly.

---

[2] The Total Fertility Rate is the number of children born to 1,000 women during their childbearing years.

[3] These data come from various sources. Data for the earliest years, 1940, 1950, and 1960, are for mothers of young children but the exact age of the children is not specified. For the rest of the years, data are for mothers of children under six years of age. See source note for full citations.

When looking at workforce participation rates, it is important to keep in mind that rates vary by age group. The line on the main chart shows a steady increase in the percentage of women in the labor market. The percentage of women with young children in the workforce (marked by squares on the chart) has also risen and in 1997 was higher than the rate of all women in the workforce. This is the result of age differences in workforce participation.

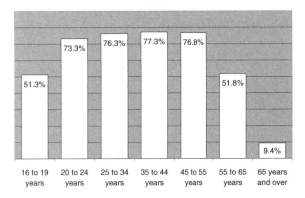

Female Participation in the Workplace by Age, 2000

Female workforce participation rates for the year 2000 are shown to the left. The highest rates are for women in the prime childbearing and child rearing years.

Our fertility rates, as we saw in the previous panel, are influenced by many factors the most prominent of which is the availability of reliable contraceptives. Another important factor is the number of alternative activities that women have to childbearing and child rearing. A woman is very unlikely to decide to have or not have a baby based solely on whether or not she is working. However, she is likely to postpone childbearing while she goes to college. Then, once she has invested time and money to obtain a college education, she may well try and work her way up to a desired job position before deciding to have a child. This postponing of childbearing leads to having fewer babies and thus a lower TFR. The later a woman starts bearing children, the fewer she is likely to have.

Articles offering advice on how best to balance work and family have grown to dominate women's magazines during the 1990s. The subject has also gained a lot of attention in the human resource departments of large organizations. Our society is in the midst of a transformation. The tasks associated with caregiving and child rearing, as well as maintaining social networks, is no longer handled primarily at the family level. Rather, it is being handled at a more institutional level. There is much debate about whether or not this is a good thing, about how it can be done most efficiently, and about how and whether government policies can or should be made to facilitate this transition. As we work these issues out, we continue to breed and raise children — just at a lower pace than in the past.

The next panel asks the question, just how much are we postponing childbearing?

Source: Fertility data are from the U.S. Department of Health and Human Services, National Center for Health Statistics (NCHS), "Vital Statistics of the United States, 1998," Volume I, *Natality*, updated from later issues of *National Vital Statistics Reports* and *Monthly Vital Statistics Reports* also published by NCHS. Workplace participation data are from the U.S. Department of Labor, "Boom in day care industry the result of many social changes," *Monthly Labor Review*, August 1995, page 7 and "Marital and Family Characteristics of the Labor Force," *Current Population Survey*, March 1997. Data were also used from a table published by Columbia University on their web site, "Mothers of Young Children in the Paid Workforce," available online at http://www.columbia.edu/itc/history/brinkley/3651/webresource/stats_mothers_workforce.htm. Data on Female participation in the workforce by age are from the U.S. Census Bureau, "Civilian Labor Force and Participation Rates with Projections: 1980 to 2008," *Statistical Abstract of the United States: 2001*, page 367.

Older Moms are Catching Up

Percentage of Babies Born to Mothers by Age of Mother, 1933 -- 2000

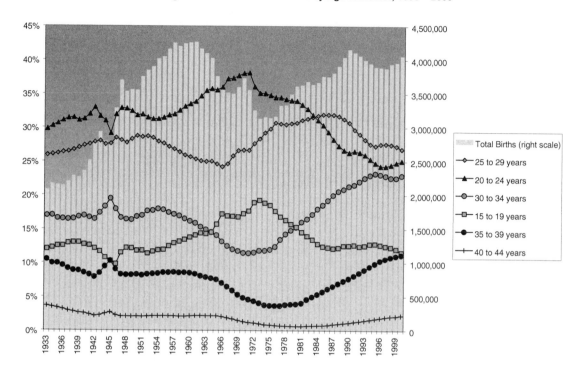

This graph presents a look at the trends in childbearing by age of the mother. As we have seen in the previous panels, the introduction of reliable birth control methods and growing participation of women in the workforce have caused many women to postpone childbearing.

The graph presents, in the form of bars, the total number of births annually from 1933 through 2000. These births are then charted as a percentage of total births by the age of the mother. The left side of the graph depicts an era before reliable birth control methods were available. The mid-1940s are a particularly volatile period as the impact of U.S. participation in World War II had a notable impact on birth rates.

The right side of the graph presents data for a period in which birth control was readily available and women were entering college and the workforce in record numbers.

The trend towards postponing childbearing until later in life is clearly visible in this graph. The higher age groups all grew in terms of their percentage of births. The younger age groups bore a smaller percentage of the babies born as we neared the turn of the century. The age group 20 to 24 has been surpassed by those aged 25 to 29. Women in there early 30s accounted for 23% of births in 2000, almost as many as the women in their early 20s who bore 25% of the babies. Women in their late 30s accounted for almost as many births (11.1%) in 2000 as women in their late teens (11.6%), an age group that has seen its percentage of births drop sharply from a high of 19.3% in 1973.

In part this birth pattern results from the dominance of the Baby Boom in all late 20th century demographic trends. There were, quite simply, more women in their 30s in the 1990s than women in their 20s.

Female Population Figures by Age Group

(2005 and 2010 are projections)

Women in their:	1970	1980	1990	2000	2005	2010
20s	**15,309,000**	**20,595,000**	19,967,000	18,017,000	*18,830,000*	*19,433,000*
30s	11,829,000	16,290,000	**21,086,000**	**20,977,000**	*18,745,000*	*18,017,000*

The trend towards childbearing later in life results from both demographic realities as well as social, cultural, and economic changes. The age at which men and women enter a first marriage has also risen during the 20th century as we have delayed the commitment to marriage and family-formation generally[4]. The question is, will this trend continue, stabilize? Or, alternately, will it prove to have been another Baby Boom-related trend that will reverse itself as the boom generation ages?

Only time will tell. During the first decade of the 21st century the youngest of the Baby Boom generation will pass out of the breeding age range, and we will then see whether the pattern they have set, of childbearing later in life, continues. Worth noting is the fact that during this same period women in their 20s will again out-number women in their 30s.

Next we turn to two trends that have emerged in the 1990s and are at least tangentially related to later childbearing: the rise in multiple birth pregnancies (twins, triplets, quadruplets, etc...) and the rise in cesarean deliveries.

Source: U.S. Department of Health and Human Services, Centers for Disease Control and Prevention, National Center for Health Statistics, Division of Vital Statistics, "Live Births by Age of Mother and Race: United States, 1933-98. For the years 1999 and 2000, and published by the same department "Births: Final Data for 2000" issued on February 12, 2002. Population by age group data is from two U.S. Census Bureau publications, *Historical Statistics of the United States, Colonial Times to 1970*, page 15, and *Statistical Abstract of the United State: 2001*, pages 14 and 15. Data on median age at first marriage are from the U.S. Census Bureau, *Current Population Report*, "American Families and Living Arrangements: March 2000" and "Census 2000 Supplemental Survey Profile," table 1.

---

[4] In 1950 the median age at which women entered a first marriage was 20.3 years. By the year 2000 that age had risen to 25.1 years. Men are also entering marriage later at the turn of the century (age 26.8 years) than they did in the middle (22.8 years).

Infertility and Its Unexpected Multiplier Effect

Rate of High Order Multiple Births (triplets and higher) by Age of Mother, 2000

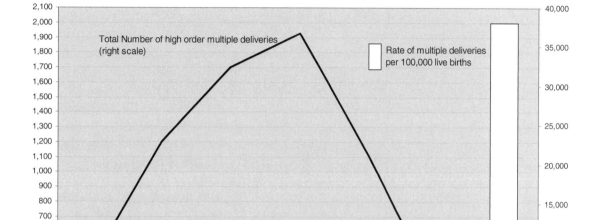

Women in their early 30s bear most of the triplets, quadruplets, and higher order multiples born in the United States. Women in their late 40s and early 50s, however, have by far the highest rate of multiple births per delivery.

In the previous panel we saw that more women are choosing to have children later in life. One of the side effects of this trend is that more couples are having difficulty conceiving and are turning to fertility treatments in greater numbers. The rising numbers of high order multiple deliveries (triplets and higher order multiples) tells us that the treatments for infertility that became available throughout the 1970s are definitely being used.

According to the National Center for Health Statistics, an estimated 80% of triplet and higher order multiples are the result of the use of assisted reproductive technologies[5] (ART) and ovulation-inducing drugs. There is a naturally higher likelihood of multiple births with increasing maternal age. However, that (natural) increase is slight and the increase we are seeing in the United States over the last decades is dramatic.

The graph shows the distribution of all higher order multiple deliveries in the year 2000 by age of mother. The rate is the number of multiple deliveries per 100,000 live births. The total number of multiple births (including twins) is shown in the form of a solid line

---

[5] This term refers to the types of treatments that assist in conception, like in vitro fertilization, and go beyond the use of drugs.

that peaks in the 30 to 34 year age group. The rates for women over 30 years of age are all higher than the average and for the oldest moms it reaches a remarkable 1,998 high order multiples per 100,000 live births.

The rates for 2000 reflect a striking rise in multiple deliveries since the 1970s[6]. There was very little change in the rate of triplet and higher order multiple births during the period 1930 through 1970. The rate remained stable at approximately 30 per 100,000 live births. The dramatic rise in this rate to 180 in 2000 illustrates the impact of ART and other in-fertility treatments.

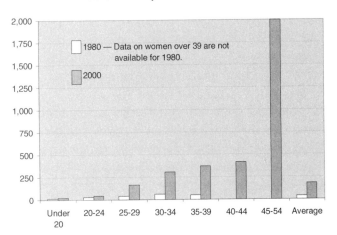

Rate of Multiples 1980 and 2000

The chart to the left shows the rates of high order multiples for the years 1980 and 2000 by maternal age group.

The postponing of childbearing clearly has an impact on the ease with which older parents enter the parenting game. Headlines about 40 something actresses giving birth creates the false impression for many women that postponing child-bearing until their late 30s or even 40s is a reasonable option.

What the headlines do not mention is the fact that women in their 40s having babies are usually doing so with donor eggs, according to Dr. David Adamson, a leading fertility specialist at Stanford University. This explains to a large degree why the rate of multiples for women over 45 shoots up dramatically from already high rates for all women over 35.

Turning back the biological clock has limits, many of which were only fully recognized in the 1990s according to Dr. Sarah Berga, a reproductive endocrinologist at the University of Pittsburgh. We may assume that unless and until new fertility treatments are found, we will not see a continued trend towards ever-greater postponement of child-bearing. And for those who have postponed a bit too long, beware what you wish for — quadruples are a handful.

Source: Center for Disease Control, *National Vital Statistics Report*, "Births: Final Data for 2000," page 87 and *Morbidity and Mortality Weekly Report*, "Contribution of Assisted Reproductive Technology and Ovulation-Inducing Drugs to Triplet and Higher-Order Multiple Births: United States, 1980-1997." Statements by Doctors Adamson and Berga are from an article by Nancy Gibbs, "Making Time for a Baby", *Time*, April 15, 2002, pages 48-54.

---

[6] Worth noting here is the birth date of Louise Joy Brown, the world's very first "test-tube baby," born on July 25, 1978 in Great Britain. A test-tube baby is a baby who results from an in vitro fertilization procedure. "In vitro," literally, means "in glass."

The Labors of Love

Rate of Cesarean Section Deliveries, 1989--2001

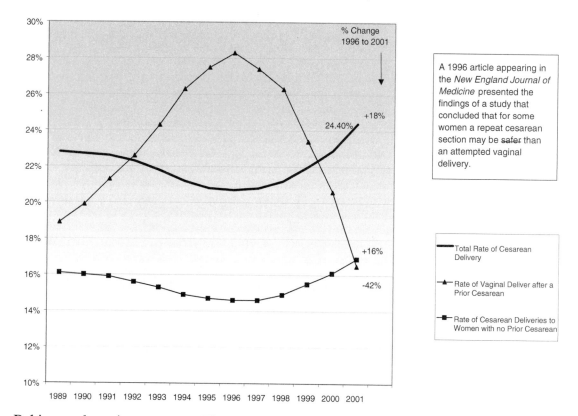

A 1996 article appearing in the *New England Journal of Medicine* presented the findings of a study that concluded that for some women a repeat cesarean section may be safer than an attempted vaginal delivery.

Total Rate of Cesarean Delivery

Rate of Vaginal Deliver after a Prior Cesarean

Rate of Cesarean Deliveries to Women with no Prior Cesarean

Babies are born in two ways. They are either brought into the world through the labor of mother and child in a "normal" vaginal delivery or they are removed from the mother's uterus in a surgical procedure called a cesarean delivery or cesarean section (C-section). The cesarean section has existed in some form since ancient times. Until the early 20th century it was used almost exclusively when the mother was already dead or dying and it was necessary to cut the baby out in order to try and salvage at least one life.

Even today, a cesarean section is a major abdominal surgery but, happily, it is one that saves the lives of many women and children during high risk and complicated deliveries. Nonetheless, according to the World Health Organization no country or region is justified in having cesarean delivery rates greater than 10% to 15%. Why then are the rates in the United States so much higher (24.4% in 2001) and why have they risen sharply in the last years of the 20th century?

The graph presents rates of cesarean deliveries, both total and primary (those to women with no previous C-section) and the rate of vaginal delivery for women with one or more previous cesarean deliveries. The percentage change from 1996 to 2001 for each of these rates is also provided. The percentage change is measured from the year 1996 because that is the year in which the lowest rates were registered for the period presented. The patterns are clear.

The rate of cesarean delivery in 1970 was approximately 5%[7]. By 1988 the rate had shot up to 24.7%. For several years thereafter it fell slightly. Then, in 1997 it began again to rise and in 2001 had almost climbed back to the 1988 peak reaching 24.4%.

There is great uncertainty as to why we deliver so many babies by C-section. Some claim that new mothers are unwilling to endure the pain and inconvenience of having a baby the "old-fashioned' way. Are some mothers today "too posh to push" as is suggested in an article by that title in *U.S. News and World Report*? Although some few cesarean deliveries probably result from this attitude, this alone can hardly explain a rise in cesarean deliveries of 400% in 30 years, or even 18% in the last 5 years presented on the graph.

C-sections have become much safer during the last 40 years but they are still serious abdominal surgery and are not undertaken lightly. The primary medical reasons given for performing a cesarean section are:

1. Dystocia or non-progressive labor. This is experienced more often when painkillers are used during labor (including epidurals), an increasingly common and popular practice. As one expectant mother put it, "Would you use breathing techniques for a root canal?"[8]

2. Breech presentation — the baby is not positioned headfirst.

3. Fetal distress.

4. Mother underwent a previous cesarean delivery.

There are many reasons for the changing rates of cesarean deliveries. It is a combination of two in particular that goes furthest in explaining the sharp increases: fear of litigation and technology.

A technology used to monitor a fetus during delivery — electronic fetal monitoring (EFM) — was introduced in the 1960s and began to be used widely in the 1970s. This technology allows obstetricians and gynecologists to monitor very closely both the mother and baby during labor and delivery.

Interestingly, when EFM is used regularly it results in much higher rates of cesarean section than are found in practices that do not regularly use EFM. The explanation for this has to do with the fact that EFM monitoring picks up on small abnormalities in fetal condition but can not accurately link these with any sort of negative outcome. This may cause a cautious physician to decide on a C-section more quickly than he or she would otherwise.

---

[7] Data were not collected on a national basis for this measure until the late 1980s. The estimate for 1970 is made by the National Institute of Health. See source note for a full citation.

[8] Quoted in an article by Jeffrey Zurlinden. See source notes for full citation.

Here is where the fear of litigation comes into the equation. The number of malpractice lawsuits filed in the United States has risen over the last decades, and during the 1990s malpractice jury awards have sky rocked. Obstetrics is a specialty that has been particularly hard hit by malpractice suits and sharply rising insurance premiums.

Physicians, concerned about the risk of lawsuits tend to practice "defensive medicine.[9]" A practitioner viewing a mildly abnormal pattern on a monitor or seeing a mother's labor slow might choose to "give it a little time." However, a physician operating under considerable fear of a malpractice lawsuit will be less willing to give it a little time and will likely practice "defensive medicine," in this case, proceed quickly to a cesarean delivery.

As Doctors A. Shinha and S. Arulkumaran state in their 1999 presentation before the First World Congress On: Controversies in Obstetrics, Gynecology & Infertility:

> "The litigious climate that has enveloped medicine in general and Obstetrics in particular has probably resulted in the universal use of EFM which perhaps increases the diagnosis of 'fetal distress' and hence cesarean section as the mode of delivery."

Will the trend towards more cesarean deliveries continue to increase? In 1990 the U.S. Department of Health and Human Services published a report entitled *Healthy People 2000* in which targets were set for a number of health care indicators. The target set for C-sections was a national rate of between 10% and 15% by the year 2000. Clearly, we did not meet that goal. The national rate of cesarean sections in 2000 was 22.9%.

The *Healthy People 2010* report has revised upwards the target rates for cesarean sections. This reflects changed thinking within the medical community on the desirability of continuing to press for reductions in cesarean delivery for women who have undergone the procedure before.

As the debate continues, studies will be made, recommendations will change as our understanding of "best practices" change, and doctors and midwives will continue to assist mothers as they give birth to new generations.

Source: U.S. Department of Health and Human Services, Centers for Disease Control, *National Vital Statistics Report*, "Births: Final Data for 2000," page 72 and "Births: Preliminary Data for 2001," page 3. The cesarean delivery rate estimate for 1970 is from the National Institute of Health, *Cesarean Section — A Brief History*, available online at http://www.nlm.nih.gov/exhibition/cesarean /cesarean_1.html. The New England Journal of Medicine article mentioned in the graphic was summarized in and article by Rhonda Rowland, "C-section or Labor," *CNN Interactive*, September 5, 1996, available online at http://cgi.cnn.com/HEALTH/9609/ 05/caesarean/. Susan Brink, "To Posh To Push," *U.S. News & World Report*, August 5, 2002, page 42-44. Jeffrey Zurlinden, RN, MS, ACRN, High-Tech Birthing is Back, Nursing Spectrum, August 26, 2002, available online at http://www.nursingspectrum.com/. A. Sinha and S. Arulkumaran, *Does Electronic Fetal Monitoring Increase CS Rates*, a paper presented at the First World Congress On: Controversies in Obstetrics, Gynecology & Infertility, Prague, Czech Republic, 1999. Centers for Disease Control, Healthy People 2000 and 2010, available online at http://www.cdc.gov/nchs/hphome.htm.

---

[9] Defensive medicine is what one calls the medicine practiced when doctors order tests, procedures, or visits, or avoid high-risk patients or procedures primarily (but not necessarily solely) to reduce their exposure to malpractice liability.

Contraceptive Use

Female Contraceptive Use by Type, 1982 and 1995

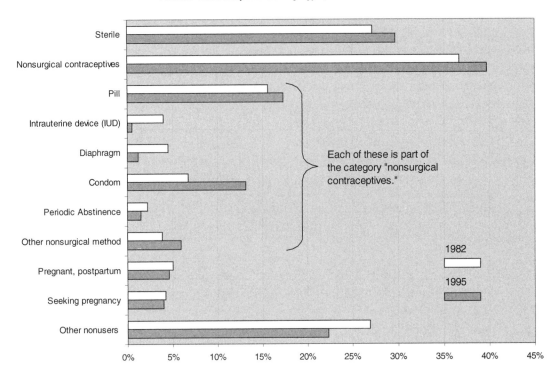

The desire to control female reproduction is nothing new. History shows us that women have taken substances in an attempt to prevent pregnancy for centuries. Happily, women no longer have to risk their health with such things as drinking mercury or gunpowder as they have in the distant past. Some would argue that new contraceptive medications may also cause their users harm, but for the most part none would argue that the modern contraceptives are as harmful as drinking mercury.

In the middle of the 20th century advances were made in the synthetic manufacture of the hormone progesterone, a female hormone that controls ovulation and thus the ability to become pregnant. In 1960 the United States Food and Drug Administration approved the first oral contraceptive for sale. It is estimated that within ten years "the pill" became the most popular nonsurgical form of contraceptive used by American women.

The graph presents information about the types of birth control methods used by woman between 15 and 44 years of age in 1982 and in 1995. These are two of the years for which data were collected in a special survey by the National Center for Health Statistics. The graph also shows the percentage of women who are not using birth control methods because they are pregnant, have just had a child, are attempting to conceive a child, or fall into the category "other nonusers." The other nonusers are women who have never had intercourse or are currently abstaining from sexual relations.

The percentages presented add to more than 100% for both years. This is because respondents may have answered with more than one type of contraceptive method used.

For example, a woman may use an intrauterine device (IUD) and also use condoms to protect against sexually transmitted disease. Or, she may use a diaphragm as well as one of the "other nonsurgical methods" like spermicidal foam.

The most popular single form of birth control, in both 1982 and 1995, was surgical sterilization. As a group, the nonsurgical methods are most popular but include a large variety of single methods. The pill is the most popular of these. Between 1982 and 1995 there was a 95% increase in the number of women using condoms as one means of birth control. This is most likely the result of the dual protection offered by the use of a condom, protection against pregnancy and against sexually transmitted disease.

The percentage of women who were not currently using a contraceptive because they were not sexually active dropped by 17% between 1982 and 1995, from 26.9% to 22.3%. The IUD and diaphragm have also declined in usage over the period shown.

Family planning has become a much easier activity in the late 20th century with the rise in availability of contraceptive methods. But, when these fail and/or are not used properly another action is available, abortion. That is what we will turn to in our next panel.

Source: U.S. Census Bureau, *Statistical Abstract of the United States 1990*, "Contraceptive Use by Women, 15—44 Years Old, by Age, Race, Marital Status, and Method of Contraception: 1982," p. 70, and *Statistical Abstract of the United States 2001*, "Contraceptive Use by Women, 15-44 Years of Age: 1995," p. 69.

The Story of Abortion in the Late 20th Century

Number of Births and Abortions, 1972 -- 1997

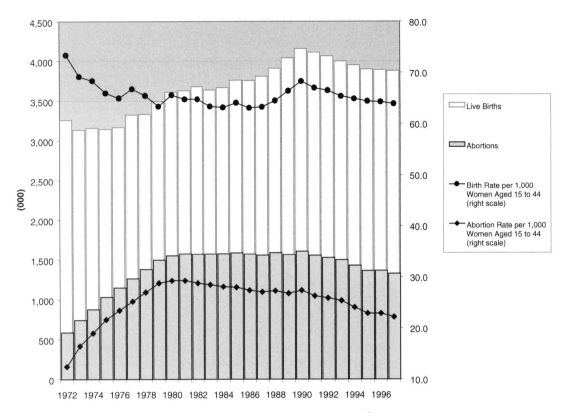

Until the U.S. Supreme Court ruled on the *Roe v. Wade*[10] case in 1973 laws regulating abortion varied widely from state to state. In some, abortion was illegal under any circumstances. In others, 14 states in all by 1972, a legal abortion could be performed if the woman and her doctor felt that it was necessary. There are, however, no reliable figures on the number of abortions performed, either legally or illegally, prior to 1975. Figures presented for 1972 through 1974 are Center for Disease Control and Prevention (CDC) estimates of the number of *legal* abortions performed annually.

The graph presents the number of babies born and the number of abortions performed each year in the United States between 1972 and 1997. The rates of birth and abortion are also charted and appear as lines. These rates are the rate of births or abortions per 1,000 women in the childbearing age cohort, 15 to 44 years. In order to assess trends it is important to use rates instead of counts so that variations in the population are eliminated.

---

[10] In the case of *Roe v. Wade* the Supreme Court ruled that most state laws on abortion were unconstitutional. This decision eliminated legislative interference in abortion matters during the first trimester of pregnancy. It also placed limits on the restrictions that states could pass on abortion in later stages of pregnancy.

The abortion rate rose sharply from the early 1970s through 1980 and 1981 when it reached a peak of 29.3 abortions for every 1,000 women of childbearing age. The legalization of abortion in 1973 was clearly a watershed event that came on the heels of the sexual revolution and ushering in an era of change. The rise in abortion was steady through 1980 and 1981. From that point on the abortion rate has fallen annually with one small up tick in 1990, a year that saw a similar up tick in the birth rate.

Clearly, despite the availability of reliable birth control methods, a great number of couples fail to prevent unwanted pregnancies. In 1997, most women who underwent an abortion:

Were under the age of 25:	52%
Were unmarried:	81%
Had never borne a child:	42%
Had never undergone a previous abortion:	51%
Underwent the procedure at less than 11 weeks gestation:	77%

Future trends in the abortion rate are difficult to predict. The most likely predictor is related to the age demographics of women since most abortions are performed on young women. The chart to the right presents a breakdown of women by age group. Each age group is shown as a percentage of the overall female population of childbearing age, 15 to 44 years. When the abortion rate was highest (1980), the youngest women made up the greatest percentage of fertile women. As the youngest age group declined as a percentage of all fertile women, the abortion rate fell. In the near future young women will again become the largest

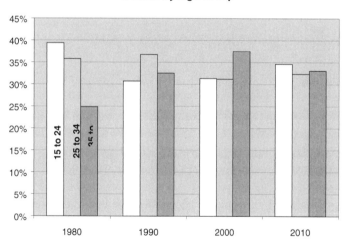

Women by Age Group

group of women in the childbearing age cohort. This suggests that the abortion rate may rise in the early 21st century, assuming there are no changes in the social, cultural, and/or legal attitudes towards abortion during the intervening time period. This is, of course, an assumption that assumes much.

Source: The data used in the graphs are from the U.S. Bureau of the Census, *Statistical Abstract of the United States, 1980*, pp. 69-70. *Statistical Abstract of the United States, 2001*, p. 71. The data are originally from the Centers for Disease Control and Prevention (CDC). The abortion data for 1972 through 1974 are CDC estimates.

The Littlest of Our Babies

Low Birth Weight (LBW) Babies, 1980 -- 2000

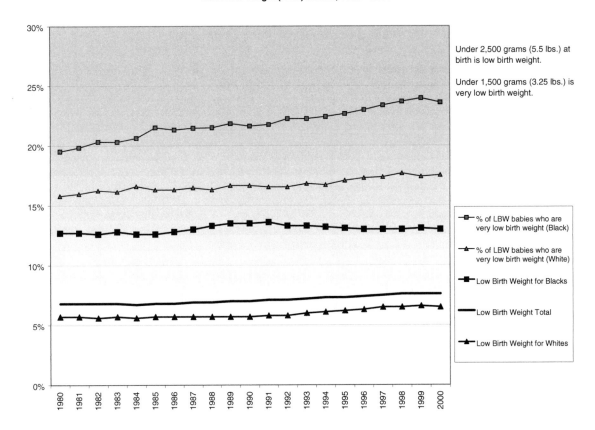

One of the earliest indicators of a baby's health is her weight at birth. Low weight at birth (less than 2,500 grams, 5 lbs. 8 oz.) is not only the cause of 70% of infant deaths and a third of all handicapped conditions, it also affects the life of the child as an adult — for the worse. Low-birth weight is usually abbreviated as LBW.

This subject has been covered in this volume already — see *Children's Health: Low-Birthweight*, in Chapter 1. Here we present somewhat more data for a shorter time span, but for every year, and also point out black and white differences in the very low birth-weight category. The data will refresh the user's memory before we conclude this chapter with a look at babies — what reproduction is all about.

A note about very low-birth weight babies. The two lines at the top of the graph show the percentage of LBW babies in that category, those under 3 lbs. 4 oz. at birth. As for LBW babies, so here again for the very tiny children, the figure for blacks (23.6%) is much higher than from whites (17.5%). Black women also have the highest rate of premature births of all racial groups (17.3%). The corresponding rate for non-Hispanic whites in 2000 was 10.4% and for Hispanics it was 11.4%.

Trends in low-weight births have risen slightly over the last 20 years in part the result of dramatic increases in multiple birth, a subject we have just covered. Among whites, 6.5% of all live births in 2000 were low-weight. Among blacks this figure was 13.0%..4% and for Hispanics it was 11.4%.

Although the trend over the period shown has been towards more LBW babies, there was a slight decline from 1999 to 2000, overall and for each racial group. It will be good news if this single year trend continues.

Sources: U.S. Department of Health and Human Services, Centers for Disease Control and Prevention "Births: Final Data for 2000," *National Vital Statistics Report,* Vol. 50, No. 5, February 12, 2002.

Birth Defects, Do We Know What the Trends Are?

Infant Mortality Resulting from Birth Defects

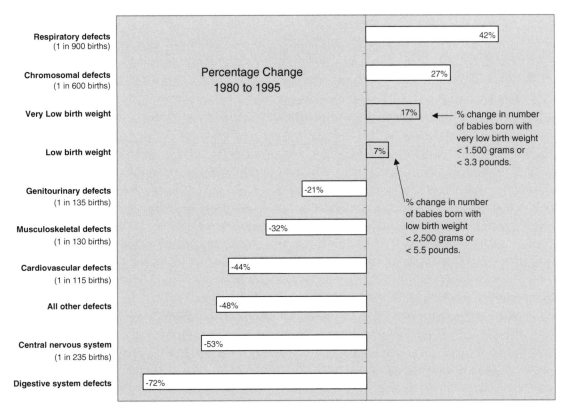

The tracking of statistics on birth defects is one area in which the United States has not excelled. There is no national clearinghouse in which data on birth defects collected at the state level is brought together. Furthermore, many states do not, or did not until the late 1990s, collect data on birth defects. In 1996, Congress directed the Center for Disease Control to establish Centers of Excellence for Birth Defects Prevention and Research. As these centers are established and efforts are made to collect data on birth defects, we will know more about whether or not birth defects are on the rise or declining.

For now, we must use what data are available to try and assess trends. The chart presents data from a Center for Disease Control report on infant mortality resulting from birth defects. The percentage changes in infant deaths attributable to birth defects between 1980 and 1995 are charted. Birth defects are the leading cause of child mortality accounting for 20% of all infant deaths. Data are presented by category of birth defects[11]. By way of ref-

---

[11] The birth defect categories have names that are reasonably self-explanatory. Clarification on two may be useful. Genitourinary defects are those related to the absence of one or both kidneys (if both are missing, death occurs shortly after birth); or those related to urinary obstruction, malformations that obstructs the passage of urine. Chromosomal defects are those related to chromosomal abnormalities that may result in conditions like Down syndrome. About 40% of babies with this condition also suffer from congenital heart defects as well as visual and hearing impairments.

erence, the incidence rate per live birth is listed under each of the largest categories. Cardiovascular defects are the most common (occurring in one infant out of every 115 newborns) and the most deadly (accounting for 31.4% of all birth defect related infant deaths in 1992, according to the American Heart Association).

One of the known risk factors associated with many birth defects is low birth weight. Therefore, included in the chart are percentage changes in the number of babies born with low birth weights and with very low birth weights. These babies have a higher risk of birth defects than babies born weighing at least 5.5 pounds. The observable trend towards greater numbers of low birth weight babies portends poorly on birth defect trends.

Six of the eight defect categories charted showed declining mortality rates over the fifteen-year period presented, from -21% for genitourinary defects to -72% for digestive system defects. This is good news, whether or not the reason for the declining mortality rates is (1) fewer children being born with life threatening abnormalities or, (2) better and more successful treatments.

Two categories that saw increased mortality were respiratory defects and chromosomal defects. Two trends that we saw earlier in this chapter may account at least in part for these increases; a higher number of premature births and a larger number of babies being born to older women. The greater the maternal age at the birth of the child, the greater the risk for chromosomal birth defects.

What we will have to await are the data that will make clear whether these changes in the numbers of infant deaths associated with birth defects are the result of fewer babies being born with abnormalities or better treatment available to care for babies who are born with birth defects. We can hope that both are true.

One thing we know to be true is that infants survive at a far greater rate now than ever before in history. The next and final panel of this chapter will address infant mortality rates and their dramatic decline in the second half of the 20th century.

Source: U.S. Center for Disease Control, Morbidity and Mortality Weekly Report, "Trends in Infant Mortality Attributable to Birth Defects — United States, 1980—1995," September 25, 1998 / 47(37); pp. 773-778, available online at http://www/cdc/gov/epo /mmwr/preview/mmwrhtml /00054921.htm. Data on the incidence rates of different birth defects are from the March of Dimes, "Leading Categories of Birth Defects," a report available online at http://www.modimes.org/344_1471.htm.

Progress Keeping our Littlest Alive

Infant Mortality, 1950 - 2000

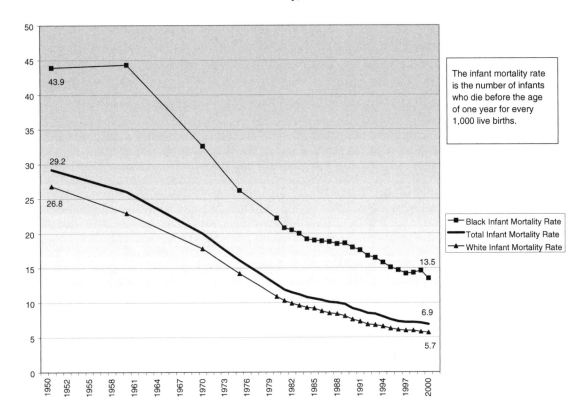

> The infant mortality rate is the number of infants who die before the age of one year for every 1,000 live births.

Legend:
- ■ Black Infant Mortality Rate
- — Total Infant Mortality Rate
- ▲ White Infant Mortality Rate

The infant mortality rate is a count of babies who die before reaching their first birthdays for every 1,000 live births. The death of an infant is a particularly painful loss so it is reassuring to see that the trend in infant mortality is sharply down. In the year 2000 fewer than 7 babies for every 1,000 born failed to reach their a first birthday.

Although this is a vast improvement over the past, it still represents a large number. A total of 27,960 babies died during their first year of life in 2000. One way to grasp the true meaning of the improvement made in infant mortality rates over the fifty years, 1950 to 2000, is to realize that had the infant mortality rate of 1950 existed in the year 2000, we would have lost 118,519 babies. The infant mortality rate in 1950 was 29.2 per 1,000 more than 4 times the rate at the turn of the 21st century, 6.8 per 1,000 live births. Great progress has been made.

Infant mortality is divided into neonatal deaths, those occurring less than 28 days after birth, and postneonatal, infants who survive the first 28 days but die before they reach their first year. More than two-thirds of infant deaths (18,733 in 2000) are neonatal. Most neonatal deaths are associated with (1) low birth weight, (2) congenital malformation, deformations, and chromosomal abnormalities, (3) conditions caused by complications in the mother's pregnancy, (4) respiratory distress, and (5) by complications of placenta, cord, and membranes. Such causes consistently account for more than 50% of all neonatal death.

One third of infant deaths (9,227 in 2000) occurred after the first 28 days of life. The leading cause of death for these infants was sudden infant death syndrome (SIDS) followed by congenital malformations, deformations, and chromosomal abnormalities. The third cause was accidents.

Race breakdowns for infant mortality are based on the mother's race. The highest rates experienced are by African Americans (13.5 per 1,000 live births in 2000), the lowest by Asians and Pacific Islanders (4.9). Whites had a rate of 5.7 in 2000. People of Hispanic origin, regardless of race, had a rate of 5.6 while American Indians and Alaskan Natives lost 8.3 babies for every 1,000 born in 2000.

The infant mortality rate experienced by blacks is still quite high, more than twice that experienced by whites. Although many attribute this difference to the lower average household income of blacks, one must ask why this reasoning does not hold for Hispanics. As the following table shows, there was no direct correlation between median household income and infant mortality rates in 2000.

Race or Ethnic Group	Median Household Income	Infant Mortality Rate
White	$44,232	5.7
Black	$30,436	13.5
Hispanic	$33,455	5.6

The causes of infant mortality are complex. According to the Centers for Disease Control and Prevention, the infant mortality rate is one of the most widely used general indices of health in both the United States and around the world. We have come a long way. But we have further to go in our efforts to keep African American babies alive and healthy.

Sources: Infant mortality data are from three reports by the U.S. Department of Health and Human Services, Centers for Disease Control, *National Vital Statistics Report*, Vol. 49, No. 8, and 11, September 21, 2001 and October 12, 2001. *National Vital Statistics Report*, Vol. 50, No. 12, August 28, 2002. U.S. Centers for Disease Control and Prevention "Current Tends in Infant Mortality – United States, 1988," *Morbidity and Mortality Weekly Report*, September 21, 1991. Income data are from the U.S. Census Bureau, *Income 2000*, Table 1. "Median Income of Households by Selected Characteristics, Race, and Hispanic Origin of Householder: 2000, 1999, and 1998," available online at http://census.gov/hhes/income/income00/inctab1.html.

Chapter 12

The Environment

Air, earth, fire, and water. The four elements of the universe according to Empedocles, a philosopher who lived in the 400s B.C.[1] Science has proven, contrary to Empedocles' theories, that matter is not made up of varying ratios of these elements. However, all living matter needs all or most of these elements to survive.

In this chapter we will discuss the quality of our air and water and how it relates to our health. The first two panels look at air pollution. First we discuss the U.S. Environmental Protection Agency's six principal pollutants. Next, we'll try to shed some light on the claims that air pollution causes asthma. Despite claims that asthma cases are rising because our air is increasingly more polluted, we'll actually see that air pollution levels are falling overall.

The next three panels look at water pollution. First we'll look at national water quality. Have things gotten better since the Clean Water Act was enacted in 1972? Can we really say that 2002 is the Year of Clean Water, as Congress declared?

Despite having some of the cleanest water in the world, our waterways do contain pollutants. Next, we'll define the top 5 water pollutants and discuss their effects on our health. Our discussion of water pollution concludes with a discussion of the quality of our drinking water. In 2000, more than 1 billion people worldwide lacked clean drinking water. In the United States, the drinking water is some of the safest in the world. However, in 2001, nearly 24 million people in the U.S. had their health threatened by contaminated drinking water. Two of the key chemicals that must be regulated in order to maintain safe drinking water are arsenic and fluoride, according to the World Health Organization. In the United States safe levels of these two chemicals have been in dispute recently. We'll touch on these issues briefly.

Bacteria are everywhere in our environment. Some are harmful; others are not. Before the advent of penicillin, the first antibiotic, bacterial diseases such as pneumonia and tuberculosis killed large numbers of people. Since the discovery of antibiotics, however, these diseases have virtually disappeared. Or have they? The final panel in this chapter discusses the threat of drug resistant bacteria to our wellbeing.

---

[1] Source: "Empedocles (fl. 450 BCE.)" *The Internet Encyclopedia of Philosophy.* Retrieved July 16, 2002 from http://www.utm.edu/research/iep/e/empedocl.htm.

Air Pollution

National Air Pollutant Emissions, 1940-1998

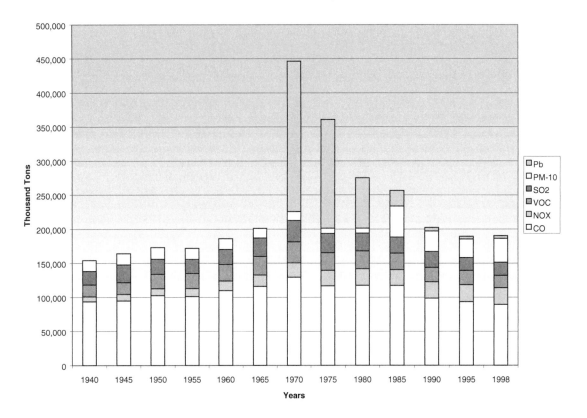

Pollution can be hazardous to your health — and it can kill. According to the World Health Organization, an estimated 3 million people die each year of air pollution. Bad air accounts for 5% of the annual deaths worldwide. The graphic shows the worst of the actors — the U.S. Environmental Protection Agency's six principal air pollutants. Please note that lead (Pb) first appears in this measurement in 1970.

Pollution emissions are down since 1970, the year when the first Clean Air Act Amendments took effect. The exception is oxides of nitrogen, usually abbreviated as NOXs. Particulate matter (dust, soot, usually reported as PM-10) went down from 1985 to 1995, but then rose again a little in 1998. The steep drop of lead in the air — it went from 220,900 tons in 1970 to 4,000 tons in 1998 — happened at the filling station. Leaded gasoline was phased out. Overall, levels of these air pollutants have been below the EPA's standards for safety since the 1970s. But some urban, industrialized cities still don't meet safety standards. In 1997, the EPA lowered the standards for ground-level ozone (source of the famous LA smog), to which volatile organic chemicals (VOCs) and NOXs are contributors. U.S. air quality continues to exceed these new standards.

What are these pollutants? What are their effects?

Lead (Pb) occurs naturally as a metal and has been used in many products. Its greatest use in modern times has been as an anti-knock component of gasoline. In 1970, 78% of lead emissions came from motor vehicles. Unleaded gasoline came to be introduced in 1975 for use with cars equipped with catalytic converters. In December 1995, EPA banned leaded gasoline altogether. From 1980 to 1999, lead emissions dropped by 94%. Currently, 52% of lead emissions come from metals-processing facilities. Urban areas with high traffic levels, trash incinerators, or industrial facilities that burn fuel still have a problem with high lead levels in the air. In 1999, 10 cities still failed to meet EPA's levels for lead.

Children and infants are most sensitive to lead in the air. They continue to have the highest lead levels in their blood among the general population. Children are also exposed to lead by ingesting paint chips, soil, food, and water contaminated with lead. Leaded paint was banned in 1978, but older homes may still have it. Lead accumulates in the blood. Continued exposure, even at low levels, can ultimately lead to organ damage, osteoporosis, and reproductive disorders. High levels of lead can lead to seizures, mental retardation, and behavior problems. Lead exposure is also implicated in high blood pressure and in heart disease, especially in men. Animals suffer as do people — and even low levels of lead can inhibit the growth of vegetation and cause reproductive and neurological damage in marine life.

Particulate matter (PM-10) is a mixture of solid particles and liquid droplets in the air. Particles 2.5 micrometers or larger are found in windblown dust and come from grinding operations. Tinier particles (2.5 micrometers or smaller) come from fuel combustion, power plants, trucks and buses burning diesel. These tiny objects are the most dangerous because they easily reach the deep recesses of the lungs. PM-10 has thus been linked to premature death, asthma, and other breathing ailments. The elderly, children, those with heart or lung disease, and asthmatics are most affected by this pollutant.

PM-10 also causes haze. In the west, natural visibility is 140 miles, but particulate pollution has reduced the range to somewhere between 33 to 90 miles. It's worse in the east. Natural visibility is 90 miles, but the current range is merely 14 to 24 miles. Thirty-three percent of the haze in the Grand Canyon is caused by PM-10 emissions from Southern California. PM-10 can also damages to buildings and erodes our monuments.

Sulfur dioxide (SO$_2$) gas is formed when coal and oil are burned. It's also found during metal smelting and other industrial processes. Exposure to this gas has been linked to breathing difficulties, lower immunity to respiratory infections, and aggravation of cardiovascular disease (if exposed in combination with PM-10). The elderly, children, those with preexisting cardiovascular and lung disease, and asthmatics are most affected by this pollutant.

SO$_2$ and acid rain are linked. The sulfur compound dissolves in the rain. The sour liquid acidifies soil, lakes, and streams. In turn this conditions kills crops and wildlife. Sulfur oxides also attack buildings and monuments. On June 24, 2002, China announced a program to reduce SO$_2$ emissions 10% by 2005 by targeting its biggest industrial polluters. The U.S. reduced SO$_2$ emissions by 18% from 1986 to 1995 (13% in 1994-1995 alone).

Volatile organic chemicals (VOCs). These chemicals are used in household products such as paints, varnishes, and cleaners. They are organic solvents. When used they spread in the air. Indoor air pollution is largely a consequence of VOCs. The EPA's studies found levels of some organic chemicals to be 2 to 5 times higher inside homes than out of doors. These chemicals can cause eye, nose, and throat irritation; headaches; nausea; and damage to liver, kidney, and the central nervous system. Some, like benzene, cause cancer in humans. Methylene chloride and perchloroethylene (used in paint strippers and dry cleaning, respectively) have been found to cause cancer in animals.

VOCs are known to contribute to the development of smog. When inhaled (even in small amounts), smog can cause respiratory problems, inflammation of lung tissue, and it reduces a person's immunity to bronchitis and pneumonia. Children and asthmatics are susceptible to the effects of smog — but so are healthy adults who moderately exercise in the summer. They can experience 15 to 20% reduction in lung function over several hours of exposure to low levels of smog.

Nitrogen oxides (NOXs) are a family of gases produced during high temperature fuel combustion (cars, utilities). They contribute to ground-level ozone (smog), acid rain, and eutrophication[2]. Nitrous oxide, one type of NOX, is a greenhouse gas. Greenhouse gases cause climate changes — global warming. NOXs irritate the lungs and lower immunity to respiratory infections. Those with respiratory problems and heart disease are most affected. But exposure to these gases may also cause these types of health problems.

Carbon monoxide (CO) is a colorless, odorless poisonous gas emitted from the incomplete combustion of hydrocarbon-based fuels (like gasoline, diesel, coal, and gas). In the U.S., 66% of the carbon monoxide emissions come from motor vehicles. In urban areas, motor vehicles contribute about 90% of the carbon monoxide. In 1992, carbon monoxide levels in 20 U.S. cities exceeded the Federal air quality standard and affected 14 million people. CO is still with us despite the fact that auto companies added catalytic converters to their passenger vehicles in the 1970s — which reduce carbon monoxide emissions by 80% per vehicle.

Carbon monoxide inhibits a person's blood from carrying oxygen to organs and tissues. The monoxide grabs hold of oxygen to form carbon dioxide, the gas we breathe out. Those with heart disease are highly susceptible to the effects of carbon monoxide and may experience chest pains if they breathe in the gas while exercising. Infants, the elderly, and people with respiratory problems also have sensitivity to CO.

Sources: Chart data for 1940-1960: U.S. Census Bureau. *Statistical Abstract of the United States, 1994*. Chart data for 1970-1998: U.S. Census Bureau. *Statistical Abstract of the United States, 2001*. "Sulfur Dioxide." Retrieved June 25, 2002 from http://www.clean airtrust.org/sulfurdioxide.html. U.S. Environmental Protection Agency data retrieved June 24-26, 2002 and July 8-10, 2002 from http://www.epa.gov. Patricia Primi and Michael H. Surgan. *Look Out For Lead!*, July 1999. Retrieved July 3, 2002 from http://www.oag.state.ny.us/envi-ronment/lead96.html. World Health Organization. "Air Pollution Fact Sheet," September 2000. Retrieved July 10, 2002 from http://www.who.int/inf-fs/en/fact187.html.

---

[2] The nutrients in a body of water increase, which leads to a reduction in the amount of oxygen in the water. As a result, fish, animal, and plant life are adversely affected.

Air Pollution and Asthma

Age-adjusted Asthma Prevalence and Total Air Pollutant Emissions, 1980-1999

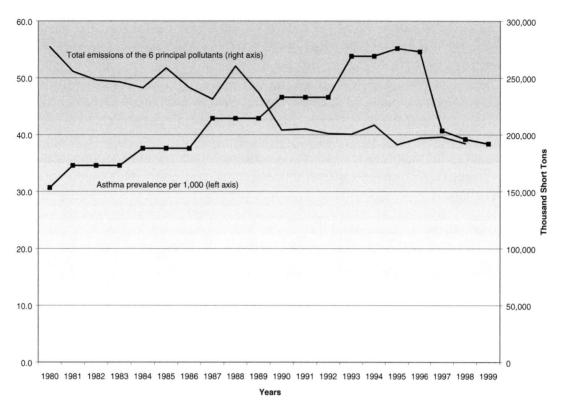

Asthma is a chronic lung disease characterized by the narrowing or blockage of the air passages aggravated by "triggers" in the air. The effects are shortness of breath, wheezing, chest tightness, and coughing. Long term effects include weakening of the heart muscle. In some cases, emergency room treatment is needed to restore normal breathing. In 2002, 17 million people in the U.S. had asthma; 5 million were children under age 18. In 1980, a total of 6.7 million had the disease. In 1999, over 4,600 people died of asthma, down from a high of 5,667 in 1996, but nearly twice the number that died in 1980.

What are the triggers of asthma? Cold air, allergens, and some types of viral infections. Those with asthma are also sensitive to air pollutants. In high concentrations, these pollutants can cause an asthma attack. The graphic shows the self-reported prevalence rate of asthma per 1,000 people[3]. From 1980 to 1996, the number of asthma cases rose dramatically. In 1997, the prevalence rate data was changed to exclude anyone that hasn't had an attack in the past 12 months. Therefore, the numbers drop significantly from 1996 to 1997, suggesting that many asthmatics have their condition under control.

---

[3] 1980-1994 asthma prevalence rate is based on 1970 population. The rate from 1995-1999 is based on 2000 population. Data from 1981-1994 were reported in 3-year intervals. The percentage of people with asthma went from 3% in 1980 to 5.5% in 1996.

Part of the drop from 1997 to 1999 may have to do with the drop in the amount of air pollutant emissions and, therefore, the reduction in at least one of the triggers for asthma. Another reason could be that more people are seeking treatment to control the disease. The rate of physician office visits for asthma was up 52.5% from 1980 to 1999. The rate of emergency room visits was up also, but not as much: 29%. Some of the downturn in active asthma cases, recently, may also be due to government programs that encourage management of the disease. In 1997, the National Asthma Education and Prevention Program outlined new guidelines for the treatment of asthma in an attempt to reduce the number of deaths and disabilities. In 1999, the Centers for Disease Control and Prevention (CDC) developed the National Asthma Control Program. Its goals are to "reduce the number of deaths, hospitalizations, emergency department visits, school or work days missed, and limitations on activity due to asthma."[4] In 2001, the CDC received $25.7 million in funding for the project, which was spent on collecting and analyzing data, implementing scientifically-proven treatments for asthma, and partnerships with state and local health departments.

Who develops asthma? Doctors don't know why some people develop asthma and others do not. Two risk factors are heredity and a disposition to allergies. Some have claimed that air pollution causes (not just triggers) asthma. How can this be when pollution levels were down (29% between 1980 and 1996), and rates of asthma were up (78%)? Some studies have shown a correlation between air pollution and childhood asthma. A study conducted by the University of Southern California followed 3,535 children living in 12 communities from 1993 to 1998. Six communities had higher than average ozone concentrations and six had lower than average ozone concentrations. The study found that children who played three or more sports (physical activity requiring the intake of more than the "normal" amount of air) in high ozone communities developed asthma at a rate 3 times higher than athletic children in low ozone communities. Another study conducted over 8 years (the results were released in January 2002) found that children who moved to communities with high levels of particulate matter (PM-10), nitrogen dioxide, and acid vapor showed decreased lung function growth compared to children who moved to communities with low levels of these pollutants. As seen previously, emissions of PM-10 and nitrogen oxides (nitrogen dioxide is one form) are increasing. Does this mean we are putting more children at risk for serious health problems?

Sources: Mannino, David M., et. al. Centers for Disease Control and Prevention. "Surveillance for Asthma -- United States, 1960-1995." *Morbidity and Mortality Weekly Report*, April 24, 1998. David M. Mannino, et. al. Centers for Disease Control and Prevention. "Surveillance for Asthma -- United States, 1980-1999." *Morbidity and Mortality Weekly Report, March 29, 2002*. Office of Air Quality Planning and Standards. U.S. Environmental Protection Agency. *National Air Pollutant Emissions Trends, 1900-1998,* March 2000. Retrieved July 2, 2002 from http://www.epa.gov/ttn/chief/trends/trends98/trends98.pdf. The Asthma and Allergy Foundation of America. "Asthma & Allergies." Retrieved July 3, 2002 from http://www.aafa.org. The Asthma and Allergy Foundation of America and the National Pharmaceutical Council. *A Closer Look at Asthma.* Retrieved July 3, 2002 from http://www.aafa.org. Centers for Disease Control and Prevention. "National Asthma Control Program." Retrieved July 3, 2002 from http://www.cdc.org. "Study Links Air Pollution and Asthma." *SinusPharmacy,* February 1, 2002. Retrieved July 3, 2002 from http://www.sinuspharmacy.com/news_childrenasthmastudy.html. U.S. Census Bureau. *Statistical Abstract of the United States, 2001.*

---

[4] Source: CDC.

Water Pollution

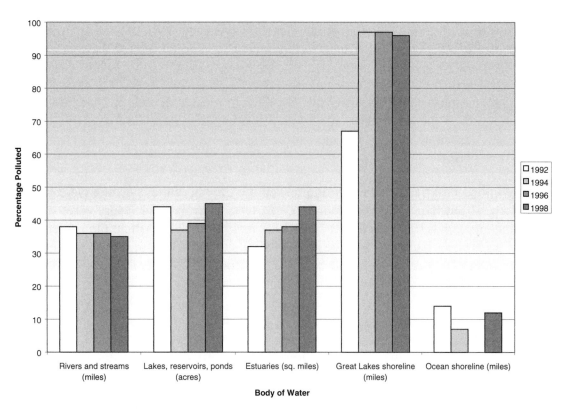

Marking the 30th anniversary of the Clean Water Act, Congress declared 2002 the Year of Clean Water. The state of the nation's waterways has improved since the 1960s when dead fish were washing ashore and lakes were catching on fire. But there is still room for improvement.

The graphic shows the percentage of waterways classified as impaired or "not attainable" for beneficial uses. Beneficial uses include aquatic life support, fish consumption, shellfish harvesting, drinking water supply, recreation, and agriculture — uses recommended by the EPA. Before 1972, some states defined one beneficial uses as "waste assimilation," making dumping legal in some cases. The Clean Water Act Banned this as an appropriate use.

"Impaired" means that some beneficial uses are only partially supported or not supported at all. The water may not be safe enough to drink, for instance. When a body of water is considered not attainable, beneficial uses are not supported at all due to one of six biological, chemical, physical, or economic and social conditions specified in Federal regulations. Some of these include naturally high concentrations of pollutants, natural physical features that make the body of water unsuitable for a habitat, or poor water quality that cannot be reversed without creating more environmental damage.

The U.S. has more than 3.5 million miles of rivers and streams, approximately 40.8 million acres of lakes, ponds, and reservoirs, over 34,000 square miles of estuaries[5], over 58,000 miles of ocean shoreline, and over 5,500 miles of Great Lakes shoreline. Under section 305(b) of the Clean Water Act, 61 states, American Indian Tribes, Territories, Interstate Water Commissions, and the District of Columbia are required to submit water quality information to the Environmental Protection Agency (EPA). The EPA then compiles the data into the *National Water Quality Inventory* report, which EPA sends to Congress.

Due to budget constraints, not all bodies of water are assessed for this biennial report. Ocean shoreline is the least represented with 5 to 9% being assessed from 1992 to 1998. The Great Lakes shoreline was the most represented with 90 to 99% being assessed during this time period.

From 1992 to 1998, pollution levels diminished. Ocean shorelines became cleaner where cleaned up — but more miles were polluted in 1998 than in 1994. More acres of lakes, reservoirs, and ponds became cleaner from 1992 to 1994, but, after that, the percentage of polluted acres rose. Estuaries and the Great Lakes shoreline became more polluted over this time span. The big jump in the percentage of polluted Great Lakes shoreline from 1992 to 1994 may have more to do with state regulations (which control what contaminants are checked for) than with a sudden mass contamination of the waters. Reporting entities have some flexibility in determining the criteria for each assessment and these criteria may change every two years. Because the reporting of quality of the Great Lakes shoreline is shared by a few states, pollution regulation in one or more states may have an exaggerated impact.

Despite the apparent rise in water pollution levels in some types of bodies of water, the state of the nation's water supply is better than it was in 1972 when the Clean Water Act was first enacted. In 1972, 33% of the nation's water was safe for fishing and swimming. By 1997, 66% was safe for fishing and swimming. Erosion of soil due to agricultural runoff (one of the major pollutants in rivers and streams) was reduced by 1 billion tons from 1972 to 1997. And, modern wastewater treatment facilities serve twice (173 million) the number of people they did in 1972.

Sources: Office of Water. U.S. Environmental Protection Agency. *Water Quality Report, 1992-1996*. Retrieved June 26, 2002 from http://www.epa.gov/305b. U.S. Census Bureau. *Statistical Abstract of the United States: 2001*. U.S. Environmental Protection Agency. "Federal Water Pollution Control Act." Retrieved June 27, 2002 from http://www.yearofcleanwater.org. U.S. Environmental Protection Agency. "Clean Water Act: A Brief History," 1997. Retrieved June 26, 2002 from http://www.epa.gov/owow/cwa/history.htm. "What is an Estuary?" Retrieved June 26, 2002 from http://www.estuaries.org/estuarywhat.html.

---

[5] An estuary is a body of water formed along the coast when fresh water from rivers flows into and mixes with salt water from the ocean. Estuaries provide an essential habitat for more than 75% of commercial fishing in the U.S. Some famous estuaries: Chesapeake Bay and Puget Sound. Source: "What is an Estuary?" Retrieved June 26, 2002 from http://www.estuaries.org/estuarywhat.html.

Leading Water Pollutants

Leading Water Pollutants, 1998

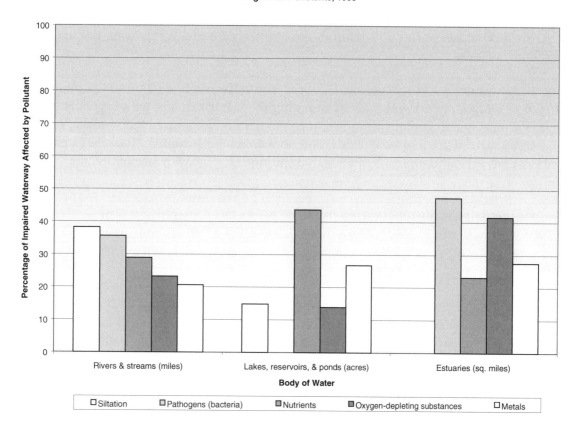

The graphic shows the percentage of impaired and not attainable waterways affected by the top 5 water pollutants. For definitions, see previous panel. We did not include data from the Great Lakes shoreline because the shoreline contains pollutants other than those listed here. PCBs, DDT and pesticides are the top pollutants on the Great Lakes shoreline. Ocean shoreline data were not included in the graph because the sample size (5%) was too small to be representative.

Siltation affected more than 111,000 miles of rivers and streams and more than 1 million acres of lakes, reservoirs, and ponds in 1998. When it rains, mineral particles wash off plowed fields, construction and logging sites, urban areas, strip-mined land, and eroded stream banks. Sediment deprives aquatic plant life of sunlight and muddies the water generally. Settling sediment suffocates fish eggs, destroys insect habitats and thus food for fish. Fish population is reduced or fish die out. Excessive sediment also hampers water treatment processes and boating.

Pathogens such as bacteria, viruses, and protozoan affected more than 103,000 miles of rivers and streams and 5,900 square miles of estuaries in 1998. Pathogens can cause illnesses (e.g. typhoid, minor respiratory and skin diseases). Many of us in the summertime probably watch for news reports of beach closings. In 2000, there were 11,270 beach closings or advisories interfered with recreation — up from 6,160 in 1999, and 484 in

1988. Is this due to increased pollution or better monitoring? It's difficult to tell. But in 2001, the National Resources Defense Council urged the Bush administration to implement improved federal water quality standards approved by the Clinton administration. Pathogens enter the waterways through inadequately treated sewage, storm water drains, septic systems, runoff from livestock pens, boats that dump sewage, and wildlife. From 1999 to 2000, there was a 40% jump in the number of beaches reporting pollution from unknown sources.

Nutrients (nitrates and phosphates[6]) occur naturally. Excessive levels stimulate the growth of aquatic weeds and algae. These clog the waterway, use up oxygen as they decompose, and block sunlight from reaching the depths. Fish and other aquatic creatures may suffocate. Swimming is impeded, and boat engines get fouled. Sources of excessive nutrients are agricultural, residential, and urban runoff; sewage treatment plants; and acid rain.

Oxygen-depleting substances have the same effect as excessive levels of nutrients. Untreated wastewater is a source. More than 67,000 miles of rivers and streams; over a million acres of lakes, reservoirs, and ponds; and more than 5,000 square miles of estuaries are affected.

Metals, such as mercury, lead[7], and cadmium[8], contaminate around 44,000 miles of rivers and streams; 2 million acres of lakes, reservoirs, and ponds; 3,000 square miles of estuaries. These naturally occurring metals in excessive amounts can pose health risks to both animals and humans. For example, when mercury enters water it turns to methyl mercury, its most toxic form. Aquatic wildlife that consumes mercury-laced plants or fish can suffer neurological damage and have difficulty with reproduction. Although scientists disagree as to what level of mercury is harmful to human health, the effects of mercury can range from paralysis to brain damage to death.

Have things gotten better? In some cases, yes. In others, no. The table on the following page shows comparisons of pullution between 1992 and 1998. Negative percentages mean that the level of the pollutant in 1998 was below the 1992 level. Positive percentages mean that the level of the pollutant in 1998 was higher than the 1992 level. NA means no data were available for one or both years.

---

[6] Nitrates are found in sewage and fertilizers and phosphates are found in detergents and fertilizers.

[7] See the panel entitled "Air Pollution" for more information on the health affects associated with lead.

[8] Cadmium accumulates in the kidneys and at very high levels can cause kidney failure. The average human daily intake of cadmium is 10 to 25 micrograms per day, far below the tolerable level of 60 to 70 micrograms per day recommended by the World Heath Organization. Source: http://www.cadmium.org.

Percentage Change of Impaired Waterway Affected By Pollutants, 1992-1998

	Rivers & streams (miles)	Lakes, reservoirs, & ponds (acres)	Estuaries (square miles)
Siltation	-6.8	-7.2	NA
Pathogens	-8.1	NA	5.4
Nutrients	8.6	3.7	-31.9
Oxygen-depleting substances	-0.8	-10.1	7.5
Metals	NA	-20.3	NA

The next panel will discuss the state of our drinking water.

Sources: U.S. Environmental Protection Agency. *National Water Quality Inventory, 1992* and *1998.* Retrieved June 26, 2002 from http://www.epa.gov/305b/. John Heilprin. "Bacteria-caused beach closings and advisories to nearly double, report says." *The Detroit News*, August 8, 2001. Guy Williams. National Wildlife Federation. "Mercury Pollution Prevention in Healthcare," July 1997. Retrieved June 27, 2002 from http://www.nwf.org/greatlakes/resources/mercury.html.

Our Drinking Water

Community Water Systems (CWS), 1993-2001

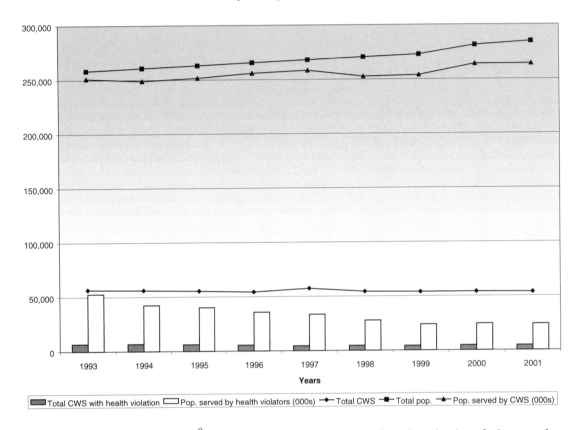

Cholera and schistosomiasis[9]. They are diseases that infect hundreds of thousands to hundreds of millions of people around the world due to lack of clean drinking water and sanitary systems (as of 2000, more than 1 billion people still lacked clean drinking water and over 2.4 billion lacked proper sanitation). These diseases are unheard of in the United States. We have one of the cleanest drinking water supplies and some of the best wastewater treatment facilities in the world. (In 2000, North America treated 90% of its wastewater. Europe: 66%; Asia: 35%; Latin America and the Caribbean: 14%; and Africa: 0%. World Health Organization).

The graphic shows the state of community water systems in America. Most people in the U.S. are served by community water systems. Since 1993, the number of people served by such systems rose and the number of systems reporting health violations decreased. However, in the year 2001, the health of more than 24 million people was still at risk due to contaminated drinking water in the U.S.

---

[9] Cholera is an illness caused by a bacterial infection of the intestine. Outbreaks in the U.S. are limited to travelers who were exposed to the disease in Asia, Africa, or Latin America and those that eat infected seafood they brought back to the U.S. Schistosomiasis is caused by parasitic worms that penetrate the skin. An estimated 200 million people are infected worldwide; however, the disease is not found in the U.S.

According to the World Health Organization (WHO), two of the key chemicals that must be regulated for safe drinking water are arsenic and fluoride. Both are naturally occurring substances, although they also enter the water via runoff from manufacturing plants, farms, and orchards. In the United States, safe levels of arsenic and fluoride in drinking water have been in dispute recently.

In October 2001, the U.S. Environmental Protection Agency (EPA) lowered the maximum contamination level standards for arsenic from 50 parts per billion to 10 ppb. What was the reasoning behind this? The National Academy of Sciences reported that 3 ppb of arsenic puts 4 to 10 people per 10,000 at risk for bladder and lung cancer. Therefore, the lower standard should save 1.5 to 11.4 million people a year. But, not all are convinced that this lower standard is going to show such dramatic results. No one disputes the health effects of high levels of arsenic in drinking water. In 2000, the WHO warned of mass arsenic poisoning of 35 to 77 million people in Bangladesh. 100,000 had already developed debilitating skin lesions and more were at risk for developing cancer, neurological disorders, and diabetes if continually exposed to drinking water with high arsenic levels (but higher than 50 ppb, surely).

The new standard mostly affects community water systems in the West where arsenic occurs naturally in the water. And the solution is not simply to filter the water. One option to extract the arsenic, called ion exchange filtering, creates wastewater that can be considered hazardous and would be costly to dispose of. Regardless of treatment option, some customers' monthly water bills could triple to pay for the equipment, treatments, and employees needed to implement the new standard. Many wonder if the old standard was good enough. "Paul Ritzma, deputy secretary of the [New Mexico] Environment Department, said department officials know of no New Mexico illnesses directly linked to arsenic in drinking water, and he expressed doubt that the new rules will lead to a drop in cancer" (Clark). Only time will tell if the new standard will save lives, or will be an unnecessary costly burden on community water systems and consumers.

Fluoride. Naturally occurring fluoride in water is less than 1 part per million (ppm) in most places. In 1945, the Dental Hygiene Unit at the National Institute of Health, studied the effects of adjusted fluoride levels (between 1.0-1.2 ppm) on children in 8 cities in the U.S. and Canada. They found that after 13 to 15 years, tooth decay was reduced 50 to 70% among children in communities with fluoridated water and the incidence of fluorosis (discoloration, pitting of enamel) was low. In 1962, the United States adopted standards that set the optimal range for fluoride concentrations at 0.7-1.2 ppm; by May 2001, the level had been raised to 4.0 ppm. After seeing the dramatic results (68% drop in tooth decay among 12-year olds since 1966), the American Dental Association, the American Medical Association, the WHO, and other professional and scientific organizations endorsed fluoridated water. Soon, fluoride was added to some brands of toothpaste and mouth rinses.

But, by the mid-1980s, children in communities with fluoridated water only had 18% less tooth decay than those in communities without. This was attributed to the widespread use of fluoridated water in bottling and packaged foods. By 1992, 56% of the population of the U.S. was receiving fluoridated water.

Although support of community fluoridation is high, the expansion of the program has been slow in recent years. Why? Some people, scientists, and policymakers may think that tooth decay is no longer a major health problem. Unlike early in the 20th century, people now take for granted that they will retain all or most of their teeth for a lifetime. (But, 94% of those 18 years old and over have tooth decay.) A second problem may be cost. Most of the water systems that are not fluoridated are small and per capita costs may be prohibitive for the consumers. A third problem: opponents to fluoridation, such as Citizens for Safe Drinking Water, who make claims that earlier research neglected to study the side effects of adding fluoride to drinking water. They claim that fluoride in the water, even at EPA "safe" levels, causes cancer, Down syndrome, heart disease, osteoporosis, and Alzheimer's disease.

And some cities are listening to their claims. From 1990 to 2000, nearly 80 cities and counties in the U. S. and Canada (and one in Australia) stopped fluoridating their water. Some, such as Kelowna and Campbell River, British Columbia fluoridated their water for 42 and 33 years, respectively, before deciding to quit the practice. In the United States, Western Nassau County, New York quit fluoridating its water after 23 years.

Sources: U.S. Environmental Protection Agency. *Factoids: Drinking Water and Ground Water Statistics, 1998-2001.* U.S. Environmental Protection Agency. Summary Inventory, Violations, and GPRA MS Excel PivotTables. All EPA data retrieved June 28, 2002 from http://www.epa.gov/safewater/. U.S. Census Bureau. *Statistical Abstract of the United States, 2001.* 2000 and 2001 total population data: U.S. Census Bureau. "Your Gateway to Census 2000." Retrieved June 28, 2002 from http://www.census.gov/main/www/ cen2000.html. Population Division. U.S. Census Bureau. "Table US2001EST-01 - Time Series of National Population Estimates: April 1, 2000 to July 1, 2001," December 27, 2001. Retrieved June 28, 2002 from http://eire.census.gov/popest/data/national/populartables/files/national01.pdf. World Health Organization. *Water for Health: WHO's Guidelines for Drinking Water Quality.* World Health Organization. *Global Water Supply and Sanitation Assessment 2000 Report.* Retrieved June 28, 2002 from http://www.who.int. Division of Bacterial and Mycotic Diseases. Centers for Disease Control. *Disease Information.* Retrieved June 28, 2002 from http://www.cdc.gov/ncidod/dbmd/diseaseinfo/. Division of Parasitic Diseases. Centers for Disease Control. "Fact Sheet: Schistosomiasis." Retrieved June 28, 2002 from http://www.cdc.gov/. World Health Organization "Researchers Warn of Impending Disaster from Mass Arsenic Poisoning," September 8, 2000. Retrieved June 28, 2002 from http://www.who.int. Heather Clark. "Small community water associations oppose new arsenic standards." *The Nando Times,* June 25, 2002. Retrieved June 27, 2002 from http://www.nandotimes.com. Centers for Disease Control. *Morbidity and Mortality Weekly Report,* October 22, 1999. "Cities Rejecting Fluoridation." Retrieved June 27, 2002 from http://www.nofluoride.com/CitiesRejecting.pdf. Emily Richmond. "Dentists spent $50,000 on Mtn. View campaign." *Palo Alto News,* August 7, 1999. Retrieved June 27, 2002 from http://www.nofluoride.com/50k_ vote.htm. *Springs/Portsmouth Water Quality Report – 2001.*

Drug Resistant Germs

Timeline of Antibiotic Resistance, 1928-2002

1928	Alexander Fleming discovered penicillin and its ability to kill bacteria.
c. 1938	British research and engineering team developed methods for large-scale production of penicillin.
1945	Discovery of penicillin-resistant strains of staphylococcus (staph) bacteria.
1950s	Penicillin-resistant staph infections rampant in hospitals that used penicillin frequently.
1959	A new antibiotic, methicillin, was introduced.
1960	Discovery of methicillin-resistant strains of staph bacteria.
1976	Rural Mississippi high school students and family members infected with multi-drug resistant tuberculosis.
1987-1992	Nearly 1,200 cases of multi-drug resistant tuberculosis occurred in the United States.
c. 1990	First case of drug-resistant meningitis discovered.
1991	More than 40% of staph infections are resistant to at least one antibiotic.
1994	15% of intensive care unit enterococcus infections are resistant to vancomycin, a "last-resort" anti-biotic. VRE, as the bacteria are called, are responsible for urinary, gastrointestinal, and pelvic infections. VRE may also infect the blood and heart.
2000	First case of multi-drug resistant streptococcus pneumoniae discovered: 11-month old child hospitalized for ear infection that did not respond to conventional treatment; Zyvox, a new antibiotic, is approved for treatment of serious infections.
2002	First case of staph bacteria fully-resistant to vancomycin is discovered in Michigan.

Survival of the Fittest. Charles Darwin's phrase to describe the process of evolution in his book *Origin of the Species* and an appropriate way to describe the evolution of the various strains of drug-resistant bacteria. When patients become ill from a bacterial infection, antibiotics (when used properly) will kill the organisms and the patient will get better. Occasionally there will be bacteria that aren't killed. These resistant bacteria then replicate and their offspring will also carry resistant genes. If all of the susceptible bacteria weren't killed, resistant bacteria may pass their resistant genes to them through the process of conjugation.[10] The process is accelerated when antibiotics are not used properly or are overused.

Dr. Jeffrey Koplan, director of the Centers for Disease Control (CDC), estimates that 50 million prescriptions a year written for antibiotics are unnecessary. In a 1997 study, 70% of U.S. doctors said that they were pressured into prescribing unnecessary antibiotics. Many patients demand antibiotics when they or their children feel ill, but taking antibiotics for colds or other viral infections does not cure these infections. Taking such drugs, however, does contribute to the development of resistant bacterial strains. A woman from Mississippi testified before a U.S. Senate committee in 2000. Her daughter "was an outgoing 13-month old who had taken antibiotics for recurrent ear infections before catching

---

[10] Plasmids (small, independently replicating DNA) with the resistant gene become incorporated into the genome of the other bacteria.

meningitis the drugs couldn't treat." In 2000, her daughter was 10 years old, in a coma, and kept alive by machines (Neergaard).

When antibiotics are appropriately prescribed, patients who stop taking them when they "feel better" are also contributing to the spread of resistant bacteria. The bacteria that were responding to the antibiotic may not have been completely killed, and resistant bacteria may pass on their resistant genes to the nonresistant bacteria. A recurrence of the illness will need stronger antibiotics to cure the patient. In some cases, incomplete treatment may not be a choice but the result of other circumstances. Poverty in many developing countries forces many to take counterfeit antibiotics (a $21 billion business worldwide).[11] As a result, not only are resistant strains increasing, but curable illnesses are going untreated.

Half of the antibiotics produced are used to treat sick animals, as growth promoters in livestock, and to remove harmful organisms in crops. This ongoing low-level dosing with antibiotics increases the possibility of resistant bacteria spreading from livestock and other food sources to humans. VRE can be traced to the use of avoparcin, an animal equivalent of vancomycin. Bacteria that may be harmless to livestock may be harmful (or fatal) to humans. But trying to eliminate it so that it doesn't spread to humans may do more harm. In 2000, in the United States, 5,000 people became ill with multi-drug resistant campylobacteriosis[12] caused by contaminated chicken. The antibiotics that failed to cure the human illness, contracted from the poultry, had been given to the poultry to prevent that illness from being spread to humans.

Is there anything being done to control this problem? In 1999, the Task Force on Antimicrobial Resistance was formed. In 2000, they, in conjunction with the CDC and other government agencies, released the report *Public Health Action Plan to Combat Antimicrobial Resistance.* Their plan included: (1) national surveillance to track outbreaks, monitor patterns of antibiotic use, and improve monitoring of antibiotic use in agricultural settings; (2) public health campaigns to educate the public and health care professionals in the proper use of antibiotics and to promote vaccinations, hygiene, and safe food handling; (3) research studying the physiology of bacteria and its mutation into drug-resistant strains, and (4) using that information to develop new and improved antibiotics for humans and animals.

Is the plan working? In 2000, the first new antibiotic in over 25 years was approved by the Food and Drug Administration (FDA). Zyvox was approved to treat VRE and methicillin-resistant staph infections along with certain types of pneumonia and skin and

---

[11] 51% of counterfeit drugs uncovered by the World Health Organization contained no active ingredient. 17% contained the wrong ingredient. 11% contained weaker than the recommended concentration of the active ingredient. And some actually contained poisons that could lead to severe disability and death. Only 4% of counterfeit drugs contained the same quantity and quality of the drug as the legal equivalent. Source: World Health Organization.

[12] Causes diarrhea, abdominal pain, and fever that may last 2-5 days. In people with suppressed immune systems, it can lead to a potentially fatal blood infection.

---

bloodstream infections. It's believed that bacteria will be less likely to develop resistance to this drug, a synthetic compound. In 2002, a new childhood vaccine for meningitis dramatically cut the disease prevalence and has lessened the spread of penicillin-resistant strains of other similar infections.

Another improvement: In 2002, a CDC study found that in the 1990s the number of anti-biotic prescriptions doctors wrote fell by 24%. But, this was not enough for the CDC. In April 2002, the CDC launched a new campaign entitled "Prevent Antimicrobial Resistance: A Campaign for Clinicians." Julie L. Gerbending, acting deputy director of the National Center for Infectious Diseases, says the problem is not that there aren't guidelines detailing the effective use of antibiotics; it's that physicians rarely read the guidelines. The new campaign will simplify the current guidelines into a 12-step program giving physicians only the information they need to know.

This campaign will also target patients so that they can do their part — a much-needed educational campaign considering that "every medicine cabinet in this country has leftover antibiotics"[13] (Neergaard). If taken properly, no antibiotics should be leftover. During the U.S. anthrax attacks in 2001, news of the improper use of Cipro was in the headlines. Some people never exposed to anthrax were taking the antibiotic thinking it would provide immunity. Others who were exposed to it stopped taking the medication before they were supposed to.

Starting in 2002, the U.S. government will hold yearly meetings to assess the effectiveness of the campaigns to combat antibiotic resistance. "The success of antibiotics in fighting diseases over the past five decades led to misplaced optimism that the 'war on infections' was nearly won. Unfortunately, …bacteria are cagey, tenacious organisms that swiftly develop resistance to antibiotics and to drug-rich environments" (Phinney).[14]

Sources: Office of Technology Assessment. U.S. Congress. *Impacts of Antibiotic-Resistant Bacteria,* September 1995. Lauran Neergaard. Associated Press. "Antibiotics Losing Their Fight." *ABCNews.com,* December 14, 2000. David Phinney. "Declaring War on Germs." *ABCNews.com,* February 25, 1999. Lisa Richwine. Reuters. "Bug Beware." *ABCNews.com,* April 18, 2000. All *ABCNews.com* data retrieved July 8-10, 2002 from http://abcnews.go.com. "New CDC campaign targets antibiotic resistance." *Infectious Disease News,* April 2002. Retrieved July 9, 2002 from http://www.infectiousdiseasenews.com/200204/cdc.asp. Lauran Neergaard. Associated Press. "Antibiotics a treasure government debates how to save." *MEDLINEplus,* June 10, 2002. Retrieved July 8, 2002 from http://www.nlm.nih.gov/medlineplus/news/fullstory_8001.html. "Infectious Diseases: Enterococcus Species." Retrieved July 9, 2002 from http://www.aventis.com/main/0,1003,EN-XX-7950-23720—FF.html. World Health Organization. *Report on Infectious Diseases 2000: Overcoming Antimicrobial Resistance,* 2000. Retrieved July 8, 2002 from http://www.who.int. Streptococcus, Staphylococcus and Campylobacteriosis information: Centers for Disease Control data retrieved July 8-10, 2002 from http://www.cdc.gov. Marisa Schulz. "Drug-resistant staph case reported." *The Detroit News,* July 4, 2002. "Plasmid." *On-line Medical Dictionary,* October 14, 1997. Retrieved July 10, 2002 from http://cancerweb.ncl.ac.uk.

[13] A quote by Lester Crawford, acting director of the FDA.

[14] A quote by Senator Bill Frist of Tennessee at a Senate subcommittee hearing on public health.

Tuberculosis

Tuberculosis Rates per 100,000 Population, 1996 and 2000

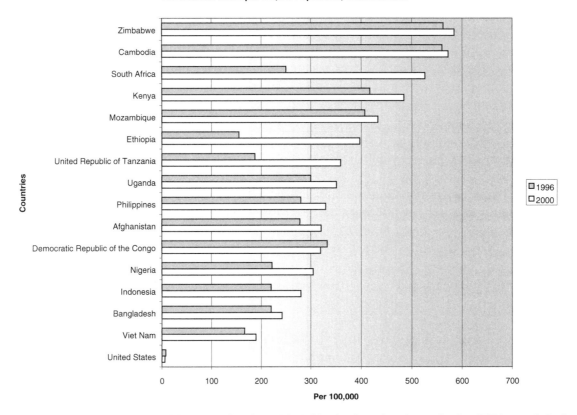

In 1993, the World Health Organization (WHO) declared tuberculosis (TB) a global emergency. What is TB? It's a contagious disease caused by the bacterium *Mycobacterium tuberculosis.* Its symptoms include a bloody cough, fever, fatigue, and weight loss. If not treated, it destroys the tissue of the organs affected (mostly the lungs). It's spread through coughing, sneezing, or talking. Those infected do not necessarily develop the disease. When the TB bacilli enter a person's system, a healthy immune system surrounds the bacilli with a thick waxy substance, protecting the person from contracting the disease. If the immune system is weakened, the bacilli cannot be put into this dormant state, and then the person contracts the contagious form of TB. WHO, in its report *Global Tuberculosis Control: WHO Report 2002,* estimates that in 2000 8.7 million people were infected with TB and 3.8 million had active cases. Thirty-four percent of the active cases worldwide can be found in the countries listed in the chart. The National Institute of Allergy and Infectious Diseases (NIAID), however, estimates that 2 billion people worldwide are infected with TB, 8 million develop active cases yearly, and 3 million die of the disease every year. These latter figures are the ones most people quote when speaking about this epidemic.

Displayed in the chart on the previous page are those countries with the highest TB rates per 100,000 people[15]. The United States was added to the chart for comparison. Excluding the United States, the only country in the chart to see a drop in the TB rate was the Democratic Republic of the Congo. Surprising, since all other African countries on the list saw their TB rates increase. In 2001, the WHO warned that TB cases in Africa were expected to double by 2010, partially due to the rise in HIV-positive cases. The chart bears this out. Between 24% and 67% of the TB cases in the African countries shown were also HIV-positive. South Africa's rate, for example, more than doubled from 1996 to 2000. By 2000, 60% of its TB cases also were HIV-positive.

This contrasted sharply with most of the other countries in the chart — where the percentage of TB with HIV-positive cases were between 0% and 1.4%. This suggests that other factors caused the numbers of TB cases to increase. Another factor could be the higher incidences of multidrug-resistant (MDR) TB. MDR TB may be more difficult to cure and may spread more rapidly if not treated promptly. In many of the non-African nations, more than 2% of their TB cases are MDR. In Afghanistan, for example, 7.3% of TB cases are MDR. Other factors contributing to the rise in TB rates are poverty (and associated poor health conditions), war (impeding the access to health care), and underfunding of health care programs.

Although the number of active TB cases in the United States has declined in the past nine years to just under 16,000, TB still remains a health threat. NIAID estimates that in 2002 10 to 15 million people in the U.S. are infected with TB. About 10% of them will develop an active case in their lifetime.

Why are so many infected and why is there an increasing risk of active cases developing? One reason is the HIV/AIDS epidemic. Those with HIV or AIDS have impaired immune systems which leaves them susceptible to developing an active case of the disease. Another reason is the number of foreign-born people living in the U.S. who come from areas where there is a high incidence of TB. About half of the TB cases are in this population. Poverty, injection drug use, and homelessness leave people susceptible to the disease. Crowded shelters and prisons have high incidences of TB transmission. As the population ages, health declines, and more people move into long-term care facilities. Those infected with the disease long ago are more likely to develop active cases and are more likely to spread the disease to others.

How does the U.S. compare to other North American and European countries? The table on the next page shows that in 2000, the U.S. rate was lower than many rates in other industrialized countries — quite an improvement since 1900, when the U.S. rate was 194 per 100,000 people.

---

[15] The 1996 data for Zimbabwe, Cambodia, Kenya, and Mozambique are actually for 1999. These countries were selected from a list of the top 22 countries with the highest number of TB cases. These 22 countries account for 79.1% of the TB cases worldwide.

TB Rates per 100,000 People for Selected

North American and European Countries, 2000

Russian Federation[16]	132.0
Hungary	31.0
Mexico	16.0
Germany	11.0
France	10.0
United Kingdom	10.0
Canada[17]	6.2
Italy	6.0
United States	**5.8**
Sweden	5.0

Sources: World Health Organization. *Global Tuberculosis Control: WHO Report, 1998, 2001*, and *2002*. Retrieved July 11, 2002 from http://www.who.int. Division of Tuberculosis Elimination. Centers for Disease Control and Prevention. *Reported Tuberculosis in the United States, 2000*. Retrieved July 9, 2002 from http://www.cdc.gov. Howard Njoo, et. al. Health Canada. *Tuberculosis in Canada – 1996*, 1998. National Institute of Allergy and Infectious Diseases. "Focus on Tuberculosis: Ancient Enemy, Present Threat." Retrieved July 8, 2002 from http://www.niaid.nih.gov/newsroom/focuson/tb02/tb.htm. World Health Organization. "HIV Causing Tuberculosis Cases to Double in Africa," April 23, 2001. Retrieved July 9, 2002 from http://www.who.int. World Health Organization. "Fact Sheet 104: Tuberculosis," April 2000. Retrieved July 8, 2002 from http://www.who.int. Centers for Disease Control and Prevention. "Achievements in Public Health, 1900-1999: Control of Infectious Diseases." *Morbidity and Mortality Weekly Review,* July 30, 1999. Retrieved July 3, 2002 from http://www.cdc.gov/mmwr/preview/mmwrhtml/mm4829a1.htm. National Institute of Allergy and Infectious Diseases. National Institutes of Health. "Fact Sheet: Tuberculosis," March 2002. Retrieved July 15, 2002 from http://www. niaid.nih.gov/factsheet/tb.htm.

---

[16] Ranked 10 in the number of TB cases in 2000. This rate is from the Country Profile section of the report *Global Tuberculosis Control: WHO Report 2002*. In the same report, the European regional section states the rate for Russian Federation as 95.

[17] The most recent year available was 1996.

Chapter 13

Medical Professionals

This chapter looks at trends in the medical professions, from physicians to physician assistants, then on to nurses and technicians, ending with virtual doctors practicing telemedicine. We look at numbers of medical professionals, trends in specialization, and the phenomenon of geographic maldistribution.

Medical professionals are overwhelmingly concentrated in metropolitan areas. What are the implications of their locational preferences? The consequences may be especially dire for the growing population of non-urban elderly, the poor, minorities, and country folk.

And if geographic maldistribution is not troubling enough, we shall see that the operative word when it comes to nearly every type of medical professional is "shortages." Healthcare workers are leaving the profession, frustrated by stagnant salaries and loss of autonomy. Smart, hard-working young people who might replace them fail to see the point of sacrificing years of their lives for little return. The finger of blame is pointed at managed care — our rapidly expanding system of health insurance, which controls costs by placing limits on physicians' fees and restricting a patient's choice of physicians. We shall see that there is a pervasive dissatisfaction among healthcare workers with the managed care system. Doctors say it is robbing them of their dignity. Nurses say cost-saving measures required by managed care are wearing them out and endangering the safety of their patients.

On the bright side, the media are full of stories these days about the wonders that rapid advances in medical knowledge have in store for us. Geographic maldistribution may become moot if doctors are able to perform surgery using robots on patients many miles away. Writing for *Futurist* in 2001, Cetron and Davies predicted that medical advances will soon have us at the point where "the need for hospital and hospice care could plummet. Except where surgery is required, most patients will be treated at home by nurse practitioners, physician's assistants, technicians, and other non-physician providers."[1] The questions we are left with: Can these medical wonders become commonplace if there are not enough healthcare workers to oversee them and no one is willing to pay for them?

---

[1] Cetron, Marvin J. and Owen Davies, "Trends Now changing the world: Technology, the Workplace,..." *Futurist*, March/April 2001, p27-42.

The Number of Doctors Is Up; Doctors Are More Diverse

Estimated Supply of Physicians: 1970-1996

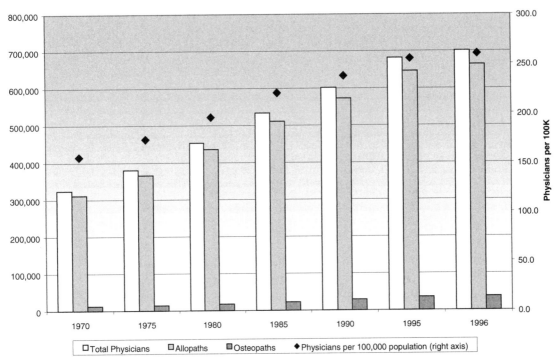

Legend: □ Total Physicians □ Allopaths ▣ Osteopaths ◆ Physicians per 100,000 population (right axis)

"In the United States, there seems to be an insatiable appetite for physicians and health care." — Biviano and Makarehchi (see Source notes)

In 1949, the United States had 191,577 doctors of medicine to serve a population of about 150 million Americans. By 1960, the number of doctors had grown 36% to 260,484.[2] The graphic shows data for the years between 1970 and 1996. In 1970 there were 323,800 practicing physicians (up 24% from 1960). The number of doctors grew 117% between 1970 and 1996, to 701,200, to serve a population of 265 million people.

The chart shows that there were 155.6 physicians per 100,000 population in 1970 and 260 in 1996, a 67% increase. For an international perspective, consider this: In the period 1990 to 1998, physicians per 100,000 population ratios for the United States, India, Philippines, and Pakistan were 270, 40, 10, and 60, respectively (Biviano and Makarehchi).

Of the 701,200 doctors practicing in 1996, 663,900 were allopaths and 37,300 were osteopaths. Allopathy can be defined as "That system of medical practice which aims to combat disease by the use of remedies which produce effects different from those produced by the special disease treated; a term invented ... to designate the ordinary practice, as opposed to homeopathy" (homeopathy is discussed in Chapter 3). Osteopathic

---

[2] *Health, United States, 1998*; see source notes.

medicine is "A system of therapy and medicine based on the theory that the normal body is a vital mechanical organism whose structural and functional states are of equal importance and is capable of making its own remedies against infections and toxic conditions when there are favourable environmental circumstances and adequate nutrition."[3] Between 1970 and 1996, allopathic physicians increased 113% and osteopathic physicians increased 196%.

Physicians 2000 by Race/Ethnicity

Race/Ethnicity	Number	Percentage
White	431,607	53.0
Black	20,464	2.5
Hispanic	28,189	3.5
Asian	72,602	8.9
American Native/Alaska Native	491	.0006
Other	20,104	2.5
Unknown	240,313	30.0
Total	**812,770**	**100.4**

Minority Physicians: The table shows physician data by ethnicity for the year 2000. The number of doctors reached 812,770 that year, up 16% over 1996. An estimated 10% of the physician workforce are underrepresented minorities (African American, Hispanic, Native American), although these groups comprise 30% of the population and will comprise 40% by 2030.

Women Physicians: More women began entering medical school in the 1970s and by the 1980s an estimated 17% of doctors were women. Today women make up more than 21% of practicing physicians. American medical schools awarded 8,314 medical degrees in 1970, of which, 699 were awarded to women (8%). Of the 15,286 medical degrees awarded in 2000 (an 84% increase), 6,525 (43%) were awarded to women.

Foreign-born doctors: More foreign-born doctors are practicing in the United States. They represented nearly 25% of all allopaths practicing in 2000. (See the panel entitled *Physician Workforce: Current Concerns* for more on this topic.)

Why do we have so many more doctors today than we ever had? Why do we have more foreign-born doctors? Do we have more doctors than we need? We will examine those questions in the next three panels.

Sources: Chart: Data estimated by Health Resources and Services Administration, Bureau of Health Professions, http://bhpr.hrsa.gov/healthworkforce/factbook.htm. Table: Total Physicians By Race/Ethnicity, 2000, American Medical Association, http://www.ama-assn.org/ama/pub/article/168-187.html. Marilyn Biviano and Farzaneh Makarehchi, *Globalization and the Physician Workforce in the United States*, Bureau of Health Professions, 2002, http://bhpr.hrsa.gov:80/healthworkforce/gpw.htm. "Women's History in America," Women's International Center, http://www.wic.org/misc/history.htm. Kreier, Rachel, "Celebrating Women Physicians," *American Medical News*, Vol. 41, No. 30, Aug. 10, 1998, http://www.ama-assn.org/sci-pubs/msjama/articles/vol_280/no_9/ art7.htm. Milani, Laura "Training for Tomorrow," *New Physician*, March 1994. Information retrieved September 30, 2002.

[3] According to Cancerweb. See http://cancerweb.ncl.ac.uk/

Is There a Doctor in the Area?

Doctors per 100,000 Population: 1998

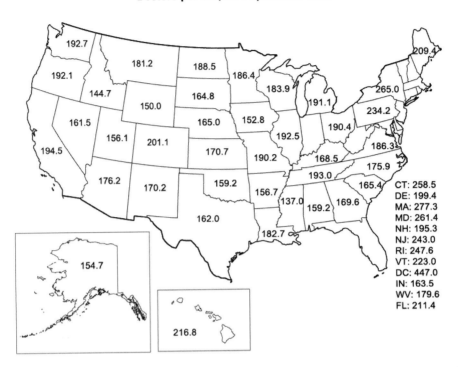

192.7
181.2
188.5
186.4
209.4
192.1
144.7
164.8
183.9
265.0
150.0
191.1
234.2
161.5
165.0
152.8
194.5
156.1
201.1
192.5
190.4
186.3
170.7
190.2
168.5
176.2
170.2
159.2
193.0
175.9
156.7
165.4
162.0
137.0
159.2
169.6
182.7

CT: 258.5
DE: 199.4
MA: 277.3
MD: 261.4
NH: 195.3
NJ: 243.0
RI: 247.6
VT: 223.0
DC: 447.0
IN: 163.5
WV: 179.6
FL: 211.4

154.7

216.8

The map shows the number of active patient care physicians per 100,000 population in 1998. That year, the national average was 198. The map shows that the District of Columbia far exceeded the national average with 447 physicians. Following were Massachusetts (277.3), New York (265), Maryland (261.4), Connecticut (258.5), Rhode Island (247.6), New Jersey (243), Pennsylvania (234.2), and Vermont (223).

Data like those on the map are assembled into 51 reports and are used by policymakers and educators in the 50 states and the District of Columbia and by the U.S. Bureau of Health Professions to analyze and interpret workforce needs. For instance, the information permits the identification of Health Professional Shortage Areas (HPSA).[4] To address shortages, incentives can be offered and new health professions programs can be developed or enrollment limited in overrepresented programs.

A look at the report for the District of Columbia reveals that of their 477 physicians per 100,000 population, 111 were active primary care physicians, compared to a national average of 59 (the remaining doctors were specialists, a topic covered in the next panel.) The federal Council on Graduate Medical Education considers 60 to 80 per 100,000 people to be desirable. The American Academy of Family Physicians recommends 76.[5]

---

[4] See http://www.bphc.hrsa.gov. A detailed listing of HPSAs is published in the Federal Register; see http://www.access.gpo.gov/su_docs/aces/aces140.html.

[5] Figures cited by Vanselow; see Source notes.

Looking at the map, one might wonder: Why are so many doctors concentrated on the East Coast?[6] One reason: Doctors tend to concentrate in urban and suburban areas. Doctors' preferences have led to a national mismatch between physician supply and need. A typical result of the mismatch is described by Roger W. Wilkins in *American Medical News*: "Medical care is still hard to find for minorities, especially if they are poor. In Harlem, there is one physician for every 7,000 people. On the east side of Manhattan, where the rich people live, there is one physician for every 600 people." Like minorities, rural residents have problems with access to health care.

It wasn't always this way. Kevin Grumbach provides historical background, hearkening back to the evolution of health care delivery in the 20th century. He writes that in 1900 America was home to 160 medical schools with more than 25,000 students. Health care was provided by "a heterogeneous mixture of minimally regulated purveyors of medical services calling themselves physicians [who] sought their livelihood in a market largely devoid of third-party payment" (and the ratio was about 175 physicians per 100,000).

Along came reformer Abraham Flexner, who stated in his influential 1910 report: "The curse of medical education is the excessive number of schools. The situation can improve only as weaker and superfluous schools are extinguished." Flexner called for stronger regulation of medical schools and stricter licensing policies for medical practitioners, a policy that resulted over the next few decades in the closing of more than 30 medical schools. Physician supply grew smaller and physicians' incomes rose. By 1930, the number had dropped to about 125 physicians per 100,000 population. Impoverished rural areas and later, inner cities, were left to fend for themselves as doctors abandoned them for more lucrative pastures. The trend toward fewer doctors reversed in the last third of the 20th century. We look at that issue next as it relates to physician specialization.

Sources: Map: National Center for Health Workforce Information and Analysis, State Health Workforce Profiles, http://bhpr.hrsa.gov/healthworkforce/profiles/default.htm; Primary source: American Medical Association. Biviano, Marilyn, and Farzaneh Makarehchi, *Globalization and the Physician Workforce in the United States*, Bureau of Health Professions, 2002, http://bhpr.hrsa.gov/healthworkforce/. Kevin Grumbach, "Fighting Hand To Hand Over Physician Workforce Policy," September/October 2002, http://www.healthaffairs.org/freecontent/v21n5/s6.htm. Vanselow, Neal A., M.D., "Are we headed for a surplus of 'generalist' healthcare providers?" *Postgraduate Medicine*, Vol 105 no 7 June 1999. Kolata, Gina, "Study finds health care spending doesn't correlate with wellness," July 21, 2002, http://seattletimes.nwsource.com/html/healthscience/134497499_care21.html. Greene, Jay "Academic Matters: Medical educators must increase diversity in medicine by recruiting strong minority students," *American Medical News*, Vol. 41, No. 46, Dec. 14, 1998, http://www.ama-assn.org/sci-pubs/msjama/articles/vol_280/no_21/ammcdive.htm.Information retrieved September 26, 2002. Information retrieved September 26,2002.

---

[6] For those who do not live on the East Coast, it may be comforting to know that life expectancy is no greater in regions that have more specialists, and Medicare surveys find that the quality of care is no better. (Gina Kolata; see Sources)

Doctors Are Specialists

Charting the Growth in Medical Specialists: 1970 to 1996

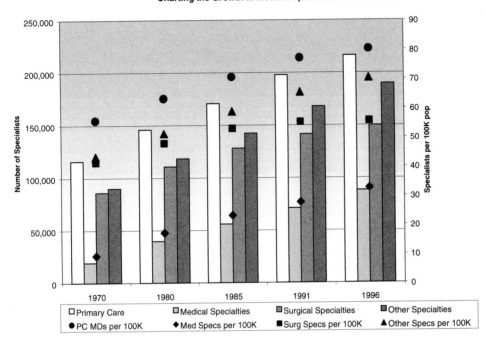

"In 1965 there were 115 practicing physicians (excluding physicians in training) for every 100,000 people. By the late 1990s there were almost 200 per 100,000, an increase of nearly 75 percent even after accounting for the underlying growth in the U.S. population. The increase in physician supply per capita occurred almost exclusively for specialists." — Kevin Grumbach

It's true that there was substantial growth in medical, surgical, and other specialties from 1970 to 1996 (chart). Medical specialties went from 9.3 to 32.6 per 100,000 population (up 250%). Surgical specialties went from 41.4 to 55.6 (up 34%). "Other" specialties went from 43.3 to 70.3 (up 62%).[7] There was also substantial growth in the number of primary care physicians (general and family practice, internal medicine, and pediatrics), from a ratio of 55.7 to 80.2 per 100,000 population (up 44%).

---

[7] Medical specialties include: Allergy & immunology, cardiovascular diseases, dermatology, family practice subspecialties, gastroenterology, internal medicine subspecialties, pediatric allergy, pediatric cardiology, other pediatric subspecialties, and pulmonary diseases. Surgical specialties include: colon/rectal surgery, general surgery, neurological surgery, obstetrics and gynecology, ophthalmology, orthopedic surgery, otolaryngology, plastic surgery, thoracic surgery, and urology. Other specialties include: aerospace medicine, anesthesiology, child psychiatry, diagnostic radiology, emergency medicine, general preventive medicine, medical genetics, neurology, nuclear medicine, occupational medicine, pathology and forensic pathology, physical medicine and rehabilitation, psychiatry, public health, radiology, radiation oncology, and other and unspecified.

Primary Care Physicians and Selected Specialists Per 100,000 Population

	1970	1980	1985	1991	1996
Primary Care	55.7	63.2	70.5	77.1	80.2
Medical Specialties					
Cardiovascular Disease	3.1	4.2	5.5	6.4	7.1
Surgical Specialties					
General Surgery	14.3	14.7	15.8	15.3	14.1
Obstetrics and Gynecology	9.1	11.4	12.8	13.7	14.2
Ophthalmology	4.8	5.6	6.1	6.4	6.6
Orthopedic Surgery	4.6	6.1	7.1	8.0	8.3
Other Specialties					
Anesthesiology	5.2	6.9	9.1	11.0	12.4
Diagnostic Radiology	0.9	3.0	5.3	6.7	7.4
Emergency Medicine	0.0	2.5	4.7	6.0	7.4
Pathology and Forensic Pathology	5.0	5.9	6.5	6.8	6.8
Psychiatry	10.2	11.9	13.3	14.2	14.2

The table shows data on the subspecialties in which the greatest number of physicians are now concentrated. What brought about this tremendous rise in the number of medical specialists? The development of modern medical techniques demanded more specialists. For example, the table shows a growth rate in anesthesiology specialists of 138%, from 5.2 per 100,000 population in 1970, to 12.4 in 1996.

Other factors contributed to a rise in specialists, including Medicare legislation of the 1960s, which focused national attention on a growing elderly population. The consensus was that there was an inadequate supply of physicians to meet their needs. According to Dr. Sidney Weissman: "The federal government intervened to increase physician supply and supported an increase in the number and size of medical schools. From the early 1960s to 1975, the number of U.S. medical school graduates rose from 8,000 to 16,000 per year." The number of geriatricians or physicians with any type of geriatric training has not grown, however, a phenomenon the Alliance for Aging Research (AAR) attributes to a lack of national resolve and age denial ("Peter Pan medicine"). According to AAR, only about 9,000 of America's 701,000+ practicing physicians are certified with added qualifications in geriatrics.

According to Grumbach, 1963 to 1990 was "the epoch of government blank checks.... Open-ended federal subsidies to teaching hospitals provided financial incentives for more specialized physician training programs. By the 1990s the federal government was spending more than $6 billion per year for graduate medical education (GME), with state governments contributing additional funds." The next thing we knew, we had too many specialists. Or did we? The next panel looks at this and other current concerns about the physician supply.

Sources: Chart: Bureau of Health Professions, *United States Health Workforce Personnel Factbook,* Table 202, http://bhpr.hrsa.gov/ healthworkforce/factbook.htm; Primary sources: American Medical Association. *Physician Characteristics and Distribution in the US 1997/98,* Chicago, 1997. Also prior annual issues (formerly titled *Physician Distribution and Medical Licensure in the U.S.*) and U.S. Bureau of the Census. *Current Population Reports.* Series P-25 Nos. 941, 943, 1023, 1036, 1049, 1075, and 1093, *Statistical Abstract of the United States: 1997* (117th edition) Washington, DC, 1997. AHRQ Focus on Research, "Rural Health Care," http://www. ahcpr.gov/news/focus/focrural.htm. U.S. General Accounting Office, *Health Workforce: Ensuring Adequate Supply and Distribution Remains Challenging,* August 1, 2001, http://www.gao.gov/. Kevin Grumbach, "Fighting Hand To Hand Over Physician Workforce Policy," September/October 2002, http://www.healthaffairs.org/freecontent/v21n5/s6.htm. Sidney Weissman, M.D., "Psychiatrists: Shortage or Surplus?" *Psychiatric Times,* October 1997, vol XIV, Issue 10, http://www.psychiatrictimes.com. Mike Mitka, As Americans Age, Geriatricians Go Missing," *JAMA Medical News & Perspectives,* http://jama.ama-assn.org. Information retrieved September 30, 2002.

The Physician Workforce: Current Concerns

Professionally Active Physicians by Place of Medical Education

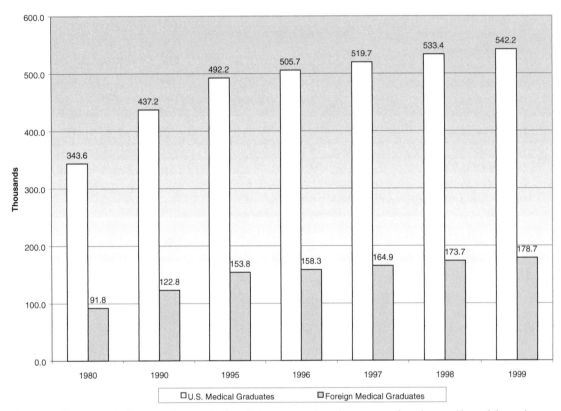

"The steady growth in numbers of physicians coming into practice is attributable primarily to ever increasing numbers of IMGs [International Medical Graduates], about which the committee is very concerned." — Committee on the U.S. Physician Supply, 1996.

Foreign-educated doctors (IMGs): The chart shows the rise in the number of practicing physicians according to their place of medical education — the United States or abroad.[8] Foreign-educated doctors who successfully complete an accredited residency or fellowship program in the United States are often recruited to remain here and serve where American doctors will not. Between 1980 and 1999, the number of IMGs practicing here nearly doubled, while the number of active native physicians rose 58%. According to a University of North Carolina at Chapel Hill study, the states with the highest

---

[8] An International Medical Graduate (IMG) is a person who has graduated from a medical school in an international state (outside the United States, Canada, and Puerto Rico) or who is otherwise qualified to practice medicine in an international state. IMGs must complete an accredited residency or fellowship program in the United States. These foreign-born physicians usually enter the country under an exchange visitor program administered by the U.S. Information Agency (USIA). Their visas (called J-1 visas) require them to leave the country when their medical training is done, but this requirement can be waived at the request of a federal agency or a state. This waiver generally requires that the physician practice for a specified period in an underserved area. The program often became a stepping stone to immigration.

rate of foreign-educated doctors are Florida and West Virginia (45%), North Dakota (40%), and Illinois (39%). States with more than 20% IMGs in rural areas are New York, Kansas, Georgia, Kentucky, Louisiana, North Carolina, and Texas.

The practice of recruiting foreign-trained doctors is controversial. Among the complaints: "...allowing foreign physicians to remain in the United States after completing their graduate medical education could contribute to a general oversupply of physicians, which could drive up medical costs" (General Accounting Office). After the September 11 terrorist attacks, the policy of granting visa waivers to foreign doctors came under scrutiny.[9]

Are There Too Many Doctors? Experts have said yes for decades. To illustrate the complexity of the issue, we offer quotes from three news reports.

(1) October 25, 2001 — Sacramento, California: "Speaking at a panel discussion Thursday, health care experts disagreed strongly about whether California is suffering from a physician shortage. The five panelists ... offered a wide range of views on the issue, ranging from accusations that managed care has eroded the state's ability to recruit the best and the brightest, to denials that there even is a shortage. However, on one key issue four of the five agreed: California does suffer from a shortage of specialists." The shortage was blamed "on warnings issued in earlier years of a surplus of specialists that influenced many medical students to pursue careers in primary care." (Silber)

(2) July 21, 2002 — New York: "Some medical specialties and geographical areas are suffering from a glut of doctors and hospitals... Supply seems to drive demand. More hospitals in an area mean many more days spent in hospitals with no discernible improvements in health. More medical specialists mean many more specialist visits and procedures." (Kolata; describing a study from Dartmouth Medical School)

(3) September 5, 2002 — New York: "A study led by Edward Salsberg, executive director of the Center for Health Workforce Studies at the University of Albany in New York, cites evidence to suggest that the nation may be facing a future doctor shortage. US medical schools produced only 12% more graduates between 1980 and 2000, while the US population grew 24%, the study finds. And minorities continue to be sorely underrepresented among medical school graduates, it said." (Pallarito)

Minorities Are Underrepresented in the Physician Workforce: Minorities make up only about 10% of practicing physicians and enrollment of minorities in medical schools has been falling, abetted by anti-affirmative-action policies adopted in some states. Minority physicians are more likely to serve patients in underserved communities and some people believe that physicians who are themselves products of a cultural tradition may be more sensitive to minority patients. Satel contends, however, that "Only a handful of studies have been devoted to the question of whether patients' outcomes are better if they

---

[9] A pre-September 11 analysis by GAO and the Appalachian Regional Commission's Inspector General found instances in which foreign physicians were not practicing at the facility where agencies believed them to be or were not practicing full-time in the underserved areas for which their waivers were granted.

and their doctors are of the same race. Many of these studies were conducted with psychiatric patients, and the majority show that the clinician's race has very little to do with how black and white patients fare in their treatment and recovery."

Geographic Maldistribution of Physicians: According to the Council on Graduate Medical Education (COGME), geographic maldistribution — the tendency for physicians to practice in affluent urban and suburban areas — leaves inner-city and rural communities struggling to attract sufficient healthcare professionals. "This is the central paradox of the American health care system: shortages amid surplus."

Who Will Care for the Elderly? The AGS Foundation for Health in Aging (which lobbies for increased funding for geriatric training) reports that the nation's need for geriatricians is critical (the elderly population, now at 12% of the total, will triple by 2050).

Physicians Against Managed Care: Kevin Grumbach describes the 1990s as "the era of the wholesale market for physician labor," a reference to the physician's changing role under managed care. Patients no longer shop for physicians, Grumbach writes; rather, HMOs act as "bulk purchasers of physician services." Physicians Who Care (http://www.hmopage.org/) complains: "HMOs have introduced a novel innovation in American Health care: incentives for physicians not to treat patients." Critics say managed care places profits before sound medical practice. With their incomes declining, doctors are fighting back. In 1999 members of the American Medical Association voted overwhelmingly to form a national doctor's union. In 2001 The Medical Society of the State of New York brought lawsuits against six of the state's largest managed care companies, charging "that the companies systematically harm both patients and physicians by systematically engaging in illegal practices and routinely breaching the terms of contracts with physicians. ... The suits specifically point to the insurance carriers' continual arbitrary denial of medically necessary care, capricious reductions in reimbursement claims," etc.[10] Dr. Donald Timmerman says the lawsuits are a way for doctors to regain "dignity and a chance of becoming an active participant in this country's healthcare system."

Sources: Chart: *Statistical Abstract of the United States: 2001*, p106; Primary source: American Medical Association, Chicago, IL, *Physician Characteristics and Distribution in the U.S.* (annual). GAO, "Foreign Physicians: Exchange Visitor Program Becoming Major Route to Practicing in U.S. Underserved Areas," and "Health Workforce: Ensuring Adequate Supply and Distribution Remains Challenging," http://www.gao.gov/. Pallarito, Karen, "US Health Worker Shortage Endangers Public," Reuters Health, Sept 5, 2002, http://www.nlm.nih.gov/medlineplus/. Kolata, Gina, "Study finds health care spending doesn't correlate with wellness," July 21, 2002, http://seattletimes.nwsource.com/. Silber, Judy, "Health Care Experts Say California Needs More Medical Specialists," *Knight Ridder/Tribune Business News*, Oct 25, 2001 p1. COGME, "Physician Distribution and Health Care Challenges in Rural and Inner-City Areas," Feb 1998, http://www.cogme.gov/. "NY Physicians Launch Major Litigation Against Managed Care Insurance Carriers," http://www.rcms.org/. Page, Leigh, "Litigious pushback," *Modern Physician*, June 2002. AGS Foundation for Health in Aging, "Public Policy: The Critical Shortage of Geriatricians," http://www.healthinaging.org/. Satel, Sally, "Health and Medical Care," in *Beyond the Color Line: New Perspectives on Race and Ethnicity in America*, Thernstrom, Abigail, and Stephan Thernstrom, eds., http://www-hoover.stanford.edu/homepage/books/fulltext/colorline/default.htm. Information retrieved September 26, 2002.

[10] See the American Medical Association's Web site for litigation updates (http://www.ama-assn.org/ama/pub/category/8100.html) or call Medical Society of the State of NY (516-488-6100, ext. 320).

Physician Assistants

Physician Assistants per 100,000 Population: 1999

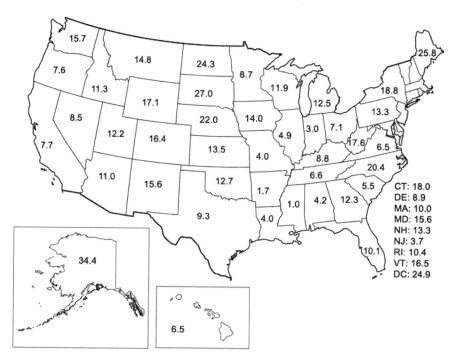

The map shows the distribution of physician assistants (PAs) per 100,000 population in 1999. The national average was 10.4.

Duke University created the first PA training program in 1965 to take advantage of the skills of medics returned from Vietnam. By 1991 there were about 20,000 PAs in clinical practice, a number that had more than doubled to about 42,708 by the beginning of 2002. According to the American Academy of Physician Assistants, there were 10,000 students enrolled in 132 accredited PA programs in 2002.

Students accepted for PA training typically hold a bachelor's degree and have some experience in a healthcare setting. Training programs are usually associated with a medical school and last a little over 2 years. Once dominated by men, the profession is now about 55% female, according to Medline. By law PAs must be supervised by a physician, and they perform many of the tasks once performed only by physicians, such as history taking, physical exams, diagnosis, and writing prescriptions. Starting salary is about $60,000.

Some doctors complain that PAs are being used by cost-conscious HMOs to replace physicians. J.D. Kleinke predicts the day will come when the managed care system will turn the practice of medicine from an art to a science and doctors will spend less time acting as clinicians and more time serving as managers of large numbers of PAs and other paraprofessionals. The result of changes like this, says Kleinke, "is paradoxical: those most bedeviled by managed care (physicians) may come to embody its essence but, one hopes, not its reputation for mean-spiritedness."

Sources: Chart: National Center for Health Workforce Information and Analysis, State Health Workforce Profiles; Primary Source: American Academy of Physician Assistants; http://bhpr.hrsa.gov/healthworkforce/profiles/default.htm. American Academy of Physician Assistants, http://www.aapa.org/glance.html. J. D. Kleinke, "The Industrialization of Health Care," Pulse — Report Vol. 278, pp. 1456-1457, Nov. 5, 1997, http://www.ama-assn.org/sci-pubs/msjama/articles/vol_278/no_17/pu145601.htm. "Physician Assistant profession," MedlinePlus Health Information, http://www.nlm.nih.gov/medlineplus/ency/article/001935.htm. Information retrieved September 30, 2002.

A Nursing Crisis

Registered Nurses (Total), RNs per 100,000, and Nursing School Graduates (RN)

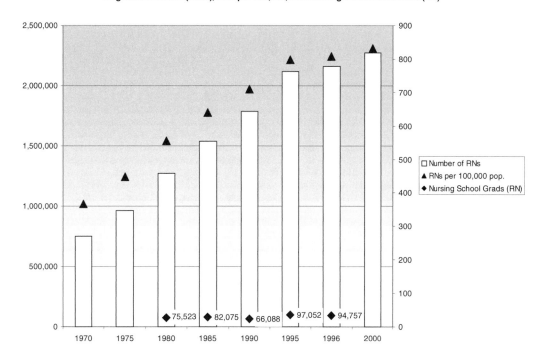

"The American health care system was built on the backs of nurses." — Lucille Joel, EdD, President, American Nurses' Association (quoted in Friedman; see Source notes)

Linda Richards qualified as America's first "trained" nurse in 1873, in a time when most nurses' training was on-the-job and nursing was little better than slave labor. Technological advances in medicine called for educated people, as outlined in the 1922 Goldmark Report, published by the Rockefeller Foundation.[11] The report advocated financial support of university-based schools of nursing. The Nursing Training Act of 1964 allocated nearly $300 million to nursing education, with $35 million designated for college-level programs. It seemed that nursing might finally be recognized as a respectable profession — albeit one dominated by women (about one in 20 nurses is male) — with all the baggage that comes with a female-dominated profession, such as low pay.

As the graphic demonstrates, in 1970 there were 750,000 registered nurses; by 2000 there were 2.3 million. The number of nursing school graduates at the baccalaureate, associate, and diploma levels rose 28%, from 75,523 in 1970 to a peak of 97,052 in 1995 (a rather steep drop in enrollment in 1990 may be attributable to the "baby bust.") Enrollment in 1996 was down to 94,757. Not shown on the chart is a reported upturn in enrollment that happened as the economy soured in 2001. According to the American Association of Colleges of Nursing, enrollment in entry-level baccalaureate programs rose 3.7% in fall

---

[11] A 500-page study formally titled *Nursing and Nursing Education in the United States*.

2001 compared to fall 2000, marking the end of a six-year period of decline. Total enrollment in all nursing programs leading to the baccalaureate degree was 106,557.

The table shows a national average of 366 nurses per 100,000 population in 1970, compared to 832 nurses in 2000, a 127% increase. Yet U.S. Health Resources and Services Administrator Elizabeth James Duke, Ph.D. noted in June 2002 that "a shortage of nurses threatens the quality of health care in communities across America." The nursing shortage is called one of the most pressing problems now facing the health care system. How can this be? For one thing, statistics for licensed registered nurses do not reflect the fact that many of those licensed nurses are no longer employed in nursing.

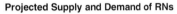

Projected Supply and Demand of RNs

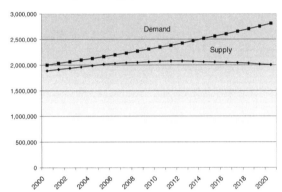

A demand for nurses that was not projected to become critical until 2007 had already become evident in 2000, as the small chart shows. The projected demand for new nurses for the period 2000-2020 is nearly 1 million more nurses than the projected supply. Factors driving the growth in demand for nurses include a growing population, a larger proportion of elderly persons who will require intensive health care services (the 65+ group is projected to grow 54% between 2000 and 2020) and medical advances that require nurses with special skills and experience. Factors affecting the supply of RNs include declining numbers of nursing school graduates, the aging of the RN workforce (average age in 1999: 45), declines in relative earnings, and the emergence of alternative job opportunities.

Like doctors, nurses complain that managed care and the pressure to cut costs have changed the profession and discourage young people from entering it. It takes a special sort of person to be a nurse. Dr. Denise Geolot, director of the division of nursing at the Bureau of Health Professions, says: "I think one of the things we have to address is the image of nursing and lack of respect that nurses experience."

Sources: Chart: Health Resources and Services Administration, *United States Health Workforce Personnel Factbook*, http://bhpr.hrsa. gov/healthworkforce/factbook.htm, and National Center for Health Statistics, *Health, United States, 2002,* Table 102. DeSales University, Significant Events in the History of Nursing," http://www4.allencol.edu/~sey0/hist1a.html.. Bureau of Health Professions, "Projected Supply, Demand and Shortages of Registered Nurses: 2000-2020," http://bhpr.hrsa.gov/healthworkforce/rnproject/default.htm. "Facts About the Nursing Shortage," http://www.nursesource.org/facts_shortage.html. Health and Human Services Administration News, "HHS Awards $30 Million to Address Emerging Nursing Shortage," June 4, 2002, http://newsroom.hrsa.gov:80/releases/2002releases/nursegrants.htm. Emily Friedman "Troubled past of 'invisible' profession," *JAMA, The Journal of the American Medical Association,* Dec 12, 1990 v264 n22 p2851(5). Melanie R. Margolis, "Nursing School Enrollment Increases," http://www.law.uh.edu/healthlawperspectives/MedicalProfessionals/020131Nursing.html. Information retrieved September 30, 2002.

Is There a Nurse in the Area?

Registered Nurses Per 100,000 Population: 1996

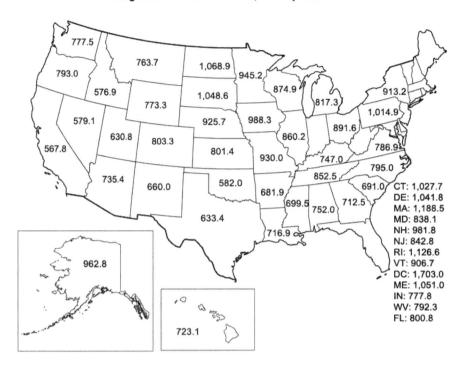

The map shows the number of registered nurses per 100,000 population in 1996. The national average that year was 808. As we saw with physicians, there is a geographic maldistribution of registered nurses. The Bureau of Health Professions points out that the national shortage of RNs is not evenly distributed across the states. Some states have experienced steeper population growth than others, leaving them with severe shortages of nurses. In 2000, 30 states were estimated to have RN shortages. By 2020, 44 states and the District of Columbia are projected to have shortages.

Notice that California ranked last in nurses per 100,000 in 1996, with Nevada and Idaho a close second- and third-to-last. These states experienced population growth between 1990-1997 of 8.3%, 39.5%, and 20.2%, respectively. Desperate for more nurses, California passed legislation in 1999 that established statewide standards for the number of patients assigned to a nurse (a too-large patient load is a common complaint among nurses). In 2002 California passed new legislation requiring the state to add 5,000 nurses by 2003. The California Nurses Association called the measure "a landmark bill that will make California the first state in the nation to require safe hospital staffing.... This is one of the most significant days in the history of nursing."

Key the name of any state on a computer, followed by the phrase "nurse shortage," and you will see that no state is immune. The consequences of a shortage of nurses are terrible to contemplate. Horror stories abound about compromised quality of care blamed on a lack of sufficient nursing staff (the nurse "struggled to give one patient blood, while another began having a heart attack and yet another strained to breathe on a respirator...").

To recruit nurses during a shortage, hospitals offer huge signing bonuses or pay two to three times the normal hourly rate for nurses to hire temporary workers. They promise lower patient-staff ratios to burned-out staff. During the nursing shortage of the 1980s, the American Nurses Association began certifying hospitals as "magnets," hospitals described as excellent places for nurses to work (in 2002, 10 hospitals qualified). One criterion for certification: the hospital must have a nurse in the top level of administration.

In July 2002, Congress passed the Nurse Reinvestment Act to help alleviate the shortage of nurses. Speaking in support of the bill, Congressman John Dingell of Michigan called nurses the "unsung heroes in health care." He noted that Detroit imports 15 to 20% of its nursing staff from Canada (which has its own nursing shortage) and that a University of Detroit-Mercy study predicted a need in Michigan by 2007 for 1.4 million registered nurses versus a predicted supply of only 656,000. The Nurse Reinvestment Act established scholarships, nurse retention, and patient safety enhancement grants, and grants for comprehensive geriatric training. It also called for public service announcements to inform "potential nurses about the resources available to them if they choose to enter this wonderful profession" (Dingell).

With reference to "this wonderful profession," it is interesting to note what Nurse Advocate has to say: "Numerous sources report that nurses and other healthcare workers are assaulted in the workplace more frequently than any other US worker group.... Nurses tend to minimize and ignore violence, and in addition, do not report violence. Nurses cite lack of employer support and fear of retaliation as common reasons for not reporting."

Sources: Map: National Center for Health Workforce Information and Analysis, State Health Workforce Profiles, http://bhpr.hrsa.gov/healthworkforce/profiles/default.htm. Bureau of Health Professions, "Projected Supply, Demand and Shortages of Registered Nurses: 2000-2020," http://bhpr.hrsa.gov/healthworkforce/rnproject/default.htm. Joan Obra, "Law intensifies the state and Valley nurse shortage," *The Fresno Bee*, Jan 23, 2002 pC1. Jodie Snyder, "Nurse Shortage Critical in State," *Arizona Republic*, Sept 1, 2002 pD1. "Looking for Quality Patient Outcomes: The American Nurses Credentialing Center's Magnet Program Recognizes Excellence," http://nursingworld.org/readroom/nti/9804nti.htm. Statement of Congressman John D. Dingell, http://www.house.gov/commerce_democrats/press/107st140.htm. Sarah A. Webster, "Stressed Nurses Quit, Hurting Patient Care," *The Detroit News*, November 18, 2001, http://www.detnews.com/specialreports/2001/nursing/sunlead/sunlead.htm. "California signs nurse-to-patient ratio bill," http://www.calnurse.org. Nurse Advocate: Nurses and Workplace Violence, http://www.nurseadvocate.org/nursewpv.html. Information retrieved September 30, 2002.

Nurse Practitioners: Where They Practice

Nurse Practitioners per 100,000 Population: 1998

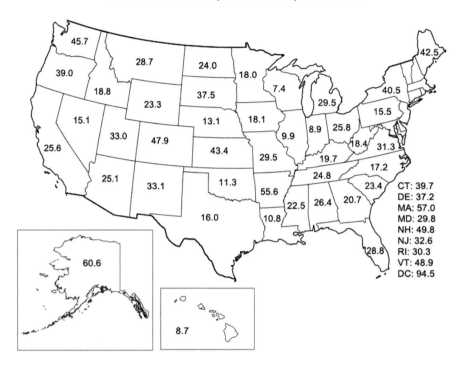

The map shows the distribution of nurse practitioners (NPs; also called advanced practice nurses) across the nation in 1996. That year, the national average was 26.3 per 100,000 population.

The 1967 establishment of a pediatric nurse practitioner program at the University of Colorado, Boulder, is said to have marked the beginning of the nurse practitioner movement. According to the Bureau of Labor Statistics: "Nurse practitioners provide basic primary health care. They diagnose and treat common acute illnesses and injuries. Nurse practitioners also can prescribe medications (but certification and licensing requirements vary by State). Other advanced practice nurses include clinical nurse specialists, certified registered nurse anesthetists, and certified nurse-midwives. Advanced practice nurses must meet higher educational and clinical practice requirements beyond the basic nursing education and licensing required of all RNs."

Advanced Practice Nurses by Specialty

Title	Number
Nurse Practitioner	48,237
Certified Nurse Midwife	7,400
Clinical Nurse Specialist	58,185
Certified Registered Nurse Anesthetist	25,238

According to NursingWorld, about 140,000 advanced practice nurses deliver health care, primarily to underserved populations (the elderly, the poor, the rural). The table shows the areas of expertise of these 140,000 nurses. NursingWorld asserts that "Some 60% to 80% of primary and preventive care traditionally done by doctors can be done by a nurse for less money" were it not for the fact that there are too many restrictions on their activities.

Nurses performing the tasks of a doctor at a lower cost seems like a concept that the health care finance people could get behind. However, Canavan reports that nurse practitioners have been stymied by physician lobbies and Medicare reimbursement policies, among other things. Even when NPs and clinical nurse specialists performed the same services as doctors, it was not until 1998 that those services became eligible for Medicare Part B coverage and direct payment, regardless of the geographic region where they were performed, if the same services were covered when provided by a physician.[12] Previously, NP services were covered only when provided in nursing homes or rural areas.

With nurses in short supply everywhere, it is not hard to imagine the value of a certified nurse midwife to the poor and to pregnant women in rural areas. Nevertheless, these professionals complain of state policies that constrain their activities: supervision requirements, lack of prescriptive authority, differing third-party reimbursement policies, restrictions on hospital privileges, and excessive malpractice premiums.

Autonomy has also been an issue for nurse anesthetists, who attend some 17 million patients per year. In 2002 President George W. Bush ended a practice dating back more than 35 years when he gave states the freedom to opt out of a Medicare rule requiring that nurse anesthetists work under the supervision of a physician. Bush's supporters pointed to the cost savings to be realized, since nurse anesthetists earn about one-half as much as anesthesiologists (who are in short supply). Critics claim the move will be hazardous to patients' health.

Sources: Map: National Center for Health Workforce Information and Analysis, State Health Workforce Profiles, http://bhpr.hrsa.gov/healthworkforce/profiles/default.htm. "Registered Nurses," http://www.bls.gov/oco/ocos083.htm. Table: "Advanced Practice Nursing: A New Age in Health Care," http://www.nursingworld.org/readroom/fsadvprc.htm. Nurse-Midwifery Position Statement, http://www.nursingworld.org/readroom/position/practice/prmidwif.htm. Kathleen Canavan, "Specialty Fields Practice Differences Spawned by Managed Care," *The American Nurse*, October 1996, http://www.nursingworld.org/readroom/mgcare5.htm. Lawrence Budd, "Some States Dropping Nurse Anesthetist Oversight Rule, *Dayton Daily News*, May 29, 2002 p1A. Information retrieved September 30, 2002.

---

[12] Effective with the passage of Public Law 105-33 (effective Jan 1, 1998). See http://www.nursing world.org/gova/medreimb.htm

LPNs: Where They Practice

LPNs per 100,000 Population: 1998

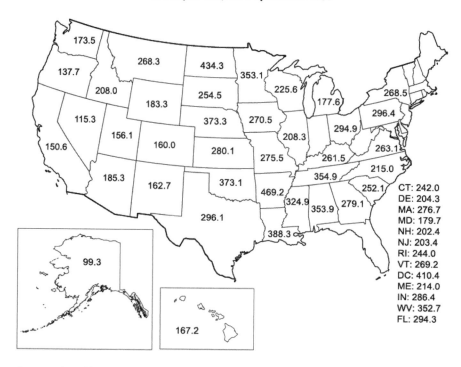

	1980	1985	1990	1995
Nursing Program Graduates: LPNs				
LPN Grads	41,892	36,955	35,417	44,234

The map shows the distribution of licensed practical nurses (LPNs) per 100,000 population across the nation in 1998. The national average that year was 249.3. The national ratio of LPNs employed for every 100 RNs that year was 32.

As we saw with registered nurses (RNs), there are severe shortages in states where the population is growing, especially in the West (California, Nevada, Alaska, and Idaho, for example).

The role of LPN developed because of nursing shortages during World War II. Unlike registered nurses, who are awarded baccalaureate degrees, the licensed practical nurse receives one year of training, usually in a vocational or technical school.[13] LPNs provide basic bedside care, including taking vital signs, treating bedsores, and administering enemas and injections. The job requirements: "Physical strength and stamina; compassion; self confidence; good judgment and decision-making skills" (Bureau of Labor Statistics). The salary range: $15,000 to $33,000 a year. The complaints: Low pay, too little time to spend on patient care, and too much paperwork.

---

[13] They are called licensed vocational nurses in California and Texas.

In 2000 29% of LPNs were employed in nursing homes. Though the pay is better in hospitals, competition for hospital jobs is keen. LPN burnout is common, as described by Cyndi Drew, an LPN from Chesapeake employed in a nursing home. She wrote to the editor of the local newspaper: "UPS [United Parcel Service] workers get paid more and have better benefits than nurses in this area and they're not responsible for people's lifes. What person in their right mind would pay for a medical education, only to be paid less than someone who loads boxes on a truck and delivers them?" What person, indeed?

Sources: Map: National Center for Health Workforce Information and Analysis, State Health Workforce Profiles, http://bhpr. hrsa.gov/healthworkforce/profiles/default.htm. Table: Health United States 2002, Table 104. National Federation of Licensed Practical Nurses, http://www.nflpn.org/. Licensed Practical and Licensed Vocational Nurses, http://www.bls.gov/oco/ocos102.htm. "Nursing Homes Take Their Toll on Nurses, Too," (Letter to the Editor), *The Virginian Pilot*, April 14, 2002 pJ3. Information retrieved September 30, 2002.

Radiologic Technologists

Radiologic Technologists per 100,000 Population: 1999

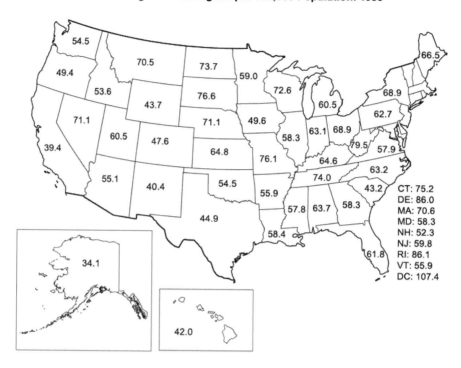

CT: 75.2
DE: 86.0
MA: 70.6
MD: 58.3
NH: 52.3
NJ: 59.8
RI: 86.1
VT: 55.9
DC: 107.4

The map shows the distribution of radiologic technologists (rad techs) per 100,000 population in 1998. The national average that year was 58.3.

According to the Bureau of Labor Statistics, among other tasks, "Radiologic technologists and technicians take x rays and administer nonradioactive materials into patients' blood streams for diagnostic purposes. Some specialize in diagnostic imaging technologies such as computed tomography (CT) and magnetic resonance imaging (MRI)." Rad techs may opt for more training and certification in the emerging field of Radiology Practitioner Assistants, a position somewhat similar to physician assistant.

The Bureau of Health Professions reports that the number of recipients of rad tech degrees per 100,000 population increased 10% from 1992 to 1997. An American Hospital Association report released early in 2002 reported a national vacancy rate for hospital radiologic technologists hovering around 15%.

Is the job dangerous? Less so now than before 1950, apparently. In a study of 69,525 female rad techs who were certified as radiation technologists between 1926 and 1982, it was found that women (who fill 75% of the jobs) who began working between 1940 and 1949 were about 2-1/2 times more likely to die of breast cancer compared with those who started working in 1960 or later. It was not until nearly 20 years after Wilhelm Conrad Roentgen's 1895 discovered the x-ray that precautions such as lead aprons and film badges started coming into widespread use. Too, lower radiation dose exposure is now recommended.[14]

Sources: Map: National Center for Health Workforce Information and Analysis, State Health Workforce Profiles, http://bhpr. hrsa.gov/healthworkforce/profiles/default.htm. "Registered Nurses," http://www.bls.gov/oco/ocos083.htm. National Society of Radiology Practitioner Assistants, http://www.RadiologyPA.org/faqs.asp. "Mortality may be tied to prolonged exposure to low-dose radiation," *Medical Letter on the CDC & FDA*, July 21, 2002 p14. Information retrieved September 30, 2002.

---

[14] An interesting history of the use of radiation technology can be found at http://www.asrt.org/other_categories/about_asrt/history.htm.

Emergency Medical Technicians

Emergency Medical Technicians per 100,000 Population: 1998

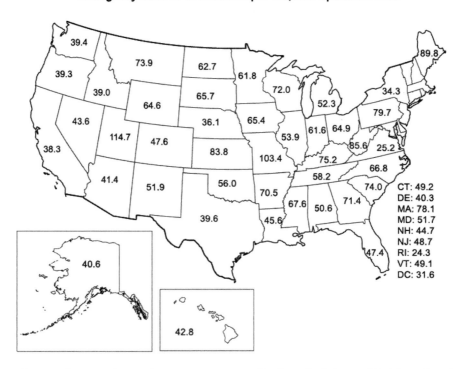

The map shows the number of emergency medical technicians (EMTs, also known as paramedics) per 100,000 population in 1998. The national ratio that year was 53.8.

An EMT is the lifesaver dispatched to your home or accident scene when 911 is called. The EMT, working under the direction of a physician (usually through radio communication), determines the nature and extent of your condition, gives you appropriate care, and if necessary transports you to a hospital. The EMT works 45 to 60 hours a week and earns $17,930 to $37,760 per year. The average length of training is 1,000 hours (American Medical Association). The National Registry of Emergency Medical Technicians (NREMT) sets the standards for the training and examination of EMTs. Between 1992 and 1997, the number of recipients of EMT degrees per 100,000 population increased by 62% (Bureau of Health Professions).

"Job stress is common due to irregular hours and treating patients in life-or-death situations" (Bureau of Labor Statistics). The job stress may be exacerbated by having one's ambulance turned away from overcrowded emergency rooms. Peter G. Gosselin described the deterioration of the nation's emergency care system in the *Los Angeles Times*: "At the great hospitals of the nation's major cities and ballooning suburbs, ambulances are being turned away and patients are stacked in hallways like so much cordwood. America's dwindling capacity for emergency care is being outstripped by Americans' demand for it." Gosselin blames the situation on "under-investment during the 1990s in the kinds of goods and services that traditionally have served as society's foundation… One result is that the country is coming off its longest economic expansion in more than a century with fewer emergency rooms than it had to begin with."

Hopson et al. interviewed 500 EMTs/paramedics for their book, *Burnout to Balance: EMS Stress*. They found emergency responders typically experience job burnout within three to five years of beginning work. Their subjects were prone to multiple marriages and suicidal thoughts.

If the personnel shortages previously described don't have you worried enough, ponder the emergency room situation the next time you feel an episode of what you think is heartburn coming on.

Sources: Chart: National Center for Health Workforce Information and Analysis, State Health Workforce Profiles; Primary Source: Bureau of the Census; http://bhpr.hrsa.gov/healthworkforce/profiles/default.htm. "Emergency Medical Technicians and Paramedics," Bureau of Labor Statistics, http://www.bls.gov/oco/ocos101.htm. NREMT, http://www.nremt.org/. AMA, http://www.ama-assn.org/ama/pub/category/4242.html. Gosselin, Peter G., "Private Prosperities, Public Breakdowns: Amid Nationwide Prosperity...," *Los Angeles Times*, August 6, 2001. Edwards, Johnny, "Medics battle burnout with stress counseling," http://www.augustachronicle.com/stories/040501/met_021-6082.000.shtml. Information retrieved September 30, 2002.

Clinical Laboratory Technologists

Clinical Laboratory Technologists per 100,000 Population: 1999

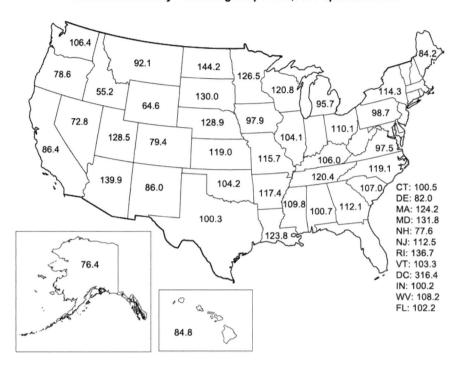

The map shows the distribution of clinical laboratory technologists (lab techs) per 100,000 population across the nation in 1998. The national ratio was 105.4.

Lab techs examine human blood, tissues, and fluids on orders from a physician. According to the Bureau of Labor Statistics: "Clinical laboratory testing plays a crucial role in the detection, diagnosis, and treatment of disease. Clinical laboratory technologists, also referred to as clinical laboratory scientists or medical technologists, and clinical laboratory technicians, also known as medical technicians or medical laboratory technicians, perform most of these tests." Most lab techs hold at least a bachelor's degree with a major in medical technology or a life science.

Lab tech earnings range from $34,220 to more than $55,560. Starting salaries cannot compete with those in the computer field, for example. The relatively low pay relative to the rigor of the training program, and the prospect of night shifts and health risks may be keeping young people from entering the field. Amy Fletcher reports that between 1985 and 2001, 186 lab technologist and 63 technician programs closed. In just two years between July 1999 and July 2001, 32 bachelor-degree lab programs and 17 technician programs closed. According to the Bureau of Health Professions, between 1992 and 1997, the number of recipients of lab tech degrees per 100,000 population increased by 36%, but spot shortages of lab techs are reported and large numbers of lab techs who trained during the peak years of 1974 to 1984 are getting ready to retire.

Not every state requires that lab techs be licensed or registered. This led to a situation in Boston in which at least two hospitals reportedly hired high school students to perform lab tests. The implications of inadequately trained personnel performing clinical tests are awful to contemplate.

Sources: Chart: National Center for Health Workforce Information and Analysis, State Health Workforce Profiles, Primary Source: Bureau of the Census; http://bhpr.hrsa.gov/healthworkforce/profiles/default.htm. BLS, "Clinical Laboratory Technologists and Technicians," http://www.bls.gov/oco/ocos096.htm. Amy Fletcher, "Workers for med labs in short supply," *Denver Business Journal*, July 13, 2001 v52 i49 p1A Michael Lasalandra, "Legislature urged to mandate lab tech licensing," *The Boston Herald*, Sept 24, 2001 p027 Pennell C. Painter, Ph.D.,"What Has Happened to All the Techs ?" http://www.ivdtrials.com/TechStaff.htm. Information retrieved September 30, 2002. Information retrieved September 30, 2002.

Virtual Doctors

The Most Common Telemedicine Activities

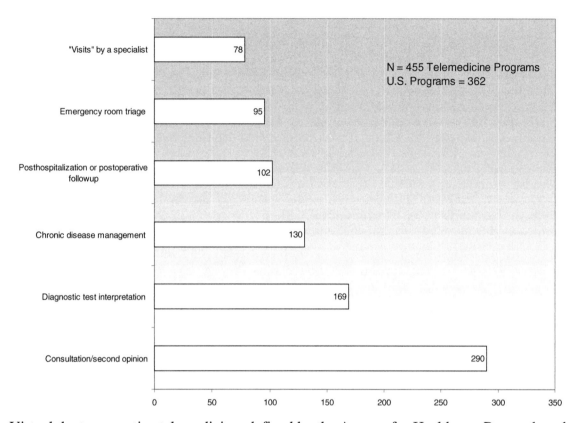

N = 455 Telemedicine Programs
U.S. Programs = 362

Activity	Value
"Visits" by a specialist	78
Emergency room triage	95
Posthospitalization or postoperative followup	102
Chronic disease management	130
Diagnostic test interpretation	169
Consultation/second opinion	290

Virtual doctors practice telemedicine, defined by the Agency for Healthcare Research and Quality (AHRQ) as: "The use of telecommunications technology for medical diagnostic, monitoring, and therapeutic purposes when distance separates the users." AHRQ's study, *Telemedicine for the Medicare Population*, identified 455 telemedicine programs in operation in 2000, 362 of which were in the United States.[15] The study was undertaken to determine telemedicine's costs and benefits because of a growing call for Medicare to pay for telemedicine services. The table shows the most common telemedicine activities being performed by the 455 programs identified. Figures inside the bars show how many of the programs were performing the named activity.[16]

---

[15] The Association of Telehealth Service Providers (ATSP) reported 206 telemedicine programs in 2000, up 724% over the 25 projects identified in 1995 and up 21% over the 170 identified in 1999. ATSP describes itself as "an international membership-based organization dedicated to improving health care through growth of the telehealth industry. See http://www.atsp.org/.

[16] Merriam-Webster online defines triage as "the sorting of and allocation of treatment to patients and especially battle and disaster victims according to a system of priorities designed to maximize the number of survivors."

Telemedicine promises better access to health care for heretofore underserved populations. Telemedicine has been around since the late 1950s and has been used successfully in rural areas, in prisons, and by the military, but technological advances and rapidly rising medical costs are hastening its widespread implementation.[17] The possibilities of telemedicine seem limitless and the potential cost savings are staggering (by one estimate, $36 billion a year).[18] The technology includes devices that can be implanted in a patient's chest to collect heart and blood pressure data and transmit it to a doctor's office over the Internet. Similar devices can monitor patients with diabetes and other chronic conditions, saving the elderly and afflicted a trip to the doctor's office. "Smart toilets" can do a urinalysis and transmit the results for study. The list goes on.

Technological advances like these are challenging the longstanding belief that doctors must interact with patients one-on-one. The big questions now are: Who will pay for telemedicine and how is it to be regulated? Recognizing the cost savings promised by telemedicine, Medicare and insurance companies slowly started coming around in the late 1990s. For example, First Health Group will pay doctors $25 for Internet consultations with patients. The 1997 Balanced Budget Act included the first Medicare telemedicine payment provisions. By September 30, 2000, Medicare had reimbursed a rather unimpressive $20,000 for 301 teleconsultation claims, but at least the debate had changed from *whether* Medicare should pay to *how* Medicare should pay (Pushkin).[19]

Telemedicine has raised concerns about the practice of medicine across state lines (some states require doctors to be licensed in every state where they provide telemedicine consulting). Proposed national licensure of physicians is opposed by the American Medical Association and others who see licensing as a states' rights issue. Other concerns involve record keeping and confidentiality. While the establishment debates these issues, contemplate the future as imagined by Maryann Karinch (*Telemedicine: What the Future Holds When You're Ill*): "Robots performing complex surgical procedures directed by medical specialists at major hospitals continents away. Dark, bubbling aquariums where babies born too soon breathe special liquids that allow their premature lungs to develop. Pocket-sized computers programming new nerve networks, so people with spinal cord injuries can walk again." And maybe, no more long hours spent sitting in waiting rooms.

Sources: Chart: Agency for Healthcare Research and Quality, *Telemedicine for the Medicare Population*, http://www.ahcpr.gov/. Maryann Karinch, *Telemedicine: What the Future Holds When You're Ill*," http://www.karinch.com/Telemedicine.html.. Nancy Brown, "What is Telemedicine?," May 3, 2002, http://trc.telemed.org/. Tom Sanders, "Virtual Doctors," April 2002, http://www. doctorandpharmacy.com/. Blanton, Thomas, et al., "Telemedicine: The Health System of Tomorrow, *Futurist*, Sept/Oct 1995. Dena S. Pushkin, "Telemedicine: Follow the Money," *Online Journal of Issues in Nursing*, September 30, 2001, http://www.nursingworld. org/. Information retrieved October 2, 2002.

---

[17] Florida was moved to initiate a prison telemedicine program in 1990 after a prison inmate sued the state over inadequate health care and won a $1 million settlement (Blanton and Balch; see Source notes).

[18] According to the consulting firm of Arthur D. Little, cited in *Futurist* (see Source notes).

[19] As of September 2002 the U.S. Congress had not yet acted on proposed legislation (Medicare Remote Monitoring Services Coverage Act) to require Medicare to pay physicians the same amount for remote monitoring of patients' conditions as they are paid for face-to-face consultations.

Chapter 14

Medical Infrastructure

The population of the United States is increasing. At the same time, the number of hospitals is decreasing. Hospital closures and mergers are creating potentially dangerous situations across the country. According to the American Civil Liberties Union (ACLU): the merger of religiously controlled (specifically Catholic) hospitals and secular hospitals present a particular threat to women's health care. But is this a Catholic vs. secular values issue or did this "threat" start long before the first merger between a Catholic and a secular hospital?

Hospice care was envisioned to be "something between a hospital and a home, with the skills of one and the hospitality, warmth, and time of the other."[1] The next two panels present the history of hospice care in America and discuss the influence government intervention has on this hospice care concept.

Both Medicare and Medicaid have been under scrutiny recently as the cost of health care soars. Will the millions of elderly and poor continue to receive health care coverage in the future?

Drug and vaccine shortages are becoming an increasing problem. The next panel discusses the consequences of drug companies halting (or slowing) the manufacture of certain drugs. We also discuss what the Food and Drug Administration is doing about these shortages. In October 2001, bioterrorism became a concern as anthrax was spread through the mail system. Will drug manufacturers be able to produce enough vaccines or antibiotics if a large-scale bioterrorism attack plagues the United States?

Before September 11, 2001, the government focused on health care reform. The skyrocketing costs and the millions of uninsured were on the minds of many. Some of those in the health care profession said that administrative costs, especially those associated with insurance company paperwork, accounted for an increasing share of a patient's health care dollar. In the final panel of this chapter we discuss the medical vs. non-medical costs of health care.

---

[1] Source: "The History of Hospice." Retrieved September 11, 2002 from http://www.cp-tel.net/pamnorth/history.htm.

Hospitals

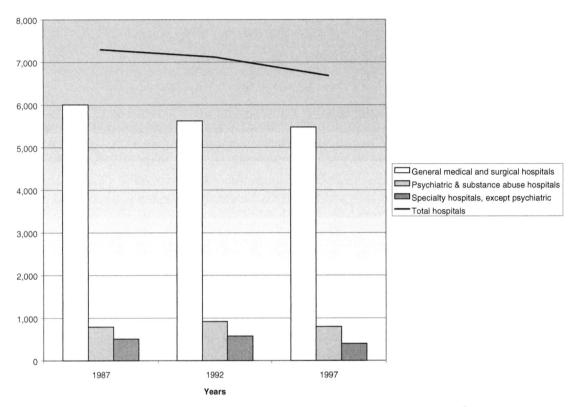

In the 1987 to 1997 decade, the number of hospitals decreased by 8.4%.[2] Only psychiatric & substance abuse hospitals (hereafter "psychiatric hospitals") gained in number during this time period.[3] There were 14 more in 1997 than were present in 1987. But, the number was greatest in 1992: 919 vs. 787 in 1987 and 801 in 1997.

The majority of hospitals are not-for-profit. The one exception to this has been psychiatric hospitals. In 1992, the number of for-profit hospitals of this type exceeded the number in the not-for-profit category. But the decline in the number of for-profit facilities in 1997 (103 vs. 15 in the not-for-profit sector) suggests that many could not make a profit and either merged or closed completely. Despite this, the number of for-profit psychiatric hospitals in 1997 continued to exceed the number in 1987. There were fewer not-for-profit facilities in this sector in 1997 than in 1987.

---

[2] In 2000, the total number of hospitals dropped 20.4% to 5,810 from 7,298 in 1987.

[3] The term "substance abuse hospitals" was included with psychiatric hospitals for the first time in the *1997 Economic Census*. The term seems to have been an added qualifier only. No additional hospitals were included in the statistics. In fact, the number of hospitals in this category fell by 14 from 1992-1997.

Specialty hospitals, except psychiatric followed a similar pattern. The number of for-profit specialty hospitals increased from 1987 to 1992, then decreased again in the five year period 1992-1997. But, despite this decrease, for-profits still outnumbered not-for-profits in 1997. Not-for-profits increased from 1987 to 1992 (just as they had done in the psychiatric hospital sector) before declining in number from 1992 to 1997. In this case, however, the biggest declines were seen in the not-for-profit sector (137 fewer of this, 43 fewer for-profits).

We see a reverse of this pattern in general medical and surgical hospitals. From 1987 to 1992, the number of for-profit hospitals declined (as did not-for-profit), but then increased in number from 1992 to 1997. However, there were fewer specialty hospitals of both types in 1997 than there had been in 1987. A majority of all hospitals were general medical & surgical hospitals (82% in 1987 and 1997, and 79% in 1992).

The table below shows the number of for-profit (taxable) and not-for-profit (exempt) hospitals over the decade.

Number of Hospitals by Tax Exempt Status, 1987-1997

	1987	1992	1997
Total hospitals			
Taxable	1,395	1,403	1,345
Exempt	5,903	5,717	5,340
General medical & surgical hospitals			
Taxable	885	704	792
Exempt	5,121	4,920	4,695
Psychiatric (& substance abuse) hospitals			
Taxable	373	492	389
Exempt	414	427	412
Specialty hospitals, except psychiatric			
Taxable	137	207	164
Exempt	368	370	233

From 1987 to 2000, the population of the United States increased 16.1%. At the same time, the number of hospitals decreased by 20.4%. The next two panels discuss the trends of hospital mergers and their impact on health care.

Sources: U.S. Census Bureau. *1992* and *1997 Economic Census*. Arsen J. Darnay. *Service Industries USA, Fourth Edition*, 1999; Original source: U.S. Census Bureau. *1987 Census of Service Industries*. U.S. Census Bureau. *Statistical Abstract of the United States: 2001*. U.S. Census Bureau. "Your Gateway to Census 2000." Retrieved September 4, 2002 from http://www.census.gov/main/ www/cen2000.html. American Hospital Association. "Fast Facts on U.S. Hospitals from *Hospital Statistics*." Retrieved September 4, 2002 from http://www.hospitalconnect.com/aha/resource_center/fastfacts/fast_facts_US_hospitals.html.

Hospital Merger Aftermath: Secular vs. Religious Values?

Hospital Mergers, 1996-2000

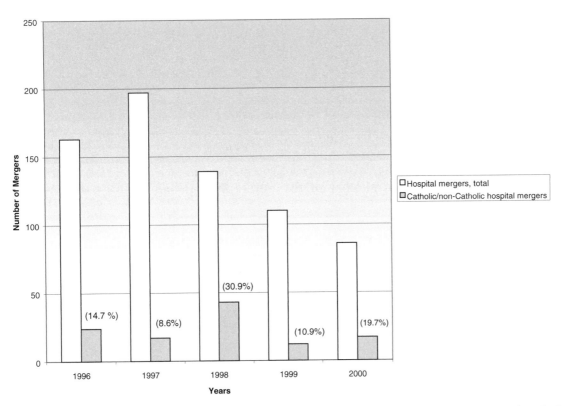

After peaking in 1997, the total number of hospital mergers and acquisitions headed downward. The number of Catholic/non-Catholic hospital mergers fluctuated between 1996 and 2000 (as did their percentage of all mergers, shown in parentheses). This type of merger peaked in 1998.

Since at least 1994, groups such as Catholics for a Free Choice, the American Civil Liberties Union (ACLU), Physicians for Reproductive Choice and Health (PRCH) and MergerWatch have been criticizing the mergers between Catholic and non-Catholic hospitals. MergerWatch is a project of the Education Fund of Family Planning Advocates of New York State, Inc. Criticism has come, specifically, about the impact of mergers on women's reproductive health care. According to the ACLU, "the problem for reproductive health care arises when a religiously controlled institution tries to impose upon its new partners its restrictions against providing certain reproductive services. As a result of these new business relationships, many hospitals no longer dispense contraceptives, provide abortions, or perform surgical sterilizations. This reorganization of health care constitutes one of the most serious and least visible threats to women's access to comprehensive reproductive health services in years."[4]

There have been mergers between secular and religiously controlled hospitals of other denominations, but those mergers haven't met with as much, if any, criticism. Why? According to PRCH and MergerWatch, other denominations such as Presbyterian, Methodist, Jewish, and Episcopalian "provide health care in a nondenominational manner, and do not use religious doctrine to limit health care services." Others, such as the Seventh Day Adventists, Church of Jesus Christ of Latter-Day Saints, and Baptist hospitals impose restrictions on reproductive health care, but Catholic hospitals tend to have the most restrictive policies, especially where abortion is concerned. Catholic hospitals also make up the majority of the religiously controlled hospitals in the U.S.. 18% of the total hospital beds in the U.S. are in religiously controlled hospitals: 15% in Catholic controlled hospitals, 3% in hospitals controlled by other denominations. (In 2000, the number of Roman Catholic controlled hospitals numbered 621 out of 5,810 hospitals total.)

But is the merging of Catholic and non-Catholic hospitals the cause of this decline in the number of hospitals performing comprehensive reproductive health care? Non-Catholic hospitals that merge with Catholic hospitals are expected to follow the tenets of the document *Ethical and Religious Directives for Catholic Health Education*, formulated by the National Conference of Catholic Bishops. This document forbids health care providers in Catholic hospitals from providing abortions, information about contraceptives and contraception (including information about AIDS and STD prevention involving condoms), fertility treatments, and sterilizations. According to Catholics for a Free Choice, "nearly half" of the 127 mergers involving Catholic and secular hospitals from 1990 to 1998 resulted in termination of all or some of their reproductive services. This leaves one to wonder about the more than half previously-secular hospitals that did not change their reproductive health policies.

The number of hospitals performing one aspect of women's reproductive health care, abortions, dropped 50% from 1982 to 1996.[5] The number of counties in the United States with an abortion provider has been decreasing since 1978 (23% in 1978 vs. 14% in 1996).[6] But, the merger "frenzy" between Catholic and non-Catholic hospitals seemed to start in 1994, when there were a total of 19 Catholic/non-Catholic hospital mergers. (From 1990 to 1993, there were a total of 3:1 in 1990 and 2 in 1992.) In comparison to other Western industrialized countries, in 1996, the abortion rate in the U.S. was still the

---

[4] Source: Reproductive Rights Freedom Network. American Civil Liberties Union. "Hospital Mergers: The Threat to Reproductive Health Services," 1997. Retrieved September 4, 2002 from http://www.aclu.org/library/hospital.html.

[5] The number of clinics performing abortions increased 10% from 1982-1996. In 1996, 70% of abortions were being performed in specialized clinics. Only 7% were being performed in hospitals. 1996 is the most recent data available.

[6] The court decision legalizing abortion, Roe v. Wade, was decided on January 22, 1973. In 1978, 1.41 million abortions were performed. In 1996, 1.37 million abortions were performed.

highest: 22.9 per 1,000 women aged 15-44. This suggests that even with the reduction of abortion services at hospitals, the United States still had the best access to these services in the industrialized world.

In terms of overall health care, "in many cities with both Roman Catholic sponsored hospitals and public or private secular hospitals, the former are often regarded as giving better quality of care."[7] What is the impact on quality of care? According to a study of hospital mergers in California (370 hospitals between 1994 and 1996), there is little impact on health care (within the hospital) when hospitals merge. The differences in length of stay and inpatient mortality varied only by fractions of a percentage point.

But, what about access to health care after hospitals merge or close? One of the criticisms levied is that some patients will lose access to health care services. The next panel will discuss this issue.

Sources: Monroe, Stephen, M. and Kathy Hammell. Irving Levin Associates. "Hospital M&A Activity Slow in 2000 As Health Care Industry Begins to Stabilize," March 28, 2001. Retrieved September 4, 2002 from http://www.levinassociates.com/pressroom/press-releases/pr2001/pr103har7.htm. Catholics for Free Choice. "Catholic Health Care." Retrieved September 4, 2002 from http://www.cath4choice.org/nobandwidth/English/healthmergers.htm. American Hospital Association. "Fast Facts on U.S. Hospitals from *Hospital Statistics*™," November 15, 2001. Retrieved September 4, 2002 from http://www.hospitalconnect.com/aha/resource_center/fast-facts/fast_facts_US_ hospitals.html. Linda Villarosa. "Newest Sill for Future Ob-Gyns: Abortion Training." *The New York Times,* June 11, 2002. Physicians for Reproductive Choice and Health and MergerWatch. *Mergers & You: The Physician's Guide to Religious Hospital Mergers*. Retrieved September 4, 2002 from http://www.prch.org/PRCH_Merger_Bro.pdf. B.A. Robinson. "Abortion and Roman Catholic Hospital Mergers," January 29, 2001. Retrieved September 4, 2002 from http://www.religioustolerance.org/abo_rcc.html. Alan Guttmacher Institute and Physicians for Reproductive Choice and Health "Abortion Rates in Western Industrialized Countries." *An Overview of Abortion in the United States,* 2002. Retrieved September 4, 2002 from http://www.agi-usa.org/pubs/abslide/abort_slides.pdf. Stanley K. Henshaw. "Abortion Incidence and Services in the United States, 1995-1996." *Family Planning Perspectives,* November/December 1998. Retrieved September 4, 2002 from http://www.agi-usa.org/pubs/journals/3026398.html. Reproductive Rights Freedom Network. American Civil Liberties Union. "Hospital Mergers: The Threat to Reproductive Health Services." Retrieved September 4, 2002 from http://www.aclu.org/library/hospital.html. Margie Manning. "Patient care unaffected by hospital mergers." *St. Louis Business Journal,* January 26, 1998. Retrieved September 4, 2002 from http://stlouis.bizjournals.com/stlouis/stories/1998/01/26/story7.html. "410 U.S. 113 Supreme Court of the United States Roe, et. al. v. Wade, District Attorney of Dallas County." Retrieved September 20, 2002 from http://members.aol.com/abtrbng/410us113.htm.

---

[7] Source: B.A. Robinson. "Abortion and Roman Catholic Hospital Mergers," January 29, 2001. Retrieved September 4, 2002 from http://www.religoustolerance.org/abo_rcc.htm.

Hospital Closures and Access to Health Care

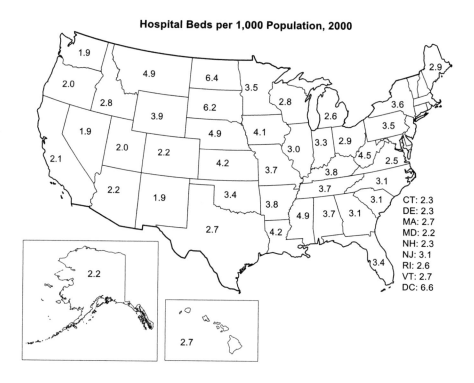

Hospital Beds per 1,000 Population, 2000

CT: 2.3
DE: 2.3
MA: 2.7
MD: 2.2
NH: 2.3
NJ: 3.1
RI: 2.6
VT: 2.7
DC: 6.6

The map shows the number of community hospital beds per 1,000 population.[8] The states with the largest populations do not have the greatest number of hospital beds per 1,000 people. The next table shows the top 5 states ranked according to hospital beds per 1,000 and total population. The national average: 3.0 beds per 1,000.

Top 5 States Ranked by Hospital Beds per 1,000 Population and Total Population

	Beds per 1,000	Population rank		Beds per 1,000	Population rank
District of Columbia	6.6	50	California	2.1	1
North Dakota	6.4	47	Texas	2.7	2
South Dakota	6.2	46	New York	3.6	3
Mississippi, Montana, Nebraska (tied)	4.9	31, 44, 38	Florida	3.4	4
West Virginia	4.5	37	Illinois	3.0	5

---

[8] According to the American Hospital Association, "community hospitals are defined as all nonfederal, short-term general, and other special hospitals. Other special hospitals include obstetrics and gynecology; eye, ear, nose, and throat; rehabilitation; orthopedic; and other individually described specialty services. Community hospitals include academic medical centers or other teaching hospitals if they are nonfederal short-term hospitals. Excluded are hospitals not accessible by the general public, such as prison hospitals or college infirmaries." There are 4,915 community hospitals in the United States. Source: American Hospital Association. "Fast Facts on U.S. Hospitals from *Hospital Statistics*™," November 15, 2001. Retrieved September 4, 2002 from http://www.hospitalconnect.com/aha/resource_center/fastfacts/fast_facts_US_hospitals.html.

Why do some of the least populated states contain the most hospital beds per 1,000? Do these states have higher hospital admissions rates? Not in every case. The next table shows the top 5 states in terms of hospital admissions per 1,000 per year. Only the District of Columbia had the same ranking in both hospital beds and in admissions.[9] West Virginia and Mississippi were in the top 5 in both of these categories.

Top 5 States Ranked by Hospital Admissions per 1,000 Population and Beds per 1,000 Ranking, 2000

	Admissions per 1,000	Beds per 1,000 ranking
District of Columbia	255	1
West Virginia	162	5
Louisiana	155	8
Alabama, Mississippi (tied)	153	14, 4
Pennsylvania	150	18

Twenty-six states had higher rankings for admissions per 1,000 than beds per 1,000, possibly suggesting that there was a shortage of beds in these states. From 1990 to 2000, approximately 500 hospitals closed nationally. In a study of hospitals in 52 mid-sized and large cities by the Robert Wood Johnson Foundation, nearly 28% of the hospital beds were eliminated from 1980 to 1997.

Massachusetts ranked 27th in hospital admissions and 32nd in beds in 2000. More than 30 hospitals closed from 1980 to 2002, and more were warning of closures in 2002. Hospital beds were reduced by 30%: from 23,000 to 16,000 (or 2.5 beds per 1,000 population). In March 2002, Holy Family Hospital in Methune, Massachusetts canceled elective surgeries for a week in order to keep beds open for a backlog of emergency room patients. The same month, the Massachusetts House adopted a resolution urging Governor Jane Swift to declare a public health emergency due to another major hospital closing: Deaconess-Waltham Hospital, a 115-year old community hospital.[10] Deaconess-Waltham expects an $8 million loss in 2002. And, it is not alone. Two thirds of the hospitals in Massachusetts are losing money (LeBlanc).

From 1980 to 2000, 45 hospitals closed in Ohio. But, in Ohio there has been debate about how much these closings truly affected quality and access to health care. "Community groups say low-income people are losing services as more urban or inner-city hospitals close. Yet health care analysts say Ohio still has more hospital capacity than people need, even after this year's closings" (Bonfield).[11] They may both be right. Avondale residents have seen two large hospitals in mostly African American communities close since 1997. One, Bethesda Oak, "was a favorite for seniors because the hospital was on a convenient

---

[9] For all states in 2000, Maine and Utah also ranked the same in both categories.

[10] If this facility closes, it would affect more than 1,200 employees and 200 doctors. "The health system would also lose 163 inpatient beds (including 43 psychiatric beds), more than 6,200 annual inpatient visits, and more than 20,000 yearly emergency visits." Source: Massachusetts Medical Society Online. "MMS Trustees Create Task Force on Hospital Closings – Vital Signs." Retrieved September 10, 2002 from http://www.massmed.org.

[11] Ohio ranked 28th in number of beds and 23rd in hospital admissions.

bus route. Other hospitals...may be close to Bethesda Oak, but getting to the appointments has become more complicated," according to Tom Jones, chairman of the neighborhood public safety task force. But, Bethesda Oak's average bed occupancy was down to 42 patients a day when it closed. Hardly enough to sustain a 450-bed hospital.

Interestingly, the predictors of hospital closures changed from the 1980s to the 1990s. To some extent, however, the predictors are the same. Low occupancy rates, low Medicare admissions, and hospitals surrounded by competitor hospitals may lead to less financially secure hospitals (a predictor from 1990 to 1997, but not from 1980 to 1990).

Predictors of Hospital Closings, 1980-1997

1980-1990	1990-1997
Hospitals with fewer beds	Hospitals with fewer beds
Hospitals in minority neighborhoods	Less financially secure hospitals
Hospitals surrounded by competitor hospitals	Less financial resources relative to patient volume
Patients' length-of-stay longer	
Low occupancy rates	
Low Medicare admissions	

In the "CGE&Y 2002 Hospital Executive Survey," top executives of healthcare facilities nationwide listed the following as the major obstacles to running a thriving hospital. Phrases in bold are terms from the survey.[12]

Inadequate reimbursement levels. Some insurance companies delay payments on valid claims, more uninsured patients are seeking care, and government and managed care reimbursements are inadequate to meet health care costs. In Massachusetts, hospitals say "the single biggest problem" is the reimbursement for Medicaid patients. The state reimburses the hospital at 71 cents on the dollar, which causes a $200 million a year loss to hospitals in that state (LeBlanc).

Severe staffing shortages. Nursing shortages have been a problem for at least 5 years. But, recently shortages in laboratory, information technology, and business office staff have been causing problems in all areas of health care by "driving up costs and threatening patient safety and health" (Lisi).

Unwieldy regulatory requirements. Hospital costs are rising due to more and more government regulation. Hospital officials fear that the new regulations under the Health Insurance Portability and Accountability Act of 1996 (HIPAA) that will take effect in 2003 will just add to the burden.

Rapidly changing patient demands. The aging population will require more specialized care, time with hospital staff, and Medicare/Medicaid resources. "Better informed patients are demanding more specialty services, greater convenience, and additional options for services" (Lisi).

---

[12] CGE&Y stands for Cap Gemini Ernst & Young U.S. LLC. The survey was conducted by Gartner Consulting. Gartner conducted "in-depth telephone interviews" with "nearly four-dozen top executives of healthcare facilities across the nation." (Lisi)

Constrained capacity. Hospital closures and an increasing population are causing more people to be serviced by fewer facilities.

Encroaching specialty facilities. Full-service hospitals are serving more and more of the uninsured and lower income patients, while more of those with health insurance and higher incomes go to specialty hospitals for their care.

Growing liability issues. Malpractice insurance premiums have skyrocketed in the last few years, causing a financial burden on hospitals as well as doctors. In some cases, even when hospitals did not close, certain departments within hospitals did due to an inability to pay for malpractice insurance. In 2002, Methodist Hospital and Mercy Hospital in Philadelphia, PA announced that they were closing their obstetrics departments. In 1999, there were 2,940 maternity units. That is 463 fewer than in 1991. For more information on this topic, see the panel entitled *Is Malpractice Litigation Hazardous to Our Health?* in Chapter 15.

Endangered capital investments. "Constraints on revenue and rising costs make it tougher for hospitals to buy new technology and infrastructure. Hospitals often need state-of-the-art technology to remain competitive and keep up with patient demands" (Lisi). But, not all hospitals see this as an obstacle to becoming financially viable. Newton-Wellesley Hospital, in Massachusetts, recorded losses of $23 million in 1998. Despite this, it invested in new radiology equipment and expanded its emergency, women's health, and pediatric departments. In 2001, it still reported a loss, but only of $5 million. Union Hospital, also in Massachusetts, invested in a new emergency room after reporting losses of $2 million in 1997. In 2001, it recorded a surplus of $5 million.

Sources: The Henry J. Kaiser Family Foundation. "State Health Facts Online." Retrieved September 4, 2002 from http:// www.state healthfacts.kff.org. U.S. Census Bureau. United States Census 2000 Summary File 3. Retrieved September 6, 2002 from http://www.census.gov. U.S. Census Bureau. *Statistical Abstract of the United States, 2001.* American College of Emergency Physicians. "Emergency Medicine Statistical Profile," July 2001. Retrieved September 6, 2002 from http://www.acep.org/. American Hospital Association. "Fast Facts on U.S. Hospitals from *Hospital Statistics*™." Retrieved September 4, 2002 from http://www.hos pital-connect.com/. Tim Bonfield. "Ohio hospitals face stress." *The Cincinnati Enquirer*, August 20, 2000. Retrieved September 6, 2002 from http://enquirer.com/. Robert Wood Johnson Foundation. "Research to Update Information on Urban Hospital Closings, Mergers, and other Reconfigurations," January 2001. Retrieved September 6, 2002 from http://www.rwjf.org. U.S. Department of Health and Human Services. "HHS Issues First Major Protections for Patient Privacy." Retrieved September 10, 2002 from http://www.hhs.gov/. New Jersey Hospital Association. "NJHA Supports Physician Call for Action on Medical Malpractice Crisis," June 13, 2002. Steve LeBlanc. "State beset by hospital closings," March 10, 2002. Retrieved September 6, 2002 from The Ad Hoc Committee to Defend Health Care web site at http://216.36.252.42/ news_state_beset.htm. Chris Lisi. "Top Hospital Executives Identify Leading Trends, Worry About Future in New National Survey," May 9, 2002. Retrieved September 10, 2002 from http://www.us.cgey.com/news/. Massachusetts Medical Society Online. "MMS Trustees Create Task Force on Hospital Closings – Vital Signs," February 25, 2002. Retrieved September 10, 2002 from http://www.massmed.org. John Seewer. "Small-town maternity wards give way to high costs, heavier competition." *The Review*, April 26, 2002. Retrieved September 10, 2002 from http://www.the-review.com. Marie McCullough. "High costs shrink maternity care." *The Philadelphia Inquirer*, July 7, 2002. Retrieved September 10, 2002 from http://www.philly.com/.

Hospice Care

Number of Hospice Patients, 1976-2001

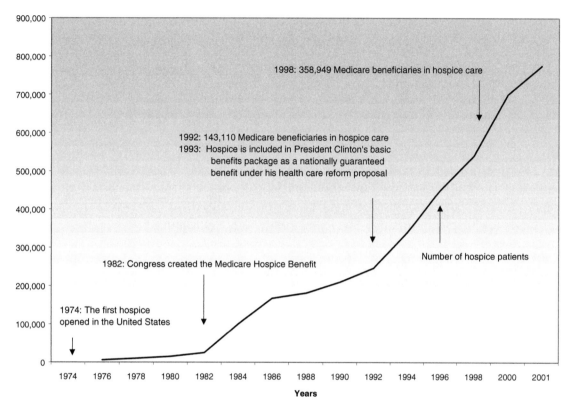

"Palliative care focuses on quality of life, control of pain and symptoms and attention to the psychosocial and spiritual experiences of adapting to advanced illness. Hospice care is a specialized and intensive form of palliative care for patients with advanced, life-threatening illnesses and for their families, emphasizing quality of life, life-closure issues and the relief of suffering" (Beresford).

In 1963, Dr. Cicely Saunders gave a lecture at Yale University on holistic hospice care to students, nurses, social workers, and chaplains. The lecture included photos of terminally ill cancer patients and their families. They showed the differences before and after such care. At the time, Dr. Saunders was in the midst of establishing the first hospice in England, St. Christopher's. In 1965, the Dean of the Yale School of Nursing invited Dr. Saunders to become a visiting faculty member for the spring term. Students who heard her lecture opened the first hospice in the United States in 1974, the Connecticut Hospice. That year, a Connecticut Hospice nurse and a volunteer made their first visit to the home of a terminally ill patient, pioneering the Hospice Home Care movement. In 1980, Connecticut Hospice opened the "first specially-designed, free-standing Hospice InPatient

Care Center in Branford, Connecticut."[13] In 1988, Connecticut Hospice opened the Hospice Cottage for homeless patients.

Why name these facilities "hospices"? According to Dr. Saunders, "'the name hospice, 'a resting place for travelers or pilgrims,' was chosen because this will be something between a hospital and a home, with the skills of one and the hospitality, warmth, and time of the other.'"[1]

In 1972, the U.S. Senate Special Committee on Aging conducted the first national hearings on the subject of death with dignity. Dr. Elisabeth Kübler-Ross, author of the internationally best-selling book *On Death and Dying*, testified saying: "We live in a very particular death-denying society. We isolate both the dying and the old, and it serves a purpose. They are reminders of our own mortality. We should not institutionalize people. We can give more help with home care and visiting nurses, giving families and the patients the spiritual, emotional, and financial help in order to facilitate the final care at home." In 1974, the first hospice legislation was introduced in Congress proposing federal funds for hospice programs. The legislation was not enacted.

In 1978, a U.S. Department of Health, Education and Welfare task force reported that "the hospice movement…is a viable concept and one which holds out a means of providing more humane care for Americans dying of terminal illness while possibly reducing costs. As such, it is the proper subject of federal support." The next year, the Health Care Financing Administration (HCFA) set out to assess the cost effectiveness of hospice care and in 1982 developed the daily reimbursement system for the Medicare Hospice Benefit.[14]

In 1989, a Government Accounting Office study found that only 35% of eligible hospices were Medicare certified. Why? The low payment rates that HCFA established. That same year, Congress gave hospices their first increase in reimbursements and changed the provisions to provide for yearly increases tied to the yearly increases in hospital reimbursements. By 1993 there were 1,288 Medicare certified hospices compared to 31 in 1984.[15] A year later, HCFA, responding to "questionable certifications and recertifications of terminal illnesses," alerted hospices that they will be denied payments if they do not improve their documentation and certification procedures.[16] The conditions of participation

---

[13] The National Cancer Institute (NCI) funded the Connecticut Hospice from 1974 to 1977 "to develop a national demonstration center for home care for the terminally ill and their families." From 1978 to 1980 they funded 26 other hospices. Source: "The History of Hospice." Retrieved September 11, 2002 from http://www.cp-tel.net/pamnorth/ history.htm.

[14] As of 2001, the name was changed to Centers for Medicare and Medicaid Services.

[15] In 2000, 2,912 hospices were Medicare certified. This represented 91% of all hospices.

[16] Medicare funding for hospice care prior to the Balanced Budget Act of 1997 was based on two 90-day benefit periods followed by a 30-day period and an unlimited fourth benefit period. After each period, physicians must certify that the patient has six months or less to live. Currently there are two initial 90-day periods followed by unlimited 60-day periods. The average length of hospice care in 1992 was 64 days. In

and reimbursement in the Medicare Hospice Benefit were rewritten by the HCFA that same year.

From 1976 to 1996, there was a 7,400% increase in the number of hospice patients. But there were still thousands of eligible patients not taking advantage of these services. In 1996, the Robert Wood Johnson Foundation funded a $1.2 million campaign to educate consumers and physicians on end-of-life issues. The Hospice Association of America participated in this campaign. In 2000, 25% of those who died in the U.S., died while receiving hospice care.

The next panel will look at hospice care for Medicare beneficiaries.

Sources: The National Hospice and Palliative Care Organization. "More Patients and Families Choose Hospital Care Each Year." Retrieved September 11, 2002 from http://www.nhpco.org. "The History of Hospice." Retrieved September 11, 2002 from http://www. cp-tel.net/pamnorth/history.htm. National Hospice and Palliative Care Organization. "NHPCO Facts and Figures." Retrieved September 11, 2002 from http://www.nhpco.org. Larry Beresford. National Hospice and Palliative Care Organization and the Center to Advance Palliative Care. *Hospital-Hospice Partnerships in Palliative Care*. Retrieved September 11, 2002 from http://www.nhpco.org. Hospice of Michigan. "Brief history of the hospice movement." Retrieved September 11, 2002 from http://www.hom.org/ movement.html. William J. Scanlon. Health, Education, and Human Services Division. United States General Accounting Office. "Medicare: More Beneficiaries Use Hospice: Many Factors Contribute to Shorter Periods of Use," September 18, 2000. Retrieved September 11, 2002 from http://www.gao.gov/new.items/he00201t.pdf.

2000, it was 48 days. Sources: "The History of Hospice." Retrieved September 11, 2002 from http://www.cp-tel.net/pamnorth/ history.htm. National Hospice and Palliative Care Organization. "NHPCO Facts and Figures." Retrieved September 11, 2002 from http://www.nhpco.org.

Hospice Care for Medicare Patients

Medicare Hospice Patients by Primary Diagnosis, 1992 and 1998

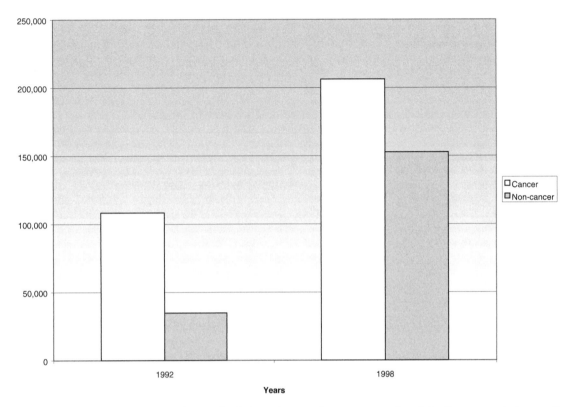

From 1992 to 1998, 58 to 67% of all hospice patients were also Medicare recipients. In 1992, 75.6% of Medicare hospice patients had a primary diagnosis of cancer. In 1998, 57.4% did. As more patients and doctors became aware of hospice services, more patients with non-cancer illnesses chose to take advantage of these services. But, as more patients took advantage of these services the average length of stay in hospice care for Medicare beneficiaries declined (from 74 days in 1992 to 59 days in 1998). Those diagnosed with illnesses other than cancer stay longer in hospice care than those with cancer. But, from 1992 to 1998, the average number of days used by non-cancer patients declined by 38%. The average number of days for cancer patients declined by 14%.

Medicare pays for hospice care when the beneficiary is expected to live 6 months or less. Once cancer patients choose hospice care over curative measures, the disease follows a progression that's fairly easy for the physician to predict. Progression of non-cancer illnesses may be less easy to predict. Those with Alzheimer's disease, for example, may be able to live for many years before the illness finally takes their lives, while others will die after a shorter period of time. The patient, his family, and his physician may postpone the decision to enter hospice care until the patient's heart is weakened or a secondary illness brings him closer to death. And by the time the patient is in that weakened condition, he may have days to live rather than months.

But there are always exceptions to the rule and some patients live longer in hospice care than what their doctor predicted — longer than the 6 months allowed by Medicare. What do hospices do then?

In 1993, the Health Care Financing Administration (HCFA) warned hospices about "questionable certifications and recertifications of terminal illnesses."[17] If they didn't improve their documentation and certification procedures, they would be denied payments.[18] Audits in Puerto Rico in the early 1990s found that hospices there were billing Medicare to take care of patients with illnesses such as obesity and arthritis. In the United States, the government found that Medicare paid out more than $83 million in fraudulent claims. As a result, in the latter part of the 1990s, the HCFA turned to United Government Services (UGS, a subsidiary of Blue Cross & Blue Shield of Wisconsin) to root out fraud.

In 1997, UGS focused its attention on Plattsburgh, N.Y. Some patients of Hospice of North County received letters informing them that they may owe the government thousands of dollars for unneeded hospice care. All the recipients of the letters were diagnosed as terminally ill, in their 80s and 90s, and had outlived the federal guidelines for the Medicare Hospice Benefit.

One woman who received the letter was Rosie DesParois, an 87-year old woman diagnosed with advanced breast and endometrial cancer when she entered hospice. Doctors thought the cancer had spread to her liver, but she was still alive four years later. The hospice was getting $88 a day from Medicare for those four years.

"Mrs. DesParois, a retired nurse…hated taking medicine and was terrified of needles. She loved the idea of spending her final days in her old house that she adored, tinkering in her flower garden, continuing her 70-year cigarette habit. Alice Ballard…[a hospice nurse] visited several times a week and, with the rest of the hospice staff, worked miracles, recalls Mrs. DesParois's granddaughter…. She remembers how hospice nurses brought coffee and doughnuts, gently coaxed her grandmother into taking pills, even hand-washed her collection of antique teacups. [After the hospice dropped Mrs. DesParois, she] couldn't remain at home, and she slid downhill…. She was sent to a hospital, then to a nursing home where she became almost unrecognizable…. She stopped eating almost completely…. Cancer spread to her pancreas and her stomach." She died on September 16, 1998, "away from her home and the hospice staff." The government's cost-saving

---

[17] In 2001, the name was changed to Centers for Medicare and Medicaid Services.

[18] Medicare funding for hospice care prior to the Balanced Budget Act of 1997 was based on two 90-day benefit periods followed by a 30-day period and an unlimited fourth benefit period. After each period, physicians must certify that the patient has six months or less to live. Currently there are two initial 90-day periods followed by unlimited 60-day periods. Sources: "The History of Hospice." Retrieved September 11, 2002 from http://www.cp-tel.net/pamnorth/ history.htm. National Hospice and Palliative Care Organization. "NHPCO Facts and Figures." Retrieved September 11, 2002 from http://www.nhpco.org.

move to stop paying for her hospice care (because "the auditor was dubious that she was that sick") ended up costing Medicare nearly twice what it was paying hospice in nursing home reimbursements.[19]

In May 1998, UGS started to seize the hospice's Medicare reimbursements. A court hearing was held in September 1998 and the hospice won. The judge determined that there had been no fraud. "The fact that some patients 'exceeded those expectations does not indicate that a fraud was perpetrated,' he wrote.[20] Rather he said, 'it suggests that health and illness, life and death, are subject to factors and influences beyond the science of medicine.'" The government appealed and lost. In March 1999, UGS returned $85,000 to the hospice. (Unfortunately, the hospice's court fees were $80,000.)

Now, fear of audits (and litigation, presumably) has changed the way the hospice does business. The hospice is more selective in admitting patients. Patients' records have to be written in such a way as to allow for the least amount of interpretation. No longer are nurses allowed to write: "The patient is stable." Instead, something similar to: "The patient is experiencing improved quality of life with hospice pain and symptom control and supportive services." And, adherence to the "six-month rule" is stricter. Mary Lou Kingsley, a North County hospice nurse, wondered if the hospice, in an attempt to comply with Medicare law, abandoned a patient with heart and lung disease. Nine months after he came to hospice (3 months longer than the 6 months allowed by Medicare) he was doing better, so the hospice discharged him. Two weeks later he was found dead. Did this hospice abandon the original hospice care concept envisioned by Dr. Cicely Saunders (see previous panel)? Are others doing the same in an attempt to ward off the auditors?

Sources: The National Hospice and Palliative Care Organization. "More Patients and Families Choose Hospital Care Each Year." Retrieved September 11, 2002 from http://www.nhpco.org. William J. Scanlon. Health, Education, and Human Services Division. United States General Accounting Office. "Medicare: More Beneficiaries Use Hospice; Many Factors Contribute to Shorter Periods of Use," September 18, 2000. Retrieved September 11, 2002 from http://www.gao.gov/new.items/he00201t.pdf. "The History of Hospice." Retrieved September 11, 2002 from http://www.cp-tel.net/pamnorth/history.htm. Lucette Lagnado. "Rules are Rules: Hospice's Patients Beat the Odds, So Medicare Decides to Crack Down – Terminally Ill Who Don't Die Within a 6-Month Period Risk Losing Coverage – Al Ouimet's 9-Year Survival." *The Wall Street Journal*, June 5, 2000. Retrieved September 11, 2002 from http://www.nhpco.org/public/articles/c025.doc.

---

[19] Source: Lagnado, Lucette. "Rules are Rules: Hospice's Patients Beat the Odds, so Medicare Decides to Crack Down – Terminally Ill Who Don't Die Within a 6-Month Period Risk Losing Coverage – Al Ouimet's 9-Year Survival." *The Wall Street Journal*, June 5, 2000. Retrieved September 11, 2002 from http://www.nhpco.org/public/articles/c025.doc.

[20] In this hospice, 4.8% lived between 7 months and a year and 3.6% lived more than a year. A study of nearly 200,000 hospice patients nationwide by Dr. Nicholas Christakis, an associate professor of medicine and sociology at the University of Chicago, found that 7.2% of hospice patients lived longer than a year.

Medicare

Enrollment in Medicare, 1966-2075

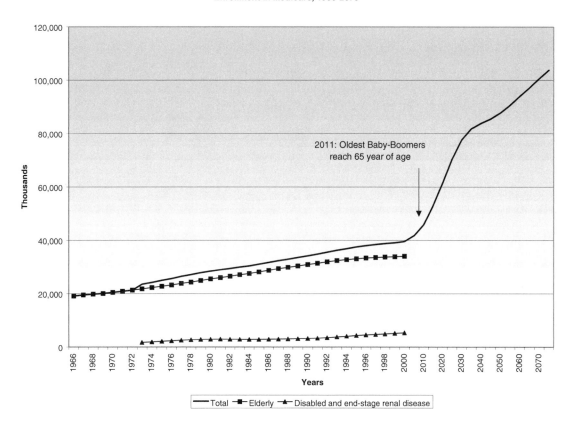

In the 1950s, the elderly were facing a health care crisis. The high cost of health care was "the greatest single cause of economic dependency in old age."[21] From 1900 to 1950, the number of elderly Americans quadrupled, from 3 million to 12 million and only 12.5% had health care coverage. Many private insurers considered the elderly a "bad risk" and would not insure them. Unions had a difficult time finding insurers to cover their retirees.

From 1950 to 1963, the number of elderly rose to 17.5 million. The cost of hospital care was rising at about 6.7% a year, much more than the cost of living. The average income of older Americans was around $1,000 a year. Insurance companies raised premiums and reduced benefits, making private insurance unaffordable or inadequate for the elderly on fixed incomes.

---

[21] Source: Medicare Rights Center. "The History of Medicare and the Current Debate." Retrieved September 13, 2002 from http://www.medicarerights.org/maincontenthistory.html. Those over 65 are eligible for Medicare if they or their spouse worked for at least 10 years in Medicare-covered employment and are a citizen or permanent resident of the United States. Source: Centers for Medicare and Medicaid Services. U.S. Department of Health and Human Services. "Who is Eligible for Medicare?" Retrieved September 16, 2002 from http://www.medicare.gov/Basics/Eli-gibility.asp.

In 1965, Medicare, a government-run insurance program "designed to provide all older adults with comprehensive health care coverage at an affordable cost," was established.[1] In 1972, people with disabilities and people with end-stage renal disease were allowed to enroll in Medicare. Until this time, these two groups were also facing the problem of finding reliable health care coverage.

In 2000, 39.6 million people were Medicare beneficiaries. The table below shows some of the characteristics of Medicare beneficiaries. Most are white, non-Hispanic women with incomes below $25,000. Of those that live alone, 72% are women, 15% are over the age of 85, and 56% have an income of less than $15,000.

Demographics of Medicare Beneficiaries, 2000

Total Medicare beneficiaries[22]	39.6 million
Disabled & end-stage renal disease	5.4 million
Elderly[23]	34.1 million
Age:	
Under 65	5.5 million
% women	44%
65-74	17.9 million
% women	54%
75-84	12.6 million
% women	59%
85+	4.7 million
% women	71%
Race/ethnicity of the elderly:	
White, non-Hispanic	81.6%
Black, non-Hispanic	8.1%
Hispanic	6.5%
Other	3.8%
Race/ethnicity of the disabled:	
White, non-Hispanic	68.1%
Black, non-Hispanic	17.1%
Hispanic	10.1%
Other	4.7%

People are living longer. Soon, the Baby-Boom generation will be eligible for Medicare. Prescription drug costs are rising and increasingly becoming unaffordable to the elderly on fixed incomes. Congress is debating whether to add a prescription drug benefit to Medicare. As a result, the solvency of the Medicare system has been of concern in recent years. The next panel will discuss this issue in more depth.

Sources: Centers for Medicare and Medicaid Services. "Medicare Enrollment: National Trends 1966-1999" and *2002 Annual Report of the Boards of Trustees of the Federal Hospital Insurance Trust and Federal Supplementary Medical Insurance Trust Funds*. Retrieved September 12, 2002 from http://cms. hhs.gov. Office of Research, Development, and Information. Centers for Medicare & Medicaid Services. "Program Information on Medicare, Medicaid, SCHIP, and other programs of the Centers for Medicare & Medicaid Services," June 2002. Retrieved September 12, 2002 from http://cms.hhs.gov/charts/default.asp. Medicare Rights Center. "The History of Medicare and The Current Debate." Retrieved September 13, 2002 from http://www.medicarerights.org/maincontenthistory.html.

---

[22] Numbers do not sum due to rounding.

[23] In November 2000, 34.9 million people were 65 years old and older.

The Solvency of Medicare

Medicare Income, Expenditures, and Trust Fund Assets, Fiscal Year, 1970-2011

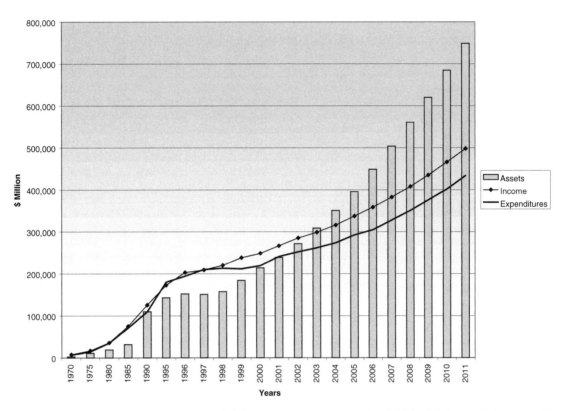

Medicare is the second largest social insurance program. In 1999, 14.1% of the population was enrolled in Medicare. The chart above shows the income, expenditures, and trust fund assets of the Medicare system. Data for 2002 to 2011 are estimates. 1995 and 1997 were the only two years when expenditures exceeded income. But, during these two years, there were more than enough assets in the trust fund to cover the extra expenses.

Medicare benefits consist of two parts: hospital insurance (HI) and medical insurance (SMI).[24] Each of these is funded differently and each fund is kept separate. SMI is funded by premiums paid by beneficiaries (in 2002, $54 a month) and by general revenues. Under current law, SMI premiums and general revenue rates are set yearly to match the projected SMI expenditures for the following year. HI income is linked to payroll tax revenues. Unfortunately, "per capita health care expenditures have increased significantly more rapidly than either wages or the economy overall."[25] As a result, when people debate the solvency of Medicare, they are essentially debating the solvency of the HI por-

---

[24] This is what is commonly known as Part A and Part B Medicare benefits, respectively.

[25] Source: Centers for Medicare and Medicaid Services. *2002 Annual Report of the Boards of Trustees of the Federal Hospital Insurance Trust and Federal Supplementary Medical Insurance Trust Funds.* Retrieved September 12, 2002 from http://cms.hhs.gov/publications/trusteesreport/default.asp.

---

tion.

The graph on the previous page may lead us to believe that income will continue to exceed expenditures, and in the event this doesn't happen (as in 1995 and 1997) there will be enough assets to draw from. But, if we look at costs and income as a percentage of

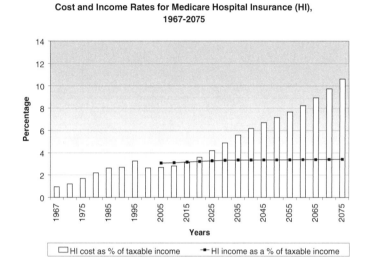

Cost and Income Rates for Medicare Hospital Insurance (HI), 1967-2075

taxable income (next chart) this may not be always the case. In fact, if the Centers for Medicare and Medicaid Services (CMS) projections are accurate (i.e. legislatures do nothing to offset rising costs), trust fund assets will have to be tapped as early as 2016. (The eldest Baby-Boomers will be turning 65 around 2011.) And, unlike previous years, CMS estimates that this withdrawal of assets will be ongoing. No longer will monies be added, and the amount gained through interest payments (assets are invested in U.S. Treasury securities) will be significantly less than what will be paid out. Some estimate that the Medicare trust fund will be insolvent by 2030.

What can be done? In anticipation of rising costs, Congress enacted the Balanced Budget Act of 1997. It created the Medicare+Choice program (M+C). Under the plan, Health Maintenance Organizations (HMOs) provide Medicare beneficiaries a more comprehensive health care coverage than Medicare at an affordable price (albeit only by doctors of and at hospitals in their network).[26] Medicare reimburses HMOs at a given rate for the service provided. This, along with new anti-fraud initiatives (discussed somewhat in the previous panel), preventative-care benefits, a simpler payment system, and establishment of medical savings accounts was expected to save Medicare $115 billion a year.

In reality, expenditures for Medicare decreased $617 million from 1997 to 1999. In 2002, 13% of Medicare beneficiaries were enrolled in M+C or other HMOs (down from 15% in 2001).

From 1999 to 2002, M+C HMOs began pulling out of the program due to inadequate reimbursements and federal regulations. According to Aetna U.S. Healthcare (Aetna), one of the HMOs that pulled out of the M+C program in certain areas, CMS "needs to provide adequate payment rates. While medical inflation increases at a double-digit rate (pharmacy costs alone are expected to rise almost 20 percent this year), the government is

---

[26] Almost all doctors and hospitals accept the Original Medicare Plan.

expected to increase payments to Medicare HMOs by about 5% in 2000." And, speaking about federal regulation, Aetna states: "…the Medicare+Choice interim final regulation is more than 90 pages and there have been more than 100 new mandates since the program's inception." HMOs also spent $95 million a year on a user fee to pay for the Medicare beneficiary information campaign.[27]

From 1999 to 2002, 2.2 million Medicare beneficiaries were affected by HMOs withdrawing from the M+C program or reducing their service areas. 327,000 no longer had access to a M+C plan. From 1999 to 2001, Medicare expenditures increased $29 billion.

In 2000, the Balanced Budget Refinement Act of 1999 (BBRA) was enacted to address the "flawed policy and excessive payment reductions resulting from the Balanced Budget Act (BBA) of 1997. It reflects the commitment of the President, Vice President, Secretary Shalala and Congress to act immediately to ensure that Medicare beneficiaries can continue to receive high-quality, accessible health care."[28] What was its effect on HMOs?

"Although the General Accounting Office and other independent experts believe that managed care plans continue to be overpaid – even after the BBA," reimbursement rates increased. BBRA also provided entry bonuses for HMOs that set up service in counties previously not serviced by HMOs and for HMOs who previously withdrew from an area but decided to provide service again. The BBRA reduced user fees, provided HMOs with greater flexibility in benefits, and reduced quality standards for HMOs. But, despite the $4 billion the BBRA allocated for HMOs, from 2000 to 2002, HMOs continued to withdraw from the M+C program or reduced benefits, affecting 1.8 million people. Will Congress do anything in the future to head off the rising costs of Medicare? Not likely any time soon. The current debate in Congress entails adding prescription drug coverage to the original Medicare plan.

Sources: Centers for Medicare and Medicaid Services. 2002 Annual Report of the Boards of Trustees of the Federal Hospital Insurance Trust and Federal Supplementary Medical Insurance Trust Funds. Retrieved September 12, 2002 from http://cms.hhs.gov/publications/trusteesreport/default.asp. Centers for Medicare and Medicaid Services. "Protecting Medicare Beneficiaries When Their Medicare+Choice Organization Withdraws," September 1, 2001. Retrieved September 12, 2002 from http://cms.hhs.gov/media/press/release.asp. David M. Walker. Comptroller General of the United States. United States Government Accounting Office. "Medicare: Financial Outlook Poses Challenges for Sustaining Program and Adding Drug Coverage," April 17, 2002. Retrieved September 12, 2002 from http://www.gao.gov/new.items/d02643t.pdf. Aetna U.S. Healthcare. "Current Medicare Issues," August 2001. Retrieved September 13, 2002 from http://www.aetna.com/public_policy_issues/medicare.htm. The Majority Staffs. House and Senate Committees on the Budget. "The Balanced Budget Act of 1997: Summary of Provisions," July 30, 1997. Retrieved September 13, 2002 from http://www.house.gov/budget/papers/mainsumm.htm. Office of Research, Development, and Information. Centers for Medicare and Medicaid Services. "Program Information on Medicare, Medicaid, SCHIP, and other programs of the Centers for Medicare & Medicaid Services," June 2002. Retrieved September 12, 2002 from http://cms.hhs.gov/charts/default.asp. Centers for Medicare and Medicaid Services. "The 2001 Medicare and Medicaid Statistical Supplement to the Health Care Financing Review." Retrieved September 12, 2002 from http://cms.hhs.gov/review/supp/table10a.pdf. The Office of Congressman Neil Abercrombie. "Balanced Budget Refinement Act of 1999: Highlights." Retrieved September 13, 2002 from http://datahub-3.datahub.com/.

---

[27] Source: Aetna U.S. Healthcare. "Current Medicare Issues," August 2001. Retrieved September 13, 2002 from http://www.aetna.com/public_policy_issues/medicare.htm.

[28] Source: The Office of Congressman Neil Abercrombie. "Balanced Budget Refinement Act of 1999: Highlights." Retrieved September 13, 2002 from http://datahub-3.datahub.com/.

Medicaid and the Uninsured

Persons Served by Medicaid, 1977-1998

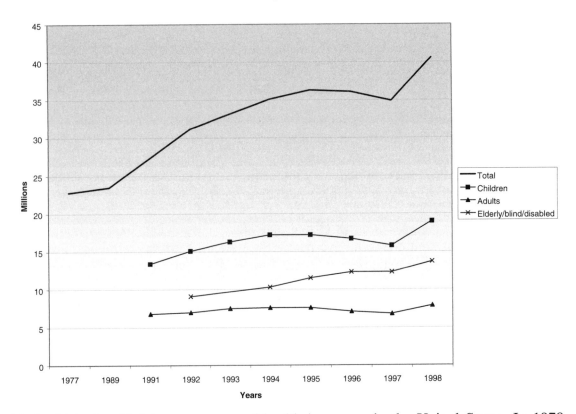

Medicaid is the third largest source of health insurance in the United States. In 1978, Medicaid covered 9.1% of the population, in 1998 12.0%. This same year, 18% of the non-elderly population had no health insurance.[29] The graph shows the number of persons for whom a Medicaid claim was paid during that year. Most of those served by Medicaid are children (in 1998, 51%).[30] 1998 was the first year those served by managed care Medicaid plans[31] were added to the statistics.

Medicaid was established in 1965 as part of the same legislation that established Medicare. Before the law passed, state and local governments, charities, and community hospitals provided health care for the poor. Starting in 1950, the federal government provided matching funds for state payments to medical providers for individuals receiving public assistance monies. In 1960, the Kerr-Mills Act established a program called

---

[29] Nearly all persons over the age of 65 are covered under Medicare.

[30] In 1998, 57% of the uninsured lived in households with children.

[31] The Balanced Budget Act of 1997 provided new managed care options for Medicaid. But managed care Medicaid plans have existed before this. In 1996, 40.1% of Medicaid recipients were in managed care plans. In 2001, 56.8% were.

"Medical Assistance for the Aged." Federal funds were given to states that covered the "medically needy" elderly: people who did not qualify for public assistance, but needed assistance with medical expenses. The Medicaid program is an extension of the Kerr-Mills Act.

Medicaid provides three types of benefits: (1) health insurance for low-income families with children and the disabled, (2) long-term care for the elderly and disabled, and (3) supplemental coverage for low-income Medicare beneficiaries for services not covered by Medicare.

Each state, under broad federal guidelines, establishes its own eligibility requirements, benefits, payment rates, and program administration for Medicaid. Not all people with low incomes are eligible. However, new eligibility requirements were drafted in the 1980s, and Medicaid program waivers allowed states to extend Medicaid benefits beyond the traditional groups (i.e. aged, blind, disabled, families with children, and pregnant women).

Federal regulations mandate that state Medicaid programs cover certain people and services. Federal regulations also provide options for extending coverage.

But, what about the 43.9 million Americans, in 1998, without health insurance coverage?[32] Why aren't they covered under Medicaid? Most are the employed and their dependents.[33] 73% live at or above the federal poverty level of about $16,450 per year for a family of four. 19% of uninsured working families work two or more full-time jobs. And, in 32 states, parents who work full-time for minimum wage ($5.15/hr or about $10,700 a year) are not eligible for Medicaid.

Why can't Medicaid be extended to cover the currently uninsured? In the next panel we'll take a look at Medicaid expenditures.

Sources: Health Care Financing Administration. U.S. Department of Health and Human Services. *Chartbook 2000: A Profile of Medicaid,* September 2000. Retrieved September 16, 2002 from http://cms.hhs.gov/charts/medicaid/2Tchartbk.pdf. Centers for Medicare and Medicaid Services. "National Summary of Medicaid Managed Care Programs and Enrollment June 30, 2001." Retrieved September 16, 2002 from http://cms.hhs.gov/medicaid/managedcare/trends01.pdf. The Henry J. Kaiser Family Foundation. The Kaiser Commission on Medicaid and the Uninsured. *Uninsured in America: Key Facts*, March 2000. Available online: http://www.pbs.org/newshour/health/uninsured/kaiserstudy/kaiser_key_facts.pdf.

---

[32] In 1988, there were 33.6 million Americans without health insurance coverage. The number of uninsured grew by 30.6% from 1988-1998.

[33] In a survey cited in *Uninsured in America* (see source), 64% of the uninsured said that the high cost of health insurance is preventing them from having coverage. In the 1990s, employees were expected to pay more and more of their health care premiums. As a result, employees paid three times as much for health care benefits in 1998 as they did in 1977.

The Solvency of Medicaid

Medicaid Enrollment, 1990-2007, and Estimated Federal Share of Medicaid Payments per Enrollee, 1996-2007

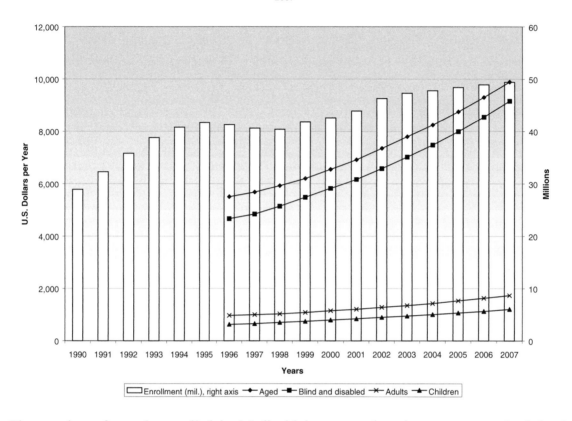

The number of people enrolled in Medicaid is expected to increase — as is federal spending per enrollee. Although 51% of Medicaid beneficiaries are children, they are the least costly (per person) to the program; children are least likely to need costly medical intervention. Adults generally require more costly medical care, therefore expenditures for this population are slightly higher. Not surprisingly, the most expensive to insure under Medicaid are the aged and the disabled. Both of these populations may require more costly medical care over a longer period of time (such as nursing home care). Some elderly Medicare beneficiaries are also eligible for Medicaid payments to help with their Medicare premiums and other health related expenses.

Despite the increase in federal Medicaid funding, states have been cutting benefits to their enrollees. Why? Pressure to balance budgets (49 states have legislation mandating a balanced budget). In 2001, states faced a total budget deficit of $40-50 billion ($4.4 billion in total Medicaid deficit alone).[34] Medicaid expenditures were the second largest state budget expenditure, next to education (15% of the average state budget in 1999).[35]

---

[34] 31 states reporting. North Dakota had the smallest Medicaid budget deficit: $1.1 million. Texas had the largest: $716.7 million. Source: National Association of State Budget Offices. National Governors Asso-

In August 2001, the Congressional Budget Office (CBO) estimated that state revenue would grow by 2.3% in the next fiscal year, but the CBO also estimated that Medicaid expenditures would grow by 9%. "That disparity is unsustainable [even] in a booming economy," according to Matt Salo, chief health lobbyist of the National Governors Association.

In the third quarter of 2001, 31 states experienced declining state and local tax revenue. By February 2002, 24 states were in and 17 states were nearing recession. Unfortunately, when states experience a recession, more people are unemployed and the numbers of those applying for Medicaid and other public assistance increases. At the same time, with fewer people working, tax revenues drop. Faced with mounting deficits in 2002, legislatures in some states cut their Medicaid programs.

In Missouri, eligibility requirements were tightened. This eliminated insurance coverage for 36,000 low-income parents.[36] Medicaid services were also cut back substantially. Health services for new mothers were reduced, affecting 160,000 women. Dental services were dropped for low-income adults, affecting 300,000 people. The state also imposed stricter limits on which drugs can be prescribed without prior authorization. These measures reduced expenditures by $360 million.

Montana increased the amount all adult, elderly, and disabled Medicaid beneficiaries must pay when they use medical services (5% of all expenses). This includes prescription drugs and doctor's office visits. The charge for hospital admission is now $200. (In order to be eligible for Medicaid in Montana, a person's income cannot be over $10,032 a year or $836 a month.[37]) Health care provider reimbursements were reduced by 2.6% also. According to the Center for Budget and Policy Priorities, increasing out-of-pocket costs for those least able to pay will lead to more beneficiaries avoiding or delaying medical care. And, reducing Medicaid reimbursements to providers may lead some to stop accepting Medicaid patients.

Besides the impact on beneficiaries, some criticize these cuts as harmful to the states' economies. For every dollar cut from the state Medicaid program, the state loses $1 to $3 in federal matching money. "For example, by cutting its Medicaid program by $66 million, … South Carolina saved $20 million in state dollars but gave up $46 million in federal matching funds that could have helped the state achieve a faster economic recovery" (Landa). Not to mention the cuts that hospitals have to make when Medicaid money is cut: according to Diane Rowland, executive Director of the Kaiser Commission on Medi-

---

ciation. *Medicaid and Other State Healthcare Issues: The Current Situation,* May 2002. Retrieved September 18, 2002 from http://www.nasbo.org/Publications/PDFs/fsmedicaidmay2002.pdf.

[35] Medicaid funds comprised 43.6% of all federal funds provided to states in 1999.

[36] Previously, the income limit for a family of three was $15,000. This was lowered to $11,600.

[37] As of July 1, 2000.

---

caid and the Uninsured, "the largest employer in most [small towns] is the health care system, either the hospital or the community health center.... Many of these centers and hospitals are highly dependent on Medicaid revenue.... In the absence of Medicaid, the patients don't go away, the revenue just goes away, and the jobs go away."

Sources: Committee on the Budget. The United States Senate. "Medicaid." Retrieved September 17, 2002 from http://www.senate. gov/~budget/republican/latest%20data/medicaid.htm. Amy Snow Landa. "Medicaid morass: States are cutting funds to make up for major revenue shortfalls." *American Medical News*, January 7, 2002. Retrieved September 18, 2002 from http://www.ama-assn.org/ sci-pubs/amnews/pick_02/gvsa0107.htm. National Association of State Budget Officers. National Governors Association. *Medicaid and Other State Healthcare Issues: The Current Situation*, May 2002. Retrieved September 18, 2002 from http://www.nasbo.org/ Publications/PDFs/fsmedicaidmay2002.pdf. Leighton Ku, et. al. Center on Budget and Policy Priorities. "State Medicaid Cutbacks and the Federal Role in Providing Fiscal Relief to States," August 2, 2002. Retrieved September 18, 2002 from http://www.cbpp.org/7 -12-02health.pdf. Mark M. Zandi. Economy.com."The Outlook for State Tax Revenues," 2002. Retrieved September 18, 2002 from http://www.nga.org/cda/files/TAXREVENUES02.pdf. Matthew Broaddus, et. al. Center on Budget and Policy Priorities. *Expanding Family Coverage: States' Medicaid Eligibility Policies for Working Families in the Year 2000*, February 13, 2002. Retrieved September 18, 2002 from http://www.cbpp.org/1-2-02health.pdf. Health Care Financing Administration. U.S. Department of Health and Human Services. *Chartbook 2000: A Profile of Medicaid,* September 2000. Retrieved September 16, 2002 from http://cms.hhs.gov/ charts/medicaid/2Tchartbk.pdf.

Drug and Vaccine Shortages

National Drug Shortages, 1980-2001

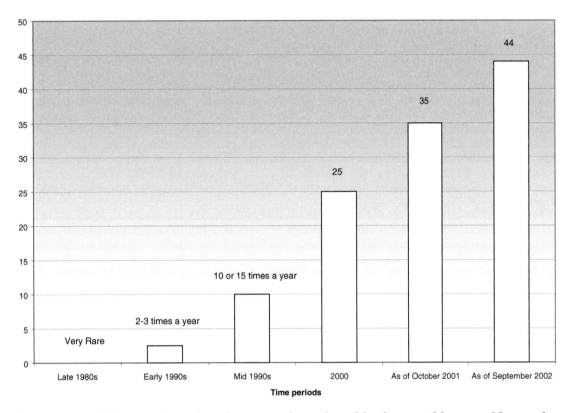

The number of drug and vaccine shortages skyrocketed in the past 20 years. No one kept an accurate track of the number of shortages until 2000 when the University of Utah's Drug Information Service began compiling Drug Product Shortages Bulletins in 2000. The U.S. Food and Drug Administration (FDA) also maintains a web site detailing the "medically necessary" drugs that are in short supply.[38] The number of drugs on these two lists varies because of the "medically necessary" condition imposed by the FDA. As of September 2002, the FDA lists 7 drug shortages and 5 drugs that have a limited distribution. In some parts of the country, the situation is worse. Tony Czaplicki, pharmacy director for Montclair Baptist Medical Center, maintains a list of 3,600 back-ordered drugs.

---

[38] According to the FDA, a drug is considered medically necessary "if it is used to treat or prevent a serious disease or medical condition, and there is no other available source of that product or alternative product that is judged by medical staff to be an adequate substitute. Patient 'inconvenience' alone is an insufficient basis to classify a product as a medical necessity." Source: Center for Drug Evaluation and Research. Food and Drug Administration. "Definition of a Medically Necessary Product," July 6, 2001. Retrieved September 18, 2002 from http://www.fda.gov/cder/drug/shortages/presentation/sld005.htm.

The most recent shortages? Anti-inflammatory steroid injections, antibiotics, and vaccines.[39]

All the data in the graph on the previous page are from the Drug Information Service (DIS) at the University of Utah Hospitals and Clinics in Salt Lake City. Data before 2000 are estimates given by Dr. Linda S. Tyler, pharmacy manager at DIS. The data includes drugs and vaccines.

Why the shortages? Manufacturing problems, supplier problems, shortage of active pharmaceutical ingredients, enforcement of FDA regulations, natural disasters that destroy raw materials, packaging difficulties, and corporate decisions to discontinue drugs all contribute to drug and vaccine shortages. Another contributor: just-in-time inventories.

Many hospitals used to keep two-week supplies of drugs. But with health care plans limiting the list of "acceptable" drugs and hospitals cutting funds for the purchase of (high cost) drugs, most hospitals only keep a three or four day supply. Some drugs have to be ordered on demand. In 2002, when a doctor at Long Island Jewish Medical Center prescribed a cancer drug for a patient undergoing a bone marrow transplant, the pharmacist, James Abberton, had to fill out a form and fax it to the drug company. "'Five years ago, I could buy 400 bottles and keep them on supply. Today, I can only get it for one patient at a time,' states Abberton." (Talan). And, that patient is lucky. In some cases, the drug that is needed is not available. As of April 2002, intravenous ganciclovir (used to treat severe infections in AIDS patients) could not be obtained.[40]

In some cases, drug manufacturers discontinue old products and replace them with new ones. Why do manufacturers discontinue effective drugs? When drug companies merge, the new corporations often trim their product lines. Also, shareholder pressures may lead executives to discontinue products that do not generate profits.

Meanwhile, the doctor, pharmacist, and patient are left to find alternatives (if they exist). Unfortunately, "certain well-established drugs have safety profiles that are just better than the alternatives," according to Joseph Deffenbaugh, professional practice associate at the American Society of Health-System Pharmacists. And switching drug therapies can have adverse effects on the patient's health. Doctors may have to use unfamiliar drugs and as a result, run the risk of giving the patient the improper dosage. The patient has to be monitored more closely to determine the alternative drug's effectiveness (and any side-effects). Then, when the original drug comes back on the market (if it wasn't discontinued), the doctor must monitor the patient's health closely in the transition back to the

---

[39] Early in 2002, 1.1 million doses each of varicella (chicken pox) and MMR (measles, mumps, rubella) vaccine were on backorder nationwide.

[40] Roche Pharmaceuticals, which manufactures this drug, wrote doctors a letter stating that this drug would be available later that spring. But as of August 2, 2002, the drug was still listed on the DIS drug shortage list.

original drug. In some cases, patient deaths can occur when drugs and vaccines are taken off the market. In 2000, Wyeth Laboratories decided to stop production of the adenovirus vaccine. That year, two U.S. Navy recruits died of adenovirus infections and thousands of others were sickened. This virus is common in boot camp barracks — but until that year every recruit was vaccinated against the illness.

And, yet, some suppliers are getting the drugs that are (supposedly) in short supply. When hospital pharmacies cannot get a drug from their usual wholesaler, and the manufacturer does not tell them when (or if) the drug will become available again, some pharmacists buy the drug from other wholesalers and distributors. And pay top dollar. In some cases, these suppliers seek out the pharmacists. Brian D. Benson, pharmacy manager for Iowa Lutheran Hospital in Des Moines, receives telephone calls and faxes from secondary wholesalers that advertise "products that are generally unavailable and have a 200% markup on the price." Benson suggests that state boards of pharmacy investigate these wholesalers "to see if hoarding is a regular practice for some companies." Unfortunately, most states do not have a lot of idle investigators just sitting around. Iowa employs only three investigators for the entire state.[41]

Can anything be done about the shortages? "The government, and specifically the FDA, cannot tell the unregulated drug companies what to do or what to produce." (Everett). In some cases, when the FDA enforces regulations governing manufacturing practices (quality control is under the FDA jurisdiction) more shortages occur. "On May 18, 2002, the FDA fined Schering-Plough $500 million for poor manufacturing practices in 90% of its drug products since 1998. The FDA fine covered 125 prescription and non-prescription drugs…. As a part of the settlement, the company was to pay an additional $175 million if it failed to improve manufacturing practices at all four of its plants. Rather than upgrade its laboratories and factories, Schering-Plough simply decided to suspend production of 73 products. As with the suspension of influenza vaccine production by two makers last year, the result is instant shortages" (Everett).

Sources: Maguire, Phyllis. "Drug shortages raise new fears about patient care." *ACP-ASIM Observer*, December 2001. Retrieved September 18, 2002 from http://www.acponline.org/journals/news/dec01/drug_shortage.htm. Drug Shortages Management Resources Center. University of Utah. "Drug Product Shortage Bulletins." Retrieved September 18, 2002 from http://www.ashp.org/shortages. Center for Drug Evaluation and Research. U.S. Food and Drug Administration. "Definition of a Medically Necessary Product" and "Drug Shortages." Retrieved September 18, 2002 from http://www.fda.gov/cder/drug/shortages/. Jamie Talan. "Doctors encounter drug shortages." *The Detroit News*, April 14, 2002. Retrieved September 18, 2002 from http://www.detnews.com/2002/health/0204/17/a03-464741.htm. Donna Young. American Society of Health System Pharmacists. "Drug Shortages Frustrate Health Care Providers," April 4, 2002. Retrieved September 18, 2002 from http://www.ashp.org. Kelly McClurg. "Pharmaceutical prices are up, availability down," *Birmingham Business Journal*, July 12, 2002. Retrieved September 18, 2002 from http://birmingham.bizjournals.com/birmingham/stories/2002/07/15/story3.html. Centers for Disease Control. "Notice to Readers: Shortage of Varicella and Measles, Mumps and Rubella Vaccines and Interim Recommendations from the Advisory Committee on Immunization Practices." *MMWR*, March 8, 2002. Retrieved September 18, 2002 from http://www.cdc.gov/mmwr/preview/mmwrhtml/mm5109a6.htm. Linda Everett. "U.S. Hospitals Face Critical Drug Shortages." *Executive Intelligence Review*, August 9, 2002. Retrieved September 19, 2002 from http://www.larouchepub.com/other/2002/2930drug_shtge_ii.html.

---

[41] Source for all quotes in this paragraph: Young, Donna. American Society of Health-System Pharmacists. "Drug Shortages Frustrate Health Care Providers," April 4, 2002. Retrieved September 18, 2002 from http://www.ashp.org.

Defending the U.S. Against Bioterrorism

Licensed vaccines, 1999	Vaccines in research and development, 1999
Anthrax	Vaccinia (cell-culture)[42]
Smallpox	Botulinum toxoids
Plague	Tularemia
	Q fever
	Venezuelan encephalitis
	Eastern equine encephalitis
	Western equine encephalitis

Federal reserves of antibiotics and vaccines	
Antibiotics to treat anthrax, 2001	Treatments for 2 million people for 60 days
Antibiotics to treat anthrax, 2002 goal	Treatments for 12 million people for 60 days
2002 budget allocation for antibiotics to treat anthrax	$643 million
Doses of smallpox vaccine, 2001	15 million
Doses of smallpox vaccine, 2002 goal	300 million
2002 budget allocation for stockpiling smallpox vaccine	$509 million

October 4, 2001. The day "bioterrorism" became reality in the United States. On this day the Palm Beach County Health Department, the Florida State Department of Health, and the Centers for Disease Control (CDC) reported that a 63-year old patient was hospitalized with inhalation anthrax. That patient later died. By December 2001, 22 cases of anthrax had been reported.

That same month, the Bush Administration asked for $1.5 billion in emergency funds for the Department of Health and Human Services (HHS) to help in their response to bioterrorism attacks. Much of the money was to go towards increasing the national supply of antibiotics to treat anthrax and increasing the national supply of the smallpox vaccine.

With the growing crisis of drug shortages in the United States (see previous panel), can America's drug companies manufacture millions of doses of antibiotics and vaccines in just one year?

In October 2001, HHS contracted with Bayer Corporation to provide the government with 100 million tablets of Cipro, an antibiotic used to treat anthrax cases. The $95 million agreement also calls for Bayer to rotate the government inventory to "assure the American public a continuously fresh supply of Cipro."[43] This increase in reserves would allow 12 million people to be treated for anthrax. The contract provides for two more orders of 100 million tablets if needed. Cipro makes up about 10% of the antibiotic reserves in the National Pharmaceutical Stockpile (NPS). Anthrax is treated with a combination of antibiotics. Cipro is used for the first 5 days in a 60-day antibiotic regimen.

---

[42] A smallpox vaccine.

[43] Source: U.S. Department of Health and Human Services. "HHS, Bayer Agree to Cipro Purchase." *HHS News,* October 24, 2001. Retrieved September 19, 2002 from http://www.hhs.gov.

In November 2001, HHS signed a $428 million fixed-price contract with Acambis Inc. (and its subcontractor Baxter International Inc.) to produce 155 million doses of the smallpox vaccine by the end of 2002. This is in addition to what was agreed upon in earlier contracts. In September 2000, the CDC contracted with Acambis to produce 40 million doses of the vaccine to be delivered by 2004. But, in September 2001, the contract was renegotiated and Acambis agreed to produce and deliver 54 million doses by late 2002. In addition to these efforts, National Institute of Allergy and Infectious Diseases studies indicate that diluting the existing supply of the vaccine (which has been stored since 1983) will create 77 million doses. All totaled, the NPS should have 286 million doses of the smallpox vaccine by the end of 2002. Nearly enough doses for everyone in the United States.[44]

Sources: Butler, Mary Ellen. "HHS To Use Emergency Funds For Bioterrorism." *U.S. Medicine*, November 2001. Retrieved September 19, 2002 from http://www.usmedicine.com/. U.S. Department of Health and Human Services. "HHS, Bayer Agree to Cipro Purchase." and "HHS Awards $428 Million Contract to Produce Smallpox Vaccine." *HHS News*, various dates. Retrieved September 19, 2002 from http://www.hhs.gov. Philip K. Russell. "Vaccines in Civilian Defense Against Bioterrorism." *Emerging Infectious Diseases*, July-August 1999. Retrieved September 19, 2002 from http://www.cdc.gov/ncidod/EID/vol5no4/pdf/russell.pdf. Centers for Disease Control. "Ongoing Investigation of Anthrax – Florida, October 2001" and "Update: Investigation of Bioterrorism-Related Anthrax – Connecticut, 2001." *MMWR*, various dates. Retrieved September 19, 2002 from http://www.cdc.gov/mmwr/.

---

[44] As of September 19, 2002, there were 288 million people in the U.S. Source: U.S. Census Bureau.

Health Services: Medical vs. Non-Medical

Health Services Employment, 1998 and 2001

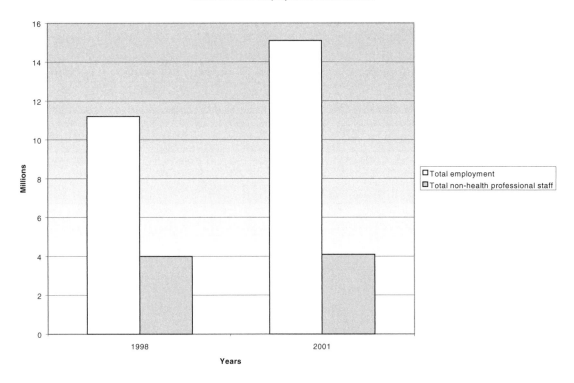

From 1998 to 2001, the number of health service employees increased by 35%, from 11.2 million to 15.1 million. The number of health professionals (hereafter "medical professionals") increased by 53%: 7.2 million to 11.0 million. The number of non-health professionals (hereafter "non-medical staff") increased by only 2.5%: from 4.0 million to 4.1 million. In 1998, non-medical staff made up 36% of the health services workforce. In 2001, 27.2%.

The smaller chart shows the number of medical professionals and the number of non-medical staff by employment location. The chart also shows their ratio. Physicians' offices have the highest percentage of non-medical staff: 46%. Home health care providers have the lowest percentage: 16%. The percentage of non-medical staff in hospitals equaled the average for all health care venues.

What about administrative expenditures? The table below lists the top 11

Health Services Employment by Location, 1998

hospital expenditures (by percentage) for 1990 and 1994 (the latest data available). The list is in 1990 ranking order. The numbers in parentheses represent the rank in 1994. The parentheses will only appear if the ranking is different than in 1990. In both cases, the largest single expenditure was for administrative and general costs. These expenditures increased and general routine care expenditures decreased. Total administrative costs accounted for 26% of hospital costs in 1994, up from 24.6% in 1990 ($78 billion and $54 billion, respectively).[45]

Top 11 Hospital Expenditures

Percentage of Total Hospital Costs, 1990 and 1994

	1990 (%)	1994 (%)
Administrative and general	14.22	15.20
Adult and pediatric general routine care	14.05	12.57
Employee benefits	6.80	7.79
Capital related costs – buildings and fixtures	5.93	5.19
Laboratory	5.31	5.05
Radiology – diagnostic	3.89	3.88
Operation of plant	3.58	(9) 3.22
Operating room	3.47	(7) 3.57
Dietary	3.38	(11) 2.81
Capital related costs – movable equipment	3.20	(8) 3.45
Drugs charged to patients	2.91	(10) 3.04

According to the American Medical Student Association (AMSA) web site, the United States spends about $1,000 per capita on administrative costs. Canada spends only $250. Many who advocate universal health care cite this disparity as a positive money-saving feature of a single-payer system of health care. With the money saved (a projected $100 billion according to the Government Accounting Office), the government can insure the currently uninsured and underinsured.

Before September 11, 2001, health care reform, including the issue of universal health care, was on the minds of lawmakers. Since then, other issues have crowded out reform. But with increasing administrative costs taking money away from clinical services, will lawmakers consider legislative measures to reverse this situation in the future?

Sources: Bureau of Health Professions. National Center for Health Workforce Information and Analysis. U.S. Department of Health and Human Services. HRSA State Health Workforce Profiles -- Alabama, December 2000. Bureau of Health Professions. "More than 1 in 10 Americans works in health care or is a health professional." Original source: Bureau of Labor Statistics. Retrieved September 20, 2002 from http://bhpr.hrsa.gov. Steffie Woolhandler, et. al. "Administrative Costs in U.S. Hospitals" and "Costs of Care and Administration At For-Profit and Other Hospitals in the United States." The New England Journal of Medicine, various dates. Retrieved September 20, 2002 from http://www.nejm.org. National Center for Health Statistics. *Health, United States, 2001 With Urban and Rural Health Chartbook,* 2001. Retrieved September 20, 2002 from http://www.cdc.gov/nchs/data/hus/hus01.pdf. American Medical Student Organization. "AMSA's Universal Health Care Initiative." Retrieved September 20, 2002 from http://www.amsa.org/hp/uhc-initiative.cfm.

---

[45] Figures were based on total non-federal hospital expenditures for 1990 and 1995. Source: National Center for Health Statistics. *Health, United States, 2001 With Urban and Rural Health Chartbook,* 2001. Retrieved September 20, 2002 from http://www.cdc.gov/nchs/. The "Administrative and general" category includes financial management and planning, accounts payable, patient billing, payroll, etc.

Chapter 15

Funding

This chapter begins by looking at some of the issues dealing with federal funding of health research and development (R&D). Growth in funding for health R&D from 1953 to the present has exceeded the growth rate of defense R&D. Does the government spend the most money researching the biggest killers of our day? Or do "special interest groups" have some influence?

Next we take a look at some of the *Healthy People 2010* goals. Since 1980, the U.S. Department of Health and Human Services has released reports detailing healthy living objectives for the decade to come. One of the main goals in *Healthy People 2010*, is to increase healthy life expectancy. In the 20th century, we have accomplished this goal. In 1900, the average life expectancy was a little over 46 years — in 2000, 76.9 years. But, what can we do to live a healthier (not just longer) life? What is the federal government doing to encourage us?

The next three panels discuss some of the leading health concerns stated in the report *Healthy People 2010: Understanding and Improving Health.* A 1993 study linked 14% of all deaths in the United States to a sedentary lifestyle and poor dietary habits. The percentage of obese people nearly doubled from 1990 to 2000. What is the government doing to encourage people to get moving? According to this report, "cigarette smoking is the single most preventable cause of disease and death in the United States." Is funding for tobacco control programs proportional to the prevalence of cigarette smoking? According to the *2000 National Survey of Substance Abuse Treatment Services,* in 1999, 14.2 million people aged 12 and older used illicit drugs and 44.6 million binged on alcohol at least once in the month prior to taking the survey. Over 1 million people were in treatment programs for substance abuse. What is the government's funding priority: prevention or treatment?

The last two panels examine funding of a different kind. Most medical students receive loans to pay for their education. Tuition, fees, and housing costs are rising and students are graduating with more and more debt. Is there anything being done at the government level to help graduates pay off this debt? The last panel examines medical malpractice insurance premiums. Doctors are leaving the profession or moving to other states where insurance premiums are lower, leaving doctor shortages in some parts of the country. What is causing the skyrocketing insurance premium rates? Is anything being done to bring rates down to affordable levels?

Government Funding Priorities

U.S. Government Research and Development Outlays, 1949-2003

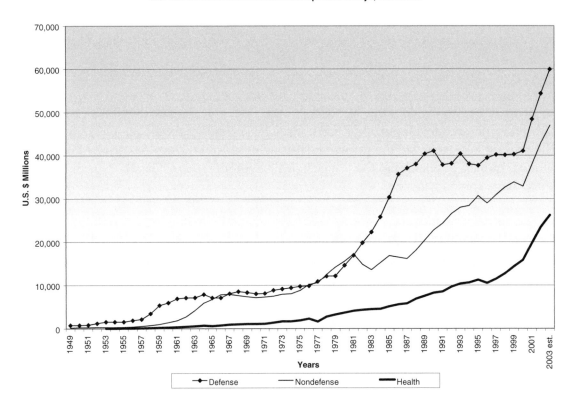

Government spending for research and development (R&D) has been and continues to be on the rise. Health R&D outlay data were first available in 1953. Since then, government funding of health R&D decreased only twice: in 1977[1] and 1996. The table below tracks the growth rate of government funding of health R&D as compared to defense and non-defense R&D funding. As the table shows, during the periods between downturns, health R&D outlays grew at a faster rate than both defense R&D and total nondefense R&D funding.[2]

Comparative Growth Rates (%) For R&D Funding

	1953-1976	1977-1995	1996-2003 est.
Defense R&D	532	247	52
Nondefense R&D	3,347	191	62
Health R&D	**4,993**	**583**	**150**

---

[1] There was a transfer quarter from October 1, 1976 to December 31, 1976, during which the fiscal year was changed from July 1-June 30 to October 1-September 30. The drop in 1977 shown in the graph could be due to this transition period. Monies allocated during the transfer quarter do not appear in the graph.

[2] Total nondefense R&D spending growth outpaced defense R&D spending growth in 29 of the 50 years shown.

But how does health R&D funding fit in with other nondefense R&D funding? Has it been getting more attention in recent years, as the dollar figures in the graph above suggest? Or does the high growth rate from the mid-1950s to the mid-1970s suggest that a higher priority was given to health R&D in this time period? The graphic below shows health R&D outlays as a percentage of total nondefense R&D outlays. Although the growth in health R&D funding was greatest from 1953 to 1976, health R&D as a percentage of total nondefense R&D was greatest in the latter half of the 1990s. Health R&D began taking up a larger and larger percentage of nondefense R&D in the mid-1960s. In 2001 health R&D funding was greater than 51% of the total funding for nondefense R&D. This upward trend is expected to continue at least until 2003.

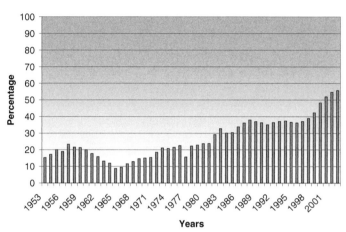

U.S. Government Health R&D Outlays as a Percentage of Total Nondefense Outlays, 1953-2003

But where specifically is the funding going? In the first chapter of this volume, we discussed the top 10 causes of death. Are these diseases getting the most attention?

We will attempt to answer these questions in the next panel.

Source: Executive Office of the President of the United States. Budget of the United States Government: Fiscal Year 2003. Historical Tables. "Table 9.8 -- Composition of Outlays for the Conduct of Research and Development: 1949-2003." Retrieved August 8, 2002 from http://w3.access.gpo.gov/usbudget/fy2003/.

Where The Funding Goes

Top 5 Institutions Funded by the National Institutes of Health (NIH), 1953-2003

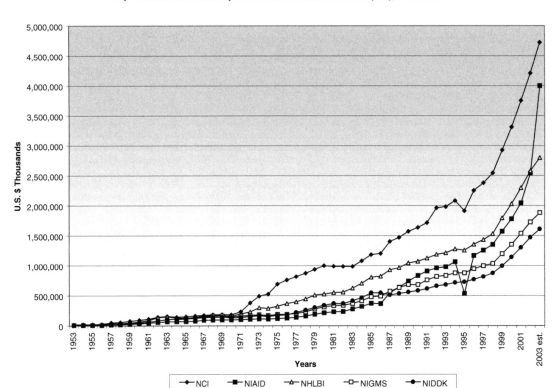

The graphic shows the National Institutes of Health (NIH) distribution of monies to various institutions. The five institutions shown received (and are expected to receive in 2003) the most allocations of money of all institutions under the NIH. NCI is the National Cancer Institute. NIAID is the National Institute of Allergies and Infectious Diseases. NHLBI is the National Heart, Lung, and Blood Institute. NIGMS stands for the National Institute of General Medical Sciences and NIDDK stands for National Institute of Diabetes & Digestive & Kidney Diseases.

Do the allocations correspond to the conditions that most threaten the health of Americans? Not necessarily. In 1996, "a blue-ribbon panel appointed by the Institute of Medicine broke down [the funding] this way: For every $10 spent per cancer death on cancer research, $110 is spent per AIDS death on AIDS research and $3 is spent per heart disease death on heart disease research." But, heart disease has been the leading cause of death since the 1920s.[3] According to Dr. Stuart Seides, a past president of the Washington American Heart Association, "those groups that speak the loudest or strike a particular note among the public or among legislators may get a proportion of the research dollar

---

[3] And the most costly in terms of health care and lost wages. According to NIH, the national cost for heart diseases was $183 billion in 2000. That's $26 billion more than cancer and $83 billion more than diabetes.

that is out of proportion to the number of victims of that particular disease."[4] As of 1998, there was no organized lobby for heart disease.

This disparity in funding is not a recent phenomenon. The graphic below[5] shows a history of 1999's top 7 causes of death. Since 1925, diseases of the heart killed the most people. From 1925 to 1955, two years after we began tracking funding, deaths from diseases of the heart increased nearly one and a half times as fast as deaths from cancer: 210.7% and 156.3%, respectively. But, funding for heart research (NHLBI) ranked 2nd to funding for cancer (NCI). From 1955 to 1985 the numbers reversed. Now, even though diseases of the heart were killing more people, the growth rate at which people were dying of cancer was nearly 3 times higher than the growth rate of people dying of diseases of the heart: 91.8% and 31.7%, respectively. From 1985 onward, the numbers of people dying of cancer continued to rise. At the same time, the number of people dying of diseases of the heart declined. And funding for cancer (NCI) remained in the lead.

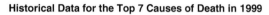

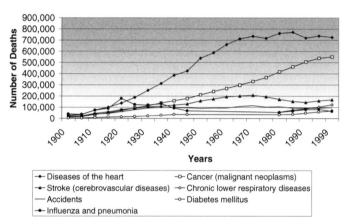

But, the NHLBI does not just research diseases of the heart, its treatments, and its cures. It also researches the causes, treatments, and cures for cerebrovascular diseases (stroke) and chronic lower respiratory diseases (asthma and emphysema), the 3rd and 4th causes of death in 1999 respectively.

Until the mid- to late-1980s, diabetes and digestive and kidney disorders (NIDDK) research was the third most funded. Diabetes was the 7th leading killer in the United States until 1999 when it became the 6th leading cause of death surpassing influenza and pneumonia. After 1987, NIDDK dropped in rank and became the 5th most funded institute under the NIH.[6] This, despite the rise in the number of diabetes cases since at least 1990.

From 1987-1988, genetic research (NIGMS) ranked third in funding. After this, however, it dropped to 4th behind allergies and infectious diseases (NIAID). Besides genetic re-

---

[4] Source for both quotes in this paragraph: Schiavone, Louise. "Cancer rally calls attention to the politics of medical spending." *CNN interactive,* September 25, 1998. Retrieved August 13, 2002 from http://www. cnn.com/HEALTH/9809/25/cancer.march.advancer/.

[5] 1950-1975 data for influenza and pneumonia and diabetes mellitus were extrapolated.

[6] In 1996, the NIAID became the 5th most funded institute. During this year total NIH funding dropped off (see previous panel), and funding to the NIAID was halved. Funding returned to normal levels in 1997.

---

search, this institute studies the interactions of biological, physiological, and pharmacological processes on diseases and other medical conditions. Therefore, its research may have an impact on every aspect of medical research done at the other NIH institutes. From 1989 onward, this institute's funding rank dropped to 4th.

Once ranked 5th, funding for allergies and infectious diseases (NIAID) moved up to 3rd place in 1990. Perhaps this was in response to the growing concern about AIDS in the U.S. and around the world. Celebrities who had the disease began speaking out. President Reagan commented on the disease for the first time in 1990.[7] That same year, nearly 200,000 people were living with HIV, an increase of nearly 1,700% since 1984, and the numbers rose for another 2 to 3 years.

NIAID is also concerned with finding the causes, treatments, and cures for new diseases, and older ones that are becoming resistant to the medicines we traditionally used to treat them.

What will happen in 2003? Why is the proposed funding for allergies and infectious diseases rising so much? (That would then rank NIAID second in the amount of funding it receives from the NIH.) Is there a new epidemic on the horizon? This $1.5 billion increase in funding[8] is due in large part to the events of September 11, 2001 and the anthrax scares in the subsequent months. This increase in funding, along with an extra $1.2 billion that NIAID expects to allocate from other funds is to go into bioterrorism research. The Institute, anticipating long-term funding, is launching research campaigns to study anthrax, tularemia, plague, botulism toxin, and hemorrhagic fever viruses. Its efforts will also go towards researching E. coli and staphylococcus bacteria. Their goal is to discover vaccines or better medications to combat these illnesses (should we ever need them).

Sources: Chart data: National Center for Health Statistics. Centers for Disease Control. U.S. Department of Health and Human Services. Historical Data Table HIST290A. Retrieved August 9, 2002 from http://www.cdc.gov/nchs/data/statab/; National Center for Health Statistics. Centers for Disease Control. U.S. Department of Health and Human Services. *National Vital Statistics Report,* Vol. 49, No. 11, October 12, 2001. Retrieved August 9, 2002 from http://www.cdc.gov/nchs/data/nvsr49/nvsr49_11.pdf. NIAID 2003 funding and research information: Dr. Anthony Fauci, MD. "An Expanded Biodefense Role for the National Institutes of Health," April 2002. Retrieved August 9, 2002 from http://www.homeland-security.org/journal/Articles/fauci.htm. Individual institute information retrieved from their respective websites: http://www.cancer..gov, http://www..niaid.nih.gov, http://www.nhlbi.nih.gov/, http://www.nigms.nih.gov, and http://www.niddk.nih. gov. Louise Schiavone. "Cancer rally calls attention to the politics of medical spending." *CNN interactive,* September 25, 1998. Retrieved August 13, 2002 from http://www.cnn.com/HEALTH/9809/25/cancer. march.advancer/. Office of the Assistant Secretary for Planning and Evaluation. U.S. Department of Health and Human Services. "Physical Activity Fundamental to Preventing Disease," June 20, 2002. Retrieved August 27, 2002 from http://aspe.hhs.gov/health/ reports/physicalactivity/.

---

[7] For more on the history of AIDS see the panel *"Two Decades of AIDS"* in Chapter 10.

[8] The largest increase in funding for a NIH institute in history. Source: http://www.homelandsecurity.org. Full citation in source note.

Healthy People 2010 Goals

Life Expectancy, 1900-2000

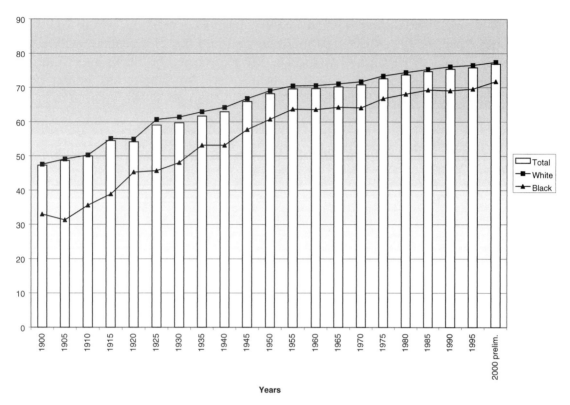

Years

The nationwide health promotion and disease prevention agenda, Healthy People, started in 1979 with a report entitled *Healthy People: The Surgeon General's Report on Health Promotion and Disease Prevention.* This report outlined five national goals for reducing premature deaths and improving the quality of life for older Americans. In 1980, *Promoting Health/Preventing Disease: Objectives for the Nation,* presented 226 health targets for the nation to achieve by 1990. *Healthy People 2000: National Disease Prevention and Health Promotion Objectives*, released in 1990, was divided into 22 priority areas with 319 objectives that were to be achieved by the year 2000.

The Healthy People Consortium, a group of 350 national organizations and 250 state public health, mental health, substance abuse, and environmental agencies under the guidance of the U.S. Department of Health and Human Services, conducted three national meetings and five regional meetings in 1998 to formulate the set of goals for the year 2010. Individuals and organizations gave testimony in the regional meetings and on two other occasions in 1997 and 1998. The public from every state, the District of Columbia, and Puerto Rico was allowed to comment (by mail or Internet) on the objectives the Consortium was formulating. Then, in January 2000, the report *Healthy People 2010: Understanding and Improving Health* was released.[9] It contained 10 leading health indi-

---

[9] In November 2000, a second edition was released.

---

cators and 28 priority areas with 467 objectives to be achieved by 2010. The primary goals of *Healthy People 2010* are to increase healthy life expectancy and eliminate health disparities.

The chart on the previous page shows one of the *Healthy People 2010* goals being met. Life expectancy increased during the 20th Century, from 47.3 years in 1900 to 76.9 years in 2000. Life expectancy is expected to increase well into the 21st century, with a projected life expectancy in 2060 of 82 years. The life expectancy of blacks and whites are also converging, suggesting that access to health care for blacks has gotten better throughout the century. However there is still a long way to go, as we've seen in earlier chapters.

The next three panels will discuss some of the leading health indicators mentioned in *Healthy People 2010*.

Sources: National Center for Health Statistics. Centers for Disease Control. *National Vital Statistics Report*, October 9, 2001 and March 21, 2002. Retrieved August 12, 2002 from http://www.cdc.gov/nchs/. U.S. Department of Health and Human Services. *Healthy People 2010: Understanding and Improving Health*, 2nd ed., November 2000. Retrieved August 27, 2002 from http://www.health. gov/healthypeople. U.S. Department of Health and Human Services. "Healthy People 2000 Fact Sheet." Retrieved August 27, 2002 from http://odphp.ososphs.dhhs.gov/pubs/hp2000/hp2kfact.htm. Capital Region Information Service. "Healthy People 2000." Retrieved August 30, 2002 from http://www.crisny.org/health/us/health7.html.

Let's Get Moving

Physical Activity and Obesity Trends, 1990-2001 and Healthy People 2010 Targets

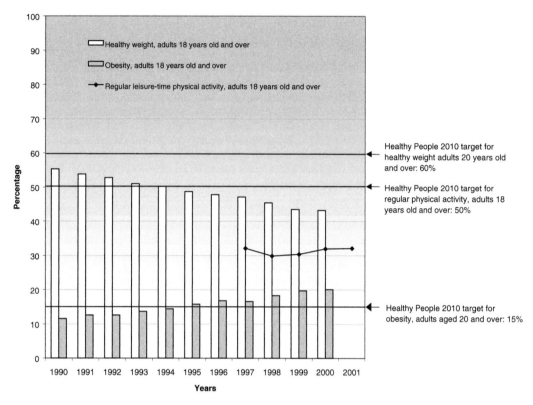

Data from a 1993 study reported on in the *Journal of the American Medical Association* showed that 14% of all deaths in the United States were due to sedentary lifestyles and poor dietary habits. High blood pressure, coronary heart disease, Type 2 diabetes, and colon cancer are just some diseases attributed to inactivity, obesity, and an unhealthy diet. In 2002, 50 million people in the U.S. had high blood pressure, 12.6 million had coronary artery disease, 17 million had diabetes (90-95% of which were Type 2), and each year 107,000 people are diagnosed with colon cancer. With inactivity comes obesity. The percentage of obese people nearly doubled in the decade from 1990-2000. It is no wonder then that *Healthy People 2010* lists physical activity and obesity (and overweight) as the top two public health concerns.

What is being done to get us moving and losing weight? A few programs funded by the federal government are presented here.

ACEs: Active Community Environments. This is a Centers for Disease Control and Prevention (CDC) initiative to promote active lifestyles within communities. The goals: "encourage development of pedestrian and bicycle friendly environments [and] promote active forms of transportation like walking and bicycling." The Task Force on Community Preventive Services recommends creating or increasing access to trails and promoting their use. Trails "represent a diversity of opportunity from the gifted athlete interested in a convenient place to train to the individuals who are looking for an aesthetically pleasing place to take an after dinner walk to a family walking to spend time together."[1]

Increased aerobic activity, like walking and bicycling, helps in weight loss. It significantly reduces blood pressure and can protect against non-insulin dependent diabetes. According to the results of some studies, this type of regular exercise can also improve the symptoms of mild-to-moderate depression and anxiety "of a magnitude comparable to that obtained with some pharmacological agents."[10]

In 2002, the U.S. Department of Health and Human Services teamed up with the National Recreation and Park Association[11] to promote the idea that parks are places where "community members can come to … exercise … and participate in other ways to make a difference in their success and well-being."[12]

Kids Walk-to-School Program. Physical fitness is not just for adults. This community-based program encourages children to walk to and from school, in groups, accompanied by adults. The program also encourages community partnerships with schools, PTA, local police departments, departments of public works, civic associations, local politicians, and businesses to create safe routes to walk or bicycle. Besides physical fitness for adults and children, additional benefits include safer, friendlier neighborhoods and less traffic congestion, according to the CDC.

This Alabama mother's quote from International Walk-to-School Day 2001 just may sum up the CDC's goals: "We walk every day regardless of the weather. It makes the day brighter to have the quality time going to and from school with [my son] Eric. He loves the sights and sounds and he is one of only 4 walkers at his school. So sad when we are so dependent on cars for our transportation and what we miss out on in nature. We do not have sidewalks but have a petition in progress to get them. We would love to get a grant to put them on our street to the school to get more kids out."[13]

The federal government also funds obesity prevention programs through individual state health departments.[14] The funding targets physical activity as well as nutrition programs.

---

[10] Source: Centers for Disease Control and Prevention. National Center for Chronic Disease Prevention and Health Promotion. "Promoting Physical Activity Through Trails." Retrieved August 27, 2002 from http://www.cdc.gov/nccdphp/dnpa/physical/trails.htm.

[11] A nonprofit association that represents over 170,000 outdoor and indoor public park and recreation facilities.

[12] A quote by Dr. Eve E. Slater, Assistant Secretary for Health. Source: "National Recreation and Park Association and U.S. Department of Health and Human Services Working for the Nation's Wellness," February 26, 2002.

[13] Source: "2001 iwalk photos and quotes." Retrieved August 27, 2002 from http://www.iwalktoschool.org/quotes/quotes4.hsql.

[14] The states that receive funding are California (15-19%), Connecticut (15-19%), North Carolina (>=20%), Massachusetts (15-19%), Rhode Island (15-19%), Texas (>=20%), Colorado (10-14%), Florida (15-19%),

California's Obesity Prevention Initiative is a partnership of state agencies. Their programs target those under 18 years old in an attempt to get the youth to start leading a healthy lifestyle that will (hopefully) carry over into adulthood. The Michigan Department of Community Health is using its funding for obesity prevention programs targeting the African American community.

Sources: Centers for Disease Control and Prevention. "Youth Risk Behavior Surveillance — United States 1993, 1995, 1997, 1999, and 2001." *MMWR*, various dates. Centers for Disease Control and Prevention. National Center for Health Statistics. "Data table for figure 7.1 Percent of adults aged 18 years and over who engaged in regular leisure-time physical activity: United States 1997-2001." Retrieved August 27, 2002 from http://www.cdc.gov/nchs/major/nhis/released200207/figures07_1-7_3.htm. Centers for Disease Control and Prevention. Nationwide Trend Data. *Behavioral Risk Factor Surveillance System.* Retrieved August 27, 2002 from http://apps.nccd.cdc.gov/brfss/Trends/trendchart.asp. U.S. Department of Health and Human Services. *Healthy People 2010: Understanding and Improving Health,* 2nd. ed., November 2000. Retrieved August 27, 2002 from http://www.health.gov/healthypeople. Centers for Disease Control and Prevention. National Center for Chronic Disease Prevention and Health Promotion. Department of Nutrition and Physical Activity. Data retrieved August 12-27, 2002 from http://www.cdc.gov/nccdphp/dnpa/. U.S. Department of Health and Human Services. "National Recreation and Park Association and U.S. Department of Health and Human Services Working for the Nation's Wellness," February 26, 2002. Retrieved August 12, 2002 from http://web.health.gov/healthypeople/Implementation/ nrpa/. "2001 iwalk photos and quotes." Retrieved August 27, 2002 from http://www.iwalktoschool.org/quotes/quotes4.html. Office of the Assistant Secretary for Planning and Evaluation. U.S. Department of Health and Human Services. *Physical Activity Fundamental to Preventing Disease,* June 20, 2002. Retrieved August 27, 2002 from http://aspe.hhs.gov/health/reports/physicalactivity/.

Michigan (>=20%), Montana (15-19%), Pennsylvania (>=20%), and Washington (15-19%). The numbers in parentheses represent the percentage of obese people in the state in 2000.

Quitting the Habit: Smoking

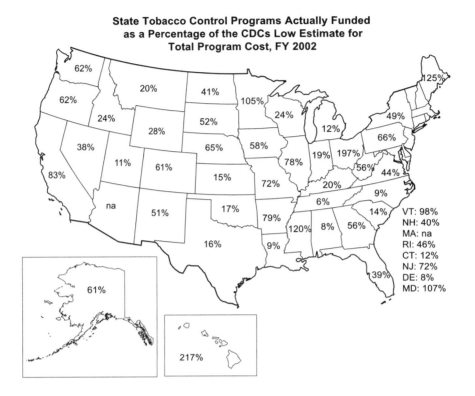

State Tobacco Control Programs Actually Funded as a Percentage of the CDCs Low Estimate for Total Program Cost, FY 2002

"Cigarette smoking is the single most preventable cause of disease and death in the United States. Smoking results in more deaths each year in the United States than AIDS, alcohol, cocaine, heroin, homicide, suicide, motor vehicle crashes, and fires — combined."[15] The medical costs of smoking are estimated at $50 billion a year. Tobacco use is the third major public health concern cited in *Healthy People 2010*.

The Centers for Disease Control and Prevention's (CDC) report *Best Practices for Comprehensive Tobacco Control Programs* outlines nine components for a comprehensive tobacco control program. These include: community programs, chronic disease programs, school programs, enforcement of existing policies, statewide programs, counter-marketing, cessation programs, surveillance and evaluation, and administration and management. This report also contains funding formulas for each of the programs. These formulas are used by the CDC in order to estimate total program costs. The estimates vary with state population size. The CDC makes two estimates, a low estimate and a high estimate. The chart above shows the percentage of the CDC's low estimate that is actually spent in each state on these programs. For example, the CDC's low estimate for total program costs in California (if they would implement all of the CDC's recommended

---

[15] Source: U.S. Department of Health and Human Services. *Healthy People 2010: Understanding and Improving Health,* 2nd ed., November 2000.

programs) was $165.1 million in fiscal year 2002, but the state actually spent $137.8 million, or 83%.[16] "na" means data were not available for that state.

State spending varies widely (from 6% in Tennessee to 217% in Hawaii). Does this variance correspond to the prevalence of smoking in each state? Not necessarily. The table below shows the states with the highest cigarette smoking prevalence and their ranking in terms of percentage spent relative to CDC recommendations.[17] Only Ohio's funding rank was higher than its adult smoking prevalence ranking. The *Healthy People 2010* goals for smoking prevalence are 12% for adults and 16% for 9-12 graders.

Top 5 States with the Highest Cigarette Smoking Prevalence, 2000 and

Rankings of Percentage Spent Relative to CDC Recommendations, 2002

State	Cigarette smoking prevalence, adults 18 years old and over (%)	Tobacco control funding rank	State	Cigarette smoking prevalence, 9-12 graders (%)	Tobacco control funding rank
Kentucky	30.5	35	North Dakota	40.6	28
Nevada	29.1	31	West Virginia	38.5	22
Missouri	27.2	12	Kentucky	37.4	35
Indiana	27.0	37	Alaska	36.5	18
Ohio	26.3	2	Louisiana	36.4	45
National	**23.3**		**National**	**28.0**	

Why isn't funding proportionate? Is it a lack of money?[18] No. From 1999-2004, most states will receive a combined average of $41 billion from settlements with the tobacco companies. The median CDC funding estimate for all the recommended programs is $14.5 billion, or 35.4%. For small states (less than 3 million people), $7-20 per person would cover the costs of implementing all of the CDC recommended programs. In large states (more than 7 million people), this cost would be lower: $5-16 per person. Perhaps funding for these programs is simply a matter of legislative priorities.

Are these programs effective? Yes. California's per capita consumption of tobacco declined by 16% from 1992 to 1996. Massachusetts's per capita consumption declined by 20% during the same time period. What worked? Raising tobacco taxes and mass-media antismoking campaigns. Tobacco use among Florida middle-schoolers and high-schoolers declined 2.5% and 2.2%, respectively. What worked with these teenagers (and

---

[16] Funding for the programs comes from state appropriations (taxes, tobacco settlement monies, and other sources), federal (CDC Office on Smoking and Health) and non-government (Robert Wood Johnson Foundation and the American Medical Association) sources.

[17] Smoking prevalence data is for 2000, the most recent year available.

[18] In many cases, states used little or no tobacco settlement monies for tobacco control programs in 2002. In 2001, Tennessee and Michigan received $151.4 million and $258.9 million, respectively, in tobacco settlement monies, but spent none of it on tobacco control programs in 2002. Hawaii, on the other hand, received $35.8 million in tobacco settlement monies in 2001and spent $22.2 million of it for tobacco control programs in 2002.

pre-teens)? Mass-media antismoking campaigns, community-based activities, education and training, and enforcement of existing laws.

The next panel discusses the prevalence of substance abuse and government funding priorities for substance abuse programs.

Sources: Tobacco Information and Prevention Source (TIPS). National Center for Chronic Disease Prevention and Health Promotion. Centers for Disease Control and Prevention. U.S. Department of Health and Human Services. "Tobacco Control Funding Summary, Fiscal Year 2002," "Current Cigarette Smoking Among Adults Aged 18 and Older, 2000," "Current Cigarette Smoking and Tobacco Use Among Youth, Grades 9-12," "Best Practices for Comprehensive Tobacco Control Programs, August 1999 Fact Sheet," and *Tobacco Control State Highlights 2002.* Retrieved August 28-29, 2002 from http://www.cdc.gov/tobacco/. U.S. Department of Health and Human Services. *Healthy People 2010: Understanding and Improving Health,* 2nd ed., November 2000.

Quitting the Habit: Substance Abuse

Percentage of the U.S. Population Reporting Binge Alcohol and Illicit Drug Use in the Past
Month, 12 years old and over, 1979-2000

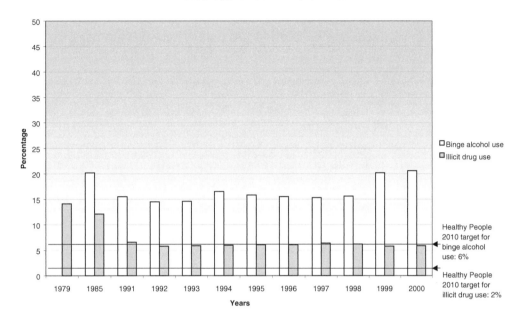

According to the *2000 National Survey of Substance Abuse Treatment Services*, in 1999, there were 14.2 million people age 12 and older using illicit drugs[19] and 44.6 million who binged on alcohol at least once in the month prior to taking the survey. Bingeing is defined as drinking five or more drinks "at the same time or within a couple of hours of each other" on at least one day in the past 30 days.[20] According to *Healthy People 2010*, "alcohol and illicit drug use are associated with child and spousal abuse; sexually transmitted diseases, including HIV infection; teen pregnancy; school failure; motor vehicle crashes;…low worker productivity; and homelessness…. Long-term heavy drinking can lead to heart disease, cancer, alcohol-related liver disease, and pancreatitis. Alcohol use during pregnancy is known to cause fetal alcohol syndrome, a leading cause of preventable mental retardation." *Healthy People 2010* lists substance abuse as the 4th leading public health concern.

The graphic shows the percentage of the population age 12 and older who binged on alcohol and who used illicit drugs, as reported in the *2000 National Survey*. Over this time period, illicit drug use was down, but binge alcohol use fluctuated. Most recently, from

[19] In 2002, 15.9 million people age 12 and older used illicit drugs according to a federal study. Source: "16 million use drugs, federal study says." *The Detroit News,* September 6, 2002.

[20] Source: Packer, Lisa E, et. al. Substance Abuse and Mental Health Services Administration. *1998 National Household Survey on Drug Abuse*, August 12, 1999. Retrieved August 28, 2002 from http://www.samhsa.gov/oas/NHDA/98DetailedTables/101112v1_2.pdf.

1999-2000, bingeing was on the rise. The chart also shows the *Healthy People 2010* goals: to reduce the prevalence of binge drinking by 14.6% and the prevalence of illicit drug use by 3.9%.

Each year, the overall budget for the Substance Abuse and Mental Health Services Administration (SAMHSA) has gone up. This allowed the Administration to allocate more and more money to state treatment and prevention programs. However, in the fiscal year 2003 budget, even though the allocations include a $57 million increase, some state programs may have to be cut. Why?

The budget calls for a $126.6 million increase for treatment programs[21], but cuts the budget for prevention programs by $45.2 million. And for the second year in a row, there is no allocation of federal monies for High Risk Youth Grants. Binge drinking among 12 to 17 year olds increased from 8% to 10.1% from 1998-1999, the last years for which data are available. That meant that a little over 2.3 million 12 to 17 year olds binged on alcohol in 1999. Illicit drug use among 12 to 17 year olds went down from 1997 and 1998, according to *Healthy People 2010*. But this report also states: "youth are experimenting with a variety of illicit drugs, including marijuana, cocaine, crack, heroin, acid, inhalants, and methamphetamines, as well as misuse of prescription drugs and other 'street' drugs. The younger a person becomes a habitual user of illicit drugs, the stronger the addiction becomes and the more difficult it is to stop use." A SAMHSA study to be released in 2002 found that High Risk Youth Demonstration Programs reduced the incidence of substance abuse among program participants by 11%. Even those who had already started using cigarettes, alcohol, or marijuana benefited from the programs. In 1999, 2.3 million 12 to 17 year olds used illicit drugs.

Sources: Office of Applied Studies. Substance Abuse and Mental Health Services Administration. U.S. Department of Health and Human Services. *National Household Survey on Drug Abuse,* 1998-2000, various publication dates. Retrieved August 28, 2002 from http://www.samhsa.gov/. U.S. Department of Health and Human Services. *Healthy People 2010: Understanding and Improving Health,* 2nd ed., November 2000. "Fiscal Year 2003 President's Budget: Substance Abuse and Mental Health Services Administration (SAMHSA)." *APA Online.* Retrieved August 30, 2002 from http://www.apa.org/ppo/funding/p03samhsabudg.html. SAMHSA. U.S. Department of Health and Human Services. "Over 1 Million People Receiving Addiction Treatment." Retrieved August 30, 2002 from http://www.samhsa.gov/news/content/ nssats_press.htm. SAMHSA. U.S. Department of Health and Human Services. *SAMHSA Fiscal Year 2003 Budget,* February 12, 2002. Retrieved August 30, 2002 from http://www.samhsa.gov/budget/content/2003/2003 budget-03.htm.

---

[21] The increase in monies for substance abuse treatment is a part of the President's Drug Treatment Initiative. President George W. Bush's "number one priority in the mental health and substance abuse area is to reduce the 'substance abuse treatment gap' and reduce the waiting list for those seeking substance abuse services." In 2000, over 1 million people received treatment for substance abuse. Source: "Fiscal Year 2003 President's Budget: Substance Abuse and Mental Health Services Administration (SAMHSA)." *APA Online.* Retrieved August 30, 2002 from http://www.apa.org. U.S. Department of Health and Human Services. "Over 1 Million People Receiving Addiction Treatment." Retrieved August 30, 2002 from http://www. samhsa.org.

Medical School Debt and Repayment

Tuition Costs in Constant 2000 Dollars, 1987-2000

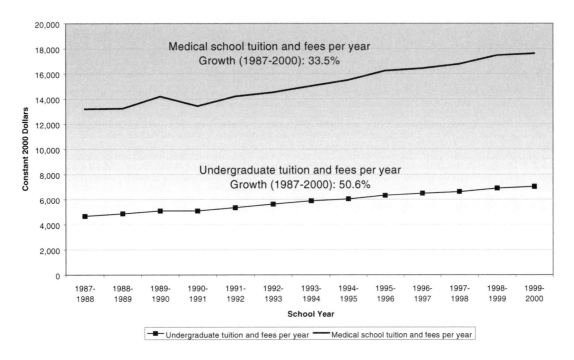

In order to become a doctor, a student must complete 4 years of college and 4 years of medical school (for starters). The graphic above charts the rise in undergraduate and medical school tuition rates. The rise in tuition rates contributes to the rise in debt for those seeking to finance their education with loans. According to the Association of American Medical Colleges, about 81% of medical students incur some educational debt. The average debt for a medical school student in 2000 was $95,000. This was a 58% increase from 1993 when the average medical school student owed $60,000.[22]

Of course, tuition isn't the only expense for future doctors. The cost of room and board has also gone up (32.5%[23] from 1992-1993 to 1999-2000). In the 1992-1993 school year, the average cost for undergraduate room and board at a 4-year college or university was $4,006 a year. By the 1999-2000 school year, the average cost rose to $5,308 a year. This expense can be alleviated if students have the luxury of living with their parents during their time in college. But, if living with mom and dad is not an option, and living in a dorm is unappealing, living in an apartment (even with a roommate sharing the expenses) may cost even more.

---

[22] In 2000 constant dollars, the increase was 34% (from $71,036 in 1993 to $95,000 in 2000).

[23] In 2000 constant dollars, the increase was 12% (from $4,743 in 1992-1993 to $5,308 in 1999-2000).

After medical students graduate, they must complete 3 to 5 years of residency, and, depending on the specialty, another 1 to 5 years of a fellowship. The good news: working on a residency pays a salary. (In 1999, the average annual salary for residents was $35,000.) The bad news: medical school debt rose an average of 6% from 1993 to 1999, but residents' salaries rose only 2% during this time period.[24] As a result, many medical school graduates deferred paying back their loans (if they could) until after they finished their residency. Unfortunately, this meant the interest on the loan kept growing, debt kept rising, and deductions for interest paid could not be taken. Since 1986, there has been a 5-year limit on this deduction, and even if graduates went into private practice before the 5-year limit was over, there was a good chance that they would be earning too much to be eligible for the deduction. The 5-year limit on tax deductions for education loans was eliminated as part of the Economic Growth and Tax Relief Reconciliation Act of 2001. The income limitations were also modified. This law took effect starting with the 2002 tax year. Therefore, it remains to be seen if this will truly help graduates pay off their loans.

In the meantime, there are other ways medical school graduates can eliminate their debt. By making a two-year commitment to serve in medically underserved areas as a part of the National Health Service Corps, primary care physicians can eliminate $50,000 in loan debt. The longer the time commitment, the greater the debt that is erased. Established physicians can join the U.S. Navy or Army Reserves. They offer loan repayment of up to $20,000. If neither public service nor the military is appealing, there is always debt consolidation. Educational consolidation loans, offered through the Federal Government, banks, and other lenders, lowers monthly payments by combining the amount owed on all loans into a single loan and charging a lower rate of interest.[25]

The next panel will discuss another large expense for new and experienced doctors alike: medical liability insurance premiums.

Sources: National Center for Education Statistics. U.S. Department of Education. *Digest of Education Statistics, 2001*. Association of American Medical Colleges. "Total Enrollment by Gender and Race/Ethnicity, 1992-2001." and "How much does medical school cost and can I afford it?" Retrieved August 12, 2002 from http://www.aamc.org/data/facts/famg82001.htm. "The Inflation Calculator." Retrieved August 13, 2002 from http://www.westegg.com/inflation. Tanya Albert. "Bills Offer Relief from Medical School Debt." *Edcuation Update Online*, April 2001. Retrieved August 20, 2002 from http://www.educationupdate.com/april01/medbills.html. Doreen Mangan. "Say goodbye to your med school debt." *Medical Economics*, December 6, 1999. Retrieved August 12, 2002 from http://www.findarticles.com. Dr. Carl Bianco, M.D. "How Becoming a Doctor Works." Retrieved August 20, 2002 from http://www.howstuffworks.com/becoming-a-doctor.htm. "Bill Summary & Status for the 107th Congress" Retrieved August 20, 2002 from http://thomas.loc.gov. "How Medicare Calculates GME Payments, Part I." *JAMA*, May 26, 1999. Retrieved August 28, 2002 from http://jama.ama-assn.org/issues/v281n20/fpdf/jrf90014.pdf.

---

[24] Since 1965, part of this salary was paid by Medicare. Direct graduate medical education payments are inflation-adjusted based on the average per-resident amount in 1984 and on the number of residents and the proportion of inpatient days used by Medicare patients. Congress has since modified the formula to reduce Medicare reimbursement payments.

[25] The interest rate is based on a weighted average of the loans being consolidated, and rounded up to the next highest one-eighth of 1%. This is a federally mandated interest rate for educational consolidation loans and will be the same whether the consolidation loan is financed through the federal government, banks, or other lenders.

Is Malpractice Litigation Hazardous to Our Health?

Top 5 States for Yearly Medical Liability Insurance Premiums, 2001

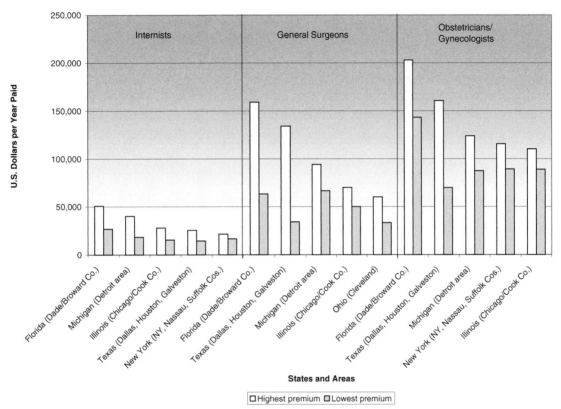

"Your loved one is seriously injured in a car wreck and needs immediate surgery to relieve swelling to the brain. You find there is only one practicing neurosurgeon left in your town and he's working in a hospital that is a two-hour drive away."[26] This scenario may take place one day (if it hasn't already) in Beaumont, Texas, where there was only one practicing neurosurgeon in 2002. But the problem of doctor shortages in certain areas is not limited to Beaumont, Texas. Across the country, doctors are leaving the profession or scaling back services because of the astronomically high malpractice insurance premiums. Rates that continue to rise:

Range of Malpractice Insurance Rate Increases, 2000-2001

	2000 (%)	2001 (%)
Internists	2.8-49.0	2.1-68.6
General surgeons	3.9-42.0	0.2-86.0
OB/Gyns	2.8-42.0	0.3-69.0

[26] Source: Lankarge, Vicki. "Doctors abandon patients as malpractice premiums soar." Retrieved August 22, 2002 from http://www.insure.com/health/medliability201.html.

Why are premiums so high? Malpractice jury awards, according to insurance companies, President George W. Bush, and the American Medical Association.[27] Every year about 10,000 medical malpractice lawsuits are filed. The average malpractice case takes nearly 4 years to resolve. According to the Health Care Liability Alliance, 43% of malpractice premiums are given out as jury awards. The other 57% are used for attorney's fees. According to insurers' figures, the average jury award in 2000 was $3.49 million, up 79% since 1993.

Other sources provide more modest figures. The graph below shows median individual awards given out by juries and settlements in malpractice cases. In 1999, the average jury award was $800,000.[28] This was 60% higher than in 1993. Settlement awards rose 63% in this time period. The median individual payment insurance companies made to cover jury awards in 2000 was $132,312, according to the Pennsylvania Medical Society.[29]

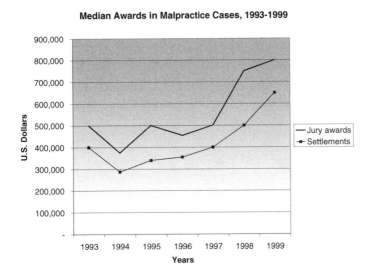

Median Awards in Malpractice Cases, 1993-1999

Insurance companies in the states with the highest malpractice insurance rates (see graph on the previous page) don't necessarily pay out the most to cover jury awards. Michigan ranked 2nd and 3rd in the amount certain physicians pay for malpractice premiums. However, Michigan ranked 12th in the total amount insurers paid to cover jury awards in malpractice cases. The table on the next page shows the rankings for both malpractice insurance premiums and total amount insurance companies pay to cover jury awards. Obstetricians/gynecologists (OB/GYN) were chosen for the table because they pay the highest premiums in relationship to the other physicians mentioned above. A possible reason for this: "medical mis-

---

[27] J. Robert Hunter, the insurance director for the Consumer Federation of America, blames insurance companies' mismanagement for high malpractice insurance premiums. The insurers agree that during the Wall Street boom times of the 1990s, they lowered premiums to attract more hospitals and doctors. Money for jury awards came from stock market profits and company reserves. But, now that the stock market is in a slump and company reserves are drying up, insurers claim that malpractice insurance premiums must be hiked in order to make up for the losses.

[28] Source: *Current Award Trends in Personal Injury, 2000 Edition*; Jury Verdict Research, Horsham, Pa.

[29] Some states have patient compensation funds (CAT). A jury award to a patient may be $1,000,000, but some of that amount may be paid from the CAT fund while the insurance company will pick up the rest. Of the states mentioned above, only Florida has such a program.

takes [in obstetric wards] have historically led to expensive jury awards and settlements." (Treaster).

Insurance Premium vs. Insurance Payment for Jury Awards Rankings, With Total Amount Paid by Insurance Companies, 2000

	Insurance premium ranking for OB/GYNs, 2001	Insurance payment rankings for jury awards	Total amount paid by insurance companies ($)
Florida	1	3	321,079,744
Texas	2	5	217,518,136
Michigan	3	12	79,040,011
New York	4	1	632,996,221
Illinois	5	4	271,050,075
Ohio	6	6	205,148,823
Nevada	7	22	37,090,955
West Virginia	8	35	19,370,928

Is anything being done to curb skyrocketing insurance premiums? Tort reform legislation is being passed by many states (and proposed in the federal government) in order to cut back on "frivolous" lawsuits. But is tort reform the answer? According to Howard A. Richter, MD, president of the Pennsylvania Medical Society, it is. He states that California OB/GYNs averaged $23,000-$72,000 in malpractice insurance premiums, while those in Florida pay between $143,000 and $203,000. California caps its jury awards, Florida does not.

What do lawyers say? Bill R. Frame, president of the West Virginia Trial Lawyers Association, states that tort reform takes "away our fundamental right to seek and obtain compensation for a wrong." Limiting jury awards, according to trial lawyers, only increases the insurer's profits and does nothing to lower malpractice premiums. Some opponents to tort reform also point to a 1999 study by the National Academy of Science's Institute of Medicine which estimated that between 44,000 and 98,000 Americans die in hospitals each year due to medical errors.[30] Therefore, some say, only a fraction of those who should seek compensation are doing so.

What do doctors say? 94% of doctors surveyed by The Harris Poll for the *Common Good Fear of Litigation Study*[31] feel that malpractice lawsuits should be settled by "a medical court presided over by independent medical professionals and other experts that would have authority to review and decide injury cases."

Tort reform has met with challenges as far back as 1980. Since then 15 state courts have limited their states' medical liability reform, including jury award caps. California's

---

[30] The study extrapolates these numbers from two studies (one in New York in 1984 and one in Colorado and Utah in 1992) and applies them to the number of patients admitted to hospitals in 1997. In New York, 3.7% of hospital admissions resulted in "injuries caused by medical management." Of this, 58% were considered preventable (i.e. medical error). In Colorado the numbers were 2.9% and 53%, respectively.

[31] A survey conducted from March 4-20, 2002 polling 300 doctors around the U.S., 73% specialists and 27% primary care physicians.

Medical Injury Compensation Reform Act of 1975 has withstood court challenges, however.

Medical review boards have met a similar fate in North Carolina. In 2001, the state Court of Appeals ruled that it was unconstitutional to require expert-witness reviews of malpractice claims before lawsuits can be filed. The court ruled that the process limited a "plaintiff's access to the courts and [violated] the equal protection clauses of the state and federal constitutions."

Nevada is the latest state to enact medical liability reform legislation with jury award caps[32] (Mississippi and New Jersey lawmakers are discussing the matter), but as of August 2002, insurance companies in Nevada had no plans of lowering their medical malpractice premiums. What will this mean for the future of accessible health care? Will more doctors move to states with lower premiums?[33] Will more patients have to drive for hours (or possibly to another state) just to see a specialist?

Sources: "Medical liability rates continue their upward swing." *Medical Liability Monitor,* October 1, 2001. Retrieved August 20, 2002 from http://www.ama-assn.org/ama/upload/mm/395/malpractice.pdf. Humphrey Taylor, et. al. *Common Good Fear of Litigation Study – The Impact on Medicine,* April 11, 2002. Rita Rubin. "You might feel a bit of a pinch." *USA Today,* December 3, 2001. Retrieved August 21, 2002 from http://www.usatoday.com/news/healthscience/health/2001-12-04-insurance-usat.htm. Tanya Albert. "Nevada enacts bold tort reforms." *AMNews,* August 26, 2002. Retrieved August 21, 2002 from http://www.ama-assn.org/sci-pubs/amnews/pick_02/gv110826.htm. "Do damage caps restrain rising professional liability damages?" *Physician's Weekly,* August 19, 2002. Retrieved August 21, 2002 from http://www.physweekly.com/. Francis X. Clines. "Insurance-Squeezed Doctors Fold Their Tents." *The New York Times,* June 13, 2002. Retrieved August 21, 2002 from http://www.nytimes.com/. Leigh Somerville. "Doctors, insurers seek to reverse ruling they believe will lead to frivolous suits." *The Business Journal,* November 9, 2001. Retrieved August 20, 2002 from http://triad.bizjournals.com/triad/stories/2001/11/12/story3.html. Mike Strobbe. "Insured at premium prices." *The Charlotte Observer,* March 17, 2002. Retrieved August 20, 2002 from http://www.charlotte.com/. Linda T. Kohn, et. al. *To Err is Human: Building a Safer Health System,* 2000. Retrieved August 21, 2002 from http?/www.nap.edu/. "Medical Malpractice Lawsuits by the Numbers." Retrieved August 22, 2002 from http://www.aahpeckochamber.tv/malpractice/numbers.htm. National Center for Policy Analysis. "Jury Awards Boost Doctors' Malpractice-Insurance Costs." *Health Issues,* September 10, 2001. Retrieved August 22, 2002 from http://www.ncpa.org/iss/hea/pd091001d.html. Vicki Lankarge. "Doctors abandon patients as malpractice premiums soar." and "State-by-state chart of medical malpractice payments," April 3, 2002. Retrieved August 22, 2002 from http://www.insure.com/health/. Tanya Albert. "Malpractice awards pushing insurance premiums higher." *AMNews,* March 5, 2001. Retrieved August 21, 2002 from http://www.ama-assn.org/sci-pubs/amnews/pick_01/prl10305.htm. Joseph B. Treaster. "Rise in Insurance Forces Hospitals to Shutter Wards." *The New York Times,* August 25, 2002.

---

[32] In July 2002, Nevada's only Level 1 trauma center closed for 10 days because physicians could not afford pay their malpractice insurance premiums. The legislation was enacted in hopes of heading off such an event in the future.

[33] By moving from Beckley, West Virginia to Blacksburg, Va. 80 miles away, orthopedic surgeon Dr. Joe Prud'homme saved $62,000 a year on his malpractice insurance. Dr. Prud'homme launched a letter-writing campaign in 2001 out of his office to urge the West Virginia legislature to pass tort reform legislation.

Part II

Data Presentation

Data used to create graphics in the first part of this book are present in Part II in tabular format. The tables are arranged by chapter and follow the same sequence as the panels in the chapters. Locating the appropriate table should, therefore, be easy.

In most instances, the data shown are the same as those used to generate the graphics. From time to time, however, additional time series are presented or data are presented for more years. For an explanation of the data, please consult the panel in which they are used. The tables carry some explanatory notes, but the relevance of the data — and the reasons they were selected — are not spelled out.

Tables carry source notes. However, for more information on the subject, including other sources of information, please consult the source notes and (if present), the footnotes shown in the relevant panel in Part I of this volume.

Chapter 1
THE STATE OF OUR HEALTH

Leading Causes of Death in 1900 and in 2000

	Deaths per 100,000 Population
1900	
Major cardiovascular diseases	345.2
Influenza and pneumonia	202.2
Tuberculosis	194.4
2000	
Diseases of the heart and stroke	317.3
Malignancies (cancer)	199.9
Chronic lower respiratory diseases	44.8

Source: For 1900 data: *Historical Statistics of the United States*, U.S. Department of Commerce, Bureau of the Census, Table B149-166, p. 58. For 2000 data: U.S. Department of Health and Human Services, Centers for Disease Control and Prevention, obtained at http://www.cdc.gov/nchs/hphome.htm.

Leading Causes of Death in 1999

	Number of Deaths
All causes	2,391,399
Diseases of the heart	725,192
Cancer (malignant neoplasms)	549,838
Stroke (cerebrovascular diseases)	167,366
Chronic lower respiratory diseases	124,181
Accidents (unintentional injuries)	97,860
Diabeters mellitus	68,399
Influenza and pneumonia	63,730
Alzheimer's disease	44,536
Nephritis, nephrotic syndrome and nephrosis	35,525
Septicemia	30,680

Source: Anderson, Robert N. *Deaths: Leading Causes for 1999.* National Vital Statistics Reports, Volume 49, Number 11, October 12, 2001. Department of Health and Human Services.

Top Ten Leading Causes of Death, Men and Women, 1999

	% of All Deaths and Rank			
	Women		Men	
	(%)	Rank	(%)	Rank
Heart disease	30.7	1	29.9	1
Cancer	21.7	2	24.3	2
Stroke	8.5	3	5.5	3
Respiratory diseases	5.1	4	5.3	5
Diabeters	3.1	5	2.7	6
Influenza/pneumonia	3.0	6	2.4	7
Accidents	2.8	7	5.4	4
Alzheimer's	2.6	8	1.1	-
Kidney diseases	1.5	9	1.4	10
Septicemia	1.4	10	1.1	-
Liver diseases	0.8	-	1.5	9
Suicide	0.5	-	2.0	8

Source: Anderson, Robert N. *Deaths: Leading Causes for 1999.* National Vital Statistics Reports, Volume 49, Number 11, October 12, 2001. Department of Health and Human Services.

Top Ten Leading Causes of Deaths by Race

Asian/PI stands for Asians and Pacific Islanders. American Indian includes Native Alaskans.

	Percent of all Deaths				Rank			
	White	African American	American Indian	Asian/ PI	White	African American	American Indian	Asian/ PI
Heart disease	30.8	27.6	21.3	27.0	1	1	1	1
Cancer	23.2	21.7	16.2	26.2	2	2	2	2
Stroke	7.0	6.6	4.8	9.2	3	3	5	3
Respiratory diseases	5.6	2.8	3.6	3.3	4	6	7	6
Accidents	4.0	4.5	11.7	4.6	5	4	3	4
Influenza/pneumonia	2.8	2.1	2.8	2.5	6	10	8	7
Diabeters	2.6	4.2	6.4	3.4	7	5	4	5
Alzheimer's	2.0	0.8	0.8	0.7	8	-	-	-
Kidney diseases	1.4	2.4	1.7	1.7	9	9	-	9
Suicide	1.3	0.7	2.6	2.0	10	-	9	8
Septicemia	1.2	2.0	1.5	1.2	-	-	-	10
Liver diseases	1.1	1.0	4.5	0.9	-	-	6	-
Homicide	0.4	2.7	2.2	1.1	-	8	10	-
HIV	0.3	2.8	0.6	0.3	-	7	-	-

Source: Anderson, Robert N. *Deaths: Leading Causes for 1999.* National Vital Statistics Reports, Volume 49, Number 11, October 12, 2001. Department of Health and Human Services.

Top Ten Leading Causes of Infant Deaths in 1999

	Percent of Deaths
Leading Causes of Death	
Congenital malformations	19.6
Death related to low birth weight	15.7
Sudden infant death syndrome	9.5
Maternal complications of pregnancy	5.0
Respirotary diseases	4.0
Complications of placenta, cord, and membranes	3.7
Accidents	3.0
Bacterial sepsis	2.5
Diseses of the circulatory system	2.4
Atelectasis	2.3
Births and Deaths	
Total births - Number	3,959,000
Deaths before age 1 - Number	27,937
Deaths before the age of 28 days	18,728
Percentiles	
Deaths before age 1 as % of all births	0.71
Deaths before age 28 days as % of all births	0.47
Death before age 28 as % of all infant deaths	67.04

Source: Anderson, Robert N. *Deaths: Leading Causes for 1999.* National Vital Statistics Reports, Volume 49, Number 11, October 12, 2001. Department of Health and Human Services.

Death Rates per 100,000 Population, 1979 to 1998, Selected Diseases

Year	Ischemic Heart Disease		Females		
	Males	Females	Fenakes Stroke	Breast Cancer	Diabetes
1979	454.7	255.5	92.3	31.2	17.3
1980	459.7	263.1	91.7	31.9	18.0
1981	440.1	250.3	85.7	32.0	17.4
1982	427.8	243.7	80.4	32.2	17.0
1983	420.6	241.8	77.4	32.1	17.6
1984	403.7	233.4	75.4	32.9	16.7
1985	393.7	227.0	73.3	33.0	17.0
1986	373.2	219.1	70.2	32.8	16.8
1987	359.7	212.5	68.8	32.7	16.9
1988	352.1	209.0	67.4	33.2	17.5
1989	337.4	200.5	64.1	33.2	19.8
1990	328.2	193.9	62.6	33.3	19.9
1991	316.7	187.8	60.3	32.8	19.8
1992	306.7	182.1	59.3	31.8	19.8

[Continued]

Death Rates per 100,000 Population, 1979 to 1998, Selected Diseases

[Continued]

Year	Ischemic Heart Disease		Females		
	Males	Females	Fenakes Stroke	Breast Cancer	Diabetes
1993	306.7	182.7	60.3	31.5	20.9
1994	295.0	176.3	60.4	31.1	21.5
1995	287.8	173.6	61.4	30.8	22.0
1996	276.9	167.7	60.8	29.8	22.4
1997	265.7	160.9	59.5	28.6	22.3
1998	254.1	155.6	58.2	27.9	22.3

Source: U.S. Department of Health and Human Services, Centers for Disease Control and Prevention, National Center for Health Statistics, National Vital Statistics System, accessed at http://www.cdc.gov/nchs/default.htm, May 29, 2002.

Death Rates of Females by Race, 1979 to 1999, Ischemic Heart Disease

	Whites	Blacks	Non-Whites
1979	255.4	255.8	242.4
1980	262.6	274.2	254.6
1981	250.2	258.1	238.5
1982	243.7	250.0	230.6
1983	241.1	254.6	235.5
1984	232.9	244.2	225.6
1985	226.3	241.2	221.9
1986	218.0	238.7	218.7
1987	211.5	232.4	212.3
1988	207.6	232.3	211.7
1989	198.5	228.7	208.0
1990	192.1	220.1	200.3
1991	185.8	218.6	196.9
1992	179.9	212.3	191.9
1993	180.3	217.4	195.3
1994	174.3	206.4	185.4
1995	171.4	205.4	183.9
1996	165.8	198.7	175.3
1997	159.1	191.7	168.1
1998	153.7	186.8	163.4
1999	152.5	192.5	167.4

Source: U.S. Department of Health and Human Services, Centers for Disease Control and Prevention, National Center for Health Statistics, National Vital Statistics System, accessed at http://www.cdc.gov/nchs/default.htm, May 29, 2002.

Obesity - 1960 to 1999

Persons 20-74 years, age adjusted to 2000 population. NA stands for Not Available. For definitions of obesity and overweight, please see text in Part I.

| | Percent Obese | | | | Percent Overweight | |
| | Men | Women | | | | |
		All Races	White	Black	All	Men
1960-1962	10.7	15.7	14.2	26.8	13.3	38.3
1971-1974	12.2	16.8	15.4	29.7	14.6	41.5
1976-1980	12.8	17.1	15.5	31.3	15.1	39.2
1988-1994	20.6	26.0	24.3	39.0	23.3	39.9
1999	NA	NA	NA	NA	27.0	NA

Source: Centers for Disease Control and Prevention, National Center for Health Statistics, Division of Health Examination Statistics. Unpublished data. Retrieved http://www.cdc.gov/ on June 1, 2002.

Mammograms and Possible Breast Cancer Relationships - Women, 1987 to 1998, Selected Years

Death rates are per 100,000 population.

| Year | % of Women Who Had Mammograms | | Breast Cancer Death Rates | |
	White	Black	White	Black
1987	29.6	24.0	32.6	36.4
1990	52.2	46.4	33.2	38.1
1991	55.6	48.0	32.6	38.2
1993	60.0	59.1	31.3	38.1
1994	60.6	64.3	30.8	37.8
1998	67.4	66.0	27.3	35.7

Source: U.S. Department of Health and Human Services, *Health United States, 2001*, p. 279, downloaded from http://www.cdc.gov/nchs/products/pubs/pubd/hus/tables/2001/01hus082

Breast Cancer Survival Rates for Women, Selected Years

Survival rates show the percent of individuals still alive five years after initial diagnosis.

	% Surviving	
	White	Black
1974-79	75.2	63.1
1980-82	77.1	65.9
1983-85	79.7	63.7
1986-88	84.6	69.6
1989-94	86.7	70.6

Source: U.S. Department of Health and Human Services, *Health United States, 2001*, p. 279, downloaded from http://www.cdc.gov/nchs/products/pubs/pubd/hus/tables/2001/01hus082.pdf. Survival rates are from National Institutes of Health, National Cancer Institute, Cancer Statistics Branch, Bethesda, Maryland 20892.

People with High Serum Cholesterol, Selected Years

	Percent with High Serum Cholesterol					
	All Races		Whites		African Americans	
	Men	Women	Men	Women	Men	Women
1960-62	30.6	35.6	31.3	36.2	26.0	31.8
1971-74	27.9	29.1	27.9	28.9	26.6	30.5
1975-80	26.4	28.8	26.4	29.2	25.8	26.2
1988-94	18.8	20.5	19.1	20.7	16.4	19.5

Source: U.S. Department of Health and Human Services, Centers for Disease Control, *Morbidity and Mortality Weekly Report*, October 31, 1997, accessed at http://www.cdc.gov/mmwr/preview/mmwrhtml/00049741.htm.

Prevalence and Incidence of Self-reported Diabetes Mellitus, by Year — United States

Age-adjustment, in this case to 1985 population structure, is conducted to make data more comparable, year to year, despite shifting age structure of the population.

Year	Prevalence			Incidence - Diagnosed in Last 12 mo.		
	Number of Existing Cases (000)	Rate per 1,000 Population	Age-Adjusted Rate per 1,000 Population	Number of Existing Cases (000)	Rate per 1,000 Population	Age-Adjusted Rate per 1,000 Population
1980	5,528	25.4	25.5	541	2.5	2.5
1981	5,645	25.1	25.3	501	2.2	2.2
1982	5,729	25.2	25.4	713	3.1	3.2
1983	5,613	24.5	24.7	690	3.0	3.0
1984	6,004	25.9	26.0	645	2.8	2.8
1985	6,134	26.2	26.2	679	2.9	2.9
1986	6,563	27.8	27.8	644	2.7	2.7

[Continued]

Prevalence and Incidence of Self-reported Diabetes Mellitus, by Year — United States

[Continued]

Year	Prevalence			Incidence - Diagnosed in Last 12 mo.		
	Number of Existing Cases (000)	Rate per 1,000 Population	Age-Adjusted Rate per 1,000 Population	Number of Existing Cases (000)	Rate per 1,000 Population	Age-Adjusted Rate per 1,000 Population
1987	6,609	27.7	27.6	715	3.0	3.0
1988	6,162	25.6	25.4	678	2.8	2.8
1989	6,467	26.6	26.3	677	2.8	2.8
1990	6,212	25.2	24.8	521	2.1	2.1
1991	7,206	29.0	28.5	672	2.7	2.7
1992	7,365	29.3	28.5	613	2.4	2.4
1993	7,783	30.6	29.7	865	3.4	3.3
1994	7,744	29.8	29.3	965	3.7	3.7

Source: U.S. Department of Health and Human Services, Centers for Disease Control, *Morbidity and Mortality Weekly Report*, October 31, 1997, accessed at http://www.cdc.gov/mmwr/preview/mmwrhtml/00049741.htm.

Maternal Mortality Rates, Selected Years

Rise in values from 1998 to 1999 in part due to redefinition of mortality codes.

Year	Deaths per 100,000 Live Births		
	All	White	Black
1950	73.7	53.1	NA
1960	32.1	22.4	92.0
1970	21.5	14.4	65.5
1980	9.4	6.7	24.9
1990	7.6	5.1	21.7
1995	6.3	3.6	20.9
1996	6.4	4.1	19.9
1997	7.6	5.2	20.1
1998	6.1	4.2	16.1
1999	8.3	5.5	23.3

Source: U.S. Department of Health and Human Services, *Health United States, 2001*, obtained from http://www.cdc.gov/ nchs/products/pubs/pubd/hus/tables/2001/01hus044.pdf.

Death Rates for Ischemic Heart Disease, 1979 to 1998

Year	Age-Adjusted Death Rates per 100,000 Population				
	All Races		Males		
	Females	Males	White	Black	Non-White
1979	255.5	454.7	462.3	315.9	377.5
1980	263.1	459.7	466.3	334.5	392.2
1981	250.3	440.1	447.4	316.2	366.2
1982	243.7	427.8	434.9	305.3	356.7
1983	241.8	420.6	427.3	308.2	354.0
1984	233.4	403.7	410.1	296.6	340.8
1985	227.0	393.7	399.3	293.4	338.4
1986	219.1	373.2	377.8	288.2	327.3
1987	212.5	359.7	363.4	281.8	322.0
1988	209.0	352.1	355.7	279.8	315.6
1989	200.5	337.4	339.6	276.1	312.3
1990	193.9	328.2	330.5	267.0	302.1
1991	187.8	316.7	318.4	264.1	296.1
1992	182.1	306.7	308.4	255.8	286.6
1993	182.7	306.7	307.8	260.5	291.0
1994	176.3	295.0	296.3	247.4	277.1
1995	173.6	287.8	288.4	247.1	276.3
1996	167.7	276.9	278.9	235.3	254.2
1997	160.9	265.7	267.1	228.3	247.6
1998	155.6	254.1	255.2	221.9	239.1

Source: U.S. Department of Health and Human Services, Centers for Disease Control and Prevention, National Center for Health Statistics, National Vital Statistics System, accessed at http://www.cdc.gov/nchs/default.htm, May 29, 2002.

Death Rates for Lung Cancer, 1979 to 1998

Year	Age-Adjusted Death Rates per 100,000 Population				
	All Races		Males		
	Females	Males	White	Black	Non-White
1979	22.4	82.9	81.6	101.7	93.4
1980	24.4	85.2	83.8	107.6	97.3
1981	25.1	85.4	83.8	109.7	94.4
1982	26.6	87.1	85.5	112.4	99.8
1983	28.3	87.1	85.5	112.6	99.9
1984	29.1	88.3	86.4	118.0	104.1
1985	30.6	88.6	86.8	117.3	103.1
1986	31.5	89.0	87.0	119.1	104.1
1987	32.9	90.0	88.0	121.6	105.5
1988	34.3	89.9	87.9	122.2	105.5
1989	35.9	89.8	87.6	124.6	106.6
1990	37.1	91.1	89.0	125.4	107.2
1991	37.8	90.2	88.2	123.0	105.1

[Continued]

Death Rates for Lung Cancer, 1979 to 1998
[Continued]

| Year | Age-Adjusted Death Rates per 100,000 Population | | | | |
| | All Races | | Males | | |
	Females	Males	White	Black	Non-White
1992	38.9	88.2	86.3	120.5	102.5
1993	39.6	87.9	85.9	121.1	103.3
1994	40.0	86.0	84.1	117.5	100.1
1995	40.7	84.7	82.9	114.8	97.4
1996	40.9	82.9	81.4	111.5	93.9
1997	41.4	81.6	80.2	108.3	91.1
1998	41.5	79.9	78.6	105.2	88.5

Source: U.S. Department of Health and Human Services, Centers for Disease Control and Prevention, National Center for Health Statistics, National Vital Statistics System, accessed at http://www.cdc.gov/nchs/default.htm, May 29, 2002.

Death Rates for Prostate Cancer, 1979 to 1998

| Year | Age-Adjusted Death Rates per 100,000 Population | | | |
	All Races	White	Black	Non-White
1979	32.1	30.1	56.3	51.0
1980	32.8	30.5	61.1	54.3
1981	32.7	30.3	62.1	54.9
1982	32.9	30.7	60.9	53.7
1983	33.4	31.1	63.0	55.0
1984	33.6	31.2	64.5	56.0
1985	33.4	30.8	65.8	57.4
1986	34.4	32.0	66.0	57.0
1987	34.6	32.1	67.8	58.0
1988	35.4	32.9	68.5	58.2
1989	36.6	34.1	70.6	59.9
1990	38.4	35.5	77.0	64.8
1991	38.9	36.2	76.6	63.8
1992	38.9	36.0	78.7	65.2
1993	39.1	36.0	80.0	67.0
1994	38.3	35.4	77.8	64.5
1995	37.1	34.2	75.7	63.1
1996	35.6	32.8	75.6	60.9
1997	33.8	31.1	71.1	56.9
1998	32.0	29.4	68.7	54.0

Source: U.S. Department of Health and Human Services, Centers for Disease Control and Prevention, National Center for Health Statistics, National Vital Statistics System, accessed at http://www.cdc.gov/nchs/default.htm, May 29, 2002.

Death Rates for Colorectal Cancer, 1979 to 1998

| Year | Age-Adjusted Death Rates per 100,000 Population | | | | |
| | All Races | | Males | | |
	Females	Males	White	Black	Non-White
1979	23.8	32.3	32.6	29.8	28.7
1980	23.8	32.8	33.0	32.4	30.5
1981	23.3	31.9	32.1	32.0	29.8
1982	23.0	31.9	32.0	32.9	30.5
1983	22.7	32.1	32.3	32.3	29.9
1984	23.1	32.1	32.2	34.0	31.1
1985	22.7	31.8	31.8	33.4	31.0
1986	21.9	31.2	31.1	34.7	31.7
1987	21.6	31.2	31.1	34.6	31.6
1988	21.2	30.4	30.3	33.8	30.5
1989	20.9	30.2	29.9	35.8	32.4
1990	20.6	30.4	30.1	37.3	33.0
1991	20.2	29.3	29.0	35.4	31.2
1992	19.9	29.0	28.7	35.8	31.4
1993	19.8	28.3	27.9	35.3	31.2
1994	19.4	28.0	27.6	35.0	30.8
1995	19.3	27.5	27.0	35.6	31.3
1996	18.7	26.5	26.1	33.6	29.1
1997	18.4	26.0	25.5	34.2	29.6
1998	18.2	25.4	24.9	32.7	28.3

Source: U.S. Department of Health and Human Services, Centers for Disease Control and Prevention, National Center for Health Statistics, National Vital Statistics System, accessed at http://www.cdc.gov/nchs/default.htm, May 29, 2002.

Death Rates from Accidents, 1979 to 1998

| Year | Age-Adjusted Death Rates per 100,000 Population | | | | |
| | All Races | | Males | | |
	Females	Males	White	Black	Non-White
1979	25.8	69.5	67.5	88.7	86.0
1980	26.1	69.0	66.9	91.0	87.0
1981	24.1	65.1	63.7	82.2	77.1
1982	22.5	59.9	58.5	75.1	71.1
1983	22.3	58.0	56.5	74.7	70.2
1984	22.2	57.6	56.3	73.1	68.0
1985	22.2	57.1	55.5	75.6	69.9
1986	22.0	57.2	55.6	75.2	69.5
1987	22.2	56.4	54.6	75.4	69.2
1988	22.8	57.0	55.0	78.6	71.6
1989	22.4	54.9	53.0	77.0	68.9
1990	21.5	52.9	51.4	69.0	63.1
1991	20.8	50.7	49.1	68.0	61.0
1992	20.0	48.6	47.4	63.2	57.1

[Continued]

Death Rates from Accidents, 1979 to 1998

[Continued]

| Year | Age-Adjusted Death Rates per 100,000 Population | | | | |
| | All Races | | Males | | |
	Females	Males	White	Black	Non-White
1993	20.7	50.1	48.6	66.9	59.5
1994	20.9	50.1	48.6	65.3	59.1
1995	21.3	50.2	48.9	64.9	58.4
1996	21.9	49.5	48.7	61.6	54.7
1997	21.8	49.2	48.4	60.3	54.2
1998	22.1	49.4	48.7	60.8	53.4

Source: U.S. Department of Health and Human Services, Centers for Disease Control and Prevention, National Center for Health Statistics, National Vital Statistics System, accessed at http://www.cdc.gov/nchs/default.htm, May 29, 2002.

Death Rates from Suicide, 1979 to 1998

| Year | Age-Adjusted Death Rates per 100,000 Population | | | | |
| | All Races | | Males | | |
	Females	Males	White	Black	Non-White
1979	6.3	19.9	20.7	12.7	13.0
1980	5.7	19.9	20.9	11.4	11.6
1981	6.0	19.8	20.9	11.4	11.5
1982	5.8	20.4	21.6	11.2	11.1
1983	5.5	20.4	21.6	11.1	11.2
1984	5.6	20.9	22.1	11.7	11.6
1985	5.2	21.1	22.4	11.9	11.7
1986	5.5	21.9	23.2	12.2	12.1
1987	5.3	21.7	23.0	12.8	12.7
1988	5.1	21.2	22.5	12.2	11.9
1989	4.9	21.0	22.3	13.0	12.4
1990	4.8	21.5	22.8	12.8	12.5
1991	4.7	21.2	22.5	13.0	12.6
1992	4.7	20.6	21.9	12.6	12.1
1993	4.6	20.9	22.1	13.0	12.6
1994	4.5	20.7	21.9	12.9	12.8
1995	4.4	20.6	21.9	12.5	12.3
1996	4.3	20.0	21.3	11.9	11.7
1997	4.4	19.4	20.6	11.4	11.7
1998	4.3	19.2	20.6	10.6	11.0

Source: U.S. Department of Health and Human Services, Centers for Disease Control and Prevention, National Center for Health Statistics, National Vital Statistics System, accessed at http://www.cdc.gov/nchs/default.htm, May 29, 2002.

Death Rates from Homicide, 1979 to 1998

Year	Age-Adjusted Death Rates per 100,000 Population				
	All Races		Males		
	Females	Males	White	Black	Non-White
1979	4.2	15.6	9.6	67.5	58.7
1980	4.4	16.6	10.4	69.4	59.2
1981	4.2	16.0	10.0	67.2	56.5
1982	4.1	14.7	9.2	60.3	50.5
1983	3.8	12.9	8.2	52.5	43.9
1984	3.8	12.4	7.9	49.8	41.1
1985	3.8	12.2	7.7	48.4	39.6
1986	4.0	13.2	8.0	53.8	43.9
1987	4.0	12.4	7.4	51.6	41.6
1988	4.0	12.9	7.4	55.2	44.1
1989	4.0	13.5	7.6	57.6	45.8
1990	4.0	14.8	8.3	63.1	49.5
1991	4.3	15.7	8.7	66.0	51.6
1992	4.0	15.1	8.5	61.7	48.0
1993	4.2	15.1	8.1	63.4	49.5
1994	3.9	14.6	8.1	59.1	46.1
1995	3.8	13.1	7.4	51.8	40.5
1996	3.5	11.9	6.6	47.1	36.5
1997	3.2	11.2	6.4	43.1	33.4
1998	3.1	10.0	5.8	38.4	29.5

Source: U.S. Department of Health and Human Services, Centers for Disease Control and Prevention, National Center for Health Statistics, National Vital Statistics System, accessed at http://www.cdc.gov/nchs/default.htm, May 29, 2002.

Suicide Rate for Males as Percent of Population

Year	Male Suicide Rate per 100,000	Males 15-24 as % of Population
1979	69.5	9.1
1980	69.0	9.1
1981	65.1	9.0
1982	59.9	8.8
1983	58.0	8.6
1984	57.6	8.4
1985	57.1	8.2
1986	57.2	8.1
1987	56.4	7.9
1988	57.0	7.7
1989	54.9	7.5
1990	52.9	7.6
1991	50.7	7.4

[Continued]

Suicide Rate for Males as Percent of Population

[Continued]

Year	Male Suicide Rate per 100,000	Males 15-24 as % of Population
1992	48.6	7.3
1993	50.1	7.2
1994	50.1	7.1
1995	50.2	7.0
1996	49.5	7.0
1997	49.2	7.0
1998	49.4	7.0

Source: U.S. Department of Health and Human Services, Centers for Disease Control and Prevention, National Center for Health Statistics, National Vital Statistics System, accessed at http://www.cdc.gov/nchs/default.htm, May 29, 2002. Population data from U.S. Bureau of the Census.

Male Suicides in 1999 by Age

Age Group	Number of Suicides	Percent of Total
10-14	192	0.8
15-19	1,347	5.7
20-24	1,979	8.4
25-34	4,194	17.9
35-44	5,019	21.4
45-54	3,854	16.4
55-64	2,255	9.6
65 and over	4,618	19.7

Source: U.S. Department of Health and Human Services, Centers for Disease Control and Prevention, National Center for Health Statistics, National Vital Statistics System, accessed at http://www.cdc.gov/nchs/default.htm, May 29, 2002. "Suicide Among Black Youths - United States, 1980-1995," *Morbidity and Mortality Weekly Report*, Centers for Disease Control, March 20, 1998.

Historical Suicide Rates per 100,000 Population, Both Sexes, All Races

Year	Suicide Rate
1900	10.2
1910	15.3
1920	10.2
1930	15.6
1940	14.4
1950	11.4

[Continued]

Historical Suicide Rates per 100,000 Population, Both Sexes, All Races

[Continued]

Year	Suicide Rate
1960	10.6
1970	11.6
1980	11.9
1990	12.4
2000	10.0

Source: U.S. Department of Health and Human Services, Centers for Disease Control and Prevention, National Center for Health Statistics, National Vital Statistics System, accessed at http://www.cdc.gov/nchs/default.htm, May 29, 2002. U.S. Bureau of the Census, *Historical Statistics of the United States*, 1975.

Suicide Rates of Whites and Blacks, Both Sexes, 1979 to 1998

Data are age-adjusted rates per 100,000 population.

Year	Suicide Rate	
	Whites	Blacks
1979	12.9	6.9
1980	12.7	6.0
1981	12.9	6.1
1982	13.2	6.0
1983	13.1	5.8
1984	13.5	6.2
1985	13.4	6.3
1986	14.0	6.5
1987	13.8	6.7
1988	13.5	6.8
1989	13.2	7.1
1990	13.5	6.9
1991	13.3	6.7
1992	13.0	6.8
1993	13.1	7.0
1994	12.9	7.0
1995	12.9	6.7
1996	12.7	6.5
1997	12.4	6.2
1998	12.4	5.7

Source: U.S. Department of Health and Human Services, Centers for Disease Control and Prevention, National Center for Health Statistics, National Vital Statistics System, accessed at http://www.cdc.gov/nchs/default.htm, May 29, 2002.

Low-Birthweight (LBW) Live Births, Selected Years

Low-birthweight babies weigh less than 2,500 grams at birth. Superlow- birthweight babies weigh less than 1,500 grams.

	LBW as % of Live Births				LBW Singletons (% of Live Birth)		
	All Races	Whites	Blacks	Superlow Births	All Races	Whites	Blacks
1970	7.93	6.85	13.90	1.17	NA	NA	NA
1975	7.38	6.27	13.19	1.16	NA	NA	NA
1980	6.84	5.72	12.69	1.15	5.96	4.90	11.46
1985	6.75	5.65	12.65	1.21	5.80	4.77	11.35
1990	6.97	5.70	13.25	1.27	5.90	4.68	11.86
1995	7.32	6.22	13.13	1.35	6.05	4.98	11.59
2000	7.80	6.70	13.10	1.45	6.00	4.99	11.15

Source: U.S. Department of Health and Human Services, Centers for Disease Control and Prevention, *Health, United States, 2001*. For 2000 data: *National Vital Statistics Report*, Vol. 50, No. 5, February 12, 2002.

Breastfeeding Rates, Selected Years

Data for 1970-71 for Whites and Blacks includes Hispanics.

	Percent of Mothers Who Breast-fed				
	Breast-fed in Hospital				Breast-fed 3 Month or More
	All Races	Non-Hispanic White	Non-Hispanic Black	Hispanic	
1970-71	24.9	26.4	10.8	NA	12.3
1972-74	30.1	32.5	12.5	33.1	18.8
1975-77	36.7	38.9	16.8	42.9	24.3
1978-80	47.5	53.2	19.6	46.3	30.7
1981-83	58.1	64.3	26.0	52.8	39.7
1984-86	54.5	59.7	22.9	58.9	34.4
1987-89	52.3	58.3	21.0	51.3	32.2
1990-92	54.2	59.1	22.9	58.8	33.1
1993-94	58.1	61.2	27.4	67.4	32.7

Source: U.S. Department of Health and Human Services, Centers for Disease Control and Prevention, data from National Survey of Family Growth, published in *Health, United States*, 1994 and 2001.

Infant Mortality Rate, 1980 to 1999

Infants are under one year of age. The rate is expressed as deaths per 1,000 live births.

Year	All Races			Both Sexes	
	Both Sexes	Girls	Boys	Whites	Blacks
1980	12.6	11.2	13.9	10.9	22.2
1981	11.9	10.7	13.1	10.3	20.8
1982	11.5	10.2	12.8	9.9	20.5
1983	11.2	10.0	12.3	9.6	20.0
1984	10.8	9.6	11.9	9.3	19.2
1985	10.6	9.3	11.9	9.2	19.0
1986	10.4	9.1	11.5	8.8	18.9
1987	10.1	8.9	11.2	8.5	18.8
1988	10.0	8.9	11.0	8.4	18.5
1989	9.8	8.8	10.8	8.1	18.6
1990	9.2	8.1	10.3	7.6	18.0
1991	8.9	7.8	10.0	7.3	17.6
1992	8.5	7.6	9.4	6.9	16.8
1993	8.4	7.4	9.3	6.8	16.5
1994	8.0	7.2	8.8	6.6	15.8
1995	7.6	6.8	8.3	6.3	15.1
1996	7.3	6.6	8.0	6.1	14.7
1997	7.2	6.5	8.0	6.0	14.2
1998	7.2	6.5	7.8	6.0	14.3
1999	7.1	6.4	7.7	5.8	14.6

Source: U.S. Department of Health and Human Services, Centers for Disease Control, *National Vital Statistics Report*, Vol. 49, No. 8 and 11, September 21, 2001 and October 12, 2001.

Infant Mortality - 50 Years of Decline

Infants are under one year of age. The rate is expressed as deaths per 1,000 live births.

Year	All races			White			Non-White			Black		
	Both	Male	Female	Both	Male	Female	Both	Male	Female	Both	Male	Female
1940	47.0	52.5	41.3	43.2	48.3	37.8	73.8	82.2	65.2	72.9	81.1	64.6
1950	29.2	32.8	25.5	26.8	30.2	23.1	44.5	48.9	39.9	43.9	48.3	39.4
1960	26.0	29.3	22.6	22.9	26.0	19.6	43.2	47.9	38.5	44.3	49.1	39.4
1970	20.0	22.4	17.5	17.8	20.0	15.4	30.9	34.2	27.5	32.6	36.2	29.0
1980	12.6	13.9	11.2	11.0	12.3	9.6	19.1	20.7	17.5	21.4	23.3	19.4
1990	9.2	10.3	8.1	7.6	8.5	6.6	15.5	17.0	14.0	18.0	19.6	16.2
1999	7.1	7.7	6.4	5.8	6.4	5.2	11.9	12.9	10.9	14.6	15.9	13.2

Source: U.S. Department of Health and Human Services, Centers for Disease Control, *National Vital Statistics Report*, Vol. 49, No. 8 and 11, September 21, 2001 and October 12, 2001.

Sudden Infant Death Syndrome (SIDS) in Decline, 1983 to 1998

Table updated from CDC sources past 1994. Data show deaths per 1,000 live birth in the year.

	White	Black
1983	1.226	2.698
1984	1.232	2.533
1985	1.237	2.332
1986	1.210	2.447
1987	1.184	2.368
1988	1.216	2.380
1989	1.182	2.402
1990	1.107	2.306
1991	1.102	2.328
1992	1.012	2.184
1993	0.970	2.189
1994	0.851	1.941
1995	0.948	2.217
1996	0.818	2.319
1997	0.804	2.172
1998	0.773	2.137

Source: "Sudden Infant Death Syndrome, United States, 1983-1994", Centers for Disease Control, National Center for Chronic Disease Prevention and Health Promotion, published in *Morbidity and Mortality Weekly Report*, Vol. 45, No. 40, October 11, 1996.

Estimated Life Expectancy at Birth in Years

	All races			White			Black[1]		
	Both sexes	Male	Female	Both sexes	Male	Female	Both sexes	Male	Female
1948	67.2	64.6	69.9	68.0	65.5	71.0	60.0	58.1	62.5
1949	68.0	65.2	70.7	68.8	66.2	71.9	60.6	58.9	62.7
1950	68.2	65.6	71.1	69.1	66.5	72.2	60.8	59.1	62.9
1951	68.4	65.6	71.4	69.3	66.5	72.4	61.2	59.2	63.4
1952	68.6	65.8	71.6	69.5	66.6	72.6	61.4	59.1	63.8
1953	68.8	66.0	72.0	69.7	66.8	73.0	62.0	59.7	64.5
1954	69.6	66.7	72.8	70.5	67.5	73.7	63.4	61.1	65.9
1955	69.6	66.7	72.8	70.5	67.4	73.7	63.7	61.4	66.1
1956	69.7	66.7	72.9	70.5	67.5	73.9	63.6	61.3	66.1
1957	69.5	66.4	72.7	70.3	67.2	73.7	63.0	60.7	65.5
1958	69.6	66.6	72.9	70.5	67.4	73.9	63.4	61.0	65.8
1959	69.9	66.8	73.2	70.7	67.5	74.2	63.9	61.3	66.5
1960	69.7	66.6	73.1	70.6	67.4	74.1	63.6	61.1	66.3
1961	70.2	67.1	73.6	71.0	67.8	74.6	64.5	62.0	67.1
1962	70.1	66.9	73.5	70.9	67.7	74.5	64.2	61.6	66.9
1963	69.9	66.6	73.4	70.8	67.4	74.4	63.7	61.0	66.6
1964	70.2	66.8	73.7	71.0	67.7	74.7	64.2	61.3	67.3

[Continued]

Estimated Life Expectancy at Birth in Years
[Continued]

	All races			White			Black[1]		
	Both sexes	Male	Female	Both sexes	Male	Female	Both sexes	Male	Female
1965	70.2	66.8	73.8	71.1	67.6	74.8	64.3	61.2	67.6
1966	70.2	66.7	73.9	71.1	67.5	74.8	64.2	60.9	67.6
1967	70.5	67.0	74.3	71.4	67.8	75.2	64.9	61.4	68.5
1968	70.2	66.6	74.1	71.1	67.5	75.0	64.1	60.4	67.9
1969	70.5	66.8	74.4	71.4	67.7	75.3	64.5	60.6	68.6
1970	70.8	67.1	74.7	71.7	68.0	75.6	64.1	60.0	68.3
1971	71.1	67.4	75.0	72.0	68.3	75.8	64.6	60.5	68.9
1972	71.2	67.4	75.1	72.0	68.3	75.9	64.7	60.4	69.1
1973	71.4	67.6	75.3	72.2	68.5	76.1	65.0	60.9	69.3
1974	72.0	68.2	75.9	72.8	69.0	76.7	66.0	61.7	70.3
1975	72.6	68.8	76.6	73.4	69.5	77.3	66.8	62.4	71.3
1976	72.9	69.1	76.8	73.6	69.9	77.5	67.2	62.9	71.6
1977	73.3	69.5	77.2	74.0	70.2	77.9	67.7	63.4	72.0
1978	73.5	69.6	77.3	74.1	70.4	78.0	68.1	63.7	72.4
1979	73.9	70.0	77.8	74.6	70.8	78.4	68.5	64.0	72.9
1980	73.7	70.0	77.4	74.4	70.7	78.1	68.1	63.8	72.5
1981	74.1	70.4	77.8	74.8	71.1	78.4	68.9	64.5	73.2
1982	74.5	70.8	78.1	75.1	71.5	78.7	69.4	65.1	73.6
1983	74.6	71.0	78.1	75.2	71.6	78.7	69.4	65.2	73.5
1984	74.7	71.1	78.2	75.3	71.8	78.7	69.5	65.3	73.6
1985	74.7	71.1	78.2	75.3	71.8	78.7	69.3	65.0	73.4
1986	74.7	71.2	78.2	75.4	71.9	78.8	69.1	64.8	73.4
1987	74.9	71.4	78.3	75.6	72.1	78.9	69.1	64.7	73.4
1988	74.9	71.4	78.3	75.6	72.2	78.9	68.9	64.4	73.2
1989	75.1	71.7	78.5	75.9	72.5	79.2	68.8	64.3	73.3
1990	75.4	71.8	78.8	76.1	72.7	79.4	69.1	64.5	73.6
1991	75.5	72.0	78.9	76.3	72.9	79.6	69.3	64.6	73.8
1992	75.8	72.3	79.1	76.5	73.2	79.8	69.6	65.0	73.9
1993	75.5	72.2	78.8	76.3	73.1	79.5	69.2	64.6	73.7
1994	75.7	72.4	79.0	76.5	73.3	79.6	69.5	64.9	73.9
1995	75.8	72.5	78.9	76.5	73.4	79.6	69.6	65.2	73.9
1996	76.1	73.1	79.1	76.8	73.9	79.7	70.2	66.1	74.2
1997	76.5	73.6	79.4	77.2	74.3	79.9	71.1	67.2	74.7
1998	76.7	73.8	79.5	77.3	74.5	80.0	71.3	67.6	74.8
1999	76.7	73.9	79.4	77.3	74.6	79.9	71.4	67.8	74.7
2000	76.9	74.1	79.5	77.4	74.8	80.0	71.8	68.3	75.0

Source: National Vital Statistics Report, Vol. 47, No. 28, December 13, 1999, National Center for Health Statistics, U.S. Department of Health and Human Services. *Notes:* 1. Prior to 1970, data for the black population are not available. Data shown for 1948-69 are for the nonwhite population.

Chapter 2
DISEASES

Rate of Sexually Transmitted Diseases per 100,000 Population

NR stands for Not Reported.

Year	Syphilis	Gonorrhea	Chlamydia	HIV/ AIDS
1941	368.2	146.7	NR	NR
1942	363.4	160.9	NR	NR
1943	447.0	213.6	NR	NR
1944	367.9	236.5	NR	NR
1945	282.3	225.8	NR	NR
1946	271.7	275.0	NR	NR
1947	252.3	270.0	NR	NR
1948	218.2	239.8	NR	NR
1949	175.3	217.3	NR	NR
1950	146.0	192.5	NR	NR
1951	116.1	168.9	NR	NR
1952	110.2	160.8	NR	NR
1953	95.9	153.9	NR	NR
1954	82.9	153.5	NR	NR
1955	76.2	147.0	NR	NR
1956	78.7	135.7	NR	NR
1957	73.5	127.4	NR	NR
1958	66.4	135.6	NR	NR
1959	69.2	137.6	NR	NR
1960	68.8	145.4	NR	NR
1961	68.8	145.8	NR	NR
1962	68.7	143.6	NR	NR
1963	66.6	149.2	NR	NR
1964	60.4	159.0	NR	NR
1965	58.9	169.6	NR	NR
1966	54.4	181.9	NR	NR
1967	52.5	207.3	NR	NR
1968	48.8	235.7	NR	NR
1969	46.3	268.6	NR	NR
1970	45.3	297.2	NR	NR
1971	46.9	327.2	NR	NR
1972	43.9	369.7	NR	NR

[Continued]

Rate of Sexually Transmitted Diseases per 100,000 Population

[Continued]

Year	Syphilis	Gonorrhea	Chlamydia	HIV/AIDS
1973	41.7	402.0	NR	NR
1974	39.6	428.2	NR	NR
1975	37.6	467.7	NR	NR
1976	33.2	464.1	NR	NR
1977	29.6	459.5	NR	NR
1978	29.4	459.7	NR	NR
1979	30.1	450.3	NR	NR
1980	30.5	445.1	NR	NR
1981	32.0	435.2	NR	NR
1982	32.9	417.9	NR	NR
1983	32.1	387.6	NR	NR
1984	29.8	374.8	NR	NR
1985	28.5	384.3	NR	NR
1986	28.3	372.8	NR	NR
1987	35.9	323.6	NR	NR
1988	42.5	300.3	NR	NR
1989	46.6	297.1	NR	13.6
1990	54.3	278.0	NR	16.7
1991	51.0	247.1	NR	17.3
1992	44.2	196.7	NR	17.8
1993	39.7	172.4	NR	40.2
1994	32.0	168.4	NR	30.1
1995	26.2	149.5	182.6	27.2
1996	20.0	122.8	188.1	25.2
1997	17.4	121.4	196.8	21.9
1998	14.2	132.9	236.6	17.2
1999	13.1	133.2	254.1	16.7

Source: Centers for Disease Control and Prevention. Data for 1999 and HIV/AIDS data from *Summary of notifiable diseases, United States, 1999.* MMWR 1999; 48 (No. 53). Data from 1941 through 1993 available at http://wonder.cdc.gov/wonder/STD/OSTD3202/Table_1.html.

AIDS Deaths by Sex and Type of Exposure to the Disease

Year	Number of Cases — By Sex — Both Sexes[1]	Men	Women	By Exposure — Men Having Sex With Men	Hetero-sexual Contact	Injecting Drug Use	Percent of Cases in Year — By Sex — Men	Women	By Exposure — Men Having Sex With Men	Hetero-sexual Contact	Injecting Drug Use	All Other Exposures
1993	45,598	38,908	6,146	27,144	4,262	12,477	85.3	13.5	59.5	9.3	27.4	3.8
1994	50,418	42,322	7,510	29,062	5,502	14,167	83.9	14.9	57.6	10.9	28.1	3.3
1995	51,117	42,434	8,144	28,471	6,388	14,668	83.0	15.9	55.7	12.5	28.7	3.1
1996	38,025	30,636	6,960	19,445	5,550	11,840	80.6	18.3	51.1	14.6	31.1	3.1
1997	21,999	17,212	4,567	10,113	3,761	7,483	78.2	20.8	46.0	17.1	34.0	2.9
1998	18,397	14,241	4,033	8,310	3,256	6,376	77.4	21.9	45.2	17.7	34.7	2.5

[Continued]

AIDS Deaths by Sex and Type of Exposure to the Disease
[Continued]

Year	Number of Cases						Percent of Cases in Year					
	By Sex			By Exposure			By Sex		By Exposure			
	Both Sexes[1]	Men	Women	Men Having Sex With Men	Hetero-sexual Contact	Injecting Drug Use	Men	Women	Men Having Sex With Men	Hetero-sexual Contact	Injecting Drug Use	All Other Exposures
1999	17,172	12,991	4,063	7,412	3,289	6,039	75.7	23.7	43.2	19.2	35.2	2.5
2000	15,245	11,514	3,656	6,559	3,117	5,213	75.5	24.0	43.0	20.4	34.2	2.3

Source: Centers for Disease Control & Prevention, National Center for HIV, STD and TB prevention, www.cdc.gov/hiv/stats/hasr 1301/table30.htm. *Notes:* 1. Both sexes includes children, not specifically shown. Number of exposures do not total to both sexes because miscellaneous exposures are not shown.

Selected Childhood Diseases

NR stands for Not Reported.

Year	Total Number of Occurrences Reported					
	Diphtheria	Measles (Rubeola)	Mumps	Pertussis (Whooping Cough)	Polio-myelitis	Rubella (German Measles)
1944	14,150	630,291	NR	109,873	19,029	NR
1945	18,675	146,013	NR	133,792	13,624	NR
1946	16,354	659,843	NR	109,860	25,698	NR
1947	12,262	222,375	NR	156,517	10,827	NR
1948	9,493	615,104	NR	74,715	27,726	NR
1949	7,969	625,281	NR	69,479	42,033	NR
1950	5,796	319,124	NR	120,718	33,300	NR
1951	3,983	530,118	NR	68,687	28,386	NR
1952	2,960	683,077	NR	45,030	57,879	NR
1953	2,355	449,146	NR	37,129	35,592	NR
1954	2,041	682,720	NR	60,886	38,476	NR
1955	1,984	555,156	NR	62,786	28,985	NR
1956	1,568	611,936	NR	31,732	15,140	NR
1957	1,211	486,799	NR	28,295	5,485	NR
1958	918	763,094	NR	32,148	5,787	NR
1959	934	406,162	NR	40,005	8,425	NR
1960	918	441,703	NR	14,809	3,190	NR
1961	617	423,919	NR	11,468	1,312	NR
1962	444	481,530	NR	17,749	910	NR
1963	314	385,156	NR	17,135	449	NR
1964	293	458,083	NR	13,005	122	NR
1965	164	261,904	NR	6,799	72	NR
1966	209	204,136	NR	7,717	113	46,975
1967	219	62,705	NR	9,718	41	46,888
1968	260	22,231	152,209	4,810	53	49,371
1969	241	25,826	90,918	3,285	20	57,686
1970	435	47,351	104,953	4,249	33	56,552
1971	215	75,290	124,939	3,036	21	45,086
1972	152	32,275	74,215	3,287	31	25,507

[Continued]

Selected Childhood Diseases
[Continued]

Year	Total Number of Occurrences Reported					
	Diphtheria	Measles (Rubeola)	Mumps	Pertussis (Whooping Cough)	Polio-myelitis	Rubella (German Measles)
1973	228	26,690	69,612	1,759	8	27,804
1974	272	22,094	59,128	2,402	7	11,917
1975	307	24,374	59,647	1,738	8	16,652
1976	128	41,126	38,492	1,010	14	12,491
1977	84	57,345	21,436	2,177	18	20,395
1978	76	26,871	16,817	2,063	15	18,269
1979	59	13,597	14,225	1,623	34	11,795
1980	3	13,506	8,576	1,730	9	3,904
1981	5	3,124	4,941	1,248	6	2,077
1982	2	1,714	5,270	1,895	8	2,325
1983	5	1,497	3,355	2,463	15	970
1984	1	2,587	3,021	2,276	8	752
1985	3	2,822	2,982	3,589	7	630
1986	-	6,282	7,790	4,195	9	551
1987	3	3,655	12,848	2,823	9	306
1988	2	3,396	4,866	3,450	9	225
1989	3	18,193	5,712	4,157	9	396
1990	4	27,786	5,292	4,570	6	1,125
1991	5	9,643	4,264	2,719	9	1,401
1992	4	2,237	2,572	4,083	6	160
1993		312	1,692	6,586	3	192
1994	2	963	1,537	4,617	8	227
1995	-	309	906	5,137	7	128
1996	2	508	751	7,796	5	238
1997	4	138	683	6,564	5	181
1998	1	100	666	7,405	1	364
1999	1	100	387	7,288	-	267

Source: Centers for Disease Control and Prevention. *Summary of notifiable diseases, United States, 1999.* MMWR 1999 and earlier years.

Historical Diseases That Still Plague Us

Year	Total Number of Occurrences Reported						
	Cholera	Leprosy	Malaria	Plague	Syphillis	Tuberculosis	Typhoid Fever
1944	-	37	57,626	1	467,755	126,294	4,599
1945	-	40	62,763	-	359,114	114,931	4,211
1946	-	43	48,610	-	963,647	119,256	3,268
1947	-	56	15,116	1	355,592	134,946	3,075
1948	-	63	9,606	-	314,313	137,006	2,840
1949	-	41	4,151	3	256,463	134,865	2,795

[Continued]

Historical Diseases That Still Plague Us
[Continued]

Year	Total Number of Occurrences Reported						
	Cholera	Leprosy	Malaria	Plague	Syphillis	Tuberculosis	Typhoid Fever
1950	-	44	2,184	3	217,558	121,742	2,484
1951	-	57	5,600	1	174,924	118,491	2,128
1952	-	57	7,023	-	167,762	86,700	2,341
1953	-	60	1,310	-	148,573	84,304	2,252
1954	-	56	715	-	130,697	79,775	2,169
1955	-	75	522	-	122,392	77,368	1,704
1956	-	52	234	1	130,201	69,895	1,700
1957	-	36	132	1	123,758	67,149	1,231
1958	-	39	85	-	113,884	63,534	1,043
1959	-	44	71	4	120,824	57,535	859
1960	-	54	72	2	122,538	55,494	816
1961	-	63	73	3	124,658	53,726	814
1962	-	80	118	-	126,245	53,315	608
1963	-	103	99	1	124,137	54,042	566
1964	-	97	93	-	114,325	50,874	501
1965	2	96	147	8	112,842	49,016	454
1966	-	109	565	5	105,159	47,767	378
1967	-	81	2,022	3	102,581	45,647	396
1968	-	123	2,317	3	96,271	42,623	395
1969	-	98	3,102	5	92,162	39,120	364
1970	-	129	3,051	13	91,382	37,137	346
1971	1	131	2,375	2	95,997	35,217	407
1972	-	130	742	1	91,149	32,882	398
1973	1	146	237	2	87,469	30,998	680
1974	-	118	293	8	83,771	30,122	437
1975	-	162	373	20	80,356	33,989	375
1976	-	145	471	16	71,761	32,105	419
1977	3	151	547	18	64,621	30,145	398
1978	12	168	731	12	64,875	28,521	505
1979	1	185	894	13	67,049	27,669	528
1980	9	223	2,062	18	68,832	27,749	510
1981	19	256	1,388	13	72,799	27,373	584
1982	-	250	1,056	19	75,579	25,520	425
1983	1	259	813	40	74,637	23,846	507
1984	1	290	1,007	31	69,888	22,255	390
1985	4	361	1,049	17	67,563	22,201	402
1986	23	270	1,123	10	68,215	22,768	362
1987	6	238	944	12	86,545	22,517	400
1988	8	184	1,099	15	103,437	22,436	436
1989	-	163	1,277	4	110,797	23,495	460
1990	6	198	1,292	2	134,255	25,701	552
1991	26	154	1,278	11	128,569	26,283	501
1992	103	172	1,087	13	112,581	26,673	414
1993	18	187	1,411	10	101,259	25,313	440

[Continued]

Historical Diseases That Still Plague Us
[Continued]

Year	Total Number of Occurrences Reported						
	Cholera	Leprosy	Malaria	Plague	Syphillis	Tubercu- losis	Typhoid Fever
1994	39	136	1,229	17	81,696	24,361	441
1995	23	144	1,419	9	68,953	22,860	369
1996	4	112	1,800	5	52,976	21,337	396
1997	6	122	2,001	4	46,540	19,851	365
1998	17	108	1,611	9	37,977	18,361	375
1999	6	108	1,666	9	35,628	17,531	346

Source: Centers for Disease Control and Prevention. *Summary of notifiable diseases, United States, 1999.* MMWR 1999 and earlier years.

Selected Diseases Identified in the Second Half of the 20th Century

Blanks are left where no data are available.

Year	Total Number of Occurrences Reported						
	AIDS	Hepatitis A	Hepatitis B	Hepatitis C	Legionaire's Disease	Lyme Disease	Toxic Shock Syndrome
1964		37,740					
1965		33,856					
1966		32,859	1,497				
1967		38,909	2,458				
1968		45,893	4,829				
1969		48,416	5,909				
1970		56,797	8,310				
1971		59,606	9,556				
1972		54,074	9,402				
1973		50,749	8,451				
1974		40,358	10,631				
1975		35,855	13,121				
1976		33,288	14,973		235		
1977		31,153	16,831		359		
1978		29,500	15,016		761		
1979		30,407	15,452		593		
1980		29,087	19,015		475		
1981		25,802	21,152		408		
1982		23,403	22,177		654		
1983		21,532	24,318	3,470	852		502
1984	4,445	22,040	26,115	3,871	750		482
1985	8,249	23,210	26,611	4,184	830		384
1986	12,932	23,430	26,107	3,634	948		412
1987	21,070	25,280	25,916	2,999	1,038		372
1988	31,001	28,507	23,177	2,619	1,085		390

[Continued]

Selected Diseases Identified in the Second Half of the 20th Century
[Continued]

Year	Total Number of Occurrences Reported						
	AIDS	Hepatitis A	Hepatitis B	Hepatitis C	Legionaire's Disease	Lyme Disease	Toxic Shock Syndrome
1989	33,722	35,821	23,419	2,529	1,190		400
1990	41,595	31,441	21,102	2,553	1,370		322
1991	43,672	24,378	18,003	3,582	1,317	9,465	280
1992	45,472	23,112	16,126	6,010	1,339	9,895	244
1993	103,533	24,238	13,361	4,786	1,280	8,257	212
1994	78,279	26,796	12,517	4,470	1,615	13,043	192
1995	71,547	31,582	10,805	4,576	1,241	11,700	191
1996	66,885	31,032	10,637	3,716	1,198	16,455	145
1997	58,492	30,021	10,416	3,816	1,163	12,801	157
1998	46,521	23,229	10,258	3,518	1,355	16,801	138
1999	45,104	17,047	7,694	3,111	1,108	16,273	113

Source: Centers for Disease Control and Prevention. *Summary of notifiable diseases, United States, 1999.* MMWR 1999 and earlier years.

Depression as Measured by Visits to Physicians

Diagnoses are not available for all the years. Drug mentions are also reported only spottily. Blanks are left where no data are available.

Year	Physician Visits			Diagnoses Recorded			Drug Mentions Recorded		
	All Causes	Depression	Depr. % of All Visits	Major depression	Neurotic Depression	Major as % of Total	Prozac	Zoloft	Anti-depressants
1989	692,702	7,350	1.06						
1990	704,604	7,000	0.99						
1991	669,689	7,060	1.05						
1992	762,045	8,344	1.09						
1993	717,191	8,758	1.22				6,462		6,462
1994	681,457	13,180	1.93				5,989		5,989
1995	697,082	9,011	1.29	6,002	2,863	66.6			
1996	734,493	8,169	1.11	5,582	2,897	68.3	6,613		6,613
1997	959,300	12,003	1.25	8,275	3,691	68.9	8,225	7,607	15,832
1998	829,280	9,708	1.17				8,152	8,364	16,516
1999	756,734	9,664	1.28				7,922	8,351	16,273
2000	823,542	10,043	1.22					9,183	9,183

Source: U.S. Department of Health and Human Services, *National Ambulatory Medical Care Survey*, 1989 through 2000, accessible at http://www.cdc.gov/nchs/about/major/ahcd/adata.htm.

Attention Deficit Disorder and Learning Disability - 1997-1998

ADD stands for Attention Deficit Disorder; LD stands for Learning Disability. - is used to indicate that data did not meet precision standards.

Characteristics	Percent of All Children 6-11 Years			Boys			Girls		
	ADD/noLD	LD/noADD	Both	ADD/noLD	LD/noADD	Both	ADD/noLD	LD/noADD	Both
Total	3.3	4.2	3.5	4.7	4.7	4.9	1.7	3.7	2.0
Age									
6 to 8	2.3	3.4	2.7	3.3	3.8	4.0	1.3	2.9	1.5
9 to 11	4.2	5.0	4.2	6.1	5.6	5.7	2.2	4.4	2.6
Race/ethnicity									
White	4.1	3.9	3.6	6.0	4.2	5.0	2.1	3.7	2.2
Black	1.8	5.4	4.1	2.7	7.6	6.5	-	3.2	-
Hispanic	1.4	4.6	2.6	1.8	4.8	3.1	-	4.5	-
Family structure									
Mother and Father	3.0	3.5	2.9	4.4	4.0	3.8	1.5	3.0	2.0
Mother only	3.8	6.1	4.6	5.4	6.6	7.0	-	5.7	2.0

Source: Pastor, P.N., Reuben, C.A. *Attention deficit disorder and learning disability: United States, 1997-98.* National Center for Health Statistics. Vital Health Statistics 10(206). 2002, accessible at http://www/cdc/gove/nchs/data/sereies/sr_10/sr10_206.pdf.

Trends in Cancer Mortality, 1979 to 1998

Data are intended to show that cancer death rates have changed very little over a span of 20 years.

Year	Age-Adjusted Death Rates per 100,000 Population								
	All Cancers	Trachea, Bronchus, Lung	Prostate	Breast (Females)	Colorectal	Lymphoid, leukemia	Ovarian	Pancreatic	Stomach
1979	204.0	47.9	32.1	31.2	27.2	18.4	9.4	10.7	7.5
1980	207.9	49.9	32.8	31.9	27.4	18.9	9.4	10.7	7.4
1981	206.4	50.3	32.7	32.0	26.7	18.5	9.3	10.7	7.2
1982	208.3	51.7	32.9	32.2	26.5	19.0	9.3	10.6	7.0
1983	209.1	52.6	33.4	32.1	26.4	19.1	9.2	10.7	6.8
1984	210.8	53.6	33.6	32.9	26.7	19.2	9.1	10.8	6.8
1985	211.3	54.6	33.4	33.0	26.3	19.5	9.1	10.6	6.5
1986	211.5	55.2	34.4	32.8	25.6	19.6	9.2	10.6	6.3
1987	211.7	56.4	34.6	32.7	25.4	19.4	9.2	10.6	6.2
1988	212.5	57.2	35.4	33.2	24.8	19.6	9.3	10.5	6.1
1989	214.2	58.1	36.6	33.2	24.6	20.2	9.3	10.6	6.2
1990	216.0	59.3	38.4	33.3	24.5	20.4	9.4	10.7	6.1
1991	215.8	59.4	38.9	32.8	23.8	20.8	9.5	10.7	6.0
1992	214.3	59.2	38.9	31.8	23.5	20.7	9.5	10.7	5.7
1993	214.6	59.5	39.1	31.5	23.2	20.9	9.1	10.7	5.7
1994	213.1	59.0	38.3	31.1	22.9	21.2	9.4	10.7	5.4
1995	211.7	58.9	37.1	30.8	22.7	21.3	9.2	10.5	5.4
1996	208.7	58.4	35.6	29.8	21.9	21.2	9.0	10.5	5.2

[Continued]

Trends in Cancer Mortality, 1979 to 1998
[Continued]

Year	Age-Adjusted Death Rates per 100,000 Population								
	All Cancers	Trachea, Bronchus, Lung	Prostate	Breast (Females)	Colorectal	Lymphoid, leukemia	Ovarian	Pancreatic	Stomach
1997	205.7	58.1	33.8	28.6	21.6	21.2	9.1	10.6	5.0
1998	202.4	57.6	32.0	27.9	21.2	20.8	8.8	10.6	4.8

Source: U.S. Department of Health and Human Services, Centers for Disease Control and Prevention, National Center for Health Statistics, National Vital Statistics System, accessed at http://www.cdc.gov/nchs/default.htm, May 29, 2002.

Five-Year Relative Cancer Survival Rates for Selected Cancer Sites

Data are based on the Surveillance, Epidemiology, and End Results Program's population-based registries in Atlanta, Detroit, Seattle-Puget Sound, San Francisco-Oakland, Connecticut, Iowa, New Mexico, Utah, and Hawaii.

Sex and site	Percent of Patients									
	White					Black				
	1974-79	1980-82	1983-85	1986-88	1989-97	1974-79	1980-82	1983-85	1986-88	1989-97
Both sexes										
All sites	50.9	52.1	53.8	56.7	62.0	39.2	39.7	39.7	42.6	49.7
Oral cavity and pharynx	54.9	55.6	55.2	55.2	57.1	36.6	31.0	35.2	34.6	33.7
Esophagus	5.5	7.3	9.3	10.8	13.8	3.3	5.4	6.2	7.2	9.0
Stomach	15.2	16.5	16.3	19.1	19.8	15.9	19.4	19.0	19.1	21.6
Colon	51.9	55.7	58.4	61.5	62.6	47.3	49.2	49.4	52.8	52.4
Rectum	49.8	53.1	55.9	59.1	61.0	40.4	38.4	43.7	51.4	53.0
Pancreas	2.4	2.8	2.9	3.2	4.2	3.2	4.5	5.2	6.0	3.9
Lung and bronchus	13.1	13.5	13.8	13.5	14.7	11.3	12.1	11.4	11.9	11.4
Urinary bladder	74.9	78.9	78.2	80.7	82.1	51.5	58.7	59.3	62.3	63.8
Non-Hodgkin's lymphoma	48.2	51.8	54.4	52.8	53.5	50.3	50.0	45.1	50.2	43.0
Leukemia	36.6	39.5	41.9	44.1	45.9	30.8	33.1	32.9	37.6	35.7
Male										
All sites	43.4	46.7	48.5	51.7	60.8	32.1	34.3	34.5	37.7	49.6
Oral cavity and pharynx	54.3	54.6	54.3	52.2	55.0	31.2	26.5	29.9	29.3	28.2
Esophagus	5.1	6.5	7.8	11.3	13.7	2.3	4.6	5.0	7.0	8.9
Stomach	13.8	15.6	14.6	16.2	17.4	15.3	18.5	18.5	15.0	20.1
Colon	51.0	56.0	58.9	62.4	63.2	45.3	46.7	48.3	52.5	52.5
Rectum	49.0	51.7	55.2	58.8	60.6	36.7	36.1	43.1	46.6	52.7
Pancreas	2.6	2.5	2.6	2.9	3.9	2.4	3.2	4.4	6.4	4.0
Lung and bronchus	11.6	12.2	12.0	12.0	13.1	10.0	10.9	10.3	11.9	10.0
Prostate gland	70.3	74.5	76.2	82.7	94.9	60.7	64.7	63.8	69.3	88.1
Urinary bladder	76.0	79.9	79.5	82.3	84.2	58.9	63.3	64.8	67.5	67.4
Non-Hodgkin's lymphoma	47.2	50.9	53.4	50.0	49.8	44.7	47.2	43.6	46.9	38.9
Leukemia	35.5	39.5	41.6	45.4	47.1	30.9	30.1	31.8	36.5	34.0
Female										
All sites	57.4	57.1	58.8	61.4	63.3	46.8	46.0	45.3	47.8	49.9
Colon	52.6	55.4	58.0	60.7	61.9	48.8	51.1	50.2	53.1	52.4
Rectum	50.8	54.6	56.7	59.5	61.5	43.8	41.3	44.2	56.2	53.3
Pancreas	2.2	3.0	3.2	3.4	4.4	4.1	5.8	5.8	5.6	3.7
Lung and bronchus	16.7	16.2	17.0	15.8	16.7	15.5	15.5	14.1	11.8	13.9
Melanoma of skin	85.8	88.3	89.3	91.2	91.8	69.9	[1]	70.1	[1]	76.2
Breast	75.4	77.1	79.2	83.9	86.6	63.1	65.9	63.4	69.3	71.7

[Continued]

Five-Year Relative Cancer Survival Rates for Selected Cancer Sites
[Continued]

Sex and site	Percent of Patients									
	White					Black				
	1974-79	1980-82	1983-85	1986-88	1989-97	1974-79	1980-82	1983-85	1986-88	1989-97
Cervix uteri	69.7	68.1	70.5	71.8	71.8	62.9	61.2	60.0	55.3	60.0
Corpus uteri	87.6	82.8	84.5	84.4	85.7	59.3	54.8	54.2	57.0	58.5
Ovary	37.2	38.7	40.2	42.0	51.0	40.3	39.1	41.2	38.6	47.4
Non-Hodgkin's lymphoma	49.2	52.8	55.4	56.1	58.0	57.5	53.3	47.0	54.4	49.9

Source: National Institutes of Health, National Cancer Institute, Surveillance, Epidemiology, and End Results (SEER)Program, shown in *Health United States 2002.*
Note: 1. Data for population groups with fewer than 25 annual cases are not shown.

Death Rates for Selected Leading Causes of Death Among Persons Age 65 or Older

Data show the diseases likely to carry off the Baby Boom Generation. Rates are age-adjusted death rates per 100,000 population.

Year	Heart Disease	Cancer	Stroke	Chronic Obstructive Pulmonary Diseases	Pneu-monia & Influenza
1980	2,629	1,052	669	179	214
1981	2,547	1,056	625	186	207
1982	2,503	1,069	587	186	181
1983	2,512	1,078	566	204	207
1984	2,450	1,087	548	211	214
1985	2,431	1,091	533	226	243
1986	2,372	1,101	508	228	245
1987	2,316	1,106	497	230	237
1988	2,306	1,114	491	240	263
1989	2,172	1,133	465	240	253
1990	2,092	1,142	449	245	258
1991	2,049	1,151	436	252	245
1992	1,995	1,154	427	253	233
1993	2,032	1,164	437	275	249
1994	1,963	1,161	437	273	239
1995	1,941	1,160	442	273	239
1996	1,894	1,150	438	278	236
1997	1,832	1,133	426	281	237
1998	1,795	1,125	414	288	248

Source: National Institute on Aging, drawing data from the National Vital Statistics System, National Center for Health Statistics, U.S. Department of Health and Human Services. NIA is accessible at http://www.nia.nih.gov/.

Death Rates from Alzheimer's Disease, 1979 to 1998

Data show that the disease came to be recognized only in the late 1980s. Rates are age-adjusted death rates per 100,000 population.

	Death Rate of those Aged:		
	65-74	75-84	85+
1979	2.1	3.0	4.3
1980	3.2	4.8	7.6
1981	3.8	7.2	12.2
1982	5.1	12.2	17.9
1983	7.8	21.4	37.8
1984	9.3	31.8	59.8
1985	10.5	42.2	86.1
1986	10.8	46.9	103.7
1987	11.1	54.7	135.4
1988	11.3	57.2	151.2
1989	10.6	58.6	170.4
1990	10.2	58.6	187.8
1991	9.9	57.4	190.7
1992	9.6	55.7	199.0
1993	9.7	63.9	227.6
1994	11.0	66.7	251.8
1995	11.1	73.4	274.7
1996	11.0	72.8	284.7
1997	10.8	73.3	299.2
1998	10.4	70.0	299.5

Source: U.S. Department of Health and Human Services, Centers for Disease Control and Prevention, National Center for Health Statistics, National Vital Statistics System, accessed at http://www.cdc.gov/nchs/default.htm, May 29, 2002.

Chapter 3
PREVENTION

Top-Selling Medicinal Herbs in the United States: 1995-99

Sales in millions of dollars.

Herb	Sales in 1995	Sales in 1999	% Change
Echinacea	170	280	65
Garlic	150	190	27
Ginkgo biloba	170	300	76
Ginseng	190	210	11
St. John's wort	10	280	2,700
Saw palmetto	40	110	175
Combinations	900	1,680	87
All other	840	1,060	26
Total	2,470	4,110	66

Source: "Alternative Medicine," *World Almanac and Book of Facts*, Annual 2001 p508; Primary Sources: National Center for Complementary and Alternative Medicine, National Institutes of Health, *Nutrition Business Journal.*

Alternative Health Care Practitioners: 1999

Practice	Licensed Practitioners
Acupuncture	5,500
Chiropractic	65,300
Homeopathy	1,700
Massage therapy	32,700
Naturopathy	2,200
Osteopathy	39,800
Traditional Oriental medicine	10,500
Total	159,600

Source: "Alternative Medicine," *World Almanac and Book of Facts*, Annual 2001 p508; Primary Sources: National Center for Complementary and Alternative Medicine, National Institutes of Health, *Nutrition Business Journal.*

NCCAM Budget Appropriations ($ Mil.): 1992-2002

NCCAM is National Center for Complementary and Alternative Medicine.

FY	$
1992	2
1998	20
1999	50
2000	69
2001	89
2002	105

Source: Budget of the United States Government, retrieved July 2, 2002, from http://www.whitehouse.gov/omb/budget/fy2003/pdf/hist.pdf.

Per Capita Consumption of Major Food Commodities, 1970-97[1]

Year	Meat, poultry, fish							Eggs
	Pounds, boneless, trimmed equivalent							
	Red meat			Poultry		Fish/shellfish	Total[4]	Number
	Beef	Pork	Total[2]	Chicken	Total[3]			
1970	79.6	48.0	131.7	27.4	33.8	11.7	177.3	308.9
1971	79.0	52.6	135.5	27.4	34.0	11.5	181.0	309.9
1972	80.3	47.8	131.8	28.3	35.4	12.5	179.7	303.0
1973	75.8	43.0	121.8	27.1	33.7	12.7	168.2	288.4
1974	80.6	46.7	130.4	27.0	33.8	12.1	176.3	283.0
1975	83.0	38.7	125.8	26.4	32.9	12.1	170.9	276.0
1976	88.8	40.3	133.0	28.5	35.5	12.9	181.4	269.8
1977	86.3	42.3	132.3	29.0	35.9	12.6	180.9	267.0
1978	82.2	42.3	127.5	30.4	37.3	13.4	178.2	271.5
1979	73.5	48.6	124.4	32.8	40.1	13.0	177.6	276.6
1980	72.1	52.1	126.4	32.7	40.8	12.4	179.6	271.1
1981	72.8	49.9	125.1	33.7	42.1	12.6	179.7	264.4
1982	72.5	44.9	119.8	33.9	42.2	12.4	174.4	264.1
1983	74.1	47.4	123.9	34.0	42.7	13.3	180.0	260.2
1984	73.9	47.2	123.7	35.3	44.0	14.1	181.7	260.1
1985	74.6	47.7	124.9	36.4	45.5	15.0	185.4	254.7
1986	74.4	45.2	122.2	37.2	47.4	15.4	184.9	253.5
1987	69.6	45.6	117.4	39.4	51.0	16.1	184.5	253.8
1988	68.6	48.8	119.5	39.6	51.9	15.1	186.6	246.6
1989	65.4	48.4	115.9	40.9	53.9	15.6	185.4	237.0
1990	63.9	46.4	112.3	42.4	56.3	15.0	183.5	234.3
1991	63.1	46.9	111.9	44.2	58.3	14.8	185.1	233.7
1992	62.8	49.4	114.1	46.7	60.8	14.7	189.5	235.0
1993	61.5	48.9	112.1	48.5	62.5	14.9	189.5	235.6
1994	63.6	49.5	114.7	49.3	63.3	15.1	193.2	237.7
1995	64.4	49.0	115.1	48.8	62.9	14.9	193.0	235.4

[Continued]

Per Capita Consumption of Major Food Commodities, 1970-97

[Continued]

Year	Meat, poultry, fish							Eggs Number
	Pounds, boneless,trimmed equivalent							
	Red meat			Poultry		Fish/shellfish	Total[4]	
	Beef	Pork	Total[2]	Chicken	Total[3]			
1996	65.0	45.9	112.8	49.8	64.4	14.7	191.8	237.1
1997	63.8	45.6	111.0	50.9	64.8	14.5	190.3	238.7
1998	64.9	49.1	115.6	51.6	65.8	14.5	195.9	243.8

Source: USDA/Center for Nutrition Policy and Promotion (CNPP), Appendix Table 1, retrieved June 5, 2002, from http://www.ers.usda.gov/publications/aib750/aib750app.pdf. *Notes:* 1. Forecast for 1998 shown for meat and eggs. 2. Includes veal, lamb, and mutton. 3. Includes turkey. 4. Computed from unrounded data.

Per Capita Consumption of Major Food Commodities, 1970-97-continued[1]

Beverage milk products measured in gallons. Fluid cream products and yogurt measured in half-pints.

Year	Dairy Products						
	Fluid Milk Products				Fluid Cream Products		
	Beverage Milk						
	Whole	Lower Fat & Fat Free	Total[4]	Yogurt	Cream[5]	Sour Cream	Total[6]
1970	25.5	5.8	31.3	1.5	7.2	2.0	9.8
1971	25.0	6.3	31.3	2.0	6.7	2.2	9.6
1972	24.1	6.9	31.0	2.4	6.4	2.4	9.7
1973	23.0	7.5	30.5	2.5	6.7	2.4	9.8
1974	21.7	7.7	29.5	2.7	6.4	2.7	9.8
1975	21.1	8.4	29.5	3.6	6.3	3.1	10.0
1976	20.4	9.0	29.3	3.9	6.3	3.0	10.1
1977	19.5	9.5	29.0	4.3	6.2	3.1	10.2
1978	18.7	9.8	28.6	4.5	6.2	3.2	10.1
1979	18.0	10.2	28.2	4.5	6.3	3.3	10.3
1980	17.0	10.5	27.6	4.6	6.3	3.4	10.5
1981	16.3	10.8	27.1	4.5	6.5	3.5	10.8
1982	15.5	10.9	26.4	4.8	6.5	3.7	11.0
1983	15.2	11.1	26.3	5.8	6.9	3.9	11.7
1984	14.8	11.6	26.4	6.6	7.6	4.2	12.7
1985	14.3	12.3	26.7	7.3	8.2	4.3	13.5
1986	13.5	13.0	26.5	7.7	8.8	4.4	14.2
1987	13.0	13.3	26.3	7.9	8.8	4.6	14.3
1988	12.3	13.5	25.8	8.2	8.7	4.6	14.3
1989	11.3	14.7	26.0	7.7	9.0	4.7	14.7
1990	10.5	15.2	25.7	7.4	8.7	4.7	14.3
1991	10.2	15.5	25.6	7.8	8.7	4.9	14.5
1992	9.8	15.6	25.3	7.8	9.1	5.1	15.0

[Continued]

Per Capita Consumption of Major Food Commodities, 1970-97-continued

[Continued]

Year	Dairy Products						
	Fluid Milk Products				Fluid Cream Products		
	Beverage Milk		Total[4]	Yogurt	Cream[5]	Sour Cream	Total[6]
	Whole	Lower Fat & Fat Free					
1993	9.3	15.4	24.8	7.9	9.2	5.1	15.1
1994	9.2	15.6	24.8	8.6	9.2	5.2	15.2
1995	8.8	15.6	24.3	9.4	9.5	5.5	15.9
1996	8.7	15.7	24.4	8.9	10.2	5.4	16.4
1997	8.5	15.5	24.0	9.5	10.7	5.6	17.0

Source: USDA/Center for Nutrition Policy and Promotion (CNPP), Appendix Table 1, retrieved June 5, 2002, from http://www.ers.usda.gov/publications/aib750/aib750app.pdf. *Notes:* 4. Computed from unrounded data. 5. Includes half and half, light cream, and heavy cream. 6. Includes eggnog.

Per Capita Consumption of Major Food Commodities, 1970-97-continued

Year	Dairy Products						
	Pounds					Frozen Dairy	
	Cheese				Cottage Cheese		
	Cheddar	Mozzarella	Cream[7]	Total[8]		Ice Cream	Total[9]
1970	5.8	1.2	0.6	11.4	5.2	17.8	28.5
1971	5.9	1.4	0.6	12.0	5.3	17.7	28.2
1972	6.0	1.6	0.6	13.0	5.4	17.6	28.0
1973	6.1	1.8	0.7	13.5	5.2	17.5	28.0
1974	6.3	1.9	0.7	14.4	4.6	17.5	27.7
1975	6.0	2.1	0.7	14.3	4.6	18.6	28.6
1976	6.4	2.3	0.8	15.5	4.7	18.0	27.5
1977	6.8	2.5	0.8	16.0	4.7	17.6	27.5
1978	6.9	2.7	0.9	16.8	4.7	17.6	27.3
1979	6.9	2.8	0.9	17.2	4.5	17.3	26.5
1980	6.9	3.0	1.0	17.5	4.5	17.5	26.4
1981	7.0	3.0	1.0	18.2	4.3	17.4	26.5
1982	8.7	3.3	1.1	19.9	4.2	17.6	26.4
1983	9.1	3.7	1.2	20.6	4.1	18.1	27.1
1984	9.5	4.0	1.2	21.5	4.1	18.2	27.2
1985	9.8	4.6	1.2	22.5	4.1	18.1	27.9
1986	9.8	5.2	1.3	23.1	4.1	18.4	27.9
1987	10.6	5.6	1.4	24.1	3.9	18.4	28.2
1988	9.5	6.0	1.5	23.7	3.9	17.3	27.7
1989	9.2	6.4	1.6	23.8	3.6	16.1	28.7
1990	9.0	6.9	1.7	24.6	3.4	15.8	28.4
1991	9.1	7.2	1.8	25.0	3.3	16.3	29.2
1992	9.2	7.7	2.0	26.0	3.1	16.3	28.9

[Continued]

Per Capita Consumption of Major Food Commodities, 1970-97-continued

[Continued]

Year	Dairy Products						
	Pounds					Frozen Dairy	
	Cheese				Cottage		
	Cheddar	Mozzarella	Cream[7]	Total[8]	Cheese	Ice Cream	Total[9]
1993	9.1	7.5	2.1	26.2	2.9	16.1	29.3
1994	9.1	7.9	2.2	26.8	2.8	16.1	29.9
1995	9.1	8.1	2.1	27.3	2.7	15.7	29.4
1996	9.2	8.5	2.2	27.7	2.6	15.9	28.6
1997	9.6	8.4	2.3	28.0	2.7	16.2	28.7

Source: USDA/Center for Nutrition Policy and Promotion (CNPP), Appendix Table 1, retrieved June 5, 2002, from http://www.ers.usda.gov/publications/aib750/aib750app.pdf. *Notes:* 7. Includes Neufchatel. 8. Excludes full-skim American and cottage, pot, and baker s cheese. 9. Includes lower fat and nonfat ice cream, sherbet, mellorine, frozen yogurt beginning 1981 and other nonstandardized frozen dairy products.

Per Capita Consumption of Major Food Commodities, 1970-97-continued

| Year | Fats and Oils | | | | | | Total Fat Content[10] |
| | Pounds | | | | | | |
	Butter	Margarine	Lard/Beef Tallow	Shortening	Salad/ Cooking Oils	Total Product Weight[10]	
1970	5.4	10.8	4.6	17.3	15.4	55.8	52.6
1971	5.2	10.9	4.2	16.8	15.6	55.0	51.8
1972	5.0	11.1	3.7	17.6	16.8	56.6	53.4
1973	4.8	11.1	3.3	17.0	17.7	56.5	53.3
1974	4.5	11.1	3.2	16.9	18.1	55.5	52.4
1975	4.7	11.0	3.2	17.0	17.9	55.8	52.6
1976	4.3	11.9	2.9	17.7	19.5	58.3	55.1
1977	4.3	11.4	2.5	17.2	19.1	56.4	53.3
1978	4.4	11.3	2.4	17.8	20.1	58.0	54.9
1979	4.5	11.2	2.9	18.4	20.8	59.5	56.4
1980	4.5	11.3	3.6	18.2	21.2	60.3	57.2
1981	4.2	11.1	3.5	18.5	21.8	60.5	57.4
1982	4.3	11.0	3.8	18.6	21.9	61.3	58.2
1983	4.9	10.4	4.1	18.5	23.6	63.1	60.0
1984	4.9	10.4	3.8	21.3	22.5	64.6	61.6
1985	4.9	10.8	3.7	22.9	23.6	67.5	64.3
1986	4.6	11.4	3.5	22.1	24.4	67.7	64.5
1987	4.7	10.5	2.7	21.4	25.6	66.2	63.2
1988	4.5	10.3	2.6	21.5	26.3	66.5	63.6
1989	4.4	10.2	2.1	21.5	24.4	63.8	60.8
1990	4.4	10.9	2.4	22.2	24.8	65.9	62.8
1991	4.4	10.6	3.1	22.4	26.7	68.4	65.4
1992	4.4	11.0	4.1	22.4	27.2	70.4	67.4

[Continued]

Per Capita Consumption of Major Food Commodities, 1970-97-continued

[Continued]

Year	Fats and Oils Pounds						Total Fat Content[10]
	Butter	Margarine	Lard/Beef Tallow	Shortening	Salad/ Cooking Oils	Total Product Weight[10]	
1993	4.7	11.1	3.9	25.1	26.8	73.3	70.2
1994	4.8	9.9	4.7	24.1	26.3	71.5	68.6
1995	4.5	9.2	4.9	22.5	26.9	69.6	66.9
1996	4.3	9.2	5.3	22.3	26.1	68.6	65.8
1997	4.2	8.6	4.7	20.9	28.7	68.2	65.6

Source: USDA/Center for Nutrition Policy and Promotion (CNPP), Appendix Table 1, retrieved June 5, 2002, from http://www.ers.usda.gov/publications/aib750/aib750app.pdf. *Notes:* 10. Includes specialty fats used mainly in confectionery products and nondairy creamers.

Per Capita Consumption of Major Food Commodities, 1970-97-continued

Year	Pounds, Fresh-Weight Equivalent						
	Fruit			Vegetables			
				Fresh		Processing Canning	
	Fresh	Process-ing[11]	Total[4]	Potatoes	Total	Tomatoes	Total
1970	101.2	136.5	237.7	61.8	152.9	62.1	100.7
1971	100.3	141.7	242.0	56.1	146.7	68.3	107.7
1972	94.8	136.8	231.5	57.9	149.9	64.9	104.5
1973	96.4	138.4	234.9	52.4	146.6	58.4	98.1
1974	95.6	138.6	234.2	49.4	144.5	61.3	99.3
1975	101.8	150.3	252.1	52.6	147.1	61.9	97.8
1976	101.5	155.5	257.0	49.4	146.4	65.7	103.3
1977	99.7	170.4	270.1	50.1	147.0	62.8	101.7
1978	103.4	154.4	257.8	46.0	141.6	58.8	96.7
1979	100.1	149.7	249.8	49.3	146.5	64.3	100.5
1980	104.8	157.5	262.4	51.1	149.3	63.6	102.7
1981	103.6	156.5	260.2	45.8	142.8	59.3	97.1
1982	107.4	154.7	262.1	47.1	148.6	60.1	95.1
1983	110.0	168.5	278.6	49.8	148.5	60.9	96.5
1984	112.6	153.5	266.0	48.3	154.0	68.5	102.6
1985	110.6	158.8	269.4	46.3	156.1	63.2	99.4
1986	117.3	159.0	276.3	48.8	156.2	63.6	99.8
1987	121.6	164.0	285.5	47.9	162.4	65.2	99.1
1988	120.9	151.9	272.8	49.6	167.4	61.3	94.8
1989	122.8	156.3	279.1	50.0	172.2	69.4	102.4
1990	116.3	157.1	273.5	46.8	167.2	75.4	110.7
1991	113.0	153.6	266.6	50.4	167.2	77.4	113.3
1992	123.5	144.5	268.0	48.6	171.1	73.7	111.6
1993	124.9	160.5	285.4	49.3	171.9	76.4	112.1

[Continued]

Per Capita Consumption of Major Food Commodities, 1970-97-continued

[Continued]

Year	Pounds, Fresh-Weight Equivalent						
	Fruit			Vegetables			
				Fresh		Processing Canning	
	Fresh	Process-ing[11]	Total[4]	Potatoes	Total	Tomatoes	Total
1994	126.5	157.8	284.3	50.3	177.4	73.6	107.8
1995	124.6	160.8	285.4	49.2	175.1	75.6	110.2
1996	129.0	160.8	289.8	50.0	181.8	74.2	108.5
1997	133.2	161.5	294.7	47.9	185.6	72.7	105.9

Source: USDA/Center for Nutrition Policy and Promotion (CNPP), Appendix Table 1, retrieved June 5, 2002, from http://www.ers.usda.gov/publications/aib750/aib750app.pdf. *Notes:* 11. Excludes wine grapes.

Per Capita Consumption of Major Food Commodities, 1970-97-continued

Year	Pounds, Fresh-Weight Equivalent							
	Vegetables						Total Vegetables[4]	Total Fruit/ Vegetables[4]
	Processing							
	Freezing		Dehydrating	Potatoes for Chips	Pulses	Total		
	Potatoes	Total						
1970	28.5	43.7	13.2	17.4	7.6	182.5	335.4	573.2
1971	30.1	45.4	13.8	17.2	7.5	191.6	338.3	580.3
1972	30.3	45.5	13.3	16.7	6.7	186.7	336.6	568.2
1973	34.2	50.5	14.3	16.3	7.9	187.1	333.8	568.6
1974	35.3	51.4	16.0	15.7	6.2	188.6	333.2	567.3
1975	37.1	52.7	16.7	15.5	7.2	189.9	337.0	589.1
1976	41.8	57.7	17.1	15.8	7.0	200.9	347.3	604.3
1977	42.2	59.4	12.7	16.2	6.9	196.9	343.9	613.9
1978	42.6	59.0	13.4	16.5	5.9	191.5	333.1	590.8
1979	38.5	55.5	13.1	16.7	6.8	192.5	339.1	588.9
1980	35.4	51.6	10.6	16.5	5.8	187.2	336.4	598.8
1981	41.5	58.3	11.6	16.6	6.0	189.6	332.4	592.6
1982	38.6	54.3	12.4	17.0	6.9	185.6	334.3	596.4
1983	39.2	55.7	11.7	17.8	7.0	188.6	337.1	615.6
1984	43.7	62.8	11.8	18.0	5.5	200.6	354.6	620.7
1985	45.4	64.5	12.8	17.6	7.6	201.9	358.1	627.5
1986	46.3	64.5	12.8	18.1	7.3	202.6	358.7	635.1
1987	47.9	67.0	12.3	17.6	5.7	201.6	364.0	649.5
1988	43.3	64.2	12.1	17.1	7.5	195.7	363.1	635.9
1989	46.8	67.6	12.4	17.4	6.3	206.0	378.2	657.3
1990	46.5	66.8	14.6	16.4	7.1	215.6	382.8	656.3
1991	51.2	72.7	15.5	17.3	7.8	226.6	393.9	660.5
1992	50.2	70.8	14.3	17.2	8.2	222.1	393.2	661.1
1993	52.9	75.1	15.5	17.5	7.7	227.9	399.8	685.1

[Continued]

Per Capita Consumption of Major Food Commodities, 1970-97-continued

[Continued]

Year	Pounds, Fresh-Weight Equivalent							Total Fruit/ Vegetables[4]
	Vegetables							
	Processing						Total Vegetables[4]	
	Freezing		Dehydrating	Potatoes for Chips	Pulses	Total		
	Potatoes	Total						
1994	57.4	79.5	14.7	17.0	8.5	227.4	404.8	689.1
1995	56.9	79.9	14.7	16.6	8.5	229.9	405.0	690.4
1996	60.4	83.9	17.6	16.4	8.0	234.5	416.2	706.1
1997	59.0	81.5	18.6	15.9	8.5	230.4	416.0	710.8

Source: USDA/Center for Nutrition Policy and Promotion (CNPP), Appendix Table 1, retrieved June 5, 2002, from http://www.ers.usda.gov/publications/aib750/aib750app.pdf. *Note:* 4. Computed from unrounded data.

How Expenditures on Many Grocery Products in High- and Low-Income Cities Vary From the U.S. Average

Items With Above-Average Household Expenditures Relative to U.S. Average	Percent	Items With Below-Average Household Expenditures Relative to U.S. Average	Percent
Low-income cities[1]		Low-income cities[1]	
Cornmeal[3]	242	Seltzers/club soda[3]	34
Canned sausage	192	Refrigerated salad dressing[3]	38
Solid shortening[3]	175	Bottled water[3]	41
Canned lunch meat	162	Miscellaneous refrigerated juices[3]	43
Flour	155	Deluxe frozen vegetables	44
Ground pepper	141	Frozen green beans[3]	47
Evaporated condensed milk	138	Frozen fish dishes	48
Refrigerated biscuits[3]	132	Frozen Italian dishes	51
Low-calorie soft drinks	131	Refrigerated yogurt[3]	52
Canned pie filling[3]	128	Refrigerated Mexican foods	53
High-Income cities[2]		High-Income cities[2]	
Seltzers/club soda[3]	197	Solid shortening[3]	48
Miscellaneous refrigerated juices[3]	171	Canned meat stew	56
Bottled water	171	Canned pie filling[3]	56
Refrigerated orange juice	160	Refrigerated biscuits[3]	57
Refrigerated drinks	155	Spoonable salad dressing	60
Frozen green beans[3]	154	Cornmeal[3]	61
Dried rice	152	Canned green beans	68
Refrigerated yogurt[3]	147	Dry toaster items	68

[Continued]

How Expenditures on Many Grocery Products in High- and Low-Income Cities Vary From the U.S. Average
[Continued]

Items With Above-Average Household Expenditures Relative to U.S. Average	Percent	Items With Below-Average Household Expenditures Relative to U.S. Average	Percent
Butter	147	Refrigerated pastries	69
Refrigerated salad dressing[3]	142	Canned poultry	69

Source: Mark D. Jekanowski and James K. Binkley,"Food Spending Varies Across the United States," *FoodReview,* Vol. 23, Issue 1, Jan-Apr 2000, pp. 38+; primary source: Compiled from data collected by Selling Area Marketing Incorporated (SAMI), 1990 *Notes:* 1. Representative low-income cities are: Scranton, Pennsylvania; Charleston,West Virginia; Shreveport, Louisiana; and El Paso, Texas. 2. Representative high-income cities are: New York City, New York; Chicago, Illinois; Miami, Florida; and San Francisco, California. 3. Items that have both the lowest (highest) indices for high-income regions, and the highest (lowest) indices for low-income regions.

Certified Organic Farmland Acreage and Livestock: 1992 to 1997

NA Not available.

Item	Unit	1992	1995	1997	Crop	Certified Organic Acreage, 1997	
						Total (1,000)	Percent of Total Cropland
Certified growers	Number	3,587	4,856	5,021	Total	1,347	0.16
					Pastureland and rangeland	496	0.11
Certified organic acreage, total	1,000	935	918	1,347	Cropland	850	0.23
Pastureland and rangeland	1,000	532	279	496			
Cropland	1,000	403	639	850	Corn	43	0.10
Certified animals					Wheat	126	0.20
Beef cows	Number	6,796	NA	4,429	Oats	30	1.10
Milk cows	Number	2,265	NA	12,897	Barley	30	0.50
Hogs and pigs	Number	1,365	NA	482	Spelt	2	36.70
Sheep and lambs	Number	1,221	NA	705	Buckwheat	8	30.10
Layer hens	Number	43,981	NA	537,826	Soybeans	82	0.10
Broilers	Number	17,382	NA	38,285	Alfalfa	62	0.30
Unclassified/other	Number	NA	NA	226,105	Grapes	19	1.90

Source: Statistical Abstract of the United States: 2001, Table 805. Primary sources: U.S. Dept. of Agriculture, Economic Research Service, "U.S. certified organic farmland acreage and livestock, 1992-97"; published April 4 2000; http://www.ers.usda.gov/whatsnew/issues/organic/table4.html; and "Certified organic and total U.S. acreage, selected crops, 1995-97"; published April 4, 2000; http://www.ers.usda.gov/whatsnew/issues/organic/table5.htm

Intake Levels and Nutrient Densities of Foods at Home and Away From Home, Individuals Age 2 and Over, 1977-95

NA Not available.

	1977-78	1987-88	1989	1990	1991	1994	1995
Calories:							
Average intake (kcal)	1,876.0	1,807.0	1,837.0	1,853.0	1,883.0	2,006.0	2,043.0
% consuming > REA	26.0	22.0	24.0	26.0	26.0	28.0	31.0
% of total calories:							
At home	82.0	73.0	73.0	74.0	71.0	69.0	66.0
Away from home[1]	18.0	27.0	27.0	26.0	29.0	31.0	34.0
Restaurants	3.0	5.0	7.0	6.0	6.0	8.0	8.0
Fast food	3.0	8.0	9.0	9.0	9.0	11.0	12.0
Schools[2]	3.0	3.0	2.0	2.0	3.0	2.0	2.0
Other public places	3.0	2.0	3.0	2.0	3.0	3.0	2.0
Others	6.0	9.0	7.0	8.0	9.0	7.0	9.0
Fat:							
Avg. intake (grams)	86.3	74.7	72.0	72.9	73.4	74.9	76.2
Avg. intake (% of cal.)	41.2	37.0	35.3	35.4	35.1	33.6	33.6
% meeting recom.	13.0	21.0	20.0	29.0	30.0	36.0	37.0
Nutrient density (% of cal.):							
Benchmark density[3]	30.0	30.0	30.0	30.0	30.0	30.0	30.0
Average nutrient density	41.2	37.0	35.3	35.4	35.1	33.6	33.6
Home foods	41.1	36.3	34.4	34.5	33.8	31.9	31.5
Away from home[1]	41.2	38.7	37.8	38.1	38.2	37.4	37.6
Restaurants	46.2	41.3	40.7	40.7	41.2	40.0	40.1
Fast food	41.6	39.7	39.7	39.6	38.8	39.9	39.3
Schools[2]	40.1	38.0	37.7	36.1	36.8	36.1	35.7
Other public places	41.4	41.2	34.8	40.9	42.3	30.3	32.6
Others	38.6	36.4	33.9	33.1	34.2	34.1	34.9
Saturated fat:							
Avg. intake (grams)	NA	27.7	25.7	26.0	26.0	25.6	26.2
Avg. intake (% of cal.)	NA	13.8	12.6	12.6	12.4	11.5	11.5
% meeting recom.	NA	17.0	29.0	29.0	31.0	40.0	39.0
Nutrient density (% of cal.):							
Benchmark density[3]	NA	10.0	10.0	10.0	10.0	10.0	10.0
Average nutrient density	NA	13.8	12.6	12.6	12.4	11.5	11.5
Home foods	NA	13.5	12.3	12.2	12.1	11.1	10.9
Away from home[1]	NA	14.7	13.5	13.8	13.3	12.4	12.8
Restaurants	NA	15.5	14.3	13.5	14.0	12.3	12.5
Fast food	NA	15.4	14.2	14.5	13.1	13.6	13.8
Schools[2]	NA	13.9	15.4	16.1	15.4	14.4	14.2
Other public places	NA	15.2	12.0	14.6	13.8	9.8	9.8
Others	NA	13.7	12.0	11.8	12.0	11.1	12.1
Cholesterol:							
Average intake (mg)	NA	286.0	282.0	272.0	265.0	260.0	268.0
% meeting recom.	NA	66.0	66.0	70.0	70.0	71.0	69.0
Nutrient density (mg/1,000 kcal):							
Benchmark density[3]	NA	166.0	163.0	162.0	159.0	150.0	147.0

[Continued]

Intake Levels and Nutrient Densities of Foods at Home and Away From Home, Individuals Age 2 and Over, 1977-95

[Continued]

	1977-78	1987-88	1989	1990	1991	1994	1995
Average nutrient density	NA	158.0	153.0	147.0	140.0	130.0	131.0
Home foods	NA	161.0	155.0	148.0	143.0	127.0	129.0
Away from home[1]	NA	151.0	149.0	143.0	143.0	134.0	134.0
Restaurants	NA	215.0	207.0	195.0	187.0	187.0	176.0
Fast food	NA	138.0	137.0	123.0	136.0	124.0	124.0
Schools[2]	NA	121.0	116.0	107.0	123.0	101.0	106.0
Other public places	NA	160.0	161.0	189.0	152.0	103.0	114.0
Others	NA	131.0	116.0	117.0	116.0	113.0	122.0
Sodium:							
Average intake (mg)	NA	3,023.0	3,090.0	3,081.0	3,168.0	3,313.0	3,348.0
% meeting recom.	NA	41.0	40.0	40.0	39.0	36.0	34.0
Nutrient density (mg/1,000 kcal):							
Benchmark density[3]	NA	1,328.0	1,307.0	1,296.0	1,275.0	1,196.0	1,175.0
Average nutrient density	NA	1,672.0	1,681.0	1,662.0	1,681.0	1,651.0	1,637.0
Home foods	NA	1,678.0	1,679.0	1,671.0	1,670.0	1,630.0	1,630.0
Away from home[1]	NA	1,656.0	1,686.0	1,638.0	1,708.0	1,695.0	1,651.0
Restaurants	NA	1,824.0	1,817.0	2,017.0	2,019.0	1,898.0	1,873.0
Fast food	NA	1,575.0	1,654.0	1,616.0	1,628.0	1,724.0	1,674.0
School[2]	NA	1,604.0	1,526.0	1,529.0	1,512.0	1,601.0	1,576.0
Other public places	NA	1,911.0	1,807.0	1,657.0	1,738.0	1,469.0	1,548.0
Others	NA	1,590.0	1,607.0	1,402.0	1,579.0	1,551.0	1,476.0
Fiber:							
Average intake (grams)	NA	12.7	13.7	13.1	14.0	15.2	15.2
% meeting recom.	NA	18.0	20.0	20.0	20.0	24.0	24.0
Nutrient density (grams per 1,000 kcal):							
Benchmark density[3]	NA	10.7	10.7	10.5	10.6	10.5	10.4
Average density	NA	7.0	7.4	7.1	7.4	7.6	7.4
Home foods	NA	7.5	7.9	7.5	7.9	8.1	8.1
Away from home[1]	NA	5.8	6.2	5.9	6.4	6.5	6.1
Restaurants	NA	5.8	6.0	6.2	6.7	7.0	6.2
Fast food	NA	5.0	5.5	5.3	5.3	5.7	5.6
Schools[2]	NA	7.6	7.5	8.0	7.6	7.1	7.1
Other public places	NA	6.9	7.2	6.1	6.3	6.5	6.8
Others	NA	5.9	6.6	5.8	6.9	6.8	6.2
Calcium:							
Average intake (mg)	743.0	756.0	773.0	791.0	785.0	794.0	813.0
% meeting recom.	31.0	32.0	33.0	36.0	33.0	35.0	36.0
Nutrient density (mg/1,000 kcal):							
Benchmark density[3]	481.0	491.0	479.0	475.0	466.0	439.0	432.0
Average nutrient density	396.0	418.0	420.0	426.0	416.0	395.0	397.0
Home foods	402.0	439.0	444.0	448.0	446.0	421.0	425.0
Away from home[1]	368.0	360.0	356.0	365.0	350.0	337.0	343.0
Restaurants	280.0	302.0	315.0	295.0	312.0	301.0	291.0
Fast food	304.0	342.0	338.0	345.0	305.0	350.0	353.0
Schools[2]	645.0	648.0	596.0	707.0	676.0	657.0	689.0

[Continued]

Intake Levels and Nutrient Densities of Foods at Home and Away From Home, Individuals Age 2 and Over, 1977-95

[Continued]

	1977-78	1987-88	1989	1990	1991	1994	1995
Other public places	341.0	346.0	430.0	368.0	316.0	302.0	317.0
Others	308.0	330.0	326.0	316.0	321.0	286.0	296.0
Iron:							
Average intake (mg)	11.3	12.9	13.5	13.6	13.7	15.1	15.7
% meeting recom.	42.0	47.0	50.0	51.0	50.0	57.0	61.0
Nutrient density (mg/1,000 kcal):							
Benchmark density[3]	6.3	6.4	6.3	6.3	6.2	5.8	5.7
Average nutrient density	6.0	7.1	7.4	7.3	7.3	7.5	7.7
Home foods	6.2	7.6	7.9	7.8	7.8	8.1	8.4
Away from home[1]	5.3	5.9	5.9	6.0	6.2	6.3	6.3
Restaurants	5.8	6.3	5.9	6.6	6.3	6.7	6.5
Fast food	5.3	5.7	6.1	6.4	6.2	6.3	6.3
Schools[2]	5.0	5.4	5.5	5.6	6.1	6.3	6.1
Other public places	5.4	6.1	5.9	5.7	5.6	5.3	5.5
Others	5.2	5.9	5.8	4.8	6.1	6.1	6.4

Source: Biing-Hwan Lin, Joanne Guthrie, and Elizabeth Frazco, *Nutrient Contribution of Food Away From Home*, Compiled by ERS from NFCS 1977-78, NFCS 1987-88, CSFII 1989-91, and CSFII 1994-95, 1-day intake data; retrieved July 3, 2002, from www.ers.usda.gov/publications/aib750/aib750l.pdf
Notes: 1. Away from home presents the aggregate of fast foods, restaurants, schools, other public places, and others. 2. Schools are classified as a separate category for children only; for adults, they are included in the others category. 3. Benchmark densities are obtained by dividing the recommended intake for each nutrient by the individual's actual food energy intake. The benchmark density for specific groups of individuals is the sum of recommended intakes for all individuals divided by the sum of their actual caloric intakes.

Physical Activity: 1998

In percent. Covers persons 18 years old and over. Based on responses to questions about physical activity in prior month from the Behavioral Risk Factor Surveillance Survey. Estimates are age-adjusted to the year 2000 standard population. Based on a survey sample of approximately 147,000 persons in 50 states and the District of Columbia in 1998.

Characteristic	Persons Who Meet Recommended Activity[1]	Persons With Insufficient Activity[2]	Persons Who Are Physically Inactive[3]
Total	25.3	45.8	28.9
Male	26.4	46.8	26.9
Female	24.4	44.8	30.8
White, non-Hispanic	26.4	47.3	26.3
Black, non-Hispanic	20.9	43.9	35.2
Hispanic	20.8	38.6	40.6
Other	25.6	44.6	29.8
Males:			
18 to 29 years old	27.7	54.2	18.1
30 to 44 years old	22.8	52.7	24.5
45 to 64 years old	25.4	44.1	30.5
65 to 74 years old	32.1	36.8	31.1
75 years old and over	32.1	26.9	41.0

[Continued]

Physical Activity: 1998
[Continued]

Characteristic	Persons Who Meet Recommended Activity[1]	Persons With Insufficient Activity[2]	Persons Who Are Physically Inactive[3]
Females:			
18 to 29 years old	24.5	50.0	25.5
30 to 44 years old	24.7	47.4	27.9
45 to 64 years old	23.9	44.7	31.4
65 to 74 years old	23.6	40.5	35.9
75 years old and over	25.3	26.8	47.9
School years completed:			
Less than 12 years	15.7	34.4	49.9
12 years	21.3	44.5	34.2
Some college (13-15 years)	26.9	48.1	24.9
College (16 or more years)	33.5	49.9	16.6
Household income:			
Less than $10,000	19.7	36.5	43.8
$10,000 to $19,999	19.3	40.5	40.2
$20,000 to $34,999	22.8	45.0	32.2
$35,000 to $49,999	26.9	48.5	24.6
$50,000 and over	33.5	49.0	17.6

Source: Statistical Abstract of the United States: 2001, Table 198. Primary source: U.S. National Center for Chronic Disease Prevention and Health Promotion, unpublished data. Notes: 1. Recommended activity is physical activity at least five times/week x 30 minutes/time or vigorous physical activity for 20 minutes at a time at least three times/week. 2. Persons whose reported physical activity does not meet recommended level. 3. Persons with no reported physical activity.

Immunization and Infectious Diseases, Healthy People Objectives

DTP is diphtheria-tetanus-pertusis. MMR is measles-mumps-rubella. Hib is Haemophilus influenzae.

Objective	Baseline Year	Percentage										
		Baseline	1990	1991	1992	1993	1994	1995	1996	1997	1998	1999
Children 19-35 months												
Diphtheria-tetanus-pertussis (3+doses)	-	-	-	69	83	88	90	95	95	95	96	96
Polio (3 or more doses)	-	-	-	53	72	79	79	88	91	91	91	90
Measles-containing	-	-	-	82	83	84	90	90	91	91	92	92
Haemophilus influenzae type b (3+doses)	-	-	-	2	28	55	75	92	92	93	93	94
Hepatitis B (3 or more doses)	-	-	-	-	16	34	68	82	84	87	88	-
4DTP/3Polio/1MMR	-	-	-	-	55	67	68	76	78	78	81	80
Children in licensed care facil.[1,2]	1987-88	94-95[3]	94-96[4]	94-96[5]	94-96[6]	95-98[7]	97-98[8]	98-99[9]	95[10]	93-95[11]	93-96[12]	93-95[13]
Children in K-postsecondary[1,2]	1987-88	97-98[3]	97-98[4]	96-98[5]	96-98[6]	92-94[7]	93-94[8]	94-95[9]	98-99[10]	95-98[11]	95-97[12]	96-99[13]

Source: National Center for Health Statistics, Healthy People 2000 Final Review, Table 20, retrieved June 13, 2002, from http://www.cdc.gov/nchs/. Notes: 1. Range of antigen-specific immunization levels. 2. Three or more doses for DTP and polio. 3. 1987-88 school year. 4. 1989-90 school year. 5. 1990-91 school year. 6. 1991-92 school year. 7. 1992-93 school year. 8. 1993-94 school year. 9. 1994-95 school year. 10. 1995-96 school year. 11. 1996-97 school year. 12. 1997-98 school year. 13. 1998-99 school year.

Vaccine-Preventable Diseases (Number of Cases), Epidemic-Related Pneumonia and Influenza Deaths Among People 65 years and Over (Per 100,000), and Percentage of Population 65 Years and Over Who Have Been Immunized

Diseases/Immunizations	1990	1991	1992	1993	1994	1995	1996	1997	1998	1999
Diphtheria to 25 years	2.0	2.0	3.0	0.0	2.0	0.0	0.0	3.0	1.0	0.0
Tetanus to 25 years	6.0	4.0	7.0	4.0	5.0	5.0	3.0	9.0	9.0	5.0
Polio (wild-type virus)	0.0	0.0	0.0	0.0	0.0	0.0	0.0	0.0	0.0	0.0
Measles	26,527.0	9,411.0	2,237.0	312.0	963.0	309.0	508.0	138.0	100.0	100.0
Rubella	1,125.0	1,401.0	160.0	192.0	227.0	128.0	238.0	181.0	364.0	267.0
Congenital Rubella Syndrome	11.0	47.0	11.0	5.0	7.0	6.0	4.0	5.0	7.0	6.0
Mumps	5,292.0	4,264.0	2,572.0	1,692.0	1,537.0	906.0	751.0	683.0	666.0	387.0
Pertussis	4,570.0	2,719.0	4,083.0	6,586.0	4,617.0	5,137.0	7,796.0	6,564.0	7,405.0	7,298.0
Pneumonia & influenza deaths (per 100k)	19.9[1]	22.6[2]	18.6[3]	20.0[4]	15.7[5]	21.0[6]	19.2[7]	17.3[8]	15.8[9]	NA
Pneumococcal immunizations										
Noninstitutionalized people 65+ (%)	NA	21.0	NA	28.0	30.0	34.0	NA	43.0	46.0	NA
Black 65 years and over (%)	NA	14.0	NA	14.0	15.0	23.0	NA	22.0	26.0	NA
Hispanic 65 years and over (%)	NA	12.0		12.0	14.0	23.0		23.0	23.0	NA
Influenza immunizations (last 12 mos)										
Noninstitutionalized people 65+ (%)	NA	42.0	NA	52.0	55.0	58.0	NA	63.0	63.0	NA
Black 65 years and over (%)	NA	27.0	NA	33.0	39.0	40.0	NA	45.0	46.0	NA
Hispanic 65 years and over (%)	NA	NA	NA	47.0	38.0	50.0	NA	53.0	50.0	NA

Source: National Center for Health Statistics, *Healthy People 2000 Final Review*, Table 20, retrieved June 13, 2002, from http://www.cdc.gov/nchs/. *Notes:* NA Not reported. 1. 1979- 80 influenza season through 1986-87 influenza season. 2. 1987 -88 influenza season through 1989-90 influenza season. 3. 1988 -89 influenza season through 1990-91 influenza season. 4. 1989 -90 influenza season through 1991-92 influenza season. 5. 1990 -91 influenza season through 1992-93 influenza season. 6. 1991 -92 influenza season through 1993-94 influenza season. 7. 1992 -93 influenza season through 1994-95 influenza season. 8. 1993 -94 influenza season through 1995-96 influenza season. 9. 1994- 95 influenza season through 1996-97 influenza season.

Estimated Growth in Community Health Care Sites: 2002-2006

X Not applicable.

Year	Added Sites	For a Total of
2001	X	3,307
2002	252	3,559
2003	430	3,737
2004	660	3,967
2005	930	4,237
2006	1,200	4,507

Source: The White House Office of Management and Budget, retrieved June 26, 2002, from http://www.whitehouse.gov/omb/budget/fy2003/bud15.html.

School-Based Health Centers-Select Operations, Services, and Policies by Grades Served, Age of Center, and Sponsorship

806 school-based health centers completed the questionnaire. STD is sexually transmitted disease.

	Grades Served			Age of SBHC				Sponsor Type				
	Elementary	Middle	High	<2 years	2-4 years	5-9 years	10+ years	Health Department	Community Health Center	School	Hospital Medical Center	University
Primary care	20	24	28	24	24	24	30	20	29	19	28	24
Mental health	12	19	23	17	14	18	30	14	18	23	16	24
Operation Hours (%)												
>30 hrs/week	57	72	78	58	62	72	88	71	72	76	65	73
Summer operations	47	48	49	42	49	45	55	48	41	41	56	54
Services On-site (%)												
Prescriptions	91	87	90	94	92	84	89	77	97	77	95	98
Medications dispensed	55	56	65	65	58	58	72	52	59	37	70	71
STD diagnose/treat	30	55	77	42	52	57	75	61	63	34	51	48
Birth control		22	28	21	19	21	41	29	22	13	25	15
Psychological development assessment	72	75	73	70	72	73	72	68	71	58	79	93
Individual substance abuse counseling	42	57	70	55	53	60	70	56	53	67	53	51
Tobacco prevention in class	45	59	57	54	51	54	52	57	41	56	51	62
Policies (%)												
Parental consent every visit	18	10	8	13	16	10	4	9	9	17	12	24
Bill third party	75	78	71	76	69	75	71	82	85	51	64	76
Chart audits	84	89	88	82	83	93	91	90	89	71	87	88
Patient survey	66	73	76	64	73	72	77	70	80	59	70	68
Acceptance of SBHC (%)												
Students enrolled	70	68	60	52	66	64	66	66	68	55	64	66
Students visited at least once	63	58	50	62	55	53	48	64	50	60	46	90

Source: National Assembly on School-Based Health Care, *Creating Access to Care for Children and Youth: School- Based Health Center Census 1998-1999*, June 2000, retrieved June 25, 2002, from http://www.nasbhc.org/.

U.S. Human Genome Project Funding

Millions of dollars. These numbers do not include construction funds, which are a very small part of the budget. The Human Genome Project is sometimes reported to have a cost of $3 billion. However, this figure refers to the total projected funding over a 15-year period (1990- 2005) for a wide range of scientific activities related to genomics. The Department of Energy (DOE) and National Institutes of Health (NIH) genome programs set aside 3% to 5% of their respective total annual budgets for the study of the project's ethical, legal, and social issues. For an explanation of the NIH budget, contact the Office of Human Genome Communications, National Human Genome Research Institute, National Institutes of Health; 301-402- 0911.

FY	DOE	NIH	U.S. Total
1988	10.7	17.2	27.9
1989	18.5	28.2	46.7
1990	27.2	59.5	86.7
1991	47.4	87.4	134.8
1992	59.4	104.8	164.2
1993	63.0	106.1	169.1
1994	63.3	127.0	190.3
1995	68.7	153.8	222.5
1996	73.9	169.3	243.2
1997	77.9	188.9	266.8
1998	85.5	218.3	303.8

[Continued]

U.S. Human Genome Project Funding

[Continued]

FY	DOE	NIH	U.S. Total
1999	89.9	225.7	315.6
2000	88.9	271.7	360.6
2001	86.4	308.4	394.8
2002	87.8	346.7	434.3
Total	948.5	2,413.0	3,361.3

Source: Human Genome Project Budget, retrieved June 26, 2002, from http://www.ornl.gov/ hgmis/project/budget.html.

Chapter 4
RISKY BEHAVIOR

Meal/Snack Eating Patterns of Americans Aged 2 and Over, and Contribution of Away-From-Home Foods, Selected Nutrients and Food Components, 1977-95

NA Not available.

Item	1977-78	1987-88	1989	1990	1991	1994	1995
			Number				
Meals/day	2.7	2.6	2.6	2.6	2.6	2.7	2.6
Snacks/day	1.1	0.9	1.2	1.2	1.4	1.5	1.6
			Percent				
Meals:							
At home	84	76	76	77	73	72	71
Away from home[1]	16	24	24	23	27	28	29
Snacks:							
At home	83	80	80	82	82	79	78
Away from home[1]	17	20	20	18	18	21	22
All eating occasions:							
At home	84	77	77	78	76	74	73
Away from home[1]	16	23	23	22	24	26	27
Restaurant	2	4	4	4	4	6	5
Fast food	3	7	7	7	7	8	9
School[2]	3	2	2	2	3	2	2
Other public	3	2	2	2	2	2	2
Others	6	8	8	7	8	8	9
Calories:							
At home	82	73	73	74	71	69	66
Away from home[1]	18	27	27	26	29	31	34
Total fat:							
At home	81	72	71	72	68	65	62
Away from home[1]	19	28	29	28	32	35	38
Saturated fat:							
At home	NA	72	71	72	69	67	63
Away from home[1]	NA	28	29	28	31	33	37
Cholesterol:							
At home	NA	74	75	75	70	68	66
Away from home[1]	NA	26	25	25	30	32	34

[Continued]

Meal/Snack Eating Patterns of Americans Aged 2 and Over, and Contribution of Away-From-Home Foods, Selected Nutrients and Food Components, 1977-95

[Continued]

Item	1977-78	1987-88	1989	1990	1991	1994	1995
Fiber:							
At home	NA	78	77	78	75	74	73
Away from home[1]	NA	22	23	22	25	26	27
Calcium:							
At home	83	77	77	78	75	74	71
Away from home[1]	17	23	23	22	25	26	29
Iron:							
At home	84	78	78	79	75	74	73
Away from home[1]	16	22	22	21	25	26	27

Source: Biing-Hwan Lin, Joanne Guthrie, and Elizabeth Frazco, *Nutrient Contribution of Food Away From Home,* Compiled by ERS from NFCS 1977-78, NFCS 1987-88, CSFII 1989-91, and CSFII 1994-95, 1-day intake data; retrieved July 3, 2002, from www.ers.usda.gov/. *Notes:* 1. Away from home presents the aggregate of fast foods, restaurants, schools, other public places, and others. 2. Schools are classified as a separate category for children only; for adults, they are included in the "others" category.

Incidence (Per 100,000 Population) of Diagnosed Infections for Pathogens by Year and Pathogen

NR Not reported. Data are from the Foodborne Diseases Active Surveillance Network for the five original sites from 1996-2000 and for all eight sites in 2000. The Foodborne Diseases Active Surveillance Network (FoodNet) is the principal foodborne disease component of CDC' s Emerging Infections Program (EIP). FoodNet is a collaborative project of the CDC, nine EIP sites (California, Colorado, Connecticut, Georgia, New York, Maryland, Minnesota, Oregon and Tennessee), the U.S. Department of Agriculture (USDA), and the Food and Drug Administration (FDA). The project consists of active surveillance for foodborne diseases and related epidemiologic studies designed to help public health officials better understand the epidemiology of foodborne diseases in the United States. The project began in five states and surveilled laboratory-confirmed cases. Each year the surveillance area, referred to as the catchment, expands. By 2002 it covered 38 million persons in nine states.

Pathogen	Original Five Sites					All Sites
	1996	1997	1998	1999[1]	2000[1]	2000
Campylobacter	23.5	25.2	21.4	17.5	20.1	15.7
Cryptosporidium	NR	3.7[2]	2.9[2]	1.8[2]	2.4[2]	1.5
Cyclospora	NR	0.4[2]	0.1[2]	0.1[2]	0.1[2]	0.1
Escherichia coli O 157	2.7	2.3	2.8	2.1	2.9	2.1
Listeria	0.5	0.5	0.6	0.5	0.4	0.3
Salmonella	14.5	13.6	12.3	13.6	12.0	14.4
Shigella	8.9	7.5	8.5	5.0	11.6	7.9
Vibrio	0.2	0.3	0.3	0.2	0.3	0.2
Yersinia	1.0	0.9	1.0	0.8	0.5	0.4

Source: Preliminary FoodNet Data on the Incidence of Foodborne Illnesses-Selected Sites, United States, 2000, *MMWR Morbidity and Natality Weekly Report,* April 6, 2001; retrieved July 9, 2002, from http://www.cdc.gov/mmwr/. *Notes:* 1. Urine isolates excluded because urine isolates were not reported before 1999. 2. Rates from 1997-2000 for Cyclospora and Cryptosporidium were calculated using the 1997 catchment area. Connecticut, Minnesota, and selected counties in California began data collection at the beginning of 1997; Oregon and other selected counties in California began this process in the middle of the year. Only full-year data are included in these rate calculations.

National School Lunch Program: Participation and Lunches Served

School lunch data as of June 24, 2002. Participation data are nine-month averages (summer months are excluded).

Fiscal Year	Millions					Free/RP Total Lunches Served	% of Total
	K-12 Enrollment	Average Participation					
		Free	Reduced Price	Full Price	Total		
1970	51.2	4.6	[1]	17.8	22.4	3,565.1	20.7
1975	49.8	9.4	0.6	14.9	24.9	4,063.0	40.3
1980	46.2	10.0	1.9	14.7	26.6	4,387.0	45.1
1981	45.5	10.6	1.9	13.3	25.8	4,210.6	48.6
1982	45.1	9.8	1.6	11.5	22.9	3,755.0	50.2
1983	44.9	10.3	1.5	11.2	23.0	3,803.3	51.7
1984	44.9	10.3	1.5	11.5	23.4	3,826.2	51.0
1985	44.9	9.9	1.6	12.1	23.6	3,890.1	49.1
1986	45.2	10.0	1.6	12.2	23.7	3,942.5	49.1
1987	45.4	10.0	1.6	12.4	23.9	3,939.9	48.6
1988	45.4	9.8	1.6	12.8	24.2	4,032.9	47.4
1989	45.8	9.8	1.6	12.9	24.3	4,004.9	47.2
1990	46.4	9.9	1.7	12.6	24.1	4,009.1	48.3
1991	47.2	10.3	1.8	12.1	24.2	4,050.9	50.4
1992	48.1	11.2	1.7	11.7	24.6	4,101.9	53.0
1993	48.9	11.8	1.7	11.3	24.9	4,137.7	54.8
1994	49.7	12.2	1.8	11.3	25.3	4,201.8	55.9
1995	50.5	12.5	1.9	11.3	25.7	4,253.4	56.4
1996	51.3	12.7	2.0	11.3	25.9	4,313.2	56.9
1997	51.9	13.0	2.1	11.3	26.3	4,409.0	57.6
1998	52.4	13.1	2.2	11.3	26.6	4,424.9	57.8
1999	52.7	13.0	2.4	11.6	26.9	4,513.2	57.6
2000	52.9	13.0	2.5	11.8	27.2	4,574.9	51.1
2001	53.1	12.9	2.6	12.0	27.5	4,583.8	56.9

Source: National School Lunch Program: Participation and Lunches Served, National School Lunch Annual Summary, from http://www.fns.usda.gov/pd/slsummar.htm. Enrollment data from *Statistical Abstract of the United States 2001*, Table 205; primary source: U.S. National Center for Education Statistics, *Digest of Education Statistics*, annual, and *Projections of Education Statistics*, annual. *Note:* 1. Included with free meals.

Drug Use (12- to 17-Year-Olds) by Type of Drug (Percent): 1985 to 1999

NA Not available. Current users are those who used a drug at least once within the month prior to the study.

Age and Type of Drug	Ever Used				Current User					
	1985	1990	1995	1998	1985	1990	1995	1997	1998	1999
12 to 17 Years Old										
Marijuana and hashish	20.1	12.7	16.2	17.0	10.2	4.4	8.2	9.4	8.3	7.0
Cocaine	4.7	2.6	2.0	2.2	1.5	0.6	0.8	1.0	0.8	0.7
Alcohol	56.1	48.8	40.6	37.3	41.2	32.5	21.1	20.5	19.1	19.0

[Continued]

Drug Use (12- to 17-Year-Olds) by Type of Drug (Percent): 1985 to 1999
[Continued]

Age and Type of Drug	Ever Used				Current User					
	1985	1990	1995	1998	1985	1990	1995	1997	1998	1999
Binge alcohol use[2]	NA	NA	NA	NA	21.9	NA	7.9	8.3	7.7	7.8
Cigarettes	50.7	45.1	38.1	35.8	29.4	22.4	20.2	19.9	18.2	15.9

Source: National Center for Education Statistics, *The Condition of Education 1999*; Primary Source: University of Michigan, Survey Research Center, Institute for Social Research, *Monitoring the Future Study*; retrieved July 15, 2002, from http://nces.ed.gov/pubs99/condition99/indicator- 27.html

Percentage of High School Seniors Who Reported Using Alcohol or Drugs Any Time During the Previous Year, by Type of Drug: School Years 1975-98

Only drug use not under a doctor's orders is included. Estimates were tabulated using restricted-use files. NA Not available.

Year	Alcohol	Marijuana	Any Illicit Drug Other Than Marijuana	Stimulants	LSD	Cocaine	Sedatives	Tranquilizer	Inhalants
1975	84.8	40.0	26.2	16.2	7.2	5.6	11.7	10.6	NA
1976	85.7	44.5	25.4	15.8	6.4	6.0	10.7	10.3	3.0
1977	87.0	47.6	26.0	16.3	5.5	7.2	10.8	10.8	3.7
1978	87.7	50.2	27.1	17.1	6.3	9.0	9.9	9.9	4.1
1979	88.1	50.8	28.2	18.3	6.6	12.0	9.9	9.6	5.4
1980	87.9	48.8	30.4	20.8	6.5	12.3	10.3	8.7	4.6
1981	87.0	46.1	34.0	26.0	6.5	12.4	10.5	8.0	4.1
1982	86.8	44.3	30.1	20.3	6.1	11.5	9.1	7.0	4.5
1983	87.3	42.3	28.4	17.9	5.4	11.4	7.9	6.9	4.3
1984	86.0	40.0	28.0	17.7	4.7	11.6	6.6	6.1	5.1
1985	85.6	40.6	27.4	15.8	4.4	13.1	5.8	6.1	5.7
1986	84.5	38.8	25.9	13.4	4.5	12.7	5.2	5.8	6.1
1987	85.7	36.3	24.1	12.2	5.2	10.3	4.1	5.5	6.9
1988	85.3	33.1	21.1	10.9	4.8	7.9	3.7	4.8	6.5
1989	82.7	29.6	20.0	10.8	4.9	6.5	3.7	3.8	5.9
1990	80.6	27.0	17.9	9.1	5.4	5.3	3.6	3.5	6.9
1991	77.7	23.9	16.2	8.2	5.2	3.5	3.6	3.6	6.6
1992	76.8	21.9	14.9	7.1	5.6	3.1	2.9	2.8	6.2
1993	72.7[1]	26.0	17.1	8.4	6.8	3.3	3.4	3.5	7.0
1994	73.0[1]	30.7	18.0	9.4	6.9	3.6	4.2	3.7	7.7
1995	73.7[1]	34.7	19.4	9.3	8.4	4.0	4.9	4.4	8.0
1996	72.5[1]	35.8	19.8	9.5	8.8	4.9	5.3	4.6	7.6
1997	74.8[1]	38.5	20.7	10.2	8.4	5.5	5.4	4.7	6.7
1998	74.3[1]	37.5	20.2	10.1	7.6	5.7	6.0	5.5	6.2

Source: National Center for Education Statistics, *The Condition of Education 1999*. Primary source: University of Michigan, Survey Research Center, Institute for Social Research, *Monitoring the Future Study*, retrieved July 19, 2002, from http://nces.ed.gov/pubs99/condition99/SupTables/supp- table-27-1.html." *Notes:* 1. In 1993, the questions regarding alcohol consumption changed; therefore, data for alcohol use from 1993 through 1998 may not be comparable to earlier years. For example, in 1993, the original wording produced an estimate of 76 percent for alcohol use. The new wording produced an estimate of 73 percent.

Drug Use by Type of Drug and Age Group: 1985 to 1999

NA Not available. Data are for adults, in percent.

Age and Type of Drug	Ever Used[1]				Current User					
	1985	1990	1995	1998	1985	1990	1995	1997	1998	1999
12 Years Old and Over										
Any illicit drug	34.4	34.2	34.2	35.8	12.1	6.7	6.1	6.4	6.2	7.0
Marijuana and hashish	29.4	30.5	31.0	33.0	9.7	5.4	4.7	5.1	5.0	5.4
Cocaine	11.2	11.2	10.3	10.6	3.0	0.9	0.7	0.7	0.8	0.8
Crack	NA	1.5	1.8	2.0	NA	0.3	0.2	0.3	0.2	0.2
Inhalants	7.9	5.7	5.7	5.8	0.6	0.4	0.4	0.4	0.3	0.3
Hallucinogens	6.9	7.9	9.5	9.9	1.2	0.4	0.7	0.8	0.7	0.7
PCP	2.0	2.0	3.2	3.5	NA	NA	NA	0.1	NA	NA
LSD	4.6	5.8	7.5	7.9	NA	NA	0.3	0.2	0.3	0.2
Heroin.	0.9	0.8	1.2	1.1	0.1	NA	0.1	0.2	0.1	0.1
Alcohol	84.9	82.2	82.3	81.3	60.2	52.6	52.2	51.4	51.7	52.0
Binge alcohol use[2]	NA	NA	NA	NA	20.2	14.4	15.8	15.3	15.6	15.1
Cigarettes.	78.0	75.4	71.8	69.7	38.7	32.6	28.8	29.6	27.7	29.7
Smokeless tobacco	NA	17.5	17.0	17.2	NA	3.9	3.3	3.2	2.0	2.2
12 to 17 Years Old										
Marijuana and hashish	20.1	12.7	16.2	17.0	10.2	4.4	8.2	9.4	8.3	7.0
Cocaine	4.7	2.6	2.0	2.2	1.5	0.6	0.8	1.0	0.8	0.7
Alcohol	56.1	48.8	40.6	37.3	41.2	32.5	21.1	20.5	19.1	19.0
Binge alcohol use[2]	NA	NA	NA	NA	21.9	NA	7.9	8.3	7.7	7.8
Cigarettes	50.7	45.1	38.1	35.8	29.4	22.4	20.2	19.9	18.2	15.9
18 to 25 Years Old										
Marijuana and hashish	57.6	50.4	41.4	44.6	21.7	12.7	12.0	12.8	13.8	16.4
Cocaine	24.3	19.3	9.8	10.0	8.1	2.3	1.3	1.2	2.0	1.9
Alcohol	(NA)	87.6	84.4	83.2	70.1	62.8	61.3	58.4	60.0	60.2
Binge alcohol use[2]	NA	NA	NA	NA	34.4	NA	29.9	28.0	31.7	31.1
Cigarettes	75.3	70.7	67.7	68.8	47.4	40.9	35.3	40.6	41.6	41.0
26 to 34 Years Old										
Marijuana and hashish	54.1	56.5	51.8	47.9	19.0	9.5	6.7	6.0	5.5	6.4
Cocaine	23.6	25.4	21.6	17.1	6.3	1.9	1.2	0.9	1.2	1.0
Alcohol	NA	NA	90.1	88.2	70.6	64.4	63.0	60.2	60.9	61.9
Cigarettes	84.7	84.1	75.8	71.8	45.7	42.4	34.7	33.7	32.5	34.4
35 Years Old and Over										
Marijuana and hashish	13.9	19.6	25.3	29.4	2.6	2.4	1.8	2.6	2.5	2.5
Cocaine	4.1	5.9	8.6	10.4	0.5	0.2	0.4	0.5	0.5	0.6
Alcohol	NA	83.5	87.1	86.6	57.5	49.5	52.6	52.8	51.7	53.4
Cigarettes.	82.2	79.0	77.5	75.2	35.5	28.9	27.2	27.9	25.1	28.5

Source: Statistical Abstract of the United States: 2001, Table 189. Primary sources, U.S. Substance Abuse and Mental Health Services Administration, National Household Survey on Drug Abuse. *Notes:* 1. Comparable data for 1999 are not available. 2. Binge use is defined as drinking five or more drinks on the same occasion on at least one day in the past 30 days. 3. Nonmedical use; does not include over-the-counter drugs.

Emergency Department Drug Episodes by Patient Demographic Characteristics: 1994-2000

Estimates for the coterminous United States by year.

Demographic characteristics	1994	1995	1996	1997	1998	1999	2000	% Change 1994-2000[1]	% Change 1998-2000[1]	% Change 1999-2000[1]
GENDER										
Male	263,823	256,049	257,490	269,919	281,263	292,018	309,607	17.4		
Female	250,182	252,137	250,826	252,035	256,211	257,983	281,793	12.6	10.0	9.2
Unknown	4,875	5,333	5,616	4,864	4,958	4,766	10,162	108.5	105.0	113.2
RACE/ETHNICITY										
White	278,747	277,538	273,690	284,026	295,346	309,964	334,819	20.1	13.4	
Black	141,351	139,388	135,303	134,895	136,474	132,981	133,735			
Hispanic	50,368	47,354	55,026	52,697	57,162	56,840	68,282	19.5	20.1	
Race/ethnicity[2]	6,038	5,533	6,020	6,097	5,382	5,585	5,160			
Unknown	42,377	43,705	43,895	49,102	48,068	49,397	59,568	40.6		
AGE										
6-17 years	61,294	62,219	65,051	63,157	60,037	53,870	64,467	19.7		
6-11 years	1,001	1,503	1,175	1,727	952	1,185	1,024			
12-17 years	60,293	60,715	63,876	61,429	59,084	52,685	63,443	20.4		
18-25 years	112,273	103,704	98,614	104,630	103,373	109,579	123,310	19.3	12.5	15.5
18-19 years	27,863	28,543	26,863	29,276	30,062	29,738	34,359	23.3	14.3	
20-25 years	84,410	75,161	71,751	75,354	73,311	79,841	88,951	21.3		
26-34 years	151,419	143,930	139,545	138,890	138,471	131,254	135,464			
26-29 years	61,825	58,796	56,006	57,044	57,332	52,900	55,151			
30-34 years	89,594	85,135	83,539	81,846	81,138	78,354	80,314			
35 years and older	190,446	202,287	209,864	218,422	239,140	259,256	277,283	45.6	16.0	
35-44 years	132,312	142,339	143,731	147,533	160,025	165,483	175,055	32.3		
45-54 years	42,012	44,752	49,379	54,388	60,200	71,699	78,808	87.6	30.9	
55 years and older	16,121	15,196	16,754	16,502	18,915	22,074	23,420	45.3	23.8	
Unknown	NA	1,379	859	1,719	1,412	809	1,038			
TOTAL DRUG ABUSE EPISODES	518,880	513,519	513,933	526,818	542,432	554,767	601,563	15.9	10.9	

Source: Emergency Department Trends from the Drug Abuse Warning Network, Preliminary Estimates January-June 2001 with Revised Estimates 1994-2000, Table 4.2.0. Primary source: Office of Applied Studies, SAMHSA, Drug Abuse Warning Network, 2001 update; retrieved July 24, 2002, from http://www.samhsa.gov/oas/dawn/TrndED/2001/Text/TrndEDtxt.PDF *Notes:* 1. This column denotes statistically significant increases and decreases between estimates for the periods noted. 2. Race/ethnicity not tabulated above.

Use of Selected Substances in the Past Month by Persons 12 Years of Age and Over, According to Age, Sex, Race, and Hispanic Origin: Selected Years 1979-99

NA Not available. Persons of Hispanic origin may be of any race. Binge alcohol means five or more drinks on the same occasion at least once in the past month. In 1999 the survey was redesigned. Estimates for 1999 presented in this table are based on a reduced sample size.

Alcohol	Percent of Population										
	1979	1985	1990	1992	1993	1994	1995	1996	1997	1998	1999
12 years and over	63	60	53	49	51	54	52	51	51	52	52
12-17 years	50	41	33	21	24	22	21	19	21	19	19
12-13 years	NA	NA	NA	NA	NA	9	8	5	7	5	NA
14-15 years	NA	NA	NA	NA	NA	22	21	19	21	21	NA
16-17 years	NA	NA	NA	NA	NA	36	34	31	33	32	NA
18-25 years	75	70	63	59	59	63	61	60	58	60	60
26-34 years	72	71	64	62	64	65	63	62	60	61	62
35 years and over	60	58	50	47	50	54	53	52	53	53	53
12-17 years:											
Male	52	44	34	22	24	22	22	19	21	19	NA
Female	47	38	31	19	23	21	20	18	20	19	NA
White, non-Hispanic	53	46	37	22	26	24	23	20	22	21	NA

[Continued]

Use of Selected Substances in the Past Month by Persons 12 Years of Age and Over, According to Age, Sex, Race, and Hispanic Origin: Selected Years 1979-99

[Continued]

Alcohol	Percent of Population										
	1979	1985	1990	1992	1993	1994	1995	1996	1997	1998	1999
Black, non-Hispanic	NA	30	21	18	18	18	15	15	16	13	NA
Hispanic	NA	27	24	20	22	18	19	20	19	19	NA
18-25 years:											
Male	NA	NA	NA	NA	NA	71	68	67	66	68	NA
Female	NA	NA	NA	NA	NA	55	55	54	51	52	NA
White,non-Hispanic	NA	NA	NA	NA	NA	68	67	65	64	65	NA
Black,non-Hispanic	NA	NA	NA	NA	NA	52	48	50	47	50	NA
Hispanic	NA	NA	NA	NA	NA	54	49	50	49	51	NA
Binge alcohol											
12 years and over	NA	20	14	15	15	17	16	15	15	16	15
12-17 years	NA	22	15	10	11	8	8	7	8	8	8
12-13 years	NA	NA	NA	NA	NA	2	2	1	1	1	NA
14-15 years	NA	NA	NA	NA	NA	8	8	6	8	8	NA
16-17 years	NA	NA	NA	NA	NA	16	15	15	16	15	NA
18-25 years	NA	34	30	30	29	34	30	32	28	32	31
26-34 years	NA	28	21	23	22	24	24	23	23	22	22
35 years and over	NA	13	8	9	10	12	12	11	12	12	11
12-17 years:											
Male	NA	29	19	13	15	9	9	9	10	9	NA
Female	NA	14	12	7	7	7	6	6	7	7	NA
White, non-Hispanic	NA	26	18	11	13	10	9	8	9	9	NA
Black, non-Hispanic	NA	6	NA	6	3	3	3	4	4	3	NA
Hispanic	NA	15	11	9	12	5	7	8	7	6	NA
18-25 years:											
Male	NA	NA	NA	NA	NA	47	41	44	39	43	NA
Female	NA	NA	NA	NA	NA	21	19	21	17	21	NA
White,non-Hispanic	NA	NA	NA	NA	NA	40	34	37	33	38	NA
Black,non-Hispanic	NA	NA	NA	NA	NA	17	16	19	13	16	NA
Hispanic	NA	NA	NA	NA	NA	26	23	25	22	25	NA
Marijuana											
12 years and over	13	10	5	5	5	5	5	5	5	5	5
12-17 years	14	10	4	3	4	6	8	7	9	8	7
12-13 years	NA	NA	NA	NA	NA	2	2	1	3	2	NA
14-15 years	NA	NA	NA	NA	NA	5	10	7	9	9	NA
16-17 years	NA	NA	NA	NA	NA	12	13	13	16	15	NA
18-25 years	36	22	13	11	11	12	12	13	13	14	16
26-34 years	20	19	10	9	8	7	7	6	6	6	6
35 years and over	3	3	2	2	2	2	2	2	3	3	3
12-17 years:											
Male	16	11	5	4	4	7	9	8	10	9	NA
Female	12	9	4	3	4	5	7	7	8	8	NA
White, non-Hispanic	16	12	5	4	4	6	8	7	10	9	NA
Black, non-Hispanic	10	6	2	2	3	5	8	7	9	8	NA

[Continued]

Use of Selected Substances in the Past Month by Persons 12 Years of Age and Over, According to Age, Sex, Race, and Hispanic Origin: Selected Years 1979-99

[Continued]

Alcohol	Percent of Population										
	1979	1985	1990	1992	1993	1994	1995	1996	1997	1998	1999
Hispanic	8	6	3	3	4	6	8	7	8	8	NA
18-25 years:											
Male	NA	NA	NA	NA	NA	16	15	17	17	17	NA
Female	NA	NA	NA	NA	NA	9	9	9	8	10	NA
White, non-Hispanic	NA	NA	NA	NA	NA	13	13	14	13	15	NA
Black, non-Hispanic	NA	NA	NA	NA	NA	12	12	14	14	15	NA
Hispanic	NA	NA	NA	NA	NA	8	7	8	8	9	NA
Cocaine											
12 years and over	2.6	3.0	0.9	0.7	0.7	0.7	0.7	0.8	0.7	0.8	0.8
12-17 years	1.5	1.5	0.6	0.3	0.4	0.3	0.8	0.6	1.0	0.8	0.7
18-25 years	9.9	8.1	2.3	2.0	1.6	1.2	1.3	2.0	1.2	2.0	1.9
26-34 years	3.0	6.3	1.9	1.5	1.0	1.3	1.2	1.5	0.9	1.2	1.0
35 years and over	0.2	0.5	0.2	0.2	0.4	0.4	0.4	0.4	0.5	0.5	0.6
12-17 years:											
Male	2.2	1.9	0.8	0.3	0.5	0.3	0.8	0.4	0.9	0.6	NA
Female	0.8	1.1	0.5	0.3	0.4	0.3	0.7	0.8	1.1	1.0	NA
White, non-Hispanic	1.4	1.5	0.4	0.2	0.4	0.3	0.9	0.5	1.1	0.9	NA
Black, non-Hispanic	NA	1.3	0.8	0.3	0.3	0.1	0.1	0.1	0.1	NA	NA
Hispanic	2.1	2.6	2.0	1.3	1.1	0.8	0.8	1.1	1.0	1.4	NA
18-25 years:											
Male	NA	NA	NA	NA	NA	1.9	1.7	2.7	1.9	2.6	NA
Female	NA	NA	NA	NA	NA	0.6	0.9	1.4	0.5	1.3	NA
White,non-Hispanic	NA	NA	NA	NA	NA	1.2	1.5	2.3	1.2	2.2	NA
Black, non-Hispanic	NA	NA	NA	NA	NA	0.7	0.7	1.1	0.9	0.6	NA
Hispanic	NA	NA	NA	NA	NA	2.2	1.1	2.1	1.5	2.7	NA

Source: Health, United States, 2001, Table 63. Primary sources: SAMHSA, NHS; retrieved July 18, 2002, from http://www.cdc.gov/.

Prescription and Over-The-Counter Drug Use by Type of Drug: 1985 to 1999

NA Not available. Data are for persons aged 12 and over.

Type of Drug	Ever Used[1]				Current User					
	1985	1990	1995	1998	1985	1990	1995	1997	1998	1999
Any illicit drug	34.4	34.2	34.2	35.8	12.1	6.7	6.1	6.4	6.2	7.0
Stimulants[2]	7.3	5.5	4.9	4.4	1.8	0.6	0.4	0.3	0.3	0.3
Sedatives[2]	4.8	2.8	2.7	2.1	0.5	0.2	0.2	0.1	0.1	0.1
Tranquilizers[2]	7.6	4.0	3.9	3.5	2.2	0.6	0.4	0.4	0.3	0.4
Analgesics	2.0	7.6	6.3	6.1	5.3	1.4	0.9	0.6	0.7	0.8

Source: Statistical Abstract of the United States: 2001, Table 189. Primary source: U.S. Substance Abuse and Mental Health Services Administration, *National Household Survey on Drug Abuse*, annual. *Notes:* 1. Comparable data for 1999 are not available. 2. Nonmedical use; does not include over-the-counter drugs.

Percentage of Smoking Prevalence Among U.S. Adults, 18 Years of Age and Older, 1955-2000

NA Not available. Estimates since 1992 incorporate some-day smokers (people who do not smoke every day).

Year	Overall Population	Males	Females	Whites	Blacks
1955	NA	56.9	28.4	NA	NA
1965	42.4	51.9	33.9	42.1	45.8
1966	42.6	52.5	33.9	42.4	45.9
1970	37.4	44.1	31.5	37.0	41.4
1974	37.1	43.1	32.1	36.4	44.0
1978	34.1	38.1	30.7	33.9	37.7
1979	33.5	37.5	29.9	33.3	36.9
1980	33.2	37.6	29.3	32.9	36.9
1983	32.1	35.1	29.5	31.8	35.9
1985	30.1	32.6	27.9	29.6	34.9
1987	28.8	31.2	26.5	28.5	32.9
1988	28.1	30.8	25.7	27.8	31.7
1990	25.5	28.4	22.8	25.6	26.2
1991	25.7	28.1	23.5	25.5	29.1
1992	26.5	28.6	24.6	26.6	27.8
1993	25.0	27.7	22.5	24.9	26.1
1994	25.5	28.2	23.1	26.3	27.2
1995	24.7	27.0	22.6	25.6	25.8
1997	24.7	27.6	22.1	25.3	26.7
1998	24.1	26.4	22.0	25.0	24.7
1999	23.5	25.7	21.5	24.3	24.3
2000	23.3	25.7	21.0	24.1	23.2

Source: Smoking Prevalence Among U.S. Adults, Centers for Disease Control, retrieved August 6, 2002, from http://www.cdc.gov/tobacco/research_data adults_prev/prevali.htm

Percentage of High School Seniors Who Smoked During the Previous 30 Days

NA Not available.

Year	Total	Males	Females	Whites	Blacks	Hispanics	Total
1976	38.8	37.7	39.1	NA	NA	NA	38.8
1977	38.4	36.6	39.6	38.3	36.7	35.7	38.4
1978	36.7	34.5	38.1	37.6	32.7	32.8	36.7
1979	34.4	31.2	37.1	36.0	30.2	26.8	34.4
1980	30.5	26.8	33.4	33.0	26.8	22.6	30.5
1981	29.4	26.5	31.6	30.5	23.7	23.2	29.4
1982	30.0	26.8	32.6	30.7	21.8	24.7	30.0
1983	30.3	28.0	31.6	31.3	21.2	24.7	30.3
1984	29.3	25.9	31.9	31.2	19.3	25.3	29.3
1985	30.1	28.2	31.4	31.3	18.1	25.5	30.1
1986	29.6	27.9	30.6	31.9	16.9	23.7	29.6
1987	29.4	27.0	31.4	32.1	14.2	22.7	29.4
1988	28.7	28.0	28.9	32.2	13.3	21.9	28.7
1989	28.6	27.7	29.0	32.2	12.6	20.6	28.6
1990	29.4	29.1	29.2	32.3	12.2	21.7	29.4
1991	28.3	29.0	27.5	32.2	10.6	24.0	28.3
1992	27.8	29.2	26.1	31.8	8.7	25.0	27.8
1993	29.9	30.7	28.7	33.2	9.5	24.2	29.9
1994	31.2	32.9	29.2	35.2	10.9	23.6	31.2
1995	33.5	34.5	32.0	36.6	12.9	25.1	33.5
1996	34.0	34.9	32.4	38.1	14.2	25.4	34.0
1997	36.5	37.3	35.2	40.7	14.3	25.9	36.5
1998	35.1	36.3	33.3	41.7	14.9	26.6	35.1

Source: Smoking status of high school seniors, United States, *Monitoring the Future Projects*, 1976-1998, retrieved August 6, 2002, from http://www.cdc.gov/tobacco/research_data/youth/.

Deaths From Invasive Melanomas of the Skin : 1975-1999

Incidence per 100,000 population by year of diagnosis.

	Males and Females	Males	Females
1975	7.9	8.5	7.5
1980	10.5	11.8	9.6
1981	11.1	12.1	10.4
1982	11.2	12.5	10.2
1983	11.1	12.6	10.0
1984	11.4	12.9	10.4
1985	12.7	15.1	11.1
1986	13.3	15.7	11.6

[Continued]

Deaths From Invasive Melanomas of the Skin : 1975-1999

[Continued]

	Males and Females	Males	Females
1987	13.6	15.9	12.1
1988	12.8	14.9	11.4
1989	13.7	16.4	11.8
1990	13.8	16.6	11.8
1991	14.6	17.5	12.5
1992	14.8	18.3	12.2
1993	14.6	18.0	12.1
1994	15.6	19.6	12.6
1995	16.4	20.2	13.7
1996	17.1	21.3	14.1
1997	17.6	21.4	14.8
1998	17.6	21.7	14.7
1999	17.4	21.7	14.2

Source: Centers for Disease Control, National Cancer Data, Table XVI, *Melanomas of Skin (Invasive), http://seer.cancer.gov/csr/1973_1999/melama.*

Hepatitis Cases Reported: 1980 to 1999

Disease	1980	1985	1990	1994	1995	1996	1997	1998	1999
Hepatitis B (serum) (1,000)	19.0	26.6	21.1	12.5	10.8	10.6	10.4	10.3	7.7
Hepatitis A (infectious) (1,000)	29.1	23.2	31.4	29.8	31.6	31.0	30.0	23.2	17.0
Hepatitis C/Non-A, non-B (1,000)[1]	[2]	4.2	2.6	4.4	4.6	3.7	3.8	3.5	3.1

Source: Statistical Abstract of the United States: 2001, Table 181 U.S. Centers for Disease Control and Prevention, Atlanta, GA, Summary of Notifiable Diseases, United States, 1999, *Morbidity and Mortality Weekly Report,* Vol. 48, No. 53, April 6, 2001. *Notes:* 1. Includes some persons positive for antibody to hepatitis C virus who do not have hepatitis. 2. Disease was not notifiable.

Chapter 5
TREATMENTS

Number of All Listed Procedures for Discharges from Short-Stay Hospitals

Data exclude Federal hospitals.

	1990	2000	Change 90-00	% of Total in 1990	% of Total in 2000
All Procedures	40,508	39,981	-527	100.0	100.0
Operations of					
Nervous system	952	1,000	48	2.4	2.5
Endocrine system	96	90	-6	0.2	0.2
Eye	350	80	-270	0.9	0.2
Ear	137	37	-100	0.3	0.1
Nose, mouth, and pharynx	585	261	-324	1.4	0.7
Respiratory system	975	969	-6	2.4	2.4
Cardiovascular	3,881	5,939	2,058	9.6	14.9
Hemic and lymphatic system	361	315	-46	0.9	0.8
Digestive system	5,271	5,145	-126	13.0	12.9
Urinary system	1,664	962	-702	4.1	2.4
Male genital organs	594	258	-336	1.5	0.6
Female genital organs	2,440	2,061	-379	6.0	5.2
Obstetrical procedures	6,792	6,209	-583	16.8	15.5
Musculoskeletal system	3,132	3,171	39	7.7	7.9
Integumentary system	1,387	1,264	-123	3.4	3.2
Miscellaneous diagnostic and therapeutic procedures - Total	11,890	12,223	333	29.4	30.6
Computerized axial tomography	1,506	754	-752	3.7	1.9
Arteriography and angiocardiography	1,735	2,005	270	4.3	5.0
Diagnostic ultrasound	1,608	886	-722	4.0	2.2
Respiratory therapy	1,164	991	-173	2.9	2.5
Insertion of endotracheal tube		429	NA		1.1
Injection/infusion of cancer chemotherapy substance		199	NA		0.5
Circulatory monitoring	724		NA	1.8	
Radioisotope scan	603		NA	1.5	
Pyelogram	291		NA	0.7	

Source: 2000 National Hospital Discharge Survey, Advanced Data from Vital and Health Statistics, Number 329, June 19, 2002. 1990 data from *National Hospital Discharge Survey: Annual Summary, 1990*, Series 13, Number 113. Vital and Health Statistics, U.S. Department of Health and Human Services.

Number of All Listed Procedures for Discharges from Short-Stay Hospitals by Age Group

Data exclude Federal hospitals.

Age of Patient Discharged	1990	2000	% of Total in 1990	% of Total in 2000
Under 15	1,960	1,951	4.8	4.9
15-44	16,186	13,518	40.0	33.8
45-64	9,052	9,775	22.3	24.4
65 and older	13,308	14,737	32.9	36.9
All Discharges	40,506	39,981	100.0	100.0

Source: 2000 National Hospital Discharge Survey, Advanced Data from Vital and Health Statistics, Number 329, June 19, 2002. 1990 data from *National Hospital Discharge Survey: Annual Summary, 1990*, Series 13, Number 113. Vital and Health Statistics, U.S. Department of Health and Human Services.

Five-Year Relative Cancer Survival Rates for Selected Cancer Sites

Data are based on the Surveillance, Epidemiology, and End Results Program's population-based registries in Atlanta, Detroit, Seattle-Puget Sound, San Francisco-Oakland, Connecticut, Iowa, New Mexico, Utah, and Hawaii. Please note: These data also appear in Chapter 2. This table is reproduced here for the user's convenience.

Sex and site	White 1974-79	White 1980-82	White 1983-85	White 1986-88	White 1989-97	Black 1974-79	Black 1980-82	Black 1983-85	Black 1986-88	Black 1989-97
Both sexes										
All sites	50.9	52.1	53.8	56.7	62.0	39.2	39.7	39.7	42.6	49.7
Oral cavity and pharynx	54.9	55.6	55.2	55.2	57.1	36.6	31.0	35.2	34.6	33.7
Esophagus	5.5	7.3	9.3	10.8	13.8	3.3	5.4	6.2	7.2	9.0
Stomach	15.2	16.5	16.3	19.1	19.8	15.9	19.4	19.0	19.1	21.6
Colon	51.9	55.7	58.4	61.5	62.6	47.3	49.2	49.4	52.8	52.4
Rectum	49.8	53.1	55.9	59.1	61.0	40.4	38.4	43.7	51.4	53.0
Pancreas	2.4	2.8	2.9	3.2	4.2	3.2	4.5	5.2	6.0	3.9
Lung and bronchus	13.1	13.5	13.8	13.5	14.7	11.3	12.1	11.4	11.9	11.4
Urinary bladder	74.9	78.9	78.2	80.7	82.1	51.5	58.7	59.3	62.3	63.8
Non-Hodgkin's lymphoma	48.2	51.8	54.4	52.8	53.5	50.3	50.0	45.1	50.2	43.0
Leukemia	36.6	39.5	41.9	44.1	45.9	30.8	33.1	32.9	37.6	35.7
Male										
All sites	43.4	46.7	48.5	51.7	60.8	32.1	34.3	34.5	37.7	49.6
Oral cavity and pharynx	54.3	54.6	54.3	52.2	55.0	31.2	26.5	29.9	29.3	28.2
Esophagus	5.1	6.5	7.8	11.3	13.7	2.3	4.6	5.0	7.0	8.9
Stomach	13.8	15.6	14.6	16.2	17.4	15.3	18.5	18.5	15.0	20.1
Colon	51.0	56.0	58.9	62.4	63.2	45.3	46.7	48.3	52.5	52.5
Rectum	49.0	51.7	55.2	58.8	60.6	36.7	36.1	43.1	46.6	52.7
Pancreas	2.6	2.5	2.6	2.9	3.9	2.4	3.2	4.4	6.4	4.0
Lung and bronchus	11.6	12.2	12.0	12.0	13.1	10.0	10.9	10.3	11.9	10.0
Prostate gland	70.3	74.5	76.2	82.7	94.9	60.7	64.7	63.8	69.3	88.1
Urinary bladder	76.0	79.9	79.5	82.3	84.2	58.9	63.3	64.8	67.5	67.4
Non-Hodgkin's lymphoma	47.2	50.9	53.4	50.0	49.8	44.7	47.2	43.6	46.9	38.9
Leukemia	35.5	39.5	41.6	45.4	47.1	30.9	30.1	31.8	36.5	34.0
Female										
All sites	57.4	57.1	58.8	61.4	63.3	46.8	46.0	45.3	47.8	49.9

[Continued]

Five-Year Relative Cancer Survival Rates for Selected Cancer Sites

[Continued]

Sex and site	Percent of Patients									
	White					Black				
	1974-79	1980-82	1983-85	1986-88	1989-97	1974-79	1980-82	1983-85	1986-88	1989-97
Colon	52.6	55.4	58.0	60.7	61.9	48.8	51.1	50.2	53.1	52.4
Rectum	50.8	54.6	56.7	59.5	61.5	43.8	41.3	44.2	56.2	53.3
Pancreas	2.2	3.0	3.2	3.4	4.4	4.1	5.8	5.8	5.6	3.7
Lung and bronchus	16.7	16.2	17.0	15.8	16.7	15.5	15.5	14.1	11.8	13.9
Melanoma of skin	85.8	88.3	89.3	91.2	91.8	69.9	[1]	70.1	[1]	76.2
Breast	75.4	77.1	79.2	83.9	86.6	63.1	65.9	63.4	69.3	71.7
Cervix uteri	69.7	68.1	70.5	71.8	71.8	62.9	61.2	60.0	55.3	60.0
Corpus uteri	87.6	82.8	84.5	84.4	85.7	59.3	54.8	54.2	57.0	58.5
Ovary	37.2	38.7	40.2	42.0	51.0	40.3	39.1	41.2	38.6	47.4
Non-Hodgkin's lymphoma	49.2	52.8	55.4	56.1	58.0	57.5	53.3	47.0	54.4	49.9

Source: National Institutes of Health, National Cancer Institute, Surveillance, Epidemiology, and End Results (SEER)Program, shown in Health United States 2002.
Notes: 1. Data for population groups with fewer than 25 annual cases are not shown.

Cigarette Consumption Per Capita (Those Aged 18 or Older), 1900 to 1998

Year	Cigarettes per Capita	Year	Cigarettes per Capita	Year	Cigarettes per Capita
1900	54	1933	1,334	1966	4,287
1901	53	1934	1,483	1967	4,280
1902	60	1935	1,564	1968	4,186
1903	64	1936	1,754	1969	3,993
1904	66	1937	1,847	1970	3,985
1905	70	1938	1,830	1971	4,037
1906	86	1939	1,900	1972	4,043
1907	99	1940	1,976	1973	4,148
1908	105	1941	2,236	1974	4,141
1909	125	1942	2,585	1975	4,122
1910	151	1943	2,956	1976	4,091
1911	173	1944	3,039	1977	4,043
1912	223	1945	3,449	1978	3,970
1913	260	1946	3,446	1979	3,861
1914	267	1947	3,416	1980	3,849
1915	285	1948	3,505	1981	3,836
1916	395	1949	3,480	1982	3,739
1917	551	1950	3,552	1983	3,488
1918	697	1951	3,744	1984	3,446
1919	727	1952	3,886	1985	3,370
1920	665	1953	3,778	1986	3,274
1921	742	1954	3,546	1987	3,197
1922	770	1955	3,597	1988	3,096
1923	911	1956	3,650	1989	2,926

[Continued]

Cigarette Consumption Per Capita (Those Aged 18 or Older), 1900 to 1998
[Continued]

Year	Cigarettes per Capita	Year	Cigarettes per Capita	Year	Cigarettes per Capita
1924	982	1957	3,755	1990	2,826
1925	1,085	1958	3,953	1991	2,720
1926	1,191	1959	4,073	1992	2,641
1927	1,279	1960	4,171	1993	2,538
1928	1,366	1961	4,266	1994	2,522
1929	1,504	1962	4,266	1995	2,515
1930	1,485	1963	4,345	1996	2,443
1931	1,399	1964	4,194	1997	2,372
1932	1,245	1965	4,258	1998	2,300

Source: U.S. Department of Agriculture (cigarette consumption). CDC Wonder data base for cancer mortality rates. Background data from American Cancer Society publications available at http://www.cancer.org, especially *Cancer Facts or Cancer Facts & Figures* for various years.

Cigarette Consumption and Male and Female Lung Cancer Rates, Selected Years, 1930 to 1998

Cigarette consumption is per capita for those 18 years old or older. Death rates are shown as deaths per 100,000 population.

Year	Per Capita Cigarette Consumption	Male Lung Cancer	Female Lung Cancer
1930	1,485	4.0	2.5
1935	1,564	6.0	3.3
1940	1,976	10.2	3.9
1945	3,449	14.3	4.2
1950	3,552	21.6	4.8
1955	3,597	30.0	5.1
1960	4,171	38.2	5.6
1965	4,258	47.4	7.5
1970	3,985	58.2	11.1
1975	4,122	65.8	15.4
1979	3,861	70.0	22.2
1980	3,849	71.9	24.3
1981	3,836	71.9	25.3
1982	3,739	73.1	27.0
1983	3,488	73.1	28.9
1984	3,446	74.1	29.9
1985	3,370	74.3	31.7
1986	3,274	74.4	32.8
1987	3,197	75.2	34.4
1988	3,096	74.9	36.0

[Continued]

Cigarette Consumption and Male and Female Lung Cancer Rates, Selected Years, 1930 to 1998

[Continued]

Year	Per Capita Cigarette Consumption	Male Lung Cancer	Female Lung Cancer
1989	2,926	74.8	38.0
1990	2,826	75.7	39.3
1991	2,720	74.7	40.3
1992	2,641	73.0	41.8
1993	2,538	72.7	42.6
1994	2,522	70.9	43.2
1995	2,515	69.6	44.1
1996	2,443	68.2	44.6
1997	2,372	66.8	45.3
1998	2,300	65.4	45.6

Source: U.S. Department of Agriculture (cigarette consumption). CDC Wonder data base for cancer mortality rates. Background data from American Cancer Society publications available at http://www.cancer.org, especially *Cancer Facts or Cancer Facts & Figures* for various years.

National Center for Complementary and Alternative Medicine (NCCAM) Clinical Trials Under Way

Subject	Number of Trials
Acupuncture	17
Chiropractic therapy	6
Massage	4
Gingu Biloba	9
St. Johns Wort	6
Meditation	4

Source: National Center for Complementary and Alternative Medicine, accessible at http://www.nccam.nih.gov/.

Chapter 6
DRUGS

Number of Top 10 Prescriptions Dispensed, 1995-2001

	Number of Prescriptions (mil.)	% of Total
1995	240	10.91
1997	270	11.25
2000	347	11.96
2001	358	11.55

Source: IMS Health. "US Top 10 Products by Prescriptions" and "Leading 10 Products by Total U.S. Dispensed Prescriptions, 2001." Retrieved July 16, 2002 from http://www.imshealth.com. Alan Cook, DC. "The Top 10" and "The Top 10 Drugs—1997." Retrieved July 16, 2002 from http://www.chiroweb.com/archives. National Institute for Health Care Management. *Prescription Drug Expenditures in 2001: Another Year of Escalating Costs*, May 6, 2002. Retrieved July 17, 2002 from http://www.nihcm.org.

Depressive Disorders, 2000-2001

Data in millions

	2000	2001
Total adults with depressive disorders	19.0	19.7
Antidepressant prescriptions dispensed	98.0	111.0

Source: IMS Health. *National Disease and Theraputic Index, 2002* and *National Prescription Audit Plus, 2002.* Retrieved July 18, 2002 from http://www.imshealth.org. Number of adults with depressive disorders extrapolated based on a figure of 9.5% of the population suffers from depressive disorders. Population data: "Projections of the Total Resident Population by 5-Year Age Groups, and Sex with Special Age Categories: Middle Series, 1999 to 2000" and "Projections of the Total Resident Population by 5-Year Age Groups, and Sex with Special Age Categories: Middle Series, 2001 to 2005." Retrieved from U.S. Census Bureau website at http://www.census.gov.

Children with ADHD and Children Taking Ritalin, 1975-2000

	1975	1988	2000
Children with ADHD	2,650,120	2,529,840	2,807,960
Children on Ritalin	150,000	1,000,000	6,000,000

Source: National Council for Community Behavioral Healthcare. National Mental Health Association. "Key Facts and Statistics." Retrieved July 18, 2002 from http://www.nmha.org/children/green/facts.cfm. Leonard Sax. "Ritalin: Better Living Through Chemistry?" *The World and I Online*, November 2000. Retrieved July 22, 2002 from http://www.worldandi.com/public/2000/November/sax.html.

Average Retail Prescription Prices, 1990-2001

	Constant 2001 Dollars		Actual Dollars	
	Brand Name	Generics	Brand Name	Generics
1990	37.25	14.11	27.16	10.29
1992	42.06	14.71	33.68	11.78
1994	43.99	16.69	37.37	14.18
1996	50.49	17.58	45.11	15.71
1998	57.17	18.52	53.51	17.33
2000	66.86	19.79	65.29	19.33
2001	71.18	21.96	71.18	21.96
% change (1990-2001)	91.10	55.60	140.40	87.90

Source: Levitt, Larry. The Henry J. Kaiser Family Foundation. *Prescription Drug Trends*, February 2001. Retrieved July 24, 2002 from http://www.kff.org. "The Inflation Calculator." Retrieved July 24, 2002 from http://www.westegg.com/inflation. National Association of Chain Drug Stores. "Industry Statistics." Retrieved August 1, 2002 from http://www.nacds.org.

Advertising Expenditures, 1996-2000

Data in $ million unless otherwise noted.

	1996	1997	1998	1999	2000
Total promotional spending on prescription drugs	9,200	11,000	12,500	13,900	15,700
Total direct-to-consumer advertising	791	1,069	1,317	1,848	2,467
Number of marketing staff	60,539	67,392	71,374	81,296	87,810

Source: National Institute for Health Care Management. *Prescription Drug Expenditures in 2001: Another Year of Escalating Costs*, May 6, 2002. Retrieved July 17, 2002 from http://www.nihcm.org. National Institute For Health Care Management. *Prescription Drugs and Mass Media Advertising, 2000*, November 2001. Retrieved July 26, 2002 from http://www.nihcm.org. Larry Levitt. The Henry J. Kaiser Family Foundation. *Prescription Drug Trends*, November 2001. Alan Sager and Deborah Socolar. Boston University School of Public Health. "Drug Industry Marketing Staff Soars While Research Staff Stagnates." *Drug Data Brief*, December 6, 2001. Retrieved July 29, 2002 from http://rxpolicy.com/studies/bu-rypromotion-v- randd.pdf.

U.S. Retail Prescription Drug Expenditures and Allocation of Monies by Percentage of Retail Sales, 1996-2001

	1996	1997	1998	1999	2000	2001
U.S. prescription drug retail sales ($ mil.)	69,100	78,900	93,400	111,100	131,900	154,500
Wholesale/retail markup (%)	6.3	9	13	8.7	12.1	15.4
R&D expenditures, domestic & foreign (%)	24.5	24	22.4	20.4	19.7	19.6
Total promotional expenditures (%)	13.3	13.9	13.4	12.5	11.9	12.3
Direct-to-consumer advertising (%)	1.1	1.4	1.4	1.7	1.9	1.7
Other expenses (%)	55.9	53.1	51.2	58.4	56.3	52.7

Source: Pharmaceutical Research and Manufacturers of America. *PhRMA Industry Profile 2002.* Retrieved August 6, 2002 from http:// www.phrma.org/publications/publications/profile02/. National Institute for Health Care Management. "Factors Affecting the Growth of Prescription Drugs Expenditures," July 1999. National Institute for Health Care Management. *Prescription Drugs and Mass Media Advertising, 2000,* November 2001. National Institute for Health Care Management. *Prescription Drug Expenditures 2001: Another Year of Escalating Costs,* May 6, 2002. All National Institute for Health Care Management data retrieved July 17-28, 2002 from http://www.nihcm.org. Larry Levitt. The Henry J. Kaiser Family Foundation. *Prescription Drug Trends,* November 2001. IMS Health. "Total U.S. Promotional Spending by Type, 2001" Retrieved July 16, 2002 from http://www.imshealth org.

U.S. Per Capita Expenditures on Health Care in Constant 2000 Dollars, 1993-2000

	1993	1994	1995	1996	1997	1998	1999	2000
Total expenditures for the three categories listed	2,626	2,631	2,662	2,681	2,709	2,783	2,882	2,983
Hospital care	1,468	1,464	1,464	1,462	1,455	1,458	1,475	1,499
Physician and clinical services	923	927	939	943	954	989	1,016	1,041
Prescription drugs	235	240	259	276	300	336	391	443

Source: Centers for Medicare & Medicaid Services. U.S. Health and Human Services. "Table 9: Personal Health Care Expenditures, by Type of Expenditure and Source of Funds: Calendar Years 1993-2000." Retrieved August 5, 2002 from http://www.cms.hhs.gov/statistics/nhe/historical/t9.asp. "The Inflation Calculator." Retrieved August 5, 2002 from http://www.westegg.com/inflation/. U.S. Census Bureau. *Statistical Abstract of The United States: 2001.*

Chapter 7
SENIOR HEALTH

Population 65 Years and Over: 1980-1990 and 1990-2000

Total and percent change, by region.

Region, Division, State	1980		1990		2000		% Change 1980-90	% Change 1990-2000
	Number	%	Number	%	Number	%		
United States	25,549,544	25.5	31,078,895	31.0	34,991,753	35.0	21.6	12.0
Northeast	6,071,865	6.0	6,948,232	6.9	7,372,282	7.3	14.4	5.4
Midwest	6,692,026	6.7	7,725,193	7.7	8,259,075	8.3	15.4	6.6
South	8,487,699	8.5	10,668,679	10.7	12,438,267	12.4	25.7	16.0
West	4,297,954	4.3	5,736,791	5.7	6,922,129	7.0	33.5	19.9

Source: U.S. Census Bureau, http://www.census.gov/population/www/socdemo/age.html; Primary sources: U.S. Bureau of the Census, unpublished data consistent with U.S. Population Estimates, by Age, Sex, Race, and Hispanic Origin: 1980 to 1991, *Current Population Reports*, P25-1095, U.S. Government Printing Office, Washington, DC, 1993, and Census 2000 Summary File 1; 1990 Census of Population, General Population Characteristics (1990 CP-1).

Homeownership Rates, Total and Householders Aged 65 and Over: 1950-1990

1950 total does not include Alaska and Hawaii.

Year	Total	65+
2000	67.4	80.4
1990	64.2	75.2
1980	64.4	70.1
1970	62.9	67.5
1960	61.9	68.8
1950	55.0	67.9

Source: U.S. Census Bureau, Historical Census of Housing Tables, Ownership Rates, Ownership Rates by Household and Structure Type, http://www.census.gov/hhes/www/housing/census/historic/ownrate.html

Nursing Home Residents 65 Years of Age and Over: 1973-74, 1985, 1995, and 1999

NA Not applicable. Excludes residents in personal care or domiciliary care homes. Age refers to age at time of interview. Rates are based on the resident population as of July 1. Starting in 1997, population figures are adjusted for net underenumeration using the 1990 National Population Adjustment Matrix from the U.S. Bureau of the Census.

Age	Residents				Residents Per 100,000 Population			
	1973-74	1985	1995	1999	1973-74	1985	1995	1999
65 years and over, age adjusted[1]	NA	NA	NA	NA	58.5	54.0	45.9	43.3
65 years and over, crude	961,500	1,318,300	1,422,600	1,469,500	44.7	46.2	42.4	42.9
65-74 years	163,100	212,100	190,200	194,800	12.3	12.5	10.1	10.8
75-84 years	384,900	509,000	511,900	517,600	57.7	57.7	45.9	43.0
85 years and over	413,600	597,300	720,400	757,100	257.3	220.3	198.6	182.5

Source: Health, United States, 2001, Table 97, http://www.cdc.gov/nchs/hus.htm. *Notes:* 1. Age adjusted by the direct method to the year 2000 population standard using the following three age groups: 65-74 years, 75-84 years, and 85 years and over.

Distribution of Older Renter Households by Age (%)

Year	Age 65-74	Age 75+
1980	56	44
1989	50	50
1993	48	52
1995	47	53

Source: "Housing Characteristics of Older Households," AARP calculations from American Housing Surveys, AARP data retrieved August 23, 2002, from http://research.aarp.org.

Reported Cases of Domestic Elder Abuse: 1986-1996

Figures collected by the National Center on Elder Abuse (NCEA) from state adult protective service agencies and state units on aging.

Year	Cases (000)
1986	117
1987	128
1988	140
1990	211
1991	213
1993	227
1994	241
1996	293

Source: National Center on Elder Abuse, Elder Abuse Information Series, www.elderabusecenter.org/.

Elder Abuse

Types of elder maltreatment substantiated by adult protective services agencies: 1996

Maltreatment	Number of Incidents	Percentages[1]
Neglect	34,525	48.7
Emotional/psychological abuse	25,142	35.4
Financial/material exploitation	21,427	30.2
Physical abuse	18,144	25.6
Abandonment	2,560	3.6
Sexual abuse	219	0.3
Other	994	1.4
Total incidents	70,942[2]	

Source: The National Elder Abuse Incidence Study; Final Report, http://www.aoa.gov/abuse/report/GFindings- 01.htm#P131_7832. *Notes:* 1. Estimated number of substantiated reports of domestic elder abuse with each type of ma2. Total incidents do not equal totals across abuse categories because more than one substantiated

Nursing Homes, Residents, and Staff

Statistics reported by Catherine Hawes, PhD, in testimony before the U.S. Senate Committee on Finance in June 2002.

Item	Amount
Homes with serious deficiencies	25%
Homes cited for abuse violations	10%
Residents w/serious cognitive impairment	66%
Residents who are married	12%
Residents surveyed who reported abuse	44%
Residents surveyed who reported rough treatment	48%
Staff surveyed who yelled at resident	51%
Median hourly earnings certified nursing assts.	$8.61
Nurse aide rank most dangerous occupations	4th

Source: Abuse In Residential Long-Term Care Facilities: What Is Known About Prevalence, Causes, And Prevention, Testimony Before the U.S. Senate Committee on Finance, Catherine Hawes, Ph.D., http://finance.senate.gov/hearings/testimony/061802chtest.pdf.

Hearing and Vision Impairments

Percentage distribution of hearing and vision limitations among adults aged >=70 years, by selected sociodemographic characteristics. United States, National Health Interview Second Supplement on Aging, 1994. Total population 8,767.

Characteristic	Vision impairment		Hearing impairment		Vision & hearing impaired	
	Population	%	Population	%	Population	%
Population aged>=70 yrs	3,652,626	18.1	6,697,497	33.2	1,724,277	8.6
Sex						
Male	1,319,000	16.4	3,214,181	40.0	726,200	9.0
Female	2,333,626	19.2	3,483,316	28.7	998,077	8.2

[Continued]

Hearing and Vision Impairments

[Continued]

Characteristic	Vision impairment		Hearing impairment		Vision & hearing impaired	
	Population	%	Population	%	Population	%
Race[1]						
White	3,246,700	17.9	6,243,983	34.5	1,588,000	8.8
Black	307,273	19.6	303,450	19.3	82,604	5.3
Other	98,653	20.6	150,064	31.3	53,673	
Hispanic ethnicity[2]						
Yes	137,787	18.7	215,513	29.3	69,401	8.2
No	3,469,017	18.1	6,405,472	33.4	1,644,370	8.6

Source: Vincent A. Campbell, Ph.D., et al., *Surveillance for Sensory Impairment, Activity Limitation, and Health-Related Quality of Life Among Older Adults United States, 1993-1997,* Tables 3 and 4, CDC, http://www.cdc.gov/mmwr/preview/mmwrhtml/ss4808a6.htm#top. *Notes:* 1. Race data are presented only for whites, blacks, and others because sample sizes for other racial groups were too small for meaningful analysis. 2. Persons of Hispanic origin can be of any race.

Self-Assessments of Health

Percentage of fair or poor self-rated health reported by older adults, by selected demographic factors. Behavioral Risk Factor Surveillance System, 1993-1997. Total population = 178,846. Persons of Hispanic origin can be of any race.

	Age Group					
	55-64 Years (n=64,919)		65-74 Years (n=67,469)		>=75 Years (n=46,458)	
	Male	Female	Male	Female	Male	Female
Total	21.1	20.8	25.9	26.5	32.8	34.4
Race						
White	19.8	18.3	24.7	24.6	32.1	33.5
Black	31.4	36.5	39.8	43.3	42.8	46.5
Asian/Pacific Islander	16.3	19.3	22.1	18.2	25.6	28.6
Native Amer/Alaskan Native	23.2	44.1	32.5	42.0	48.7	38.9
Hispanic ethnicity						
Yes	33.9	37.3	32.7	39.3	39.5	45.8
No	20.3	19.7	25.5	25.9	32.6	34.0
Educational level						
Less than h.s. graduate	42.2	43.5	40.7	42.4	43.3	44.8
High school graduate	21.7	19.5	25.9	24.9	30.7	32.7
Some college	17.9	14.4	22.1	19.2	29.0	27.2
College graduate	9.6	8.5	13.3	13.1	23.1	22.3
Annual household income						
<$15,000	51.1	44.3	42.8	38.1	42.9	41.6
$15,000-$24,999	28.8	22.5	30.3	25.7	34.2	31.7
$25,000-$34,999	21.2	16.1	19.6	18.0	25.3	25.5
$35,000-$49,999	14.4	10.5	13.6	13.8	24.6	22.5
>=$50,000	10.8	13.3	17.3	26.3	27.3	32.2
Marital status						
Married	19.2	17.6	24.1	24.0	32.0	32.8
Divorced	28.8	25.1	30.3	28.4	37.7	35.6
Widowed	32.9	28.7	34.8	29.6	34.3	35.3

[Continued]

Self-Assessments of Health

[Continued]

	Age Group					
	55-64 Years (n=64,919)		65-74 Years (n=67,469)		>=75 Years (n=46,458)	
	Male	Female	Male	Female	Male	Female
Separated	29.7	40.4	39.1	47.1	37.5	35.1
Never married	28.1	23.9	30.5	25.8	34.2	31.4

Source: Vincent A. Campbell, Ph.D, et al., *Surveillance for Sensory Impairment, Activity Limitation, and Health- Related Quality of Life Among Older Adults-United States, 1993-1997,* Tables 3 and 4, CDC, http://www.cdc.gov/mmwr/preview/mmwrhtml/ss4808a6.htm#top.

Medicare Benefits: 1980 to 2000

NA Not available. In millions of dollars. By type of provider. 23,776 represents $23,776,000,000. For years ending Sept. 30.

Type of Provider	1980	1990	1995	1996	1997	1998	1999	2000
Hospital insurance benefits, total	23,776	65,721	113,394	123,908	136,007	134,321	129,107	125,992
Inpatient hospital	22,860	57,012	81,095	84,513	88,541	86,942	85,696	86,566
Skilled nursing facility	392	2,761	8,683	10,416	12,388	13,377	11,488	10,593
Home health agency	524	3,295	15,715	17,157	17,938	14,115	8,994	4,552
Hospice	NA	318	1,854	1,969	2,082	2,080	2,494	2,818
Managed care	NA	2,335	6,047	9,853	15,059	17,807	20,435	21,463
Supplementary ins. benefits, total	10,144	41,498	63,490	67,165	71,117	75,782	79,151	88,876
Physician fee schedule	NA	NA	31,110	31,569	31,958	32,338	33,379	35,947
Durable medical equipment	NA	NA	3,576	3,785	4,112	4,104	4,278	4,573
Carrier lab[1]	NA	NA	2,819	2,654	2,414	2,166	2,085	2,201
Other carrier[2]	NA	NA	4,513	4,883	5,452	5,854	6,400	7,164
Hospital[3]	NA	NA	8,448	8,683	9,251	8,977	8,473	8,439
Home health	NA	NA	223	236	246	189	405	4,570
Intermediary lab[4]	NA	NA	1,437	1,338	1,419	1,478	1,517	1,622
Other intermediary[5]	NA	NA	5,110	5,664	6,372	6,543	5,642	6,013
Managed care	NA	NA	6,253	8,353	9,893	14,132	16,970	18,348

Source: Statistical Abstract of the United States, 2001, Table 135; primary source: U.S. Centers for Medicare & Medicaid Services, unpublished data. *Notes:* 1. Lab services paid under the lab fee schedule performed in a physician' s office lab or an independent lab. 2. Includes free-standing ambulatory surgical centers facility costs, ambulance, and supplies. 3. Includes the hospital facility costs for Medicare Part B services that are predominantly in the outpatient department. The physician reimbursement associated with these services is included on the Physician Fee Schedule line. 4. Lab fee services paid under the lab fee schedule performed in a hospital outpatient department. 5. Includes ESRD free-standing dialysis facility payments and payments to rural health clinics, outpatient rehabilitation facilities, psychiatric hospitals, and federally qualified health centers.

Current Risk Behaviors, Elderly Persons: Various Years

NA Not available.

Behavior, Sex, and Race Cigarette Smoking	Percent of Population											
	1965	1974	1979	1983	1985	1990	1992	1994	1995	1997	1998	1999
All males												
65 years and over	28.5	24.8	20.9	22.0	19.6	14.6	16.1	13.2	14.9	12.8	10.4	10.5
White male												
65 years and over	27.7	24.3	20.5	20.6	18.9	13.7	14.9	11.9	14.1	11.5	10.0	9.9
Black male												
65 years and over	36.4	29.7	26.2	38.9	27.7	21.5	28.3	25.6	28.5	26.0	16.3	16.8

[Continued]

Current Risk Behaviors, Elderly Persons: Various Years

[Continued]

| Behavior, Sex, and Race | Percent of Population | | | | | | | | | | | |
Cigarette Smoking	1965	1974	1979	1983	1985	1990	1992	1994	1995	1997	1998	1999
All females												
65 years and over	9.6	12.0	13.2	13.1	13.5	11.5	12.4	11.1	11.5	11.5	11.2	10.7
White female												
65 years and over	9.8	12.3	13.8	13.2	13.3	11.5	12.6	11.1	11.7	11.7	11.2	10.4
Black female												
65 years and over[1]	7.1	8.9	8.5	13.1	14.5	11.1	11.1	13.6	13.3	10.7	11.5	13.6
High Serum Cholesterol												
Male[2]												
65-74 years	38.0	34.7	31.7	NA	NA	21.9	NA	NA	NA	NA	NA	NA
75 years and over	NA	NA	NA	NA	NA	20.4	NA	NA	NA	NA	NA	NA
Female[2]												
65-74 years	68.5	57.7	51.6	NA	NA	41.3	NA	NA	NA	NA	NA	NA
75 years and over	NA	NA	NA	NA	NA	38.2	NA	NA	NA	NA	NA	NA
Overweight												
Male[2]												
65-74 years	47.8	54.6	54.2	NA	NA	NA	NA	NA	NA	NA	NA	NA
Female[2]												
65-74 years	60.9	55.9	59.5	NA	NA	NA	NA	NA	NA	NA	NA	NA
Visited Dentist in Last Year												
Male 65 years and over	NA	NA	NA	NA	NA	NA	NA	NA	NA	55.4	57.8	54.7
Female 65 years and over	NA	NA	NA	NA	NA	NA	NA	NA	NA	54.4	55.4	55.2
Mammogram in last 2 years												
Female												
65-74 years	NA	NA	NA	NA	NA	48.7	55.7	64.2	63.0	69.4	NA	NA
75 years and over	NA	NA	NA	NA	NA	35.8	37.8	41.0	44.6	57.2	NA	NA
Pneumococcal immuniz.[2,3]												
65 years and over	NA	NA	NA	NA	NA	21.0	28.0	30.0	34.0	43.0	46.0	NA
Influenza immuniz. in last year[2,3]												
65 years and over	NA	NA	NA	NA	NA	42.0	52.0	55.0	58.0	63.0	63.0	NA

Source: Healthy People 2000, Final Review, Table 20; *Health, United States, 2001,* Tables 60, 68, 69, 80, 82; Primary sources: (Smoking data) CDC, National Center for Health Statistics (NCHS), National Health Interview Survey; (Cholesterol, smoking, obesity data) CDC, NCHS, Division of Health Examination Statistics. Unpublished data. (Dental and mammogram data) CDC, NCHS, National Health Interview Survey. *Notes:* 1. Some estimates are considered unreliable (standard error of 20-30%). 2. Years do not correspond precisely to smoking years; for general comparison purposes only. 3. Noninstitutionalized population.

Medicare Outlays and Enrollment

Net outlay in billions, 1995 constant dollars. Elderly persons enrolled, in millions.

Fiscal Year	Net Outlay	Elderly Enrolled
1967	11.1	19.1
1970	21.9	20.5
1975	32.8	22.8
1980	57.1	25.5

[Continued]

Medicare Outlays and Enrollment
[Continued]

Fiscal Year	Net Outlay	Elderly Enrolled
1985	90.2	28.2
1990	112.8	30.9
1991	117.2	31.5
1992	128.5	32.0
1993	137.1	32.4
1994	147.6	32.8
1995	159.9	33.0
1996	170.6	33.3

Source: Medicare and Health Care Chartbook, U.S. House of Representatives, Committee on Ways and Means, February 27, 1997, http://www.access.gpo.gov/congress/house/ways-and- means/.

Age and Prime-Time Television: Fall 2000

Age distribution of characters featured on prime-time television. Total = 2,251.

Character	Number
Child	72
Adolescent	174
Young Adult (approx. 19-29)	414
Adult (approx. 30-39)	727
Settled Adult (approx. 40-49)	473
Older Adult (approx. 50-69)	310
Elderly (over 70)	67
Don't Know/Can't Tell	14

Source: Maria D. Vesperi, *Media, Marketing, and Images of the Older Person in the Information Age*, http://www.generationsjournal.org/gen25-3/intro.html.

Chapter 8
DISABILITY

Disabled Population as a Percentage of the Total Population in 1991, 1994, and 1997

Population numbers are in thousands.

Population Segment	1991-2		1994-5		1997	
	Number	% of Total	Number	% of Total	Number	% of Total
Total Population	251,796		261,749		267,655	
Population with a Severe Disability	24,117	9.58	25,968	9.92	32,970	12.32
Population with a Non-severe Disability	24,819	9.86	27,938	10.67	19,626	7.33
Population with No Disability	202,860	80.57	207,842	79.41	215,059	80.35

Source: U.S. Bureau of the Census, *Americans with Disabilities, 1997*, Table 1, "Prevalence of Disability by Age, Sex, Race, and Hispanic Origin: 1997," February 2001, p. 10.

Disabled Population by Age Group in 1997

Population numbers are in thousands.

	Total Population	Disabled Population		Severely Disabled Population		Severely Disabled
		Number	As % of Total	Number	As % of Total	As % of All Disabled
Under 3 years	11,619	233	2.01	58	0.50	24.89
Under 15 years	59,606	4,661	7.82	2,256	3.78	48.40
15 to 24 years	36,897	3,961	10.74	1,942	5.26	49.03
25 to 44 years	83,887	11,200	13.35	6,793	8.10	60.65
45 to 54 years	33,620	7,585	22.56	4,674	13.90	61.62
55 to 64 years	21,591	7,708	35.70	5,223	24.19	67.76
65 years and over	32,064	17,480	54.52	12,073	37.65	69.07

Source: U.S. Bureau of the Census, *Americans with Disabilities, 1997*, Table 1, "Prevalence of Disability by Age, Sex, Race, and Hispanic Origin: 1997," February 2001, p. 10.

Leading Causes of Disability Among Persons Aged 15 Years and Older, 1991-92

	Number of Cases (000)	Percent of Total Cases
Arthritis or rheumatism	7,200	17.10
Back or spine problems	5,700	13.50
Heart trouble	4,600	11.10
Lung or respiratory trouble	2,800	6.80
High blood pressure (hypertension)	2,200	5.10
Stiffness or deformity of limb	2,000	4.80
Diabetes	1,600	3.90
Blindness or other visual impairment	1,500	3.50
Deafness or serious trouble hearing	1,100	2.60
Stroke	1,100	2.50
Cancer	896	2.10
Broken bone / fracture	830	2.00
Mental or emotional problems	784	1.90
Paralysis of any kind	716	1.70
Head or spinal cord injury	592	1.40

Source: U.S. Department of Health, Centers for Disease Control, "Prevalence of Disability and Associated Health Conditions, United States, 1991-1992," *Mortality and Morbidity Weekly Report*, 1994, Volume 43, Number 40, available online at http//www.cdc.gov/ mmwr/preview/mmwrhtml/ 00033002.htm.

Leading Causes of Disability Among Persons Aged 17 Years or Younger, 1991-92

	Number of Cases	Percent of All Cases
Autism	48,000	1.00
Missing limb, finger or toes	70,000	1.40
Paralysis of any kind	73,000	1.50
Hay fever or other respiratory allergies	76,000	1.60
Tonsilitis or repeated ear infection	80,000	1.60
Deafness or serious trouble hearing	116,000	2.40
Impairment deformity of back, foot or leg	121,000	2.50
Epilepsy or seizure disorder	128,000	2.60
Cerebral palsy	129,000	2.70
Blindness or other visual impairment	144,000	3.00
Mental or emotional problems	305,000	6.30
Asthma	311,000	6.40
Mental retardation	331,000	6.80

[Continued]

Leading Causes of Disability Among Persons Aged 17 Years or Younger, 1991-92

[Continued]

	Number of Cases	Percent of All Cases
Speech problems	634,000	13.10
Learning disability	1,435,000	29.50

Source: U.S. Department of Health, Centers for Disease Control, "Prevalence of Disability and Associated Health Conditions, United States, 1991-1992," *Mortality and Morbidity Weekly Report*, 1994, Volume 43, Number 40, available online at http//www.cdc.gov/ mmwr/preview/mmwrhtml/ 00033002.htm.

Children and Youths with Disabilities Served by Selected Programs for the Disabled, 1977-2000

For the years 1977 through 1988 the data are for all children aged 3 to 21 years. From 1989 through 2000 the age range covered is 6 to 21 years. Numbers are in thousands.

Year	Population Aged 6-20 Years	All Children Served	Children Served by Type of Disability								
			Speech Impaired	Learning Disabled	Mentally Retarded	Emotionally Disturbed	Deaf or Hearing Impaired	Visually Impaired	Orthopedic Impairment	Austims	All Other Disabilities
1977	NA	3,722	1,309	800	972	284	90	38	-	-	-
1978	NA	3,777	1,227	969	945	289	87	36	-	-	-
1979	NA	3,889	1,213	1,132	902	299	86	31	70	-	156
1980	66,080	4,005	1,185	1,278	869	328	80	32	64	-	164
1981	65,283	4,142	1,168	1,462	828	348	79	33	58	-	165
1982	64,578	4,198	1,133	1,620	785	340	76	29	59	-	151
1983	64,061	4,255	1,132	1,740	757	353	72	30	55	-	115
1984	63,657	4,298	1,126	1,805	726	361	73	30	56	-	116
1985	63,336	4,315	1,126	1,830	695	371	69	30	56	-	138
1986	63,173	4,317	1,127	1,861	661	376	65	26	56	-	142
1987	63,259	4,374	1,128	1,907	656	381	66	70	57	-	148
1988	63,529	4,446	1,031	2,090	649	405	62	27	49	-	133
1989	52,962	4,173	NA	NA	NA	NA	NA	NA	NA	NA	NA
1990	53,445	4,219	NA	NA	NA	NA	NA	NA	NA	NA	NA
1991	53,506	4,362	988	2,144	552	391	59	24	49	NA	154
1992	53,777	4,459	NA	NA	NA	NA	NA	NA	NA	NA	NA
1993	54,314	4,586	NA	NA	NA	NA	NA	NA	NA	NA	NA
1994	55,086	4,779	1,018	2,428	554	415	65	25	57	19	198
1995	55,975	4,908	1,020	2,510	571	428	65	25	61	23	204
1996	56,954	5,079	1,027	2,602	586	439	68	26	63	29	239
1997	57,971	5,231	1,049	2,674	594	446	69	26	66	34	271
1998	58,728	5,397	1,064	2,755	603	454	70	26	67	43	314
1999	59,410	5,539	1,074	2,816	611	463	71	26	69	54	355
2000	59,891	5,683	1,090	2,872	614	470	72	27	71	65	400

Source: Data in this tables are from five different editions of a book produced annually by the U.S. Bureau of the Census, *Statistical Abstract of the United States*, editions 1980, p. 363; 1990, p. 146; 1995, p. 171; 1999, p. 186; and 2000, p. 175. Note: NA means that data were not available for those years. A dash (-) means data were not yet collected for the category.

Number of Workers on Disability Benefits and Total Benefits Paid, 1970-2001

The count of workers on disability benefits is as of December 31 for each year listed.

Year	Disabled Workers Receiving Disability Benefits	Total Benefits Paid to Disabled Workers ($ mil.)	Average Benefits Paid Annually to Each Beneficiary (2000 Dollars)	Civilian Labor Force (000)	Disability Beneficiaries per 1,000 Workers in the Labor Force
1970	1,493,316	2,448	6,963	78,594	19.00
1971	1,647,696	3,028	7,369	80,471	20.48
1972	1,832,916	3,626	7,556	83,400	21.98
1973	2,016,884	4,676	8,270	86,401	23.34
1974	2,236,928	5,662	8,203	86,144	25.97
1975	2,488,951	6,908	8,354	86,665	28.72
1976	2,670,244	8,190	8,148	89,803	29.73
1977	2,834,432	9,456	8,214	94,105	30.12
1978	2,879,828	10,315	8,238	97,581	29.51
1979	2,870,411	11,333	8,261	99,933	28.72
1980	2,861,253	12,816	8,672	99,645	28.71
1981	2,776,519	14,379	9,222	99,032	28.04
1982	2,603,713	14,811	9,583	102,996	25.28
1983	2,568,966	15,196	9,765	106,223	24.18
1984	2,596,535	15,623	9,683	108,216	23.99
1985	2,656,500	16,483	9,691	110,728	23.99
1986	2,727,386	17,409	9,757	113,793	23.97
1987	2,785,885	18,053	9,712	116,104	23.99
1988	2,830,284	19,165	9,825	117,830	24.02
1989	2,895,364	20,314	9,908	118,241	24.49
1990	3,011,294	22,113	10,115	117,466	25.64
1991	3,194,938	24,738	10,094	117,466	27.20
1992	3,467,783	27,856	10,143	118,997	29.14
1993	3,725,966	30,913	10,212	121,464	30.68
1994	3,962,954	33,711	10,276	124,721	31.77
1995	4,185,263	36,610	10,204	125,088	33.46
1996	4,385,623	39,625	10,242	127,860	34.30
1997	4,508,134	41,083	10,072	130,679	34.50
1998	4,698,319	43,467	9,947	132,577	35.44
1999	4,879,455	46,459	9,948	134,513	36.27
2000	5,042,334	49,848	9,886	135,888	37.11
2001	5,274,183	54,246	10,234	134,055	39.34

Source: U.S. Social Security Administration, Social Security Beneficiary Statistics, "Number of Beneficiaries Receiving Benefits on December 31, 1970-2001," published online in December 2001, available online at http://www.ssa.gov/OACT/ProgData/benefits/html. Labor force figures are from the U.S. Bureau of Labor Statistics, Office of Employment and Unemployment Statistics, Division of Labor Force Statstics, Washington, DC. Per capita data on benefits paid to beneficiaries have been normalized to the base year 2000.

New Disability Beneficiaries by Diagnostic Group, 1960-2000 by Decade

Diagnostic Group	1960	1970	1981	1990	2000
Total New Beneficiaries	207,805	350,384	351,847	467,977	610,700
Musculoskeletal system	17,124	52,086	58,639	74,501	153,600
All mental disorders	17,287	38,406	36,318	105,173	143,200
Circulatory diseases	55,855	108,906	85,994	73,585	75,400
Neoplasms	17,739	36,095	56,410	65,939	63,600
Nervous system diseases	32,105	22,575	28,516	37,737	50,100
Injuries	NA	28,231	20,868	22,315	28,700
Respiratory diseases	16,489	24,254	21,520	22,158	26,200
Endocrine diseases	5,406	13,141	14,768	16,255	17,100
Genito-urinary system	1,077	2,912	6,230	10,294	14,900
Digestive system diseases	3,575	9,051	7,363	7,431	12,700
Infectious diseases	10,903	8,760	2,596	22,023	10,700
All Others	28,475	2,370	7,220	7,455	10,600
Skin diseases	463	NA	1,345	866	1,700
Diseases of the blood	442	NA	942	1,734	1,500
Congenital anomolies	865	3,597	3,118	511	700

Source: U. S. Social Security Administration, *Annual Statistical Report on the Social Security Disability Insurance Program, 2000*, Table 18, "Awards to Disabled Workers by Diagnostic Group, 1960-2000," September 2001, p. 56.

All Social Security Disability Beneficiaries, by Diagnostic Group in 2000

Diagnostic Group	Number of Cases	Percent of All Cases
Total	5,042,333	100.00
Musculoskeletal system	1,152,231	22.85
All mental disorders	1,618,758	32.10
Circulatory diseases	532,998	10.57
Neoplasms	136,404	2.71
Nervous system diseases	479,246	9.50
Injuries	231,066	4.58
Respiratory diseases	166,054	3.29
Endocrine diseases	244,456	4.85
Genito-urinary system	84,687	1.68
Digestive system diseases	69,735	1.38
Infectious diseases	97,919	1.94
Skin diseases	12,351	0.24
Diseases of the blood	12,070	0.24
Congenital anomolies	8,540	0.17
All Other and Unknown	195,818	3.88

Source: U. S. Social Security Administration, *Annual Statistical Report on the Social Security Disability Insurance Program, 2000*, Table 4, "All Disabled Beneficiaries by Diagnostic Group and Sex, December 2000," September 2001, pp. 32-33.

Highest Level of Education Attained in the General Population and Among Disability Beneficiaries

Data for the general population are for 2000. Data for disability beneficiaries are for 1998.

Highest Educational Level Completed	General Population Aged 25 Years or Older		Disability Beneficiaries	
	Number	% of Total	Number	% of Total
Less than 9th grade	13,755,477	7.5	642,331	12.5
9th to 12th, no diploma	21,960,148	12.1	916,855	17.8
High school graduate	52,168,981	28.6	1,863,777	36.1
Some college	38,351,595	21.0	1,179,585	22.9
Associate degree	11,512,833	6.3	NA	NA
Bachelor's or higher degree	44,462,605	24.4	546,823	10.6

Source: U.S. Social Security Administration, *Annual Statistical Report on the Social Security Disability Insurance Program, 2000*, September 2001, Table 45, available online at http://www.ssa.gov/statistics/di_asr/2000/sect6.html. Note: The educational level of 0.2% of disability beneficiaries is unknown for 1998.

Population Aged 16 to 64 Years by Highest Level of Education Attained and Disability Status, 1995 and 2001

All figures are in thousands.

	Total Population	Highest Level of Education Attained				
		8th Grade or Less	Up to 12th Grade but no Diploma	High School Graduate	Some College	Bachelor's or Higher Degree
General Population						
In 1995	166,756	8,688	23,471	53,448	45,252	35,894
In 2001	178,202	7,949	23,827	54,158	49,343	42,924
Severely Disabled Population						
In 1995	10,376	1,978	2,440	3,681	1,663	613
In 2001	11,645	1,544	2,339	4,369	2,464	928

Source: U.S. Bureau of the Census, *Disability: Selected Characteristics of Persons 16 to 74: 2001*, Table 1., "Selected Characteristics of Civilians 16 to 74 Years Old with a Work Disability, by Educational Attainment and Sex: 2001," October 2000, available online at http://www.census.gov/hhes/www/disable/cps/cps101.html.

Disability Status, Employment Rate, and Annual Rate of Earnings for Individuals 21 to 64 Years Old in 1997

Numbers are in thousands unless otherwise specified.

Persons with:	Total Number	Number Employed	% of Total Employed	Median Earnings	Mean Earnings
No disability	125,084	105,624	84.44	23,654	31,053
Non-severe disability	10,393	8,527	82.05	20,457	26,412
Severe disability	17,409	5,464	31.39	13,272	18,631

Source: U.S. Bureau of the Census, *Americans with Disabilities: 1997*, Table 4, "Disability Status, Employment, and Annual Rate of Earnings: Individuals 21 to 64 Years Old: 1997," February 2001, available online at http://www.census.gov/hhes/www/disable/sipp /disab97/ds97t4.html.

Chapter 9
OUR MENTAL HEALTH

Estimated Annual Number of Americans, Age 18-54, with Illness.

Disorder	Number
Suicides (1999 data)	29,199
Anorexia nervosa	100,000
Bulimia nervosa	360,000
Suicide attempts	730,000
Autism	1,000,000
Schizophrenia	2,200,000
Bipolar disorder	2,300,000
Alzheimer's Disease	4,000,000
Major depression	9,900,000
Depression	18,800,000
Anxiety disorders	19,100,000

Source: Chart data are estimates. Data for bulimia refers to college age women. *The Numbers Count: Mental Disorders in America.* Retrieved May 2, 2002 from http://www.nimh.gov.

Americans with a Mood Disorder

Figures show millions of people thought to be suffering from each disorder.

Disorder	Millions
Bipolar disorder	2.3
Panic disorder	2.4
Agoraphobic	3.2
Obsessive-compulsive disorder	3.3
Generalized anxiety disorder	4.0
Post-traumatic stress disorder	5.2
Social anxiety disorder	5.3
Possess a specific phobia	6.3

Source: Chart figures come from the National Institute of Mental Health located at http://www.nimh.nih.gov.

Cases of Autism

Number of cases logged by California Department of Developmental Services.

Year	Cases
1987	3,864
1993	4,911
1998	11,995
Jul-01	15,441
Jul-02	18,460

Source: California Health and Human Services Agency, *Department of Developmental Services: Changes in the Population of Persons with Autism and Pervasive Developmental Disorders in California' s Developmental Services System,* March 1, 1999.

Suicide Rates for Selected Groups

Rate is per 100,000 people of the population.

	1990	1991	1992	1993	1994	1995	1996	1997	1998	1999
85+	22.2	24	21.9	22.8	23.0	21.6	20.2	20.8	21	19.2
65+	20.5	19.7	19.1	19.0	18.1	18.1	17.3	16.8	16.9	15.9
25-34	15.2	15.2	14.5	15.1	15.4	15.4	14.5	14.3	13.8	13.5
Total	12.4	12.2	12.0	12.1	12.0	11.9	11.6	11.4	11.3	10.7
Men	20.4	20.1	19.6	19.9	19.8	19.8	19.3	18.7	18.6	17.6
Women	4.8	4.7	4.6	4.6	4.5	4.4	4.4	4.4	4.4	4.1
White	13.5	13.3	13.0	13.1	12.9	12.9	12.7	12.4	12.4	11.7
Nonwhite	7.0	6.8	6.8	7.1	7.2	6.9	6.7	6.5	6.2	6.0

Source: USA Suicide Official Final Data Retrieved August 22, 2002 from http://www.suicidology.org.

Who Visits Psychiatrists

Data are shown by age group for 1989-1990.

Age	Percent
Under 15	5.0
15-24	7.9
25-44	48.2
45-64	31.7
65+	7.2

Source: Schappert, Susan M. *Office Visits to Psychiatrists: United States, 1989-90.* U.S. Department of Health and Human Services, National Ambulatory Medical Survey.

Number of Mental Health Facilities

	1970	1976	1980	1986	1990	1992	1994	1998
Non-Federal general hospitals with separate psychiatric services	797	870	923	1,351	1,674	1,616	1,612	1,707
Residential treatment centers for emotionally disturbed children	261	331	368	437	501	497	459	461
Private psychiatric hospitals	150	182	184	314	462	475	430	348
State and county mental hospitals	310	303	280	285	273	273	256	229
VA medical centers	115	126	136	139	141	162	161	145

Source: Chapter 14 of *Mental Health in the United States, 2000* by the U.S. Department of Health and Human Services located at http://www.mentalhealth.org.

Chapter 10
SEXUALITY

Attitudes about Premarital Sex

Data show attitudes about premarital sex, based on a Gallup poll survey. Figures are in percent.

	Not wrong	Wrong
1969	21	68
1973	43	47
1985	52	39
1987	48	46
1991	54	40
1996	55	40
1998	56	40
2001	60	38

Source: Majority Considers Sex Before Marriage Morally Okay. Available online from http://www.gallup.com.

Adult Sexual Activity, 1994

Figures show percentage of adults identifying the level of their sexual activity.

	None	Few Times per Year	Few Times per Month	2 or 3 Times per Week	4 Times per Week
Men 18-24	14.7	21.1	23.9	28.0	12.4
Men 25-29	6.7	14.8	31.0	36.2	11.4
Men 30-34	9.7	16.7	34.7	31.5	7.4
Men 35-39	6.8	12.6	40.0	35.3	5.3
Men 40-44	6.7	16.9	44.4	26.4	5.6
Men 45-49	12.7	19.8	33.3	27.8	6.3
Men 50-54	7.8	19.6	45.1	22.5	4.9
Men 55-59	15.7	24.7	41.6	16.9	1.1
Women 18-24	11.2	16.1	31.5	28.8	12.4
Women 25-29	4.5	10.3	38.1	36.8	10.3
Women 30-34	8.1	16.6	34.6	32.9	7.8
Women 35-39	10.8	15.7	37.8	32.5	3.2
Women 40-44	14.6	15.5	46.1	16.9	6.8
Women 45-49	16.1	16.1	41.0	23.6	3.1
Women 50-54	19.3	20.7	40.0	17.8	2.2
Women 55-59	40.8	22.4	29.6	4.8	2.4

[Continued]

Adult Sexual Activity, 1994

[Continued]

	None	Few Times per Year	Few Times per Month	2 or 3 Times per Week	4 Times per Week
All Men	9.8	17.6	35.5	29.5	7.7
All Women	13.6	16.1	37.2	26.3	6.7

Source: U.S. Department of Health and Human Services, *Report to Congress on Out-of-Wedlock Child-bearing,* September 1995, Table IV and Laumann, E.O. et al. 1994. *The Social Organization of Sexuality.*

Sexual Fantasies and Behaviors

Figures based on percent of survey respondents.

	Would Like To	Have Done
Engaged in sado-masochistic sex	5	7
Had sex on a plane or train	44	11
Used an aphrodisiac	15	12
Had sex with someone of the same sex	7	17
Had "cybersex" on the Internet	7	23
Had sex at the office	19	23
Had sex with more than one person at same time	27	24
Had an extramarital affair	4	28
Had sex with someone 10 or more years younger/older	13	40
Had sex in a public place	10	48
Had sex with married person	5	56
Had a one night stand	9	57
Had sex in a car	7	80

Source: Love and Lust: A Euro RSCG Global Study. available online from http://www.eurorscg.com.

How Americans Describe Themselves Sexually

Figures are percent of survey respondents.

	Percent
Prude/uptight about sex	3.0
Promiscuous	4.0
Obsessed with sex	7.0
Voyeur	8.0
Not very interested in sex	11.0
Sexually frustrated	14.0
Dissatisfied with sex life	20.0
Sexy	28.0
Sexually adventurous	32.0

[Continued]

How Americans Describe Themselves Sexually

[Continued]

	Percent
Skilled lover	32.0
Romantic	61.0

Source: Love and Lust: A Euro RSCG Global Study. Available online from http://www.eurorscg.com.

Viagra Prescriptions

Data are in thousands.

	Percent
Jul-98	517
Jan-99	268
Jan-01	1,150
Jan-02	1,000

Source: Chamberlain, Claudine. "Happy Birthday, Viagra." Rose Pike. "Better than Cigars" both Retrieved August 6, 2002 from http://www.abcnews.go.com; "All Signs are Good for OTC Sales in Wake of Huge Viagra Success." *Drug Store News,* June 22, 1998, p. 53. Andrew Humphreys. "Marketer of the Year." *Med Ad News,* March 2002, p. 6; Frank Scussa "Making History." *Med Ad News.*

Top Cosmetic Treatments for Men

Figures show the number of men having each procedure.

	1998	2001	% change
Eyelid surgery	15,564	44,726	187.3
Laser skin resurfacing	4,522	19,122	322.8
Ear surgery	3,663	17,555	379.2
Dermabrasion	2,082	12,235	487.6
Fibril injection	70	414	491.4
Chin augmentation	1,218	9,561	684.9
Nose reshaping	13,143	136,009	934.8
Collagen injection	4,067	48,400	1,090.0
Hair transplantation	2,146	27,817	1,196.2
Chemical peels	3,287	168,093	5,013.8

Source: Data come from the American Society of Plastic Surgeons, located at http://www.plasticsurgery.org.

What Teenagers Know About Sex

Figures show percent of correct responses among teenagers surveyed. "T" or "F" indicates true or false statement.

	Percent
A pap smear test is used to check for cancer of the cervix (T)	18
Young people can never choose to be abstinent once they have sexual intercourse (F)	27
A teenage girl who has had an abortion will have difficulty getting pregnant when she wants to have a baby (F)	27
Fertilization of the egg occurs in the vagina (F)	27
Douching is a method of birth control (F)	30
The male hormone is called testosterone (T)	33
Once you have a STD, you cannot get the same one again (F)	37
If a girl has sexual intercourse during her period, she can still get pregnant (T)	48

Source: Knowledge about Reproduction, Contraception, and Sexually Transmitted Infections among Young Adolescents in American Cities. Social Policy, Spring 2000, p. 41.

Teenagers Who Have Had Sex

Figures show percent of teenagers who have had intercourse. Those who remain sexually active are included.

	1993	1995	1997	1999	2001
Total	53.0	53.1	48.4	49.9	45.6
All females	50.2	52.1	47.7	47.7	42.9
All males	55.6	54.0	48.9	52.2	48.5
Whites, total	48.4	48.9	43.6	45.1	43.2
Blacks, Non-Hispanic, total	79.7	73.4	72.7	71.2	60.8
Hispanics, total	56.0	57.6	52.2	54.1	48.4
Whites, females	47.4	49.0	44.0	44.8	41.3
Blacks, Non-Hispanic, females	70.4	67.0	65.5	66.9	53.4
Hispanics, females	48.3	53.3	45.7	45.5	44.0
Whites, males	49.3	48.9	43.3	45.4	45.1
Blacks, Non-Hispanic, males	89.2	81.0	80.3	75.7	68.8
Hispanics, males	63.5	62.0	57.7	62.9	53.0
Total currently sexually active	37.6	37.9	34.8	27.3	33.4
Total males, currently sexually active	37.5	35.5	33.4	30.5	33.4
Total females, currently sexually active	37.5	40.4	46.5	23.9	33.4

Source: "Youth Risk Behavior Surveillance." Centers for Disease Control and Prevention, Surveillance Summaries, June 28, 2002.*MMWR* 2002: 51 (No. ss-4)."

HIV/AIDS Cases in the United States

	1980	1981	1982	1983	1984	1985	1986	1987	1988	1989	1990	1991	1992
Cases diagnosed	99	335	1,201	3,153	6,360	12,026	19,372	29,070	36,064	43,399	49,446	60,472	79,477
Deaths	30	129	466	1,512	3,518	6,997	12,154	16,456	21,189	27,767	31,734	36,959	41,480

Source: Chart data from United States of America Epidemiological Fact Sheets on HIV/AIDS and Sexually Transmitted Infections, 2002 Update, *HIV/AIDS Surveillance Report,* Vol. 11 no. 2, table 22. 1980 figure is actually for total cases pre-1980."

New HIV Cases by Race

Figures are annual estimates.

	Percent
Black	54.0
White	26.0
Hispanics	19.0
Other	1.0

Source: "New CDC Studies Shed Light on Factors Underlying High HIV Infection Rates Among Gay and Bisexual Men. " available online from http://www.cdc.gov.

Chapter 11
REPRODUCTION

Live Births, Birth Rates and Fertility Rates Over the 20th Century

Birth rate is the number of births per 1,000 population. The fertitlity rate is the number of births per 1,000 women of childbearing age, 15 to 44 years.

Year	Number of Live Births	Birth Rate	Fertility Rate
1909	2,718,000	30.0	126.8
1910	2,777,000	30.1	126.8
1915	2,965,000	29.5	125.0
1920	2,950,000	27.7	117.9
1925	2,909,000	25.1	106.6
1930	2,618,000	21.3	89.2
1935	2,377,000	18.7	77.2
1940	2,559,000	19.4	79.9
1945	2,858,000	20.4	85.9
1950	3,632,000	24.1	106.2
1955	4,097,000	25.0	118.3
1960	4,257,850	23.7	118.0
1965	3,760,358	19.4	96.3
1970	3,731,386	18.4	87.9
1975	3,144,198	14.6	66.0
1980	3,612,258	15.9	68.4
1985	3,760,561	15.8	66.3
1990	4,158,212	16.7	70.9
1995	3,899,589	14.8	65.6
2000	4,064,948	14.8	67.6

Source: U.S. Department of Health and Human Services, Center for Disease Control and Prevention, *National Vital Statistics Report*, Vol. 49, No. 1, April 17, 2001, p. 25.

Fertility Rates and Infant Mortality Rates, 1940-2000

The total fertility rate is the number of children born to 1,000 women during the childbearing years, age 15- 44. The infant mortality rate is the number of infants who die before reaching one year of age per 1,000 live births.

	Total Fertility Rate	Infant Mortality Rate
1940	2,301.3	47.0
1941	2,399.1	45.3
1942	2,628.2	40.4
1943	2,718.3	40.4
1944	2,567.6	39.8
1945	2,491.2	38.3
1946	2,942.7	33.8
1947	3,273.5	32.2
1948	3,108.6	32.0
1949	3,110.1	31.2
1950	3,090.5	29.2
1951	3,269.3	28.4
1952	3,358.4	28.4
1953	3,424.1	27.8
1954	3,542.6	26.6
1955	3,578.5	26.4
1956	3,689.0	26.0
1957	3,767.0	26.3
1958	3,700.5	27.1
1959	3,712.4	26.4
1960	3,653.6	26.0
1961	3,620.3	25.3
1962	3,461.3	25.3
1963	3,318.8	25.2
1964	3,190.5	24.8
1965	2,912.6	24.7
1966	2,721.4	23.7
1967	2,557.7	22.4
1968	2,464.2	21.8
1969	2,455.5	20.9
1970	2,480.0	20.0
1971	2,266.5	NA
1972	2,010.0	NA
1973	1,879.0	NA
1974	1,835.0	NA
1975	1,774.0	16.1
1976	1,738.0	NA
1977	1,789.5	NA
1978	1,760.0	13.8
1979	1,808.0	13.1
1980	1,839.5	12.6
1981	1,812.0	11.9

[Continued]

Fertility Rates and Infant Mortality Rates, 1940-2000
[Continued]

	Total Fertility Rate	Infant Mortality Rate
1982	1,827.5	11.5
1983	1,799.0	11.2
1984	1,806.5	10.8
1985	1,844.0	10.6
1986	1,837.5	10.4
1987	1,872.0	10.1
1988	1,934.0	10.0
1989	2,014.0	9.8
1990	2,081.0	9.2
1991	2,073.0	8.9
1992	2,065.0	8.5
1993	2,046.0	8.4
1994	2,036.0	8.0
1995	2,019.0	7.6
1996	2,027.0	7.3
1997	2,032.5	7.2
1998	2,058.5	7.2
1999	2,075.0	7.1
2000	2,133.5	6.9

Source: U.S. Department of Health and Human Services, National Center for Health Statistics (NCHS), *Vital Statistics of the United States, 1998*, Volume I, Natality, updated from later issues of *National Vital Statistics Reports* and *Monthly Vital Statistics Reports* also published by NCHS.

Fertiltiy Rate and Percentage of Females in the Workplace, Selective Years, 1940-2000

The total fertility rate is the number of children born to 1,000 women during their childbearing years, age 15-44.

	Total Fertility Rate	Percent of Women in the Workforce	
		Total	Mothers with Young Children
1940	2,301.3	27.0	8.0
1950	3,090.5	33.3	12.0
1960	3,653.6	37.6	20.0
1970	2,480.0	43.3	NA
1975	1,774.0	NA	33.0
1980	1,839.5	51.3	42.0
1990	2,081.0	58.0	54.0
1993	2,046.0	NA	53.0

[Continued]

Fertiltiy Rate and Percentage of Females in the Workplace, Selective Years, 1940-2000

[Continued]

	Total Fertility Rate	Percent of Women in the Workforce	
		Total	Mothers with Young Children
1997	2,032.5	NA	65.0
2000	2,133.5	60.9	NA

Source: U.S. Department of Health and Human Services, National Center for Health Statistics (NCHS), *Vital Statistics of the United States, 1998*, Volume I, and updated from later issues of *National Vital Statistics Reports* and *Monthly Vital Statistics Reports* also published by NCHS. Workplace participation data are from the U.S. Department of Labor, "Boom in day care industry the result of many social changes," *Monthly Labor Review*, August 1995, page 7 and "Marital and Family Characteristics of the Labor Force," *Current Population Survey*, March 1997. Data were also used from a table published by Columbia University on their web site, "Mothers of Young Children in the Paid Workforce," available online at http://www.columbia.edu/itc/History/brinkley/3651/web- resource/stats_mothers_workforce.htm.

Female Participation in the Civilian Laborforce, by Age, 2000

Age	Percent Participating
16 to 19 years	51.3
20 to 24 years	73.3
25 to 34 years	76.3
35 to 44 years	77.3
45 to 55 years	76.8
55 to 65 years	51.8
65 years and over	9.4

Source: U.S. Census Bureau, "Civilian Labor Force and Participation Rates with Projections: 1980 to 2008," *Statistical Abstract of the United States: 2001*, page 367.

Live Births by Age of Mother, 1933-2000

Only registered births are listed. No adjustments have been made for the underregistration of births.

	Total Number of Births	Percentage of Births by Age Group of Mother at Time of Birth							
		15 Years or Under	15-19 Years	20-24 Years	25-29 Years	30-34 Years	35-39 Years	40-44 Years	45 Years and Over
1933	2,081,232	0.13	12.07	29.81	25.93	16.98	10.49	3.66	0.36
1934	2,167,636	0.13	12.28	30.29	26.06	17.02	9.94	3.52	0.34
1935	2,155,105	0.15	12.54	30.64	26.19	16.59	9.94	3.38	0.33
1936	2,144,790	0.14	12.55	31.10	26.38	16.50	9.61	3.19	0.32
1937	2,203,337	0.14	12.94	31.42	26.49	16.44	9.14	2.96	0.30
1938	2,286,962	0.14	13.04	31.50	26.72	16.50	8.86	2.81	0.28
1939	2,265,588	0.15	13.04	31.08	27.04	16.80	8.82	2.64	0.27

[Continued]

Live Births by Age of Mother, 1933-2000

[Continued]

	Total Number of Births	Percentage of Births by Age Group of Mother at Time of Birth							
		15 Years or Under	15-19 Years	20-24 Years	25-29 Years	30-34 Years	35-39 Years	40-44 Years	45 Years and Over
1940	2,360,399	0.14	12.74	31.28	27.36	16.96	8.52	2.58	0.24
1941	2,513,427	0.14	12.60	32.01	27.55	16.71	8.23	2.40	0.21
1942	2,808,996	0.13	12.15	33.02	27.86	16.46	7.87	2.17	0.18
1943	2,934,860	0.13	11.71	31.69	28.02	17.39	8.48	2.26	0.17
1944	2,794,800	0.13	10.77	31.02	27.52	18.32	9.43	2.51	0.18
1945	2,735,456	0.13	10.27	29.13	27.61	19.46	10.26	2.69	0.21
1946	3,288,672	0.11	9.80	31.97	28.48	17.91	9.01	2.28	0.17
1947	3,699,940	0.12	11.51	32.88	28.12	16.66	8.25	2.09	0.15
1948	3,535,068	0.14	12.22	32.81	27.75	16.42	8.19	2.11	0.15
1949	3,559,529	0.14	12.17	32.44	28.30	16.33	8.18	2.09	0.15
1950	3,554,149	0.14	11.80	31.83	28.75	16.82	8.26	2.10	0.14
1951	3,750,850	0.14	11.83	31.97	28.59	16.99	8.13	2.09	0.13
1952	3,846,986	0.13	11.39	31.51	28.70	17.66	8.27	2.09	0.13
1953	3,902,120	0.14	11.68	31.28	28.47	17.71	8.36	2.13	0.13
1954	4,017,362	0.15	11.90	31.29	27.93	17.94	8.39	2.16	0.13
1955	4,047,295	0.15	11.96	31.48	27.65	17.85	8.53	2.16	0.13
1956	4,163,090	0.15	12.50	31.84	27.18	17.44	8.53	2.16	0.12
1957	4,254,784	0.16	12.93	32.00	26.81	17.18	8.59	2.13	0.12
1958	4,203,812	0.16	13.18	32.54	26.38	16.93	8.53	2.11	0.12
1959	4,244,796	0.16	13.45	33.13	25.91	16.51	8.55	2.11	0.12
1960	4,257,850	0.16	13.79	33.51	25.67	16.15	8.45	2.15	0.12
1961	4,268,326	0.17	14.10	33.86	25.34	15.87	8.33	2.20	0.12
1962	4,167,362	0.18	14.40	34.67	25.08	15.32	8.03	2.20	0.12
1963	4,098,020	0.19	14.31	35.47	24.99	14.89	7.86	2.17	0.12
1964	4,027,490	0.19	14.54	35.74	25.01	14.53	7.69	2.18	0.12
1965	3,760,358	0.21	15.71	35.56	24.62	14.08	7.52	2.17	0.12
1966	3,606,274	0.23	17.23	35.99	24.20	13.16	7.00	2.06	0.12
1967	3,520,959	0.24	16.94	37.22	24.64	12.48	6.46	1.90	0.12
1968	3,501,564	0.27	16.89	37.32	25.81	11.99	5.88	1.73	0.11
1969	3,600,206	0.29	16.79	37.68	26.59	11.77	5.27	1.51	0.09
1970	3,731,386	0.31	17.28	38.03	26.66	11.47	4.83	1.34	0.08
1971	3,555,970	0.33	17.66	38.10	26.63	11.43	4.57	1.21	0.07
1972	3,258,411	0.37	18.91	36.04	27.63	11.51	4.34	1.13	0.07
1973	3,136,965	0.41	19.26	35.10	28.32	11.79	4.04	1.02	0.06
1974	3,159,958	0.40	18.84	35.07	29.22	11.80	3.74	0.88	0.05
1975	3,144,198	0.40	18.52	34.78	29.79	11.94	3.67	0.84	0.05
1976	3,167,788	0.38	17.64	34.46	30.69	12.37	3.65	0.77	0.05
1977	3,326,632	0.34	16.81	34.46	30.55	13.44	3.63	0.72	0.04
1978	3,333,279	0.32	16.30	34.19	30.46	14.23	3.79	0.68	0.04
1979	3,494,398	0.31	15.72	34.02	30.60	14.80	3.87	0.66	0.03
1980	3,612,258	0.28	15.29	33.95	30.68	15.24	3.90	0.64	0.03
1981	3,629,238	0.27	14.53	33.40	31.09	16.02	4.02	0.64	0.03
1982	3,680,537	0.27	13.96	32.77	31.30	16.45	4.56	0.67	0.03
1983	3,638,933	0.27	13.45	31.89	31.54	17.16	4.96	0.71	0.03

[Continued]

Live Births by Age of Mother, 1933-2000
[Continued]

	Total Number of Births	Percentage of Births by Age Group of Mother at Time of Birth							
		15 Years or Under	15-19 Years	20-24 Years	25-29 Years	30-34 Years	35-39 Years	40-44 Years	45 Years and Over
1984	3,669,141	0.27	12.80	31.11	31.77	17.95	5.34	0.73	0.03
1985	3,760,561	0.27	12.43	30.35	31.95	18.52	5.70	0.75	0.03
1986	3,756,547	0.27	12.30	29.34	31.93	19.20	6.13	0.79	0.03
1987	3,809,394	0.27	12.14	28.24	31.92	19.97	6.51	0.91	0.04
1988	3,909,510	0.27	12.24	27.30	31.70	20.55	6.89	1.01	0.04
1989	4,040,958	0.28	12.53	26.67	31.26	20.85	7.27	1.10	0.04
1990	4,158,212	0.28	12.55	26.30	30.71	21.31	7.64	1.17	0.04
1991	4,110,907	0.29	12.64	26.51	29.68	21.52	8.05	1.27	0.04
1992	4,065,014	0.30	12.43	26.33	29.01	22.02	8.48	1.37	0.05
1993	4,000,240	0.31	12.53	25.95	28.22	22.53	8.93	1.48	0.06
1994	3,952,767	0.33	12.79	25.33	27.55	22.93	9.40	1.61	0.06
1995	3,899,589	0.31	12.82	24.76	27.27	23.20	9.84	1.72	0.07
1996	3,891,494	0.29	12.63	24.29	27.53	23.07	10.27	1.85	0.08
1997	3,880,894	0.26	12.45	24.27	27.56	22.85	10.56	1.96	0.09
1998	3,941,553	0.24	12.30	24.49	27.48	22.56	10.78	2.06	0.10
1999	3,959,417	0.23	12.02	24.80	27.23	22.54	10.97	2.10	0.11
2000	4,058,814	0.21	11.55	25.08	26.79	22.90	11.14	2.22	0.11

Source: U.S. Department of Health and Human Services, Centers for Disease Control and Prevention, National Center for Health Statistics, Division of Vital Statistics, "Live Births by Age of Mother and Race: United States, 1933-98." For the years 1999 and 2000, "Births: Final Data for 2000," issued on February 12, 2002.

Multiple Births by Race and Age Group of Mother, 2000

Race and Number of Babies per Delivery	All Births by Category	Age Group of Mother							
		Under 15	15-19	20-24	25-29	30-34	35-39	40-44	45-54
Total, All Races	4,058,814	8,519	468,990	1,017,806	1,087,547	929,278	452,057	90,013	4,604
White, total	3,194,005	4,439	333,013	772,811	874,180	764,708	368,711	72,414	3,729
White, non-Hispanic	2,362,968	1,840	204,056	523,971	651,445	617,371	302,576	58,631	3,078
Black, total	622,598	3,808	118,954	202,596	141,968	94,808	49,295	10,699	470
Black, non-Hispanic	604,346	3,736	116,019	197,190	137,545	91,477	47,577	10,347	455
Hispanic	815,868	2,638	129,469	247,552	218,167	141,493	62,993	12,987	569
Singleton Deliveries									
All Races	3,932,573	8,401	461,430	994,973	1,055,143	892,549	430,743	85,568	3,766
White, total	3,094,219	4,383	328,163	757,193	848,539	733,674	350,728	68,552	2,987
White, non-Hispanic	2,281,129	1,824	200,935	512,693	630,695	590,506	286,845	55,230	2,401
Black, total	601,451	3,750	116,434	196,054	136,595	90,808	47,035	10,345	430
Black, non-Hispanic	583,667	3,680	113,530	190,773	132,299	87,577	45,391	10,001	416
Hispanic	798,739	2,596	127,765	243,274	213,457	137,593	60,922	12,607	525
Twin Deliveries									
All Races	118,916	115	7,452	22,383	30,628	33,873	19,648	4,071	746
White, total	93,235	56	4,765	15,289	24,046	28,407	16,486	3,522	664
White, non-Hispanic	76,018	16	3,071	11,023	19,339	24,486	14,365	3,103	615
Black, total	20,626	55	2,500	6,444	5,250	3,841	2,165	340	31
Black, non-Hispanic	20,173	53	2,469	6,319	5,123	3,744	2,103	332	30
Hispanic	16,470	42	1,669	4,204	4,545	3,682	1,953	341	34
High Order Deliveries									
All Races	7,325	3	108	450	1,776	2,856	1,666	374	92
White, total	6,551	-	85	329	1,595	2,627	1,497	340	78

[Continued]

Multiple Births by Race and Age Group of Mother, 2000

[Continued]

Race and Number of Babies per Delivery	All Births by Category	Age Group of Mother							
		Under 15	15-19	20-24	25-29	30-34	35-39	40-44	45-54
White, non-Hispanic	5,821	-	50	255	1,411	2,379	1,366	298	62
Black, total	521	3	20	98	123	159	95	14	9
Black, non-Hispanic	506	3	20	98	123	156	83	14	9
Hispanic	659	-	35	74	165	218	118	39	10

Source: Center for Disease Control, *National Vital Statistics Report*, "Births: Final Data for 2000," p. 87.

Rate of High Order Multiple Births by Age of Mother, 1980 and 2000

High order multiples include triples, quadruplets and higher number multiple deliveries. The rates listed here are the number of high order multiples per 100,000 live births.

Mother's Age Group	1980	2000
Under 20	14.8	23.0
20-24	31.4	44.2
25-29	42.8	163.3
30-34	58.3	307.3
35-39	47.6	368.5
40-44	NA	415.5
45-54	NA	1,998.3
Average	37.0	180.5

Source: Center for Disease Control, *National Vital Statistics Report*, "Births: Final Data for 2000," page 87 and *Morbidity and Mortality Weekly Report*, "Contribution of Assisted Reproductive Technology and Ovulation-Inducing Drugs to Triplet and Higher-Order Multiple Births: United States, 1980-1997."

Child Deliveries by Method, Number and Percent, 1989-2001

Rates are number per 100 live births.

Years	All Births	Births by Method of Delivery						Cesarean Delivery Rate		Rate of Vaginal Birth After Prev. C-Section
		Vaginal		Cesarean			Not Stated			
		Total	After Prev. C-Section	Total	Primary	Repeat		Total	Primary	
1989	3,798,734	2,793,463	71,019	826,955	521,873	305,082	178,316	22.8	16.1	18.9
1990	4,110,563	3,111,421	84,299	914,096	575,066	339,030	85,046	22.7	16.0	19.9
1991	4,110,907	3,100,891	90,690	905,077	569,195	335,882	104,939	22.6	15.9	21.3
1992	4,065,014	3,100,710	97,549	888,622	554,662	333,960	75,682	22.3	15.6	22.6
1993	4,000,240	3,098,796	103,581	861,987	539,251	322,736	39,457	21.8	15.3	24.3
1994	3,952,767	3,087,576	110,341	830,517	520,647	309,870	34,674	21.2	14.9	26.3
1995	3,899,589	3,063,724	112,439	806,722	510,104	296,618	29,143	20.8	14.7	27.5
1996	3,891,494	3,061,092	116,045	797,119	503,724	293,395	33,283	20.7	14.6	28.3
1997	3,880,894	3,046,621	112,145	799,033	502,526	296,507	35,240	20.8	14.6	27.4
1998	3,941,553	3,078,537	108,903	825,870	519,975	305,895	37,146	21.2	14.9	26.3
1999	3,959,417	3,063,870	97,680	862,086	542,080	320,006	33,461	22.0	15.5	23.4

[Continued]

Child Deliveries by Method, Number and Percent, 1989-2001
[Continued]

| Years | All Births | Births by Method of Delivery | | | | | | Cesarean Delivery Rate | | Rate of Vaginal Birth After Prev. C-Section |
| | | Vaginal | | Cesarean | | | Not Stated | | | |
		Total	After Prev. C-Section	Total	Primary	Repeat		Total	Primary	
2000	4,058,814	3,108,188	89,978	923,991	577,638	346,353	26,635	22.9	16.1	20.6
2001	4,040,121	3,054,331	NA	985,790	NA	NA	NA	24.4	16.9	16.5

Source: U.S. Department of Health and Human Services, Centers for Disease Control and Prevention, *National Vital Statistics Report*, "Births: Final Data for 2000," p. 72 and "Births: Preliminary Data for 2001," p. 3.

Child Deliveries by Method and Age Group of Mother, 2000

Rates are number per 100 live births.

| Mother's Age Group | All Births | Births by Method of Delivery | | | | | | Cesarean Delivery Rate | | Rate of Vaginal Birth After Prev. C-Section |
| | | Vaginal | | Cesarean | | | Not Stated | | | |
		Total	After Prev. C-Section	Total	Primary	Repeat		Total	Primary	
Total	4,058,814	3,108,188	89,978	923,991	577,638	346,353	26,635	22.9	16.1	20.6
< 20 years	477,509	400,130	2,678	74,587	66,048	8,539	2,792	15.7	14.2	23.9
20-24 years	1,017,806	821,844	17,300	189,595	130,169	59,426	6,367	18.7	13.9	22.5
25-29 years	1,087,547	836,437	25,199	243,911	151,334	92,577	7,199	22.6	15.7	21.4
30-34 years	929,278	680,240	27,102	242,681	136,977	105,704	6,357	26.3	17.3	20.4
35-39 years	452,057	309,497	14,819	139,355	73,647	65,708	3,205	31.0	20.0	18.4
40-54 years	94,617	60,040	2,880	33,862	19,463	14,399	715	36.1	25.4	16.7

Source: U.S. Department of Health and Human Services, Centers for Disease Control and Prevention, *National Vital Statistics Report*, "Births: Final Data for 2000," p. 72.

Contraceptive Use by Women 15 to 44 Years of Age: 1982 and 1995

All figures are percentages.

Contraceptive Status and Method	1982	1995	% Change 1982 to 1995
Sterile	27.2	29.7	9.2
Nonsurgical contraceptives	36.7	39.7	8.2
Pill	15.6	17.3	10.9
Intrauterine device (IUD)	4.0	0.5	-87.5
Diaphram	4.5	1.2	-73.3
Condom	6.7	13.1	95.5
Periodic Abstinence	2.2	1.5	-31.8
Other nonsurgical method	3.8	5.9	55.3
Pregnant, postpartum	5.0	4.6	-9.2
Seeking pregnancy	4.2	4.0	-4.8
Other nonusers	26.9	22.3	-17.1

Source: U.S. Census Bureau, *Statistical Abstract of the United States 1990*, "Contraceptive Use by Women, 15-44 Years Old, by Age, Race, Marital Status, and Method of Contraception: 1982," p. 70, and *Statistical Abstract of the United States 2001*, "Contraceptive Use by Women, 15- 44 Years of Age: 1995," p. 69.

Birth and Abortion Rates by Race: 1972-1997

Year	Rate per 1,000 Women Aged 15 to 44 Years			
	Births	Abortions		
	All Races	All Races	Whites	Non-Whites
1972	73.4	12.5	NA	NA
1973	69.2	16.5	NA	NA
1974	68.4	19.0	NA	NA
1975	66.0	21.7	17.2	49.3
1976	65.0	23.5	18.9	51.0
1977	66.8	25.3	20.6	52.8
1978	65.5	27.0	22.3	54.5
1979	63.4	28.8	24.0	56.2
1980	65.6	29.3	24.3	56.5
1981	64.8	29.3	24.3	55.9
1982	64.8	28.8	23.8	55.5
1983	63.4	28.5	23.3	55.5
1984	63.2	28.1	23.1	54.3
1985	64.1	28.0	22.6	55.5
1986	63.1	27.4	21.8	55.9
1987	63.3	27.1	21.1	56.0
1988	64.5	27.3	21.2	57.3
1989	66.4	26.8	20.9	54.7
1990	68.3	27.4	21.5	54.4
1991	67.0	26.3	20.3	53.8
1992	66.5	25.9	19.6	53.9
1993	65.4	25.4	18.9	53.5
1994	64.9	24.1	17.9	51.1
1995	64.4	22.9	17.0	48.1
1996	64.3	22.9	16.6	49.2
1997	63.9	22.2	16.1	47.8

Source: U.S. Census Bureau, *Statistical Abstract of the United States, 2001*, Table 92, p. 71. Date are originally from the Centers of Disease Control. Abortions in 1983 and 1986 are extrapolations.

Low Birth Weight Babies by Race: 1980-2000

All figures are percentages.

Years	Low birth weight (<2,500 grams)			Very low birth weight (<1,500 grams)		
	Total	Black	White	Total	Black	White
1980	6.80	12.70	5.70	1.15	2.48	0.90
1981	6.80	12.70	5.70	1.16	2.52	0.91
1982	6.80	12.60	5.60	1.18	2.56	0.91
1983	6.80	12.80	5.70	1.19	2.60	0.92
1984	6.70	12.60	5.60	1.19	2.60	0.93
1985	6.80	12.60	5.70	1.21	2.71	0.93
1986	6.80	12.80	5.70	1.21	2.73	0.93
1987	6.90	13.00	5.70	1.24	2.79	0.94

[Continued]

Low Birth Weight Babies by Race: 1980-2000

[Continued]

Years	Low birth weight (<2,500 grams)			Very low birth weight (<1,500 grams)		
	Total	Black	White	Total	Black	White
1988	6.90	13.30	5.70	1.24	2.86	0.93
1989	7.00	13.50	5.70	1.28	2.95	0.95
1990	7.00	13.50	5.70	1.27	2.92	0.95
1991	7.10	13.60	5.80	1.29	2.96	0.96
1992	7.10	13.30	5.80	1.29	2.96	0.96
1993	7.20	13.30	6.00	1.33	2.96	1.01
1994	7.30	13.20	6.10	1.33	2.96	1.02
1995	7.30	13.10	6.20	1.35	2.97	1.06
1996	7.40	13.00	6.30	1.37	2.99	1.09
1997	7.50	13.00	6.50	1.42	3.04	1.13
1998	7.60	13.00	6.50	1.45	3.08	1.15
1999	7.60	13.10	6.60	1.45	3.14	1.15
2000	7.60	13.00	6.50	1.43	3.07	1.14

Source: U.S. Department of Health and Human Services, Centers for Disease Control and Prevention, "Births: Final Data for 2000," *National Vital Statistics Report*, Vol. 50, No. 5, February 12, 2002.

Infant Mortality Rates by Race, 1950-2000 Selected Years

The rate is the number of infants who die before they reach one year of age per 1,000 live births.

Years	Infant Mortality Rates		
	Total	Black	White
1950	29.2	43.9	26.8
1960	26.0	44.3	22.9
1970	20.0	32.6	17.8
1975	16.1	26.2	14.2
1980	12.6	22.2	10.9
1981	11.9	20.8	10.3
1982	11.5	20.5	9.9
1983	11.2	20.0	9.6
1984	10.8	19.2	9.3
1985	10.6	19.0	9.2
1986	10.4	18.9	8.8
1987	10.1	18.8	8.5
1988	10.0	18.5	8.4
1989	9.8	18.6	8.1
1990	9.2	18.0	7.6
1991	8.9	17.6	7.3
1992	8.5	16.8	6.9
1993	8.4	16.5	6.8
1994	8.0	15.8	6.6
1995	7.6	15.1	6.3

[Continued]

Infant Mortality Rates by Race, 1950-2000 Selected Years

[Continued]

Years	Infant Mortality Rates		
	Total	Black	White
1996	7.3	14.7	6.1
1997	7.2	14.2	6.0
1998	7.2	14.3	6.0
1999	7.1	14.6	5.8
2000	6.9	13.5	5.7

Source: U.S. Department of Health and Human Services, Centers for Disease Control and Prevention, "Births: Final Data for 2000," *National Vital Statistics Report*, Vol. 50, No. 5, February 12, 2002.

Rates of Specific Organ System Defects Associated with Infant Deaths, 1980 and 1995

Rates are the number of infant deaths associated with specific organ system defects at birth per 100,000 live births.

Organ Systems	1980	1995	% Change 1980 to 1995
Cardiovascular defects	105.5	58.8	-44.3
Central nervous system defects	46.7	21.9	-53.1
Chromosomal defects	18.1	23.0	26.8
Respiratory defects	17.8	25.2	42.2
Musculoskeletal defects	17.8	12.1	32.1
Genitourinary defects	12.5	10.0	-20.5
Digestive system defects	8.0	2.2	-71.9
All other defects	28.7	14.9	-48.2
Total	255.2	168.1	-34.2

Source: U.S. Centers for Disease Control, *Morbidity and Mortality Weekly Report*, "Trends in Infant Mortality Attributable to Birth Defects - United States, 1980- 1995," September 25, 1998, pp. 773-778, available online at http://www/cdc/gov/epo/mmwr/preview/mmwrhtml/00054921.htm.

Chapter 12
THE ENVIRONMENT

National Air Pollutant Emissions, 1940-1998

Thousand tons.

	CO	NOX	VOC	SO2	PM-10	Pb	Total
1940	93,616	7,374	17,161	19,952	15,957	NA	154,060
1945	94,825	9,548	17,308	26,007	16,545	NA	164,233
1950	102,609	10,093	20,936	22,357	17,133	NA	173,128
1955	101,281	11,563	21,973	20,883	16,245	NA	171,945
1960	109,745	14,140	24,249	22,227	15,558	NA	185,919
1965	115,928	16,579	27,630	26,750	14,198	NA	201,085
1970	129,444	20,928	30,982	31,161	13,042	220,869	446,426
1975	116,757	22,632	26,079	28,011	7,671	159,659	360,809
1980	117,434	24,384	26,336	25,905	7,119	74,153	275,331
1985	117,013	23,198	24,428	23,658	45,445	22,890	256,632
1990	98,523	24,049	20,936	23,660	29,962	4,975	202,105
1995	93,353	24,921	20,817	19,181	27,070	3,929	189,271
1998	89,454	24,454	17,917	19,647	34,741	3,973	190,186

Source: Office of Air Quality Planning and Standards. U.S. Environmental Protection Agency. *National Air Pollutant Emissions Trends, 1900-1998*, March 2000. Retrieved July 2, 2002 from http://www.epa.gov/ttn/chief/trends/trends98/trends98.pdf. *Note:* NA stands for data not available.

National Water Quality: Percentage of Polluted Bodies of Water, 1992-1998

	1992	1994	1996	1998	% of Total Assessed			
					1992	1994	1996	1998
Rivers and streams (miles)	38	36	36	35	18	17	19	23
Lakes, reservoirs, ponds (acres)	44	37	39	45	46	42	40	42
Estuaries (sq. miles)	32	37	38	44	75	78	72	32
Great Lakes shoreline (miles)	67	97	97	96	99	94	94	90
Ocean shoreline (miles)	14	7	NA	12	6	9	6	5

Source: Office of Water. U.S. Environmental Protection Agency. *Water Quality Report, 1992-1996.* Retrieved June 26, 2002 from http://www.epa.gov/305b. U.S. Census Bureau. *Statistical Abstract of the United States: 2001. Notes:* NA stands for not available.

Leading Water Pollutants, 1998

Percentage of miles, acres, or square miles of impaired waterway affected by the pollutant.

	Rivers & Streams (miles)	Lakes, Reservoirs, & Ponds (acres)	Estuaries (sq. miles)	Great Lakes Shoreline (miles)
Siltation	38.2	14.8	NA	NA
Pathogens (bacteria)	35.6	NA	47.4	3.9
Nutrients	28.9	43.7	23.1	4.9
Oxygen-depleting substances	23.2	13.9	41.5	3.7
Metals	20.6	26.7	27.5	3.0
Suspended solids	NA	10.2	NA	NA
Thermal modifications	12.8	NA	17.8	NA
Priority toxic organic chemicals	NA	NA	6.5	29.2
Pesticides	15.3	NA	NA	21.4
Nonpriority organic chemicals	NA	NA	NA	21.4

Source: U.S. Environmental Protection Agency. *1998 National Water Quality Inventory.* Retrieved June 26, 2002 from http://www.epa.gov/305b/98report/. *Note:* NA stands for data not available.

Community Water Systems (CWS), 1993-2001

	1993	1994	1995	1996	1997	1998	1999	2000	2001
Total CWS	56,483	56,133	55,427	54,340	57,425	54,367	53,923	54,067	53,783
Total pop. (000)	258,119	260,637	263,082	265,502	268,048	270,509	272,945	281,421	284,797
Pop. served by CWS (000)	250,967	248,852	251,450	255,871	258,307	252,530	253,795	263,926	264,145
Total CWS with health violation	6,778	6,736	6,097	5,434	4,594	4,613	4,164	4,617	4,583
Pop. served by health violators (000)	52,703	42,305	40,232	35,822	33,580	27,722	23,990	24,640	24,217
Arsenic violations	10	10	9	19	13	14	24	14	27
Fluoride violations	118	93	87	92	65	81	64	49	143

Source: U.S. Environmental Protection Agency (EPA). *Factoids: Drinking Water and Ground Water Statistics, 1998-2001.* U.S EPA. Summary Inventory, Violations, and GPRA MS Excel PivotTables. All EPA data retrieved June 28, 2002 from http://www.epa.gov/ safewater/. U.S. Census Bureau. *Statistical Abstract of the United States, 2001.* 2000 and 2001 total population data: U.S. Census Bureau. "Your Gateway to Census 2000." Retrieved June 28, 2002 from http://www.census.gov/main/www/cen2000.html. Population Division. U.S. Census Bureau. "Table US2001EST-01 - Time Series of National Population Estimates: April 1, 2000 to July 1, 2001," December 27, 2001. Retrieved June 28, 2002 from http://eire.census.gov/popest/data/national/populartables/files/national01.pdf.

Chapter 13
MEDICAL PROFESSIONALS

Physician Supply

Estimated supply of physicians and physician-to-population ratios.

Year	Physicians	Allopathic (MD)[1]	Osteopathic (DO)[2]
1970	323,800	311,200	12,600
1975	380,400	366,400	14,000
1980	453,100	435,500	17,600
1985	533,600	511,100	22,500
1990	601,700	572,700	29,000
1995	681,700	646,000	35,700
1996	701,200	663,900	37,300
Percent Change			
1970-1996	116.6	113.3	196.0
1970-1975	17.5	17.7	11.1
1975-1980	19.1	18.9	25.7
1980-1985	17.8	17.4	27.8
1985-1990	12.8	12.1	28.9
1990-1995	13.3	12.8	23.1
1995-1996	2.9	2.8	4.5
Total per 100,000 Pop.			
1970	155.6	149.6	6.1
1975	173.5	167.1	6.4
1980	195.9	188.3	7.6
1985	220.5	211.2	9.3
1990	237.6	226.1	11.5
1995	255.1	241.8	13.4
1996	260.0	246.1	13.8
% Change per 100,000 Pop.			
1970-1996	67.1	64.5	126.2
1970-1975	11.5	11.7	4.9
1975-1980	12.9	12.7	18.8
1980-1985	12.6	12.2	22.4
1985-1990	7.8	7.1	23.7
1990-1995	7.4	6.9	16.5
1995-1996	1.9	1.8	3.0

Source: Data estimated by Health Resources and Services Administration, Bureau of Health Professions, http://bhpr.hrsa.gov/healthworkforce/factbook.htm.

Medical Personnel Per 100,000 Population

Doctor, nurse practitioner, and emergency medical technician data are for 1998. Physician assistant and radiologic technologist data are for 1999. RN data are for 1996.

	Doctors	Physician Assistant	Nurse Practitioners	Registered Nurses	Licensed Practical Nurses	Emergency Medical Technicians	Clinical Laboratory Technicians	Radiologic Technologists
Alabama	159.2	4.2	26.4	752.0	353.9	50.6	100.7	63.7
Alaska	154.7	34.4	60.6	962.8	99.3	40.6	76.4	34.1
Arizona	176.2	11.0	25.1	735.4	185.3	41.4	139.9	55.1
Arkansas	156.7	1.7	55.6	681.9	469.2	70.5	117.4	55.9
California	194.5	7.7	25.6	567.8	150.6	38.3	86.4	39.4
Colorado	201.1	16.4	47.9	803.3	160.0	47.6	79.4	47.6
Connecticut	258.5	18.0	39.7	1,027.7	242.0	49.2	100.5	75.2
Delaware	199.4	8.9	37.2	1,041.8	204.3	40.3	82.0	86.0
Florida	211.4	10.1	28.8	800.8	294.3	47.4	102.2	61.8
Georgia	169.6	12.3	20.7	712.5	279.1	71.4	112.1	58.3
Hawaii	216.8	6.5	8.7	723.1	167.2	42.8	84.8	42.0
Idaho	144.7	11.3	18.8	576.9	208.0	39.0	55.2	53.6
Illinois	192.5	4.9	9.9	860.2	208.3	53.9	104.1	58.3
Indiana	163.5	3.0	8.9	777.8	286.4	61.6	100.2	63.1
Iowa	152.8	14.0	18.1	988.3	270.5	65.4	97.9	49.6
Kansas	170.7	13.5	43.4	801.4	280.1	83.8	119.0	64.8
Kentucky	168.5	8.8	19.7	747.0	261.5	75.2	106.0	64.6
Louisiana	182.7	4.0	10.8	716.9	388.3	45.6	123.8	58.4
Maine	209.4	25.8	42.5	1,051.0	214.0	89.8	84.2	66.5
Maryland	261.4	15.6	29.8	838.1	179.7	51.7	131.8	58.3
Massachusetts	277.3	10.0	57.0	1,188.5	276.7	78.1	124.2	70.6
Michigan	191.1	12.5	29.5	817.3	177.6	52.3	95.7	60.5
Minnesota	186.4	8.7	18.0	945.2	353.1	61.8	126.5	59.0
Mississippi	137.0	1.0	22.5	699.5	324.9	67.6	109.8	57.8
Missouri	190.2	4.0	29.5	930.0	275.5	103.4	115.7	76.1
Montana	181.2	14.8	28.7	763.7	268.3	73.9	92.1	70.5
Nebraska	165.0	22.0	13.1	925.7	373.3	36.1	128.9	71.1
Nevada	161.5	8.5	15.1	579.1	115.3	43.6	72.8	71.1
New Hampshire	195.3	13.3	49.8	981.8	202.4	44.7	77.6	52.3
New Jersey	243.0	3.7	32.6	842.8	203.4	48.7	112.5	59.8
New Mexico	170.2	15.6	33.1	660.0	162.7	51.9	86.0	40.4
New York	265.0	18.8	40.5	913.2	268.5	34.3	114.3	68.9
North Carolina	175.9	20.4	17.2	795.0	215.0	66.8	119.1	63.2
North Dakota	188.5	24.3	24.0	1,068.9	434.3	62.7	144.2	73.7
Ohio	190.4	7.1	25.8	891.6	294.9	64.9	110.1	68.9
Oklahoma	159.2	12.7	11.3	582.0	373.1	56.0	104.2	54.5
Oregon	192.1	7.6	39.0	793.0	137.7	39.3	78.6	49.4
Pennsylvania	234.2	13.3	15.5	1,014.9	296.4	79.7	98.7	62.7
Rhode Island	247.6	10.4	30.3	1,126.6	244.0	24.3	136.7	86.1
South Carolina	165.4	5.5	23.4	691.0	252.1	74.0	107.0	43.2
South Dakota	164.8	27.0	37.5	1,048.6	254.5	65.7	130.0	76.6
Tennessee	193.0	6.6	24.8	852.5	354.9	58.2	120.4	74.0
Texas	162.0	9.3	16.0	633.4	296.1	39.6	100.3	44.9
Utah	156.1	12.2	33.0	630.8	156.1	114.7	128.5	60.5
Vermont	223.0	16.5	48.9	906.7	269.2	49.1	103.3	55.9
Virginia	186.3	6.5	31.3	786.9	263.1	25.2	97.5	57.9
Washington	192.7	15.7	45.7	777.5	173.5	39.4	106.4	54.5

[Continued]

Medical Personnel Per 100,000 Population

[Continued]

	Doctors	Physician Assistant	Nurse Practitioners	Registered Nurses	Licensed Practical Nurses	Emergency Medical Technicians	Clinical Laboratory Technicians	Radiologic Technologists
West Virginia	179.6	17.6	18.4	792.3	352.7	85.6	108.2	79.5
Wisconsin	183.9	11.9	7.4	874.9	225.6	72.0	120.8	72.6
Wyoming	150.0	17.1	23.3	773.3	183.3	64.6	64.6	43.7
District of Columbia	447.0	24.9	94.5	1,703.0	410.4	31.6	316.4	107.4

Source: National Center for Health Workforce Information and Analysis, State Health Workforce Profiles, http://bhpr.hrsa.gov/healthworkforce/profiles/default.htm. Primary Sources: Division for Nursing; Bureau of Labor Statistics; American Medical Association; American Dental Association; American Academy of Physician Assistants;National Council of State Boards of Nursing; Bureau of the Census.

Active Physicians

Number of active physicians (MDs) and physician-to- population ratios by specialty, largest specialty groups: selected years 1970 to 1996

Type of Practice	1970		1980		1991		1996	
	Active MDs	Per 100K Pop	Active MDs	Per 100K Pop	Active MDs	Per 100K Pop	Active MDs	Per 100K Pop
Estimated Active	311,203	149.6	435,545	188.3	594,697	231.8	663,943	246.2
Primary Care[1]	115,822	55.7	146,093	63.2	197,719	77.1	216,446	80.2
General and Family Practice	57,948	27.9	60,049	26.0	71,687	27.9	78,910	29.3
Internal Medicine	39,924	19.2	58,462	25.3	85,839	33.5	92,321	34.2
Pediatrics	17,950	8.6	27,582	11.9	40,193	15.7	45,215	16.8
Medical Specialties	19,340	9.3	39,711	17.2	71,021	27.7	88,027	32.6
Cardiovascular Disease	6,476	3.1	9,823	4.2	16,478	6.4	19,237	7.1
Dermatology	4,003	1.9	5,660	2.4	7,912	3.1	8,854	3.3
Gastroenterology	2,010	1.0	4,046	1.7	7,946	3.1	9,718	3.6
Pulmonary Diseases	2,315	1.1	3,715	1.6	6,337	2.5	6,824	2.5
Surgical Specialties	86,042	41.4	110,778	47.9	141,560	55.2	149,857	55.6
General Surgery	29,761	14.3	34,034	14.7	39,211	15.3	37,943	14.1
Obstetrics and Gynecology	18,876	9.1	26,305	11.4	35,273	13.7	38,424	14.2
Ophthalmology	9,927	4.8	12,974	5.6	16,433	6.4	17,777	6.6
Orthopedic Surgery	9,620	4.6	13,996	6.1	20,640	8.0	22,521	8.3
Otolaryngology	5,409	2.6	6,553	2.8	8,373	3.3	9,028	3.3
Urology	5,795	2.8	7,743	3.3	9,452	3.7	10,021	3.7
Other Specialties	89,999	43.3	118,334	51.2	167,808	65.4	189,625	70.3
Anesthesiology	10,860	5.2	15,958	6.9	28,148	11.0	33,318	12.4
Diagnostic Radiology	1,968	0.9	7,048	3.0	17,253	6.7	20,043	7.4
Emergency Medicine	0	0.0	5,699	2.5	15,470	6.0	20,030	7.4
Neurology	3,074	1.5	5,685	2.5	9,742	3.8	11,585	4.3
Pathology and Forensic Pathology	10,483	5.0	13,642	5.9	17,428	6.8	18,457	6.8
Psychiatry	21,146	10.2	27,481	11.9	36,405	14.2	38,417	14.2
Radiology	10,524	5.1	11,653	5.0	7,848	3.1	8,181	3.0

Source: Bureau of Health Professions, United States Health Workforce Personnel Factbook, Table 202, http://bhpr.hrsa.gov/healthworkforce/factbook.htm; Primary sources: American Medical Association. *Physician Characteristics and Distribution in the US 1997/98*, Chicago, 1997. Also prior annual issues (formerly titled *Physician Distribution and Medical Licensure in the U.S.*) and U.S. Bureau of the Census. *Current Population Reports*. Series P-25 Nos. 941, 943, 1023, 1036, 1049, 1075, and 1093, *Statistical Abstract of the United States: 1997* (117th edition) Washington, DC, 1997. *Notes:* 1. Includes General and Family Practice, Internal Medicine, and Pediatrics.

Physicians by Place of Medical Education: 1980 to 1999

Professionally active physicians, in thousands. Includes Puerto Rico and outlying areas.

Activity	1980	1990	1995	1996	1997	1998	1999
Doctors of medicine, total	467.7	615.4	720.3	737.8	756.7	777.9	797.6
Professionally active	435.5	560.0	646.0	663.9	684.6	707.0	720.9
Place of medical education:							
U.S. medical graduates	343.6	437.2	492.2	505.7	519.7	533.4	542.2
Foreign medical graduates[1]	91.8	122.8	153.8	158.3	164.9	173.7	178.7

Source: U.S. Bureau of the Census, *Statistical Abstract of the United States: 2001.*121st ed. Washington, DC: U.S. Government Printing Office, 2001, p. 106; Primary source: American Medical Association, Chicago, IL, *Physician Characteristics and Distribution in the U.S.* (annual). *Notes:* 1. Foreign medical graduates received their medical education in schools outside the Unit

Registered Nurses

- Not available. Number of RNs, percent change, RNs per 100,000 population, and percent change in number of RNs per 100,000 population.

Year	Number of RNs	% Change	RNs Per 100,000 Pop.	% Change
1970	750,000	-	366	-
1975	961,000	-	449	-
1980	1,272,900	-	555	-
1985	1,538,100	-	640	-
1990	1,789,600	-	710	-
1995	2,115,800	-	798	-
1996	2,161,700	-	808	-
2000	2,271,300	-	832	-
1970-1996	-	188.2	-	120.8
1970-1975	-	28.1	-	22.7
1975-1980	-	32.5	-	23.6
1980-1985	-	20.8	-	15.3
1985-1990	-	16.4	-	10.9
1990-1995	-	18.2	-	12.4
1995-1996	-	2.2	-	1.3

Source: Health Resources and Services Administration, *United States Health Workforce Personnel Factbook,* http://bhpr.hrsa.gov/healthworkforce/factbook.htm, and National Center for Health Statistics, *Health, United States, 2002,* Table 102.

Nursing School Graduates

NA Not available.

Specialty	1980	1985	1990	1995	2000
Licensed practical	41,892	36,955	35,417	44,234	NA
Registered, total	75,523	82,075	66,088	97,052	94,757
Baccalaureate	24,994	24,975	18,571	31,254	32,413
Associate degree	36,034	45,208	42,318	58,749	56,641
Diploma	14,495	11,892	5,199	7,049	5,703

Source: Health Resources and Services Administration, *United States Health Workforce Personnel Factbook*, http://bhpr.hrsa.gov/healthworkforce/factbook.htm, and National Center for Health Statistics, *Health, United States, 2002*, Table 102.

The Most Common Telemedicine Activities

The number of telemedicine programs that were performing the named activity. The Agency for Healthcare Research and Quality (AHRQ), which conducted the study, identified 455 telemedicine programs in operation in 2000, 362 of which were in the United States.

Activity	Number
Consultation/second opinion	290
Diagnostic test interpretation	169
Chronic disease management	130
Posthospitalization or postoperative followup	102
Emergency room triage	95
Visits by a specialist	78

Source: Agency for Healthcare Research and Quality, *Telemedicine for the Medicare Population,* http://www.ahcpr.gov/.

Chapter 14
MEDICAL INFRASTRUCTURE

Number of Hospitals, 1987-1997

	1987	1992	1997
Total hospitals	7,298	7,120	6,685
General medical and surgical hospitals	6,006	5,624	5,477
Psychiatric & substance abuse hospitals	787	919	801
Specialty hospitals, except psychiatric	505	577	397

Source: U.S. Census Bureau. *1992* and *1997 Economic Census.* Arsen J. Darnay. *Service Industries USA, Fourth Edition,* 1999; Original source: U.S. Census Bureau. 1987 Census of Service Industries.

Hospital Mergers, 1996-2000

	Hospital Mergers, Total	Catholic/ Non-Catholic Hospital Mergers	Catholic/ Non-Catholic Hospital Mergers as % of Total
1996	163	24	14.7
1997	197	17	8.6
1998	139	43	30.9
1999	110	12	10.9
2000	86	17	19.7

Source: Monroe, Stephen, M. and Kathy Hammell. Irving Levin Associates. "Hospital M&A Activity Slow in 2000 As Health Care Industry Begins to Stabilize," March 28, 2001. Retrieved September 4, 2002 from http://www.levinassociates.com/pressroom/pressreleases/pr2001/pr103har7.htm. Catholics for Free Choice. "Catholic Health Care." Retrieved September 4, 2002 from http://www.cath4choice.org/nobandwidth/English/healthmergers.htm.

Number of Hospice Patients, 1976-2000

	Hospice Patients
1974	NA
1976	6,000
1978	10,000
1980	15,000

[Continued]

Number of Hospice Patients, 1976-2000

[Continued]

	Hospice Patients
1982	25,000
1984	100,000
1986	167,000
1988	181,000
1990	210,000
1992	246,000
1994	340,000
1996	450,000
1998	540,000
2000	700,000
2001	775,000

Source: The National Hospice and Palliative Care Organization. "More Patients and Families Choose Hospital Care Each Year." Retrieved September 11, 2002 from http://www.nhpco.org. *Note:* NA stands for data not available.

Medicare Hospice Patients, 1992 and 1998

	1992	1998
Cancer	108,232	206,190
Non-cancer	34,878	152,759

Source: William J. Scanlon. Health, Education, and Human Services Division. United States General Accounting Office. "Medicare: More Beneficiaries Use Hospice; Many Factors Contribute to Shorter Periods of Use," September 18, 2000. Retrieved September 11, 2002 from http://www.gao.gov/new.items/he00201t.pdf.

Enrollment in Medicare, 1966-2075

	Total	Elderly	Disabled and End-stage Renal Disease
1966	19,109	19,109	NA
1967	19,521	19,521	NA
1968	19,821	19,821	NA
1969	20,103	20,103	NA
1970	20,491	20,491	NA
1971	20,915	20,915	NA
1972	21,332	21,332	NA
1973	23,545	21,815	1,731
1974	24,201	22,273	1,928
1975	24,959	22,790	2,168
1976	25,663	23,271	2,392
1977	26,458	23,838	2,619

[Continued]

Enrollment in Medicare, 1966-2075
[Continued]

	Total	Elderly	Disabled and End-stage Renal Disease
1978	27,164	24,371	2,793
1979	27,859	24,948	2,911
1980	28,478	25,515	2,963
1981	29,010	26,011	2,999
1982	29,494	26,540	2,954
1983	30,026	27,109	2,918
1984	30,455	27,571	2,884
1985	31,083	28,176	2,907
1986	31,750	28,791	2,959
1987	32,411	29,380	3,031
1988	32,980	29,879	3,102
1989	33,579	30,409	3,171
1990	34,203	30,948	3,255
1991	34,870	31,485	3,385
1992	35,579	32,011	3,569
1993	36,306	32,462	3,844
1994	36,935	32,801	4,135
1995	37,535	33,142	4,393
1996	38,064	33,424	4,640
1997	38,445	33,630	4,815
1998	38,825	33,802	5,023
1999	39,140	33,929	5,212
2000	39,579	34,100	5,400
2005	41,834	NA	NA
2010	45,878	NA	NA
2015	52,830	NA	NA
2020	61,359	NA	NA
2025	70,355	NA	NA
2030	77,639	NA	NA
2035	81,850	NA	NA
2040	83,896	NA	NA
2045	85,537	NA	NA
2050	87,784	NA	NA
2055	90,671	NA	NA
2060	94,058	NA	NA
2065	97,199	NA	NA
2070	100,633	NA	NA
2075	103,799	NA	NA

Source: Centers for Medicare and Medicaid Services. *2002 Annual Report of the Boards of Trustees of the Federal Hospital Insurance Trust and Federal Supplementary Medical Insurance Trust Funds.* Retrieved September 12, 2002 from http://cms.hhs.gov/publications/trusteesreport/default.asp. *Note:* NA stands for data not available.

Medicare Income, Expenditures, and Trust Fund Assets, Fiscal Year, 1970-2011

	Income	Expenditures	Assets
1970	7,490	7,149	2,734
1975	16,890	14,782	11,294
1980	35,690	35,025	19,022
1985	75,510	71,384	31,923
1990	125,701	109,709	110,158
1995	173,016	180,096	143,394
1996	203,160	194,263	152,291
1997	209,354	210,389	151,256
1998	220,158	213,412	158,002
1999	238,293	211,959	184,336
2000	248,920	219,276	213,980
2001	266,350	241,175	239,154
2002	285,265	252,376	272,043
2003	298,878	262,214	308,707
2004	316,102	273,852	350,957
2005	337,451	292,669	395,739
2006	358,269	304,883	449,125
2007	382,386	327,899	503,612
2008	407,971	350,692	560,891
2009	435,050	375,546	620,395
2010	465,858	401,545	684,708
2011	498,223	433,986	748,945

Source: Centers for Medicare and Medicaid Services. *2002 Annual Report of the Boards of Trustees of the Federal Hospital Insurance Trust and Federal Supplementary Medical Insurance Trust Funds.* Retrieved September 12, 2002 from http://cms.hhs.gov/publications/trusteesreport/default.asp.

Cost and Income Rates for Medicare Hospital Insurance (HI), 1967-2075

	HI Cost as a % of Taxable Income	HI Income as a % of Taxable Income
1967	0.94	NA
1970	1.20	NA
1975	1.69	NA
1980	2.19	NA
1985	2.62	NA
1990	2.69	NA
1995	3.25	NA
2000	2.64	NA
2005	2.67	3.07
2010	2.81	3.10

[Continued]

Cost and Income Rates for Medicare Hospital Insurance (HI), 1967-2075
[Continued]

	HI Cost as a % of Taxable Income	HI Income as a % of Taxable Income
2015	3.12	3.16
2020	3.59	3.22
2025	4.19	3.27
2030	4.89	3.32
2035	5.58	3.34
2040	6.18	3.34
2045	6.70	3.35
2050	7.16	3.35
2055	7.64	3.36
2060	8.22	3.38
2065	8.92	3.39
2070	9.74	3.40
2075	10.61	3.41

Source: Centers for Medicare and Medicaid Services. *2002 Annual Report of the Boards of Trustees of the Federal Hospital Insurance Trust and Federal Supplementary Medical Insurance Trust Funds.* Retrieved September 12, 2002 from http://cms.hhs.gov/publications/trusteesreport/default.asp. *Note:* NA stands for data not available.

Persons Served by Medicaid, 1977-1998

Data are in millions.

	Total	Children	Adults	Elderly/ Blind/ Disabled
1977	22.8	NA	NA	NA
1989	23.5	NA	NA	NA
1991	NA	13.4	6.8	NA
1992	31.2	15.1	7.0	9.1
1993	NA	16.3	7.5	NA
1994	35.1	17.2	7.6	10.3
1995	36.3	17.2	7.6	11.5
1996	36.1	16.7	7.1	12.3
1997	34.9	15.8	6.8	12.3
1998	40.6	19.0	7.9	13.7

Source: Health Care Financing Administration. U.S. Department of Health and Human Services. *Chartbook 2000: A Profile of Medicaid*, September 2000. Retrieved September 16, 2002 from http://cms.hhs.gov/charts/medicaid/2Tchartbk.pdf. Centers for Medicare and Medicaid Services. "National Summary of Medicaid Managed Care Programs and Enrollment June 30, 2001." Retrieved September 16, 2002 from http://cms.hhs.gov/medicaid/managedcare/trends01.pdf. *Notes:* NA stands for data not available.

Medicaid Enrollment, 1990-2007, and Estimated Federal Share of Medicaid Payments per Enrollee, 1996-2007

Data in U.S. dollars, except where indicated.

	Aged	Blind and Disabled	Children	Adults	Average	Enrollment (mil.)
1990	NA	NA	NA	NA	NA	28.9
1991	NA	NA	NA	NA	NA	32.3
1992	NA	NA	NA	NA	NA	35.8
1993	NA	NA	NA	NA	NA	38.8
1994	NA	NA	NA	NA	NA	40.8
1995	NA	NA	NA	NA	NA	41.7
1996	5,500	4,660	630	970	1,850	41.3
1997	5,680	4,840	660	1,000	1,940	40.6
1998	5,930	5,140	710	1,030	2,040	40.4
1999	6,200	5,480	750	1,090	2,160	41.8
2000	6,550	5,820	800	1,150	2,310	42.6
2001	6,920	6,170	850	1,210	2,460	43.9
2002	7,350	6,580	900	1,280	2,630	46.3
2003	7,800	7,020	950	1,350	2,820	47.3
2004	8,240	7,480	1,010	1,430	3,020	47.8
2005	8,750	7,990	1,070	1,530	3,240	48.4
2006	9,300	8,550	1,130	1,630	3,490	48.9
2007	9,890	9,160	1,210	1,730	3,750	49.4

Source: Committee on the Budget. The United States Senate. "Medicaid." Retrieved September 17, 2002 from http://www.senate.gov/~budget/republican/latest%20data/medicaid.htm. Amy Snow Landa. "Medicaid morass: States are cutting funds to make up for major revenue shortfalls." American Medical News, January 7, 2002. Retrieved September 18, 2002 from http://www.ama-assn.org/sci- pubs/amnews/pick_02/gvsa0107.htm. *Note:* NA stands for data not available.

National Drug Shortages, 1980s-2001

	Drug and Vaccine Shortages
Late 1980s	Very rare
Early 1990s	2 to 3
Mid 1990s	10 or 15
2000	25
As of October 2001	35
As of September 2002	44

Source: Maguire, Phyllis. "Drug shortages raise new fears about patient care." *ACP-ASIM Observer*, December 2001. Retrieved September 18, 2002 from http://www.acponline.org/ journals/news/dec01/drug_shortage.htm. Drug Shortages Management Resources Center. University of Utah. "Drug Product Shortage Bulletins." Retrieved September 18, 2002 from http://www.ashp.org/shortages.

Health Services Employment, 1998 and 2001

Data are in millions.

	1998	2001
Total employment	11.2	15.1
Total non-health professional staff	4.0	4.1

Source: Bureau of Health Professions. National Center for Health Workforce Information and Analysis. U.S. Department of Health and Human Services. *HRSA State Health Workforce Profiles—Alabama*, December 2000. Bureau of Health Professions. "More than 1 in 10 Americans works in health care or is a health professional." Original source: Bureau of Labor Statistics. Retrieved September 20, 2002 from http://bhpr.hrsa.gov.

Health Services Employment by Location, 1998

Data are in millions.

	Total Employment	Non-health Professional Employment
Hospitals	5.0	1.8
Nursing homes	1.9	0.6
Home health care	0.7	0.1
Physician offices & clinics	1.8	0.8
Dentist offices & clinics	0.6	0.2
Other offices & clinics	0.5	0.2

Source: Bureau of Health Professions. National Center for Health Workforce Information and Analysis. U.S. Department of Health and Human Services. *HRSA State Health Workforce Profiles—Alabama*, December 2000. Original source: Bureau of Labor Statistics. Retrieved September 20, 2002 from http://bhpr.hrsa.gov.

Chapter 15
FUNDING

U.S. Government Research and Development Outlays, 1949-2003

Data in millions of dollars.

	Defense	Nondefense	Health
1949	762	178	NA
1950	772	282	NA
1951	846	279	NA
1952	1,204	291	NA
1953	1,553	295	45
1954	1,551	297	51
1955	1,550	345	69
1956	1,898	428	81
1957	2,134	577	134
1958	3,459	729	157
1959	5,364	1,020	216
1960	5,937	1,385	277
1961	6,922	1,864	330
1962	7,090	2,747	434
1963	7,144	4,221	551
1964	7,865	5,931	703
1965	7,077	6,763	590
1966	7,097	7,821	738
1967	8,068	7,894	905
1968	8,544	7,628	983
1969	8,314	7,346	1,073
1970	8,021	7,132	1,073
1971	8,108	7,301	1,123
1972	8,837	7,466	1,375
1973	9,139	7,896	1,659
1974	9,406	8,028	1,658
1975	9,715	8,821	1,889
1976	9,819	10,169	2,292
1977	10,874	10,569	1,649
1978	12,077	12,455	2,764
1979	12,129	14,196	3,240
1980	14,643	15,592	3,682
1981	16,937	17,231	4,084
1982	19,809	14,850	4,341

[Continued]

U.S. Government Research and Development Outlays, 1949-2003

[Continued]

	Defense	Nondefense	Health
1983	22,298	13,602	4,461
1984	25,765	15,221	4,560
1985	30,360	16,856	5,131
1986	35,656	16,485	5,574
1987	37,097	16,159	5,811
1988	38,032	18,068	6,872
1989	40,366	20,394	7,546
1990	41,078	22,732	8,253
1991	37,887	24,296	8,528
1992	38,170	26,558	9,656
1993	40,396	27,982	10,374
1994	38,055	28,397	10,628
1995	37,699	30,733	11,260
1996	39,428	29,011	10,498
1997	40,177	30,896	11,458
1998	40,141	32,662	12,718
1999	40,276	33,860	14,333
2000	41,050	32,897	15,878
2001	48,444	37,953	19,709
2002 est.	54,346	42,934	23,431
2003 est.	59,939	47,009	26,201

Source: Executive Office of the President of the United States. *Budget of the United States Government: Fiscal Year 2003.* Historical Tables. "Table 9.8—Composition of Outlays for the Conduct of Research and Development: 1949-2003." Retrieved August 8, 2002 from http:// w3.access.gpo.gov/usbudget/fy2003/. *Note:* NA stands for data not available.

U.S. Government Health R&D Outlays as a Percentage of Total Nondefense Outlays, 1953-2003

	Health Outlays as a % of Nondefense Outlays
1953	15.3
1954	17.2
1955	20.0
1956	18.9
1957	23.2
1958	21.5
1959	21.2
1960	20.0
1961	17.7

[Continued]

U.S. Government Health R&D Outlays as a Percentage of Total Nondefense Outlays, 1953-2003

[Continued]

	Health Out-lays as a % of Nondefense Outlays
1962	15.8
1963	13.1
1964	11.9
1965	8.7
1966	9.4
1967	11.5
1968	12.9
1969	14.6
1970	15.0
1971	15.4
1972	18.4
1973	21.0
1974	20.7
1975	21.4
1976	22.5
1977	15.6
1978	22.2
1979	22.8
1980	23.6
1981	23.7
1982	29.2
1983	32.8
1984	30.1
1985	30.4
1986	33.8
1987	36.1
1988	38.0
1989	37.0
1990	36.3
1991	35.1
1992	36.4
1993	37.1
1994	37.4
1995	36.6
1996	36.2
1997	37.1
1998	38.9
1999	42.3
2000	48.3
2001	51.9

[Continued]

U.S. Government Health R&D Outlays as a Percentage of Total Nondefense Outlays, 1953-2003

[Continued]

	Health Out-lays as a % of Nondefense Outlays
2002 est.	54.6
2003 est.	55.7

Source: Executive Office of the President of the United States. *Budget of the United States Government: Fiscal Year 2003.* Historical Tables. "Table 9.8—Composition of Outlays for the Conduct of Research and Development: 1949-2003." Retrieved August 8, 2002 from http://w3.access.gpo.gov/usbudget/fy2003/.

Top 5 Institutions Funded by the National Institutes of Health (NIH), 1953-2003

Data in thousands of dollars.

	NCI	NIAID	NHLBI	NIGMS	NIDDK
1953	17,887	5,534	12,000	NA	4,335
1954	20,237	5,738	15,168	NA	7,000
1955	21,737	6,180	16,668	NA	8,270
1956	24,978	7,775	18,898	NA	10,840
1957	48,432	13,299	33,396	NA	15,885
1958	56,402	17,400	35,936	NA	20,385
1959	75,268	24,071	45,613	NA	31,215
1960	91,257	34,054	62,237	NA	46,862
1961	111,000	44,000	86,900	NA	61,200
1962	142,836	56,091	132,912	NA	81,831
1963	155,742	66,142	147,398	NA	103,388
1964	144,340	68,723	132,404	104,460	113,679
1965	150,011	69,847	124,824	113,718	113,051
1966	163,768	77,987	141,462	127,188	123,203
1967	175,656	90,670	164,770	145,113	135,687
1968	183,356	94,422	167,954	160,284	143,954
1969	185,150	96,841	166,928	163,514	143,888
1970	181,454	97,342	160,634	148,294	131,761
1971	233,160	102,368	194,925	160,194	137,986
1972	378,794	109,117	232,627	173,474	153,337
1973	492,205	113,414	300,000	183,171	167,316
1974	527,486	111,089	289,550	168,329	153,561
1975	691,666	119,452	324,630	187,400	173,514
1976	761,727	126,852	370,013	187,312	179,516
1977	815,000	141,000	396,661	205,000	219,600
1978	872,388	162,341	447,909	230,796	260,253
1979	937,129	191,328	510,526	277,628	302,767
1980	999,869	215,364	527,488	312,768	341,206

[Continued]

Top 5 Institutions Funded by the National Institutes of Health (NIH), 1953-2003
[Continued]

	NCI	NIAID	NHLBI	NIGMS	NIDDK
1981	989,355	232,077	549,693	333,764	368,191
1982	986,617	235,895	559,637	339,862	368,188
1983	987,642	279,129	624,259	369,813	413,492
1984	1,081,581	319,596	704,939	415,937	464,026
1985	1,183,806	370,965	805,269	482,260	543,576
1986	1,203,369	366,964	822,292	492,630	544,858
1987	1,402,837	545,523	930,001	570,916	511,124
1988	1,469,327	638,800	965,536	632,676	534,733
1989	1,570,349	740,257	1,045,509	682,213	559,494
1990	1,634,332	832,977	1,072,354	681,782	581,477
1991	1,714,784	906,251	1,126,942	760,010	615,272
1992	1,962,587	959,082	1,188,593	816,844	658,925
1993	1,981,351	979,471	1,214,793	832,581	681,342
1994	2,082,267	1,065,583	1,277,880	875,511	716,054
1995	1,913,819	535,199	1,257,374	876,778	726,949
1996	2,254,940	1,168,483	1,354,946	946,896	770,582
1997	2,381,149	1,256,659	1,432,529	998,387	815,607
1998	2,547,314	1,351,655	1,531,061	1,035,947	873,860
1999	2,927,187	1,570,102	1,793,697	1,197,825	994,218
2000	3,314,554	1,778,038	2,029,424	1,354,420	1,141,476
2001	3,754,456	2,041,698	2,298,512	1,535,378	1,302,684
2002	4,209,700	2,542,400	2,581,600	1,726,500	1,470,800
2003 est.	4,724,500	3,999,400	2,798,200	1,881,400	1,609,300

Source: National Institutes of Health. U.S. Department of Health and Human Services. *NIH Almanac.* Publication No. 01-5, December 2001. Retrieved August 8, 2002 from http://www.nih.gov/about/almanac/. 2002 and 2003 estimated appropriations data: John Dimitri Moteff. Resources, Science, and Industry Division. Congressional Research Service. "Federal Research and Development Funding: FY2003," June 7, 2002. Retrieved August 5, 2002 from http://www.cnie.org/nle/crsreports/legislative/leg-44.pdf. *Note:* NA stands for data not available.

Historical Data for the Top 7 Causes of Death in 1999

	Diseases of the Heart	Cancer (Malignant Neoplasms)	Stroke (Cerebrovascular Diseases)	Chronic Lower Respiratory Diseases	Accidents	Diabetes Mellitus	Influenza and Pneumonia
1900	27,427	12,769	21,353	NA	14,429	2,187	40,362
1905	35,252	15,983	23,062	NA	17,701	3,066	36,855
1910	75,429	36,193	45,461	NA	39,971	7,252	73,983
1915	101,429	49,935	58,460	NA	45,504	10,914	90,330
1920	137,374	71,756	80,019	NA	60,225	13,898	178,438
1925	188,554	93,905	91,290	NA	78,230	17,112	124,122
1930	251,153	114,186	104,345	NA	93,505	22,345	120,171
1935	312,333	137,649	109,058	NA	99,064	28,364	132,625
1940	385,191	158,335	119,753	NA	96,885	35,015	92,525
1945	424,328	177,464	129,144	NA	95,918	35,160	68,386

[Continued]

Historical Data for the Top 7 Causes of Death in 1999
[Continued]

	Diseases of the Heart	Cancer (Malignant Neoplasms)	Stroke (Cerebrovascular Diseases)	Chronic Lower Respiratory Diseases	Accidents	Diabetes Mellitus	Influenza and Pneumonia
1950	537,629	210,733	156,751	NA	91,249	NA	NA
1955	585,751	240,681	174,142	NA	93,443	NA	NA
1960	661,712	267,627	193,588	NA	93,806	NA	NA
1965	712,087	297,588	201,057	NA	108,004	NA	NA
1970	735,542	330,730	207,166	NA	114,638	NA	NA
1975	716,215	365,693	194,038	NA	103,030	NA	NA
1980	761,085	416,509	170,225	56,050	105,718	34,851	54,619
1985	771,169	461,563	153,050	74,662	93,457	36,969	67,615
1990	720,058	505,322	144,088	86,679	91,983	47,664	79,513
1995	737,563	538,455	157,991	102,899	93,320	59,254	82,923
1999	725,192	549,838	167,366	124,181	97,860	68,399	63,730
2000 prelim.	709,984	551,833	166,028	123,550	93,592	68,662	67,024

Source: National Center for Health Statistics. Centers for Disease Control. U.S. Department of Health and Human Services. Historical Data Table HIST290A. Retrieved August 9, 2002 from http://www.cdc.gov/nchs/data/statab/. National Center for Health Statistics. Centers for Disease Control. U.S. Department of Health and Human Services. *National Vital Statistics Report*, Vol. 49, No. 11, October 12, 2001. Retrieved August 9, 2002 from http://www.cdc.gov/nchs/data/nvsr49/nvsr49_11.pdf. *Note:* NA stands for not available.

Life Expectancy, 1900-2000

Data for 1900-1925 are for death registration states only. Before 1970, black includes total non-white population.

	Total	White	Black
1900	47.3	47.6	33.0
1905	48.7	49.1	31.3
1910	50.0	50.3	35.6
1915	54.5	55.1	38.9
1920	54.1	54.9	45.3
1925	59.0	60.7	45.7
1930	59.7	61.4	48.1
1935	61.7	62.9	53.1
1940	62.9	64.2	53.1
1945	65.9	66.8	57.7
1950	68.2	69.1	60.8
1955	69.6	70.5	63.7
1960	69.7	70.6	63.6
1965	70.2	71.1	64.3
1970	70.8	71.7	64.1
1975	72.6	73.4	66.8
1980	73.7	74.4	68.1
1985	74.7	75.3	69.3
1990	75.4	76.1	69.1

[Continued]

Life Expectancy, 1900-2000

[Continued]

	Total	White	Black
1995	75.8	76.5	69.6
2000 prelim.	76.9	77.4	71.8

Source: National Center for Health Statistics. Centers for Disease Control. *National Vital Statistics Report*, October 9, 2001 and March 21, 2002. Retrieved August 12, 2002 from http://www.cdc.gov/nchs.

Physical Activity and Obesity Trends, 1990-2001 and Healthy People 2010 Targets

Data in percent.

	Adults 18 Years Old and Over		
	Regular Leisure-time Physical Activity	Healthy Weight	Obese
1990	NA	55.3	11.6
1991	NA	53.8	12.6
1992	NA	52.8	12.6
1993	NA	51.0	13.7
1994	NA	50.2	14.4
1995	NA	48.7	15.8
1996	NA	47.8	16.8
1997	32.1	47.1	16.6
1998	29.9	45.4	18.3
1999	30.4	43.5	19.7
2000	32.0	43.2	20.1
2001	32.1	NA	NA
2010 goal	50.0	60.0	15.0

Source: Centers for Disease Control and Prevention. "Youth Risk Behavior Surveillance—United States 1993, 1995, 1997, 1999, and 2001." *MMWR*, various dates. Centers for Disease Control and Prevention. National Center for Health Statistics. "Data table for figure 7.1 Percent of adults aged 18 years and over who engaged in regular leisure-time physical activity: United States 1997-2001." Retrieved August 27, 2002 from http://www.cdc.gov/nchs/major/nhis/released200207/figures07_1-7_3.htm. Centers for Disease Control and Prevention. Nationwide Trend Data. Behavioral Risk Factor Surveillance System. Retrieved August 27, 2002 from http://apps.nccd.cdc.gov/brfss/Trends/trendchart.asp. *Note:* NA stands for data not available.

Percentage of the U.S. Population Reporting Binge Alcohol and Illicit Drug Use in the Past Month, 12 Years Old and Over, 1979-2000

Illicit drug use numbers for 1999 and 2000 are for those 18 years old and over.

	Binge Alcohol Use	Illicit Drug Use
1979	NA	14.1
1985	20.2	12.1
1991	15.5	6.6
1992	14.5	5.8
1993	14.6	5.9
1994	16.5	6.0
1995	15.8	6.1
1996	15.5	6.1
1997	15.3	6.4
1998	15.6	6.2
1999	20.2	5.8
2000	20.6	5.9

Source: Substance Abuse and Mental Health Services Administration. Office of Applied Studies, *National Household Survey on Drug Abuse, 1998-2000*, various publication dates. Retrieved August 28, 2002 from http://www.samhsa.gov/. U.S. Department of Health and Human Services. *Healthy People 2010: Understanding and Improving Health*, 2nd ed., November 2000. *Note:* NA stands for data not available.

Enrollment and Tuition Costs in Medical School, 1987-2000

	Degrees Conferred	Enrollment	Actual Dollars		Constant 2000 Dollars	
			Undergraduate Tuition & Fees Per Year	Medical School Tuition & Fees Per Year	Undergraduate Tuition & Fees Per Year	Medical School Tuition & Fees Per Year
1987-1988	15,358	NA	3,201	9,034	4,677	13,200
1988-1989	15,460	NA	3,472	9,439	4,873	13,248
1989-1990	15,075	NA	3,800	10,597	5,089	14,193
1990-1991	15,043	NA	4,009	10,571	5,094	13,432
1991-1992	15,243	NA	4,385	11,646	5,347	14,202
1992-1993	15,531	65,575	4,752	12,265	5,626	14,521
1993-1994	15,368	66,175	5,119	13,074	5,884	15,028
1994-1995	15,537	66,788	5,391	13,834	6,040	15,499
1995-1996	15,341	66,942	5,786	14,860	6,324	16,242
1996-1997	15,571	66,926	6,118	15,481	6,492	16,428
1997-1998	15,424	66,896	6,351	16,075	6,627	16,773
1998-1999	15,562	66,539	6,723	17,011	6,905	17,470
1999-2000	15,286	66,377	7,044	17,627	7,044	17,627

Source: National Center for Education Statistics. U.S. Department of Education. *Digest of Education Statistics, 2001.* Association of American Medical Colleges. "Total Enrollment by Gender and Race/Ethnicity, 1992- 2001." Retrieved August 12, 2002 from http://www.aamc.org/data/facts/famg82001.htm. "The Inflation Calculator." Retrieved August 13, 2002 from http://www.westegg.com/inflation. *Notes:* NA stands for data not available.

Top 5 States for Yearly Medical Liability Insurance Premiums, 2001

Data in U.S. dollars.

	Highest Premium	Lowest Premium
Internists		
Florida (Dade/Broward Co.)	50,774	26,896
Michigan (Detroit area)	40,233	18,376
Illinois (Chicago/Cook Co.)	28,153	15,539
Texas (Dallas, Houston, Galveston)	25,563	14,552
New York (NY, Nassau, Suffolk Cos.)	21,648	16,751
General surgeons		
Florida (Dade/Broward Co.)	159,166	63,189
Texas (Dallas, Houston, Galveston)	133,957	34,306
Michigan (Detroit area)	94,195	66,611
Illinois (Chicago/Cook Co.)	70,178	50,021
Ohio (Cleveland)	60,021	33,397
Obstetricians/Gynecologists		
Florida (Dade/Broward Co.)	202,949	143,249
Texas (Dallas, Houston, Galveston)	160,746	69,918
Michigan (Detroit area)	123,890	87,444
New York (NY, Nassau, Suffolk Cos.)	115,429	89,317
Illinois (Chicago/Cook Co.)	110,091	88,926

Source: "Medical liability rates continue their upward swing." *Medical Liability Monitor*, October 1, 2001.

KEYWORD INDEX

This index allows users to locate all subjects, issues, government agencies, companies, programs, associations, schools, educational institutions, books, reports, personal names, and locations cited in *Social Trends & Indicators USA: Health & Sickness*. Page references do not necessarily identify the page on which a topic begins. In the cases where the topic spans two or more pages, page numbers point to where the index term appears-which may be the second or subsequent page on the topic. Cross-references have been added to index citations for ease in locating related topics.

AARP, p. 194
— home ownership, p. 192
— prescription drugs, p. 220
Abandonment of elders, p. 199
Abortion rates, pp. 306-307, 367-368
Abortions, pp. 306, 367
Abstention, pp. 304-305
Acambis, Inc., p. 393
Accidents
— causes of death, pp. 4, 8, 10, 32-33, 401, 430*t*-431*t*
— causes of disability, p. 228
Acquired immunodeficiency syndrome
— *See:* AIDS
ACT UP, p. 287
Active Community Environments
— Centers for Disease Control, p. 405
— obesity, p. 406
Active physicians, p. 522*t*
Activities of daily living, pp. 203-204, 225
Acupuncture, pp. 78, 82, 162-163
AD
— *See:* Alzheimer's Disease
ADD
— *See:* Attention Deficit Disorder
Adderall, p. 129
ADHD
— *See:* Attention Deficit/Hyperactivity Disorder
Administration on Aging, pp. 204, 206
Adrenal gland surgery, p. 151
Adult immunizations, p. 98
Adult Protective Services, p. 199
Adult smoking, pp. 121, 135, 138
Adult substance use, pp. 121-122
Advance directives
— *See:* Living wills
Advanced practice nurses, pp. 351-352

Advanced practice nurses continued:
— *See also:* Nurse practitioners
Advertising expenditures, p. 483*t*
Advertising expenditures on prescription drugs, pp. 177-178
Afghanistan, p. 332
African Americans
— *See also:* Blacks
— causes of death, pp. 8, 31, 33, 35-36, 43
— heart disease, p. 14
— hospital closings, p. 370
— infant mortality, p. 313
— measles, p. 97
— obesity, p. 17
African wastewater treatment, p. 326
Age groups
— abortion rates, p. 307
— depression, p. 64
— disabled population, p. 226
— psychiatric treatment, p. 262
— sexual activity, p. 270
— suicides, p. 261
— workforce participation, p. 296
Agency for Healthcare Research and Quality, p. 361
Aging population, pp. 203-204, 485*t*
— *See also:* Elderly population
— *See also:* Senior citizens
— Behavioral Risk Factor Surveillance System, p. 205
— causes of disability, p. 228
— instrumental activities of daily living, pp. 203-204
— Medicaid, p. 386
— National Institute on Aging, p. 204
— National Long-Term Care Surveys, p. 204
— suicides, p. 204
Aging population diseases
— Alzheimer's Disease, p. 204
— chronic illnesses, p. 204

Aging population diseases continued:
— dementia, p. 204
— depression, p. 204
— diabetes, p. 203
— hearing limitations, p. 203
— heart disease, p. 203
— hypertension, p. 203
— vision limitations, p. 203
Aging population lifestyles
— home ownership, pp. 191-192
— living arrangements, p. 192
— perceptions of quality of life, pp. 205-206
— quality of life, pp. 203, 205
Agoraphobia, pp. 252-253
The AGS Foundation for Health in Aging, p. 344
AIDS, pp. 51-52, 54, 61-62, 95, 287, 444t-445t
— ACT UP, p. 287
— by race/ethnicity, pp. 52, 54
— cases, pp. 286, 506t
— causes of death, pp. 53, 131, 440t-441t
— CD4 lymphocyte, p. 53
— Centers for Disease Control, p. 287
— deaths, p. 286
— disability benefits, p. 243
— funding, pp. 400-402
— heterosexuals, p. 53
— Highly Active Anti-Retroviral Therapy, p. 54
— homosexuals, p. 54
— National Institutes of Health, p. 287
— needle use, p. 54
— treatment, p. 286
— tuberculosis, pp. 3, 333
AIDS Coalition to Unleash Power
— *See:* ACT UP
Air pollution, pp. 316, 518t
— asthma, pp. 319-320
— carbon monoxides, pp. 316, 318
— lead, pp. 316-317
— nitrogen oxides, pp. 316, 318
— particulate matter, pp. 316-317
— sulfur dioxide, pp. 316-317
— volatile organic chemicals, pp. 316, 318
Air Rage: Crisis in the Skies, p. 140
Airplane crashes, p. 4
Alabama, p. 370
Alaska, p. 409
Alaska Natives
— HIV, pp. 288-289
— low birth weight, p. 40
— physicians, p. 337
— smoking, p. 136
Albuterol, p. 167
Alcohol
— adults, p. 121
— causes of death, pp. 125, 131
— cirrhosis, pp. 6, 108
— illicit substance use, teenagers, pp. 117-118
— mouth cancer, p. 161
— North America, p. 64

Alcohol continued:
— substance abuse, pp. 108, 411
Allegra, p. 178
Allergies (respiratory) in children, p. 229
Alliance for Aging Research, p. 341
Allopaths, p. 336
Alternative medicine practitioners, pp. 75, 78-82, 162-163, 450t
Altruistic suicides, p. 35
Alzheimer's Disease, p. 5
— aging population, p. 204
— causes of death, pp. 4, 7-8, 71-72
— death rates, p. 449t
— disability benefits, p. 243
— disabled population, p. 225
— fluoride, p. 328
— hormone replacement therapy, p. 168
— hospice care, p. 376
— mental illnesses, pp. 248-249
American Academy of Dermatology, p. 147
American Academy of Family Physicians, p. 339
American Academy of Pediatrics, pp. 46, 96
American Association of Colleges of Nursing, p. 347
American Association of Retired Persons
— *See:* AARP
American Attitudes Toward Physical Activity & Fitness, p. 93
American Civil Liberties Union
— hospital closings, p. 363
— women's reproductive health care, p. 366
American Dietetic Association, p. 84
American Hospital Association, p. 82
American Housing Survey, p. 191
American Indians
— causes of death, pp. 8, 27
— HIV, pp. 288-289
— low birth weight, p. 40
— smoking, p. 136
American Medical Association, pp. 75, 79, 82
— community health centers, p. 101
— elder abuse, p. 197
— emergency medical technicians, p. 357
— medical malpractice jury awards, p. 416
— physician-assisted suicide, p. 216
American Medical Student Association, p. 395
American Nurses Association, p. 350
American Psychiatric Association, pp. 170, 251
American Society of Health-System Pharmacists, p. 390
American Society of Plastic Surgeons, p. 277
Americans with Disabilities Act, pp. 223, 245
Amino acid dietary supplements, p. 75
Amoxil, pp. 166-167
Amphetamines, p. 125
Amyl nitrite, p. 120
Analgesics, p. 128
Androstenedione, p. 130
Anemia, pp. 39-40
Anesthesiology, p. 341
Angiocardiography, p. 152
Angioplasty, balloon, pp. 25, 151

Anomic suicides, p. 35

Anorexia nervosa, pp. 115, 248-249, 256-257

Anthrax, p. 392

Anti-inflammatory steroid injections, p. 390

Antibiotics, pp. 166, 329-331, 390-392

Antidepressants, pp. 63-64, 165, 169-170, 445t

Anxiety disorders, pp. 247-248, 250, 252, 262

Apples, p. 87

Arsenic, pp. 315, 327

Arteriography, p. 152

Arthritis, pp. 227-228

Asians, p. 52

— causes of death, pp. 8, 27, 43

— HIV, p. 289

— low birth weight, p. 40

— physicians, p. 337

— sexually transmitted diseases, p. 52

Asperger's Disorder, pp. 258-259

Aspirin, p. 130

Assisted living facilities, p. 194

Assisted Living Federation of America, p. 194

Assisted reproductive technology, pp. 291, 299-300

Assisted-suicide movement, p. 213

Association for the Advancement of Retired Persons
— See: AARP

Asthma, pp. 3, 229, 231, 315, 319-320

Atelectasis, p. 10

Atherosclerosis, p. 2

Atkins, Dr., p. 90

Atomic bombs, p. 105

Attention Deficit Disorder, pp. 65-66, 446t
— See also: Attention Deficit/Hyperactivity Disorder

Attention Deficit/Hyperactivity Disorder, pp. 65-66, 165, 171-174, 483t
— See also: Attention Deficit Disorder

Autism, pp. 229, 231, 243, 247-249, 255, 258-259, 500t

AZT, p. 286

Baby Boom generation, p. 187
— breastfeeding, p. 41
— causes of death, pp. 69-70
— fertility rates, pp. 293-294
— heart disease, p. 69
— Medicare, pp. 380, 382
— psychiatric treatment, p. 262
— reproduction, p. 291
— stroke, p. 69
— television programs, p. 222

Bachelor's Degrees, p. 42

Back problems, pp. 227-228

Bacteria, pp. 315, 323

Bacterial food-borne illnesses, pp. 111-112

Bacterial infections
— antibiotics, pp. 329-330
— causes of death, p. 2
— VRE, p. 330

Bacterial sepsis, p. 10

Balanced Budget Act, p. 382

Balanced Budget Refinement Act, p. 383

Balloon angioplasty, pp. 25, 151

Bangladesh, p. 332

Bayer Corporation, pp. 392-393

Behavioral Risk Factor Surveillance System, p. 205

Best Practices for Comprehensive Tobacco Control
  Programs, p. 408

Bethesda Oak (OH), pp. 370-371

Binge eating, pp. 249, 251, 256

Bioterrorism, pp. 88, 392-393

Bipolar disorder, pp. 247-248, 251-252, 254

Birth control, pp. 102, 104, 294

Birth defects, pp. 310-311

Birth rates, pp. 292, 306, 507t, 515t

Birth weight, low
— See: Low birth weight

Births, pp. 292, 306, 507t, 510t-512t

Blacks
— See also: African Americans
— activities of daily living, p. 204
— AIDS, pp. 52, 54
— Attention Deficit Disorder, p. 66
— breastfeeding, p. 41
— cancer, pp. 18, 28
— cancer survival rates, pp. 156-158
— causes of death, pp. 8-9, 24-27, 30, 32, 34, 37-38, 44
— childbirth, p. 23
— cholesterol levels, p. 20
— cocaine use, p. 127
— crib death, pp. 45-46
— death rates, pp. 15, 18
— heart diseases, p. 14
— HIV, pp. 54, 288-289
— illicit substance use, p. 126
— immunizations, p. 99
— life expectancy, pp. 47-48, 403-404
— low birth weight, pp. 308-309
— mammograms, p. 18
— maternal mortality, pp. 22-23
— Medicare, p. 380
— multiple births, p. 39
— obesity, p. 16
— physicians, p. 337
— prostate cancer, p. 28
— sexually transmitted diseases, p. 52
— smoking, pp. 135-137
— suicides, pp. 260, 434t

Bladder cancer, p. 156

Blindness, p. 386
— causes of disability, p. 227
— children, pp. 229, 231

Blood clots, p. 168

BMI, p. 16

Body Mass Index
— See: BMI

Bones, broken, p. 227

Botanicals, p. 75

Botox, p. 279

Botulinum toxoids, p. 392

Bowling Alone, p. 93

Brand-name prescription drugs, pp. 175-176, 179

Breakfast, pp. 139-140

Breast cancer
— causes of death, pp. 3, 12-13, 67-68
— death rates, p. 18
— Fred Hutchinson Cancer Research Center, p. 144
— hormone replacement therapy, p. 168
— survival rates, pp. 19, 158, 426*t*
— work-related stress, p. 144

Breastfeeding, pp. 41-42, 435*t*

Broken bones, p. 227

Bronchial cancer
— causes of death, p. 67
— survival rates, pp. 156, 158

Bronchitis, p. 3

Bulimia nervosa, pp. 115, 248-249, 256-257

Bureau of Education of the Handicapped, p. 232

Bureau of Health Professions, pp. 338, 349, 355

Bureau of Labor Statistics, pp. 141, 146, 351

Bush administration (President George W.)
— Human Genome Project, p. 106
— medical malpractice jury awards, p. 416

Bypass, coronary
— *See:* Coronary bypass

Cadmium, p. 324

California, pp. 190, 349, 369, 409

California Department of Developmental Services, p. 258

California Obesity Prevention Initiative, p. 407

Calorie Control Council, p. 115

Calories, pp. 89-90

CAM
— *See:* Complementary and alternative medicine

Cambodia, p. 332

Camel cigarettes, p. 138

Campylobacter infections, p. 111

Canada, p. 334

Cancer, pp. 3, 5
— *See also:* Malignancies
— *See also:* Melanomas
— *See also:* Neoplasms
— *See also:* Specific cancers
— by race/ethnicity, p. 18
— causes of death, pp. 2-4, 8-9, 67, 69-70, 401
— causes of disability, p. 227
— cigarette smoking, p. 68
— contraceptives (oral), p. 161
— deaths, pp. 446*t*-447*t*
— diet, p. 161
— digestive organs, p. 3
— elderly population, p. 210
— exercise, p. 161
— fluoride, p. 328
— hormone replacement therapy, p. 161
— hospice care, p. 376
— obesity, pp. 160-161
— stress, p. 161

Cancer detection, p. 156

Cancer funding, pp. 400-401

Cancer survival rates, pp. 19, 156-158, 478*t*-479*t*

Cancer treatment, p. 159

Cannabis sativa
— *See:* Marijuana

Carbon monoxide, pp. 316, 318

Cardiac catheterization, p. 151

Cardiovascular disease, p. 310
— *See also:* heart disease
— causes of death, p. 2
— elderly population, p. 210
— hormone replacement therapy, p. 168
— obesity, p. 405
— physicians, by specialization, p. 341
— surgical procedures, p. 150

Caribbean wastewater treatment, p. 326

Carpal Tunnel Syndrome, p. 236

Carrots, p. 87

CAT scans, p. 155

Catheterization, cardiac
— *See:* Cardiac catheterization

Catholic hospitals
— abortions, p. 367
— mergers, p. 366

Catholics for a Free Choice, pp. 366-367

Causes of death
— accidents, pp. 1-2, 4, 6, 8-9, 12, 31-34, 69-70, 401, 421*t*-422*t*, 536*t*-537*t*
— AIDS, pp. 53, 131
— alcohol, pp. 125, 131
— Alzheimer's Disease, pp. 4, 6-8, 71-72
— asthma, p. 3
— atherosclerosis, p. 2
— bacterial diseases, p. 2
— breast cancer, pp. 3, 12-13, 67-68
— bronchial cancer, p. 67
— bronchitis, p. 3
— by race/ethnicity, pp. 8-9
— by sex, pp. 6-7, 43
— cancer, pp. 2-4, 6, 8-9, 67, 69-70, 401
— cardiovascular disease, p. 2
— cerebrovascular disease, pp. 2, 4
— cervical cancer, p. 68
— cigarette smoking, p. 125
— cirrhosis, p. 6
— colorectal cancer, pp. 30, 67-68
— diabetes, pp. 4, 6, 8-9, 12-13, 69-70, 401
— drownings, p. 4
— drug abuse, p. 131
— elderly population, p. 448*t*
— emphysema, pp. 3, 6
— fires, p. 4
— heart attacks, p. 3
— heart disease, pp. 4, 6, 8-9, 12, 24-25, 69, 401
— heart failure, pp. 3, 12
— Hepatitis, p. 6
— HIV, pp. 8, 53
— homicides, pp. 4, 8-9, 131
— hypertension, p. 2
— influenza, pp. 2, 4, 6, 8-9, 69-70, 99, 401
— kidney disease, pp. 6, 8
— leukemia, pp. 3, 67-68

Causes of death continued:
— liver disease, pp. 6, 8-9
— lower respiratory diseases, pp. 3-4, 401
— lung cancer, pp. 3-4, 13, 26-28, 67
— lymphoid cancer, pp. 67-68
— malignancies, pp. 2-4
— melanomas, pp. 475t-476t
— motor vehicle accidents, pp. 4, 32, 131
— murders, pp. 36-38
— neoplasms, pp. 3-4
— nephritis, p. 4
— nephrosis, p. 4
— nephrotic syndrome, p. 4
— ovarian cancer, pp. 67-68
— pancreatic cancer, pp. 67-68
— perinatal conditions, p. 9
— pneumonia, pp. 2, 4, 6, 8-9, 69-70, 99, 401
— prostate cancer, pp. 28-29, 67-68
— pulmonary diseases, pp. 69-70
— renal disease, p. 2
— respiratory diseases, pp. 6, 8-9
— septicemia, pp. 4, 6-8
— shootings, p. 4
— smoking, pp. 4, 131
— stomach cancer, pp. 67-68
— stroke, pp. 2-4, 6, 8-9, 12-13, 69, 401
— suicides, pp. 4, 6, 8, 34-36, 131
— tracheal cancer, p. 67
— tuberculosis, pp. 2-3
— uterine cancer, p. 68
Causes of disability, p. 228
— accidents, p. 228
— aging, p. 228
— arthritis, p. 228
— back problems, pp. 227-228
— blindness, p. 227
— broken bones, p. 227
— cancer, p. 227
— deafness, p. 227
— deformities of limbs, p. 227
— disabled population, p. 227
— emotional problems, p. 227
— head injuries, p. 227
— hearing impairments, p. 227
— heart diseases, p. 227
— high blood pressure, pp. 227-228
— hypertension, p. 227
— injuries, p. 228
— lung diseases, pp. 227-228
— mental problems, p. 227
— paralysis, p. 227
— poor diet, p. 228
— respiratory disease, p. 228
— respiratory diseases, p. 227
— rheumatism, pp. 227-228
— smoking, p. 228
— spine problems, pp. 227-228
— stiffness of limbs, p. 227
— stroke, p. 227

Causes of disability continued:
— vision impairments, p. 227
CD4 lymphocyte
— AIDS, p. 53
— HIV, p. 53
Celebrex, pp. 178, 275
Celera Genomics, p. 105
Center for Budget and Policy Priorities, p. 387
Centers for Disease Control, pp. 16, 36, 43, 49, 66, 95, 97-99
— abortions, p. 306
— active community environments, pp. 405-406
— AIDS, p. 287
— antibiotics, pp. 329, 331
— *Best Practices for Comprehensive Tobacco Control, Programs*, p. 408
— bioterrorism, pp. 392-393
— birth defects, p. 310
— food poisoning, pp. 111-112
— HIV, p. 288
— infant mortality, p. 310
— Kids Walk-to-School Program, p. 406
— maternal mortality, p. 23
— obesity, pp. 109, 161
— sexual activity of teenagers, p. 284
— smoking, p. 135
— tanning, p. 147
Centers for Medicare and Medicaid Services, p. 382
Central nervous system defects, p. 310
Cereals, p. 83
Cerebral palsy, pp. 229, 231
Cerebrovascular disease, pp. 2, 4
— *See also:* Stroke
Certified nurse midwife, p. 351
Certified nurse specialist, p. 351
Certified registered nurse anesthetist, p. 351
Cervical cancer
— causes of death, p. 68
— hormone replacement therapy, p. 168
— survival rates, pp. 19, 158
Cesarean sections, pp. 151, 301
— electronic fetal monitoring, p. 302
— rates, pp. 301-302
Cheese, p. 83
Chemical peels, pp. 277-279
Chemotherapy, pp. 152, 159
Chicken pox, p. 96
Childbirth
— by age of mother, pp. 297-298
— by method of delivery, pp. 513t-514t
— Cesarean sections, pp. 301-302
— oxytocin, p. 23
— surgical procedures, p. 154
Childhood diseases, pp. 55-57, 441t-442t
Childhood Immunization Act, p. 97
Children
— *See also:* Infants
— ADHD, p. 483t
— Attention Deficit Disorder, p. 65
— Attention Deficit/Hyperactivity Disorder, p. 65

Children continued:
— autism, p. 258
— breastfeeding, p. 41
— disabilities, pp. 229-231, 494*t*
— emotional problems, p. 230
— learning disabilities, pp. 65, 229-231
— low birth weight, p. 39
— Medicaid, p. 386
— Ritalin, p. 483*t*
Children Now, p. 221
Chin augmentation, pp. 277-279
Chinese population, pp. 40, 42-43
Chiropractic care
— alternative medicine practitioners, pp. 78-79, 82, 162
Chlamydia, pp. 51-52, 95
Chloroform, p. 120
Cholera, pp. 58-59, 326, 442*t*-444*t*
Cholesterol levels, pp. 14, 20, 83, 426*t*
— elderly population, p. 210
— heart diseases, p. 12
Chromosomal defects, pp. 310, 312
Chronic illnesses, p. 204
Cigarette smoking, pp. 64, 107, 479*t*-481*t*
— adults, pp. 121, 135
— Camels, p. 138
— cancer, p. 68
— causes of death, p. 125
— low birth weight, p. 40
— Lucky Strikes, p. 136
— lung cancer, p. 160
— Philip Morris, p. 136
— prevalence, p. 409
— school-based health centers, p. 104
— teenagers, pp. 117-118
— Virginia Slims, p. 136
Cipro, p. 392
Circulatory system diseases
— causes of death, infants, p. 10
— disability benefits, pp. 235-238
Circulatory systems monitoring, p. 152
Cirrhosis, p. 6
— *See also:* Liver disease
Citizens for Safe Drinking Water, p. 328
Claritin, pp. 167, 178, 276
Clean Air Act, p. 316
Clean Water Act, pp. 315, 321
Clinical laboratory technologists, pp. 359-360
Clinical nurse specialists, p. 351
Clinton administration, p. 106
Club drugs, p. 120
CO
— *See:* Carbon Monoxide
Cocaine, p. 127
— emergency room visits, p. 124
— illicit substance use, adults, p. 121
— illicit substance use, by race/ethnicity, pp. 126-127
— illicit substance use, teenagers, pp. 117-119
— school-based health centers, p. 104
Coffee consumption, p. 139

Collagen injections, pp. 277-279
Colonoscopy, p. 31
Colorectal cancer
— causes of death, pp. 30-31, 67-68
— colonoscopy, p. 31
— death rates, p. 430*t*
— double-contrast barium enema, p. 31
— fecal occult blood test, p. 31
— obesity, p. 405
— screening, p. 211
— sigmoidoscopy, p. 31
— survival rates, pp. 156, 158
Commission on Pornography, p. 280
Common Good Fear of Litigation Study, p. 417
Community health centers, pp. 100-101, 436*t*
Community water systems, pp. 326-327, 519*t*
Commuting, p. 140
Complementary and alternative medicine, pp. 74, 82
Computed tomography, p. 355
Computerized axial tomography, p. 152
— *See also:* CAT scans
Condoms, pp. 104, 304-305
Congenital malformations
— causes of death, pp. 10, 312
— disability benefits, p. 236
Congressional Budget Office, p. 387
Connecticut Hospice, pp. 373-374
Connecticut physicians, p. 338
Continuing care retirement communities, p. 194
Contraceptive practices, pp. 161, 304-305, 514*t*
Cornell University, p. 195
Coronary bypass, p. 25
Cosmetic surgery, pp. 179, 277-279, 504*t*
Cough syrup, p. 130
Council on Graduate Medical Education, p. 344
County mental hospitals, p. 264
Cream products, p. 83
Creatine, p. 130
Crib death, pp. 45-46
— *See also:* SIDS
— *See also:* Sudden Infant Death Syndrome
D.A.R.E., pp. 133-134
Date-rape drug
— *See:* Rohypnol
DAWN
— *See:* Drug Abuse Warning Network
DCBE
— *See:* Double-Contrast Barium Enema
DDT, p. 323
Deaconess-Waltham Hospital (MA), p. 370
Deafness, pp. 227, 229
Death rates, pp. 15, 18, 423*t*-424*t*, 428*t*-433*t*, 449*t*
Death With Dignity Law, p. 216
Deaths, pp. 1-2
Defense research and development, p. 398
Deformities of limbs, p. 227
Dementia, pp. 71, 198, 204, 243
Democratic Republic of the Congo, pp. 332, 334
Dental screenings, pp. 103, 210

Dentists, p. 79

Department of Health and Human Services, p. 63

Depression, pp. 445*t*, 482*t*
— age groups, p. 262
— cases, pp. 247-248
— herbal treatments, pp. 75-76
— medications, p. 64
— prescription drugs, p. 169
— senior citizens, p. 204
— visits to physicians, p. 63

Dermabrasion, pp. 277-278

Detroit Receiving Hospital (MI), p. 265

Diabetes
— Baby Boom generation, pp. 69-70
— cause of death, pp. 4-5, 8-9
— elderly population, p. 203
— funding, p. 401
— obesity, p. 405
— prevalence, pp. 426*t*-427*t*
— women, pp. 12-14, 21

Diagnostic and Statistical Manual of Mental Disorders, p. 115, 170, 236, 251, 254-255

Diagnostic procedures, pp. 152-154, 341

Diaphragms, pp. 304-305

Diet, pp. 108, 115
— Atkins, Dr., p. 90
— cancers, p. 161
— causes of disability, p. 228
— fats, pp. 20-21
— salts, pp. 20-21
— sugars, pp. 20-21
— supplements, p. 75

Diet pills, p. 130

Dietary fat, p. 29

Dietary Guidelines for Americans, p. 114

Dietary Supplement Health and Education Act, p. 76

Digestive system diseases, pp. 3, 150, 155, 236, 310

Digital rectal exam, p. 31

Dining out, p. 109

Diphtheria, pp. 55-56, 94-95

Diphtheria, Tetanus, and Pertussis
— *See:* DTP

Disability benefits, pp. 235-239, 241, 243, 495*t*-496*t*

Disabled population, pp. 224-227, 492*t*-494*t*, 497*t*-498*t*
— Americans with Disabilities Act, p. 223
— children, p. 229
— educational attainment, pp. 240-242
— Medicaid, p. 386
— special education programs, pp. 230-231
— workforce population, pp. 233-234, 244-245

Diseases, p. 49
— *See also:* Infectious diseases

Diseases, infectious
— *See:* infectious diseases

District of Columbia, pp. 338, 369-370

Doctors of Medicine, pp. 210, 336, 340-341
— *See also:* Physicians

Doctors, virtual
— *See:* Telemedicine

Dominican Republic, p. 42

Double-contrast barium enema, p. 31

Down's Syndrome, p. 328

DRE
— *See:* Digital Rectal Exam

Drinking (alcohol), p. 104

Drinking water, pp. 326-328

Drion, Hulb, p. 218

Drownings, p. 4

Drug abuse, pp. 108, 128-131

Drug Abuse Resistance Education
— *See:* D.A.R.E.

Drug Abuse Warning Network, p. 124

Drug Enforcement Agency, p. 130

Drug Information Service, p. 390

Drug Price Competition and Patent Term Restoration Act, p. 176

Drug Product Shortages Bulletin, p. 389

Drug-resistant bacteria, p. 329

Drug shortages, pp. 389-391, 530*t*

Drug use, pp. 468*t*-470*t*

DrugFreeTeenagers.com, p. 133

DTP, p. 96

Duke University
— physician assistants, p. 345
— studies of St. John's Wort and depression, p. 81

Duke University Medical Center, p. 237

Durex [company], pp. 271, 273

Durkheim, Emile, p. 35

Dying patients, p. 212

Dyslexia, p. 243

Ear infections, p. 229

Ear surgery, pp. 150, 277-279

Earnings, pp. 244-245, 498*t*

Eastern equine encephalitis, p. 392

Eating habits, pp. 466*t*-467*t*
— disease prevention, p. 90
— eating disorders, pp. 256-257
— mental health, p. 247
— stress, pp. 139-140
— U.S. Surgeon General's recommendations, p. 83
— weight, pp. 89, 115-116

Ebola virus, pp. 62, 95

Echinacea, p. 75

Ecstasy
— emergency room visits, p. 124
— illicit substance use, teenagers, pp. 119-120

Ectopic pregnancy, p. 23

Education for All Handicapped Children Act, p. 232

Education of the Handicapped Act, p. 232

Educational attainment
— breastfeeding mothers, p. 42
— disabled population, p. 497*t*
— exercise habits, p. 92
— smoking, p. 136

Eggs, p. 83

Egoistic suicides, p. 35

Elder abuse, pp. 197-200, 486*t*-487*t*
— Adult Protective Services, p. 199

Elder abuse continued:
— American Medical Association, p. 197
— nursing homes, pp. 201-202
— perpetrator, p. 200
Elderly population, pp. 189, 196
— cancer, p. 210
— cardiovascular diseases, p. 210
— causes of death, p. 448*t*
— cholesterol, p. 210
— colorectal cancer screening, p. 211
— dental screenings, p. 210
— doctor visits, p. 210
— geographic distribution, pp. 189-190
— health care, p. 379
— immunizations, p. 463*t*
— living wills, p. 211
— mammograms, p. 210
— Medicare benefits, p. 207
— obesity, p. 210
— overweight, p. 210
— rental households, p. 195
— smoking, p. 210
Elders, Jocelyn, p. 107
Electronic fetal monitoring, p. 302
Eli Lilly & Co., p. 170
Emergency medical technicians, pp. 357-358
Emergency medicine physicians, p. 341
Emergency room visits, pp. 124-125, 130, 471*t*
Emotional abuse of elderly, p. 199
Emotional problems, pp. 227, 229-231, 264
Emphysema, pp. 3, 5-6
Employment
— disabled workers, pp. 233-234, 244-245, 498*t*
— health services, pp. 394, 531*t*
— stress, pp. 141-143
EMTs
— *See:* Emergency medical technicians
End-stage renal disease, p. 380
Endocrine system
— disability benefits, p. 236
— surgical procedures, pp. 150-151
Endometrial cancer
— *See:* Uterine cancer
Endoscopy, p. 151
Endotracheal tube insertion, p. 152
Enrollment
— Medicaid, p. 386
— Medicare, pp. 490*t*-491*t*, 526*t*-527*t*
Environment, p. 315
Environmental Protection Agency, pp. 322, 327
Epidemic-related influenza deaths, p. 463*t*
Epidemic-related pneumonia deaths, p. 463*t*
Epilepsy, pp. 229, 231
Episiotomy, p. 151
Erectile dysfunction treatments, pp. 275-276
Escherichia coli infections, p. 111
Esophageal cancer
— obesity, p. 161
— survival rates, p. 156

Estuaries, pp. 323, 325
Ether, p. 120
Ethical and Religious Directives for Catholic Health
Education, p. 367
Ethiopia, p. 332
Ethnicity
— *See:* Race/ethnicity
Euro RSCG [company], pp. 271, 273
Europe's wastewater treatment, p. 326
Euthanasia, pp. 214-215, 218
— *See also:* Physician-assisted suicide
Exercise habits, p. 92
— cancer, p. 161
— obesity, pp. 20-21
Expenditures
— fast food, p. 109
— health care, p. 484*t*
— Medicare, pp. 490*t*-491*t*, 528*t*
— prescription drugs, p. 484*t*
— psychotherapy, p. 263
— restaurant, p. 109
Eyelid surgery, pp. 277-279
Eyes, p. 150
Family Violence Prevention and Services Act of 1992, p. 199
Farmers' markets, p. 87
Farmlands, p. 458*t*
Fast-food expenditures, pp. 109-110
Fast Food Nation, pp. 110, 112
Fat injections, p. 279
Fatalistic suicides, p. 35
Fats, pp. 20-21, 83
Fecal occult blood test, p. 31
Federal grants, p. 100
Females, pp. 137, 150, 154, 304
— *See also:* Women
Fertility rates, pp. 292-295, 507*t*-510*t*
Fibril injections, pp. 277-278
Filipinos, p. 40
Financial exploitation of elderly, p. 199
Fires, p. 4
Florida, pp. 190, 369, 409, 415, 417
Florida State Department of Health, p. 392
Flour, p. 83
Fluid cream products, p. 83
Fluoride, pp. 315, 327-328
FOBT
— *See:* Fecal occult blood test
Food and Drug Administration
— antibiotics, p. 330
— drug shortages, pp. 389-391
— prescription drug prices, p. 176
Food Guide Pyramid, p. 83
Food poisoning, pp. 111-112
FoodNet, p. 111
Foods
— bioterrorism, p. 88
— consumption, pp. 451*t*-457*t*
— nutrient levels, pp. 459*t*-461*t*
— pesticide use, pp. 87-88

Foods continued:
— phytochemicals, p. 90
Foods, organic
— *See:* organic foods
Forehead lifts, p. 279
Foreign-born physicians, p. 337
Foreign-educated physicians
— *See:* IMGs
Forensic pathology physicians, p. 341
France, pp. 42, 334
Fraud, p. 376
Fred Hutchinson Cancer Research Center, p. 144
Fruits, p. 83
GAD
— *See:* Generalized Anxiety Disorder
Gallbladder cancer, p. 161
Garlic, p. 75
Gasoline, p. 120
Gastroesophageal Reflux Disease, p. 167
— *See also:* GERD
Gays, p. 54
— *See also:* Homosexuals
— *See also:* Lesbians
General surgeons medical malpractice premiums, p. 415
Generalized Anxiety Disorder, p. 252
Generic prescription drug prices, p. 175
Genetic engineering, pp. 105-106
Genital cancer, p. 3
Genital herpes, p. 95
Genital surgery, pp. 150-151
Genitourinary system diseases, pp. 236, 310
Genome research centers, p. 105
Geographic distribution of elderly population, pp. 189-190
Geographic distribution of population, p. 189
Geographic maldistribution of physicians, p. 344
GERD, p. 167
— *See also:* Gastroesophageal Reflux Disease
German measles, p. 57
— *See also:* Rubella
Germany, p. 334
Ginkgo Biloba, p. 75
— *See also:* Ginkgu Biloba
Ginkgu Biloba, pp. 162-163
— *See also:* Ginkgo Biloba
Ginseng, p. 75
Glandular surgery, p. 151
Global Tuberculosis Control: WHO Report 2002, p. 332
Glucophage, p. 167
Gonad surgery, p. 151
Gonorrhea, pp. 51-52
Government funding
— defense research and development, pp. 398, 532*t*-535*t*
— health research and development, pp. 397-399, 532*t*-535*t*
— Human Genome Project, pp. 464*t*-465*t*
— National Institutes of Health, pp. 400-401, 535*t*-536*t*
— nondefense research and development, pp. 398-399, 532*t*-534*t*
Grants for community health centers, p. 100
Grapes, p. 87
Great Britain, p. 42

Great Lakes water pollution, p. 321
Grocery expenditures, pp. 85-86, 457*t*-458*t*
Gynecologists, pp. 341, 415
Hair transplantation for men, pp. 277-278
Hanta virus, pp. 62, 95
Happy Meals, p. 110
Hard Pack, p. 138
Harvard Mental Health Letter, p. 135
Harvard School of Public Health Department of Nutrition, p. 109
Harvard University, p. 75
Hashish
— emergency room visits, p. 124
— illicit substance use, adults, p. 121
— illicit substance use, teenagers, pp. 117-118
Hay fever in children, p. 229
Hayflick Limit, p. 48
Hazelden Foundation, p. 123
HBV immunizations, p. 97
HDL, p. 20
— *See also:* High-Density Lipoprotein
Head injuries, pp. 227, 243
Heaemophilus influenzae type b
— *See:* Hib
Health assessments, pp. 488*t*-489*t*
Health care, pp. 379, 484*t*
Health Care Financing Administration, p. 374
Health Maintenance Organizations
— *See:* HMOs
Health Professional Shortage Areas, p. 338
Health research and development, pp. 397-399, 532*t*-535*t*
Health services administrative costs, pp. 394-395
Health services employment, pp. 394, 531*t*
Health violations in community water systems, p. 326
Healthy Eating Index, p. 84
Healthy People, p. 403
Healthy People 2000, pp. 73, 303
Healthy People 2010, pp. 303, 404, 408
Healthy People Consortium, p. 403
Hearing impairments, pp. 203, 227, 229, 487*t*-488*t*
Hearing screenings in school-based health centers, p. 103
Heart attacks, pp. 3, 275-276
Heart disease, pp. 5, 14
— *See also:* Cardiovascular disease
— aging population, p. 203
— Baby Boom generation, p. 69
— balloon angioplasty, p. 25
— causes of death, pp. 4, 6, 8-9, 12, 24-25, 69, 401
— causes of disability, p. 227
— cholesterol, p. 12
— coronary bypass, p. 25
— fluoride, p. 328
— funding, pp. 400-401
— MIDCAB, p. 25
— smoking, p. 136
— stents, p. 25
— surgical procedures, p. 155
Heart failure
— causes of death, pp. 3, 12

Hemic system surgical procedures, pp. 150-151
Hemorrhages in maternal mortality, p. 23
Hepatitis, pp. 6, 61, 96, 148, 444*t*-445*t*, 476*t*
Herbal therapies, pp. 75, 77, 82, 450*t*
Herbs, medicinal
— *See:* medicinal herbs
Heroin in emergency room visits, pp. 124-125
Herpes, genital
— *See:* Genital herpes
Heterosexuals, pp. 53, 289
Hib vaccinations for children, pp. 96-97
High blood pressure
— *See also:* Hypertension
— causes of disability, pp. 227-228
— obesity, p. 405
High-Density Lipoprotein, p. 21
— *See also:* HDL
Highly Active Anti-Retroviral Therapy
— AIDS, p. 54
— HIV, p. 54
Hispanics
— Attention Deficit Disorder, p. 66
— breastfeeding, p. 41
— causes of death, pp. 8-9
— causes of infant mortality, pp. 44, 313
— death rates, p. 15
— HIV, p. 289
— immunizations, p. 99
— low birth weight, p. 309
— measles, p. 97
— Medicare, p. 380
— physicians, p. 337
— smoking, p. 137
Historical diseases, pp. 442*t*-443*t*
HIV, pp. 51, 54, 286, 289-290
— by race/ethnicity, pp. 54, 288-290
— causes of death, pp. 8, 53
— CD4 lymphocyte, p. 53
— Centers for Disease Control, p. 288
— gays, p. 54
— heterosexuals, pp. 53, 289
— Highly Active Anti-Retroviral Therapy, p. 54
— homosexuals, p. 53
— lesbians, p. 54
— men, pp. 54, 288
— needle use, p. 54
— number of cases, p. 506*t*
— tuberculosis, pp. 3, 333
HMOs, pp. 345, 382-383
Holland, p. 215
Holy Anorexia, p. 115
Home health agencies, pp. 207-209, 393
Home ownership
— AARP, p. 192
— aging population, pp. 191-192
— rates, p. 485*t*
Homeopathy
— alternative medicine practitioners, pp. 78, 80, 82

Homicides
— causes of death, pp. 4, 8-9, 131
— death rates, p. 432*t*
Homosexuals
— *See also:* Gays
— *See also:* Lesbians
— AIDS, p. 287
— HIV, p. 53
Honest Cannabis Information Foundation, p. 134
Hormone replacement therapy, pp. 161, 168
Hospice care, pp. 213, 363, 373, 375
— Alzheimer's Disease, p. 376
— cancer, p. 376
— fraud, p. 376
— Health Care Financing Administration, p. 374
— Hospice Home Care movement, p. 373
— Kubler-Ross, Elisabeth, pp. 212, 374
— Medicare, pp. 214, 374, 376-378
— pain control, pp. 213-214
— patients, pp. 525*t*-526*t*
— Saunders, Dr. Cicely, pp. 376, 378
— United Government Services, pp. 377-378
Hospitals, pp. 212, 264, 364-365, 525*t*
— *See also:* Catholic hospitals
— admissions, pp. 369-370
— closings, pp. 363, 367, 369-372
— expenditures, p. 395
— medical procedures, pp. 477*t*-478*t*
— mergers, pp. 366, 525*t*
Hot Network, p. 280
House Select Committee on Aging, p. 198
Household income and infant mortality, p. 313
HRT
— *See:* Hormone replacement therapy
Human Genome Project, pp. 105-106, 464*t*-465*t*
Human immunodeficiency virus
— *See:* HIV
Hungary, p. 334
Hydrocodone/APAP, p. 167
Hypertension, p. 14
— *See also:* High blood pressure
— aging population, p. 203
— causes of death, p. 2
— causes of disability, p. 227
— low birth weight, pp. 11, 40
— maternal mortality, p. 23
Hyperthyroidism and Synthroid, p. 168
Hypothalamus gland surgery, p. 151
Idaho, p. 349
IHD
— *See:* Ischemic heart disease
Illicit substance use, pp. 126, 411-412, 539*t*
— alcohol, p. 118
— cigarettes, pp. 117-118
— cocaine, pp. 117-119, 126
— Ecstasy, pp. 119-120
— emergency room visits, p. 124
— hashish, pp. 117-118
— inhalants, pp. 119-120

Illicit substance use continued:
— LSD, p. 119
— marijuana, pp. 117-118, 126
— Rohypnol, p. 120
— sedatives, p. 119
— stimulants, p. 119
— teenagers, pp. 117, 120, 134
— tranquilizers, p. 119
Illinois, pp. 190, 369, 415, 417
IMGs, pp. 342-343
Immunizations, pp. 94, 96, 99, 103, 462*t*
— adults, p. 98
— chicken pox, p. 96
— elderly population, p. 463*t*
— HBV, p. 97
— Hepatitis, p. 96
Income
— exercise habits, p. 92
— grocery expenditures, p. 86
— Medicare, p. 528*t*
India, p. 42
Indiana, p. 409
Indians, p. 52
Individuals with Disabilities Education Act, pp. 232, 258
Indonesia, p. 332
Infant mortality
— birth defects, pp. 310-311
— causes, pp. 10-11, 423*t*, 436*t*, 508*t*-509*t*, 516*t*-517*t*
— rates, pp. 43, 312-313
— selected years, pp. 44-45
Infants, pp. 10-11
— breastfeeding, p. 41
Infectious diseases, pp. 94, 236, 462*t*
— *See also:* Diseases
Infertility, p. 299
Influenza, p. 5
— causes of death, pp. 2, 4, 8-9, 69-70, 99, 401
— epidemic of 1918, pp. 2, 94
— immunizations, pp. 96, 98-99
Inhalants, pp. 119-120
Injuries, pp. 228, 235, 238
Inpatient hospitals, pp. 207-209
Instrumental activities of daily living, pp. 203-204
Insurance companies, p. 416
Integrative medicine, p. 82
Integumentary system, pp. 150-151
International Classification of Diseases, p. 22
International Task Force on Euthanasia and Assisted Suicide, p. 217
Internists' medical malpractice premiums, p. 415
Intrauterine Devices
— *See:* IUDs
Ireland, p. 42
Iron lung, p. 95
Irradiation, p. 112
Ischemic heart disease, pp. 4, 8
— death rates, pp. 424*t*, 428*t*
Islands of Langerhans surgery, p. 151
Italy, p. 334

IUDs, pp. 304-305
Jails, pp. 265-266
Japanese, p. 43
Joe Camel, p. 138
Journal of the American Medical Association, p. 81
— hormone replacement therapy, p. 168
— obesity, p. 405
— sexuality, pp. 273-274
Kanner, Leo, p. 259
Kennedy School of Government, p. 75
Kentucky, p. 409
Kenya, p. 332
Kerr-Mills Act, p. 384
Kevorkian, Dr. Jack, p. 216
Kidney diseases
— *See also:* Nephritis
— *See also:* Nephrosis
— *See also:* Nephrotic syndrome
— cancer, p. 161
— causes of death, p. 8
— low birth weight, p. 40
Kids Walk-to-School Program, p. 406
Kubler-Ross, Elisabeth, pp. 212, 374
Laboratory technologists
— *See:* Clinical laboratory technologists
Lakes and water pollution, pp. 323, 325
Lanoxin, p. 167
Laser skin resurfacing, pp. 277-279
Latin America's wastewater treatment, p. 326
LDL
— *See:* Low-Density Lipoprotein
Lead, pp. 316-317, 324
Learning disabilities in children, pp. 65, 229-231, 446*t*
Legionnaire's Disease, pp. 61, 95, 444*t*-445*t*
Leprosy, pp. 58, 60, 442*t*-444*t*
Lesbians
— *See also:* Gays
— *See also:* Homosexuals
— AIDS, p. 54
— HIV, p. 54
Lettuce, p. 87
Leukemia, p. 3
— causes of death, pp. 3, 67-68
— survival rates, p. 156
Licensed practical nurses, pp. 353-354
Life expectancy, pp. 47-48
— Baby Boom generation, p. 187
— Hayflick Limit, p. 48
— *Healthy People 2010*, pp. 404, 437*t*-438*t*, 537*t*-538*t*
— Healthy People Consortium, p. 403
Lipitor, pp. 167, 176, 276
Listening to Prozac, p. 64
Listeria infections, p. 111
Lithium, pp. 64, 251
Liver disease
— *See also:* Cirrhosis
— cancer, p. 161
— causes of death, pp. 8-9
Livestock, p. 458*t*

Living arrangements, p. 192
Living to 100, p. 73
Living wills, pp. 211, 215
La Leche League, pp. 41-42
Looking Fit Tanning Book 2002-2003, p. 147
Louisiana, pp. 370, 409
Low birth weight, pp. 39-40, 308-310, 435*t*, 515*t*-516*t*
— causes of death, pp. 10, 312
— hypertension, pp. 11, 40
— kidney diseases, p. 40
— sexually transmitted diseases, pp. 40, 52
— singletons, p. 39
— smoking, p. 40
Low-Density Lipoprotein, p. 20
Low-fat milk, p. 83
Lower respiratory diseases, pp. 3-5, 401
LPNs
— *See:* Licensed practical nurses
LSD, p. 119
Lucky Strike cigarettes, p. 136
Lung cancer, p. 160
— cause of death, pp. 3-4, 13, 26-28, 67
— death rates, p. 428*t*
— smoking, pp. 3-4, 26, 136, 160
— survival rates, pp. 19, 156, 158
Lung diseases, p. 228
— causes of disability, p. 227
Lyme Disease, pp. 61-62, 95, 444*t*-445*t*
Lymphatic system diseases, pp. 67-68, 150-151, 156
Making Weight, p. 116
Malaria, pp. 58-59, 442*t*-444*t*
Males, pp. 137, 150-151
— *See also:* Men
Malignancies, pp. 2-4
— *See also:* Cancer
— *See also:* Neoplasms
Mammograms, pp. 18, 156, 210, 425*t*
Managed care, pp. 207-209, 344
Manhattan Project, p. 105
Manic depression
— *See:* Bipolar disorder
Marijuana, pp. 126, 133
— adults, p. 121
— emergency room visits, p. 124
— teenagers, pp. 117-118, 132
Marijuana use, p. 104
Married population and sexual activity, pp. 269-270
Maryland, p. 338
Massachusetts, pp. 338, 370, 409
Massage therapy, pp. 78-79, 162
Material exploitation of elderly population, p. 199
Maternal age at conception, p. 40
Maternal complications of pregnancy, p. 10
Maternal mortality, pp. 22-23, 427*t*
McDonald's restaurants, p. 110
Measles, pp. 55, 94-95, 97
Measles, German
— *See:* German measles

Measles, Mumps, and Rubella vaccine
— *See:* MMR
Meats, p. 83
Media images, p. 221
Medicaid, pp. 220, 363, 384-388, 529*t*-530*t*
Medical ethics, p. 188
Medical hospitals, pp. 364-365
Medical Injury Compensation Reform Act (CA), p. 418
Medical liability reform legislation, p. 418
Medical malpractice jury awards, pp. 416-417
Medical malpractice litigation, p. 303
Medical malpractice premiums, pp. 415, 417, 540*t*
Medical procedures, pp. 477*t*-478*t*
Medical professionals, pp. 335, 520*t*-522*t*
Medical review boards, p. 418
Medical school graduates, p. 414
Medical schools, pp. 82, 413, 539*t*
Medical technologists
— *See:* Clinical laboratory technologists
Medicare, pp. 219, 341, 363, 374, 376-379
— Baby Boom generation, pp. 380, 382
— benefits, pp. 207-209, 214, 489*t*
— expenditures, pp. 380-382, 490*t*-491*t*, 526*t*-528*t*
— income, p. 381
Medicare+Choice program, pp. 382-383
Medications and school-based health centers, p. 102
Medicinal herbs, p. 75
Medicine, alternative
— *See:* Alternative medicine
Meditation, pp. 162-163
Melanomas, pp. 147-148, 476*t*
— *See also:* Cancer
— *See also:* Skin cancer
Men
— *See also:* Males
— activities of daily living, p. 204
— anxiety disorders, p. 247
— bipolar disorder, p. 247
— cancer survival rates, p. 158
— causes of death, pp. 6-7, 12, 24-26, 30, 32, 34, 37-38, 53, 422*t*
— cholesterol levels, p. 20
— cosmetic surgery, pp. 277-278, 504*t*
— diabetes, p. 13
— disabled, pp. 225, 236
— eating disorders, p. 116
— HIV, pp. 54, 288
— life expectancy, p. 47
— living arrangements, p. 192
— lung cancer, p. 160
— Medicare, p. 380
— melanomas, p. 147
— obesity, p. 16
— overweight, p. 17
— prostate cancer, p. 28
— psychiatric treatment, p. 262
— schizophrenia, p. 249
— sexual activity, pp. 269-270
— smoking, pp. 135-136
— suicide rates, pp. 432*t*, 434*t*

Men continued:
— suicides, pp. 260, 433t
Mental health, pp. 103, 107, 247
Mental health facilities, pp. 264-265, 501t
Mental Health Systems Act, p. 251
Mental hospitals (county), p. 264
Mental hospitals (state), p. 264
Mental illnesses, p. 499t
— children, pp. 229, 231
— disabilities, pp. 227, 235, 248-251, 265-266
— educational attainment, p. 241
— workforce disabilities, pp. 238-239
Mental retardation, pp. 229-231, 243
Mental Retardation Facilities and Community Mental Health Centers Construction Act, p. 265
Mercury, p. 324
MergerWatch, p. 366
Metals, pp. 323-325
Methamphetamines, pp. 124-125, 129
Mexico, p. 334
Michigan, pp. 190, 216, 415-417
Michigan Department of Community Health, p. 407
MIDCAB
— *See:* Minimally Invasive Direct Coronary Artery Bypass
Midwestern United States, p. 189
Milk, low-fat, p. 83
Milk, whole, p. 83
Minimally Invasive Direct Coronary Artery Bypass, p. 25
Mississippi, pp. 369-370, 418
Missouri, pp. 387, 409
MMR, pp. 57, 96
Monitoring the Future, pp. 118-119, 132, 137
Monoamine oxidase inhibitors, p. 64
Montana, pp. 369, 387
Mood disorders, pp. 251-252, 499t
Morphine, p. 124
Mortality, maternal
— *See:* maternal mortality
Mother-father families, p. 66
Mother-only families, p. 66
Motor vehicle accidents, pp. 4, 32, 131
Mouth cancer, pp. 150, 161
Mozambique, p. 332
Multinational Monitor, p. 138
Multiple births, pp. 39, 299-300, 512t-513t
Multiple sclerosis, p. 225
Mumps, pp. 55-56, 94-95
Murders, pp. 36-38
Musculoskeletal system diseases, pp. 150, 155, 235, 238, 310
A Nation At Risk, p. 174
National Academy of Science
— drinking water, p. 327
— recommendations about salt in diet, p. 21
National Alliance for the Mentally Ill, p. 251
National Ambulatory Medical Care Survey, p. 63
National Assembly on School-Based Health Care, p. 102
National Association of Anorexia Nervosa and Associated Disorders, p. 257
National Cancer Institute, pp. 31, 400-401

National Center for Chronic Disease Prevention & Health Promotion, p. 90
National Center for Complementary and Alternative Medicine, pp. 76, 80-81, 162-163
— budget appropriations, p. 451t
— clinical trials, p. 481t
National Cholesterol Education Program, p. 167
National Conference of Catholic Bishops, p. 367
National Elder Abuse Incidence Study, pp. 199-200
National Governors Association, p. 387
National Health and Nutrition Examination Survey, p. 16
National Heart, Lung, and Blood Institute, pp. 400-401
National Hospital Discharge Survey, p. 152
National Institute for Occupational Safety and Health, p. 141-142
National Institute of Allergies and Infectious Diseases, p. 332
— bioterrorism, p. 393
— funding, National Institutes of Health, pp. 400-402
National Institute of Child Health and Human Development, p. 45
National Institute of Diabetes & Digestive & Kidney Diseases
— *See:* NIDDK
National Institute of General Medical Sciences, pp. 400-401
National Institute of Mental Health, pp. 116, 172, 248, 255-256
National Institute on Aging, pp. 148, 204
National Institute on Drug Abuse, p. 128
National Institutes of Health, pp. 3, 28, 76, 143, 163, 167
— funding, pp. 400-402, 535t-536t
— Human Genome Project, p. 105
National Long-Term Care Surveys, p. 204
National Pharmaceutical Stockpike, p. 392
National Public Radio, p. 75
National Registry of Emergency Medical Technicians, p. 357
National School Lunch Program, pp. 113-114, 468t
National Sleep Foundation, pp. 140, 143
National Vaccine Injury Compensation Program, p. 97
National Water Quality Inventory, p. 322
Native Americans, p. 337
Naturopathy, pp. 78, 80
NCCAM
— *See:* National Center for Complementary and Alternative
Nebraska, p. 369
Needle use
— AIDS, p. 54
— exchange programs, community health centers, p. 101
— HIV, p. 54
Neglect of elderly, p. 199
Neonatal deaths, pp. 10, 312
Neoplasms
— *See also:* Cancer
— *See also:* Malignancies
— causes of death, pp. 3-4
— disability benefits, pp. 235-236, 238
Nephritis, pp. 4-5
— *See also:* Kidney diseases
Nephrosis, pp. 4-5
— *See also:* Kidney diseases
Nephrotic syndrome, pp. 4-5
— *See also:* Kidney diseases

Nervous disorders, p. 262
Nervous system diseases
— disability benefits, pp. 235-236, 238
— surgical procedures, p. 150
Nevada, pp. 349, 409, 417-418
New Jersey, pp. 190, 338, 418
New York, pp. 190, 338, 369, 415, 417
Newton-Wellesley Hospital (MA), p. 372
NIDDK, pp. 400-401
Nigeria, pp. 42, 332
Nitrogen oxides
— air pollution, pp. 316, 318
— inhalants, p. 120
Nondefense research and development, pp. 398-399, 532t-535t
Nonsurgical contraceptives, pp. 304-305
North America wastewater treatment, p. 326
North Dakota, pp. 369, 409
Northeast United States, p. 189
Norvasc, p. 167
Nose reshaping, pp. 150, 277-279
NOX
— See: Nitrogen Oxides
Nurse practitioners, p. 351
— See also: Advanced practice nurses
Nurse Reinvestment Act, p. 350
Nurses, licensed practical
— See: Licensed practical nurses
Nurses, registered
— See: Registered nurses
Nursing facilities, pp. 207-209
Nursing Facility Sourcebook, p. 194
Nursing homes
— elder abuse, pp. 201-202
— licensed practical nurses, p. 354
— Medicare benefits, p. 208
— residency, pp. 193-194, 486t
— staff, p. 487t
Nursing school graduates, pp. 347, 524t
Nutrients, pp. 323-325
Obesity, pp. 16-17, 21, 90, 107, 109, 425t
— Centers for Disease Control, pp. 109, 161
— diseases, pp. 160-161, 405
— elderly population, p. 210
— Journal of the American Medical Association, p. 405
— lifestyle, pp. 20-21, 109, 115, 538t
— prevention programs, p. 407
Obsessive-compulsive disorder, pp. 247, 250, 252-253
Obstetricians, pp. 150, 303, 341, 415
Office of Alternative Medicine, p. 81
Ohio, pp. 190, 367, 409, 417
Oils, p. 83
On Death and Dying, pp. 212, 374
Ophthalmologists, p. 341
Oral cavity cancers, p. 156
Oral contraceptives, p. 161
Oregon, p. 216
Organic foods, pp. 87-88, 458t
Oriental medicine (traditional), pp. 78, 80
Orthopedic surgeons, p. 341

Osteopaths, pp. 78-79, 336
Osteoporosis
— fluoride, p. 328
— hormone replacement therapy, p. 168
Ovarian cancer
— causes of death, pp. 67-68
— survival rates, pp. 19, 158
Ovarian surgeries, p. 151
Over-the-counter medications, pp. 128, 474t
Overweight, pp. 90, 107
— by sex, p. 17
— elderly population, p. 210
Oxycodone, p. 130
Oxycontin, pp. 129-130
Oxygen-depleting substances, pp. 323-325
Oxytocin, p. 23
Pacific Islanders
— causes of death, pp. 8, 43
— HIV, p. 289
— low birth weight, p. 40
Pain control, pp. 213-214
Palliative care
— See: Hospice care
Palm Beach County Health Department (FL), p. 392
Pancreas surgeries, p. 151
Pancreatic cancer
— causes of death, pp. 67-68
— obesity, p. 161
— survival rates, pp. 156, 158
Panic disorders, pp. 252-253
Pap smears, p. 156
Paraguay, p. 42
Paralysis
— causes of disability, p. 227
— children, p. 229
Paramedics
— See: Emergency medical technicians
Parathyroid gland surgeries, p. 151
Parkinson's Disease, pp. 225, 243
Particulate matter, pp. 316-317
Partnership for A Drug-Free America, p. 132
Pathogens, pp. 323, 325, 467t
Pathologists, p. 341
Pathologists (forensic), p. 341
Patients' Rights Movement, p. 215
Paxil, p. 76
Pb
— See: Lead
PCBs, p. 323
Pennsylvania, pp. 190, 338, 370
Pennsylvania Medical Society, p. 416
Percodan, p. 129
Perinatal conditions, p. 9
Perls, Dr. Thomas, p. 73
Pertussis, pp. 55-56, 94-95
— See also: Whooping Cough
Pervasive Developmental Disorder, p. 255
Pesticide use, pp. 87-88

Pfizer
— prescription drugs, p. 167
— Viagra, p. 276
Pharmaceutical Research and Manufacturers of America
— *See:* PhRMA
Pharmacy Today, p. 140
Pharynx cancer, p. 156
Pharynx surgeries, pp. 150-151
Philip Morris cigarettes, p. 136
Philippines, p. 332
Phobias, pp. 252-253
PhRMA, pp. 175, 179
Physical abuse of elderly, p. 199
Physical activity, pp. 405, 461*t*-462*t*, 538*t*
Physical Activity and Health, p. 93
Physical deformities, p. 229
Physical education classes, p. 104
Physician assistants, p. 345
Physician-assisted suicide, pp. 215-216
— *See also:* Euthanasia
Physicians, pp. 337-338, 341, 344, 394, 520*t*, 522*t*
— *See also:* Doctors of Medicine
— geographic maldistribution, p. 344
— place of medical education, pp. 342, 523*t*
— specialization, p. 341
Physicians for Reproductive Choice and Health, p. 366
Phytochemicals, p. 90
The Pill, pp. 304-305
Pineal gland surgeries, p. 151
Pituitary gland surgeries, p. 151
Placebos, p. 76
Plague, pp. 58, 60, 392, 442*t*-444*t*
Plastic surgery
— *See:* Cosmetic surgery
The Playboy Channel, p. 280
PM-10
— *See:* Particulate matter
PMDD
— *See:* Premenstrual dysphoric disorder
Pneumonia, p. 5
— causes of death, pp. 2, 4, 8-9, 69-70, 99, 401
— immunizations, pp. 96, 98-99
Polio, pp. 55-56, 94-96
Pollutants, p. 315
Pollution
— drinking water, pp. 326-328
— World Health Organization, p. 316
Ponds, pp. 323, 325
Pornography, pp. 280-281
Post-traumatic stress disorder, pp. 247, 252-253
Postneonatal deaths, p. 312
Poultry, p. 83
Pregnancy, ectopic
— *See:* Ectopic pregnancy
Premarin, p. 167
Premarital sex, pp. 267-268, 502*t*
Premenstrual dysphoric disorder (PDD), p. 170
Prescription drugs, p. 75
— AARP, p. 220

Prescription drugs continued:
— abuse, p. 128
— advertising, p. 178
— advertising expenditures, pp. 177-178
— antidepressants, p. 169
— Attention Deficit/Hyperactivity Disorder, p. 171
— depression, p. 169
— expenditures, p. 484*t*
— Food and Drug Administration, p. 176
— men, pp. 275-276
— numbers dispensed, pp. 165-167
— prices, p. 179
— research and development, p. 176
— Ritalin, p. 171
— school-based health centers, p. 102
— shortages, p. 389
— use, pp. 474*t*, 482*t*-483*t*, 504*t*
Prevention research centers, p. 211
Preventive services at school-based health centers, p. 103
Prilosec, p. 167
Procardia XL, p. 167
Promoting Health/Preventing Disease: Objectives for the Nation, p. 403
Prostate cancer, pp. 18, 28
— causes of death, pp. 28-29, 67-68
— death rates, p. 429*t*
— dietary fat, p. 29
— PSA, p. 28
— survival rates, p. 158
Prostate-Specific Antigen
— *See:* PSA
Proventil-Aerosol, p. 167
Prozac, p. 445*t*
— depression, pp. 63-64, 76, 169, 262
— Eli Lilly & Co., p. 170
— mental illnesses, p. 251
— prescription drugs, p. 167
PSA, p. 28
Psychiatric treatment, pp. 262, 264, 500*t*
Psychiatrists, p. 341
Psychological abuse of elderly, p. 199
Psychological development assessment, p. 102
Psychotherapy
— *See also:* Psychiatric treatment
— depression, p. 169
— expenditures, p. 263
Public health, p. 101
Public Health Action Plan to Combat Antimicrobial Resistance, p. 330
Public Health Threats and Emergencies Act of 2000, p. 101
Pulmonary diseases, pp. 69-70
Q fever, p. 392
Quadruplets, p. 39
Quality of life, pp. 203, 205, 210
Quinlan, Karen Ann, p. 188
Race/ethnicity
— cholesterol levels, p. 20
— crib death, p. 45
— death rates, p. 15

Race/ethnicity continued:
— exercise habits, p. 92
— illicit substance use, p. 126
— life expectancy, p. 47
— mammograms, p. 18
— maternal mortality, p. 22
— physicians, p. 337
— sexually transmitted diseases, p. 52
Race/ethnicity and cancer survival rates
— cancer survival rates, pp. 156, 158
Race/ethnicity and causes of death, pp. 8, 28, 30, 32, 34, 43, 422t
Race/ethnicity and infant mortality, pp. 313, 517t
Race/ethnicity and low birth weight babies, pp. 308-309, 516t
Race/ethnicity and lung cancer, p. 26
Radiation, p. 105
Radiation therapy, p. 159
Radioisotope scans, p. 152
Radiologic technologists, p. 355
Recommended Energy Allowance, p. 89
Rectal cancers
— obesity, p. 161
— survival rates, p. 156
Red meat, p. 83
Registered nurses, pp. 347-349, 523t
Rehabilitation Act, p. 232
Renal disease
— causes of death, p. 2
— Medicare enrollment, p. 380
Rental households, pp. 195, 486t
Repetitive-strain injuries, p. 236
Report on Smoking and Health, pp. 107, 136
Reproduction, p. 291
Research grants, p. 81
Reservoirs, pp. 323, 325
Residential treatment centers, p. 264
Respiratory diseases, p. 5
— birth defects, p. 310
— causes of death, pp. 3-4, 8-10
— causes of disability, pp. 227-228, 235-236, 238
— children, p. 229
— surgical procedures, p. 150
— therapeutic procedures, p. 152
Restaurant expenditures, pp. 109-110
Rett's Syndrome, p. 258
Rheumatism, pp. 227-228
Rhode Island, p. 338
Risk behaviors, pp. 489t-490t
Ritalin, p. 165
— ADHD, pp. 172-174
— children, p. 483t
— drug abuse, p. 129
— prescription drugs, p. 171
River water pollution, pp. 323, 325
R.J. Reynolds, p. 138
Road rage, p. 140
Robert Wood Johnson Medical School, p. 167
Rocky Mountain Spotted Fever, p. 95
Roe v. Wade, p. 306
Rohypnol, p. 120

Rubella, pp. 55-56, 94-95
— *See also:* German measles
Rubeola, p. 56
Russian Federation, p. 334
SAD
— *See:* Social anxiety disorders
St. John's Wort, pp. 75-76, 81, 87, 162-163
Salaries of medical school graduates, p. 414
Salk, Dr. Jonas, p. 95
Salmonella infections, p. 111
Salts, pp. 20-21
Sarafem, p. 170
Saunders, Dr. Cicely, pp. 376, 378
Saw palmetto, p. 75
Schistosomiasis, p. 326
Schizophrenia, pp. 247-249
Schlosser, Eric, p. 110
School-based health centers, pp. 102-104, 464t
Seconal, p. 129
Sedatives
— abuse, p. 128
— teenagers, p. 119
Seizure disorders, pp. 229, 231
Senior citizens, pp. 187-188
— *See also:* Aging population
— *See also:* Elderly population
— living arrangements, pp. 193-194
— media images, p. 221
— Medicaid expenditures, p. 220
— Medicare payments, p. 219
— quality of life, p. 210
— risk behaviors, pp. 489t-490t
— suicides, p. 260
— television programs, pp. 221-222
Sepsis, bacterial
— *See:* Bacterial sepsis
September 11, 2001
— food-borne terrorism, p. 112
— genetic engineering, p. 106
Septicemia, pp. 4-5, 7-8
Sex education, p. 103
Sex information, pp. 282-283, 505t
Sexual abuse of elderly, p. 199
Sexual activity, pp. 269-273, 275, 284-285, 502t-503t, 505t
Sexual fantasies, pp. 271-272, 503t
Sexual intercourse, pp. 304-305
Sexuality, pp. 267-268, 273, 503t-504t
Sexually transmitted diseases, pp. 40, 51-52, 102, 439t-440t
Shalala, Donna, p. 107
Shift Work Sleep Disorder, p. 144
Shootings, p. 4
SIDS, pp. 11, 45-46, 313
— *See also:* Crib death
— *See also:* Sudden Infant Death Syndrome
Sierra Club, p. 114
Sigmoidoscopy, p. 31
Silent Spring, p. 87
Siltation, pp. 323, 325
Singletons, p. 39

Skeptic's Dictionary, p. 76
Skilled nursing facilities, pp. 207-209
Skin cancer, p. 148
— *See also:* Cancer
— *See also:* Melanomas
— survival rates, p. 13
— tanning, p. 147
Skin diseases, p. 236
Sleep disorders, p. 143
Smallpox, pp. 94-95, 392
Smoking, pp. 5, 108, 136
— adults, pp. 135-138, 474*t*
— causes of death, pp. 4, 131
— causes of disability, p. 228
— Centers for Disease Control, p. 135
— educational attainment, p. 136
— elderly population, p. 210
— emphysema, p. 3
— *Healthy People 2010*, p. 408
— heart disease, p. 136
— high school seniors, p. 475*t*
— income levels, p. 136
— low birth weight, p. 40
— lung cancer, pp. 3-4, 26, 136
— teenagers, pp. 137-138
Social anxiety disorders, pp. 252, 255
— *See also:* Social phobias
The Social Organization of Sexuality, p. 269
Social phobias, p. 247
— *See also:* Social anxiety disorders
Social Security disability benefits, pp. 233-234, 496*t*
SOu2U
— *See:* Sulfur Dioxide
South Africa, pp. 332, 334
South Carolina, p. 387
South Dakota, p. 369
Special Committee on Aging, p. 374
Specialty hospitals, p. 365
Speech impairments, pp. 229-231
Speed, p. 124
The Spice Channel, p. 280
Spinal problems, pp. 227-228
Stanford Sleep Disorders Clinic, p. 144
State mental hospitals, p. 264
STDs
— *See:* Sexually transmitted diseases
Stents, pp. 25, 151
Sterilization, pp. 304-305
Steroid use, p. 104
Stimulants
— ADHD, p. 173
— drug abuse, p. 128
— teenagers, p. 119
Stomach cancer
— causes of death, pp. 67-68
— survival rates, p. 156
Streams, pp. 323, 325
Stress, pp. 108, 139-145, 161

Stroke
— *See also:* Cerebrovascular disease
— Baby Boom generation, p. 69
— causes of death, pp. 2-5, 8-9
— disabilities, pp. 227, 243, 401
— women, pp. 12-13
Student loans, p. 414
Substance abuse, pp. 411, 471*t*-473*t*
— alcohol, p. 411
— counseling, p. 102
Substance Abuse and Mental Health Services Administration, p. 412
Substance use
— adults, pp. 121-122
— Hazelden Foundation, p. 123
Sudden Infant Death Syndrome, pp. 10, 437*t*
— *See also:* Crib death
— *See also:* SIDS
Sudden Sniffing Death Syndrome, p. 120
Sugars, pp. 20-21
Suicide, p. 35
Suicide rates, pp. 433*t*-434*t*, 500*t*
Suicides, pp. 431*t*-433*t*
— aging population, pp. 204, 261
— cause of death, pp. 4, 8
— causes of death, p. 131
— men, pp. 34-36, 260
— mental health, pp. 248-249
— school-based health centers, p. 103
Suicides, altruistic
— *See:* Altruistic suicides
Suicides, anomic
— *See:* Anomic suicides
Suicides, egoistic
— *See:* Egoistic suicides
Suicides, fatalistic
— *See:* Fatalistic suicides
Sulfa drugs, p. 2
Sulfur dioxide, pp. 316-317
Surgeon General of the United States, pp. 83, 403
Surgeons, p. 341
Surgeons (orthopedic), p. 341
Surgical hospitals, pp. 364-365
Surgical procedures, pp. 150-151, 154-155
Survival rates for cancers, pp. 13, 19, 447*t*-448*t*, 478*t*-479*t*
Sweden, pp. 42, 334
Synthroid, pp. 167-168
Syphilis, pp. 51-52, 58, 442*t*-443*t*
Talking Back to Prozac, p. 64
Tanning, p. 147
Task Force on Antimicrobial Resistance, p. 330
Tattooing, p. 148
TB
— *See:* Tuberculosis
Teenagers
— illicit substance use, pp. 117-120, 134
— marijuana, p. 132
— sedatives, p. 119
— sex information, pp. 282-283, 505*t*

Teenagers continued:
— sexual activity, pp. 284-285, 505*t*
— smoking, pp. 137-138
Telemedicine, pp. 361-362, 524*t*
Telemedicine: What the Future Holds When You're Ill, p. 362
Television programs, pp. 221-222, 280, 491*t*
Testes, p. 151
Testosterone levels, pp. 6, 29
Tetanus, pp. 94-95
Texas, pp. 190, 369, 415, 417
Thailand, p. 42
Therapeutic procedures, pp. 152-154
They Say You're Crazy, p. 170
Thompson, Tommy, pp. 73, 112
Thyroid gland surgeries, p. 151
Tobacco advertising, p. 138
Tobacco control programs, pp. 408-409
Tobacco prevention, p. 102
Tomatoes, p. 87
Tonsillitis, p. 229
Tort reform, p. 417
Total Fertility Rate, p. 295
Toxemia, p. 23
Toxic Shock Syndrome, pp. 61-62, 444*t*-445*t*
Tracheal cancer, p. 67
Tranquilizers
— drug abuse, p. 128
— teenagers, p. 119
Trans fat, p. 109
Tricyclic antidepressants, p. 64
Trimox, pp. 166-167
Triplets, pp. 39, 299-300
Trust fund assets of Medicare, p. 528*t*
Tuberculosis, pp. 2-3, 58-59, 332-334
— AIDS, p. 333
— cases and rates, pp. 442*t*-444*t*
— foreign countries, pp. 332, 334
— HIV, p. 333
— World Health Organization, p. 332
Tufts University Center for the Study of Drug Development, p. 175
Tuition and fees, pp. 413, 539*t*
Tularemia, p. 392
Twins, pp. 39, 299-300
Typhoid fever, pp. 58-59, 442*t*-444*t*
Uganda, p. 332
Ultrasound, p. 152
Umbilical cord complications, p. 10
Uninsured population, pp. 384-385
United Government Services, pp. 377-378
United Kingdom, p. 334
United Nations Human Rights Committee, p. 218
United Republic of Tanzania, p. 332
U.S. Administration on Aging, p. 199
U.S. Department of Energy, p. 105
U.S. Office of Dietary Supplements, p. 75
U.S. Surgeon General, p. 107
University of Michigan, p. 257

University of Utah Drug Information Service, p. 389
Urinary tract cancer, pp. 3, 156
Urinary tract surgeries, p. 150
Urologists, p. 275
USDA, pp. 84, 89-90
— National School Lunch Program, p. 113
— obesity, p. 109
— organic foods, pp. 87-88
Uterine cancer, p. 68
— hormone replacement therapy, p. 168
— obesity, p. 161
— survival rates, pp. 19, 158
Vacations, pp. 145-146
Vaccinations, pp. 94-95
Vaccine-preventable diseases, p. 463*t*
Vaccines, pp. 389-392
Vaccinia (cell culture), p. 392
Valium, p. 129
Vancomycin-Resistant Enterococci
— *See:* VRE
Varicella, p. 96
Vasotec, p. 167
Vegetables, p. 83
Venezuelan encephalitis, p. 392
Vermont, p. 338
Very-low birth weight, p. 310
Veterans Administration hospitals, p. 264
Viagra, pp. 267, 275-276, 504*t*
Vietnam, p. 332
Vioxx, p. 178
Viral hepatitis, p. 61
Virginia Slims cigarettes, p. 136
Virtual doctors
— *See:* Telemedicine
Viruses, p. 323
Vision impairments, pp. 487*t*-488*t*
— aging population, p. 203
— causes of disability, p. 227
— children, pp. 229, 231
Vision screenings, p. 103
Vitamins, p. 75
VOC
— *See:* Volatile Organic Chemicals
Volatile organic chemicals, pp. 316, 318
VRE, p. 330
War on Drugs, p. 118
Wastewater treatment
— Africa, p. 326
— Caribbean, p. 326
— Europe, p. 326
— Latin America, p. 326
— North America, p. 326
— United States, p. 326
Water pollution, pp. 315, 321-325, 518*t*-519*t*
Waterways, pp. 321-322
Weight-control habits, p. 115
West Virginia, pp. 369-370, 409, 417
Western equine encephalitis, p. 392
Western United States, p. 189

Whites, p. 28
— activities of daily living, p. 204
— AIDS, pp. 52, 54
— Attention Deficit Disorder, p. 66
— breast cancer, p. 18
— breastfeeding, p. 41
— cancer, pp. 18, 28
— cancer survival rates, pp. 156-158
— causes of death, pp. 8-9, 24-27, 32, 34, 36, 43-44
— childbirth, p. 23
— chlamydia, p. 52
— cholesterol levels, p. 20
— cocaine use, p. 127
— crib death, pp. 45-46
— death rates, pp. 15, 18
— depression, p. 64
— gonorrhea, p. 52
— heart diseases, p. 14
— HIV, pp. 54, 288-290
— illicit substance use, p. 126
— infant mortality, p. 313
— life expectancy, pp. 47-48, 403-404
— low birth weight, pp. 40, 308-309
— mammograms, p. 18
— maternal mortality, p. 22
— Medicare, p. 380
— obesity, pp. 16-17
— physicians, p. 337
— prostate cancer, p. 28
— smoking, pp. 135-136
— suicide rates, p. 434*t*
— suicides, p. 260
— syphilis, p. 52
Whole milk, p. 83
Whooping Cough, p. 56
Willett, Dr. Walter C., pp. 90, 109-110
Women
— *See also:* Females
— activities of daily living, p. 204
— anxiety disorders, p. 247
— bipolar disorder, p. 247
— breast cancer, p. 18
— cancer, p. 18
— cancer survival rates, p. 158
— causes of death, pp. 6-7, 12, 24, 26, 30, 32, 34, 36, 53, 422*t*
— cholesterol levels, p. 20
— contraceptive practices, p. 514*t*
— cosmetic surgery, pp. 277, 279
— death rates, pp. 15, 424*t*
— depression, p. 64
— diabetes, p. 13
— disability benefits, p. 236
— disabled population, p. 225
— eating disorders, p. 116
— elderly population, p. 196
— fertility rates, p. 295
— heart diseases, p. 14
— HIV, pp. 54, 289-290
— life expectancy, p. 47

Women continued:
— living arrangements, p. 192
— lung cancer, p. 160
— mammograms, p. 18
— Medicare, p. 380
— melanomas, p. 147
— obesity, pp. 16-17
— overweight, p. 17
— physicians, p. 337
— psychiatric treatment, p. 262
— rental households, p. 195
— schizophrenia, p. 249
— sexual activity, pp. 269-270
— smoking, pp. 135-136
— suicide rates, p. 434*t*
— suicides, p. 260
— surgical procedures, p. 154
— Total Fertility Rate, p. 295
— workforce participation, pp. 296, 509*t*-510*t*
Women's reproductive health care, p. 366
Workforce participation, pp. 295-296, 509*t*-510*t*
World Health Organization
— pollution, p. 316
— tuberculosis rates, p. 332
Yoga, p. 163
Zantac, p. 167
Zimbabwe, p. 332
Zoloft, pp. 63-64, 167, 170, 276, 445*t*

CUMULATIVE KEYWORD INDEX

This index allows users to locate all subjects, issues, government agencies, companies, programs, associations, schools, educational institutions, books, reports, personal names, and locations cited in *Social Trends & Indicators USA: Work & Leisure*; *Social Trends & Indicators USA: Community & Education*; *Social Trends & Indicators USA: Health & Sickness*; and *Social Trends & Indicators USA: Crime & Justice.* Page references do not necessarily identify the page on which a topic begins. In cases where the topic spans two or more pages, page numbers point to where the index term appears-which may be the second or subsequent page on the topic. Cross-references have been added to index citations for ease in locating related topics.

419 Fraud
— *See:* Nigerian Letter Fraud Scheme
AARP
— *See:* Association for the Advancement of Retired Persons
Abandonment of elders, p. III:199
Abortions, pp. II:321*t*
— by age group, pp. III:306-307
— by race/ethnicity, pp. II:10-13
— Catholic hospitals, pp. III:367-368
Abstention, pp. II:15, III:304-305
Acambis, Inc., p. III:393
Accidents, pp. II:21, III:430*t*
— by race/ethnicity, p. III:8
— by race/ethnicity and sex, pp. III:32-33
— causes of death, p. III:4
— causes of disability, p. III:228
— infant mortality, p. III:10
— research funding, p. III:401
Accommodations and food services, pp. I:104-105
Accountability in education, p. II:166
Acquired immunodeficiency syndrome
— *See:* AIDS
ACT scores, pp. II:173, II:369*t*
ACT UP, p. III:287
Active Community Environments, pp. III:405-406
Active physicians, p. III:522*t*
Activities of daily living, pp. III:203-204, III:225
Acupuncture, pp. III:78, III:82, III:162-163
AD
— *See:* Alzheimer's Disease
ADD
— *See:* Attention Deficit Disorder
Adderall, pp. II:303, III:129
Adelphia, p. IV:85
ADHD
— *See:* Attention Deficit/Hyperactivity Disorder

Adidas, p. IV:100
Administration on Aging, pp. III:204, III:206, IV:240
Administrative and managerial occupations
— *See:* Executive, administrative, managerial occupations
Administrative support occupations, pp. I:20, I:69-70, I:104-105, I:296*t*
Adoption assistance, p. I:134
Adrenal gland surgery, p. III:151
Adult education, p. I:233
— attainment levels, pp. I:264-265, I:332*t*
— by sex, pp. I:262, I:375*t*
— job advancement, pp. I:260-261
Adult immunizations, p. III:98
Adult leisure activities, pp. I:221, I:234, I:242, I:245-246
Adult literacy, p. II:156
Adult Protective Services, p. III:199
Adult religious affiliation, pp. II:131, II:135
Adult smoking, pp. III:121, III:135, III:138
Adult substance use, pp. III:121-122
Advance directives
— *See:* Living wills
Advanced classes, pp. II:259, II:392*t*
Advanced degree recipients, p. II:295
Advanced Fee Fraud
— *See:* Nigerian Letter Fraud Scheme
Advanced mathematics classes, pp. II:259-260
Advanced practice nurses, pp. III:351-352
— *See also:* Nurse practitioners
Advanced sciences classes, p. II:260
Advertising and public relations managers
— *See:* marketing, advertising, public relations managers
Advertising expenditures, pp. III:177-178, III:483*t*
Aerobics instructors
— *See:* fitness trainers and aerobics instructors
Afghanistan, p. III:332
African-Americans, p. IV:205

African-Americans continued:
— *See also:* Blacks
— arrests, p. IV:53
— births, pp. II:6, II:321*t*
— causes of death, pp. III:8, III:31, III:33, III:35-36, III:43
— diseases, pp. III:14, III:97
— employment, p. I:16
— families, pp. II:53, II:62
— homicides, pp. IV:217-218
— hospital closings, p. III:370
— income, p. II:21
— infant mortality, pp. II:21, III:313
— law enforcement personnel, p. IV:204
— life expectancy, p. II:20
— population, pp. II:24, II:70-71, II:345*t*
— population mobility, p. II:39
— risk behaviors, p. III:17
— single-parent households, p. II:61
— specialized museums, p. I:229
— Total Fertility Rates, p. II:8
African wastewater treatment, p. III:326
Age-based discrimination, pp. I:161, I:163, I:167
Age groups
— abortion rates, p. III:307
— book purchases, p. I:220
— death rates, 1917-1918, p. II:17
— depression, p. III:64
— disabled population, p. III:226
— employment, pp. I:20, III:296
— first marriages, p. II:338*t*
— high-school completion rates, p. I:39
— illegal labor, pp. I:43, I:301*t*
— Internet use, pp. I:272-273, I:378*t*
— mathematics proficiency, p. II:161
— population, p. I:345*t*
— psychiatric treatment, p. III:262
— reading proficiency, p. II:159
— retirement, pp. I:139, I:344*t*
— sexual activity, p. III:270
— suicides, p. III:261
— volunteering, pp. I:239-240, I:370*t*
— voter turnout, p. II:104
— work hours, p. I:44
Agency for Healthcare Research and Quality, p. III:361
Aggravated assaults, p. IV:135
— by sex, pp. IV:36, IV:38
— juveniles arrested, pp. IV:133, IV:137-138
— recidivism, p. IV:260
— reported, p. IV:5
— victimization, p. IV:31
Aging population, p. III:485*t*
— *See also:* Elderly population
— *See also:* Senior citizens
— causes of disability, p. III:228
— health problems, pp. III:203-204
— living arrangements, pp. III:191-192
— Medicaid, p. III:386
— perceptions of quality of life, pp. III:205-206
Agoraphobia, pp. III:252-253

Agriculture, pp. II:256-257, II:262
— child labor, p. I:46
— employment, pp. I:3-4, I:291*t*
— workplace injuries, p. I:156
The AGS Foundation for Health in Aging, p. III:344
Aides
— *See:* personal home care aides
AIDS
— attendant diseases, pp. III:3, III:61, III:333
— by race/ethnicity, pp. III:52, III:54
— causes of death, pp. III:53, III:131, III:440*t*
— Centers for Disease Control and Prevention (CDC), p. III:287
— cyclical patterns, p. III:51
— disability benefits, p. III:243
— funding, pp. III:400-402
— new cases, p. III:506*t*
— origins, pp. III:62, III:95
— total occurrences reported, pp. III:444*t*
— treatment, p. III:286
AIDS Coalition to Unleash Power
— *See:* ACT UP
Air pollution, pp. III:316-320, III:518*t*
Air Rage: Crisis in the Skies, p. III:140
Aircraft hijacking, p. IV:245
Aircraft pilots and flight engineers, pp. I:27-28
— *See also:* airline pilots
Airline passenger screening, pp. IV:232-234, IV:367*t*
Airline pilots, pp. I:22, I:296*t*
— *See also:* aircraft pilots and flight engineers
Airplane crashes, p. III:4
al-Rahman, Abd, p. IV:184
Alabama, pp. II:246, IV:284, III:370
Alaska, pp. IV:121, II:217, III:409
Alaska Natives, pp. IV:159-160
— diseases, pp. III:288-289
— educational attainment, pp. II:258-259, II:287-290
— low birth weight, p. III:40
— physicians, p. III:337
— population, pp. II:70-72
— risk behaviors, p. III:136
Albuterol, p. III:167
Alcohol
— adults, p. III:121
— cirrhosis, pp. III:6, III:108
— mouth cancer, p. III:161
— North America, p. III:64
— teenagers, pp. III:117-118
Alcohol consumption, pp. III:108, IV:173, IV:352*t*
Alcohol-related arrests, pp. IV:112, IV:334*t*
Alcohol-related crimes, p. IV:334*t*
— crime rate, p. IV:10
— Prohibition era, p. IV:29
— public-order crimes, pp. IV:101, IV:104, IV:111-112
— rate fluctuation, p. IV:174
Alcohol-related deaths, pp. IV:115-116, III:125, III:131, IV:174, IV:335*t*
Aleuts, p. II:24
All Handicapped Children Act, p. II:299
Allegra, p. III:178

Allergies, p. III:229
Alliance for Aging Research, p. III:341
Allopaths, p. III:336
Alternative medicine practitioners
— by specialization, pp. III:78-82, III:450t
— clinical trials, pp. III:162-163
— herbal medicines, p. III:75
Altruistic suicides, p. III:35
Alzheimer's Disease (AD), p. III:5
— aging population, p. III:204
— causes of death, pp. III:4, III:7-8, III:71-72, III:449t
— disabled population, pp. III:225, III:243
— fluoride, p. III:328
— hormone replacement therapy, p. III:168
— hospice care, p. III:376
— mental illnesses, pp. III:248-249
Amber, pp. IV:142-143
American Academy of Arts and Sciences, p. II:293
American Academy of Dermatology, p. III:147
American Academy of Family Physicians, p. III:339
American Academy of Pediatrics, pp. III:46, III:96
American Association of Colleges of Nursing, p. III:347
American Association of Law Libraries, p. IV:96
American Attitudes Toward Physical Activity & Fitness, p. III:93
American Bar Association, p. IV:284
American Booksellers Association, p. I:220
American Civil Liberties Union (ACLU)
— hate crimes, p. IV:287
— hospital closings, p. III:363
— prison population, p. IV:247
— single-sex education, p. II:308
— use of force by police, p. IV:214
— women's reproductive health care, p. III:366
American College Testing program
— See: ACT
American Dietetic Association, p. III:84
American Federation of Teachers, pp. II:231-232, II:240
American Front Skinheads, p. IV:181
American Hospital Association, p. III:82
American Housing Survey, p. III:191
American Indians, p. II:343t
— abortions, pp. II:12-13
— births, pp. II:10, II:321t
— causes of death, pp. III:8, III:27
— drug arrests, p. IV:161
— drug use, pp. IV:159-160
— educational attainment, pp. II:151, II:258-259, II:287-290
— health problems, pp. III:40, III:288-289
— juveniles arrested, p. IV:137
— law enforcement personnel, p. IV:203
— population, pp. II:24, II:70-72, II:347t
— risk behaviors, p. III:136
— Total Fertility Rates, p. II:8
American Medical Association, pp. III:75, III:79, III:82, II:250, IV:276
— community health centers, p. III:101
— elder abuse, p. III:197
— emergency medical technicians, p. III:357

American Medical Association continued:
— medical malpractice jury awards, p. III:416
— physician-assisted suicide, p. III:216
American Medical Student Association, p. III:395
American Nurses Association, p. III:350
American Psychiatric Association, pp. III:170, III:251, II:302
American Psychological Association, p. IV:290
American Society of Criminology, p. IV:243
American Society of Health-System Pharmacists, p. III:390
American Society of Plastic Surgeons, p. III:277
Americans with Disabilities Act, pp. III:223, III:245
America's Missing: Broadcast Emergency Response, p. IV:141
America's Most Wanted, p. IV:142
Amharic, p. II:76
Amino acid dietary supplements, p. III:75
Amnesty International, p. IV:248
Amoxil, pp. III:166-167
Amphetamines, p. III:125
Amputations, p. I:155
Amusement industries, p. I:7
Amyl nitrite, p. III:120
Anabolic steroids, p. IV:153
Analgesics, p. III:128
Analytic geometry, p. II:259
Androstenedione, p. III:130
Anemia, pp. III:39-40
Anesthesiology, p. III:341
Angiocardiography, p. III:152
Angioplasty, balloon, pp. III:25, III:151
Anglicans, pp. II:130-133, II:135
Animal Liberation Front, p. IV:181
Annual Report on Eating Patterns in America, p. I:180
Anomic suicides, p. III:35
Anorexia nervosa, pp. III:115, III:248-249, III:256-257
Anthrax, p. III:392
Anti-Defamation League, p. IV:287
Anti-inflammatory steroid injections, p. III:390
Antibiotics, pp. III:166, III:329-331, III:390-392
Antidepressants, pp. III:63-64, III:165, III:169-170, III:445t
Antiques, p. I:286
Antitrust violations sentencing, p. IV:108
Anxiety disorders, pp. III:247-248, III:250, III:252, III:262
AOL, p. I:282
Apache Indian tribe, pp. II:72-73
Apples, p. III:87
Aquariums, p. I:229
Arabic, p. II:76
Arabs, p. IV:184
Archer, Dennis, p. IV:288
Architecture-related occupations, p. II:296
Arizona, pp. II:63-64, IV:121, IV:277
Arizona State University, p. IV:118
Armed Forces of Puerto Rican Liberation, p. IV:181
Armed robbery, pp. IV:36, IV:38
Armenia, p. II:163
Arrests, pp. IV:294t
— alcohol-related crimes, pp. IV:112-113
— Border Patrol, pp. I:49, I:302t
— by race/ethnicity, p. IV:53

Arrests continued:
— crime index, pp. IV:330*t*
— crimes cleared, pp. IV:268-269
— homicides, p. IV:39
— justice system employment, p. IV:266
— larceny, p. IV:322*t*
— lesser offenses, pp. IV:102-103
— not included in crime rate, p. IV:9
— property crime, pp. IV:67-68
Arsenic, pp. III:315, III:327
Arsinger v Hamlin, p. IV:282
Arson, pp. IV:63, IV:68, IV:79-81
Art museums, p. I:229
Art purchases, pp. I:218-219
Arteriography, p. III:152
Arthritis, pp. III:227-228
Arthur Andersen, p. IV:85
Arthur Ashe Academy for Boys, p. II:309
Artificial-wall climbing, pp. I:200-201
Arts and entertainment, pp. I:104-105
Arts, culture, and humanities, pp. I:242, I:244-246
Aryan Nation, p. IV:181
Asian-Americans
— *See:* Asians
Asian Indians
— *See:* Asians
Asians
— births, pp. II:10, II:12-13, I:40, II:321*t*
— causes of death, pp. III:8, III:27, III:43
— diseases, pp. III:52, III:289
— drug arrests, p. IV:161
— drug use, pp. IV:159-160
— educational attainment - college, pp. II:151-153, II:287-290
— educational attainment - high school and above, pp. I:118-119
— educational attainment - vocational education, pp. II:258-259
— employment, pp. I:35, I:37
— income, pp. I:75, I:82
— Internet use, pp. I:270-271
— interracial marriages, p. II:55
— juveniles arrested, p. IV:137
— law enforcement personnel, p. IV:203
— low birth weight, p. III:40
— percentage of total population, pp. II:24, II:70-71, II:74-75, II:344*t*
— percentage of workforce population, p. I:41
— physicians, p. III:337
— population mobility, p. II:38
— salaries, p. I:38
— single-parent households, p. II:61
— Total Fertility Rates, pp. II:6-8
Asians and Pacific Islanders
— *See:* Asians
Asperger's Disorder, pp. III:258-259
Aspirin, p. III:130
Assaults
— alcohol-related crimes, p. IV:104
— domestic violence, pp. IV:25-26
— household income, p. IV:31
— *National Crime Victimization Survey*, pp. IV:4, IV:10

Assaults continued:
— perpetrators, pp. IV:36, IV:38
— population density, p. IV:58
— workplace, pp. I:151, I:157
Assemblers and inspectors
— *See:* machine operators, assemblers, and inspectors
Assemblies of God, pp. II:132-138
Assigned counsel, p. IV:281
Assisted living facilities, p. III:194
Assisted Living Federation of America, p. III:194
Assisted reproductive technology, pp. III:291, III:299-300
Assisted-suicide movement, p. III:213
Associated Press, p. I:45
Associate's degrees, pp. I:57, I:61, I:94, I:264-265, II:283
Association for the Advancement of Retired Persons (AARP), p. IV:83, III:192, III:194, III:220
Asthma, pp. III:3, III:229, III:231, III:315, III:319-320
Atelectasis, p. III:10
Atherosclerosis, p. III:2
Athletes, p. I:204
Atkins, Dr., p. III:90
Atomic bombs, p. III:105
Attendance at entertainment events, pp. I:210, I:222, I:224-225, I:363*t*
Attendance at religious services, pp. I:249, I:372*t*
Attendants
— *See:* nursing aides, orderlies, and attendants
Attention Deficit Disorder (ADD), p. III:446*t*
— National Health Interview Survey, pp. III:65-66
— Ritalin, p. II:302
Attention Deficit/Hyperactivity Disorder (ADHD), p. III:483*t*
— National Health Interview Survey, pp. III:65-66
— Ritalin, pp. III:165, III:171-174, II:302
Attitudes About Work and Leisure in America, p. I:178
Attitudes toward religion, pp. I:250-251, I:373*t*
Auctions, p. I:286
Audio products, p. I:185
Audiologists, p. I:52
Auditing clerks
— *See:* bookkeeping, accounting, and auditing clerks
Austin (TX), p. I:50
Australia, pp. II:163-165
Austria, pp. II:163, II:165
Autism, pp. III:247, III:255, III:259, III:500*t*
— California Department of Mental Health services, p. III:258
— home schooling, p. III:234
— mental illnesses, pp. III:248-249
— school performance, pp. III:229, III:231
— special education, p. II:298
Automated Data Processing Inc., p. I:172
Automated Data Processing Inc. (ADP), p. I:171
Automated Meter Reading (AMR), p. I:55
Automobiles, pp. I:7, IV:71-72, I:286, IV:324*t*
Azerbaijan, p. II:163
AZT, p. III:286
Baby Boom generation, pp. IV:29-30, IV:43, III:187
— age at first marriage, p. II:51
— attendance at performing arts, p. I:224
— breastfeeding, p. III:41

Baby Boom generation continued:
— causes of death, pp. III:69-70
— dependency ratio, p. I:141
— elderly population, p. I:53
— employment, p. I:19
— fertility rates, pp. III:293-294
— home purchases, p. I:195
— income, p. I:77
— Medicare, pp. III:380, III:382
— psychiatric treatment, p. III:262
— reproduction, p. III:291
— retirement, pp. I:21-23, I:24, I:27
— television programs, p. III:222
Bach, Robert, p. I:50
Bachelor's degrees, pp. III:42, I:264-265, II:401*t*
— by race/ethnicity and residency, pp. II:287-288
— by sex, p. II:283
— by specialization, p. II:284
— earnings, p. II:295
— income, p. I:94
— job openings, p. I:61
— student loans, p. II:275
Back problems, pp. III:227-228
Back to Basics Movement, pp. II:167, II:204-205
Bacteria, pp. III:315, III:323
— antibiotics, pp. III:329-330
— causes of death, p. III:2
— food-borne illnesses, pp. III:111-112
— sepsis, p. III:10
— VRE, p. III:330
Baggage screeners, pp. IV:232-233
Baha'i, pp. II:134-135, II:140-141, I:252-253
Balanced Budget Act, p. III:382
Balanced Budget Refinement Act, p. III:383
Ballet, p. I:216
Balloon angioplasty, pp. III:25, III:151
Bangladesh, p. III:332
Banking, p. I:273
Bankruptcy, p. IV:85
Baptists, pp. II:130-132, II:135
Barbers, p. I:54
Barbiturates, p. IV:11
Baseball, p. I:202
Basketball, pp. I:202, I:208-209
Bates, Brian, p. IV:125
Baxter, Clifford, p. IV:85
Bayer Corporation, pp. III:392-393
Beginning to Read, p. II:201
Behavioral Risk Factor Surveillance System, p. III:205
Belarus, p. II:163
Belgium, pp. II:163-165
Benefits, pp. I:127, I:242, I:341*t*
Bergen, Candice, p. II:62
Best Practices for Comprehensive Tobacco Control Programs, p. III:408
Bethesda Oak (OH), pp. III:370-371
Bias-related crimes, p. IV:206
— *See also:* Hate crimes
Bicycling, p. I:200

Bilingual education, p. II:307
Binge eating, pp. III:249, III:251, III:256
Biological sciences, p. II:284
Bioterrorism, pp. III:88, III:392-393
Bipolar disorder, pp. III:247-248, III:251-252, III:254
Birth control, pp. III:102, III:104, III:294
Birth defects, pp. III:310-311
Birth weight, low
— *See:* Low birth weight
Births, pp. II:315*t*
— Baby Boom generation, p. II:2
— by age group, pp. III:292, II:322*t*
— by race/ethnicity, pp. II:6, II:10, II:319*t*
— selected years, p. III:306
Black Liberation Army, p. IV:181
Black-white death rate ratio, p. II:327*t*
Black, Roy, p. IV:279
Blacks
— *See also:* African-Americans
— abortions, pp. II:10, II:12-13, III:321*t*
— activities of daily living, p. III:204
— births, pp. II:10, III:39, I:40, II:319*t*
— breastfeeding, p. III:41
— cancer survival rates, pp. III:156-158
— causes of death, pp. III:8-9, II:21
— childbirth, p. III:23
— computer learning opportunities, p. II:263
— crib death, pp. III:45-46
— deaths, pp. III:15, III:18, II:21
— diseases, pp. III:14, III:18, III:28, III:52, III:54, II:70-71, III:288-289
— drug arrests, pp. IV:161, IV:164
— drug convictions, p. IV:164
— drug sentences, pp. IV:165-166
— drug use, pp. IV:53, III:126-127, IV:159-160
— earnings, p. I:71
— educational attainment - college, pp. II:151-153, II:287-290
— educational attainment - high school, p. I:39
— educational attainment - high school and more, pp. I:112, I:118-119
— educational attainment - murders, p. IV:53
— educational attainment - vocational education, pp. II:258-259
— employment, pp. I:16, I:35-37, I:41, I:67-68
— families, p. I:38
— homicides, pp. IV:52-53
— housing, p. II:35
— immunizations, p. III:99
— income, pp. I:82-83
— Internet use, pp. I:270-271
— interracial marriages, pp. II:54-55
— juveniles arrested, pp. IV:137-138
— law enforcement personnel, p. IV:203
— learning disabilities, p. III:66
— life expectancy, pp. III:47-48, III:403-404
— literacy, pp. II:154, II:159
— low birth weight, pp. III:44, III:308-309
— mammograms, p. III:18
— marriages, pp. II:52-53
— maternal mortality, pp. II:21, III:22-23, II:24, II:25-27, III:30,

Blacks continued:
III:32, III:34, IV:53
— mathematics proficiency, pp. II:161-162
— Medicare, p. III:380
— murders, pp. III:37-38
— physicians, p. III:337
— political-party affiliation, p. II:108
— Population Replacement Rate, p. II:6
— poverty, p. IV:53
— racial profiling, p. IV:222
— risk behaviors, pp. III:16, III:135-137
— risk factors, p. III:20
— single-parent households, p. II:61
— suicides, pp. III:260, III:434*t*
— Total Fertility Rates, pp. II:6-7
— unemployment, p. IV:53
— volunteering, p. I:241
— voter turnout, p. II:106
Bladder cancer, p. III:156
Blindness, pp. III:227, III:229, III:231, III:386
Blood-alcohol concentration (BAC), p. IV:115
Blood clots, p. III:168
Body Mass Index (BMI), p. III:16
Bok, Sissela, p. IV:145
Bombs, p. II:245
Bones, broken, p. III:227
Bookkeeping, accounting, and auditing clerks, pp. I:61-62
Bookmobiles, pp. I:254, I:374*t*
Books, pp. I:185, I:220-221, I:268, I:286, I:366*t*
Border Patrol, pp. IV:24, I:49
Born Again Christians, pp. II:132-133
Boston College, p. II:294
The Boston Globe, p. II:293
Boston Public Schools, p. IV:131
Boston University, p. II:294
Botanicals, p. III:75
Botox, p. III:279
Botulinum toxoids, p. III:392
Bowling, p. I:200
Bowling Alone, p. III:93
Box-office revenues, pp. I:222, I:366*t*
Boy Scouts, p. I:205
Brady Handgun Violence Prevention Act, pp. IV:46-47
Brady, James, p. IV:46
Branch libraries, p. I:254
Brand-name prescription drugs, pp. III:175-176, III:179
Breakfast, pp. III:139-140
Breast cancer
— causes of death, pp. III:3, III:12-13, III:18, III:67-68
— Fred Hutchinson Cancer Research Center, p. III:144
— hormone replacement therapy, p. III:168
— survival rates, pp. III:19, III:158, III:426*t*
— work-related stress, p. III:144
Breastfeeding, pp. III:41-42, III:435*t*
Bribery sentencing, p. IV:108
Britney Spears, p. I:283
Broadway shows, pp. I:224-225
Broken bones, p. III:227
Bronchial cancer, pp. III:67, III:156, III:158

Bronchitis, p. III:3
Broward County (FL), p. IV:267
Brown University, p. II:294
Bruises, p. I:155
BuddhaNet, p. II:145
Buddhism, pp. II:132-135, I:252-253
— Internet, p. II:145
— non-Christian houses of worship, pp. II:140-141
Bulgaria, pp. II:5, II:163-164
Bulimia nervosa, pp. III:115, III:248-249, III:256-257
Bullying, pp. II:249-250
Bureau of Alcohol, Tobacco, and Firearms, pp. IV:24, IV:227
Bureau of Diplomatic Security, p. IV:227
Bureau of Education of the Handicapped, p. III:232
Bureau of Health Professions, pp. III:338, III:349, III:355
Bureau of Justice Assistance, p. IV:266
Bureau of Justice Statistics, pp. IV:243, IV:272, IV:283
Bureau of Labor Statistics, pp. I:54, III:141, III:146, III:351
Bureau of Prisons, p. IV:227
Bureau of the Census, p. IV:159
Burglaries
— arrests, p. IV:67
— by location, pp. IV:73-74
— by time of day, p. IV:325*t*
— corrections expenditures, p. IV:249
— decrease in rates, p. IV:65
— reported to police, pp. IV:4, IV:7-8, IV:77, IV:373*t*
Burns, p. I:155
Bush administration (President George W.), pp. III:106, II:242, III:416
Business
— education, pp. II:256-257, II:262
— productivity, pp. I:122, I:326*t*
— profits, p. I:122
— salaries and wages, pp. I:122, II:296
Business management and administrative services, p. II:284-285
Business services, p. I:7
Business trips, pp. I:190-191, I:359*t*
Businesses
— *See:* Home-based businesses
— home-based,
Butchers and meat cutters, p. I:54
Bypass, coronary
— *See:* Coronary bypass
Cable television, p. I:226
Cadmium, p. III:324
Cafeteria plans, p. I:135
Calculus, p. II:259
California
— Asian population, p. II:75
— cigarette smoking, p. III:409
— class size reduction programs, p. II:196
— community hospital beds, p. III:369
— distribution of elderly population, p. III:190
— expulsions from school, p. II:246
— gay-couple households, pp. II:63-64
— hate crimes, p. IV:290
— law enforcement deaths, p. IV:211

California continued:
— nursing legislation, p. III:349
— prison population, p. IV:248
— racial profiling, p. IV:223
— sex offender registry, p. IV:122
— vacation time, p. I:190
— youth gangs, p. IV:138
California Business Roundtable, p. II:262
California Department of Developmental Services, p. III:258
California Highway Patrol, pp. IV:200, IV:202, IV:223
California Institute of Technology, p. II:280
California Obesity Prevention Initiative, p. III:407
Calorie Control Council, p. III:115
Calories, pp. III:89-90
CAM
— *See:* Complementary and alternative medicine
Cambodia, p. III:332
Cambodian population, p. II:74
Camel cigarettes, p. III:138
Campylobacter infections, p. III:111
Canada, pp. I:47, IV:125, II:254, III:334
— literacy, p. II:163
— mathematics class characteristics, p. II:165
— mathematics proficiency, p. II:164
— mathematics scores, TIMSS, p. II:254
Cancer, pp. III:3, III:5, II:18
— *See also:* Malignancies
— *See also:* Melanomas
— *See also:* Neoplasms
— *See also:* Specific cancers
— by race/ethnicity, p. III:18
— causes of death, pp. III:2-4, III:8-9, III:67, III:69-70, III:401
— causes of disability, p. III:227
— contributing factors, pp. III:68, III:160-161, III:328
— deaths, pp. III:446*t*
— detection, p. III:156
— digestive organs, p. III:3
— elderly population, p. III:210
— funding, pp. III:400-401
— hospice care, p. III:376
— survival rates, pp. III:19, III:156-158, III:478*t*
— treatment, p. III:159
Cannabis sativa, p. IV:153
— *See:* Marijuana
Capital punishment
— *See:* Death penalty
Capitol Police, pp. IV:226-227
Car-rental firms, p. I:196
Carbon monoxide (CO), pp. III:316, III:318
Cardiac catheterization, p. III:151
Cardiovascular disease, pp. III:2, III:150, III:168, III:210, III:310, III:341, III:405
— *See also:* heart disease
Caribbean wastewater treatment, p. III:326
Carpal Tunnel Syndrome, pp. I:155, III:236
Carrots, p. III:87
Cars, p. I:190
Case resolutions, pp. I:163, I:167-168, I:353*t*
Cashiers, pp. I:61-62

CAT
— *See:* Computerized axial tomography
Catheterization, cardiac
— *See:* Cardiac catheterization
Catholic Church, p. IV:56
Catholic Family and Human Rights Institute, p. IV:125
Catholic hospitals, pp. III:366-367
Catholics, pp. II:110, II:130-133, II:135
Catholics for a Free Choice, pp. III:366-367
Cats, p. I:191
Caucasians, pp. II:24-25
Causes of death
— accidents, pp. III:1-2, III:4, III:32
— alcohol, pp. III:125, III:131
— Baby Boom generation, pp. III:69-70
— black-white death ratio, p. II:21
— by race/ethnicity, pp. III:8-9, III:31
— by sex, pp. III:6-7, III:12, III:32-34, III:43
— diseases, pp. III:3, III:53, III:67-72, III:475*t*
— elderly population, p. III:448*t*
— government health funding, p. III:401
— heart failure, pp. III:3, III:12
— homicides, pp. III:4, III:8-9, III:36-38, III:131
— immunizations, p. III:99
— leading causes by year, pp. III:421*t*
— leading causes, by sex, pp. III:6-7, III:13, III:24-30
— perinatal conditions, p. III:9
— research funding, p. III:401
— risk behaviors, pp. III:4, III:125, III:131
— shootings, p. III:4
— suicides, pp. III:4, III:6, III:8, III:34-36, III:131
Causes of disability, pp. III:227-228
CD4 lymphocyte, p. III:53
CDC
— *See:* Centers for Disease Control
Celebrex, pp. III:178, III:275
Celera Genomics, p. III:105
Cendant Corp., p. IV:84
Center for Budget and Policy Priorities, p. III:387
Center for Nutrition Policy and Promotion, pp. II:66-67
Centers for Disease Control, pp. III:16, III:36, III:43, III:49, III:66, III:95, III:97-99, IV:190
— abortions, p. III:306
— active community environments, pp. III:405-406
— antibiotics, pp. III:329, III:331
— *Best Practices for Comprehensive Tobacco Control, Programs*, p. III:408
— bioterrorism, pp. III:392-393
— birth defects, p. III:310
— diseases, pp. III:109, III:161, III:287-288
— food poisoning, pp. III:111-112
— infant mortality, p. III:310
— maternal mortality, p. III:23
— risk behaviors, pp. III:135, III:147
— sexual activity of teenagers, p. III:284
Centers for Medicare and Medicaid Services, p. III:382
Central America, p. I:47
Central cities, pp. II:27-28
Central Intelligence Agency (CIA), pp. IV:186, IV:188-189,

Central Intelligence Agency (CIA) continued:
IV:227
Central libraries, p. I:254
Central nervous system defects, p. III:310
Ceramics, p. I:218
Cereals, p. III:83
Cerebral palsy, pp. III:229, III:231
Cerebrovascular disease, pp. III:2, III:4
— *See also:* Stroke
Certification of teachers
— *See:* Teacher certification
Certifications of nurses, p. III:351
Cervical cancer, pp. III:19, III:68, III:158, III:168
Cesarean sections, pp. III:151, III:301-302
Character education, pp. II:206-207
Charismatics, pp. II:130-131, II:134-135
Charitable giving, pp. I:233-235, I:242-244, I:369*t*
Charter schools, pp. II:231-232
Chat, p. I:282
Chat rooms, p. I:282
Cheese, p. III:83
Chemical burns, p. I:155
Chemical peels, pp. III:277-279
Chemistry, p. II:194
Chemists, pp. I:22, I:24-25
Chemotherapy, pp. III:152, III:159
Cherokee Indian tribe, pp. II:70, II:72
Chicago (IL) law enforcement personnel, p. IV:203
Chicken pox, p. III:96
Child abuse, pp. IV:10, IV:139-140, IV:206
Child Abuse Prevention and Treatment Act, p. IV:107
Child care, pp. II:66-67, I:135, II:262, II:341*t*
Child Care Bureau, p. II:227
Child labor, pp. I:45-46
Child rape, p. IV:245
Childbirth
— by age of mother, pp. III:297-298
— by method of delivery, pp. III:513*t*
— Cesarean sections, pp. III:301-302
— oxytocin, p. III:23
— surgical procedures, p. III:154
Childhood diseases, pp. III:55-57, III:441*t*
Childhood Immunization Act, p. III:97
Children, p. IV:127
— *See also:* Infants
— *See also:* Juveniles
— *See also:* Teenagers
— Attention Deficit/Hyperactivity Disorder (ADHD), pp. III:65, III:483*t*
— attitudes toward religion, p. I:251
— autism, p. III:258
— breastfeeding, p. III:41
— disabilities, pp. III:229-231, III:494*t*
— eating habits, p. II:211
— emotional problems, p. III:230
— employment, p. II:149
— family households, pp. II:44, II:333*t*
— federally funded special education programs, p. II:298
— homicides, p. II:243

Children continued:
— illegal labor, p. I:45
— Internet use, pp. I:278-279, I:379*t*
— learning disabilities, pp. III:65, III:229-231
— living arrangements, pp. II:46, II:58-59, II:61, II:334*t*
— low birth weight, p. III:39
— married-couple households, p. II:46
— Medicaid, p. III:386
— multiple disabilities, p. II:298
— museums, p. I:229
— participation in sports, p. I:204
— poverty, p. I:92
— programs, p. I:258
— Ritalin, p. III:483*t*
— single-parent households, pp. II:46, II:340*t*
— soda consumption, p. II:311
— suicides, p. II:243
— time spent with parents, pp. I:183-184, I:357
— two-parent households, p. II:46
— video games, p. IV:144
Children Now, p. III:221
Chin augmentation, pp. III:277-279
Chin, Vincent, pp. IV:286, IV:288
China, pp. II:5, II:30
Chinese (language), pp. II:76-77
Chinese population, pp. III:40, III:42-43, II:74
Chippewa Indian tribe, pp. II:72-73
Chiropractic medicine, pp. III:78-79, III:82, III:162, II:286, II:290
Chlamydia, pp. III:51-52, III:95
Chloroform, p. III:120
Choctaw Indian tribe, pp. II:72-73
Cholera, pp. III:58-59, III:326, III:442*t*
Cholesterol levels, pp. III:12, III:14, II:18, III:20, III:83, III:210, III:426*t*
Christian houses of worship, pp. II:136-138
Christianity, pp. I:252-253
Christians, pp. II:132-135
Christiansen/Cummings Associates, p. IV:117
Chromosomal defects, pp. III:310, III:312
Chronic illnesses, p. III:204
Church Arsons Prevention Act, p. IV:287
Church of God, pp. II:132-133
Church of Jesus Christ of the Latter-Day Saints, pp. II:136-138
Churches, p. II:360*t*
Churches of Christ, pp. II:130-138
Cigarette smoking, pp. III:64, III:107, IV:173, III:479*t*
— adults, pp. III:121, III:135
— brands, pp. III:136, III:138
— causes of death, p. III:125
— diseases, pp. III:68, III:160
— low birth weight, p. III:40
— prevalence, p. III:409
— school-based health centers, p. III:104
— teenagers, pp. III:117-118
Cincinnati (OH), pp. IV:204, IV:215
Cipro, p. III:392
Circulatory system diseases, pp. III:10, III:152, III:235-238
Cirrhosis, p. III:6
— *See also:* Liver disease

Cisco Systems Inc., p. I:59
Cities, central, p. II:27
Citizens for Safe Drinking Water, p. III:328
Citizenship, p. II:349*t*
Civil liberties, p. IV:185
Civil Rights Act, p. IV:284
Civil Rights movement, p. IV:286
Civil rights violations, pp. IV:108-110
Civil Unions Law, p. II:65
Civilian employment, p. I:13
Claritin, pp. III:167, III:178, III:276
Class Size Reduction Program, pp. II:195-197
Classical music, p. I:218
Clean Air Act, p. III:316
Clean Water Act, pp. III:315, III:321
Clergy, p. II:143
Cleveland Scholarship and Tutoring Program, p. II:240
Clinical laboratory technologists, pp. III:359-360
Clinical nurse specialists, p. III:351
Clinton administration, pp. IV:95, III:106, IV:128, I:166
A Clockwork Orange, p. I:231
Clothing, pp. II:66-67
Club drugs, pp. III:120, IV:154
Clubs, p. I:185
CO
— *See:* Carbon Monoxide
— *See:* Carbon monoxide (CO)
Coaches' salaries, pp. I:206-207
Coalition Against Insurance Fraud, p. IV:94
Coalition for the Prevention of Economic Crime, p. IV:91
Coast Guard Law Enforcement Detachments, p. IV:24
Coca-Cola, p. II:310
Cocaine, p. IV:147
— arrests, p. IV:11
— emergency room visits, p. III:124
— illicit substance use, adults, p. III:121
— lifetime use reported, pp. IV:151-152
— school-based health centers, p. III:104
— trafficking, pp. IV:167-168
— use by race/ethnicity, pp. III:126-127
— use by teenagers, pp. III:117-119
— youth gangs, p. IV:34
Code Red, p. I:280
Coffee consumption, p. III:139
Cohabitation, pp. II:51, II:57-58, II:338*t*
Collagen injections, pp. III:277-279
Collectibles, p. I:286
College, p. II:151
College affordability, pp. II:275-276
College athletics, p. I:363*t*
College Board, pp. II:172, II:293, II:295
College completion rates, p. I:300*t*
College costs, pp. II:271-273, II:275, II:395*t*
College degrees, pp. I:24, I:57, I:61, I:114-116
College education, pp. I:51, I:67, I:94, I:264-265
College enrollment, pp. II:150-151
College preparatory curricula, pp. II:261-262
College sports, pp. I:199, I:206, I:208
Colonoscopy, p. III:31

Colorado, pp. II:63-64
Colorectal cancer, pp. III:67-68, III:430*t*
— causes of death, p. III:30
— obesity, p. III:405
— screening, pp. III:31, III:211
— survival rates, pp. III:156, III:158
Columbia University, p. II:294
Columbine High School, p. II:243
Commerce, p. I:280
Commercial Alert, p. II:265
Commercial participant amusements, p. I:185
Commercialized vice, p. IV:136
Commission on Pornography, p. III:280
Common Good Fear of Litigation Study, p. III:417
Communications, p. II:284
Communications Industry Forecast, p. I:268
Community foundations, pp. I:242, I:245-246
Community health centers, pp. III:100-101, III:436*t*
Community Learning Centers, pp. II:226-227
Community Protection Act (Washington state), p. IV:121
Community water systems, pp. III:326-327, III:519*t*
Commuting, pp. I:135, III:140
Complementary and alternative medicine (CAM), pp. III:74, III:82
Compliance officers, p. I:45
Comprehensive Drug Abuse and Control Act, pp. IV:12, IV:149
Computed tomography, p. III:355
Computer cracker, p. I:281
Computer hacking, pp. IV:92, I:280-281, I:379*t*
Computer learning opportunities, pp. II:263, II:393*t*
Computer products, p. I:185
Computer-related occupations, pp. I:32, I:52, I:54-55, I:58-59, I:61-62, II:296
Computer systems administrators
— *See:* Network and computer systems administrators
Computer use, p. II:264
Computer viruses, p. I:280
Computer worms, p. I:280
Computerized axial tomography, p. III:152
— *See also:* CAT scans
Computerized axial tomography (CAT) scans, p. III:152
Computerized Axial Tomography (CAT) scans, p. III:155
Computers, p. I:286
Concerts, p. I:216
The Condition of America's Schools: 1999, p. II:199
Condoms, pp. II:15, III:104, III:304-305
Congenital malformations, pp. III:10, III:236, III:312
Congregationals, pp. II:132-135, II:144
Congressional Budget Office, p. III:387
Connecticut, pp. II:217, III:338, III:373-374
Conservatives, p. II:114
Construction, p. II:32
— employment, p. I:34
— injuries in the workplace, p. I:156
— occupational fatalities, p. I:151
— productivity, pp. I:104-107, I:329*t*
Consumer Research Study on Book Purchasing, p. I:220
ConsumerSentinel, p. IV:82
Continuing care retirement communities, p. III:194

Contraceptive practices, pp. II:14-15, III:161, III:304-305, II:323*t*

Contracts, p. I:14

Contusions, p. I:155

Convict labor, pp. IV:254-255

Conyers, Jr., John, p. IV:287

Cook County (IL), pp. IV:266-267

Copyright infringement, pp. IV:95-97, IV:328*t*

Cornell University, pp. III:195, II:294

Coronary bypass, p. III:25

Corporate profits, pp. I:122, I:124, I:339*t*

Correctional population, pp. IV:19-20, IV:299*t*

Corrections Corporation of America (CCA), pp. IV:251-252

Corrections system employment, pp. IV:21-22

Corrections system expenditures, pp. IV:249-250, IV:373*t*

Cosmetic surgery, pp. III:179, III:277-279, III:504*t*

Cough syrup, p. III:130

Coughlin, Lt. Paula, p. I:166

Council on Graduate Medical Education, p. III:344

Counterfeiting, pp. IV:88-89, IV:99-100, IV:105, IV:108, IV:327*t*

County mental hospitals, p. III:264

Court trials, pp. IV:273-274

Crack cocaine, pp. IV:151, IV:162

Cream products, p. III:83

Creatine, p. III:130

Creative writing, pp. I:218-219

Creditcards.com, p. IV:91

Creek Indian tribe, pp. II:72-73

Creole, French
— *See:* French Creole

Crib death, pp. III:45-46
— *See also:* Sudden Infant Death Syndrome (SIDS)

Crime Act, p. IV:206

Crime and Punishment: Women in Prison, p. IV:243

Crime control costs, pp. IV:23-24

Crime Index, pp. IV:3, IV:6, IV:14

Crime prevention, p. IV:206

Crime rate
— arrests, pp. IV:102, IV:149, IV:175-176, IV:354*t*
— history, p. IV:15
— justice system employment, p. IV:21

Crimes Against Children, p. IV:139

Crimes against the family, p. IV:136

Crimes cleared by arrest, p. IV:379*t*

Crimes in schools, pp. II:245, II:387*t*

Croatia, p. II:163

Crocheting, p. I:218

Cross-country sports, pp. I:208-209

Cruises, p. I:196

Crystal Cathedral, p. II:145

Cuba, p. II:163

Culture and humanities
— *See also:* arts, culture, and humanities p. I:242

Curfew violations, pp. IV:106-107, IV:136

Curriculum specialization, p. II:261

Cuts, p. I:155

Cyberchurches, p. II:145

Cyberstalking, p. IV:120

Czech Republic, pp. II:163-165, I:187

Dance, pp. I:218-219

Danish, pp. II:76-77

D.A.R.E.
— *See:* Drug Abuse Resistance Education

Database administrators, p. I:52

Date-rape drugs, pp. IV:56, IV:154
— *See also:* Rohypnol

Dating online, pp. I:284-285

DAWN
— *See:* Drug Abuse Warning Network

DCBE
— *See:* Double-Contrast Barium Enema
— *See:* Double-contrast barium enema (DCBE)

DDT, p. III:323

Deaconess-Waltham Hospital (MA), p. III:370

Dead Rabbits, p. IV:43

Deafness, pp. III:227, III:229, II:298

Death penalty, pp. IV:245-246

Death row inmates, pp. IV:244, IV:246, IV:371*t*

Death With Dignity Law, p. III:216

Deaths
— by cause, pp. III:1-2
— by race/ethnicity, p. II:21
— diseases, pp. III:15, III:18, III:423*t*
— influenza epidemic, p. II:17
— life expectancy, pp. II:324*t*
— police officers, pp. IV:210-212, IV:217-218, IV:361*t*
— schools, p. II:243
— terrorism, pp. IV:190-191, IV:358*t*

Defense Department, pp. I:13, I:293*t*

Defense research and development, p. III:398

Degree completion, pp. I:260-262, I:265

Degrees conferred, pp. I:58, II:283, I:296*t* II:399*t*

Degrees conferred, professional
— *See:* professional degrees conferred

Deism, pp. II:134-135, I:252-253

Delaware, pp. II:64, II:187, II:217

Dementia, pp. III:71, III:198, III:204, III:243

Democratic Republic of the Congo, pp. III:332, III:334

Democrats, p. II:98

Denmark, p. IV:125

Dental care benefits, pp. III:103, I:131, I:133, III:210

Dentists, pp. III:79, IV:93, II:286, II:290

Department of Education, pp. IV:290, II:304

Department of Health and Human Services, p. III:63

Department of Justice, pp. IV:203, IV:207, IV:270, IV:290

Department of Labor, p. I:45

Dependency ratio, pp. II:22, I:141

Depressants, p. IV:153

Depression, pp. III:445*t*
— age groups, p. III:262
— cases, pp. III:247-248
— senior citizens, p. III:204
— treatment, pp. III:63-64, III:169
— treatments, pp. III:75-76

Dermabrasion, pp. III:277-278

Desktop publishers, p. I:52

Detective supervisors
— *See:* police and detective supervisors
Detroit (MI), pp. IV:72, IV:124, IV:215
Detroit Receiving Hospital (MI), p. III:265
Developmental delay, p. II:298
Dewey, John, p. II:203
Dexedrine, p. II:303
Diabetes
— Baby Boom generation, pp. III:69-70
— cause of death, pp. III:4-5, III:8-9
— elderly population, p. III:203
— funding, p. III:401
— obesity, p. III:405
— prevalence, pp. III:426*t*
— women, pp. III:12-14, III:21
Diagnostic and Statistical Manual of Mental Disorders, p. III:115, III:170, III:236, III:251, III:254-255
Diagnostic procedures, pp. III:152-154, III:341
Diallo, Amadou, p. IV:204
Diaphragms, pp. II:15, III:304-305
Diet, pp. III:108, III:115
— Atkins, Dr., p. III:90
— cancers, p. III:161
— causes of disability, p. III:228
— pills, p. III:130
— recommended intake, pp. III:20-21, III:29
— supplements, p. III:75
Dietary Guidelines for Americans, p. III:114
Dietary Supplement Health and Education Act, p. III:76
Dieter, Richard C., p. IV:244
Digestive system diseases, pp. III:3, III:150, III:155, III:236, III:310
Digital rectal exam (DRE), p. III:31
Digital television sets, p. I:227
Dining at home, p. I:180
Dining out, pp. III:109, I:187, I:358*t*
Diphtheria, pp. III:55-56, III:94-95
Diptheria, Tetanus, and Pertussis (DTP), p. III:96
Direct Instruction Movement, p. II:202
Disability-based discrimination, pp. I:161, I:167
Disability benefits, pp. III:235-239, III:241, III:243, III:495*t*
Disability insurance, p. I:128
Disability payments, p. I:29
Disabled population, pp. III:224-227, III:492*t*
— Americans with Disabilities Act, p. III:223
— children, pp. III:229, II:298
— educational attainment, pp. III:240-242
— Medicaid, p. III:386
— special education programs, pp. III:230-231
— workforce population, pp. III:233-234, III:244-245
Discrimination cases
— by category, pp. I:161, I:163
— merit resolutions, pp. I:167-169, I:352*t*
— workplace, pp. I:149, I:159
Diseases, p. III:49
— *See also:* Infectious diseases
Disorderly conduct, pp. IV:105, IV:112
Disposable income, p. I:347*t*
Distance education, pp. II:291-292, II:404*t*

District of Columbia, pp. II:217, IV:248, III:338, III:369-370
Dividend income
— *See:* interest and dividend income
Diving, pp. I:208-209
Divorced parents, p. II:59
Divorces, pp. II:48-49, II:335*t*
DNA testing, p. IV:245
Doctoral degrees conferred, pp. I:94, II:285, II:289-290, II:403*t* 404*t*
Doctors of Medicine, pp. IV:93, III:210, II:277-278, III:336, III:340-341
— *See also:* Physicians
Doctors, virtual
— *See:* Telemedicine
Dogs, p. I:191
Domestic abuse, pp. IV:106-107
Domestic partners, pp. II:120, I:136, II:357*t*
Domestic violence, pp. IV:10, IV:47-49, IV:206
Dominican Republic, pp. III:42, I:47
Double-contrast barium enema (DCBE), p. III:31
Down's Syndrome, p. III:328
Dragonball, p. I:283
Drawing, p. I:218
DRE
— *See:* Digital Rectal Exam
— *See:* Digital rectal exam (DRE)
Drinking (alcohol), p. III:104
Drinking water, pp. III:326-328
Drion, Hulb, p. III:218
Driving under the influence (DUI), pp. IV:112-114
Drope v Missouri, p. IV:277
Drownings, pp. III:4, II:18
Drug abuse, pp. IV:12, III:108, III:128-131
Drug Abuse Resistance Education
— *See:* D.A.R.E.
Drug Abuse Resistance Education (D.A.R.E.), pp. III:133-134
Drug Abuse Warning Network (DAWN), p. III:124
Drug-control legislation timeline, p. IV:195
Drug education, p. IV:206
Drug Enforcement Administration (DEA), pp. III:130, IV:155-156, IV:223, IV:226-227, II:303
Drug expenditures, pp. IV:349*t*
Drug Free Schools and Communities Act, p. IV:129
Drug-Induced Rape Prevention and Punishment Act, p. IV:56
Drug Information Service, p. III:390
Drug Price Competition and Patent Term Restoration Act, p. III:176
Drug-related arrests, pp. IV:296*t* 354*t*
— by presidential administration, pp. IV:149-150
— by race/ethnicity, pp. IV:161-163, IV:165-166
— convictions and sentencing, pp. IV:158, IV:164, IV:348*t*
— crime rate, pp. IV:14, IV:175-176
— effect on drug use, pp. IV:157-158
— incarcerations, p. IV:13
— juveniles, p. IV:149
— not included in crime rate, p. IV:10
— possession, p. IV:11
— sentencing, p. IV:108

Drug-related arrests continued:
— trafficking, p. IV:245
Drug-related crimes, pp. IV:101-104
— Baby Boom generation, p. IV:29
— firearms-related crimes, p. IV:40
— not included in crime rate, p. IV:10
— possession and trafficking, p. IV:109
— recidivism, p. IV:260
— state prisons population, pp. IV:236-237
Drug-resistant bacteria, p. III:329
Drug shortages, pp. III:389-391, III:530t
Drug treatment programs, p. IV:263
Drug use, pp. IV:157-158, IV:345t
— by race/ethnicity, pp. IV:159, IV:162
— by type of drug, pp. IV:169-170
DrugFreeTeenagers.com, p. III:133
Drugs distributed, pp. IV:349t
Drunk driving, pp. IV:101, IV:104, IV:206
— *See also:* Driving under the influence
DTP, p. III:96
— *See:* Diphtheria, Tetanus, and Pertussis (DTP)
DUI
— *See:* Driving under the influence
— *See:* Driving under the influence (DUI)
DUKE NUKEM, p. IV:145
Duke University, pp. III:81, I:171, III:237, II:294, III:345
Durable goods, p. I:102
Durex [company], pp. III:271, III:273
Durham versus United States, p. IV:276
Durkheim, Emile, p. III:35
Dutch, p. II:77
DVD players, p. I:227
Dyslexia, p. III:243
E-learning, p. II:292
E-mail, pp. I:273, I:278
E-tailers, p. I:284
Ear infections, p. III:229
Ear surgery, pp. III:150, III:277-279
Earnhardt, Dale, p. I:211
Earnings, p. III:498t
— by educational attainment and sex, p. II:295
— by race/ethnicity and sex, p. I:71
— by sex, pp. I:318t
— college degrees, pp. I:114-116
— disabilities, pp. III:244-245
— doctoral degrees, p. II:404t
— householders, pp. I:322t
— independent contractors, pp. I:71, I:307t
— workforce, p. I:342t
Earth First!, pp. IV:177, IV:181
Earth Liberation Front, p. IV:181
Eastern equine encephalitis, p. III:392
Eating habits, pp. II:211, III:466t
— disease prevention, p. III:90
— eating disorders, pp. III:256-257
— mental health, p. III:247
— stress, pp. III:139-140
— U.S. Surgeon General's recommendations, p. III:83
— weight, pp. III:89, III:115-116

eBay, pp. IV:100, I:282, I:380t
Ebola virus, pp. III:62, III:95
Echinacea, p. III:75
Eckankar, pp. II:134-135, I:252-253
Economic Growth and Tax Relief Reconciliation Act of 2001, p. II:278
Economic sectors, pp. I:3, I:104, I:291t
Ecstasy, pp. III:119-120, III:124, IV:147, IV:153
Ectopic pregnancy, p. III:23
Edison project, p. II:233
Education
— accountability, p. II:166
— adults, p. I:233
— attainment, pp. II:284-285
— charitable giving, pp. I:242-244
— college preparatory, p. II:262
— costs of universities, p. II:281
— elementary and secondary, pp. II:189-190
— employment, pp. I:1, I:10-12
— enrollment, p. I:292t
— expenditures, p. II:399t
— funding, pp. II:377t
— grants, p. II:273
— job advancement, pp. I:260-262
— volunteering, pp. I:245-246
Education administrators, pp. I:22, I:24-25, I:58-59
Education assistance, p. I:135
Education budget, p. II:384t
Education for All Handicapped Children Act, p. III:232
Education of the Handicapped Act, p. III:232
Education revenues, pp. II:212, II:279, II:397t
Educational achievements, pp. II:293, II:369t
Educational attainment, pp. IV:53, I:56, IV:264, I:335t
— adults, pp. I:264-265, I:332t
— Asians, pp. I:118-119
— blacks, pp. I:112, I:118-119
— breastfeeding mothers, p. III:42
— disabled population, p. III:497t
— earnings, pp. I:114-116, II:295, I:318t 405t
— exercise habits, p. III:92
— Hispanics, pp. I:112, I:118-119
— householders, pp. I:322t
— income, pp. I:94-95, II:177
— labor force, p. I:304t
— literacy, p. II:155
— men, p. I:94
— productivity, pp. I:110-111
— race/ethnicity, pp. II:152-153
— smoking, p. III:136
— teachers, pp. II:184-185
— volunteering, pp. I:238, I:370t
— whites, pp. I:112, I:118-119
— women, p. I:94
— workforce, p. I:56
Educational services, pp. I:104-105
EEOC
— *See:* Equal Employment Opportunity Commission (EEOC)
Eggs, p. III:83

Egoistic suicides, p. III:35
Eight-ball chicks, p. IV:134
El Salvador, p. I:47
E.L.A., p. II:169
Elder abuse, pp. IV:10, III:198, III:486t
— Adult Protective Services, p. III:199
— American Medical Association, p. III:197
— nursing homes, pp. III:201-202
— perpetrators, p. III:200
Elderly population, pp. II:22, II:35, IV:83, III:189, III:196, IV:241
— causes of death, p. III:448t
— diseases, p. III:210
— geographic distribution, pp. III:189-190
— health care, p. III:379
— health problems, pp. III:210-211
— immunizations, p. III:463t
— living arrangements, p. III:195
— living wills, p. III:211
— Medicare benefits, p. III:207
— prisoners, pp. I:141, IV:240
Elders, Jocelyn, p. III:107
Electrical and electronics engineers, p. I:58
Electronic commerce, pp. I:196, I:280
Electronic Communications Privacy Act, p. IV:229
Electronic fetal monitoring, p. III:302
Electronic surveillance
— *See:* wiretapping
Electronics, pp. I:286, I:367t
Electronics engineers
— *See:* electrical and electronics engineers
Electronics purchases, p. I:227
Elementary and Secondary Education Act, p. II:199
Elementary education, pp. I:11, II:189-190, I:292t
Elementary school principals, p. II:308
Elementary school teachers
— job openings, pp. I:24-25, I:58, I:61-62
— retirement, pp. I:22-23
— worker shortages, p. I:59
Eli Lilly & Co., p. III:170
Eligibility clerks, p. I:27
Elliptical motion trainers, p. I:200
Embezzlement, pp. IV:105, IV:108, IV:136
Eme Edict, p. IV:40
Emergency medical technicians (EMTs), pp. III:357-358
Emergency medicine physicians, p. III:341
Emergency room visits, pp. III:124-125, III:130, III:471t
Emory University, p. II:280
Emotional abuse of elderly, p. III:199
Emotional problems, pp. III:227, III:229-231, III:264
Emotionally disturbed children, pp. II:298-299
Emphysema, pp. III:3, III:5-6
Employee benefits, pp. I:127-130, I:133, I:135-138
Employee contributions, p. I:132
Employees, pp. I:127, I:296t
Employer costs, pp. I:127-128, I:131
Employment, pp. I:1, I:16, IV:22
— administrative support occupations (including clerical), pp. I:20, I:296t
— by industry, pp. I:1, I:3-7, I:9-14, I:20, I:34, III:141-143, III:234,

Employment continued:
III:244-245, I:291t
— by race/ethnicity and sex, p. I:16
— disabled workers, p. III:233
— Fair Labor Standards Act, p. II:146
— high school diplomas, p. II:177
— high school education, pp. I:11-12
— justice system, p. IV:21
— literacy, pp. II:157-158
Employment-practice liability cases, p. I:170
EMTs
— *See:* Emergency medical technicians
— *See:* Emergency medical technicians (EMTs)
End-stage renal disease, p. III:380
Endocrine system, pp. III:150-151, III:236
Endometrial cancer
— *See:* Uterine cancer
Endoscopy, p. III:151
Endotracheal tube insertion, p. III:152
Endowments, p. II:279
Engineering occupations, pp. II:284-285, II:296
Engineering services, p. I:7
Engineers, p. I:32
— *See also:* computer engineers
Engineers (industrial), pp. I:22-25, I:296t
England, pp. IV:125, II:165
English language, p. II:284
English Language Arts test
— *See:* E.L.A.
English literature, p. II:284
English, honors
— *See:* Honors English
Enrollment, pp. II:222-223, II:231
— elementary education, p. I:292t
— high school sports, pp. I:204-205
— Medicaid, p. III:386
— Medicare, pp. III:490t
Enron Corp., pp. IV:85, IV:109
Entertainment, p. I:268
— *See also:* arts and entertainment
Environment, pp. I:242-246, III:315
Environmental crimes and sentencing, p. IV:108
Environmental interest organizations, p. IV:181
Environmental Protection Agency, pp. III:322, III:327
Epidemic-related deaths, p. III:463t
Epilepsy, pp. III:229, III:231
Episcopalians, pp. II:130-133, II:135-138
Episiotomy, p. III:151
Equal Employment Opportunity Commission (EEOC), p. I:159, I:163, I:165, I:167, I:169, I:353t
Equipment and software, p. I:102
Equipment cleaners and laborers
— *See:* handlers, equipment cleaners, and laborers
Erectile dysfunction treatments, pp. III:275-276
Escherichia coli infections, p. III:111
Eskimos, p. II:24
Esophageal cancer, pp. III:156, III:161
Estonia, p. II:163
Estrogen, p. II:18

Estuaries, pp. III:323, III:325

Ether, p. III:120

Ethical and Religious Directives for Catholic Health Education, p. III:367

Ethiopia, p. III:332

Ethnicity, pp. II:10, II:12-13
— *See also:* Race/ethnicity
— abortions, pp. II:10, II:12-13, II:321*t*
— advanced classes, p. II:259
— Bachelor's Degree recipients, pp. II:287-288
— births, pp. II:10, II:321*t*
— college enrollment, p. II:151
— computer learning opportunities, p. II:263
— doctoral degrees conferred, pp. II:289-290
— educational attainment, pp. II:152-153
— fertility rates, p. II:321*t*
— home ownership, p. II:35
— honors English classes, p. II:259
— population, pp. II:24, II:70, II:343*t*
— Population Replacement Rate, p. II:8
— reading proficiency, p. II:159
— single-parent households, p. II:61
— Total Fertility Rates, pp. II:6-8
— vocational education credits accumulated, p. II:258

Euro RSCG [company], pp. III:271, III:273

Europe, pp. II:5, II:24, I:41, III:326

Euthanasia, pp. III:214-215, III:218
— *See also:* Physician-assisted suicide

Evaluation and the Academy: Are We Doing the Right Thing?, pp. II:293-294

Evangelicals, pp. II:132-133, II:136-138

Excessive force, pp. IV:213-214, IV:363*t*

Executive, administrative, managerial occupations, pp. I:20, I:69-70, I:296*t*

Exercise habits, pp. III:20-21, III:92, III:161, I:203

Expenditures, pp. II:215-217
— defense of the indigent, pp. IV:283-284
— drug control, pp. IV:171-172
— fast food, p. III:109
— health care, pp. I:130, III:484*t*
— Medicare, pp. III:490*t*
— prescription drugs, p. III:484*t*
— psychotherapy, p. III:263
— restaurant, p. III:109
— worker's compensation claims, p. I:153

Expulsions from school, pp. II:245-246

Extortion and sentencing, p. IV:108

Eye treatments, pp. III:150, III:277-279

Fabricators and laborers
— *See:* Operators, fabricators, and laborers

Fair Labor Standards Act (FLSA), pp. I:43, II:146

Families
— income, pp. I:92, II:264
— leisure time, p. I:173
— mealtimes, p. I:180
— poverty rates, pp. I:92-93, I:315*t*

Family and Medical Leave Act (FMLA), pp. I:137-138, I:344*t*

Family entertainment concerns, p. I:231

Family households, pp. II:42, II:44, II:53, II:333*t*

Family leave, pp. I:135, I:137

Family Violence Prevention and Services Act of 1992, p. III:199

Fanning, Shawn, p. IV:95

Farmers and ranchers, p. I:54

Farmers' markets, p. III:87

Farming, forestry, and fishing occupations, pp. I:20, I:31, I:69-70, I:200, I:296*t*

Farmlands, p. III:458*t*

Fast-food expenditures, pp. III:109-110

Fast Food Nation, pp. III:110, III:112, II:310-311

Fast-pitch softball, p. I:200

Fat injections, p. III:279

Fatalistic suicides, p. III:35

Fatalities, pp. I:149, I:151, I:156

Fathers, pp. II:53, II:62, I:183

Fats, pp. III:20-21, III:83

Fecal occult blood test (FOBT), p. III:31

Federal appropriations, p. II:279

Federal Aviation Administration, p. IV:232

Federal Bureau of Investigation (FBI)
— arrests, p. IV:272
— arson, p. IV:81
— burglaries, pp. IV:73-74
— crime index, pp. IV:9-10, IV:14, IV:293*t*
— curfew violations, p. IV:107
— federal law enforcement, pp. IV:226-227
— hate crimes, pp. IV:289-290
— property crime index, p. IV:8
— terrorism, pp. IV:180-181, IV:186, IV:188-189
— *Uniform Crime Report*, pp. IV:3, IV:5

Federal Bureau of Prisons, p. IV:226

Federal Correctional Institute Morgantown, p. IV:248

Federal financial aid, pp. II:211, II:226-227, II:273-274

Federal Firearms Act, p. IV:46

Federal government employment, pp. I:1, I:9-10, I:13, I:292*t* 293*t*

Federal government funding, p. I:256

Federal government grants and contracts, pp. III:100, II:279

Federal Interstate Anti-Stalking Law, p. IV:120

Federal law enforcement personnel, pp. IV:226-227, IV:365*t*

Federal Prison Industries, p. IV:255

Federal prisons, pp. IV:237, IV:245, IV:248, IV:370*t*

Federal Protective Service, p. IV:227

Federal Trade Commission, pp. IV:82, IV:90-91

Federal Wire Act, p. IV:118

Felony defendants
— released or detained until case disposition, pp. IV:379*t*
— trial dates, pp. IV:270-274

Female-male teacher ratio, pp. II:182-183

Females, pp. III:137, III:150, III:154, III:304, II:322*t*
— *See also:* Women
— athletes, p. I:204
— childbearing years, p. II:21
— gangsters, p. IV:135
— larcenies, p. IV:136
— law enforcement personnel, p. IV:203
— murdered, pp. IV:314*t*
— prisoners, p. IV:17

Females continued:
— violent crimes, pp. IV:135-136
— vocational education, pp. II:258-259
Fertility rates
— birth rate, pp. III:507*t*
— by decade, pp. II:2, II:4
— by race/ethnicity, p. I:40
— European community, p. II:5
— live births, pp. II:315*t*
— population replacement rates, p. II:4
— reproductive patterns, pp. III:292-295
Fibril injections, pp. III:277-278
Fiction, p. I:220
Filipinos, pp. III:40, II:74
Finance, insurance, and real estate, pp. I:6, I:104-105, I:292*t*
Financial aid, p. II:273
Financial Executives International, pp. IV:84, I:171
Financial exploitation of elderly, p. III:199
Financial managers, pp. I:22, I:24-25, I:58
Financial restatements, p. IV:84
Finland, p. II:163
Finnish, p. II:76
Firearms, p. II:245
Firearms-related crimes, pp. IV:45, IV:47-48, IV:314*t*
Fires, p. III:4
First Church of Cyberspace, p. II:145
First-line supervisors and managers, pp. I:61-62
First marriages, p. II:338*t*
Fishing occupations
— *See:* farming, forestry, and fishing occupations
Fitness centers, p. I:135
Fitness trainers and aerobics instructors, p. I:52
Five Point Gang, p. IV:43
The Fix, p. IV:30
Flexible spending accounts, p. I:136
Flexible workplace, p. I:135
Flight engineers
— *See:* aircraft pilots and flight engineers
Florida
— gay-couple households, pp. II:63-64
— geographic distribution of elderly population, p. III:190
— hate crimes, p. IV:289
— hospital beds, p. III:369
— malpractice litigation, pp. III:415, III:417
— sex offender registries, pp. IV:121-122
— smoking prevalence, p. III:409
— vacation travel, p. I:190
— youth gangs, p. IV:138
Florida State Department of Health, p. III:392
Flour, p. III:83
Flowers, pp. I:185, I:284
FLSA
— *See:* Fair Labor Standards Act
— *See:* Fair Labor Standards Act (FLSA)
Flu epidemic
— *See:* influenza epidemic
Fluid cream products, p. III:83
Fluoride, pp. III:315, III:327-328

FOBT
— *See:* Fecal occult blood test
— *See:* Fecal occult blood test (FOBT)
Food and Drug Administration, pp. III:176, III:330, III:389-391
Food Guide Pyramid, p. III:83
Food poisoning, pp. III:111-112
Food preparation workers, pp. I:61-62
Food services, p. II:262
— *See:* accommodations and food services
FoodNet, p. III:111
Foods, pp. II:66-67
— bioterrorism, p. III:88
— consumption of major commodities, pp. III:451*t*
— nutrient levels, pp. III:459*t*
— pesticide use, pp. III:87-88
— phytochemicals, p. III:90
Foods, organic
— *See:* organic foods
Fools Gold: A Critical Look at Computers in Childhood, p. II:265
Football, p. I:209
Foreign-born physicians, p. III:337
Foreign-born population, pp. I:301*t*
Foreign-educated physicians
— *See:* IMGs
Foreign Intelligence Surveillance Act (FISA), p. IV:230
Foreign languages used in the United States, pp. II:76-77, II:344*t*
Forensic pathology physicians, p. III:341
Forestry and fishing occupation
— *See:* farming, forestry, and fishing occupations
Forestry and fishing occupations
— *See:* farming, forestry, and fishing occupations
Forgery, pp. IV:105, IV:108
Fortune 500 firms, p. II:120
Foundations, pp. I:242, I:245-246
Fourth graders, p. II:200
Fractures, p. I:155
France
— breastfeeding, p. III:42
— duration of school year, p. II:254
— entertainment, p. I:187
— literacy, pp. II:163-165
— prostitution, p. IV:125
— terrorism, p. IV:184
— tuberculosis, p. III:334
— vacation time, p. I:192
Franklin W. Olin College of Engineering, p. II:280
Fraternal organizations, p. I:185
Fraud, pp. IV:64, IV:82, IV:85, IV:101, IV:104-105, III:376
Fred Hutchinson Cancer Research Center, p. III:144
Free weights, p. I:202
French, p. II:76
French (language), p. II:77
French Creole, p. II:77
Fresno (CA), p. IV:72
Friends Don't Let Friends Drive Drunk, p. IV:113
Frost & Sullivan, p. IV:117
Fruits, p. III:83
Funding, pp. II:211, II:224-225, I:256, II:377*t*

Fuqua School of Business, p. I:171
G-ratings, p. I:230
GAAP
— *See:* Generally Accepted Accounting Principles (GAAP)
GAD
— *See:* Generalized Anxiety Disorder
Gallbladder cancer, p. III:161
Gambling, pp. IV:10, IV:101, IV:105, IV:108
Games, p. I:282
Gangs, pp. IV:39, IV:43, IV:206, IV:313*t*
— *See also:* Street gangs
— *See also:* Youth gangs
Garlic, p. III:75
Gasoline, p. III:120
Gastroesophageal Reflux Disease (GERD), p. III:167
Gays, pp. III:54, II:63-64, II:122, I:191, II:342*t*
— *See also:* Homosexuals
— *See also:* Lesbians
GDP
— *See:* Gross Domestic Product
GEDs
— *See:* General equivalency diplomas (GEDs)
General equivalency diploma
— *See:* GED
General Equivalency Diplomas (GEDs), p. I:264
General managers and top executives, pp. I:58, I:61-62
General office clerks, pp. I:61-62
The General Social Survey, p. II:295
General surgeons' medical malpractice premiums, p. III:415
Generalized Anxiety Disorder (GAD), p. III:252
Generally Accepted Accounting Principles (GAAP), p. IV:85
Generic prescription drug prices, p. III:175
Genetic engineering, pp. III:105-106
Genital cancer, p. III:3
Genital herpes, p. III:95
Genital surgery, pp. III:150-151
Genitourinary system diseases, pp. III:236, III:310
Genome research centers, p. III:105
Geographic distribution of population, pp. III:189-190
Geographic maldistribution of physicians, p. III:344
Geometry, analytic
— *See:* Analytic geometry
Georgia, pp. I:50, II:63-64, II:163, II:246, IV:248, IV:284
German (language), p. II:76
German measles, p. III:57
— *See also:* Rubella
Germany, pp. II:163, I:187, II:254, III:334
Getting America's Students Ready for the 21st Century, p. II:263
Ghettos, p. IV:162
GI Bill, pp. II:273-274
— *See also:* Serviceman's Readjustment Act
Gideon v Wainwright, p. IV:281
Gift shopping, p. I:284
Gifted children, pp. II:304-305, II:406*t*
Ginkgo Biloba, p. III:75
Ginseng, p. III:75
Girl Scouts, p. I:205
Giuliani, Mayor Rudy, p. IV:216

Glandular surgery, p. III:151
Global Tuberculosis Control: WHO Report 2002, p. III:332
Glucophage, p. III:167
Golf, pp. I:200, I:211
Gonorrhea, pp. III:51-52
Goods-producing industries, p. I:291*t*
Government, p. II:193
Government drug-control budget, pp. IV:350*t*
Government expenditures on crime control, p. IV:24
Government funding, p. I:256
— Human Genome Project, pp. III:464*t*
— National Institutes of Health, pp. III:400-401, III:535*t*
— research and development, pp. III:397-399, III:532*t*
Grade inflation, p. II:293
Grandtravel, p. I:191
Grants, pp. III:100, II:273
Grapes, p. III:87
Great Britain, pp. III:42, I:187, I:192
Great Lakes water pollution, p. III:321
Greek (language), p. II:76
Greeting cards, p. I:284
Grenades, p. II:245
Griffin v Illinois, p. IV:282
Grocery expenditures, pp. III:85-86, III:457*t*
Gross Domestic Product (GDP), pp. I:102, I:143, I:328*t*
Grossman, Lt. Colonel David, p. IV:145
Groundskeeping laborers
— *See also:* landscaping and groundskeeping laborers p. I:61
Guards and watch guards, pp. I:61-62
Guatemala, p. I:47
Gun Control Act, p. IV:46
Gun-Free Schools Act, pp. IV:129-132, II:245-246
Gun-related homicide arrests, pp. IV:311*t*
Gun-related violent crime, pp. IV:39, IV:45, IV:47
Guyana, p. II:163
Gym classes
— *See:* physical education classes
Gynecologists, pp. III:341, III:415
H-1B visas, p. I:59
Hacking, p. I:208
Hair salons, p. I:54
Hair transplantation for men, pp. III:277-278
Haiti, p. I:47
Hallucinogens, pp. IV:151-153
Hamm, Mia, p. I:209
Hand packers and packagers, pp. I:61-62
Handguns, pp. IV:40, II:245
Handlers, equipment cleaners, and laborers, pp. I:20, I:296*t*
Hanta virus, pp. III:62, III:95
Happy Meals, p. III:110
Harassment, pp. I:19, I:149, I:159, I:161, I:163, I:169, I:353*t*
Hard Pack, p. III:138
Harrison Act, p. IV:12
Harry Potter and the Sorcerer's Stone, pp. I:221, I:283
Harvard Mental Health Letter, p. III:135
Harvard School of Public Health Department of Nutrition, p. III:109
Harvard University, pp. III:75, II:293
Harvest Christian Fellowship, p. II:144

Hashish, pp. III:118, III:121, III:124, IV:152
— illicit substance use, teenagers, p. III:117
Hate crimes, pp. IV:286-290, IV:382t
— *See also:* Bias-related crimes
Hawaii, p. II:64
Hawaiian Natives, p. II:72
Hay fever, p. III:229
Hayflick Limit, p. III:48
Hazelden Foundation, p. III:123
HBV immunizations, p. III:97
HDL
— *See:* High-Denisty Lipoprotein (HDL)
Head injuries, pp. III:227, III:243
Head Start, pp. II:222-225, II:383t
Heaemophilus influenzae type b
— *See:* Hib
Health assessments, pp. III:488t
Health care, pp. I:242-244, III:484t
— costs for children, pp. II:66-67
— employment, pp. I:7, I:34
— expenditures, p. I:342t
— fraud, pp. IV:93-94, IV:328t
— Medicare enrollment, p. III:379
— productivity, pp. I:104-105
— vocational education, pp. II:256-257, II:262
— volunteering, pp. I:245-246
Health Care Financing Administration, p. III:374
Health clubs, pp. I:200-201
Health information technicians
— *See:* medical records and health information technicians
Health insurance, p. I:131
— employee benefits, pp. I:128-130, I:132
— independent contractors, p. I:72
— same-sex partners, p. I:136
Health Maintenance Organizations (HMOs), pp. III:345, III:382-383
Health Professional Shortage Areas, p. III:338
Health professions, p. II:284
Health sciences, p. II:284
Health services, pp. III:394-395, III:531t
Health violations in community water systems, p. III:326
Healthy Eating Index, p. III:84
Healthy People, pp. III:73, III:303, III:403-404, III:408
Hearing impairments, pp. III:203, III:227, III:229, II:298, III:487t
Hearing screenings, p. III:103
Heart attacks, pp. III:3, III:275-276
Heart disease, pp. III:5, III:14, II:18
— *See also:* Cardiovascular disease
— aging population, p. III:203
— Baby Boom generation, p. III:69
— causes of death, pp. III:4, III:6, III:8-9, III:12, III:24-25, III:69, III:401
— causes of disability, p. III:227
— funding, pp. III:400-401
— risk behaviors, p. III:136
— risk factors, pp. III:12, III:328
— treatments, pp. III:25, III:155
Heat burns, p. I:155

Hebrew, p. II:77
Helpers and laborers, p. I:43
Hemic system surgical procedures, pp. III:150-151
Hemorrhages in maternal mortality, p. III:23
Henderson, Charles, p. II:145
Hepatitis, pp. III:6, III:61, III:96, III:148, III:444t
Herbal therapies, pp. III:75, III:77, III:82, III:450t
Herbs, medicinal
— *See:* medicinal herbs
Hero Syndrome, p. IV:81
Heroin, p. IV:147
— control legislation, p. IV:11
— description, pp. IV:151-152
— emergency room visits, pp. III:124-125
— trafficking, pp. IV:12, IV:167-168
Herpes, genital
— *See:* Genital herpes
Heterosexuals, pp. III:53, III:289
Hib vaccinations for children, pp. III:96-97
High blood pressure
— *See also:* Hypertension
— causes of disability, pp. III:227-228
— obesity, p. III:405
High-Density Lipoprotein (HDL), pp. III:20-21
High school
— diplomas, pp. I:39, II:148, II:177, I:300t
— dropouts, pp. II:148-149
— sports, pp. I:199, I:204-205, I:362
— students, pp. I:250-251
— vocational education, pp. II:256-257, II:260-262, II:363t
High school education
— adults, p. I:264
— earnings, pp. I:114-116
— employment, pp. I:11-12
— enrollment, pp. I:292t
— income, p. I:94
— staff, p. I:292t
— workforce, p. I:57
High-speed pursuits, pp. IV:219, IV:364t
Highly Active Anti-Retroviral Therapy, p. III:54
Hill, Anita, pp. I:162, I:165
Hinckley, John, pp. IV:277, IV:280
Hindi (language), p. II:76
Hinduism, pp. II:134-135, II:140-141, I:252-253
Hispanics, p. I:47
— abortions, pp. II:12-13
— births, pp. II:10, I:40, II:321t
— breastfeeding, p. III:41
— causes of infant mortality, pp. III:44, III:313
— computer learning opportunities, p. II:263
— deaths, pp. III:8-9, III:15
— diseases, pp. III:97, III:289
— drug use, pp. IV:159-160
— earnings, p. I:71
— education, pp. II:161-162, II:259
— educational attainment, pp. I:39, I:112, I:118-119, II:151-153, II:258, II:287-290
— employment, pp. I:16, I:30, I:37, I:67-68
— families, p. I:38

Hispanics continued:
— federal law enforcement officers, p. IV:227
— housing, p. II:35
— immunizations, p. III:99
— income, pp. I:82-83
— Internet use, pp. I:270-271
— law enforcement personnel, pp. IV:203-204
— learning disabilities, p. III:66
— literacy, p. II:159
— low birth weight, p. III:309
— Medicare, p. III:380
— physicians, p. III:337
— population, pp. II:24-25, II:39, II:70-71, II:346t
— risk behaviors, p. III:137
— single-parent households, p. II:61
— Total Fertility Rates, pp. II:6-8
— volunteering, p. I:241
— voter turnout, p. II:106
— youth gangs, p. IV:43
Historical diseases, pp. III:442t
History museums, p. I:229
HIV, pp. III:51, III:286, III:288-290
— attendant diseases, pp. III:3, III:333
— by race/ethnicity and sex, p. III:54
— Centers for Disease Control, p. III:288
— deaths, pp. III:8, III:53, III:289
— number of cases, p. III:506t
Hmong population, p. II:74
Hobson, Senator Cal, p. IV:253
Holidays, p. I:133
Holland, p. III:215
Holy Anorexia, p. III:115
Home-based businesses, pp. I:51, I:73-74, I:308t
Home care aides, p. I:53
— *See also:* personal home care aides
Home-cooked meals, p. I:357t
Home-entertainment products, p. I:226
Home health agencies, pp. III:207-209, III:393
Home health aides, p. I:52
Home health care, p. I:131
Home ownership, pp. II:35, III:191-192, I:194-195, II:331t
Home School Legal Defense Association, p. II:235
Home security, p. I:171
Home theatre in a box, p. I:227
Homeland Defense, p. IV:357t
Homeland Security Council, p. IV:187
Homelessness, p. IV:7
Homeopathy, pp. III:78, III:80, III:82
Homes, p. I:194
Homeschooling, p. II:234
Homework, pp. II:252-253, I:278, II:390t
Homicides, p. IV:41
— *See also:* Murders
— by age, pp. IV:308t
— by location, p. IV:319t
— by race/ethnicity, pp. IV:52-53, IV:217-218
— by sex, pp. II:18, IV:35, IV:310t
— children, p. II:243
— Columbine High School, p. II:24

Homicides continued:
— deaths, pp. III:4, III:8-9, II:21, III:131, III:432t
— domestic, pp. IV:48-49
— firearms-related, pp. IV:45, IV:311t
— incarcerations, pp. IV:306t
— population density, pp. IV:57-58
— rate fluctuation, pp. IV:28-30
— recidivism, p. IV:260
— reported to the police, pp. IV:4, IV:6
— students at school, p. II:243
— terrorism, pp. IV:190-191
— victims, pp. IV:34, IV:315t
Homosexuals, pp. III:53, III:287
— *See also:* Gays
— *See also:* Lesbians
— *See also:* Same-sex partners
Honda Accord, p. IV:71
Honduras, p. I:47
Honest Cannabis Information Foundation, p. III:134
Hong Kong, pp. II:5, II:31, II:163-165, I:187
Honolulu, p. II:75
Honor graduates, pp. II:293-294
Honors English, p. II:259
Hormone replacement therapy (HRT), pp. III:161, III:168
Horoscopes, p. I:282
Hospice care, pp. III:213, III:363, III:373, III:375
— diseases, p. III:376
— Hospice Home Care movement, p. III:373
— Kubler-Ross, Elisabeth, pp. III:212, III:374
— Medicare, pp. III:214, III:374, III:377-378
— pain control, pp. III:213-214
— patients, pp. III:525t
— Saunders, Dr. Cicely, pp. III:376, III:378
— United Government Services, pp. III:377-378
Hospitality, p. II:262
Hospitals, pp. I:131, III:212, III:264, III:364-365, III:525t
— *See also:* Catholic hospitals
— admissions, pp. III:369-370
— closings, pp. III:363, III:367, III:369-372
— expenditures, p. III:395
— medical procedures, pp. III:477t
— mergers, pp. III:366, III:525t
Hosting meals, pp. I:187, I:358t
Hot Network, p. III:280
Hotels and lodging, pp. I:7, I:196
Hotmail, p. I:282
House Select Committee on Aging, p. III:198
Household activities, pp. I:181-182, I:357
Household expenditures, pp. I:145, I:347t
Household income, pp. I:309t
— benefits, p. I:145
— college tuition, pp. II:271-272
— infant mortality, p. III:313
— Internet use, pp. I:270, I:378t
— life expectancy, p. II:21
— victimization rates, pp. IV:31-32
— weekend travel, p. I:192
Household service occupations, pp. I:20, I:32, I:296t
Households, pp. II:42-43, II:45, II:333t

Households continued:
— charitable giving, p. I:234
— earnings, pp. I:322*t*
Houses of worship, p. II:361*t*
Housing, pp. II:66-67
Housing stock, pp. II:32-34, II:330*t*
Houston (TX), p. II:30
Howard, Dennis, p. I:213
HRT
— *See:* Hormone replacement therapy
Human Genome Project, pp. III:105-106, III:464*t*
Human immunodeficiency virus
— *See:* HIV
Human resources occupations, pp. I:22, I:296*t*
Human Rights Campaign Foundation, p. II:65
Human Rights Watch, p. IV:248
Human services, pp. I:242, I:244-246
Human services assistants
— *See also:* social and human services assistants p. I:52
Humanism, pp. II:134-135, I:252-253
Humanities, p. II:285
— *See also:* arts, culture, and humanities p. I:242
Hungarian, p. II:76
Hungary, pp. II:163, II:165, III:334
Hydrocodone/APAP, p. III:167
Hyperkinetic Disorder of Children, p. II:302
Hypertension, p. III:14
— *See also:* High blood pressure
— aging population, p. III:203
— causes of death, p. III:2
— causes of disability, p. III:227
— low birth weight, pp. III:11, III:40
— maternal mortality, p. III:23
Hyperthyroidism and Synthroid, p. III:168
Hypothalamus gland surgery, p. III:151
Iceland, pp. II:163-164
Idaho, pp. II:187, IV:276, III:349
Identity theft, pp. IV:82, IV:90-92, IV:328*t*
Identity Theft and Assumption Deterrence Act, p. IV:92
IHD
— *See:* Ischemic heart disease
Illegal aliens, pp. I:49, IV:251
Illegal drug consumption, pp. IV:148, IV:167-168, IV:346*t*
Illegal gambling profits, p. IV:117
Illegal labor, p. II:349*t*
— age group, p. I:301*t*
— arrests, pp. I:49, I:302*t*
— country of origin, p. I:302*t*
— foreign countries, p. I:47
— minors, p. I:302*t*
— *Operation Child Watch*, p. I:45
— teenagers, p. I:43
Illicit substance use, pp. IV:350*t*
— Baby Boom generation, p. III:134
— by race/ethnicity, p. III:126
— emergency room visits, p. III:124
— inhalants, pp. III:119-120
— public health concerns, pp. III:411-412
— youth, pp. III:117-120

Illinois, pp. IV:248, IV:290, III:415, III:417
— gay-couple households, p. II:63
— geographic distribution of elderly population, p. III:190
— hospital beds, p. III:369
— teacher certification, p. II:187
— vacation time, p. I:190
— youth gangs, p. IV:138
IMGs, pp. III:342-343
Immigrants, pp. I:41, I:47, II:349*t*
Immigration and Naturalization Service, pp. I:47, I:49, IV:188, IV:226-227, IV:251
Immigration crimes and sentencing, p. IV:108
Immunizations, pp. III:94, III:99, III:103, III:462*t*
— adults, p. III:98
— diseases, p. III:96
— elderly population, p. III:463*t*
— HBV, p. III:97
Implants, p. II:15
Improving Teacher Quality State Grants, p. II:225
In-line skating, p. I:202
Incarceration rates, p. IV:30
Income
— Baby Boomers, pp. I:75-78
— charitable giving, pp. I:234-235
— educational attainment, pp. I:94-95
— exercise habits, p. III:92
— families, p. I:92
— grocery expenditures, p. III:86
— household, pp. I:80-81, I:85-87, II:177, II:370*t*
— Internet use, pp. I:274-275
— Medicare, p. III:528*t*
— minimum wage, p. I:90
— productivity, p. I:120
— race/ethnicity, pp. I:38, I:75, I:82-83, I:211*t*
— sex, pp. I:84, I:94, I:312*t*
Income, supplemental
— *See:* supplemental income
Independent contractors
— characteristics, p. I:307*t*
— earnings, p. I:71
— educational attainment, p. I:67
— health insurance, p. I:72
— marital status, p. I:68
— occupations, pp. I:69-70, I:307*t*
— part-time employment, p. I:68
Independents, p. II:98
India, pp. II:5, III:42, I:187
Indiana, pp. II:63, III:409
Indians, p. III:52
Indigent defendants, pp. IV:283-285, IV:381*t*
Individuals with Disabilities Education Act, pp. III:232, III:258, II:299-300
Indonesia, pp. I:187, III:332
Indoor track, p. I:208
Industrial engineers, pp. I:22-25, I:296*t*
Industry, pp. II:256-257, II:262
Infant mortality, p. II:21
— birth defects, pp. III:310-311
— causes, pp. III:10-11, III:423*t*

Infant mortality continued:
517*t*
— rates, pp. III:43, III:312-313
— selected years, pp. III:44-45
Infants, pp. III:10-11, III:41
— *See also:* Children
— *See also:* Juveniles
— *See also:* Teenagers
— *See also:* Youth
Infectious diseases, pp. III:94, III:236, III:462*t*
— *See also:* Diseases
Infertility, p. III:299
Influenza, p. III:5
— causes of death, pp. III:2, III:4, III:8-9, III:69-70, III:99, III:401
— epidemic of 1918, pp. III:2, II:17, II:20, III:94
— immunizations, pp. III:96, III:98-99
Information clerks
— *See:* receptionists and information clerks
Information scientists (research)
— *See also:* computer and information scientists p. I:52
Information services, pp. I:104-105
Information systems managers
— *See:* computer and information systems managers
Information technology, p. IV:188
Inglewood Unified School District (CA), p. IV:131
Inhalants, pp. III:119-120, IV:151
Injectables, p. II:15
Injuries, pp. I:153, III:228, III:235, III:238
Ink jet printers and counterfeiting, p. IV:88
Inpatient hospitals, pp. III:207-209
INS
— *See:* Immigration and Naturalization Service
Insanity defense, pp. IV:275, IV:277-280, IV:381*t*
Insanity Defense Reform Act, p. IV:277
Inspectors
— *See:* machine operators, assemblers, and inspectors
Instant messaging, p. I:278
Institute on Race and Poverty, p. IV:222
Instrumental activities of daily living, pp. III:203-204
Insurance
— *See:* finance and insurance
Insurance claims and policy processing clerks, p. I:54
Insurance companies, p. III:416
Insurance fraud, p. IV:80
Insurance Information Institute, p. IV:79
Integrative medicine, p. III:82
Integumentary system, pp. III:150-151
Intellectual property, p. IV:97
Interest and dividend income, pp. I:145-146
Internal Revenue Service (IRS), pp. IV:91, IV:226, I:283
International Anti-Counterfeiting Coalition, p. IV:100
International Chamber of Commerce, p. IV:100
International Classification of Diseases, p. III:22
International Intellectual Property Association, p. IV:97
International Parental Kidnapping Crime Act, p. IV:141
International Task Force on Euthanasia and Assisted Suicide, p. III:217
Internet
— *See also:* Worldwide Web

Internet continued:
— charitable giving, p. I:235
— computer hacking, p. I:280
— counterfeiting, p. IV:100
— dating, pp. I:284-285
— entertainment, pp. I:226, I:233, I:268
— missing children, p. IV:143
— online travel spending, p. I:196
— productivity, p. I:97
— religion, pp. II:142-143, II:145
— schools, p. II:264
— search terms, pp. I:282-283, I:379*t*
— volunteering, p. I:246
Internet copyright piracy, pp. IV:95, IV:98
Internet fraud, pp. IV:82, IV:91
Internet gambling, pp. IV:101, IV:117-118
Internet Public Library, pp. I:257-258
Internet use, pp. I:276, I:377*t*
— age groups, p. I:378*t*
— by race/ethnicity and sex, pp. I:270-276, I:377*t*
— children, pp. I:278, I:379*t*
— household income, p. I:378*t*
Internists' medical malpractice premiums, p. III:415
Interracial marriages, pp. II:54-55, II:339*t*
Interuterine devices (IUDs), pp. II:15, III:304-305
Interviewers and clerks
— *See:* loan interviewers and clerks
Intrauterine Devices
— *See:* IUDs
Iowa, p. II:218
Ireland, pp. III:42, II:163-165
Irish gangs, p. IV:43
Iron lung, p. III:95
Iroquois, pp. II:72-73
Irradiation, p. III:112
IRS, p. I:283
Is Love Colorblind?, p. II:55
Is Single Gender Schooling Viable in the Public Sector?, p. II:309
Ischemic heart disease (IHD), pp. III:4, III:8, III:424*t*
Islam, pp. II:140-141
— fastest-growing religions, pp. I:252-253
— increase/decrease in membership, pp. II:132-135
— terrorism, p. IV:184
Israel, pp. II:164, IV:184
Italian (language), p. II:76
Italian gangs, p. IV:43
Italy, pp. II:163, I:187, I:192, III:334
Items stolen, p. IV:326*t*
Jackson-Lee, Sheila, p. IV:287
Jacob Wetterling Act, p. IV:121
Jails, pp. III:265-266
Japan, pp. II:5, II:163-165, I:187, II:254
Japanese, pp. III:43, II:74, II:76-77
Jazz concerts, p. I:216
Jehovah's Witnesses, pp. II:132-133, II:136-138
Jenkins, Henry, p. IV:145
Jewelry making, p. I:218
Jewish Defense League, p. IV:181

Jewish gangs, p. IV:43

Jews, pp. II:110, II:145

Jobs, pp. I:52-53
— advancement, pp. I:260-262, I:265
— college education, pp. I:51, I:58, I:61-62
— entrants, p. I:37
— gains, pp. I:32-33, I:299t
— leavers, p. I:37
— losses, pp. I:33, I:299t
— openings, pp. II:189-190, I:296t
— satisfaction, p. II:295
— training, pp. I:260-262
— worker supply, pp. I:24-25, I:27-28

Joe Camel, p. III:138

Jogging, p. I:202

Johns Hopkins University, p. II:294

Joint Legislative Task Force on Government Oversight, p. IV:223

Jones, Paula, p. I:166

Jonesboro (AR), p. IV:129

Jordan, Michael, p. I:211

Journal of the American Medical Association, pp. III:81, III:168, III:273-274, III:405

Judaism, pp. II:130-133, II:135, II:140-141

Judges, p. I:32

Jupiter Communications, p. I:196

Jury awards, p. I:170

Justice Policy Institute, pp. IV:129, IV:134, IV:237

Justice system employment
— arrests, pp. IV:266, IV:378t
— by government level, p. IV:302t
— crime rate, pp. IV:21-23

Justice system expenditures, pp. IV:303t

Justifiable homicides, pp. IV:217, IV:363t

Juveniles, pp. IV:39-40, IV:70, IV:101, I:221
— *See also:* Children
— *See also:* Infants
— *See also:* Teenagers
— *See also:* Youth
— arrests by race/ethnicity, pp. IV:133-137
— by sex, pp. IV:340t
— drugs, p. IV:149
— poverty, p. IV:134
— special units of police departments, p. IV:206
— violent crimes, pp. IV:340t

Kaczynski, Theodore, p. IV:181

Kaiser Family Foundation, p. I:231

Kanner, Leo, p. III:259

Kansas, p. IV:276

Kanzai, Amil, p. IV:182

Kazakhstan, p. II:163

Kennedy School of Government, p. III:75

Kennedy, President John F., p. IV:46

Kennedy, Robert F., p. IV:46

Kentucky, pp. II:187, III:409

Kenya, p. III:332

Kerr-Mills Act, p. III:384

Ketamine, p. IV:154

Kevorkian, Dr. Jack, p. III:216

Kidnapping, pp. IV:142, IV:245, IV:260

Kidney diseases, pp. III:8, III:40, III:161
— *See also:* Nephritis, nephrosis, and nephrotic syndrome

Kids Walk-to-School Program, p. III:406

Kilpatrick, William Heard, p. II:204

King, Jr., Dr. Martin Luther, p. IV:46

King, Rodney, pp. IV:204, IV:288

KKK
— *See:* Ku Klux Klan

Klaas, Polly, p. IV:142

Koppel, Ted, p. IV:243

Korea, pp. II:164-165, II:195, II:254

Korean population, pp. II:74, II:76-77

Kozol, Jonathan, p. II:221

Kru, p. II:77

Ku Klux Klan (KKK), pp. IV:181, IV:286

Kubler-Ross, Elisabeth, pp. III:212, III:374

Kurdistan Workers Party, p. IV:183

Kyrgyzstan, p. II:163

Labor force distribution, pp. I:299t

Labor law violations, p. I:45

Labor relations managers
— *See:* personnel and labor relations managers

Laboratory animal caretakers
— *See:* veterinary assistants and laboratory animal caretakers

Laboratory technologists
— *See:* Clinical laboratory technologists

Lacerations, p. I:155

Lakes and water pollution, pp. III:323, III:325

Landscaping and groundskeeping laborers, pp. I:61-62

Language-impaired children, pp. II:298-299

Lanoxin, p. III:167

Laotian population, p. II:74

Larcenies
— arrests, pp. IV:68-69
— by type, pp. IV:322t
— corrections system expenditures, p. IV:249
— females, p. IV:136
— property crime, pp. IV:7-8
— reported to police, p. IV:373t

Larsen, Elena, p. II:142

Las Vegas (NV), p. IV:124

Laser skin resurfacing, pp. III:277-279

Last Tango in Paris, p. I:231

Latin America, pp. II:25, I:47, III:326

Latinos, pp. I:41, II:70-71

Latter-Day Saints, pp. II:130-131

Latvia, pp. II:5, II:163-164

Law, pp. II:286, II:290

Law enforcement, pp. IV:30, I:157-158, IV:201-202, IV:205
— by race/ethnicity and sex, pp. IV:203-204, IV:360t
— deaths, pp. IV:361t
— departments, p. IV:199
— employment, p. IV:359t
— salaries, p. IV:209
— timeline, pp. IV:197-198

Lawyers, pp. I:22-25, I:32, I:58

LDP
— *See:* Low-Density Lipoprotein

Lead, pp. III:316-317, III:324

Learning disabilities in children
— Attention Deficit/Hyperactivity Disorder, p. III:65
— by cause, pp. III:229-231
— demographics, p. III:446*t*
— special education programs, pp. II:298-303

Leavenworth (KS), p. IV:24

Legal occupations, pp. I:7, IV:281-282, II:296

Legionnaire's Disease, pp. III:61, III:95, III:444*t*

Leisure activities, pp. I:176-177, I:356*t*
— by type, pp. I:216-218, I:365*t*
— families, p. I:173
— sports, p. I:199
— travel, p. I:191

Leon County (FL), p. IV:274

LEP, pp. II:306-307

Leprosy, pp. III:58, III:60, III:442*t*

Lesbians, pp. III:54, II:63-64, I:191
— *See also:* Gays
— *See also:* Homosexuals
— *See also:* Same-sex partners

Lettuce, p. III:87

Leukemia, pp. III:3, III:67-68, III:156

Liberal arts, p. II:194

Liberals, p. II:114

Libraries, pp. I:233, I:254, I:256-259, I:374*t*

Licensed practical nurses (LPNs), pp. I:58-59, I:62, III:353-354

Life expectancy
— Baby Boom generation, p. III:187
— births and deaths, pp. II:324*t*
— by decade, pp. II:16-20
— by race/ethnicity and sex, pp. III:47-48
— Hayflick Limit, p. III:48
— *Healthy People*, pp. III:403-404, III:437*t*
— Social Security, pp. I:143-144

Life insurance, pp. I:128, I:133

Life sciences, pp. II:284-285

Lightner, Candy, p. IV:113

Limited English Proficiency, pp. II:306-307, II:407*t*
— *See also:* LEP

Lindbergh Law, p. IV:142

Lipitor, pp. III:167, III:176, III:276

Liquid Candy, p. II:311

Liquor-law violations, pp. IV:112, IV:136

Listening to Prozac, p. III:64

Listeria infections, p. III:111

Literacy
— adults, p. II:156
— by educational attainment, pp. IV:263, II:365*t*
— by race/ethnicity, pp. II:154-155
— employment, pp. II:157-158
— international comparisons, p. II:163

Literacy surveys, p. I:221

Literature, p. I:216

Lithium, pp. III:64, III:251

Lithuania, p. II:163

Littleton (CO), pp. IV:129, II:243

Live births, pp. II:10, II:315*t*

Liver disease, pp. III:8-9, III:161

Liver disease continued:
— *See also:* Cirrhosis

Lives on the Boundary, p. II:155

Livestock, p. III:458*t*

Living arrangements, pp. II:46, II:58, II:61, III:192, II:341*t*

Living to 100, p. III:73

Living wills, pp. III:211, III:215

La Leche League, pp. III:41-42

Loan interviewers and clerks, p. I:54

Local Education Foundations, p. II:212

Local government, pp. I:1, I:9, II:211, I:256, I:292*t*

Lodging
— *See:* Hotels and lodging

Logan International Airport, p. IV:232

Loitering, pp. IV:106-107, IV:136

LoJack Corporation, p. IV:71

Long-term-care insurance, p. I:135

Look-say method, pp. II:200-201

Looking Fit Tanning Book 2002-2003, p. III:147

Los Angeles, pp. II:30, II:75

Los Angeles (CA), pp. IV:40-41, IV:203

Los Angeles County Sheriff's Department, p. IV:200

Los Angeles Police Department, pp. IV:201, IV:211

Los Angeles Unified School District, p. IV:131

Lost work time, p. I:350*t*

Louima, Abner, p. IV:204

Louisiana, pp. III:370, III:409

The Love Bug, p. I:280

Low birth weight
— by race/ethnicity, pp. III:308-310, III:515*t*
— causes of death, pp. III:10, III:312
— hypertension, pp. III:11, III:40
— kidney diseases, p. III:40
— live births, p. III:435*t*
— sexually transmitted diseases, pp. III:40, III:52
— singletons, pp. III:39-40
— smoking, p. III:40

Low-Density Lipoprotein (LDP), p. III:20

Low-fat milk, p. III:83

Lower respiratory diseases, pp. III:3-5, III:401

LPNs
— *See:* Licensed practical nurses
— *See:* Licensed practical nurses (LPNs)

Lucky Strike cigarettes, p. III:136

Lumbee Indian tribe, pp. II:72-73

Lung cancer, p. III:160
— by sex, pp. III:13, III:26-28
— death rates, pp. III:67, III:428*t*
— risk behaviors, pp. III:3-4, III:26, III:136, III:160
— survival rates, pp. III:19, III:156, III:158

Lung diseases, pp. III:227-228

Lutherans, pp. II:130-133, II:135

Lyme Disease, pp. III:61-62, III:95, III:444*t*

Lymphatic system diseases, pp. III:67-68, III:150-151, III:156

Lysergic acid diethylamide (LSD), pp. III:119, IV:151, IV:153, IV:162

Macao, p. II:30

Machine feeders and offbearers, p. I:54

Machine operators, assemblers, and inspectors, pp. I:20, I:32,

Machine operators, assemblers, and inspectors continued:
  I:296*t*
MADD
— *See:* Mothers Against Drunk Driving (MADD)
Mail and message distributing occupations, p. I:32
Maine, pp. II:64, II:218
Major League Baseball (MLB), pp. I:210-211
Making Weight, p. III:116
Malaria, pp. III:58-59, III:442*t*
Malaysia, pp. II:5, I:187
Malcolm X, p. IV:46
Male-female teacher ratio, pp. II:182-183
Males, pp. IV:17, IV:136, III:137, III:150-151, I:204
— *See also:* Men
Malignancies, pp. III:2-4
— *See also:* Cancer
— *See also:* Neoplasms
Mammograms, pp. III:18, III:156, III:210, III:425*t*
Managed care, pp. III:207-209, III:344
Management analysts, pp. I:22-25, I:296*t*
Managerial and professional specialty occupations, pp. I:31-32
Managerial occupations
— *See:* executive, administrative, managerial occupations
Manhattan Project, p. III:105
Manic depression
— *See:* Bipolar disorder
Manslaughter, p. IV:135
Manufacturing
— compensation, p. I:326*t*
— employees, pp. I:329*t*
— employment, p. I:34
— income, p. I:120
— injuries in the workplace, p. I:156
— productivity output, pp. I:98-99, I:104-105
Maps, p. I:185
Marihuana Tax Act, p. IV:12
Marijuana, pp. III:126, III:133, IV:173
— adults, p. III:121
— consumption, p. III:104
— drug-related arrests, pp. IV:11, IV:147, IV:175
— emergency room visits, p. III:124
— lifetime drug use reported, pp. IV:151-153
— teenagers, pp. III:117-118, III:132
— trafficking, pp. IV:167-168
Marital status, pp. I:65-68
Marketing, pp. II:256-257, II:262
Marketing, advertising, public relations managers, p. I:58
Marriage, pp. II:48-49, II:335*t*
— age at first marriage, p. II:50
— Baby Boom generation, p. II:51
— by race/ethnicity, pp. II:52-54
Married-couple households, pp. II:45-47, I:92, III:269-270, I:315*t*
Maryland, pp. II:63-64, IV:223, III:338
The Maryland Report, p. II:304
Massachusetts, pp. II:63-64, IV:121, II:217, IV:287, II:305, III:338, III:370, III:409
Massachusetts Institute of Technology, p. IV:145
— *See:* MIT

Massachusetts Institute of Technology (MIT)
— grade inflation, p. II:293
— honor graduates, p. II:294
— private gifts, p. II:280
— tuition costs, p. II:268
Massage therapy, pp. III:78-79, III:162
Master's degrees, pp. I:94, II:283
Match.com, p. I:284
Matchmaker.com, p. I:284
Material exploitation of elderly population, p. III:199
Material moving occupations
— *See also:* transportation and material moving occupations
Maternal age at conception, p. III:40
Maternal complications of pregnancy, p. III:10
Maternal mortality, pp. II:21, III:22-23, IV:53, III:427*t*
Maternity leave, p. I:137
Mathematics, p. II:392*t*
— achievement, pp. II:390*t*
— class characteristics, pp. II:165, II:195
— doctoral degrees conferred, p. II:285
— proficiency, pp. II:161-162, II:164, II:203, II:237, II:366*t*
  II:386*t*
— salaries, p. II:194
— scores, p. II:254
Mathematics-related occupations, p. II:296
Mayhem: Violence as Public Entertainment, p. IV:145
MBA, p. I:212
McDonald's restaurants, pp. III:110, IV:184
McNaughtan, Daniel
— *See:* M'Naghten, Daniel
McVeigh, Timothy, pp. IV:179-181
Mealtimes, p. I:180
Measles, pp. III:55, III:94-95, III:97
Measles, German
— *See:* German measles
Meat cutters
— *See:* butchers and meat cutters
Meats, p. III:83
Media images, p. III:221
Medicaid
— elderly population, pp. III:220, III:363
— enrollment, pp. III:529*t*
— fraud, p. IV:94
— health care expenditures, p. I:131
— nonelderly population, pp. III:384-388
Medical assistants, pp. I:52-53
Medical care, p. I:133
Medical ethics, p. III:188
Medical hospitals, pp. III:364-365
Medical Injury Compensation Reform Act (CA), p. III:418
Medical liability reform legislation, p. III:418
Medical malpractice, pp. III:303, III:415-417, III:540*t*
Medical procedures, pp. III:477*t*
Medical professionals, pp. IV:93, I:157-158, III:520*t*
Medical records and health information technicians, pp. I:52-53
Medical review boards, p. III:418
Medical schools, pp. III:82, II:277, II:396*t*
Medical technologists
— *See:* Clinical laboratory technologists

Medicare
— Baby Boom generation, pp. III:380, III:382
— benefits, pp. III:207-209, III:214, III:489t
— elderly population, p. III:219
— enrollment, pp. III:380, III:527t
— expenditures, p. III:528t
— fraud, pp. IV:93-94
— hospice care, pp. III:374, III:376-379, III:526t
— income, p. III:381
— legislation, p. III:341
— medical infrastructure, p. III:363
— per-capita expenditures, p. I:131
— risk behaviors, p. III:490t
— solvency, pp. III:381-382
Medicare+Choice program, pp. III:382-383
Medications, pp. III:102, II:301-302
Medicine, pp. III:75, II:286, II:290
Medicine, alternative
— *See:* Alternative medicine
Medicine, chiropractic
— *See:* Chiropractic medicine
Medicine, veterinary
— *See:* Veterinary medicine
Meditation, pp. III:162-163
Megan's Law, p. IV:121
Melanomas, pp. III:147-148, III:476t
— *See also:* Cancer
— *See also:* Skin cancer
Melissa, p. I:280
Membership organizations, pp. I:7, I:205, I:247-249, I:371t
Men
— *See also:* Males
— accidents, p. II:18
— activities of daily living, p. III:204
— age at first marriage, p. II:50
— art purchases, p. I:219
— athletic programs, p. I:206
— cancer survival rates, p. III:158
— causes of death, pp. III:6-7, III:12, II:18, II:21, III:24-26, III:30, III:32, III:34, III:37-38, III:53, III:422t
— coaches' salaries, pp. I:206-207
— cosmetic surgery, pp. III:277-278, III:504t
— creative writing, p. I:219
— disabled, pp. III:225, III:236
— diseases, pp. III:13, II:18, III:28, III:54, III:116, III:147, I:155, III:160, III:247, III:249, III:262, III:288
— domestic homicides, pp. IV:48-49
— earnings, p. I:71
— education, pp. II:259, I:262
— educational attainment, pp. I:94, II:258, II:283, II:285
— employment, pp. I:16, I:29-30, I:33, I:65-67, I:69, I:174-175
— homicides, p. II:18
— household activities, pp. I:181-182
— income, pp. I:84, I:94
— injuries at work, pp. I:155-156
— Internet use, p. I:276
— job training, p. I:262
— life expectancy, pp. II:18-19, III:47
— living arrangements, p. III:192

Men continued:
— Medicare, p. III:380
— modern dance, p. I:219
— occupational fatalities, p. I:156
— occupations, pp. I:31-32, I:156
— online shopping, p. I:277
— police officers, p. IV:200
— political-party affiliation, pp. II:100-101
— pottery, p. I:219
— prisoners, pp. IV:18, IV:238-239
— risk behaviors, pp. III:16-17, III:135-136
— risk factors, pp. II:18, III:20
— sexual activity, pp. III:269-270
— Social Security benefits, p. I:29
— sports scholarships, p. I:206
— suicides, pp. II:18, III:260, III:432t
— teachers, p. II:182
— violent crime, pp. IV:35-38
— volunteering, pp. I:236-237
— writing, p. I:219
Mental health, pp. III:103, III:107, III:247
— facilities, pp. III:264-265, III:501t
— professionals, pp. I:157-158
— services, p. I:131
Mental Health Systems Act, p. III:251
Mental illness, p. III:499t
— disabilities, pp. III:227, III:235, III:248-251, III:265-266
— educational attainment, p. III:241
— workforce disabilities, pp. III:238-239
Mental retardation, pp. III:229-231, III:243
Mental Retardation Facilities and Community Mental Health Centers Construction Act, p. III:265
Mercury, p. III:324
MergerWatch, p. III:366
Merit resolutions, pp. I:167-168
Message distributing occupations
— *See:* Mail and message distributing occupations
Metals, pp. III:323-325
Metalworking, p. I:218
Meter readers, pp. I:54-55
Meth Tour, p. IV:156
Methadone Control Act, p. IV:12
Methamphetamines, pp. III:124-125, III:129
— drug-related arrests, pp. IV:11, IV:147
— drug trafficking, pp. IV:167-168
— laboratories, pp. IV:155-156
— lifetime use reported, pp. IV:151-153
Methodists, pp. II:130-133, II:135
Methylphenidate, p. II:302
Metropolitan areas, pp. II:27-28, II:30, II:330t
Metropolitan Statistical Areas (MSAs), p. II:29
Mexican Mafia, p. IV:40
Mexico, pp. I:47, III:334
Miami (FL), p. IV:72
Miao, p. II:77
Michigan
— gay-couple households, p. II:63
— geographic distribution of elderly population, p. III:190
— insanity defense, p. IV:277

Michigan continued:
— litigation for school funding, pp. II:220-221
— medical liability insurance premiums, pp. III:415-417
— NAEP rankings, p. II:217
— physician-assisted suicide, p. III:216
— prison population, p. IV:248
— sex offender registries, p. IV:121
— uncertified teachers, p. II:187
Michigan Department of Community Health, p. III:407
Michigan Educational Assessment Program test, p. II:169
Microsoft Corporation, p. I:59
MIDCAB
— *See:* Minimally Invasive Direct Coronary Artery Bypass
Midwestern United States, p. III:189
Migrant workers, p. I:46
Military, pp. II:122, II:357*t*
Militia, p. IV:181
Milk, low-fat, p. III:83
Milk, Mayor Harvey, p. IV:276
Milk, whole, p. III:83
Million Man March, p. II:61
Minimally Invasive Direct Coronary Artery Bypass
  (MIDCAB), p. III:25
Minimum wage, pp. I:90-91, I:316*t*
Mining, pp. I:104-106, I:156
Minnesota, pp. II:187, II:218
Missing children, pp. IV:141-143, IV:206, IV:342*t*
Mississippi, pp. IV:286, III:369-370, III:418
Missouri, pp. II:63, II:246, III:387, III:409
MMR, pp. III:57, III:96
— *See:* Measles, Mumps, and Rubella vaccine
M'Naghten, Daniel, p. IV:275
Moderates, p. II:114
Modern dance, pp. I:218-219
Moldova, p. II:163
Mon-Khmer (language), p. II:77
Monaco, p. II:30
Monetary damages, pp. I:165-166, I:169
Money-related crimes, pp. IV:10, IV:105, IV:108
Mongolia, p. II:30
Monitoring the Future, pp. III:118-119, III:132, III:137
Monk Eastman Gang, p. IV:43
Monoamine oxidase inhibitors, p. III:64
Montana, pp. II:75, II:218, IV:276, IV:290, III:369, III:387
Montana v Cowan, p. IV:276
Mood disorders, pp. III:251-252, III:499*t*
Morehouse College, pp. II:53, II:61
Mormons, pp. IV:12, II:130-133
Morning-after pill, p. II:15
Morphine, p. III:124
Mortality, maternal
— *See:* maternal mortality
Mothers, p. I:183
Mothers Against Drunk Driving (MADD), pp. IV:113, IV:207
Motor vehicle accidents, pp. III:4, II:21, III:32, III:131
Motor vehicle thefts, pp. IV:7, IV:65, IV:67, IV:76-77
Mouth cancer, pp. III:150, III:161
Movie admissions, pp. I:185, I:222
Movie ratings, pp. I:230-231, I:368*t*

Movie releases, p. I:230
Movie rentals, pp. I:187-188, I:358*t*
Movies, pp. I:222, I:286, I:366*t*
Mozambique, p. III:332
MP3, pp. I:227, I:282
MSAs, p. II:29
Multifactor Productivity, pp. I:108-109
Multinational Monitor, p. III:138
Multiple births, pp. III:39, III:299-300, III:512*t*
Multiple jobs, pp. I:63-64, I:306*t*
Multiple sclerosis, p. III:225
Multipurpose Arcade Combat Simulator (MACS), p. IV:145
Mumps, pp. III:55-56, III:94-95
Municipal government, p. I:9
Murders, pp. III:36-38
— *See also:* Homicides p. IV:5
— by age group, p. IV:33
— by race/ethnicity, p. IV:52
— by race/ethnicity, sex, and marital status, pp. IV:50-51
— crime index, p. IV:6
— death penalty, p. IV:245
— firearms-related, pp. IV:39, IV:312*t*
— juveniles, pp. IV:33, IV:133, IV:135, IV:137-138
— rate fluctuation, pp. IV:25-26
— victimization, p. IV:38
Murphy Brown, p. II:62
Murray, John, p. IV:144
Musculoskeletal system diseases, pp. III:150, III:155, III:235, III:238, III:310
Museums, pp. I:7, I:216, I:228-229, I:368*t*
Music, pp. I:218, I:268, I:286
Musical plays, p. I:216
Muslims, pp. II:132-135, II:145, IV:224
NAACP Legal Defense Fund, p. IV:244
Najim, Eyad Mahmoud Ismail, p. IV:184
Nandrolone, p. IV:153
Napster, pp. IV:95, I:283
Narcotics, pp. IV:12, IV:153
NASCAR, pp. I:211, I:283
— *See:* National Association for Stock Car Auto Racing
A Nation At Risk, pp. II:162, II:167, III:174, II:176, II:199, II:204
A Nation Online, pp. I:273, I:278
National Academy of Science, pp. III:21, III:327
National Adult Literacy Survey, pp. II:156-157
National Alliance for the Mentally Ill, p. III:251
National Ambulatory Medical Care Survey, p. III:63
National Assembly on School-Based Health Care, p. III:102
National Assessment of Educational Progress (NAEP), p. II:159, II:162, II:203, II:235-236
National Assessment of Educational Progress (NAEP) rankings, pp. II:217-218, II:376*t*
National Association for Stock Car Auto Racing (NASCAR), p. I:211, I:283
National Association of Anorexia Nervosa and Associated Disorders, p. III:257
National Association of Bilingual Education, p. II:307
National Association of Gifted Children, p. II:304
National Association of Police Organizations, p. IV:224

National Association of Realtors, p. I:194

National Association of School Nurses, p. II:303

National Basketball Association (NBA), p. I:210

National Burglar and Fire Alarm Association, p. IV:73

National Cancer Institute, pp. III:31, III:400-401

National Center for Chronic Disease Prevention & Health Promotion, p. III:90

National Center for Complementary and Alternative Medicine, pp. III:76, III:80-81, III:162-163, III:451*t*

National Center for Education Statistics, pp. II:234-235, II:269

National Center for Missing and Exploited Children, p. IV:141

National Center for Policy Analysis, p. IV:250

National Center for State Courts, p. IV:273

National Center on Addiction and Substance Abuse (CASA), p. IV:155

National Center on Institutions and Alternatives, p. IV:248

National Child Abuse and Neglect Data System, p. IV:139

National Cholesterol Education Program, p. III:167

National Coalition for Parent Involvement in Education, p. II:198

National Collegiate Athletic Association (NCAA), p. IV:118

National Commission on Excellence in Education, p. II:257

National Conference of Catholic Bishops, p. III:367

National Consumer League, p. IV:83

National Council of Teachers of Mathematics, p. II:205

National Crime Victimization Survey
— actual crimes reported, pp. IV:4, IV:6-9
— crimes reported, p. IV:294*t*
— gangs in schools, p. IV:42
— property crime, p. IV:65
— rate fluctuation, p. IV:26
— victimization of children, p. IV:139

National Data Collection - Police Use of Force, p. IV:214

National Defense Act, p. II:204

National Education Association, p. I:221

National Elder Abuse Incidence Study, pp. III:199-200

National Electronic Injury Surveillance System, p. I:205

National Endowment for the Arts, p. I:218

National Firearms Act, p. IV:46

National Football League (NFL), pp. I:210-212

National Fraud Information Center, p. IV:83

National Gambling Impact Study Commission, p. IV:117

National Governors Association, p. III:387

National Health and Nutrition Examination Survey, p. III:16

National Health Care Anti-Fraud Association, p. IV:93

National health care expenditures, p. I:342*t*

National Health Service Corps, p. II:278

National Heart, Lung, and Blood Institute, pp. III:400-401

National Highway Traffic Safety Administration, pp. IV:115, IV:219

National Hockey League (NHL), p. I:210

National Home Builders Association, p. IV:63

National Hospital Discharge Survey, p. III:152

National Instant Criminal Background Check System, p. IV:46-47

National Institute for Occupational Safety and Health, p. III:141-142

National Institute of Allergies and Infectious Diseases
— *See:* NIAID

National Institute of Child Health and Human Development, p. III:45, II:201

National Institute of Diabetes & Digestive & Kidney Diseases
— *See:* NIDDK

National Institute of General Medical Sciences, pp. III:400-401

National Institute of Justice, pp. IV:132, IV:220

National Institute of Mental Health, pp. III:116, III:172, III:248, III:255-256, II:302

National Institute on Aging, pp. III:148, III:204

National Institute on Drug Abuse, p. III:128

National Institutes of Health, pp. III:3, III:28, III:76, III:105, III:143, III:163, III:167, III:400-402, III:535*t*

National Insurance Crime Bureau, p. IV:71

National Literacy Act, p. II:191

National Long-Term Care Surveys, p. III:204

National Longitudinal Study on Adolescent Health, p. IV:136

National Longitudinal Survey of Youth, p. IV:134

National Medical Care [company], p. IV:94

National Office of Drug Policy, p. IV:168

National origin-based discrimination, pp. I:161, I:163, I:167

National Park Service, p. IV:227

National Pharmaceutical Stockpike, p. III:392

National Prosecutors Survey, p. IV:282

National Public Radio, p. III:75

National Reading Panel, pp. II:201-202

National Registry of Emergency Medical Technicians, p. III:357

National School Lunch Program, pp. III:113-114, III:468*t*

National School Safety Center, pp. II:247-248

National Sleep Foundation, pp. III:140, III:143

National Survey on Drug Abuse, p. IV:157

National Tactical Officers Association, p. IV:211

National Vaccine Injury Compensation Program, p. III:97

National Water Quality Inventory, p. III:322

Native American religion, pp. II:134-135

Native Americans, pp. II:55, I:252-253, III:337

Native Hawaiians, pp. II:70-71

Native North Americans, pp. II:6-7, II:24

Natural history museums, p. I:229

Naturopathy, pp. III:78, III:80

Navajo Indian tribe, pp. II:72-73

Navigators, pp. I:22, I:296*t*

NBA, pp. I:211-212
— *See also:* National Basketball Association
— *See:* National Basketball Association (NBA)

NC-17, p. I:231

NCAA, p. I:363*t*
— *See:* National Collegiate Athletic Association (NCAA)

NCCAM
— *See:* National Center for Complementary and Alternative

Nebraska, pp. II:218, III:369

Needle use, pp. III:54, III:101

Neglect of elderly, p. III:199

Neonatal deaths, pp. III:10, III:312

Neoplasms, pp. III:3-4, III:235-236, III:238
— *See also:* Cancer
— *See also:* Malignancies

Nephritis, nephrosis, and nephrotic syndrome, pp. III:4-5
— *See also:* Kidney diseases

Nervous disorders, p. III:262

Nervous system diseases, pp. III:150, III:235-236, III:238

Netherlands, pp. II:163-165

Network and computer systems administrators, p. I:52

Nevada, pp. II:64, IV:125, III:349, III:409, III:417-418

Never-married parents, pp. II:59-60

Never-married population, p. II:339t

New Age religion, pp. II:134-135, I:252-253

New Basics curriculum, pp. II:257, II:259

New Hampshire, pp. II:64, II:187, II:218

New Jersey
— gay-couple households, p. II:63
— geographic distribution of elderly population, p. III:190
— hate crimes, p. IV:287
— indigent defense, p. IV:284
— medical liability legislation, p. III:418
— NAEP rankings, p. II:217
— physicians, p. III:338
— racial profiling, p. IV:223
— sex offender registries, p. IV:122
— uncertified teachers, p. II:187

New Math movement, p. II:204

New Mexico, p. II:64

New York
— Asian population, p. II:75
— emergency room drug episodes, p. IV:124
— hospital beds, p. III:369
— medical malpractice litigation, pp. III:415, III:417
— physicians, p. III:338
— police department, pp. IV:200-201, IV:203-204, IV:215
— population density, p. II:30
— travel destinations, p. I:190

New York (state), pp. II:36, IV:122, IV:131, II:217, IV:248, IV:284
— Asian population, p. II:75
— expulsions from school, p. II:246
— gay-couple households, pp. II:63-64
— NAEP rankings, p. II:217

New York Knicks, p. I:213

New York University, p. II:280

New Zealand, pp. II:163-164

Newspapers, p. I:268

Newton-Wellesley Hospital (MA), p. III:372

NFL
— See: National Football League

NHL, pp. I:211-212
— See also: National Hockey League

NIAID, pp. III:332, III:393, III:400-402

Nicaragua, p. I:47

Nichols, Terry, pp. IV:179, IV:181, IV:285

Nickelodeon/Talking with Kids National Survey of Parents and Kids, p. II:249

NIDDK, pp. III:400-401

Nielsen ratings, p. I:211

Niger, p. II:5

Nigeria, pp. III:42, III:332

Nigerian Letter Fraud Scheme, pp. IV:86-87

Nightline, p. IV:243

Nitrogen oxides (NOX), pp. III:120, III:316, III:318

Nixon, President Richard M., pp. IV:12, IV:30, IV:149

No Child Left Behind Act
— class size, p. II:195
— Head Start program, p. II:225
— reading proficiency, p. II:202
— school problems, p. II:199
— school safety, p. IV:129
— single-sex education, p. II:308
— standardized tests in schools, p. II:169

No Electronic Theft (NET) Act, p. IV:95

Non-Christian houses of worship, pp. II:140-141

Nondefense research and development, pp. III:398-399, III:532t 535t

Nondurable goods, p. I:102

Nonfamily households, p. II:42

Nonfatal crimes in schools, p. II:245

Nonmetropolitan areas, pp. II:27-28, II:30, II:330t

Nonresident aliens, pp. II:287, II:289-290

Nonsurgical contraceptives, pp. III:304-305

Nonworking mothers, p. I:183

North America wastewater treatment, p. III:326

North Carolina, pp. II:63, II:246, IV:284

North Dakota, pp. II:75, II:218, III:369, III:409

North Korea, p. II:163

Northeast United States, p. III:189

Northwestern University, p. IV:118

Norvasc, p. III:167

Norway, pp. II:163-164

Nose reshaping, pp. III:150, III:277-279

Nostradamus, p. I:283

Not guilty by reason of insanity, pp. IV:275-278

NOX
— See: Nitrogen Oxides

Nurse practitioners, p. III:351
— See also: Advanced practice nurses

Nurse Reinvestment Act, p. III:350

Nurses
— by specialty, pp. I:22, III:524t
— degrees conferred, p. I:58
— job openings, pp. I:24-25, I:61-62
— nursing school graduates, p. III:347
— retirement, p. I:23
— shortages, p. I:59

Nurses, licensed practical
— See: Licensed practical nurses

Nurses, registered
— See: Registered nurses

Nursing Facility Sourcebook, p. III:194

Nursing homes
— elder abuse, pp. III:201-202
— health care costs, p. I:131
— licensed practical nurses, p. III:354
— quality of life, pp. III:207-209
— residency, pp. III:193-194, III:486t
— staff, p. III:487t

Nutrients, pp. III:323-325

Obesity, pp. III:161, III:538t
— children, p. I:203
— diseases, pp. III:160-161, III:405

Obesity continued:

— eating habits, p. III:90

— elderly population, p. III:210

— *Journal of the American Medical Association*, p. III:405

— prevention programs, p. III:407

— risky behaviors, pp. III:20-21, III:107, III:109, III:115, III:425t

— women's health, pp. III:16-17, III:21

Obsessive-compulsive disorder, pp. III:247, III:250, III:252-253

Obstetricians, pp. III:150, III:303, III:341, III:415

Occupational fatalities, pp. I:149, I:151, I:156, I:349t

Occupational Safety and Health Administration, pp. I:153-154

Occupational therapy aides, p. I:53

Occupations, p. II:296

— decline, pp. I:51, I:54-55, I:303t

— degrees conferred, pp. I:296t

— growth rate, p. I:303t

— illegal labor, p. I:43

— independent contractors, pp. I:69, I:307t

— job declines, p. I:303t

— job openings, pp. I:296t

— retirement, p. I:296t

— workplace violence, pp. IV:60-61, I:351t

O'Connor, Justice Sandra Day, pp. IV:96, IV:246

Offbearers

— *See also:* machine feeders and offbearers p. I:54

Office clerks (general), pp. I:61-62

Office machine operators, pp. I:54-55

Office of Alternative Medicine, p. III:81

Office of Homeland Security, pp. IV:187-189

Office of Juvenile Justice and Delinquency Prevention, p. IV:136, IV:142

Office of National Drug Control Policy, pp. IV:174, IV:263

Ohio, pp. II:63, IV:138, III:190, III:367, III:409, III:417

Oils, p. III:83

Oklahoma City, pp. I:229, IV:285

Older Americans Act, p. IV:107

On Death and Dying, pp. III:212, III:374

On Killing: The Psychological Cost of Learning to Kill in War and Society, p. IV:145

Oneandonly.com, p. I:284

Online auctions, p. I:286

Online banking, p. I:273

Online churches, pp. II:144, II:362t

Online dating services, pp. I:284, I:380t

Online gambling, p. IV:335t

Online search terms, pp. I:282-283, I:379t

Online shopping, pp. I:273, I:277, I:279

Online travel spending, pp. I:196-197, I:360t

Opera, pp. I:185, I:216, I:224-225

Operation Child Watch, p. I:45

Operation Pipeline, pp. IV:223-224

Operators, p. I:54

Operators, fabricators, and laborers, pp. I:31-32, I:43, I:69-70

Ophthalmologists, p. III:341

Opium Poppy Control Act, p. IV:12

Optometry degrees conferred, pp. II:286, II:290

Oral cavity cancers, p. III:156

Oral contraceptives, p. III:161

Order Clerks, pp. I:54-55

Orderlies and attendants

— *See:* nursing aides, orderlies, and attendants

Oregon, pp. II:64, III:216, IV:277

Organic foods, pp. III:87-88, III:458t

Oriental medicine (traditional), pp. III:78, III:80

Orthopedic surgeons, p. III:341

Osama bin Laden, p. I:283

Osteopaths, pp. III:78-79, II:286, II:290, III:336

Osteoporosis, pp. III:168, III:328

Out of Control: Seattle's Flawed Response to Protests Against the World Trade Organization

— 214,

Outdoor track, p. I:208

Ovarian cancer, pp. III:19, III:67-68, III:158

Ovarian surgeries, p. III:151

Over-the-counter medications, pp. III:128, III:474t

Overweight, pp. III:17, III:90, III:107, III:210

Oxycodone, p. III:130

Oxycontin, pp. III:129-130

Oxygen-depleting substances, pp. III:323-325

Oxymetholone, p. IV:153

Oxytocin, p. III:23

P-notes, p. IV:88

Pacific Islanders

— *See also:* Asians and Pacific Islanders

— abortions, pp. II:10, II:12-13

— advanced classes, p. II:259

— Bachelor's Degrees conferred, pp. II:287-288

— causes of death, pp. III:8, III:43

— doctoral degrees conferred, pp. II:289-290

— drug arrests, p. IV:161

— drug use, pp. IV:159-160

— educational attainment, pp. II:152-153

— fertility rates, p. II:321t

— HIV, p. III:289

— income, pp. I:75, I:82

— Internet use, pp. I:270-271

— interracial marriages, p. II:55

— law enforcement personnel, p. IV:203

— live births, pp. II:10, II:321t

— low birth weight, p. III:40

— population, pp. II:24, II:71, II:347t

— population mobility, p. II:38

— salaries, p. I:38

— single-parent households, p. II:61

— Total Fertility Rates, pp. II:6, II:8

— vocational education credits accumulated, p. II:258

Packagers

— *See:* hand packers and packagers

Paid leave, pp. I:129, I:133

Pain, p. I:155

Pain control, pp. III:213-214

Paintball, pp. I:200-201

Painting, p. I:218

Pakistani population, p. II:74

Palliative care

— *See:* Hospice care

Palm Beach County Health Department (FL), p. III:392

Pancreas surgeries, p. III:151

Pancreatic cancer
— causes of death, pp. III:67-68
— obesity, p. III:161
— survival rates, pp. III:156, III:158
Panic disorders, pp. III:252-253
Pap smears, p. III:156
Paraguay, p. III:42
Paralysis, pp. III:227, III:229
Paramedics
— *See:* Emergency medical technicians
Parathyroid gland surgeries, p. III:151
Parents, pp. I:183-184
Parents, divorced
— *See:* Divorced parents
Parents, never married
— *See:* Never-married parents
Parents, widowed
— *See:* Widowed parents
Parkinson's Disease, pp. III:225, III:243
Parks, p. I:216
Parolees, pp. IV:18, IV:20
Part-time employment, pp. I:65-66, I:68, I:306*t*
Particulate matter (PM-10), pp. III:316-317
Partnership for A Drug-Free America, p. III:132
Paternity leave, p. I:137
Pathogens, pp. III:323, III:325, III:467*t*
Pathologists, p. III:341
Patients' Rights Movement, p. III:215
Patrick Henry College, p. II:235
PATRIOT Act, p. IV:186
Patriot groups, p. IV:181
Paxil, p. III:76
Payzant, Thomas, pp. IV:131-132
Pb
— *See:* Lead
PCBs, p. III:323
PCP, pp. IV:151-154
PCs
— *See:* Personal computers
Peace Officer Standards and Training Commission, p. IV:211
Pearl (MS), p. IV:129
Pell Grants, p. II:273
Pennsylvania
— expulsions from school, p. II:246
— gay-couple households, p. II:63
— geographic distribution of elderly population, p. III:190
— NAEP rankings, pp. II:217, IV:287, III:338, III:370
— population, p. II:36
Pennsylvania Medical Society, p. III:416
Pensions, p. I:145
Pentecostals, pp. II:130-135
Pepsi, p. II:310
Per-pupil expenditures, pp. II:217, II:281-282, II:367*t* 382*t*
Percodan, p. III:129
Performing arts, pp. I:216-217, I:224, II:284, I:367*t*
Perinatal conditions, p. III:9
Perjury causing execution, p. IV:245
Perls, Dr. Thomas, p. III:73

Personal computers
— *See:* PCs
Personal computers (PCs), pp. I:226-227
Personal home care aides, p. I:52
Personal leave, p. I:133
Personal relationships, p. I:284
Personal Responsibility Work Opportunities Reconciliation Act, p. II:60
Personal savings rate, pp. I:147-148
Personal services, p. I:7
Personnel and labor relations managers, pp. I:24-25
Pertussis, pp. III:55-56, III:94-95
— *See also:* Whooping Cough
Pervasive Developmental Disorder, p. III:255
Pesticide use, pp. III:87-88
Pets, p. I:191
Pew Internet & American Life Project, p. II:142
Pew Research Center, p. IV:185
Pfizer, pp. III:167, III:276
Pharmaceutical Research and Manufacturers of America
— *See:* PhRMA
Pharmaceutical Research and Manufacturers of America (PhRMA), pp. III:175, III:179
Pharmacy degrees, pp. II:286, II:290
Pharmacy Today, p. III:140
Pharynx cancer, p. III:156
Pharynx surgeries, pp. III:150-151
Philip Morris cigarettes, p. III:136
Philippines, pp. I:47, III:332
Phobias, pp. III:252-253
Phoenix (AZ), p. IV:72
Phonics, systematic
— *See:* Systematic phonics
Photography, pp. I:22, I:24-25, I:218, I:296*t*
PhRMA
— *See:* Pharmaceutical Research and Manufacturers of
Physical abuse of elderly, p. III:199
Physical activity, pp. III:405, III:461*t*
Physical Activity and Health, p. III:93
Physical deformities, p. III:229
Physical education classes, pp. III:104, I:203
Physical sciences degrees, p. II:285
Physical therapist assistants, pp. I:52-53
Physician assistants, pp. I:52-53, III:345
Physician-assisted suicide, pp. III:215-216
— *See also:* Euthanasia
Physicians
— *See also:* Doctors of Medicine
— by race/ethnicity, p. III:337
— by specialty, pp. III:341, III:522*t*
— by state, p. III:338
— geographic maldistribution, p. III:344
— office staff, p. III:394
— place of medical education, pp. III:342, III:523*t*
— specialization, p. III:341
— supply, p. III:520*t*
— workplace discrimination, p. I:59
— workplace violence, p. I:58
Physicians for Reproductive Choice and Health, p. III:366

Phytochemicals, p. III:90
Piaget, Jean, p. II:203
The Pill, pp. II:15, III:304-305
Pineal gland surgeries, p. III:151
Pipefitters and steamfitters
— *See:* plumbers, pipefitters, and steamfitters
Pistols, p. II:245
Pituitary gland surgeries, p. III:151
Placebos, p. III:76
Plague, pp. III:58, III:60, III:392, III:442*t*
Planes, p. I:190
Plants, p. I:185
Plastic surgery
— *See:* Cosmetic surgery
The Playboy Channel, p. III:280
Plays (nonmusical), p. I:216
Playstation 2, p. I:283
Plug Uglies, p. IV:43
Plumbers, pipefitters, and steamfitters, pp. I:22, I:27-28
PM-10
— *See:* Particulate matter
— *See:* Particulate matter (PM-10)
PMDD
— *See:* Premenstrual dysphoric disorder
Pneumonia, pp. III:5, II:22
— Baby Boom generation, pp. III:69-70
— by century, p. III:2
— by race/ethnicity, pp. III:8-9
— childhood immunizations, pp. III:96, III:98
— funding, p. III:401
— immunizations, p. III:99
— leading diseases, p. III:4
Pocket-picking, p. IV:69
Podiatry degrees conferred, pp. II:286, II:290
Pokemon, p. I:283
Poland, pp. I:47, II:163, I:187
Police and detective supervisors, pp. I:22-23, I:27
Police department technology, pp. IV:208-209
Police forces, pp. IV:23, IV:43-44
— by sex, p. IV:200
— deaths, pp. IV:210-212, IV:217-218
— employment, pp. IV:21-22
— excessive force, pp. IV:213-214
Police pursuits, pp. IV:220-221
Police shootings, pp. IV:363*t*
Policy processing clerks
— *See:* insurance claims and policy processing clerks
Polio, pp. III:55-56, III:94-96
Polish, p. II:76
Political organizations, pp. I:245-246
Political-party affiliation, pp. II:99, II:350*t*
— by party, pp. II:98, II:114
— by race/ethnicity, p. II:108
— by sex, pp. II:100-101
Pollution, pp. III:315-316, III:326-328
Ponds, pp. III:323, III:325
Population, pp. II:70-72, II:343*t*
— births, p. II:4
— by sex, p. II:323*t*

Population continued:
— central cities, pp. II:27-28
— dependency ratio, p. II:22
— foreign-born, pp. II:348*t*
— geographic distribution, pp. II:24-25, II:30, II:36, II:331*t*
— growth rates, pp. II:37, I:302*t*
— households, pp. II:333*t*
— metropolitan areas, pp. II:27-28, II:330*t*
— Metropolitan Statistical Areas (MSAs), p. II:29
— MSAs, p. II:29
— never-married adults, p. II:339*t*
— nonmetropolitan areas, pp. II:27, II:330*t*
— over age 65, p. I:347*t*
— rural areas, p. II:329*t*
— suburban areas, pp. II:27-28, II:329*t*
— Total Fertility Rates, p. II:4
— urban areas, p. II:329*t*
— youth, pp. II:327*t*
Population changes in geographic areas, p. II:39
Population density, pp. II:30-31, IV:57-58, II:330*t*
Population mobility, pp. II:38-39, II:331*t*
Population Replacement Rate, pp. II:4, II:6, II:8
Pornography, pp. IV:108, III:280-281, I:282
Portland (OR), p. IV:124
Portuguese (language), p. II:76
Posse Comitatus Act of 1878, p. IV:24
Post-traumatic stress disorder, pp. III:247, III:252-253
Postal Inspection Service, p. IV:227
Postal Service clerks, pp. I:1, I:13, I:22-23, I:27-28, I:293*t*
Postneonatal deaths, p. III:312
Pottery, p. I:218
Poultry, p. III:83
Poverty rate
— by race/ethnicity, p. IV:53
— children, p. II:335*t*
— family demographics, pp. I:315*t*
— juveniles arrested, p. IV:134
— living arrangements, p. II:47
— minimum wage, p. I:91
— single-parent households, p. II:60
— U.S. Government definition, pp. I:88-89
— working families, pp. I:92-93
Powdered cocaine, p. IV:162
Powell v Alabama, p. IV:281
Precision, production, craft, repair occupations, pp. I:20, I:31, I:43, I:69-70, I:296*t*
Pregnancy-based discrimination, pp. I:161, I:164, I:167
Pregnancy, ectopic
— *See:* Ectopic pregnancy
Premarin, p. III:167
Premarital sex, pp. III:267-268, III:502*t*
Premenstrual dysphoric disorder (PMDD), p. III:170
Prepress technicians and workers, p. I:54
Preprimary schools, pp. II:222-223, II:382*t*
Presbyterian Church (U.S.A.), pp. II:136-138
Presbyterians, pp. II:130-133, II:135
Preschool teachers, pp. I:58-59
Prescription drug plans, p. I:133
Prescription drugs, p. III:75

Prescription drugs continued:
— AARP, p. III:220
— abuse, p. III:128
— advertising, pp. III:177-178
— antidepressants, p. III:169
— expenditures, p. III:484*t*
— numbers dispensed, pp. III:165-167
— prices, p. III:179
— research and development, p. III:176
— Ritalin, p. III:171
— school-based health centers, p. III:102
— shortages, p. III:389
Presidential elections, p. II:350*t*
Prevention research centers, p. III:211
Preventive care, pp. III:103, I:131
Priests and sexual assaults, p. IV:56
Prilosec, p. III:167
Princeton University, p. II:294
Principles and Standards for School Mathematics, p. II:205
Printer notes, pp. IV:88-89
Prison industries, p. IV:254
Prison Industries Reform Act, p. IV:255
Prisoners, p. IV:235
— by offense committed, pp. IV:13, IV:15-16, IV:236, IV:297*t*
— by race/ethnicity, pp. IV:238-239, IV:242
— by sex, pp. IV:18, IV:238-239, IV:242
— prison capacity, p. IV:372*t*
Privacy issues, p. IV:357*t*
Private attorneys, p. IV:281
Private community foundations, pp. I:242, I:245-246
Private gifts to institutions of higher education, pp. II:279-280
Private household service occupations, pp. I:20, I:32, I:296*t*
Private prisons, pp. IV:251, IV:374*t*
Private schools, pp. II:148, II:150, II:195, II:237
Private universities, pp. II:269, II:281-282
Probationers, pp. IV:18, IV:20
Procardia XL, p. III:167
Procurement clerks, pp. I:54-55
Productivity
— business, pp. I:122, I:236*t*
— construction, pp. I:106-107, I:330*t*
— corporate profits, p. I:124
— earnings, p. I:114
— educational attainment, pp. I:110-111
— employees, pp. I:104-105, I:328*t*
— Gross Domestic Product, p. I:102
— growth rates, pp. I:100-101
— income, p. I:120
— manufacturing, pp. I:97-99, I:326*t*
— stock performance, p. I:103
— technology, pp. I:102-103
— wages, pp. I:336*t*
Professional and Amateur Sports Protection Act, p. IV:118
Professional degrees conferred, pp. I:94, II:286
Professional specialties, pp. I:20, I:69-70, I:296*t*
Professional sports, pp. I:199, I:210-212, I:363*t*
Professional, scientific, and technical services, pp. I:104-105
Project Censored, p. IV:252
Project method (of teaching), p. II:204

Project STAR, p. II:196
The Promise Keepers, p. II:61
Promoting Health/Preventing Disease: Objectives for the Nation, p. III:403
Property crime, p. IV:104
— actual crimes, pp. IV:7-9
— arrests, p. IV:67
— by selected demographics, p. IV:66
— crime index, p. IV:4
— prisoners, pp. IV:236-237, IV:260
— rate fluctuation, pp. IV:63, IV:65
— recidivism, pp. IV:261, IV:266, IV:273, IV:321*t*
— reported to police, pp. IV:77-78
— teenage victims, p. IV:75
— victimization rates, p. IV:32
Proposition 13, pp. II:214, II:219
Proposition 227, p. II:307
Proprietors
— *See:* sales supervisors and proprietors
Prosecutors, p. IV:206
Prostate cancer, pp. III:18, III:28-29, III:67-68, III:158, III:429*t*
Prostate-Specific Antigen, p. III:28
— *See:* PSA
Prostitute Education Network, p. IV:124
Prostitution, pp. IV:10, IV:101, IV:106, IV:125, IV:136
— arrests, p. IV:124
— sentencing, p. IV:108
Protective services, pp. I:32, IV:139
Protestants, pp. II:110, II:132-133, II:135
Proventil-Aerosol, p. III:167
Prozac, p. III:445*t*
— depression, pp. III:63-64, III:76, III:169, III:262
— Eli Lilly & Co., p. III:170
— mental illnesses, p. III:251
— prescription drugs, p. III:167
PRWORA, p. II:60
PSA
— *See:* Prostate-Specific Antigen
Psilocybe, p. IV:153
Psychiatric treatment, pp. III:262, III:264, III:341, III:500*t*
— *See also:* Psychotherapy
Psychological abuse of elderly, p. III:199
Psychological development assessment, p. III:102
Psychologists, pp. I:22, I:24-25
Psychology degree recipients, pp. II:284-285
Psychotherapy, pp. III:169, III:263
— *See also:* Psychiatric treatment
Public Agenda survey, p. II:168
Public assistance, p. I:145
Public defenders, p. IV:281
Public education, pp. I:10, I:12
Public Health Action Plan to Combat Antimicrobial Resistance, p. III:330
Public Health Institute, p. II:310
Public Health Threats and Emergencies Act of 2000, p. III:101
Public libraries, pp. I:233, I:254, I:256, I:258-259, I:374*t*
Public-order crimes, pp. IV:236-237, IV:260
Public schools, pp. I:34, II:215-216
— class size, p. II:195

Public schools continued:
— college enrollment, p. II:150
— funding, pp. II:211, II:213
— graduates, p. II:148
— mathematics proficiency, p. II:237
Public universities, pp. II:269, II:279, II:281
Public utilities
— *See:* transportation and public utilities
Publishers (desktop), p. I:52
Pueblo Indian tribe, pp. II:72-73
Pulmonary diseases, pp. III:69-70
Punctures, p. I:155
Pupil-teacher ratio, pp. II:180, II:371*t*
Purse-snatching, pp. IV:69-70
Q fever, p. III:392
Quadruplets, p. III:39
Quayle, Dan, p. II:62
Quilting, p. I:218
Quinlan, Karen Ann, p. III:188
R-rated movies, p. I:230
Race-based discrimination, pp. I:161, I:167
Race/ethnicity
— abortions, pp. II:12-13, II:321*t*
— births, pp. II:10, I:40, II:319*t*
— cancer survival rates, pp. III:156, III:158
— causes of death, pp. III:8, II:21, III:28, III:30, III:32, III:34, III:43, III:422*t*
— computer learning opportunities, p. II:263
— correctional population, pp. IV:19-20
— crib death, p. III:45
— death row inmates, p. IV:244
— deaths, pp. III:15, II:21
— diseases, pp. III:26, III:52
— domestic homicides, pp. IV:48-49
— drug arrests, pp. IV:161-162
— drug use, p. IV:162
— earnings, p. I:71
— educational attainment, pp. I:39, I:112, I:118, II:151-152, II:258-259, II:287-290, I:300*t*
— employment, pp. I:35, I:37, I:299*t*
— exercise habits, p. III:92
— federal law enforcement officers, p. IV:227
— hate crimes, p. IV:290
— health problems, p. III:20
— housing, p. II:35
— illicit substance use, p. III:126
— income, pp. I:82, I:311*t*
— infant mortality, pp. III:313, III:517*t*
— Internet use, pp. I:270-272, I:377*t*
— law enforcement, pp. IV:203, IV:360*t*
— life expectancy, pp. II:20, III:47
— literacy, pp. II:154, II:159
— live births, pp. II:10, II:321*t*
— low birth weight, pp. III:308-309, III:516*t*
— mammograms, p. III:18
— marriage, pp. II:52-53
— maternal mortality, p. III:22
— mathematics proficiency, p. II:161
— mobility, p. II:38

Race/ethnicity continued:
— murder, p. IV:52
— physicians, p. III:337
— political-party affiliation, p. II:108
— population, pp. II:24, II:70, II:343*t*
— Population Replacement Rate, pp. II:6, II:8
— poverty, p. IV:53
— prisoners, pp. IV:238-239, IV:242
— single-parent households, p. II:61
— Total Fertility Rates, pp. II:6, II:8
— volunteering, pp. I:241, I:370*t*
— voter turnout, p. II:106
— youth gangs, pp. IV:43-44
Racial discrimination, p. IV:162
Racial profiling, pp. IV:222-225, IV:365*t*
Racketeering and sentencing, p. IV:108
Radiation, pp. III:105, III:159
Radioisotope scans, p. III:152
Radiologic technologists, p. III:355
Railroad brake, signal, and switch operators, pp. I:54-55
Railroad conductors and yardmasters, p. I:54
Ranchers
— *See:* farmers and ranchers
Rape, pp. IV:55-56, IV:58, IV:318*t*
— actual crimes reported, p. IV:5
— household income, pp. IV:31, IV:38
— juveniles arrested, pp. IV:133, IV:135, IV:137-138
— rate fluctuation, pp. IV:25-26
— recidivism, p. IV:260
Reading proficiency, pp. II:159-160, II:163, II:200-202, II:366*t*
Reagan, President Ronald, pp. IV:46, IV:277
Real estate, p. I:292*t*
Real estate, rental, and leasing services, pp. I:104-105
Reality Check, pp. II:170, II:177
Receptionists and information clerks, pp. I:61-62
Recidivism
— by race, p. IV:166
— by type of crime committed, pp. IV:260-261, IV:263
— prison industries, pp. IV:256-259
— state prisoners, pp. IV:374*t*
Recommended Energy Allowance, p. III:89
Recreation, pp. I:185, I:242, I:244-246, I:357*t*
Recreational time
— *See:* leisure time
Recreational vehicles (RVs), p. I:190
Rectal cancers, pp. III:156, III:161
Red meat, p. III:83
Registered nurses, p. III:523*t*
— growing occupations, p. I:58
— job openings, pp. I:24-25, I:61-62
— nursing school graduates, pp. III:347-348
— retirement, pp. I:22-23
— supply, p. III:349
— worker shortages, p. I:59
Rehabilitation Act, p. III:232
Rehabilitation programs, p. IV:263
Relationship Web sites, pp. I:284, I:380*t*
Religion-based discrimination, pp. I:161, I:167
Religion surfers, pp. II:142, II:361*t*

Religions, pp. II:358t
— attendance at services, pp. I:233, I:249-250, I:343t
— Christian churches, p. II:134
— gains/losses in membership, pp. II:359t
— membership, pp. I:252-253, II:358t
— traditional denominations, pp. II:130-133
— volunteering, pp. I:242, I:244-246
— voting preferences, p. II:110
Religious activities, p. II:142
Religious diversity, p. I:164
Religious organizations, pp. I:247-249, I:371t
Renal disease, pp. III:2, III:380
Reno, Janet, p. I:50
Rensselaer Polytechnic Institute, p. II:280
Rental households, pp. II:35, III:195, II:331t
Repair occupations
— *See:* precision, production, craft, repair occupations
Repeat offenders, p. IV:206
Repetitive-strain injuries, p. III:236
Report on Smoking and Health, pp. III:107, III:136
Reproduction, p. III:291
Republicans, p. II:98
Research grants, p. III:81
Reservoirs, pp. III:323, III:325
Residency, pp. II:287-290
Residential treatment centers, p. III:264
Resistance machines, pp. I:200, I:202
Respiratory diseases, p. III:5
— birth defects, p. III:310
— causes of death, pp. III:3-4, III:8-10
— causes of disability, pp. III:227-228, III:235-236, III:238
— children, p. III:229
— surgical procedures, p. III:150
— therapeutic procedures, p. III:152
Restaurant dining, pp. I:180, I:357t
Restaurant expenditures, pp. III:109-110
Retail buyers
— *See:* wholesale and retail buyers
Retail trade, pp. I:6, I:61, I:104-105, I:157-158, I:292t
Retirement, pp. I:23, I:344t
— age group, pp. I:22, I:24, I:27, I:127, I:139, I:344t
— dependency ratio, p. I:142
— employee benefits, p. I:136
— household expenses, p. I:145
— income, pp. I:128-129, I:133
— occupations, pp. I:22-23, I:296t
Rett's Syndrome, p. III:258
Rheumatism, pp. III:227-228
Rhode Island, pp. II:64, II:217, IV:224, III:338
Ridge, Tom, p. IV:188
Rifles, p. II:245
Riley, Richard, p. II:263
Risk behaviors, pp. III:489t
Ritalin, pp. III:129, III:165, III:171-174, II:302-303, II:407t
   III:483t
River water pollution, pp. III:323, III:325
R.J. Reynolds, p. III:138
Road rage, p. III:140
Robbery, p. IV:373t

Robbery continued:
— corrections expenditures, p. IV:249
— household income, pp. IV:31, IV:38
— juveniles arrested, pp. IV:133, IV:135, IV:137-138
— murders, p. IV:58
— rate fluctuation, pp. IV:25-26
— recidivism, p. IV:260
Robert Wood Johnson Medical School, p. III:167
Rockets, p. II:245
Rocky Mountain Spotted Fever, p. III:95
Roe v. Wade, p. III:306
Rohypnol, pp. III:120, IV:154
Roman Catholic Church, pp. II:136-138, II:242
Romania, p. II:163
Room and board, pp. II:271, II:277
Roosevelt, President Franklin D., p. IV:230
Roper Starch Worldwide, p. I:187
Rose, Mike, p. II:155
Rowing, p. I:208
Rubella, pp. III:55-56, III:94-95
— *See also:* German measles
Rubeola, p. III:56
Rudolph, Eric Robert, p. IV:181
Runaways, pp. IV:101, IV:136
Running, p. I:202
Running on Ritalin, p. II:303
Rural population, pp. II:27, II:329t
Russia, pp. II:5, I:187
Russian (language), pp. II:76-77
Russian Federation, pp. II:163-165, III:334
RVs, p. I:190
— *See:* Recreational vehicles (RVs)
Sacramento (CA), p. IV:72
SAD
— *See:* Social anxiety disorders
Safety in schools, pp. II:247-248
Safety issues, pp. I:171-172
Sailer, Steven, p. II:55
St. John's Wort, pp. III:75-76, III:81, III:87, III:162-163
Salaries
— athletes, pp. I:212, I:364t
— baggage screeners, p. IV:233
— law enforcement personnel, p. IV:209
— medical school graduates, p. III:414
— net worth, p. I:38
— productivity, p. I:120
— teachers, pp. II:182, II:193-194
— weekly, p. I:128
Sales occupations, pp. I:20, I:32, I:61-62, I:69-70, I:296t
Sales of educational services, p. II:279
Salk, Dr. Jonas, p. III:95
Sally Ride Academy for Girls, p. II:309
Salmonella infections, p. III:111
Salts, pp. III:20-21
Same-sex partners, pp. II:64, I:136
— *See also:* Gays
— *See also:* Homosexuals
— *See also:* Lesbians
Sarafem, p. III:170

Satellite television receivers, p. I:227

SATs, pp. II:166, II:171, II:217, II:293, II:368*t*

Saudi Arabia, p. IV:184

Saum, William, p. IV:118

Saunders, Dr. Cicely, pp. III:376, III:378

Savage Inequalities: Children in America's Schools, p. II:221

Savings, pp. I:347*t*

Savings & loans fraud, p. IV:109

Saw palmetto, p. III:75

Schistosomiasis, p. III:326

Schizophrenia, pp. III:247-249

Schlafly, Phyllis, p. II:223

Schlosser, Eric, p. III:110

Scholastic Aptitude Test
— *See:* SATs

Scholastic Assessment Test
— *See:* SATs

School-based health centers, pp. III:102-104, III:464*t*

School choice, pp. II:239-240

School finances, pp. II:220-221, II:379*t*

School performance, p. II:385*t*

School-to-Work Opportunities Act, p. II:262

School vending machines, p. II:310

School vouchers, pp. II:241-242

School-year duration, p. II:254

Schools, p. I:34
— bullying, pp. II:249-250
— by type, pp. II:211, II:222-223, II:231, II:233, II:237
— crime, pp. IV:128, IV:130, II:245
— expulsions, pp. IV:131-132
— problems perceived by teachers, p. II:198
— problems perceived by the general public, p. II:199
— youth gangs, pp. IV:42-43

Schools and Staffing Survey, pp. II:191, II:198

Science museums, p. I:229

Sciences, advanced
— *See:* Advanced sciences

Scientific and technical services
— *See:* professional, scientific, and technical services

Scientology, pp. II:134-135, I:252-253

Scofflaws, p. IV:266

Search engines, p. I:278

Seasonal workers, p. I:46

Seconal, p. III:129

Second homes, p. I:194

Secondary education, pp. I:11, II:189-190

Secondary school teachers, pp. I:58-59, I:61-62

Secret Service, p. IV:228

Secretaries, stenographers, and typists, pp. I:32, I:61-62

Secularism, pp. I:252-253

Securities and Exchange Commission, pp. IV:84-85, IV:109

Security measures, p. I:281

Sedatives, pp. III:119, III:128

Seeds, p. I:185

Segregation, p. II:345*t*

Seizure disorders, pp. III:229, III:231

Self-employment income, p. I:145

Senior citizens, pp. III:187-188

Senior citizens continued:
— *See also:* Aging population
— *See also:* Elderly population
— living arrangements, pp. III:193-194
— media images, pp. III:221-222
— Medicaid expenditures, p. III:220
— Medicare expenditures, p. III:219
— quality of life, p. III:210
— risk behaviors, pp. III:489*t*
— suicides, p. III:260

Sentencing, pp. IV:108-110, IV:333*t*

SEOG, p. II:273

Sepsis, bacterial
— *See:* Bacterial sepsis

September 11, 2001
— airline passenger screening, p. IV:232
— corporate responses, p. I:171
— deaths, p. IV:190
— food-borne terrorism, p. III:112
— genetic engineering, p. III:106
— Immigration and Naturalization Service, p. IV:227
— racial profiling, p. IV:224
— terrorism, pp. IV:177, IV:182
— timeline, pp. IV:192-194
— workplace safety, p. I:150

Septicemia, pp. III:4-5, III:7-8

Service occupations
— employment, pp. I:31-32, I:291*t*
— independent contractors, pp. I:69-70
— injuries in the workplace, p. I:156

Serviceman's Readjustment Act, pp. II:150, II:273
— *See also:* GI Bill

Services industry, pp. II:256-257, II:262
— employment, pp. I:1, I:3-4, I:6
— productivity, p. I:102

Seventh Day Adventists, p. II:132

Severance pay, p. I:134

Sewing, p. I:218

Sewing machine operators, p. I:54

Sex-based crimes, pp. IV:10, IV:101

Sex-based discrimination
— case resolutions, pp. I:163, I:167
— charges filed with the EEOC, p. I:161

Sex education, p. III:103

Sex information, pp. III:282-283, III:505*t*

Sex offenders, pp. IV:121, IV:336*t*

Sex on TV, p. I:231

Sexes
— *See also:* Females
— *See also:* Males
— *See also:* Men
— *See also:* Women
— deaths, pp. II:17, II:21
— earnings, pp. I:71, II:295
— educational attainment, pp. II:258-259, I:262, II:283, II:285, I:318*t*
— employment, pp. I:65-67, I:69, I:174, I:298*t* I:355*t*
— high school athletes, p. I:362*t*

Sexes continued:
— household activities, pp. I:181-182
— income, pp. I:84, I:94, I:312t
— Internet use, pp. I:276, I:378t
— marriage, pp. II:52-53
— occupational fatalities, pp. I:156, I:349t
— online search term, p. I:282
— political-party affiliation, p. II:100
— retirement, pp. I:139, I:344t
— teachers, p. II:182
— volunteering, pp. I:236-237
— workplace injuries, pp. I:155-156
Sexual abuse of elderly, p. III:199
Sexual activity, pp. III:304-305, III:502t
— frequency, pp. III:269-273
— teenagers, pp. III:284-285
— Viagra, p. III:275
Sexual assaults, pp. IV:36, IV:55-56, IV:245, IV:260
Sexual fantasies, pp. III:271-272, III:503t
Sexual harassment
— case resolutions, pp. I:165-167
— EEOC, pp. I:161, I:354t
— workplace, p. I:149
Sexuality, pp. III:267-268, III:503t
Sexually transmitted diseases, pp. III:40, III:51-52, III:102, III:439t
San Francisco (CA), p. II:75
Shalala, Donna, p. III:107
Shannon v United States, p. IV:277
Shift Work Sleep Disorder, p. III:144
Shootings, pp. III:4, IV:129
Shoplifting, pp. IV:69-70
Shopping online, pp. I:273, I:276, I:279
Shotguns, p. II:245
Sick leave, p. I:128
SIDS, pp. III:11, III:45-46, III:313
— *See also*: Crib death
— *See also*: Sudden Infant Death Syndrome
Sierra Club, p. III:114
Sigmoidoscopy, p. III:31
Signal and switch operators
— *See*: railroad brake, signal, and switch operators
Sikhism, pp. II:134-135, II:140-141, I:243, I:252
Silent Spring, p. III:87
Siltation, pp. III:323, III:325
Silverthorn, Dr. Persephanie, p. IV:136
Singapore, pp. II:163-165, II:188
Single-parent households, pp. II:45, II:67, II:340t
— children, p. II:46
— marital status of parents, pp. II:59-60
— poverty rates, p. II:47
— race/ethnicity, p. II:61
Single-sex education, pp. II:308-309
Singletons, p. III:39
Sioux Indian tribe, pp. II:72-73
Sixth Amendment, p. IV:281
San Jose (CA), p. II:75
Skateboarding, p. I:202
Skating, p. I:202

Skeptic's Dictionary, p. III:76
Skilled nursing facilities, pp. III:207-209
Skilling, Jeffrey, p. IV:85
Skin cancer, pp. III:13, III:147-148
— *See also*: Cancer
— *See also*: Melanomas
Skin diseases, p. III:236
Sleep disorders, p. III:143
Slovak Republic, pp. II:164-165
Slovenia, pp. II:163, II:165
Smallpox, pp. III:94-95, III:392
Smith, Benjamin, pp. IV:286, IV:288
Smock, Pamela J., p. II:57
Smoking
— cause of death, pp. III:3-5, III:26, III:108, III:131, III:135-138, IV:174, III:228, III:474t
— causes of disability, p. III:228
— diseases, p. III:3
— educational attainment, p. III:136
— elderly population, p. III:210
— *Healthy People 2010*, p. III:408
— heart disease, p. III:136
— high school seniors, p. III:475t
— income levels, p. III:136
— low birth weight, p. III:40
— teenagers, pp. III:137-138
Snowboarding, pp. I:200-202
Snowshoeing, p. I:200
SO
— *See*: Sulfur Dioxide
Soccer, pp. I:202, I:208-209
Social and human services assistants, p. I:52
Social anxiety disorders, pp. III:252, III:255
— *See also*: Social phobias
The Social Organization of Sexuality, p. III:269
Social phobias, p. III:247
— *See also*: Social anxiety disorders
Social sciences degree recipients, pp. II:284-285
Social Security, pp. I:29, I:143-145, I:346t
Social Security disability benefits, pp. III:233-234, III:496t
Social services, pp. I:7, I:34
Social welfare eligibility clerks, pp. I:22, I:296t
Social workers, pp. I:22-25
Soda consumption, p. II:311
Softball, pp. I:200, I:202, I:208-209
Software
— *See also*: equipment and software p. I:102
Solicitation, p. IV:245
Solutions to Tragedies of Police Pursuits (STOP), p. IV:219
South Africa, pp. III:332, III:334
South Carolina, p. III:387
South Dakota, p. III:369
South Korea, pp. II:163, I:187
Southern Baptist Convention, pp. II:136-138
Southern Poverty Law Center, p. IV:288
Spain, p. II:163
Spanish (language), pp. II:76, II:307
Special Committee on Aging, p. III:374
Special education programs, pp. II:189-190, II:298-299, II:406t

Special education programs continued:
  407*t*
Special education teachers, pp. I:22, I:24-25, I:58
Special units of police departments, pp. IV:206-207
Special weapons and tactics (SWAT), p. IV:211
Specialized museums, p. I:229
Specialty hospitals, p. III:365
Speech impairments, pp. III:229-231, II:298-299
Speed, p. III:124
Spending on sports, p. I:206
The Spice Channel, p. III:280
Spinal problems, pp. III:227-228
Sponges, p. II:15
Sports, pp. I:199-200
— high school athletes, p. I:204
— injuries, p. I:205
— marketing, p. I:213
— online auctions, p. I:286
— professional, p. I:210
— scholarships, p. I:206
— supplies, p. I:185
— teenagers, pp. I:201-202, I:361*t*
— television, p. I:211
Sports Illustrated, p. I:213
Spouse abuse, p. IV:10
Sprains, p. I:155
Springfield (OR), p. IV:129
Stalking, pp. IV:119-120, IV:336*t*
Standardized tests, pp. II:168, II:170, II:218, II:367*t*
Stanford Sleep Disorders Clinic, p. III:144
Stanford University, pp. II:268, II:280, II:294
Starter pistols, p. II:245
State and local grants, p. II:279
State Department, p. IV:183
State government, pp. I:1, I:9-10, II:211, I:256, I:292*t*
State mental hospitals, p. III:264
State prisoners, pp. IV:236, IV:369*t*
State University of New York at Buffalo, p. II:292
STDs
— *See:* Sexually transmitted diseases
Steamfitters
— *See:* plumbers, pipefitters, and steamfitters
Stenographers and typists
— *See:* Secretaries, stenographers, and typists
Stents, pp. III:25, III:151
Sterility, p. II:14
Sterilization, pp. III:304-305
Steroid use, p. III:104
Stimulants, pp. IV:11, III:119, III:128, IV:151-152, III:173
Stock performance, p. I:103
Stomach cancer, pp. III:67-68, III:156
Streams, pp. III:323, III:325
Street gangs, p. IV:44
Street, Picabo, p. I:209
Stress
— cancer, p. III:161
— morning habits, pp. III:139-140
— nighttime habits, pp. III:143-144
— noonday habits, pp. III:141-142

Stress continued:
— risk behaviors, p. III:108
— vacations, p. III:145
Strikes, p. I:210
Strokes, p. II:18
— *See also:* Cerebrovascular disease
— Baby Boom generation, p. III:69
— causes of death, pp. III:2-5, III:8-9
— disabilities, pp. III:227, III:243, III:401
— women, pp. III:12-13
Students
— *See also:* Children
— *See also:* Juveniles
— *See also:* Teenagers
— *See also:* Youth
— deaths in school, pp. II:243-244
— disabilities, p. II:258
— financial assistance, pp. II:395*t*
— indebtedness, pp. II:275, II:277-278, III:414
— LEP, pp. II:306-307
— limited English proficiency, p. II:306
Students Against Drunk Driving, p. IV:113
Subsidized commuting, p. I:135
Substance abuse, pp. IV:53, III:102, III:411, III:471*t*
**Substance Abuse and Mental Health Services Administration
    (SAMHSA)**, pp. IV:157, IV:159, III:412
Substance use, pp. III:121-123
Suburbs, pp. II:27-28, II:30, II:329*t*
Sudden Infant Death Syndrome, pp. III:10, III:437*t*
— *See also:* Crib death
— *See also:* SIDS
Sudden Sniffing Death Syndrome, p. III:120
Sugars, pp. III:20-21
Suicide, p. III:35
Suicides, pp. III:431*t*
— aging population, pp. III:204, III:261
— causes of death, pp. III:4, III:8, II:21, III:131
— Columbine High School, p. II:243
— firearms-related, p. IV:39
— men, pp. II:18, III:34-36, III:260
— mental health, pp. III:248-249
— school-based health centers, p. III:103
— terrorists, p. IV:190
Suicides, altruistic
— *See:* Altruistic suicides
Suicides, anomic
— *See:* Anomic suicides
Suicides, egoistic
— *See:* Egoistic suicides
Suicides, fatalistic
— *See:* Fatalistic suicides
Sulfa drugs, pp. III:2, II:22
Sulfur dioxide, pp. III:316-317
Sunbeam Corp., p. IV:84
Super Nintendo, p. IV:145
Supplemental Educational Opportunity Grants
— *See:* SEOG
Supplemental income, p. II:183
Supplemental pay, p. I:129

Support staff
— *See:* teachers and support staff
Suppositories, p. II:15
Supreme Court, pp. IV:24, IV:277, IV:281-282
Surfing, p. I:200
Surgeon General of the United States, pp. III:83, III:403
Surgeons
— *See:* Physicians and Surgeons
— *See:* physicians and surgeons
Surgical hospitals, pp. III:364-365
Surgical procedures, pp. III:150-151, III:154-155
Survival rates for cancers, pp. III:13, III:19, III:447t
  III:478t
Sweden, pp. III:42, II:163-164, III:334
Swedish (language), p. II:77
Swimming, pp. I:200, I:208-209
Switch operators
— *See:* railroad brake, signal, and switch operators
Switchboard operators (including answering service)
— occupations in decline, p. I:54
Switzerland, pp. II:163-165
Symbionese Liberation Army, p. IV:181
Symphonies, pp. I:224-225
Synthroid, pp. III:167-168
Syphilis, pp. III:51-52, III:58, III:442t
Systematic phonics, pp. II:200-202
Systems analysts, pp. I:58-59, I:61-62
— *See also:* computer systems analysts
Tagalog, pp. II:76-77
T'ai chi, pp. I:200-201
Tailhook, pp. I:162, I:166
Taiwanese population, p. II:74
Tajikistan, p. II:163
Talking Back to Prozac, p. III:64
Tanning, p. III:147
Taoism, pp. II:134-135, II:140-141, I:252-253
Task Force on Antimicrobial Resistance, p. III:330
Tattoos, pp. III:148, I:283
Tax evasion and sentencing, p. IV:108
Taxes, pp. II:211, II:213
TB
— *See:* Tuberculosis
Teacher Followup Survey, p. II:191
Teacher-pupil ratio, pp. II:180, II:371t
Teachers, p. II:371t
— by sex, pp. II:182, II:372t
— certification, pp. II:186, III:373t
— dissatisfaction, p. II:374t
— educational attainment, pp. II:184-185, II:373t
— elementary schools, pp. I:24-25, I:58, I:61-62
— preschool, pp. I:58-59
— problems perceived in schools, p. II:198
— retirement, pp. I:22-23
— salaries, pp. II:182, II:193-194, II:374t
— secondary schools, pp. I:58-59, I:61-62
— shortages, p. II:189
— Singapore, p. II:188
— special education, pp. I:22, I:24-25, I:58, I:296t
— supplemental income, p. II:183

Teachers continued:
— turnover, pp. II:191-192
— uncertified, p. II:187
— worker shortages, p. I:59
— workplace assaults, pp. I:157-158
Teachers' aides, pp. I:22-23, I:296t
Teachers and support staff, p. I:11
Team Marketing Report, p. I:212
Technical and related support occupations, pp. I:20, I:296t
Technical services
— *See:* professional, scientific, and technical services
Technical, sales, and administrative support occupations, p. I:31-32
Technicians and related support occupations, pp. I:32, I:69
Technology and communications, pp. II:256-257, II:262
Teenagers, pp. IV:33, IV:75, IV:106, IV:325t
— *See also:* Children
— *See also:* Juveniles
— *See also:* Students
— *See also:* Youth
— illegal labor, p. I:43
— illicit substance use, pp. III:117-120, III:132, III:134
— Internet use, pp. I:278-279, I:379
— physical education classes, p. I:203
— reading habits, p. I:221
— religious services attendance, p. I:373t
— sedatives, p. III:119
— sexual activity, pp. III:282-285, III:505t
— smoking, pp. III:137-138
— sports, pp. I:199, I:201-202, I:204
Telemarketing, p. IV:82
Telemedicine, pp. III:361-362, III:524t
Telephone operators, p. I:54
Television, pp. III:221-222, I:226-227, I:231, I:268, III:280, III:491t
Tellers, p. I:54
Tendinitis, p. I:155
Tennessee, pp. II:63, II:196, II:246
Tennis, pp. I:202, I:208-209
Terrorism
— civil liberty, p. IV:185
— deaths, pp. IV:183, IV:190-191, IV:356t
— domestic, pp. IV:180, IV:182
— global, p. IV:177
— timeline, pp. IV:178-179
Terrorism Information and Prevention System (TIPS), p. IV:186
Test scores, pp. II:171-175
Testosterone levels, pp. III:6, III:29, III:151, IV:153
Tests, standardized
— *See:* standardized tests
Tetanus, pp. III:94-95
Texas, pp. IV:122, IV:284, III:415, III:417
— Asian population, p. II:75
— education for gifted children, p. II:305
— expulsions from school, p. II:246
— gay-couple households, pp. II:63-64
— geographic distribution of elderly population, p. III:190
— hospital beds, p. III:369

Texas continued:
— standardized tests, p. II:218
— vacation spending, p. I:190
— youth gangs, p. IV:138
Thai population, p. II:74
Thailand, p. III:42
Theatres, pp. I:185, I:217, I:224-225
Theft, p. II:245
— arrests, pp. IV:68-70
— by property stolen, p. IV:76
— correction expenditures, p. IV:249
— crimes reported to the police, p. IV:373t
— juveniles, p. IV:136
— property crime, pp. IV:4, IV:7-8
Theology degrees conferred, pp. II:286, II:290
Therapeutic procedures, pp. III:152-154
They Say You're Crazy, p. III:170
Third International Mathematics and Science Study
— *See:* TIMSS
Third National Incidence Study of Child Abuse and Neglect, p. IV:107
Thomas, Clarence, pp. I:162, I:165
Thomas, Timothy, p. IV:204
Thompson, Tommy, pp. III:73, III:112
Thyroid gland surgeries, p. III:151
Ticket prices, pp. I:212-213, I:222, I:364t
Time for Kids, p. II:249
Time for Life: Surprising Ways Americans Use Their Time, p. I:181
Timelines
— drug-control legislation, p. IV:12
— hate crimes, p. IV:286
— law enforcement, pp. IV:197-198
— September 11, 2001, pp. IV:192-194
— terrorism, pp. IV:178-179
TIMSS, pp. II:188, II:195, II:253-254
Title IX, pp. I:204, II:308
Tobacco advertising, p. III:138
Tobacco consumption, pp. IV:12, IV:148, IV:352t
Tobacco control programs, pp. III:102, III:408-409
Tomatoes, p. III:87
Tonsillitis, p. III:229
Tort reform, p. III:417
Total Fertility Rate, p. III:295
Total Fertility Rates, pp. II:5-8
Touch football, p. I:202
Toxemia, p. III:23
Toxic Shock Syndrome, pp. III:61-62, III:444t
Toyota Camry, p. IV:71
Toys, pp. II:66, I:286
Toys and sports supplies, p. I:185
Tracheal cancer, p. III:67
Track and field, p. I:209
Trade, pp. I:6, II:256-257, II:262
Traditional workers, pp. I:71-72
Traffic deaths, pp. II:18, IV:115-116
Train robbery, p. IV:245
Tranquilizers, pp. III:119, III:128, IV:151
Trans fat, p. III:109

Transportation
— assaults in the workplace, pp. I:157-158
— child rearing costs, pp. II:66-67
— college costs, p. II:271
— injuries in the workplace, p. I:156
— occupational fatalities, p. I:151
Transportation and material moving occupations, pp. I:20, I:43, I:296t
— *See also:* material moving occupations
Transportation and public utilities, pp. I:6, I:292t
Transportation and warehousing, pp. I:104-105
Transportation Security Administration, p. IV:233
Traumatic brain injury, p. II:298
Travel, pp. I:190-192
Travel agencies, pp. I:194, I:196-197, I:360t
Treadmill exercise, p. I:200
Treason, p. IV:245
Tricyclic antidepressants, p. III:64
Trigonometry, p. II:259
Trimox, pp. III:166-167
Trinidad and Tobago, p. II:163
Triplets, pp. III:39, III:299-300
Truancy, p. IV:101
The Truly Disadvantaged, p. II:53
Trust fund assets of Medicare, p. III:528t
Tuberculosis, pp. III:2-3, III:58-59
— cases and rates, pp. III:442t
— foreign countries, pp. III:332-334
Tufts University, pp. III:175, II:294
Tuition and fees, pp. II:151, II:269-270, II:272, II:394t III:539t
— Consumer Price Index, p. II:268
— medical school, p. II:277
— public universities, p. II:279
Tularemia, p. III:392
Turkey, p. I:187
Turkmenistan, p. II:163
Turning the Corner on Father Absence in Black America, p. II:53
Twinkie Defense, p. IV:276
Twins, pp. III:39, III:299-300
Two-parent households, pp. II:46, II:67
Typhoid fever, pp. III:58-59, III:442t
Typists
— *See also:* word processors and typists p. I:54
U. S. Customs Service, p. IV:329t
Uganda, p. III:332
Ukraine, p. II:163
Ultrasound, p. III:152
Umbilical cord complications, p. III:10
Uncertified teachers, p. II:187
Underemployment, p. I:57
Unemployment, pp. IV:53, I:145
UNESCO, p. II:250
UNICOR, p. IV:255
Uniform Crime Report, pp. IV:3-5, IV:7, IV:9, IV:14, IV:139
Uninsured population, pp. III:384-385
Unions, pp. I:1, I:14, I:16, I:294t
Unitarian Universalism, pp. II:134-135, I:252-253

United Church of Christ, pp. II:132-135
United Government Services, pp. III:377-378
United Kingdom, pp. II:163, III:334
United Methodist Church, pp. II:136-138
United Nations building, p. IV:184
United Nations Human Rights Committee, p. III:218
United Republic of Tanzania, p. III:332
U.S. Administration on Aging, p. III:199
U.S. Army, p. II:292
U.S. Army Reserves, p. II:278
U.S. Customs Service, pp. IV:99, IV:226-227
U.S. Department of Education, p. I:61
U.S. Department of Energy, p. III:105
U.S. Department of Justice, p. IV:3
U.S. Navy, p. II:278
U.S. Office of Dietary Supplements, p. III:75
U.S. Surgeon General, p. III:107
University of Colorado system, p. II:280
University of Michigan, pp. II:57, I:183, III:257
University of Utah Drug Information Service, p. III:389
Unsafe School Choice Option, p. IV:129
Up the IRS, Inc., p. IV:181
Urban Policy Institute, p. IV:134
Urban population, pp. II:27, II:329t
Urdu, p. II:76
Urinary tract cancer, pp. III:3, III:156
Urinary tract surgeries, p. III:150
Urologists, p. III:275
Uruguay, p. II:163
USDA, pp. III:84, III:87-90, III:109, III:113
Usef, Ramzi, p. IV:183
Utah, p. IV:276
Uterine cancer, pp. III:19, III:68, III:158, III:161, III:168
Utilities, pp. I:104-105
Uzbekistan, p. II:163
Vacation homes, pp. I:194, I:359t
Vacation spending, p. I:190
Vacation time, pp. I:128, I:133, I:187, I:189, I:191-192, I:359t
Vacations, pp. III:145-146
Vaccinations, pp. III:94-95
Vaccines, pp. III:389-392, III:463t
Vaccinia (cell culture), p. III:392
Vagrancy, pp. IV:101, IV:106-107, IV:112
Valium, p. III:129
Valley State Prison, p. IV:243
Vancomycin-Resistant Enterococci
— See: VRE
Vandalism, pp. IV:80, IV:105
Vanderbilt University, p. II:280
Varicella, p. III:96
Vasotec, p. III:167
VCRs, p. I:226
Vegetables, p. III:83
Venezuelan encephalitis, p. III:392
Vermont, pp. II:64-65, III:338
Very-low birth weight, p. III:310
Veterans, p. II:150
Veterans Administration, pp. I:131, III:264
Veterinary assistants and laboratory animal caretakers, p. I:52

Veterinary medicine degrees conferred, pp. II:286, II:290
Viagra, pp. III:267, III:275-276, III:504t
Victim assistance, p. IV:206
Victimization
— by race/ethnicity, pp. IV:316t
— by sex, race/ethnicity, and income, pp. IV:309t
— children, pp. IV:136, IV:139-140, IV:337t
— homicides, p. IV:35
— household income, pp. IV:31-32
— workplace, p. IV:320t
Video games, pp. IV:144-145, I:227, I:231, I:268, IV:342t
Video products, p. I:185
Video rentals, pp. I:222, I:366t
Video Vigilante, p. IV:125
Videocassette recorders
— See: VCRs
Vietnam, p. III:332
Vietnamese (language), pp. II:76-77
Vietnamese population, p. II:74
Violence in schools, pp. IV:128, II:245
Violent crime, pp. I:151-152, I:351t
— actual crimes reported, pp. IV:4-6
— arrests, pp. IV:16, IV:266, IV:273
— by race/ethnicity, p. IV:52
— by sex, pp. IV:35, IV:135
— crimes reported to the police, p. IV:77
— drug-related, p. IV:13
— firearms-related, p. IV:39
— household income, p. IV:31
— juveniles, p. IV:133
— not included in crime index, pp. IV:9-10
— prisoners, pp. IV:236-237
— rate fluctuation, pp. IV:26-27
— recidivism, p. IV:260
— victimization rates, p. IV:305t
Violent Crime Control and Law Enforcement Act, p. IV:47
Violent Offender Incarceration and Truth-in-Sentencing
  Incentive Grant (VOITIS) program, pp. IV:250, IV:252
Vioxx, p. III:178
Viral hepatitis, p. III:61
Virginia, pp. II:63, II:187, II:246
Virginia Slims cigarettes, p. III:136
Virtual doctors
— See: Telemedicine
Virtual libraries, p. I:257
Virtual volunteering, p. I:246
Viruses, pp. I:280, III:323
Vision care, p. I:133
Vision impairments, pp. III:203, III:227, III:229, III:231, II:298, III:487t
Vision screenings, p. III:103
Visual arts, p. II:284
Vitamins, p. III:75
VOC
— See: Volatile Organic Chemicals
Vocational education, pp. IV:264, II:392t
— adult education, pp. II:256-257, I:264-265
— by specialization, pp. II:261-262
— credits accumulated, p. II:258

Volatile organic chemicals, pp. III:316, III:318
Volleyball, pp. I:202, I:208-209
Volpe, Justin, p. IV:204
Volunteering, pp. I:233-234, I:369t
— age group, pp. I:239-240, I:370t
— by organization type, pp. I:245-246, I:370t
— by sex, pp. I:236-237
— educational attainment, p. I:238
— race/ethnicity, pp. I:241, I:370t
— work-related organizations, pp. I:245-246
Voter registration, p. II:352t
Voter turnout, pp. II:112, II:355t
— age, pp. II:104, III:353t
— presidential elections, pp. II:96, II:350t
— race/ethnicity, pp. II:106, II:353t
— religion, pp. II:110, II:354t
— women, p. II:102
Vouchers, school, pp. II:241-242
VRE, p. III:330
Wackenhut Corrections, pp. IV:251-253
Wages, pp. I:16, I:120, I:122, I:128, I:295t
— by occupational group, p. II:296
— manufacturing, pp. I:336t
Waiters and waitresses, pp. I:61-62
Wakeboarding, pp. I:200-201
Walking
— 200,
The Wall.org, p. II:145
Walsh, Adam, p. IV:142
War on Drugs
— arrests by race/ethnicity, p. IV:163
— murders, pp. IV:28, IV:30
— Nixon, President Richard, p. IV:147
— timeline, p. IV:12
— wiretapping, p. IV:230
— youth, p. III:118
Washington (DC), pp. II:64, IV:124, IV:132, IV:215
Washington (State), pp. II:63-64, II:246
Waste Management Inc., pp. IV:84, IV:109
Wastewater treatment in selected countries, p. III:326
Watch guards
— See also: guards and watch guards p. I:61
Water pollution, pp. III:315, III:321-325, III:518t
Waterways, pp. III:321-322
Weapons crimes, pp. IV:10, IV:101, IV:104
Weather Underground, p. IV:181
Weaving, pp. I:218-219
Weekend travel, p. I:192
Weight-control habits, p. III:115
Weight machines, pp. I:200, I:202
Welfare clerks, p. I:296t
Welfare Reform Act, p. II:47
Wellness programs, p. I:135
Wesleyans, pp. II:130-131, II:135
West Germany (former), p. II:254
West Paducah (KY), p. IV:129
West Virginia, pp. II:75, II:187, III:369-370, III:409, III:417
Western equine encephalitis, p. III:392
Western Sahara, p. II:30

Western United States, p. III:189
What Works? Questions and Answers About Prison Reform, p. IV:262
White-black death rate ratio, p. II:327t
White collar crime, pp. IV:108-109
White families, p. I:38
White House budget, p. IV:188
White, Dan, p. IV:276
Whites, p. III:28
— abortions, pp. II:12-13, II:321t
— activities of daily living, p. III:204
— arrests, p. IV:53
— births, pp. II:10, III:23, I:40, II:319t
— breastfeeding, p. III:41
— cancer survival rates, pp. III:156-158
— causes of death, pp. III:8-9, II:21, III:24-27, III:32, III:34, III:36, III:43-44
— computer learning opportunities, p. II:263
— correctional population, p. IV:19
— crib death, pp. III:45-46
— deaths, pp. III:15, III:18, II:21
— diseases, pp. III:14, III:18, III:28, III:52, III:54, III:64, III:288-290
— drug arrests, pp. IV:161, IV:163-164
— drug convictions, pp. IV:164-166
— drug use, pp. III:126-127, IV:159-160
— earnings, p. I:71
— educational attainment, pp. I:39, I:112, I:118-119, II:151-153, II:258-259, II:287-290
— employment, pp. I:16, I:30, I:37, I:67-68
— family net worth, p. I:38
— gender distribution, p. II:339t
— homicides, pp. IV:52, IV:217-218
— housing, p. II:35
— income, pp. II:21, I:82-83
— infant mortality, pp. II:21, III:313
— Internet use, pp. I:270-271
— interracial marriages, pp. II:54-55
— juveniles arrested, p. IV:137
— learning disabilities, p. III:66
— life expectancy, pp. II:20, III:47-48, III:403-404
— literacy, pp. II:154, II:159
— low birth weight, pp. III:40, III:308-309
— mammograms, p. III:18
— marriage, pp. II:52-53
— maternal mortality, pp. II:21, III:22
— mathematics proficiency, pp. II:161-162
— Medicare, p. III:380
— physicians, p. III:337
— political-party affiliation, p. II:108
— population, pp. II:24-25
— population mobility, p. II:39
— Population Replacement Rate, p. II:6
— risk behaviors, pp. III:16-17, III:135-136
— risk factors, p. III:20
— single-parent households, p. II:61
— suicides, pp. III:260, III:434t
— Total Fertility Rates, pp. II:6-8
— volunteering, p. I:241

Whites continued:
— voter turnout, p. II:106
Whole language movement, p. II:201
Whole Math Movement, p. II:205
Whole milk, p. III:83
Wholesale and retail buyers (except farm products), p. I:54
Wholesale trade, pp. I:6, I:104-105, I:156, I:292*t*
Whooping Cough, p. III:56
Whyos, p. IV:43
Wiccan, pp. II:134-135
Widowed parents, p. II:59
Willett, Dr. Walter C., pp. III:90, III:109-110
Wilson, Dr. James Q., pp. IV:52, IV:137-138
Wilson, Dr. William Julius, p. II:53
Wiretapping, pp. IV:229-231, IV:366*t*
Wisconsin, pp. IV:122, II:218
Women, p. I:298*t*
— *See also:* Females
— activities of daily living, p. III:204
— age at first marriage, p. II:50
— art purchases, p. I:219
— births, p. III:295
— cancer survival rates, p. III:158
— causes of death, pp. III:6-7, III:12, III:24, III:26, III:30, III:32, III:34, III:36, III:53, III:422*t*
— contraceptive practices, pp. II:14-15, III:514*t*
— cosmetic surgery, pp. III:277, III:279
— creative writing, p. I:219
— deaths, pp. III:15, III:424*t*
— disabled population, pp. III:225, III:236
— diseases, pp. III:13-14, III:18, III:54, III:64, III:116, III:147, III:154, III:160, III:247, III:249, III:262, III:289-290, III:366
— domestic homicides, pp. IV:48-49
— earnings, p. I:71
— educational attainment, pp. I:94, I:262, II:283, II:285
— elderly population, p. III:196
— employment, pp. I:16, I:29-33, I:36, I:65-67, I:69, I:156, I:174-175, II:182, I:262, III:296, III:509*t*
— estrogen, p. II:18
— federal law enforcement personnel, p. IV:226
— household activities, pp. I:181-182
— housing, p. III:195
— income, pp. I:84, I:94
— injuries in the workplace, pp. I:155-156
— Internet use, p. I:276
— life expectancy, pp. II:18-19, III:47
— living arrangements, p. III:192
— mammograms, p. III:18
— Medicare, p. III:380
— modern dance, p. I:219
— occupational fatalities, p. I:156
— online shopping, p. I:277
— physicians, p. III:337
— police officers, p. IV:200
— political-party affiliation, pp. II:100-101
— poverty, pp. I:92-93
— prisoners, pp. IV:18, IV:242
— risk behaviors, pp. III:16-17, III:135-136

Women continued:
— risk factors, p. III:20
— sexual activity, pp. III:269-270
— single-parent households, pp. II:46-47
— specialized museums, p. I:229
— sports, pp. I:206-209, I:363*t*
— state prisons, p. IV:371*t*
— sterility, p. II:14
— suicides, pp. III:260, III:434*t*
— Total Fertility Rate, p. III:295
— violent crime, pp. IV:35-38
— volunteering, pp. I:236-237
— voting in presidential elections, pp. II:102-103
— weaving, p. I:219
Women's Rights Movement, p. I:30
Women's Sports Foundation, p. I:207
Woods, Tiger, p. I:211
Word processors and typists, pp. I:54-55
Work activities, p. I:358*t*
Work hours, pp. I:176-177, I:356*t*
— age groups, p. I:43
— by sex, pp. I:174-175, I:355*t*
— foreign countries, p. I:187
— illegal labor, p. I:43
Work-related injuries and illnesses, p. I:350*t*
Work-related organizations, pp. I:245-246
Work-study programs, p. II:273
Worker shortages, p. I:59
Worker's compensation, pp. I:145, I:153
Workforce participation, pp. III:295-296, I:298*t*
Workforce population
— age groups, p. I:20
— Baby Boomers, p. I:21
— by sex, pp. I:29-30
— earnings, p. I:342*t*
— educational attainment, p. I:56
— fertility rates, p. I:40
— foreign-born, p. I:41
— high school education, p. I:57
— national health care expenditures, p. I:342*t*
— race/ethnicity, pp. I:29-30, I:35, I:41
— unions, p. I:294
Working for Children and Families, p. II:226
Working parents, p. I:183
Workplace assaults, pp. I:157-158
Workplace discrimination, pp. I:158-159
Workplace harassment, p. I:159
Workplace illnesses, pp. I:153, I:349*t*
Workplace injuries, pp. I:153, I:155-156, I:349*t*
Workplace issues, pp. I:164-165, I:351*t*
Workplace safety, pp. I:151-152, I:351*t*
World Church of the Creator, p. IV:288
World Health Organization, pp. III:316, III:332
World Sports Exchange, p. IV:118
World Trade Center, pp. IV:179, IV:183-184, IV:195, I:283
World Trade Organization, p. I:192
WorldCom, p. IV:85
Worldwide Web, pp. I:97, I:233, I:280
Worms, p. I:280

Writing, pp. I:218-219

Wrongful termination, p. I:162

WWF, p. I:283

www.buddhanet.org, p. II:145

www.godweb.org, p. II:145

Wyoming, pp. II:75, IV:278

X-rated movies, p. I:231

Yahoo!, p. I:282

Yale University, p. II:294

Yates, Andrea, p. IV:279

Yiddish, pp. II:76-77

Yoga, pp. III:163, I:200-201

Young Adult Literacy Survey, p. II:154

Youth, pp. II:22, I:141, I:242, I:244-246

— *See also:* Children

— *See also:* Infants

— *See also:* Juveniles

— *See also:* Teenagers

Youth gangs, pp. IV:137, IV:206, IV:313*t*

— *See also:* Gangs

— *See also:* Street gangs

— by race/ethnicity, pp. IV:40-43

— cocaine, p. IV:34

— selected states, p. IV:138

Zantac, p. III:167

ZapMe! Corp., pp. II:264-265

Zero tolerance, p. IV:195

Zimbabwe, p. III:332

Zoloft, pp. III:63-64, III:167, III:170, III:276, III:445*t*

Zoological gardens, p. I:7